Going Global features articles that highlight real issues from a global perspective. Reflect on the related questions and connect the challenges posed in each article to the chapter content and your own experiences.

>>

Thinking Critically

>> Energy Crisis on the Horizon

As long ago as 2000, Canadian economist Jeff Rubin began to forward predictions that oil prices would increase dramatically in the future, and in 2007, he got more specific about it. Predicting that they would top $100 per barrel. Despite the fact that it subsequently dropped significantly from its peak levels, Rubin has predicted that the price will rise again and will wreak even worse havoc on the economy at that point, including ending the practice of global outsourcing as we know it today.

According to Rubin, the price of oil will accelerate as oil supplies continue to be depleted and demand from developing countries increases. As the price rises, transportation costs will skyrocket, and it will no longer be prudent for people to trade internationally—or even travel among borders as they do today. As a result, nations will become less interdependent and technology will stagnate. Food, rather than oil, will become scarce. Governments will be forced to innovate and spend to transition their infrastructure to new sources of energy.

There are some positive notes in Rubin's bleak forecast. He goes on to predict that industries that have suffered with the rise of globalization and competition from foreign nations will prosper. As the world becomes less dependent on petroleum and other fossil fuels, the environmental damage they cause will lessen. Governments will be forced to innovate and spend to transition their infrastructure to new sources of energy.

In Rubin's opinion, however, those nations' citizens will have to make the greatest changes. Rubin cautions that each and every person must dramatically change their ways and reduce their consumption of energy—and he believes they'll actually do it. He adds, "Don't be surprised if the new, smaller world that emerges isn't a lot more livable and enjoyable than the one we are about to leave behind."

Source: Adapted from Mohammed Hazbullah, "The Coming Oil Crisis," Newsweek, June 22, 2009.

QUESTIONS

1. In your opinion, what are the roles or responsibilities of businesses in light of the fossil fuel crisis Rubin has predicted for the future?
2. How have escalating oil prices created a need for governments to invest more heavily in improving their infrastructure? What does that mean for businesses?

<<

Thinking Critically includes a current business article in each chapter, designed to give you a look into the real world of business and spark discussion in your class. Case questions encourage you to think in depth about the article and chapter concepts.

>>

- How has business evolved, and in what areas are jobs plentiful today?
- How do external environment factors affect business?
- Why should you study business?

<<

As You Read provides a quick summary of the overall questions you should consider as you study each chapter.

Brief

BUSconnections questions save you study time! We know your time is valuable—these strategically-placed questions give you the chance to pause and evaluate your own progress through each chapter and reinforce your understanding of the Learning Outcomes as you go.

>>

[BUS] connections

1. In what ways can governments make things easier for businesspeople? Do you think the government should do more? Why or why not?
2. Imagine you own a shoe-repair business in a town near a military base. How might a war affect your business?
3. What is free trade, and how does free trade affect businesses competing overseas?

Career-Focused

Career PERSPECTIVES

THE WORLD OF ACCOUNTING

As you'll learn in this chapter, there are several types of accounting in which you can be involved. What's important is that you choose the area that holds the most interest for you. Like the field of information systems, accounting is expected to grow faster than most industries well into the next decade. That's great news for those of you who may choose accounting as a future career!

A relatively new accounting field called *forensic accounting* entails investigating possible securities fraud, contract disputes, and other complex and possibly criminal financial transactions, such as money laundering. Forensic accountants have an accounting background but also have experience in law.

One salary survey concluded that accountants and auditors with less than a year of experience earn between $28,250 and $45,000 a year. Those with one to three years of experience earn between $33,000 and $52,000. Senior accountants and auditors earn between $40,750 and $69,750; managers, between $48,000 and $90,000; and directors of accounting and auditing, between $64,750 and $200,750. This wide range of salaries reflects differences in size of firm, location, level of education, and professional credentials.

If you want to succeed in business, you need to know about accounting. It's almost impossible to run any business, regardless of size, or understand business operations without being able to read, understand, and analyze accounting reports and financial statements. Accounting reports and financial statements reveal as much about a business's health as pulse rate and blood pressure readings describe a person's health.

Do you think accounting might be right for you? Does the idea of forensic accounting intrigue your inner detective? Would you rather work as a private accountant and focus on a single business? Perhaps you're interested in becoming a public accountant—either running your own business or working for a large accounting firm. Accounting provides countless options for anyone embarking on a new career.

Entrepreneurs are always on the lookout for an acceptable ROI, which is the money gained from taking on a business risk.

Study Alert

<<

Study Alerts highlight key concepts throughout each chapter at a glance.

<<

Career Perspectives help you answer the question, "How will the concepts I am learning in class relate to my future career?" Located in each chapter, this feature incorporates short, question-based overviews that tie business concepts to real-world career examples and a variety of professions!

BusinessNow

MCGRAW-HILL TEAM

VICE PRESIDENT, EDITOR IN CHIEF **Elizabeth Haefele**
VICE PRESIDENT, DIRECTOR OF MARKETING **John E. Biernat**
SENIOR SPONSORING EDITOR **Alice Harra**
DIRECTOR OF DEVELOPMENT **Sarah Wood**
DEVELOPMENTAL EDITOR **Jenae Grossart**
EDITORIAL COORDINATOR **Vincent Bradshaw**
SENIOR MARKETING MANAGER **Keari Green**
LEAD MEDIA PRODUCER **Damian Moshak**
DIGITAL DEVELOPMENTAL EDITOR **Kevin White**
DIRECTOR, EDITING/DESIGN/PRODUCTION **Jess Ann Kosic**
PROJECT MANAGER **Jean R. Starr**
DIGITAL PRODUCTION MANAGER **Janean A. Utley**
SENIOR DESIGNER **Anna Kinigakis**
SENIOR PHOTO RESEARCH COORDINATOR **Lori Kramer**
DIGITAL PRODUCTION COORDINATOR **Brent dela Cruz**
TYPEFACE **11/13 Minion Pro**
EDITORIAL SERVICES **Agate Publishing, Inc.**
PRINTER **World Color Press Inc.**
COVER CREDITS **Front cover: Handshake, © White Packert/ Getty Images; Flash drives, © Photodisc/Getty Images; Currency, © Stockbyte/PunchStock Back cover: Credit cards, © Mark Viker/Getty Images Recycle, © Geir Pettersen/Getty Images**
CREDITS **The credits section for this book begins on page 423 and is considered an extension of the copyright page.**

AUTHOR

Amit J. Shah, DBA *Frostburg State University*

CAREER BOARD CONTRIBUTORS

Robert J. Abadie, Jr. *National College*
Laura Portolese Dias, DBA *Shoreline Community College*
Frances R. Green *Everest University*
Diane A. Hagan *Ohio Business College*
Linda A. Rose, Ph.D. *Westwood College*
Scott T. Warman, MSB *ECPI Technical College*

Library of Congress Cataloging in Publication Data

Library of Congress Control Number: 2009940089

The Internet addresses listed in the text were accurate at the time of publication. The inclusion of a Web site does not indicate an endorsement by the authors or McGraw-Hill, and McGraw-Hill does not guarantee the accuracy of the information presented at these sites.

www.mhhe.com

Ch. 3
ENTREPRENEURSHIP
AND STARTING A
SMALL BUSINESSS

BUSINESS IN
GLOBAL MARKETS

Ch. 11

Ch. 5 >
HUMAN
RESOURCE
MANAGEMENT

**Bonus
Chapter**
MANAGING YOUR
FINANCES

BusinessNow

BRIEF TABLE OF CONTENTS

9 > Management: Functions and Styles 237

*Bonus Chapter >
Managing Your Finances 361

1

THE WORLD OF
BUSINESS
AND ITS ENVIRONMENTS

LEARNING OUTCOMES

After reading this chapter, you will be able to:

1. Define and explain business and its basic terms.
2. Explain the evolution of business in the United States.
3. Describe different classifications of business.
4. Describe the five elements of the business environment.
5. Understand your options in the world of business in the future.

DARRYL ALEXANDER AND MEMPHIS BEST BBQ

Have you ever thought about starting a company to provide a product or service? Have you ever wondered how a business begins? How it grows?

As he began to contemplate his future following a distinguished career as a U.S. Marine, Darryl Alexander became increasingly curious about the answers to these questions. For years, he had dreamed of owning a barbecue restaurant in his adopted new home of Buckeye, Arizona.

Alexander began by writing down a few notes about his business plan. He then met with Jim Batz of SCORE, a nonprofit affiliate of the U.S. Small Business Administration (SBA) that is "dedicated to educating entrepreneurs and the formation, growth, and success of small business nationwide."[1] Batz offered free business mentoring services and shared his own ideas.

Batz began by asking Alexander many questions about his business proposal—questions to which Alexander quickly discovered he had no answers. "[Batz] felt my passion and sincerity, but he was very frank in telling me that I was way off-base," Alexander remarked. "He started 'red-inking' my notes and asking questions that I couldn't answer."[2]

In order to learn more about business, Alexander enrolled in a 10-week business course at a community college and continued to discuss his evolving strategies for pricing, expenses, site location, and other foundations of the business plan with Batz. Batz helped Alexander develop a sound strategy and a business plan.

Once Alexander finished his plan, he shared it with Batz, who encouraged him to take the next step approaching a bank for a loan. His hard work paid off: the bank approved a $250,000 SBA-backed loan, which left him ready to find just the right location for his restaurant. He preferred to buy a home and convert it into a restaurant, but no such sites were available. Alexander then looked into the possibility of building from scratch, but no contractor would take on the job.

Needless to say, Alexander was frustrated. An acquaintance who happened to be a member of Buckeye's Chamber of Commerce recommended a vacant restaurant location in downtown Buckeye. As soon as Alexander saw it, he knew the site was perfect.[3]

Memphis Best BBQ opened in 2007. After a full year in business, the restaurant exceeded Alexander's first-year revenue projections. Darryl Alexander understands the environment in which he operates his business. He understands the basic business terms and models, and he has successfully put them to use. He continues to learn each day, and sees endless possibilities for his business.

Questions

1. What do you think were some of the questions Batz asked Alexander that he couldn't answer?
2. Why was the location of his restaurant so important to Alexander?
3. What should Alexander do to either grow his business or continue to stay in business during tough economic times?
4. What resources within your community could assist you in starting your own business?

Sources: Adapted from "Success Stories," SCORE, http://www.score.org/success_memphis_bbq.html (accessed June 25, 2009), and the Memphis Best BBQ Web site, http://www.bestbbqofmemphis.com/history.php (accessed June 25, 2009).

As You READ >>

- How has business evolved, and in what areas are jobs plentiful today?
- How do external environment factors affect business?
- Why should you study business?

Memphis Best BBQ is an excellent example of a successful business in action. Business owners, whether they do business in New York City or Buckeye, Arizona, must have business plans and an awareness of the environmental factors that affect their business operations. Understanding these factors allows their businesses to be more agile and able to adapt to changes based on the needs of their customers and their changing environmental conditions.

>> What Is Business?

Welcome to the dynamic and exciting world of business. Examples of businesses are around us everywhere, such as a McDonald's franchise on a highway exit, a mom-and-pop corner grocery store, a nationwide chain of medical testing laboratories, or a local auto repair shop. Businesses vary in size, but large or small, they all have a significant effect on our economy and our lives.

DEFINING BUSINESS

A **business** is a person, partnership, or corporation that seeks to provide goods and services to others at a profit. **Goods** are tangible products (i.e., products that can be touched), such as cameras, food, computers, clothing, and cars. Businesses that provide goods are considered to be in the manufacturing sector of the economy. **Services** are intangible products (i.e., products that cannot be touched), such as education, insurance, and travel. Businesses that provide services are considered to be in the service sector of the economy. By purchasing the goods and services we need and want, we all participate in business.

Businesses allow people to achieve their goals in life and fulfill their dreams, including the opportunity to become wealthy. If you are willing to be an **entrepreneur** and start your own business, it could happen to you. Entrepreneurs are always on the lookout for an acceptable **return on investment (ROI)**, which is the money gained from taking on a business risk. In addition to money, investment of time is also an important consideration for entrepreneurs.

One such entrepreneur is Michael Dell, founder and chief executive officer (CEO) of Dell, Inc., a computer manufacturing company. Dell started his business in 1984 out of his dorm room with a $1,000 investment. He is now one of the richest people in America, with an estimated net worth of more than $17 billion.[5]

But most people who enter the business world have

Business A person, partnership, or corporation that seeks to provide goods and services to others at a profit.

Goods Tangible products, such as cameras, food, computers, clothing, and cars.

Services Intangible products, such as education, insurance, and travel.

Entrepreneur A person who risks time and money to start and manage a business.

Return on investment (ROI) The money gained from taking on a business risk.

Michael Dell is a success, but Bill Gates, who started the computer software giant Microsoft, has been even more successful. He is one of the richest people in the world and was estimated to be worth about $40 billion in 2008. Gates's business success has allowed him to focus on giving back. Gates is pictured here with his wife, Melinda, with whom he manages the Bill and Melinda Gates Foundation, and a group of Moroccan children who participated in the foundation's vaccination program for children in developing nations.[6]

Real World Apps

Jennifer Pierce is going to college to earn a degree in medical administration, and an Introduction to Business class is part of her degree's curriculum. The evening before the first day of her Intro to Business class, she reflects for a moment and wonders why she needs a business course, anyway. After all, she wants a career in hospital administration, and she won't be making or selling anything.

"The medical field isn't as fast-paced as the business world," Jennifer thinks. "Hospitals don't care about profits instead, they choose to focus on helping people."

The next day, as Jennifer participates in the class discussion, she slowly begins to realize that she may have been wrong. She learns that a business can either produce a tangible product or an intangible service, such as health care. In fact, as she begins to read the first chapter of her text later that evening, she discovers that her career in medical administration will be in the service sector of business, which makes up roughly 70 percent of the economy of the United States!

more modest—and realistic—goals, like supporting their families and funding their children's education. You can start your own business or work for an existing business and still meet these goals.

UNDERSTANDING BASIC BUSINESS TERMS

In the business world, there are probably many terms you're already familiar with. There are probably quite a few you'll learn about here that will be new to you. As you read this book, you will see key terms that appear in bold throughout the text. Their definitions are provided in the margins and in the back of the book to help reinforce their meaning. Understanding

these key terms will help you excel in the business world. We'll start with some of the most basic business terms in the pages that follow.

Put yourself in the entrepreneurial hot seat for a moment. If you were to start a part-time business selling hot dogs and sodas (let's call your business Hearty Hot Dogs), one of your first considerations would be to think about how much money you would earn from selling your hot dogs and sodas and how much money you'd have to spend to buy the goods and services necessary to provide those hot dogs and sodas.

For example, you'll have to buy or rent a cart or a stand. You'll also have to buy sodas, napkins, straws, buns, hot dogs, and condiments, and you'll have to hire someone to help you sell or prepare the hot dogs (since you won't be able to be there all the time). In addition, there are taxes to be paid on your sales. After you've accounted for all these costs—paid your employee and yourself for your time; purchased the supplies, food, and beverages; paid the rent on the cart; and paid the taxes due on your sales—any money you've got left over is yours to keep.

Therefore, **revenue**, which is also known as sales, is the *total* amount of money a business takes in during a given period as a result of selling its goods or services. **Expenses** are the costs of purchasing the goods and services that are needed to operate a business. **Profit**, which is also known as net income, is the amount of money a business earns beyond what it spends for goods, services, salaries, and other expenses. Keep in mind that profit is over and above the money you pay yourself in salary and the government for taxes. You may use your profits to rent or buy a second cart or hire more employees. As your business grows, you may eventually have several carts employing dozens of workers. Figure 1.1 shows a simple example of revenue, expenses, and profit for Hearty Hot Dogs.

A **loss** occurs when a business's expenses exceed its revenues. In the previous example, if you end up spending more than $4,000 for hot dogs, cart rental fees, salaries, and other expenses, Hearty Hot Dogs will incur a loss. If a business continually suffers losses, it will likely have to close. That's why risk is a factor. Starting a business always involves some degree of

> **Revenue** The total amount of money a business takes in during a given period as a result of selling its goods or services.
>
> **Expenses** The costs of purchasing the goods and services that are needed to operate a business.
>
> **Profit** The amount of money a business earns above and beyond what it spends for goods, services, salaries, and other expenses.

Figure 1.1 Hearty Hot Dogs's Revenue, Expense, and Profit Statement

Revenue Breakdown

Hot dog sales	$3,000
Soda sales	1,000
Total revenue (all sales):	$4,000

Expense Breakdown

Cost of hot dogs	$155
Cost of buns	165
Cost of condiments	100
Cost of soda	250
Cost of employee's salary	450
Cost of your salary	1,000
Cost of cart rental	900
Total expenses (all costs):	**$3,020**
Before-tax profit ($4,000 − $3,020)	$980
Total taxes:	196
Total after-tax profit (net income):	**$784**

Loss When a business's expenses are more than its revenues.

Risk The chance an individual or organization takes of losing time and money on a business that may not prove profitable.

risk, which is the chance an individual or organization takes of losing time and money on a business that may not prove profitable. Even among companies that are profitable, not all are profitable at the same level.

As Apple has found (see photo and caption below), sometimes risk taking pays off, and sometimes it doesn't. The Colgate–Palmolive Company, manufacturer of Colgate toothpaste, decided to extend its brand to launch a line of frozen dinners called Colgate's Kitchen Entrées. If the name Colgate makes you think first of toothpaste, wouldn't you be concerned that your chicken dinner might taste refreshingly minty? Needless to say, Colgate's Kitchen Entrées did not take off.[10]

Forbes magazine publisher Steve Forbes once remarked, "Risk taking is the crucial element for improving our standard of living."[12] The term **standard of living** refers to the amount of goods and services people can buy with the money they have. For example, the United States has long been known for having one of the highest standards of living in the world. However, the recession that began in 2008 led many Americans to dramatically alter their spending habits—because their respective standards of living had been reduced.[13]

If you are contemplating starting your own business, you must first do a great deal of research—for example, interviewing other businesspeople in the same industry, reading business publications, or talking to customers—to find the balance of risk and profit that's right for you. In order to decide what's right for you, you must calculate the risks

Standard of living The amount of goods and services people can buy with the money they have.

In some cases, companies that take on the most risk make the most profit. For example, Apple, Inc., the manufacturer of iMac and MacBook computers, iPods, and iPhones, has launched many failed products, including its "hockey puck" style mouse and the Apple Newton (shown), a personal digital assistant (PDA) device introduced in 1993.[8] However, Apple's failures are a clear indication of the company's willingness to take risks and in return reap huge rewards when a product is successful—like the iPod.[9]

[BUS] connections

1. Define business and risk. Are you willing to take risks in order to own your own business? Why or why not?
2. Describe the differences between revenue and profit and how the two are related.
3. What factors do you think can contribute to a high standard of living? A low standard of living?

and potential rewards of each decision. Different individuals have different tolerances for risk. Remember, it's possible to turn something you love doing into a real business. Interests in photography or working on cars could become business ventures like a photo studio or an auto repair shop.

>> The Evolution of Business in America

Over the years, businesses in the United States have become very productive. Advances in technology, transportation, and global competition have affected businesses' abilities to become or remain competitive and profitable; in turn, these factors have also affected the future employment and income levels of these businesses—and that affects you as a future employee or owner of a business. Where will the best jobs be when you graduate? The following section will briefly explore the progress of business in the U.S. economy.

PROGRESS IN THE AGRICULTURAL INDUSTRIES

Before the 1700s, most people were self-sustaining, meaning that they raised their own food and made their own clothing. In rural areas, families produced as much food and clothing as they could, and any excess was traded in exchange for items they could not produce themselves. The Industrial Revolution, which took place from the late 1700s to the mid-1800s in Western cultures, changed all that by mechanizing much of the necessary labor of farming and food and clothing production. As a result, farmers were able to produce much more than they needed to sustain themselves, and food and clothing became more widely available for purchase.[15] Today, the agricultural industry provides food for most of the world, and relatively few people in developed countries produce their own food or clothing.

With advances in technology, the modern farming industry has become so efficient that the number of farmers has dropped from about 33 percent of the population to less than 2 percent in the United States.[16] However, the loss of farm workers over the past century is not a negative sign for the economy overall, since it means that U.S. agricultural workers are among the most productive in the world. Technology is expected to continue to play an important role in the agricultural industry. For example, development of genetically modified grains and seeds and biofuels—both of which fall under the category of grains and oilseeds—dominate modern farming, as you can see in Figure 1.2, and they will continue to be growth industries in the coming years.[17]

Entrepreneur Kenny Burts decided to take a risk and make a business out of something he loved. For years, Burts had enjoyed making key lime pies for his friends and family. After being told countless times that his pies were every bit as good as pies sold in bakeries and restaurants, Burts did his own research into starting a business and decided to take the plunge in 1989. By 2007, Burts's company, Kenny's Great Pies, Inc., was producing approximately 1,500 pies per day and expected to hit an annual sales level of about $2 million.[14]

1-800-Flowers.com CEO Jim McCann has found success when taking risks with product diversification. Diversifying his company's product line has allowed McCann to meet the ever-changing needs of his customers. Traditionally, the company had focused on selling flower arrangements for special occasions. The company recognized a new market for occasions where flowers were an inappropriate choice, so it decided to market other gift items, such as tins of flavored popcorn and balloons. Expanding the company's product line was a risk, because there was no guarantee that buyers would be receptive to the company's new products. However, the risk has proven beneficial to the company—in 2008, the company made an additional $919 million in revenue over the previous year.[11]

Figure 1.2 Changes in Sales by Agricultural Industry, from 2002 to 2007

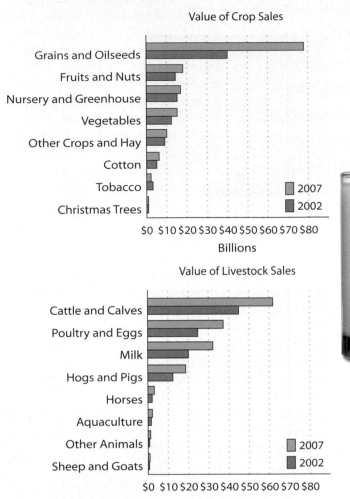

Value of Crop Sales

- Grains and Oilseeds
- Fruits and Nuts
- Nursery and Greenhouse
- Vegetables
- Other Crops and Hay
- Cotton
- Tobacco
- Christmas Trees

■ 2007
■ 2002

$0 $10 $20 $30 $40 $50 $60 $70 $80
Billions

Value of Livestock Sales

- Cattle and Calves
- Poultry and Eggs
- Milk
- Hogs and Pigs
- Horses
- Aquaculture
- Other Animals
- Sheep and Goats

■ 2007
■ 2002

$0 $10 $20 $30 $40 $50 $60 $70 $80

Source: U.S. Department of Agriculture, *2007 Census of Agriculture: Farm Numbers,* http://www.agcensus.usda.gov/Publications/2007/Online_Highlights/Fact_Sheets/economics.pdf (accessed June 9, 2009).

PROGRESS IN THE MANUFACTURING INDUSTRIES

Many farmers who lost their jobs went to work in factories, but like farming, the manufacturing industry has used technology to become more productive. As technology has increased, many of the jobs those farmers moved into in the industrial sector have been eliminated as well, and those workers have had to transition yet again, this time to jobs in the service sector.[19] As of May 2009, there were about 12 million individuals employed by the manufacturing industry, compared with 17.3 million in May 1999.[20] The loss to society is minimal if the wealth created by increased productivity and efficiency creates new jobs elsewhere—and that's exactly what has happened over the past 50 years.

The U.S. economy is increasingly shifting from a manufacturing economy to a service- and knowledge-based economy. In the past, the dominant industries in the United States produced goods, such as steel, cars, machine tools, clothing, and so on. Today, many of the dominant industries are focused on services, such as health care, telecommunications, entertainment, and financial consulting.

In their ever-increasing quest to produce goods at a lower cost, many U.S.-based manufacturers have moved their factories to countries where labor and other factors of production are cheaper or suffered the consequences, such as a loss in market share to other businesses that are either more innovative or more resourceful.

The modern automotive industry offers a prime example. In the 1950s, General Motors (GM) was the world's largest automaker. GM's then-president Charles Wilson once stated, "What's good for General Motors is good for America."[22] Things have changed drastically since then: in the midst of a massive recession in June 2009, GM filed for bankruptcy. As a result, tens of thousands of GM employees lost their jobs, helping the national unemployment rate skyrocket to 9.4 percent (that's 14.5 million people out of work).[23] As a result of GM's bankruptcy, approximately 3 million other Americans who worked in the auto industry lost their jobs or will lose them in the future as more companies turn to **outsourcing**.[24] In 2008, for the first time in the 78 years GM had existed, the Japanese automaker Toyota beat GM in global sales.[25]

Outsourcing Assigning various functions, such as accounting, production, security, maintenance, and legal work, to outside organizations.

In 2008, the agricultural industry generated close to $300 billion in sales and there were 2.2 million farms in the United States.[18]

The other side of the outsourcing coin is *insourcing*. Many foreign companies are setting up design and production facilities here in the United States. For example, Korea-based Hyundai operates design and engineering headquarters in Detroit, Michigan, and produces cars in Montgomery, Alabama. Japanese automakers Honda and Toyota have been producing cars in the United States for years. Insourcing creates many new U.S. jobs and helps offset those being outsourced.

PROGRESS IN THE SERVICE INDUSTRIES

Many workers who have lost their jobs to technological advances or outsourcing in the manufacturing sector have been able to find jobs in the service industry. In recent times, service-sector growth has slowed, but it remains the largest growth area in the U.S. economy.[26]

Today, service industries make up nearly 70 percent of the country's economic activity, with wholesale and retail trade as the leading areas in the service sector.[27] Chances are very high that you may work in such a job at some point in your career. As Figure 1.3 shows, during the period from 2006 through 2016, it is estimated that a total of 15.7 million new jobs will be created in the service sector.[28]

Figure 1.3 Changes in the Service Sector of the U.S. Economy

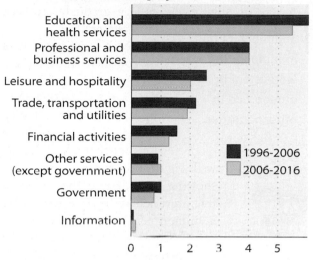

Numeric change in wage and salary employment, service-providing industry division, 1996-2006 and projected 2006-2016

Legend: 1996-2006, 2006-2016

Categories (top to bottom): Education and health services; Professional and business services; Leisure and hospitality; Trade, transportation and utilities; Financial activities; Other services (except government); Government; Information

Horizontal axis: 0 1 2 3 4 5

Source: *Occupational Outlook Handbook 2008–2009*, Bureau of Labor Statistics, U.S. Department of Labor, http://www.bls.gov/oco/oco2003.htm (accessed June 10, 2009).

Figure 1.4 What Is the Service Sector?

There's much talk about the service sector, but few discussions actually list what it includes. Here's a representative list of services as classified by the government:

LODGING SERVICES
Hotels, rooming houses, and other lodging places
Sporting and recreation camps
Trailer parks and camp sites for transients

PERSONAL SERVICES
Laundries
Linen supply
Diaper service
Carpet cleaning
Photographic studios
Health clubs
Child care
Shoe repair
Funeral homes
Tax preparation
Beauty shops

BUSINESS SERVICES
Accounting
Ad agencies
Collection agencies
Commercial photography
Commercial art
Stenographic services
Window cleaning
Consulting
Equipment rental
Exterminating
Employment agencies
Computer programming
Research and development labs
Management services
Public relations
Detective agencies
Interior design
Web design

FINANCIAL SERVICES
Banking
Insurance
Real estate agencies
Investment firms (brokers)

AMUSEMENT AND RECREATION SERVICES
Dance halls
Symphony orchestras
Pool halls
Bowling alleys
Fairs
Botanical gardens
Video rentals
Racetracks
Golf courses
Amusement parks
Carnivals
Ice skating rinks
Circuses
Infotainment

HEALTH SERVICES
Medical Assistants
Nurses
Chiropractors
Nursery care
Medical labs
Dental labs

LEGAL SERVICES

EDUCATIONAL SERVICES
Libraries
Schools
Computer schools

SOCIAL SERVICES
Child care
Job training
Family services

AUTOMOTIVE REPAIR SERVICES AND GARAGES
Auto rental
Truck rental
Parking lots
Paint shops
Tire retreading
Exhaust system shops
Car washes
Transmission repair

The U.S. economy is increasingly shifting from a manufacturing economy to a service- and knowledge-based economy, and much of the manufacturing work is being outsourced to other countries.

Study Alert

Figure 1.4 lists many service-sector jobs; look it over to see where the careers of the future are likely to be. Retailers, such as Kohl's and Target, are leaders in the service sector and are good places for college graduates to seek employment.

Here's some good news to consider: Today, there are more job openings in the service sector than in the goods-producing sector, and most of those jobs offer higher pay as well. Figure 1.5 illustrates this point, showing that despite the recession that prevailed at the time, there were 3 million U.S.-based job vacancies in February 2009. More than 96 percent of these openings were in the service sector.[29] In order to take advantage of these and similar opportunities for your own career, focus on learning more about—and then obtaining—the education or training they require.

A major advancement in the manufacturing industry has been the ability to mass-produce goods. In 1913, Henry Ford built a conveyor belt that allowed him to pull cars down an assembly line, thus eliminating the need for employees to move from one car assembly to another. By bringing the cars to the employees rather than the other way around, Ford was able to manufacture automobiles at a much faster rate. He achieved a 90 percent gain in productivity, which allowed him to increase worker wages, decrease the length of the workday, and cut the price of his vehicles.[21]

Figure 1.5 Jobs Employers Can't Fill

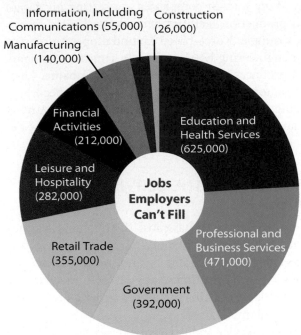

- Information, Including Communications (55,000)
- Construction (26,000)
- Manufacturing (140,000)
- Financial Activities (212,000)
- Education and Health Services (625,000)
- Leisure and Hospitality (282,000)
- **Jobs Employers Can't Fill**
- Retail Trade (355,000)
- Professional and Business Services (471,000)
- Government (392,000)

Source: Bureau of Labor Statistics

[BUS] connections

1. In your opinion, what is the biggest change in the business world that has been discussed in this section? What other changes are occurring?
2. Agriculture is no longer a viable industry as a business. Do you agree or disagree with this statement? Explain your response.
3. Among the service-sector jobs listed in Figure 1.4, which would be the top three you'd prefer to have, and why?

>> The Types of Business

Businesses can be classified under various categories. The following sections will discuss classifications by size, profit motive, and sector (such as manufacturing or service).

MICROENTERPRISES, SMEs, AND LARGE BUSINESSES

Businesses are often classified according to their size. When determining a particular business's size, the number of its employees is a primary criterion. Some commonly known descriptors are microenterprises, small and medium-sized businesses or enterprises (known as SMEs), and large businesses.

Microenterprises

Microenterprises, or microbusinesses, are typically very small. They are usually owned by a single individual and may be home- or farm-based or occupy a small storefront. Most have fewer than five employees.[30] Microenterprises comprise more than half of all small businesses in the United States today. As you might think, most businesses begin as microenterprises.

Small and Medium-Sized Enterprises

Of course, the term "small business" applies to microenterprises, but its definition varies widely, with some claiming that the term "small business" could be applied to any company with fewer than 100 employees, and others including businesses with fewer than 500 employees.[31] Katz and Green define **small and medium-sized enterprises** as follows: small enterprises employ 50 or fewer people and are managed by their owners on a day-to-day basis, and medium-sized enterprises have 51 to 500 employees.[32]

> **Small and medium-sized enterprises** Small enterprises employ 50 or fewer people and are managed by their owners on a day-to-day basis, and medium-sized enterprises have 51 to 500 employees.

If you're wondering whether small businesses are really important to the U.S. economy, consider the following facts. According to the SBA, small firms[33]

- Represent 99.7 percent of all employer firms

- Employ half of all employees in the private sector

- Are responsible for 45 percent of the total U.S. private payroll

- Have generated 60 percent to 80 percent of net new jobs annually over the last decade

- Are 53 percent home-based and 3 percent franchise-based

- Comprise 97 percent of all exporters

Figure 1.6 The Top Five Fastest-Growing Entrepreneurial Firms, 2008

Rank	Name	Location	Sales (in millions)*	No. of full-time employees**
1	Simply Self Storage	Orlando, FL	$109.1	486
2	Blue Star Energy Services	Chicago, IL	171.5	61
3	Bills.com	San Mateo, CA	43.5	320
4	HemCon Medical Technologies	Portland, OR	39.5	110
5	Global Water Resources	Phoenix, AZ	26.0	106

*2008 figures from *Entrepreneur*; **2009 figures from finance.yahoo.com.

As you can see, small businesses play a very large role in the U.S.'s economic and entrepreneurial vitality. Also, remember that microbusinesses are counted as part of these small businesses. Figure 1.6 shows the top five fastest-growing entrepreneurial companies in America in 2008, according to *Entrepreneur* magazine.[34]

Many microenterprises are home-based, particularly in their first years of operation.

Figure 1.7 The Top Five Largest U.S. Businesses, 2008

Rank	Name	Location	Sales (in millions)*	No. of full-time employees**
1	ExxonMobil	Irving, TX	$442,851	104,700
2	Walmart Stores	Bentonville, AR	405,607	2,100,000
3	Chevron	San Ramon, CA	263,159	67,000
4	ConocoPhillips	Houston, TX	230,764	33,800
5	General Electric	Fairfield, CT	183,207	323,000

*2008 figures from *Fortune*; **2009 figures from finance.yahoo.com.

As you can see from the numbers of employees in Figure 1.6, all of these companies would be classified as medium-sized enterprises. However, all five of the companies are relatively new, and four of them started with only two employees. Thus, the majority began as microenterprises.

Large Businesses

As firms grow in size, they become classified as large businesses by virtue of their number of employees (more than 500). Large businesses may have a domestic (meaning that they operate only in their home countries) or a global (operating in multiple countries) market presence. Every year, *Fortune* magazine publishes a list of the 500 largest U.S. corporations by sales. Figure 1.7 shows *Fortune*'s list of the five largest U.S. corporations in 2008, including their annual sales volume and number of employees.[35] By any measure, these businesses are very large, and all of them operate globally.

PROFIT MOTIVE: FOR-PROFIT AND NONPROFIT ORGANIZATIONS

Organizations are often classified according to their profit motive. By definition, **for-profit organizations** are motivated to earn profits; organizations that are not driven to garner profits are classified as nonprofit organizations. In many cases, **nonprofit organizations** do strive for financial gains, but these gains are used to finance the stated social or educational goals of the organization.[36] Despite their efforts to satisfy all their **stakeholders** (any people or organizations who stand to gain or lose from the activities of a business), for-profit businesses cannot provide all that is needed to fully benefit the communities in which they operate. Nonprofit organizations, such as public schools, civic associations, and charities, step in to make major contributions to the welfare of society.

The Howard Hughes Medical Institute (HHMI), a good example of a nonprofit organization in action, is committed to improving the human condition. This organization conducts biomedical research and provides the means necessary, such as education, to help develop some of the nation's most gifted researchers. HHMI "commits almost $700 million a year for research and distributes more than $80 million in grant support for science education."[37]

MANUFACTURING AND SERVICE BUSINESSES

Sometimes businesses are classified as operating in a manufacturing or a service industry. As you learned earlier in the chapter, manufacturing firms produce tangible products. One such manufacturer is HemCon Medical Technologies, which was identified by *Entrepreneur* magazine as one of the fastest-growing businesses in the country (see Figure 1.6). HemCon is a medical device manufacturer that creates innovative dressings for the acute wound care market. Much of the company's rapid growth has been due to contracts it has with the U.S. Army to supply dressings for soldiers wounded in the Iraq and Afghanistan wars.[38]

Likewise, service businesses produce intangible products, like counseling, banking, or auto repairs.

For-profit organizations Organizations that are motivated to earn profits.

Nonprofit organizations Organizations that are not driven to garner profits.

Stakeholders Any people or organizations who stand to gain or lose from the activities of a business.

Financial counseling is just one of the many service businesses that flourish in the U.S. economy today.

Bills.com, which was also recognized by *Entrepreneur* magazine, is a service business that provides a free online portal for consumers who wish to learn about complex personal finance issues and comparison shop for products and services. The company also manages consumer debt.[39]

>> The Business Environment

The business environment consists of the surrounding factors that either help or hinder the development of businesses. Failing to understand or ignoring these factors is like flying an airplane without a weather report, clearance to take off and land, or an understanding of how to navigate. Large businesses have plenty of resources for monitoring these external and internal forces, but most of the businesses in the United States are small. In order to be successful, these businesses must be acutely aware of the environments in which they operate.

A small business owner or manager can keep abreast of changes in the business environment by paying close attention to local and world news and reading business publications—particularly ones that are specific to her industry. Businesspeople who are unaware of the factors in the business environment will not be as successful. Figure 1.8 shows the five elements of the business environment:

1. The economic environment and legal environment
2. The technological environment
3. The competitive environment
4. The social environment
5. The global environment

Figure 1.8 Today's Dynamic Business Environment

GLOBAL BUSINESS ENVIRONMENT

The Economic and Legal Environment
1. Unemployment & interest rates
2. Laws & regulations
3. Freedom of ownership
4. Tradable currency
5. Elimination of corruption

The Technological Environment
1. Information technology
2. Databases
3. Bar codes
4. The Internet
5. Social networking

BUSINESS GROWTH AND JOB CREATION

The Competitive Environment
1. Customer service
2. Value
3. Employee empowerment

The Social Environment
1. Diversity
2. Demographic changes
3. Family changes

GLOBAL COMPETITION   FREE TRADE   THE QUALITY IMPERATIVE

THE ECONOMIC AND LEGAL ENVIRONMENT

Businesses do not operate in a vacuum. Instead, they must operate within a framework of laws and economic forces. People are willing to start and operate their businesses if they believe that they can make a decent living from it and achieve their goals—and that the risks they will take on are not insurmountable. Governments can encourage business development in many ways, including providing tax incentives, establishing a tradable currency, permitting private ownership of business, minimizing corruption, and loosening restrictions on commerce.

The business environment consists of the surrounding factors that either help or hinder the development of businesses. The five elements of the business environment are the economic and legal environment, the technological environment, the competitive environment, the social environment, and the global environment.

Study Alert

There are quite a few economic elements and laws that affect businesses (see Figure 1.9); some key variables that business owners and managers must understand and monitor include the unemployment rate, job outlook, the rate of inflation, interest rates, and availability of credit.

Figure 1.9 The Economic and Legal Environment

The Economic and Legal Environment
1. Unemployment & interest rates
2. Laws & regulations
3. Freedom of ownership
4. Tradable currency
5. Elimination of corruption

For example, in 2009, the "equal-opportunity recession," as it was called by *Fortune* magazine, forced its way into every aspect of the U.S. economy.[40] The unemployment rate spiraled upward, and people in all types of industries faced the possibility of job loss. At that time, the job outlook had reached its lowest point since it was first tracked in December 2000. Interest rates hit at an all-time low, enabling people and businesses to borrow money at a lower cost—but at the same time, bankers became more hesitant to lend than they had been in years. As banks became reluctant to issue loans, many companies considered resorting to credit cards. Sensing an opportunity, credit companies began to raise interest rates on credit cards, with some reaching as high as 30 percent.[41] Conditions such as these make it difficult for business owners to start or expand their businesses. If they are unable to obtain credit, they're less likely to be able to hire employees, ramp up product development, or otherwise operate the business successfully.

Laws and Regulations

Laws and regulations at all levels, including federal, state, county, and city, affect businesses because they determine what organizations can and cannot do. Some of the key legislations that must be enforced when operating a business include:

- *Licenses and permit regulations.* All businesses require licenses and permits from different governmental agencies in order to operate. A local restaurant will need a business license from its county government, license/permit from the local health department, and registration with the state as well as employer and tax ID numbers from the federal government.

- *Laws to protect workers.* Laws such as the Equal Pay Act, minimum wage regulations at federal and state levels, and the laws that led to the establishment of the Occupational Health and Safety Administration (OSHA) exist to protect the rights of employees. Under OSHA law, for example, employers must provide a workplace free from serious recognized hazards.

- *Contract laws.* A **contract** is a legally enforceable agreement between two or more parties. Contracts attempt to resolve issues regarding what constitutes a legally binding agreement.

- *Bankruptcy laws.* **Bankruptcy** is the legal process by which an individual or business unable to meet financial obligations can seek court protection under these laws and can be relieved of those debts by a court. In 2008, more than 1 million people filed for bankruptcy.[42]

> **Contract** A legally enforceable agreement between two or more parties.
>
> **Bankruptcy** The legal process by which an individual or business unable to meet financial obligations can seek court protection under these laws and can be relieved of those debts by a court.

- *Tax laws.* Government gets its money from taxing individuals and businesses. In addition to income and sales taxes, there may be consumption taxes, inheritance taxes, value-added taxes, and property taxes, just to name a few. For example, in the United States, tobacco products are heavily taxed, and as of April 2009, at least 25 states proposed raising sales taxes on tobacco even further.[43]

The quality of a state's tax system plays a big role in creation of an entrepreneurial business environment. According to the Tax Foundation's 2009 State Business Tax Climate Index, the states with the best business tax climate include Oregon, Montana, Wyoming, Nevada, South Dakota, Alaska, Texas, New Hampshire, Delaware, and Florida.[44] It's a safe bet that these states also lead the nation in entrepreneurial businesses.

What Can Government Do to Promote Business?

One way government can actively promote entrepreneurship is by allowing private ownership of businesses. In some countries, the government owns most businesses, so there is little incentive for people to work hard or create profit. All around the world today, many governments that owned most of their nations' businesses are creating wealth by selling those businesses to private individuals. For example, China has adopted a gradual approach to privatization, permitting only certain industries to become privately owned. On the other hand, Russia followed a "big bang" approach, permitting mass privatization of previously government-run businesses.[45] One of the best things governments of developing countries can do is to minimize the interference with the free exchange of goods and services.

Governments can also lessen the risks of entrepreneurship by passing laws that enable businesspeople to write contracts that are enforceable in court. The Uniform Commercial Code (UCC), for example, covers items like contracts and warranties. The lemon law that applies to vehicles is one example of the UCC. Under this law, a car can be defined as a lemon if it has serious problems that cannot be fixed, even after multiple attempts.[46] In countries that do not yet have such codes, the risks of starting a business are much greater.

A government can also establish a currency that is easily tradable in world markets, which means that you can buy and sell goods and services anywhere in the world using that currency. The U.S. dollar, for example, is a **tradable currency**. Figure 1.10 shows the five most tradable currencies in the world.[47]

> **Tradable currency** One country's money that is allowed to be exchanged for another country's money.

Figure 1.10 Top Five Most Tradable Currencies

1. U.S. dollar (USD)
2. European Union euro (EUR)
3. Japanese yen (JPY)
4. British pound (GBP)
5. Swiss franc (CHF)

Governments can also help businesses by minimizing corruption in business and in their own ranks. When most people

---

WHAT SHOULD MIKE DO?

Mike Ambrosino recently earned his degree in business. Shortly after graduation, Mike ran into his friend Sarah Viscardi, who owns a successful automobile dealership. Sarah told him about an open position at the dealership for a finance manager. Mike knew he would enjoy the challenges of the position and was confident that working for a growing dealership would be a smart career move. After being offered the job, he happily accepted. Once at the dealership, Mike quickly proved his ability as Sarah continued to expand her business. In time, she opened a second dealership and offered Mike the position of company controller.

Because of Sarah's reputation for honest deals and good customer service, her dealerships were respected by their stakeholders. However, increased competition from other dealers and a downturn in the economy caused Sarah's sales to fall, and the dealerships soon faced financial difficulties. Eventually, Sarah was forced to sell to a new owner, Greg Bartell. Greg immediately made radical changes in order to turn the business around.

In order to increase revenue, Greg made a number of decisions that Mike believed were ethically questionable. For example, if customers said they could not afford the dealership's "Tier One" warranty, which covered all repair costs, the sales people were required to aggressively encourage them to purchase a new "Tier Two" warranty, which covered few repairs. At the same time, Greg raised the prices of both levels of warranties. During an audit of some of the service department's paperwork, Mike also noticed that several jobs Greg had personally overseen seemed outrageously expensive—and Mike believed the work may not have been necessary at all.

ETHICAL ← → **DILEMMA**

In a tough economy, if you feel you have to lie to keep an important customer and you believe the customer will never know, what would you do?

QUESTIONS

1. Do you agree with Mike that these situations are ethically questionable? Why or why not?
2. What are Mike's options in this situation?
3. If you were Mike, what would you do?

think of corruption in business, they think of it as being a problem for large companies—but this is not always the case. Smaller businesses are just as prone to theft and corruption—for example, a convenience store where an employee steals money from the cash register or gives free food to her friends. When economic conditions worsen, corruption and fraud in business generally increase. In fact, between 2005 and 2008, the incidence of corporate fraud increased by 22 percent among a group of leading U.S. corporations.[48]

The **capitalist system** relies heavily on honesty, integrity, and high ethical standards. Failure to adhere to those fundamental standards can weaken the entire system, as the world discovered when scandals caused the worldwide economy to falter in 2001. The capitalist system is one in which the companies and businesses are owned by the citizens instead of the government. Given that a capitalist system relies on high ethical standards, it is easy to see the damage caused to the system by the poor moral and ethical behavior of some businesspeople.

> **Capitalist system** A system in which companies and businesses are owned by citizens instead of the government.

THE TECHNOLOGICAL ENVIRONMENT

Figure 1.11 The Technological Environment

The Technological Environment
1. Information technology
2. Databases
3. Bar codes
4. The Internet
5. Social networking

Since prehistoric times, humans have always felt the need to create tools to make their jobs easier. Businesses always have been affected and even transformed by technological developments. Various tools and machines developed throughout history have dramatically changed the business environment, but few technological changes have had a more compre-

hensive and lasting impact on businesses than the recent emergence of information technology, which includes computers, modems, the Internet, cell phones, and so on.

Chief among these developments is the Internet. Although many Internet firms failed in the early 2000s, the Internet is now a major force in business and will continue to be in the future.[49] Today, more than a billion people use computers to access the Internet, and another billion do so via their cell phones.[50] This section discusses particular issues and concerns that businesspeople face regarding technology.

Increased Productivity

When you think about technology, you might first think of fast computers or the latest cell phone. Technology has a much broader definition, as it includes everything from medical imaging devices to the various software programs that make business processes more *effective*, *efficient*, and *productive*. **Effectiveness** means producing the desired result, **efficiency** means producing goods using the least amount of **resources**, and **productivity** is the amount of output generated given a particular amount of an input (for instance, hours worked).

> **Effectiveness** Producing the desired results.
>
> **Efficiency** Producing goods using the least amount of resources.
>
> **Resource** An input used to produce a good.
>
> **Productivity** The amount of output generated given a particular amount of an input.

The more you can produce in any given period of time, the more valuable you are to companies. Tools and technology greatly improve productivity. For example, computer-aided design is used to automate many tasks that would take people much more time to accomplish in a more traditional manner. Architecture firms now use computer-aided design software to create drawings that were formerly done by hand. This innovation allows firms to deliver drawings much faster than ever before and makes alterations much easier to make.[51]

Technology affects people in all industries, including farming. Illinois farmer Bill Butler works land that has been in his family for several generations, but he has moved considerably beyond the pitchfork and plow his grandfather used. Butler relies on technological advances like global positioning system mapping and proprietary software that can analyze soil to produce more crops—and therefore make a higher profit.[52]

The costs of labor and productivity go hand in hand. Other countries may offer less expensive labor, but that labor is not necessarily as productive as domestic options may be. Likewise, increased productivity can result in labor shifts or job losses. As you learned earlier in the chapter, as machines that improve processes are invented, fewer human beings are needed to do the work. As these changes take place, businesses must evolve to adapt to the new challenges.

Making Buying and Selling Easier

A critical environmental change of interest to businesspeople is the growth of **e-commerce**, or the buying and selling of goods over the Internet.[53] There are two major types of e-commerce transactions: **business-to-consumer (B2C)** and **business-to-business (B2B)**. As important as the Internet has become to consumers, it has become even more important in the B2B market; in fact, its share of the total e-commerce market is five times that of B2C e-commerce.[54] While the potential of the B2C e-commerce market is measured in billions of dollars, B2B e-commerce is said to be measured in trillions.

E-commerce The buying and selling of goods over the Internet.

Business-to-consumer (B2C) A business that produces products to sell directly to the consumer.

Business-to-business (B2B) A business that produces products to sell to another business.

Just as is the case with traditional businesses, not every online business succeeds. Success comes to e-commerce businesses that offer quality products, good prices, great service, and a twist of innovation. Many companies, such as Walmart and Target, have combined their traditional brick-and-mortar operations with Internet sites in order to remain more competitive.

The video and DVD rental industry offers a great example of the impact of technology on their business model. Traditionally, Blockbuster Video operated storefronts, but its business model has been forced to evolve. Its competitor Netflix allows consumers to go online to rent and reserve movies, and recently it has begun to expand into online movie downloads.[55] Blockbuster was forced to compete in this new way; it has responded by shuttering many of its storefront locations.[56]

Technology has helped agricultural operations become more productive and has made farmers more efficient.

Companies use social networking sites like MySpace to communicate directly with consumers.

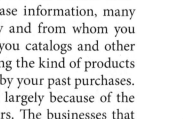

Redbox has used technology with a twist of innovation to carve a niche in this industry. Redbox, which is owned by change-machine giant Coinstar, offers customers $1 DVD rentals from its red boxes, which are conveniently located near the front of grocery and discount stores like Walmart. The boxes are the cutting-edge technology; with the swipe of a credit or debit card, customers can rent a DVD, which can be returned later to any Redbox. In 2008, Redbox's sales increased by 180 percent over the previous year—a great illustration of a company that's used technology to adapt to its changing environment.

Responsiveness to Customers

A major theme of this text is that businesses that are the most responsive to customer wants and needs will succeed. That realization points to one way in which even traditional retailers can use Internet technology. For example, businesses use bar codes to identify products you buy and their size, quantity, and color. The scanner at the checkout counter identifies the price but can also put all your purchase information into a **database**, an electronic storage file for information.

Database An electronic storage file for information.

Databases enable stores to carry only the merchandise their local population wants. But because companies routinely trade database information, many retailers know what you buy and from whom you buy it. Thus, they can send you catalogs and other direct-mail advertising offering the kind of products you might want, as indicated by your past purchases.

Businesses succeed or fail largely because of the way they treat their customers. The businesses that are most responsive to customer wants and needs are more likely to succeed; those that do not respond to their customers may be doomed to failure.

Social networking sites, such as MySpace, Facebook, and Twitter, are a great way for companies to become more aware of their customers' needs and wants and to subsequently respond to them. An industry that barely existed five years ago is now alive with individuals of all ages who are actively engaged in social networking, and traditional businesses are taking advantage of all this consumer activity on Web sites. For example, coffee giant Starbucks and fast-food chain Arby's have created Facebook pages to attract their "fans." The companies use this direct connection to their customers to send out coupons, announce menu changes, and otherwise maintain a day-to-day relationship.[57] Dell, the computer manufacturer, is among the first companies to prove it has profited from activity on Twitter. In June 2009, Dell announced that it made more than $3 million from its Twitter followers who clicked through its Twitter "tweets" to its Web site in order to make purchases.[58]

Social networking sites can even help you to land a job offer. The professional networking site LinkedIn is a great destination for connecting or reconnecting with friends, classmates, and colleagues. In addition, many companies use LinkedIn to recruit new employees. In the first three quarters of 2008, LinkedIn added approximately 1 million users each month. In the beginning of the fourth quarter—just as more and more people began to lose their jobs due to the ongoing recession—the site's activity exploded, with a million new members being added *every two weeks*.[59]

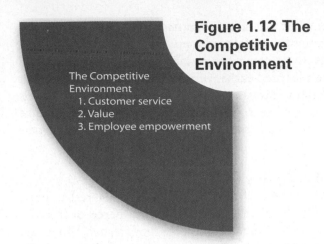

Figure 1.12 The Competitive Environment

The Competitive Environment
1. Customer service
2. Value
3. Employee empowerment

allow a company to stay competitive in world markets. Companies must offer both high-quality products and outstanding service at competitive prices—this is what is meant by the term **value**. Businesspeople must remain aware of what their competitors are doing *and* constantly improve their own products and processes in order to meet customer expectations. A businessperson who is acutely aware of his competitors and his customers is more likely to be successful. See Figure 1.12.

> **Value** Good quality at a fair price.

BUS connections

1. What types of technology exist today that didn't exist when you were in kindergarten? In high school?
2. How do you use the Internet to make purchasing decisions? Discuss your answer with some of your classmates. How does your response differ from theirs?
3. How many social networking sites do you belong to, and which of them do you prefer? What do you see as the benefits of these sites?

THE COMPETITIVE ENVIRONMENT

Competition among businesses has always existed. Some companies have found their own competitive edge by focusing on quality. Arguably, the goal for most companies is zero defects, or no mistakes at all, when making their products.[60]

Some companies, such as Motorola in the United States, have come close to meeting that standard. But simply making a high-quality product isn't enough to

Customer-Driven Organizations

Customers demand high quality and high value. For example, Southwest Airlines works very hard to ensure that its customers feel very comfortable when flying Southwest but especially when its flights are delayed. In 2009, *BusinessWeek* rated the following companies as the top five brands with the best customer service[61]:

- Online retailer Amazon.com
- USAA, which provides insurance, banking, and investment services to members of the military and their families
- Jaguar, an auto brand owned by Tata
- Lexus, an auto brand owned by Toyota
- Ritz-Carlton hotels, a hospitality brand owned by Marriott International

Each of these companies offers high value to its customers. Large and small businesses alike can succeed by providing outstanding customer service. Have you ever done business with any of these companies? What was your experience? Consider an auto repair shop that makes sure staff members know its customers by name, or a paralegal who makes sure he returns clients' phone calls the same day. Great customer service keeps customers coming back, time and again.

Employee Empowerment

In order to best meet the needs of customers, firms must give their frontline workers—office clerks, hotel front-desk staff, salespeople, people who take orders at fast-food drive-throughs, and so on—the responsibility, authority, freedom, training, and equipment they need to respond quickly to customer requests. They must also empower these staff members to make other decisions essential to producing quality goods and providing good service.

Empowerment Giving frontline workers the responsibility, authority, and freedom to respond quickly to customer requests.

To implement a policy of **empowerment**, managers must train their frontline people to make decisions without consulting managers. You'll learn more about empowerment and management in Chapters 9 and 10.

Clearly, one aspect of empowerment has been the elimination of levels of management and a redistribution of workload. Companies expect a lot more from lower-level workers than they have in the past. Because they have less supervision and more responsibility, workers need more education. Furthermore, empowered employees need to be treated as important, valuable partners in the business's efforts. Many companies have learned that it can take years to restructure an organization, so managers are willing to give up some authority and employees are willing to assume more responsibility.

THE SOCIAL ENVIRONMENT

The U.S. population is going through major changes that significantly affect how Americans live, where they live, what they buy, and how they spend their time. For ex-

Businesses big and small depend on returning customers; as a result, they should go out of their way to make customers feel as if they are number one. It is always more expensive to get a new customer than to retain an existing one.

Figure 1.13 The Social Environment

The Social Environment
1. Diversity
2. Demographic changes
3. Family changes

ample, many Americans are becoming increasingly concerned about the nutritional value of the foods they eat. As a result, Massachusetts now requires its fast-food restaurants to post nutritional data, including calorie counts, on their menus.[62] Businesspeople must be aware of these shifts in society in order to better meet the needs of their customers. See Figure 1.13. The good news is that the social environment is also a fun and interesting area to study.

Managing Diversity

Creating and managing **diversity** is an important concern in the business world. Diversity efforts now include seniors, disabled people, homosexuals, atheists, extroverts, introverts, married people, singles, and the devout. It also means dealing sensitively with workers and cultures from around the world. Legal and illegal immigrants have had a dramatic effect on many cities. Some local governments are making every effort to adapt, including changing signs, brochures, Web sites, and forms to include other languages. Has your city experienced such changes? What are some of the impacts you've noticed?

Diversity Broad differences among a group of people, including their ethnicity, sex, color, sexual orientation, body size, age, and so on.

In 2008, the minority portion of the U.S. population reached 34 percent—about 104.6 million individuals.[63] According to the U.S. Census Bureau, by the year 2050, non-Hispanic whites will be a slim majority, and the nation's Hispanic and Asian populations will triple over the next half-century. See Figure 1.14 for more about these trends.[64]

Businesses are concerned about having diverse workforces for two main reasons. First, a business can better serve customers if it has a diverse workforce. Second, a diverse work environment brings about fresh ideas and perspectives. Any person in the world of business will work with people of various ages, races, and backgrounds. Gaining a solid understanding of the importance of diversity now will result in a greater ability to work with others later on.

Figure 1.14 Diversity in America

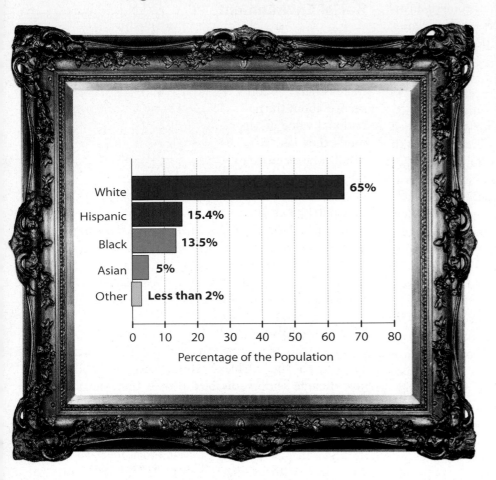

White — 65%
Hispanic — 15.4%
Black — 13.5%
Asian — 5%
Other — Less than 2%

Percentage of the Population

Source: Les Christie, "Census: U.S. Becoming More Diverse," *CNNMoney.com*, May 14, 2009, http://money.cnn.com/2009/05/14/real_estate/rising_minorities/index.htm (accessed June 9, 2009).

Managing diverse groups—whether their differences are rooted in race, sex, age, sexual orientation, country of origin, religion, or some other classification—can be difficult. It becomes even more difficult as businesses operate in different countries, and their managers must respond to all the cultural, political, and social issues that are specific to each country in which they operate. As a future manager or business owner, you will discover that hiring and retaining a diverse workforce is key to a successful business.

So which companies are the most diverse? A recent study identified PricewaterhouseCoopers, IBM Corp., Procter & Gamble, Cisco Systems, and PepsiCo as the most diversity-friendly companies in the nation. These global companies value diversity and actively work to combat oppression.[65]

The demographic group of people aged 45 to 64 is currently the richest group in U.S. society.[66] They spend more than any other age group on everything except health care and thus represent a lucrative market for restaurants, transportation, entertainment, and education.

A Rapidly Aging Population

Another social issue of concern is that huge numbers of Americans are nearing, reaching, or already past retirement age. As millions of Americans retire, there will be more jobs available than people qualified to fill them.

By 2050, the number of United States citizens aged 65 and over will more than double.[67] What do these **demographics** mean for you, and for businesses, in the future? Think of the products and services that these millions of senior citizens will want and need—travel, medicine, assisted-living facilities, adult day care, home health care, and recreation—and you'll see opportunities for successful businesses. And as these older people begin to retire, more job opportunities will arise for younger generations.

Demographics Statistics about the human population with regard to its size, density, and other characteristics.

Dual-Income Families

Dual-income families also play a role in societal changes in the United States. In a dual-income family, both adult members of the household have jobs. Approximately 80 percent of married couples living in the United States are dual-income earners.[68] Several factors have led to a dramatic growth in two-income families in the United States. The high costs of housing and of maintaining a comfortable lifestyle, the high level of taxes, and a cultural emphasis on "having it all" have made it difficult, if not impossible, for many households to live on just one income. Furthermore, many parents simply want a career outside the home.

As a result of this trend, many companies have implemented a host of programs and benefits to respond to the needs of busy two-income families. IBM and Procter & Gamble, for example, each offer employees pregnancy benefits, parental leave, flexible work schedules, and childcare and eldercare programs. Some companies offer referral services that provide counseling to parents in search of childcare or eldercare. Such trends are creating many new opportunities for graduates in human resource management and related areas of study.

Single Parents

The rapid growth of the percentage of U.S. households headed by a single parent has had a major effect on businesses as well. It is a tremendous task to work full-time and raise a family on your own. Many of these single parents are also going to school at the same time—a very tough workload to manage!

Many single parents struggle with maintaining a healthy work–life balance, and they have encouraged their employers to implement programs, such as family leave (where workers can take time off to care for a sick child) and flextime (where workers can come in or leave at selected times), that address their specific needs. These options have helped the plight of the single parent, but work–life balance remains a challenge.

THE GLOBAL ENVIRONMENT

Figure 1.15 The Global Environment

The global environment of business is so important that we show it as surrounding all the other environmental influences (see Figure 1.15). Global business will be discussed in much greater detail in Chapter 12, but here we will focus on important environmental changes in recent years, including the growth of global competition and the increase of free trade among nations and war and terrorism.

Free Trade and Globalization

Free trade is the movement of goods and services among nations without political or economic barriers; a good ex-

> **Free trade** The movement of goods and services among nations without political or economic barriers.

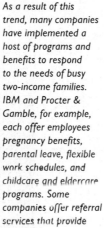

Career PERSPECTIVES

CAREER TO BE DETERMINED

A degree in business can apply to almost any career, and the possibilities are endless. First, a future businessperson should choose an industry that sounds interesting to her. Some of the possibilities in the service industry are listed in this chapter. For example, let's say you're interested in the automotive industry, but you're not interested in actually working on cars. If you're more interested in the financial side of business, you could work in the accounting department of a dealership. Other areas of expertise might include management, information technology, economics, operations, international trade, or international business, just to name a few. Every type of business in every type of industry has jobs in these areas.

Each chapter in this book will include a career focus. If a chapter is interesting to you personally, be sure to read its Career Perspectives box to explore the possible career options in that field. Of course, your instructors and advisors are also good people to connect with to discuss career choices.

What type of business do you think will be right for you? What industries do you find most interesting?

Thinking Critically

>> Energy Crisis on the Horizon

As long ago as 2000, Canadian economist Jeff Rubin began to forward predictions that oil prices would increase dramatically in the future, and in 2007, he got more specific about it, predicting that they would top $100 per barrel. Despite the fact that it subsequently dropped significantly from its peak levels, Rubin has predicted that the price will rise again and will wreak even worse havoc on the economy at that point, including ending the practice of global outsourcing as we know it today.

According to Rubin, the price of oil will accelerate as oil supplies continue to be depleted and demand from developing countries increases. As the price rises, transportation costs will skyrocket, and it will no longer be prudent for people to trade internationally—or even travel among borders as they do today. As a result, nations will become less interdependent and technology will stagnate. Food, rather than oil, will become scarce.

There are some positive notes in Rubin's bleak forecast. He goes on to predict that industries that have suffered with the rise of globalization and competition from foreign nations will prosper. As the world becomes less dependent on petroleum and other fossil fuels, the environmental damage they cause will lessen. Governments will be forced to innovate and spend to transition their infrastructure to new sources of energy.

In Rubin's opinion, however, those nations' citizens will have to make the greatest changes. Rubin cautions that each and every person must dramatically change their ways and reduce their consumption of energy—and he believes they'll actually do it. He adds, "Don't be surprised if the new, smaller world that emerges isn't a lot more livable and enjoyable than the one we are about to leave behind."[69]

Source: Adapted from Mohammed Herzallah, "The Coming Oil Crisis," *Newsweek*, June 22, 2009.

QUESTIONS

1. In your opinion, what are the roles or responsibilities of businesses in light of the fossil fuel crisis Rubin has predicted for the future?

2. How have escalating oil prices created a need for governments to invest more heavily in improving their infrastructure? What does that mean for businesses?

ample would be the elimination of taxes on goods imported from other countries. The development of efficient distribution systems,

Globalization The worldwide integration of government policies, cultures, social movements, and financial markets through trade and the exchange of ideas.

expansion of worldwide travel, and communication advances, such as the Internet, have led to the rise of **globalization**. Globalization has greatly improved living standards around the world; specifically, the rapid growth of the economies of China and India has been remarkable. Lenovo, a Chinese firm, recently bought IBM's computer-making operations. The majority of products available for sale at the retail level in the U.S. are manufactured in other countries, and many U.S. companies outsource jobs to other countries as well. If you call a U.S. company's customer service number, you might find yourself speaking to a representative on the other side of the world.

War and Terrorism

The wars in Iraq and Afghanistan have drawn billions of dollars from the U.S. economy. Some companies—such as those that make bullets, tanks, and uniforms—have benefited from the conflict. Others have lost trusted employees who have been called up by the armed forces for service. Other businesses, such as those that provide social services, have suffered because the government has redistributed money previously dedicated to them to the war effort.

The threat of terrorism also adds greatly to organizational costs, including the cost of insurance. In fact, some firms are finding it difficult to insure against terrorist attacks (see the Going Global box on this page). Security is very costly as well. Airlines, for example, have had to retrofit their planes with stronger cockpit doors, and airports have been forced to add more passenger screening devices.

Just like everyone else, businesspeople benefit from a peaceful and prosperous world. One way to lessen international tensions is to foster global economic growth among both profit-making and nonprofit organizations. Many argue that the quickest route to peace is through free and unrestrained trade.

Going GLOBAL

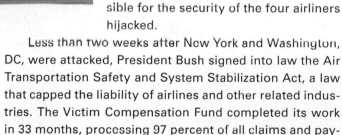

Is Terrorism a Clear and Present Danger for Insurers?

Terrorism could devastate any organization. An attack on, or near, a business's facilities could result in loss of life, property damage, denial of access, and business interruption. Of course, liability is also a major concern.

Insurers never anticipated the September 11, 2001 terrorist attacks on the World Trade Center (WTC), which are among the largest insured losses in history. The WTC's insurers had not charged the building or its tenants for the terrorism risk or received additional premiums to cover losses.

In the aftermath of the 2001 attacks, policymakers have become increasingly aware of the important role of insurance in reducing vulnerability, promoting preparedness, and encouraging prevention against terrorism. Insurance has been proven to help secure vital economic interests, and the insurance industry has begun to recognize its interdependence on government security policies.

The U.S. Congress promptly enacted legislation aimed at trying to ease the pain of both victims and the airline industry. The September 11th Victim Compensation Fund of 2001 was created to handle claims by victims of the terrorist attacks as part of this legislation aimed at providing relief to the airline industry. Prior to the 2001 terrorist attacks, the airline industry was on shaky financial ground. Survivors and their families wanted to identify and punish those within the system who had been responsible for the security of the four airliners hijacked.

Less than two weeks after New York and Washington, DC, were attacked, President Bush signed into law the Air Transportation Safety and System Stabilization Act, a law that capped the liability of airlines and other related industries. The Victim Compensation Fund completed its work in 33 months, processing 97 percent of all claims and paying out more than $7 billion to victims and their families.

Source: Adapted from X. Chen, H. Doerpinghaus, B.-X. Lin, and T. Yu, "Catastrophic Losses and Insurer Profitability: Evidence from 9/11."*Journal of Risk and Insurance*, March 2008, http://find.galegroup.com/ips/start.do?prodId=IPS (accessed June 29, 2009).

Questions

1. How can a business predict a threat that is unpredictable?

2. Should businesses rely on the federal government to stabilize the terrorism insurance market?

How Global Changes Affect You

As businesses expand to serve global markets, new jobs will be created in both manufacturing and service industries. Global trade also means global competition. The students who will prosper are those who will be prepared for the markets of tomorrow. Rapid change creates a need for continuous learning, so be prepared to continue your education throughout your career. You'll have every reason to be optimistic about job opportunities in the future if you prepare yourself well.

A FINAL THOUGHT ON ENVIRONMENT: STAKEHOLDER RECOGNITION

As mentioned earlier, stakeholders are all the people and organizations who stand to gain or lose from the activities of a business. These include customers, employees, stockholders, suppliers, lenders, special-interest groups, citizens of the surrounding community, and elected government leaders, among others (see Figure 1.16). All of these groups are affected by the products, policies, and practices of businesses, and their concerns need to be addressed.

You are a stakeholder in many businesses. For example, if you shop at Walmart, you are a stakeholder of Walmart. If you don't shop at Walmart, but you live in Bentonville, Arkansas, where Walmart's corporate headquarters are located, you are also a Walmart stakeholder, because Walmart affects the community in which you live.

The challenge for organizations is to balance—as much as possible—the needs of all their stakeholders. For example, the need for a business to make profits may be balanced against the needs of its employees to earn sufficient income. The need to stay competitive may call for moving a business's operations overseas, but that might do great harm to the business's current community. Would moving be best for everyone? Business leaders must make decisions based on all factors, including the need to make a profit. As you can imagine, pleasing all stakeholders is not easy.

[BUS] connections

1. In what ways can governments make things easier for businesspeople? Do you think the government should do more? Why or why not?
2. Imagine you own a shoe-repair business in a town near a military base. How might a war affect your business?
3. What is free trade, and how does free trade affect businesses competing overseas?

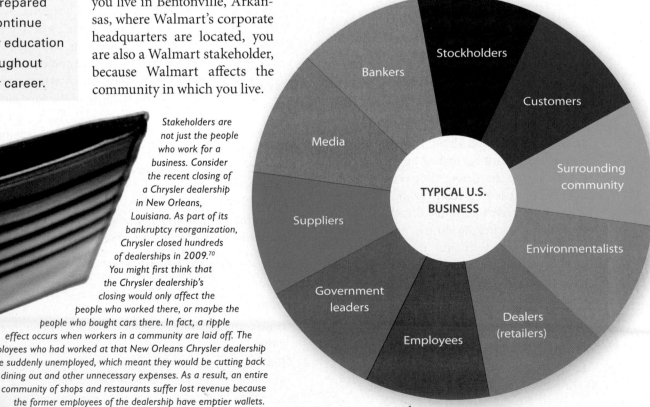

Figure 1.16 The Stakeholders of a Business

STAKEHOLDERS

TYPICAL U.S. BUSINESS

- Stockholders
- Customers
- Surrounding community
- Environmentalists
- Dealers (retailers)
- Employees
- Government leaders
- Suppliers
- Media
- Bankers

Stakeholders are not just the people who work for a business. Consider the recent closing of a Chrysler dealership in New Orleans, Louisiana. As part of its bankruptcy reorganization, Chrysler closed hundreds of dealerships in 2009.[70] You might first think that the Chrysler dealership's closing would only affect the people who worked there, or maybe the people who bought cars there. In fact, a ripple effect occurs when workers in a community are laid off. The employees who had worked at that New Orleans Chrysler dealership were suddenly unemployed, which meant they would be cutting back on dining out and other unnecessary expenses. As a result, an entire community of shops and restaurants suffer lost revenue because the former employees of the dealership have emptier wallets.

>> Your Future in Business

We are in the midst of an information-based global revolution that will alter all sectors of the economy—agricultural, manufacturing, and service. It is exciting to think of the role you will play in that revolution. As you embark on a career in business, you have several choices. You can either start your own business, or you can work for someone else. If you choose to work for someone else, it could be a large or small business, a nonprofit organization, or a government agency.

ENTREPRENEURSHIP VERSUS WORKING FOR OTHERS

There are two ways to succeed in business. Either path can lead to a happy and fulfilling career. One is to work for others, get experience and skills, and rise up through the ranks. In such a situation, someone else is assuming the entrepreneurial risk, paying you a salary, and providing benefits. Most people choose this option.

The other path is to be an entrepreneur and start your own business. As described in the case at the beginning of this chapter, Darryl Alexander started a barbecue restaurant because he dreamed about being his own boss. Making barbecue was his passion, and he was committed to making his livelihood from doing something he loved. Of course, entrepreneurs don't get paid vacations and sick leave from their bosses—they have to provide those benefits for themselves, and that means making sure someone else can take care of the business when they can't. But entrepreneurs reap the rewards for the risks they take; some, like Bill Gates, become very wealthy through hard work and the application of sound business prin-

Women now own about 40 percent of all privately held businesses in the United States.[75] According to the National Women's Business Council, one in every 18 U.S. women owns her own business.[76]

ciples—the same principles that you will be learning throughout this book.

Working for Other Businesses

Most people follow the path of working for someone else. Since you will probably be (at least at some point) looking for a job working for someone else, you'll probably be happy to know that the earning power of a college graduate far outpaces that of less-educated individuals.[71] If your focus is on growth and advancement, with the potential to move higher within the same company, it might be wise for you to choose a company that is medium-sized or large. However, if you are looking for job diversity, flexibility, and the chance to develop a broad set of skills, you might be better off at a small entrepreneurial firm, where employees might have more variety and latitude in decision making. Once you gain experience working for other firms, you'll be more ready to start your own business, if that is your dream.

Diversity and the Entrepreneurial Challenge

Millions of people from all over the world have taken the entrepreneurial challenge and succeeded. For example, the number of Hispanic-owned businesses in the United States is growing at a pace three times the national average.[72] Within the next six years, the number of Hispanic-owned businesses in the United States is forecasted to grow to 4.3 million.[73] There is also rapid growth in businesses owned by Asian Americans, African Americans, Pacific Islanders, Native Americans, and Alaskan Natives.[74]

Women have the same opportunity to engage in entrepreneurship as men, and entrepreneurship is an attractive career path for an increasing number of women. The number of women business owners has dramatically increased in the last 20 years. In 1980, there were about 3 million women business owners; by 2009, that number had grown to more than 10 million. Old assumptions that women don't like to take risks have been proven untrue: according to a survey conducted by the Simmons School of Management, "businesswomen are highly likely to take risks related to business or professional opportunities."[77] You may be familiar with some of these famous female entrepreneurs: Oprah Winfrey, Donna Karan, Lillian Vernon, and Estée Lauder—to name only a few.

Why Entrepreneurship Is Key to Wealth Creation

Factors of production The resources used to create wealth: land, labor, capital, entrepreneurship, and knowledge.

Have you ever wondered why some countries are relatively wealthy and others poor? Over time, economists have developed the following five **factors of production** that seem to contribute to a nation's wealth (see Figure 1.17):

- Land or natural resources
- Labor
- Access to capital (items used in the production of goods other than money)
- Entrepreneurship
- Knowledge

If you were to analyze rich countries versus poor countries to see what causes the differences in their levels of wealth, you would consider the factors of production in each country. Russia and China, for example, have vast areas of land with many resources, but they are not "rich" countries—yet. In contrast, Japan and Germany are relatively rich countries, but they are poor in land and other natural resources. Therefore, land is not the critical element for wealth creation. Many poor countries have massive labor pools. So labor isn't the primary source of wealth either. Finally, capital, such as machinery and tools, is widely available in world markets today, and so access to capital is not the missing element.

What makes rich countries rich is a combination of entrepreneurship and the effective use of knowledge. Entrepreneurship also makes some states and cities in the United States rich, while others remain relatively poor; different areas' business environments either encourage or discourage entrepreneurship.

Study Alert!

Entrepreneurship, one of the five factors of production (the other four are land, labor, capital, and knowledge) that lead to wealth creation, is arguably one of the most important for building a wealthy society.

WORKING FOR A NONPROFIT ORGANIZATION OR A GOVERNMENT AGENCY

Your interests may lead you to work for a nonprofit organization or a government agency, but you should know by now that doesn't mean you don't need to study business. On the contrary, if you want to work for a nonprofit organization or join a government agency, you will need business skills just as much as you would anywhere else. The concepts and principles that make businesses more effective and efficient

Figure 1.17 The Factors of Production

Land

Land and other natural resources are used to make homes, cars, and other products.

Labor

People have always been an important resource in producing goods and services, but many people are now being replaced by technology.

Capital

Capital includes machines, tools, buildings, and other means of manufacturing.

Entrepreneurship

All the resources in the world have little value unless entrepreneurs are willing to take the risk of starting businesses to use those resources.

Knowledge

Information technology has revolutionized business, making it possible to quickly determine wants and needs and to respond with desired goods and services.

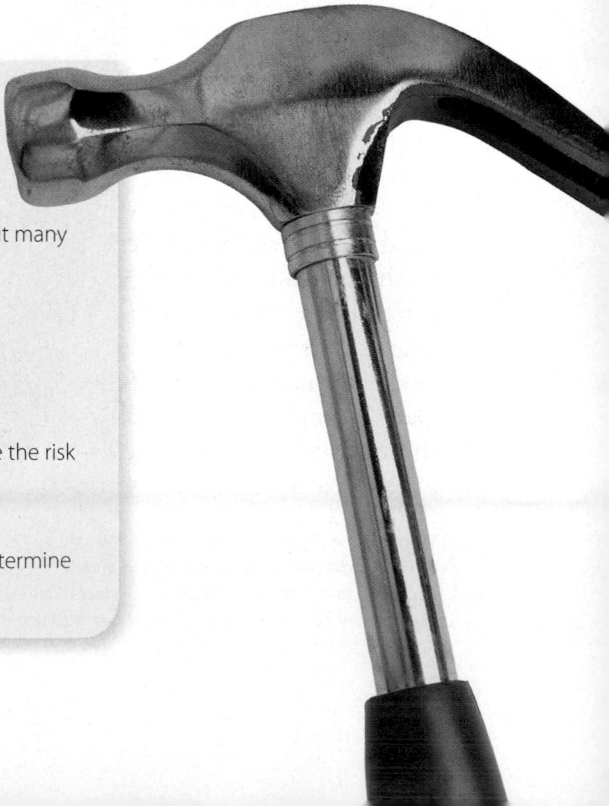

Real World Apps

After her first day in her Introduction to Business class, Jennifer Pierce learned a lot about the business world that she'd never understood before. Not only was she wrong about the definition of a business, she now realizes that there are environmental forces at play on the operations of all businesses, whether they are manufacturing or service oriented. The environmental factors that surround a business affect how it operates on a daily basis. These factors include the technology in place at the business, the diversity of the workplace, competitors, the employees, and other stakeholders.

Now that Jennifer is aware of the all-encompassing boundaries of business, she can clearly differentiate between entrepreneurship and working for others, and for profit and nonprofit businesses. She now realizes that hospitals are interested in profit and return on investment; if they weren't, they would not be able to grow and adapt to the environmental forces that affect them.

are applicable in government agencies and nonprofit organizations as well. The knowledge and skills you acquire in this and other business courses will be useful in any kind of organization.

WHY STUDY BUSINESS?

Business is all around us and affects our daily lives. Many of you may become or already are business majors. With a business degree, your options are endless. Even if you are not a business major, this textbook will give you insight into the process by which services and goods are provided to customers, and you'll learn business concepts you can apply to what-

Even pretzel carts are businesses. Business is everywhere, from the mall to Main Street to the financial districts of big cities.

ever career you choose. In it, you'll explore many areas of business and learn how businesses operate and affect your life. Understanding business can:

- Help you land a good job and set you on the path to a long and fulfilling career.
- Improve your standard of living and quality of life.
- Help you achieve your goals and fulfill your dreams.
- Help you become a more informed consumer.
- Help you become an entrepreneur.
- Help you create wealth.

This is an introductory business text, so we will tend to focus on for-profit business. Nonetheless, we will remind you periodically that you can apply the concepts you are learning to any career path.

[BUS] connections

1. What are some of the advantages of working for others? What could you gain, and what could you lose, by becoming an entrepreneur?
2. What are the five factors of production? Which of them are keys to wealth creation?
3. How can the study of business help you in your own career?

For REVIEW >>

1. Define and explain business and its basic terms.
   - A business is a person, partnership, or corporation that seeks to provide goods and services to others at a *profit*. This chapter provided an introduction to business, including defining business and explaining basic business terms like revenue, expense, profit, loss, risk, services, stakeholders, and standard of living.

2. Explain the evolution of business in the United States.
   - Advances in technology, transportation, and global competition have affected businesses' abilities to become or remain competitive and profitable. Initially, people raised their own food and made their own clothing. Over the last 200 years, the United States has moved away from manufacturing and agriculture toward a service-driven economy. Much of this change is due to the development of new technology.

3. Describe different classifications of business.
   - Businesses can be classified in various ways, including by size (microenterprises, small and medium-sized businesses, and large businesses), profit motive (for-profit or nonprofit), or whether they are manufacturing or service businesses. Differentiating businesses by size generally means noting their variances in terms of sales volume and number of employees. For-profit organizations are motivated to earn profits; organizations that are not driven to garner profits are classified as nonprofit. Manufacturing firms produce tangible products, like furniture, and service businesses produce intangible products, like legal advice.

4. Describe the five elements of the business environment.
   - The business environment consists of the surrounding factors that either help or hinder the development of businesses. The five elements of the business environment are the economic environment and legal environment, the technological environment, the competitive environment, the social environment, and the global environment. The economic and legal environment affects businesses because they must operate within a framework of laws and economic forces. The technological environment affects business through new technologies that may make jobs easier—or even obsolete. As a business's social environment constantly changes, it must respond by creating the new or different products its customers demand; as demographics change, managing diversity and being able to quickly attend to the needs of new groups of customers have become increasingly important as well. The global environment—including such pivotal issues as free trade, the effects of globalization, war, and terrorism—affects every business and every person by creating new opportunities and challenges. The more understanding businesspeople have of these five environments, the more successful they will be.

5. Understand your options in the world of business in the future.
   - The endless possibilities of your future in business were presented in the last section. Entrepreneurship, which means starting your own business, is risky but can lead to great reward, and it is an option increasingly being chosen by women and minorities in the United States. Entrepreneurship is one of the five factors of production (the other four are land, labor, capital, and knowledge) that lead to wealth creation. However, most people choose to work for other businesspeople and allow them to assume the risk of entrepreneurship. Either path can lead to a happy and fulfilling career.
   - The study of business—whether you plan to work for yourself, a for-profit business owned by someone else, a nonprofit organization, or even a government agency—is an extremely valuable tool. Understanding business can help you land a good job, set you on the path to a long and fulfilling career, improve your standard of living and quality of life, help you achieve your goals and fulfill your dreams, help you become a more informed consumer, and help make you financially secure.

Key Terms

bankruptcy	e-commerce	globalization	revenue
business	effectiveness	goods	risk
business-to-business (B2B)	efficiency	loss	services
business-to-consumer (B2C)	empowerment	nonprofit organizations	small and medium-sized enterprises
capitalist system	entrepreneur	outsourcing	stakeholders
contract	expenses	productivity	standard of living
database	factors of production	profit	tradable currency
demographics	for-profit organizations	resource	value
diversity	free trade	return on investment (ROI)	

<< Think AND DISCUSS

1. This chapter discusses two primary options in the business world: entrepreneurship or working for an existing business. Which would you prefer? Why?

2. What do you want to learn from the study of business? What questions do you have about business?

3. What are some other benefits, besides those listed in the chapter, of studying business?

4. List the possible types of expenses you might incur while running each of the following businesses:

   - A retail clothing store
   - A cabinetmaking business
   - A house-painting business
   - A convenience store

5. Break into groups and consider the following question: What are some of the factors that could cause a country's standard of living to go down? As a group, select five factors and discuss them with the rest of the class.

6. In groups, brainstorm a list of five service businesses in your neighborhoods.

INTERNET IN >> Action

1. Visit http://www.bls.gov and review historical data for unemployment rates. Then answer the following questions:

   a. What was the unemployment rate last month? What about the same month last year? The same month 10 years ago?

   b. What factors can cause unemployment to rise? What factors can cause it to go down? List at least five factors each.

2. Use your favorite search engine to search for the terms "nonprofit groups" and "social interest groups." What types of groups can you find? Name at least five and discuss their missions.

3. Many companies have diversity policies in place. They are clear, measurable ways to see how a particular company has addressed the issue of diversity and how serious the company is about maintaining a fair and diverse workplace.

   a. Visit http://www.nikebiz.com/careers/diversity.html, http://www.mcdonalds.com/usa/work/diversity.html, and http://www.coldstonecreamery.com/jobs/jobs_embracing_diversity.html to review and compare the diversity policies of Nike, McDonald's, and Cold Stone Creamery, respectively. Are the policies effective? Why or why not? How are they similar, and how are they different?

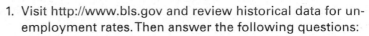

Self-Assessment Exercises

BUSINESS CAREER QUIZ

Which Business Emphasis Should You Choose?

Which area of business might interest you most? Mark your interest level for each question, with 5 being most interested and 1 being least interested.

1.	I like being creative.	5	4	3	2	1
2.	I am a good salesperson.	5	4	3	2	1
3.	I am excellent with numbers.	5	4	3	2	1
4.	I like to see how everything fits together.	5	4	3	2	1
5.	I am a people person.	5	4	3	2	1
6.	I am good at computers.	5	4	3	2	1
7.	I speak more than one language.	5	4	3	2	1
8.	I usually take a leadership role with my friends.	5	4	3	2	1
9.	I have a strong sense of fairness.	5	4	3	2	1
10.	I like learning about other cultures.	5	4	3	2	1
11.	I like to "run the show."	5	4	3	2	1

If you marked high numbers for 1, 2, and 5, you might be right for a career in marketing.

If you marked high numbers for 3 and 4, a career in finance or accounting might be right for you.

If you marked high numbers for 7 and 10, you might like a career in international business.

If you marked a high number for 9, human resource management might be a good career direction for you.

If you marked a high number for 6, a career in computer information systems is worth considering.

If you marked high numbers for 8 and 11, a leadership role might be in your future.

DIVERSITY AWARENESS QUIZ

8 = Strongly agree   6 = Agree   4 = Neutral   2 = Disagree   1 = Strongly disagree

_____ I feel comfortable spending time with people whose religious beliefs and practices are different from my own.

_____ I can tolerate or put up with people who speak a different language.

_____ Family ways of living that are different from my own are as important and valid as mine.

_____ It is essential that I consider, analyze, and challenge my own cultural experiences in order to better understand and analyze those of others.

_____ I respect and value religious beliefs and practices different from my own.

_____ I take advantage of opportunities to meet and learn from people who are different.

_____ I think learning about people who are different is very important.

_____ I feel comfortable spending time with people with values different from my own.

_____ I respect and value other languages.

_____ I think ideas about the world that are different from mine are acceptable.

_____ My experiences with different religious beliefs and practices have been an essential part of my own personal growth.

_____ I welcome opportunities to meet and learn from people who are different.

_____ I feel comfortable spending time with people whose ideas about the world are different from mine.

_____ I can tolerate people who have different religious beliefs and practices.

_____ Other spoken languages different from my own are as valid as my own.

_____ I think religious beliefs and practices different from my own are acceptable.

_____ I think the use of a language different from my own is acceptable.

_____ I respect and value family ways of living different from mine.

_____ I can tolerate people who have different ideas about how the world should work.

_____ I accept responsibility for challenging hatred and mistreatment of people of other races.

_____ I can tolerate people whose values are different from my own.

_____ My efforts to learn other languages have been an essential part of my own personal growth.

_____ Other religious beliefs and practices are as valid as my own.

_____ I can tolerate spending time with people whose lifestyles are different from mine.

_____ I feel comfortable spending time with people whose lifestyles are different from mine.

_____ I think different ways of family life are acceptable.

_____ I feel comfortable spending time learning and understanding languages different from my own.

_____ I respect, value, and seek to understand ideas and social concerns different from my own.

My experiences with different ways of family life have been an important part of my own personal growth.

_____ Conflict is inevitable when basic values differ between persons; however, I accept such conflict as an essential part of my learning.

Next, add up your total score and review your level of awareness for diversity issues.

Intolerant Level of Awareness (50–58):

You have little or no interest in acknowledging or interacting with persons different from yourself. You do not care to spend time with people whose values, family lifestyle, world view, and/or language are different from your own.

Tolerant Level of Awareness (59–75):

You have the capacity to put up with people who are different, even though you may find it unpleasant. You are willing to endure, but you do not embrace others.

Acceptance Level of Awareness (76–100):

You acknowledge others' differences without denying their importance; you acknowledge other lifestyles and values of groups other than your own; you have some sensitivity and understanding of others who are different; and you see others who are different as a resource for learning.

Respect Level of Awareness (101–134):

You admire the differences of others; you seek out frequent and positive interactions with others who are different; you understand different perspectives and social concerns; you welcome opportunities to take part in activities that reflect social concerns. Your worldview has been expanded as a benefit of your culturally diverse interactions.

Affirmation, Solidarity, and Critique Level of Awareness (135–210):

You engage in positive interactions with others who are different; you accept other cultures, languages, and family style as legitimate; and you embrace differences among people as a vehicle for learning and development. You understand that conflict is inevitable, because basic values differ, and you consider such conflicts to be learning opportunities.

2

HOW ECONOMIC
AFFECTS BUSINESS

After reading this chapter, you will be able to:

1 Understand the basics of economics, including supply and demand.

2 Describe free-market capitalism and degrees of competition.

3 Understand the differences between socialism and communism.

4 Discuss the major indicators of economic conditions.

AMILYA ANTONETTI AND SOAPWORKS

Believe it or not, a difficult challenge in your personal life could possibly lead to a multimillion dollar business. If you have a need, it's entirely possible that other people have that need, too. You can capitalize on that need, create a solution to it, make enough of that solution to sell to others, and then market it to the public, creating a supply and demand effect in the economy.

Amilya Antonetti and her husband were thrilled about the arrival of their son, David. However, shortly after his birth, David developed health issues. "When I was breast-feeding him, his lips would turn blue, his eyes would roll back into his head, and I would rush him off to the emergency room," Antonetti said.[1] He suffered from frequent rashes and labored breathing as well.

Frantic to find a solution, Antonetti began to take detailed notes about her son's every waking and sleeping moment in an effort to identify a cause or trigger of his symptoms. Eventually, she noticed a pattern—David's symptoms would peak after she finished her housecleaning regimen each Tuesday. Antonetti decided that ingredients in household cleaning supplies could be the culprit.

She started her quest for a solution by researching what chemicals were in the supplies she routinely used; many contained caustic chemicals. Antonetti threw out all the cleaning supplies that contained these ingredients—and David immediately got better. It occurred to Antonetti that if her son was allergic to these ingredients, others probably were, too. She decided to create her own cleaning products made from natural, vegetable-based ingredients and enlisted her grandmother to help.[2]

"I didn't really think about formulating, I just needed a soap that worked. I never really decided to start a soap-making business. I saw how many other mothers were in the same position I was in; they also said, 'You need to get this soap out to others.'" Antonetti said.[3]

Next, Antonetti focused on supply. She had been making the soap in her garage, but it was very hard to make enough to meet the needs of customers and keep costs low. She obtained a Small Business Administration (SBA) loan in order to expand the business and move production outside her home.

Antonetti wrote a book, *Why David Hates Tuesdays*, to stir up more demand and spark the interest of other mothers of children who were sensitive to chemicals. She also did a lot of face-to-face networking with other mothers and online marketing.

As a result, Antonetti built a strong business that was responsive to customer demand. She also created channels (both online and at the retail level) where her customers could purchase her product.

Questions

1. Imagine a product you'd like to create. List the things you would need to consider in order to find out if there is a demand for the product, and describe how you would ensure that you could create an adequate supply of the product to meet that demand.

2. Where else, besides retail stores and online, could Antonetti have marketed her product to further increase demand for her products?

3. Research other types of funding besides a small business loan. Discuss the types of funding you find with your classmates.

Sources: Adapted from Colleen Weinkam, "Keynote Speaker Amilya Antonetti," *Cincy.* October 2008. http://www.cincylifemagazine.com/ME2/dirmod.asp?sid=2CE771F28E0D4281817E2E034A9C57C6&nm=Arc hive&type=Publishing&mod=Publications::Article&mid=61465020993F438B9FCD60C66CC58CDC&tier=4&id =C85A796AE06649F2ABC19F66EC9652AB (accessed July 29, 2009); and Isabel Isidro, "Soapworks: How a Family Need Spurred a Profitable Business," Powerhomebiz.com. http://www.powerhomebiz.com/vol135/ soapworks.htm (accessed July 29, 2009).

S >>

- Why do we study economics, and how does it affect our daily lives?
- Are consumers and businesses better off in a capitalist, a socialist, or a mixed economic system?
- How do different economic indicators affect business?

Antonetti's success story illustrates how economics influences businesses and individuals. Owners and managers in every business, from small to large, must be aware of the economic factors that affect it.

>> Understanding Economics

A peasant couple dancing.

Imagine the world centuries ago, when kings and other landowners had most of the wealth and most people were peasants. Peasants often had large families, and it may have seemed a natural conclusion that there would soon be too many people and not enough food and other resources to support them. English economist Thomas Malthus made just this argument in the late 1700s and early 1800s: He believed that the masses would end up starving to death because there simply wouldn't be enough food to go around. In response to Malthus's theory and the views of other economists who predicted a dark future, Scottish historian Thomas Carlyle called economics "the dismal science."

If economics is a dismal science, why should we care about studying and understanding it? It's simple—economics affects us on an individual level every day. Every time you buy something, you're applying economics. If you choose not to purchase something because its price is too high, that's a decision based on economics. Economics also affects every business, no matter its size. Business owners and managers must be aware of economics, its key indicators, and its impact on their business. This chapter will provide an overview of the study of economics and how it relates to business.

Real World Apps

Jim Lewis, a busy college student, has just enrolled in an economics course. He's a little worried about how he'll do in the class, because he doesn't really know anything about economics. Jim doesn't read the newspaper and hates watching the news because he finds it too depressing. Of course, he knows that the U.S. economy is in recession—after all, everyone is talking about it. He just doesn't think it really has any effect on him personally, since he's a student.

Jim is interested in buying a new car, and since the automotive industry is in shambles, he figures he can't go wrong—bargains should be everywhere. He's very confident that he'll be able to get a great deal, but Jim does have a concern: He checked in with his lender about his student loan for the upcoming year and was told that the bank was under new ownership and that he wouldn't qualify for a new loan. Jim wonders if he'll have to put his new car on hold because of this new wrinkle.

THE BASICS OF ECONOMICS

Have you ever wondered why some countries are wealthy and others are poor? In the last chapter, you learned that the five factors of production play a role in the creation of wealth. In this chapter, we will explore the various economic systems of the world and how they either promote or hinder business growth, the creation of wealth, and a higher quality of life.

The differences in wealth among nations are great: In Sri Lanka, the average annual income is $818 per year; in Spain, the average is $14,576; and in Switzerland, the average is $36,988.[4] Almost half of the world's population survives on only $2.50 per day.[5]

Economics, the study of how individuals and society choose to use scarce resources to produce goods and services and distribute them for consumption, deals with understanding the choices that people make. Three items from this definition need further clarification: choice, scarce, and resources.

> **Economics** The study of how individuals and society choose to use scarce resources to produce goods and services and distribute them for consumption.
>
> **Opportunity cost** Refers to what you give up (your next best choice) in order to do or get something else (your chosen decision).

- *Choice* creates an **opportunity cost**, which refers to what you give up (your next best choice) in order to do or get something else (your chosen decision). For example, you have a choice to study or go to the movies. If you choose to study, your opportunity cost is giving up going to the movies (by the way, excellent choice).

- *Scarce* means limited. The resources used to produce goods and services are necessarily limited, and they should be conserved whenever possible.

- *Resources*: As you learned in Chapter 1, resources—land, labor, capital, entrepreneurship, and knowledge—are the factors of production.

MICROECONOMICS AND MACROECONOMICS

There are two basic types of economic study: macro and micro. First, the term *macro* refers to something very big in scale. Therefore, **macroeconomics** explores and studies the operation of a nation's economy as a whole. **Microeconomics**, on the other hand, examines the behavior of people and organizations in particular markets. While a macroeconomist would study how many jobs exist in the whole economy, a microeconomist would examine how many people are being hired in a particular industry or in a certain region of the country. In Chapter 1, Figure 1.7 showed that there were 3 million jobs that employers cannot fill nationwide—a macro view. A microeconomic perspective would take a deeper analysis, perhaps identifying how many of these jobs are in nursing or health care in Chicago, Illinois.

> **Macroeconomics** The study of the operation of a nation's economy as a whole.
>
> **Microeconomics** The study of the behavior of people and organizations in particular markets.

Macroeconomics examines larger, broader issues. Consider Malthus's belief that there were too many people in the world and not enough food to feed them. Recent statistics have shown that the world population is actually growing more slowly than expected, and in some industrialized countries, such as Japan, Germany, Italy, and Russia, population

One resource is labor, and there are certainly scarcities of labor. For example, there is a shortage of skilled nurses in the United States today. If current trends continue, about 1.1 million new nurses will need to be trained and educated by 2012 to keep up with demand.[6] Can you imagine the situation as the baby boomers age and the need for health care grows?

growth may be so slow that there will soon be too many old people and not enough young people to care for them.[7]

Although growth has slowed in some areas, the world's population is projected to grow from 6.8 billion in 2009 to more than 9 billion by 2050. The largest growth will come from developing nations; in fact, the populations of some of the world's poorest countries are projected to almost triple.[8] This sort of study—research about the effects of population growth on the world's economy—is a critical part of macroeconomics. Macroeconomists attempt to determine what makes some countries relatively wealthy and other countries relatively poor, and then they advise the nations' leaders to implement policies and programs that can lead to increased prosperity.

Naturally, the pace of population growth has a direct effect on resources. As mentioned earlier, economics deals with allocation of "scarce" resources. For example, citizens in industrialized countries like the United States and Australia have easy access to drinking water, but people living in the African country of Rwanda do not. They often have to travel across hilly terrain for hours in order to reach fresh water. Even then, the water may be contaminated.[9] Some economists believe that these resources need to be carefully divided among people, usually by the government.

A recent solution to the challenge of scarce resources has been the development of genetically modified foods (GMF). GMF seeds are said to require less water and to produce larger crops on smaller pieces of land.[12] Additionally, the crops they yield are pest resistant and can be modified to contain more essential vitamins and minerals than non-GMF produce.[13]

What can be done about resource scarcity? The answer is **resource development**. Resource development is the study of how to increase resources and create the conditions that will make better use of those resources. Outside of government, businesses may contribute to an economic system by inventing products that increase available resources. For example, businesses may discover new energy sources, new ways of growing food, and new ways of creating goods and services.[10] One business in the Netherlands has developed an innovative way of creating energy. Club WATT uses a technology that converts the crowd's movement on a club's dance floor into electricity that powers the club's speakers and other electronics.[11]

> **Resource development** The study of how to increase resources and create the conditions that will make better use of those resources.

Some macroeconomists believe that a large population, especially an educated one, can be a valuable resource. You've probably heard the saying "Give a man a fish and you feed him for a day, but teach a man to fish and you feed him for a lifetime." You can add to that: "Teach a person to start a fish farm, and he or she will be able to feed a village for a lifetime." The secret to economic development is contained in this last statement. Business owners provide jobs and economic growth for their employees and communities, as well as for themselves.

ADAM SMITH, FATHER OF MODERN ECONOMICS

Eighteenth-century Scottish economist Adam Smith was one of the first to imagine a system for creating wealth and improving the lives of everyone. Rather than believing that resources had to be divided among competing groups and individuals—the prevailing belief in 1776—Smith envisioned creating more resources in order to make everyone wealthier. Smith's book, *An Inquiry into the Nature and Causes of the Wealth of Nations*, "was the first and remains the most important book on the subject of political economy until this present day."[14] Smith is known as the "father of modern economics."[15]

The basis of his general economic theory was a desire for improving one's own condition in life. According to Smith, as long as farmers, laborers, and businesspeople (entrepreneurs) could see economic rewards for their efforts (receiving enough profits to support their families, for instance), they would work long and hard to achieve those rewards. As a result of their efforts, the economy as a whole would prosper—with plenty of food and products available to everyone.

Under Adam Smith's theory, businesspeople don't necessarily deliberately set out to help others. They work primarily for their own prosperity and growth. Yet, as individuals try to improve their own situation in life, Smith said, their efforts serve as a guiding "invisible hand" that helps the larger economy grow and prosper. Thus, the **invisible hand** turns self-directed gain into social and economic benefits for all. Of course, business owners must meet the needs of customers when producing their products, or this wealth cannot spread throughout the community. That's where the concepts of supply and demand come into play.

Invisible hand A phrase coined by Adam Smith to describe the process that turns self-directed gain into social and economic benefits for all.

The growth of microbreweries in the United States is a good example of Smith's invisible hand at work. Many people who felt passionate about beer began to brew their own craft beers, and the industry has taken off. In 1978, there were only 42 craft breweries in the U.S.; in 2008, there were 1,390.[16]

SUPPLY AND DEMAND

Supply refers to the quantity of products manufacturers or owners are willing to sell at different prices at a specific time. Generally speaking, the amount of a product supplied will increase as its price increases, because sellers can make more money at a higher price. For example, if a 40-inch high-definition television (HDTV) were priced at only $100 per unit, manufacturers might be willing to supply only 50 of them. On the other hand,

Supply The quantity of products manufacturers or owners are willing to sell at different prices at a specific time.

Smith's invisible hand theory suggests that efforts by one person to better his or her situation in life can benefit others as well.

Study Alert

if manufacturers could get $1,000 for an HDTV, they might be willing to supply 500 of them. Economists show this relationship between quantity supplied and price on a graph (see Figure 2.1). For this discussion, understanding the definition of supply is most important.

Figure 2.1 The Supply Curve at Various Prices

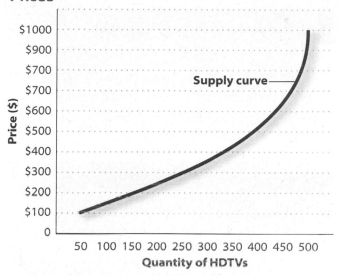

Supply curve

Figure 2.2 The Demand Curve at Various Prices

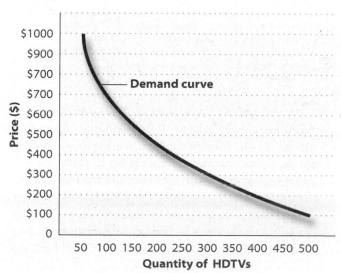

Demand curve

Demand refers to the quantity of products people are willing and able to buy at different prices at a specific time. Generally speaking, the quantity of a product demanded will increase as its price decreases. For example, if the HDTV were priced at $100, most families would be willing to buy one—perhaps more than one. However, if its price were

Demand The quantity of products people are willing and able to buy at different prices at a specific time.

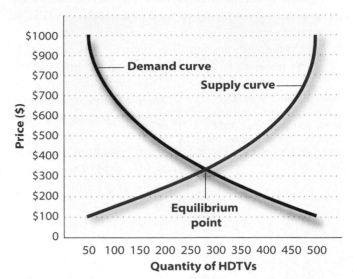
$1,000, far fewer people would buy the HDTV, and they'd probably only buy one. In other words, as the price increases, the demand for the product decreases, and vice versa (see Figure 2.2).

Yet another example of supply and demand can be found in the market for swimming pool chemicals and pool toys. In the hot summer months, demand for these products is high; therefore, the prices are high and discounts are infrequent. In fall and winter, most stores reduce the price of their pool-related products in an effort to liquidate their supply as demand falls.

As you can see from the example, supply and demand are closely related. If demand goes up, supply will go up—at least in an ideal world. If supply does not go up and demand remains high, the price will increase, because there isn't enough product to meet customers' needs. Consider the 2008 holiday season. Fisher Price's Elmo Live, Disney/Pixar's Ultimate Wall-E, and Hasbro's U-Dance were among the hottest toys available.[17] Since these toys were in high de-

Figure 2.3 The Equilibrium Point

Demand curve
Supply curve
Equilibrium point

Price ($): $1000, $900, $700, $700, $600, $500, $400, $300, $200, $100, 0

Quantity of HDTVs: 50 100 150 200 250 300 350 400 450 500

mand, it was not uncommon for stores to quickly run out of them. Many people who were able to buy them resold them on auction Web sites, such as eBay, for a tidy profit. Supply and demand can also dramatically affect an entire industry. In 2009, many people tightened their wallets and chose not to buy costlier items, such as automobiles. As a result, demand for steel in Europe declined by 15 percent.[18]

The ideal economic situation is when the economy is at an **equilibrium point**, the point at which the amount of goods sought by buyers is equal to the amount of goods produced by suppliers (see Figure 2.3). The airline and hotel industries offer good examples of supply and demand in action. As the seats on a flight or hotel rooms fill up, the price per ticket or room goes up.[19]

> **Equilibrium point** The point at which the amount of goods sought by buyers is equal to the amount of goods produced by suppliers.

Before we go further into economic theory, it is important to define the **business cycle**. The business cycle denotes a common pattern where there is a period of rapid growth (recovery and prosperity) in the economy when supply and demand stimulate each other, alternating with a period of decline (contraction or recession) with diminishing demand and supply. The business cycle is also called the *economic cycle*. See Figure 2.4.

> **Business cycle** A common pattern in which there is a period of rapid economic growth (recovery and prosperity) when supply and demand stimulate each other, alternating with a period of decline (contraction or recession) with diminishing demand and supply.

Figure 2.4 The Business/Economic Cycle

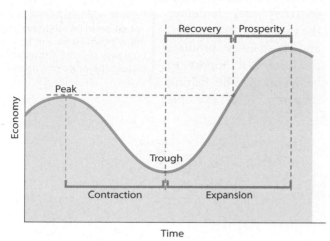

1. The right to own private property.

2. The right to own a business and keep all of that business's profits.

3. The right to freedom of competition.

4. The right to freedom of choice.

One benefit of capitalism is that it creates a **free market** in which people are willing to take more risks than they otherwise might. In a free market, decisions about what to produce and in what quantities are made by the market—that is, by buyers and sellers negotiating prices for goods and services. Consumers in the United States and in other free-market countries send signals to producers about what to make, how many of them to make, in what colors, and so on by choosing to buy (or not to buy) certain products and services.

> **Free market** A system in which decisions about what to produce and in what quantities are made by the market.

For example, if everyone decided they wanted HDTVs, the electronics industry would respond in certain ways. First, manufacturers and retailers would increase the price of HDTVs because they know people are willing to pay more for them. Next, the manufacturers would realize they could make more money by making more HDTVs. In order to build more HDTVs, the companies would have an incentive to pay their workers to start work earlier and end later. All of this activity would also spur competition, so the number of companies in the business of making HDTVs would increase.

Thus, how many HDTVs are made depends on how many we buy. The prices and quantities change as the number of HDTVs that are bought rises and falls. Consumers have immense power to determine the price of items and the availability of items in a free market, as they ultimately decide what is produced. In the next section, we'll discuss the four types of competition, a major force in a free-market system.

BUS connections

1. How are macroeconomics and microeconomics different? Are there similarities between the two?

2. What theory did Adam Smith develop? Describe it in your own words.

3. How are supply and demand interconnected? Give an example of a time when you wanted a product or a service, but it was not available for purchase. Explain.

>> Free-Market Capitalism

The economic system that has led to wealth creation in much of the world is known as **capitalism**. Under capitalism, all or most of the factors of production and distribution—such as land, factories, railroads, and stores—are owned by individuals and businesses. They are operated for profit, and businesspeople, not government officials, decide what to produce, how much of it to produce, what to charge for it, and how much to pay their workers.

> **Capitalism** An economic system in which all or most of the factors of production and distribution are privately owned and operated for profit.

Of course, no society is purely capitalist. Often, the government gets involved in certain issues, such as determining minimum wages, providing health care for certain groups of people, and lending money to key businesses if they are failing—as is the case in the United States. But capitalism is the *foundation* of the U.S. economic system.

People who live in a free-market capitalist society have four basic rights:

In a free market, decisions about what to produce and in what quantities are made by the market—that is, by buyers and sellers negotiating prices for goods and services. Consumers in the United States and in other free-market countries send signals to producers about what to make, how many of them to make, in what colors, and so on by choosing to buy (or not to buy) certain products and services.

Study Alert

COMPETITION IN FREE MARKETS

There are four commonly recognized degrees of competition: (1) perfect competition, (2) monopolistic competition, (3) oligopoly, and (4) monopoly.

Perfect competition exists when there are many businesses in a market and no one business is large enough to dictate the price of a product. Under perfect competition, it is relatively easy to enter the industry or market, and businesses produce products that appear to be identical. The fishing industry is an example

> **Perfect competition** A market condition in which there are many businesses and no one business is large enough to dictate the price of a product.

Thinking Critically

>> When Will Consumers Start Spending Again?

Have the current economic problems adversely affected your spending habits? Some experts believe that Americans are feeling somewhat positive about the economy and are more willing to open their pocketbooks. However, according to the article that follows by Ben Steverman, this muted enthusiasm about an economic recovery is balanced with considerable concern about the unemployment rate.

For the first time in a while, there is some good news for the U.S. consumer and for companies that rely on consumer spending. One booster is the rapid recovery in stock prices, with the Standard & Poor's 500 index jumping 47 percent since its low point in early March.

"Clearly, there is a wealth effect," says Keith Hembre, chief economist at First American Funds. As Americans feel wealthier, they may be more willing to spend. On Aug. 4, the Commerce Dept. said consumer spending rose 0.4 percent, after a revised 0.1 percent increase in May. The rise was boosted by spending on nondurable goods, which were up 1.7 percent in June.

Another positive for the U.S. consumer is efforts by the federal government to stimulate spending. Ford Motor said Aug. 3 that the "cash-for-clunkers" program was a big factor in its first monthly sales increase in almost two years. Ford's total sales (including fleet) rose 2 percent for July.

The problem with all this optimism about the U.S. consumer, however, is that it runs into a depressing reality: Americans are still losing their jobs, so they have less money to spend. When it comes to the economy, notes Michele Gambera, chief economist at Ibbotson Associates, a subsidiary of Morningstar, "the worry is that employment will not pick up anytime soon."

Gary Wolfer, chief economist with Univest Wealth Management, agrees. The unemployment rate will probably hit 10 percent by early 2010, he says. "I don't see those jobs coming back very quickly," Wolfer says, adding, "When jobs do come back, they're going to be totally different."

Source: Ben Steverman, "When Will Consumers Start Spending Again?" *BusinessWeek*, August 4, 2009 http://www.businessweek.com/investor/content/aug2009/pi2009084_745224.htm (accessed August 9, 2009). Reprinted with permission.

QUESTIONS

1. In your opinion, which is a more accurate indicator of economic conditions: consumer spending or unemployment? Why?

2. How have unemployment rates in your own community been affected by the economic downturn? How does the downturn affect the community at large?

of pure competition. Trout caught and sold in a lake in Minnesota are virtually identical to trout caught and sold in Michigan. As water temperature and disease influence the number of trout that are fished in a particular area, the price for this product will increase or decrease according to the law of supply and demand.

You should know, however, that there are no true examples of perfect competition. In the U.S. today, government price supports and drastic reductions in the total number of farms make it hard to argue that even farming is an example of perfect competition.

Monopolistic competition exists when a large number of businesses produce products that are very similar but are perceived by buyers as different (for example, hot dogs, candy, personal computers, or T-shirts). Actually, the competing products may even be interchangeable. Under monopolistic competition (not to be confused with monopoly, discussed later in this section), it is somewhat difficult to enter the industry or market, and **product differentiation** (an attempt to make buyers think similar products are different in some way) is a key to success. Think about what that means for just a moment. Through tactics like advertising, branding, and packaging, businesses signal to buyers that their products are different from those of competitors and, thus, they have some control over the prices they can charge. (We will discuss more about these differentiation methods in Chapter 4.) The pricing battles among restaurants in the fast-food industry offer a good example of monopolistic competition.

True perfect competition is almost impossible. Agricultural products (for example, apples, corn, or potatoes) are close, but government subsidies and consolidation have reduced the competitive market in agriculture.

ETHICAL **DILEMMA**

If you found that you could save money by hiring illegal immigrants and believed you could keep it a secret, what would you do?

Monopolistic competition A market condition in which a large number of businesses produce products that are very similar but are perceived by buyers as different.

Product differentiation An attempt to make buyers think similar products are different in some way.

Oligopoly A form of competition in which just a few businesses dominate a market.

An **oligopoly** is a form of competition in which just a few businesses dominate a market. Oligopolies exist in industries that produce products like breakfast cereal, tobacco, automobiles, soft drinks, steel, and cellular phone service. One reason some industries remain in the hands of just a few businesses is that the initial investment required to enter the industry is tremendous.

In an oligopoly, prices for products from different companies tend to be about the same. The reason why is simple: Intense price competition would lower profits for all competitors, since a price cut on the part of one producer would likely be matched by the others. As in monopolistic competition, product differentiation, rather than price, is usually the major factor in market success under oligopoly. For example, most cereals are priced similarly, as are soft drinks. Thus, advertising is a major factor in determining which of the few available brands consumers buy, because advertising can call attention to these differences—or even create them.

Perfect competition exists when there are many businesses in a market and no one business is large enough to dictate the price of a product. Monopolistic competition exists when a large number of businesses produce products that are very similar but are perceived by buyers as different (for example, hot dogs, candy, or T-shirts). An oligopoly occurs when just a few businesses dominate a market, and a monopoly occurs when only one business controls the total supply of a product and its price.

Study Alert

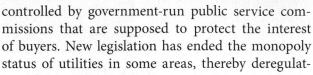

Another example of deregulation can be found in the cable industry. Most communities have only one cable provider because of the high cost of infrastructure. As a result, cable companies are carefully monitored to ensure their prices are fair to consumers. Also, it is illegal for cable companies to enter into exclusive agreements with apartment building owners. The Federal Communications Commission (FCC) now allows companies such as AT&T and Verizon to offer cable services. Such a law allows consumers more competitive choices.[23]

Pharmaceutical company GlaxoSmithKline was also accused of operating under a monopoly. According to the lawsuit, the company would not permit generic versions of its antidepressant, Paxil, to be produced. Although it still denies the allegations, the company agreed to pay a settlement of $14 million.[22]

Dr. Pepper recently introduced Dr. Pepper Cherry to its line of soft drinks. In the commercials for the drink, veteran rocker Gene Simmons of the 1970s band KISS introduces it as having just a "kiss" of cherry flavor.[20] Such an advertising campaign is an attempt to get consumers to identify a difference between Dr. Pepper Cherry and other cherry-flavored beverages, such as Coca-Cola Cherry and Pepsi Wild Cherry.

A **monopoly** occurs when only one business controls the total supply of a product and its price. In the United States, laws prohibit the creation of monopolies, which is one reason Microsoft was sued by the government in the 1990s—it appeared to be exerting monopoly power in the market for computer operating systems and Internet browsers (the case was settled in 2001).[21]

The U.S. legal system has permitted monopolies in public utilities markets that sell natural gas, water, and electric power. These utility companies' prices and profits usually have been monitored and controlled by government-run public service commissions that are supposed to protect the interest of buyers. New legislation has ended the monopoly status of utilities in some areas, thereby deregulating them. **Deregulation** refers to removal of government control and strict oversight in a market that thereby opens the market for others to enter. As a result, consumers in those areas are able to choose among utility providers. The intention of this deregulation is to increase competition among utility companies and, ultimately, lower prices for consumers. Figure 2.5 compares the four types of competition.

Monopoly A form of competition in which only one business controls the total supply of a product and its price.

Deregulation The removal of government control and strict oversight in a market that thereby opens the market for others to enter.

THE BENEFITS AND LIMITATIONS OF FREE MARKETS

A free market allows open competition among companies and encourages efficiency and effectiveness. Businesses in a free market must provide customers with high-quality products at fair prices with good

Figure 2.5 The Four Types of Competition

	Pure Competition	Monopolistic Competition	Oligopoly	Monopoly
Number of businesses competing	Numerous	Many	Few	One
Difficulty of entering the market	Easy	Somewhat difficult	Very difficult	Government regulated
Product similarity	Fairly identical	Fairly similar; perceived differences generated through marketing	Similar; perceived differences generated through marketing	Unique
Freedom in setting prices	Very little	Some	Some	Government regulated
Examples	Agricultural products	Retail clothing stores, fast-food restaurants	Automotive and steel industries	Public utilities (natural gas, electric)

service; if they don't, they'll lose customers to businesses that do. Free markets also allow the poor an opportunity to work their way out of poverty.

However, there are downsides to a free-market system. For example, some people let greed dictate how they behave in a free market.[24] For example, financier Bernard Madoff had given his investors unbeatable returns for more than 20 years. In December 2008, it was revealed that Madoff had been in effect stealing from his investors, to the tune of some $65 billion.[25]

[BUS] connections

1. What is a free-market system?
2. What are the four types of competition? Do you think one type of competition would be better than another in developing countries? Why or why not?
3. What companies in your community operate in perfect competition? Monopolistic competition? Which are parts of an oligopoly or are a monopoly? Does your opinion of these companies change because of the differences?

>> Socialism and Communism

SOCIALISM

Socialism is an economic system based on the premise that some, if not most, basic businesses—such as steel mills, coal mines, and utilities—should be owned by the government so profits can be evenly distributed among all people, perhaps through health care or retirement benefits.

Socialism An economic system based on the premise that some, if not most, basic businesses should be owned by the government so profits can be evenly distributed among all people.

As discussed in Chapter 1, high income or sales taxes in a country or state can discourage entrepreneurship. As you can imagine, under a socialist system, private businesses and individuals are taxed relatively steeply to pay for these social programs. Within the United States, state income taxes vary as well. The states with the highest state income tax rates are Hawaii, California, Rhode Island, Vermont, and Oregon.[26] Sales taxes are also a factor: The average American pays about 5 to 6 percent in sales taxes,[27] but many socialist countries charge a value-added tax (a type of sales tax) of 15 to 20 percent on most goods. [28]

Socialists acknowledge that their system can limit the major benefit of capitalism—wealth creation—but they believe that wealth should be more evenly distributed and that the government should be the agency that carries out that distribution. That's why government owns many of the factors of production in socialist nations.

Socialism has become the guiding economic platform for many countries in Europe, Africa, and much of the rest of the world. Socialist nations tend to rely heavily on the government to provide education, health care, retirement benefits, unemployment benefits, and other social services. However, some countries, such as France, are subtly moving away from socialism and leaning more to a hybrid of capitalism and socialism to get their economics moving faster.

Today, around 46 million Americans lack health insurance. If the health-care industry undergoes a reform that creates universal health insurance for U.S. citizens, 17 percent of the national economy would be socialized.[31]

The administration of U.S. president Barack Obama has endured criticism for what some say is an attempt to move the United States toward socialism. The administration plans to tax the wealthiest individuals in the country and use that money to pay for programs, such as education, climate change research, alternative energy development, and health care.[30]

In many socialist countries, the top tax rate is very high. For instance, the individual top income tax rate in Sweden is 57 percent and in Norway it is 49 percent.[29] This photo shows the Swedish capital of Stockholm.

Socialism has been more successful in some countries than in others. This photo shows Denmark's clean and modern public transportation system. In France, on the other hand, street riots erupted when young people protested legislation that would have allowed businesses to fire younger workers, and the legislation was withdrawn. What other factors might lead to slower growth in socialist countries?

The Benefits and Limitations of Socialism

The major benefit of socialism is supposed to be social equality, because income is taken from the wealthier people in the form of taxes and redistributed to the poorer members of the population through various government programs. Programs that provide free education, health care, and child care are among the benefits socialist governments distribute to citizens using tax revenues. Workers in socialist countries also usually get longer vacations than workers in capitalist countries, work fewer hours per week, and have more employee benefits, such as sick leave.

Socialism may create more equality than capitalism, but it also takes away some incentives to work hard. It can also take away the incentive to start new businesses or market new ideas. Today, many professionals living in socialist countries are subject to very high tax rates (often above 50 percent). As a consequence, many leave socialist countries for more capitalistic countries with lower taxes, such as the United States. This loss of the best and brightest people to other countries is called a **brain drain**.

Brain drain The loss of the best and brightest people to other countries.

Imagine if there were a socialist structure in your own class. After the first exam, everyone with grades of 90 and above would have to give some of their points to those with grades of 70 and below, until everyone ended up with grades in the 80s. Would the people who got perfect scores on the first exam study as hard for the next one? What about the students who got grades below 70? Would they work less hard if they knew they'd get extra points, even if they didn't do well? Can you see why workers may

not work as hard or as well if they all get the same benefits regardless of how hard they work?

Socialist systems tend to discourage the best from working as hard as they can. In the business world, socialism also results in fewer inventions and less innovation because those who come up with new ideas usually don't receive as much reward as they would in a capitalist system. As a result, people may not be motivated to try new ideas. It is important, however, not to confuse socialism with communism.

COMMUNISM

Communism is an economic and political system in which the government makes almost all economic decisions and owns almost all the major factors of production. It intrudes further into the lives of people than socialism does. For example, some communist countries have not allowed their citizens to practice certain religions, change jobs, or move to the town of their choice.

Communism An economic and political system in which the state (the government) makes almost all economic decisions and owns almost all the major factors of production, including housing for its people.

One problem with communism is that the government has no way of knowing what to produce, because prices don't reflect supply and demand as they do in free markets. The government must guess what the people need. As a result, shortages of many items, including food and clothing, may develop. Another problem is that communism doesn't inspire businesspeople to work hard because the incentives are not there. Therefore, communism is slowly disappearing as an economic form.

Most communist countries today are suffering severe economic depression. In North Korea, many people are starving. In Cuba, people are suffering from a lack of goods and services readily available in most other countries, and some people fear the gov-

Communism and socialism are different concepts. Communism is an economic and political system in which the state makes almost all economic decisions and owns almost all the major factors of production, and socialism is an economic system based on the premise that some, if not most, businesses should be owned by the government so profits can be evenly distributed.

Study Alert

ernment. During the fiscal year 2007, the U.S. Coast Guard caught 2,656 people trying to cross the sea to gain entry into the United States.[32]

Some parts of the former Soviet Union remain governed under communist concepts, but the movement there is toward free markets. In fact, Russia now has a flat tax of 13 percent for individuals and 20 percent for corporations,[33] much lower than the tax rate in the United States. When Russia introduced its flat tax, its tax revenues jumped by nearly 30 percent because most people no longer tried to avoid them. There are several advantages to a flat tax. These include simplicity and transparency. People have more of an incentive to work, and corrupt practices, such as trading on the black market, are diminished.

The trend toward freer markets in communist countries is also appearing in Vietnam and parts of China. The regions in China that are most free have prospered, while the rest of the country has grown relatively slowly.

Adam Boyle owns a restaurant. Today, Adam has a meeting at the restaurant with Leah Hess, a sales representative for one of his food suppliers. Over the years, Adam's and Leah's working relationship has grown into a friendship. Adam's restaurant is located just blocks away from an automobile plant that recently closed. Many of Adam's regular customers were workers from the plant. In addition to coming in for their lunch hour, many of them lived in the area and visited the restaurant with their families in the evenings and on weekends.

As he talks about the business with Leah, Adam mentions that although his business is not directly related to the automobile, housing, or oil industries, his sales have been dramatically affected by economic problems in those industries. Leah agrees, adding that her company has been forced to once again increase prices because high gasoline prices have had a huge impact on their distribution costs.

Adam says, "I'm not surprised. This recession has been a real nightmare. The unemployed plant workers can't afford to eat out much anymore. Many of them are moving out of the area because they can't afford to stay in their homes. My highest cost—my employees' wages—is probably going to have to rise because it's so expensive for them to drive here now that gas is so expensive."

Leah replies, "What are you going to do? Ask the government for financial assistance?"

Adam thinks for a moment before responding. "Considering that I've had such a large drop in business, it is getting extremely challenging to meet our financial obligations and still provide a quality product and good service." He leans closer to Leah and confides, "A friend of mine has started hiring people illegally and paying them in cash only. I'm considering doing it, too, just to keep afloat."

Leah nods. She understands where Adam is coming from, but as his friend, she is concerned about the consequences he might suffer if he gets caught.

If you found that you could save money by hiring illegal immigrants and believed you could keep it a secret, what would you do?

QUESTIONS

1. Describe the ethical issues in this situation. If you were Leah, what suggestions would you offer Adam to help him confront and deal with these issues?

2. Do you think the government should become more involved in assisting businesses that are affected by recessions and other economic downturns? Explain your response.

Many Eastern European countries are moving toward a flat tax, and China is also considering adopting one.[34] This photo shows Beijing, China's capital city. Countries with low flat tax rates are competing to lower their rates. Estonia dropped its flat tax rate from 26 percent to 22 percent, and by 2011, it will drop again, to 18 percent. The rate in Macedonia is expected to drop to 10 percent next year. Montenegro will have the world's lowest flat tax rate in 2010 at 9 percent.[35]

THE TREND TOWARD MIXED ECONOMIES

The nations of the world have largely been divided between those that have followed the concepts of capitalism and those that have adopted the concepts of communism or socialism. Thus, the two primary economic systems that have emerged are:

1. **Free-market economies**, which exist when the market largely determines what goods and services get produced, who gets them, and how the economy grows. *Capitalism* is the popular term used to describe this economic system.

2. **Command economies**, which exist when the government largely decides what goods and services get produced, who gets them, and how the economy grows. *Socialism* and *communism* are the popular terms used to describe variations of this economic system.

Historically, neither free-market nor command economies have resulted in optimal economic conditions. Free-market economies haven't been responsive enough to the needs of individuals who are poor, elderly, and disabled, and many believe that they don't adequately care for people who may need the most help.

On the other hand, socialist and communist countries haven't always created enough jobs or wealth to keep their economies growing fast enough. As a consequence, communist governments are disappearing, and socialist governments have begun to cut back on social programs and lower taxes on businesses and workers. The idea is to generate more business growth and thus generate more revenue.[36]

The economic picture we see in the real world today, thus, is more mixed. The trend has been for traditionally capitalist countries to move toward a more socialist system—to provide programs to take care of disadvantaged people and to better safeguard the environment—while some socialist and communist countries have adopted elements of capitalism. In a given society, this blend is called a mixed economy.

Mixed economies exist where some allocation of resources is made by the market and some is by the government. If the dominant way of allocating

> **Free-market economies** Economic systems in which the market largely determines what goods and services get produced, who gets them, and how the economy grows.
>
> **Command economies** Economic systems in which the government largely decides what goods and services will be produced, who will get them, and how the economy will grow.

Figure 2.6 Comparisons of Key Economic Systems

	Capitalism	Socialism	Communism	Mixed Economy
Type of ownership	Private ownership of land and business	Public ownership of major businesses	Public ownership of all businesses	Private ownership of land and business with government regulation
Motivation of workers	High	Little	Very little	Similar to capitalism except in government-owned enterprises, which may have fewer incentives
Government control over markets	None	Some	Total	Some
Choices in the market	Wide variety	Varies from country to country	Very little	Similar to capitalism
Social freedoms	High level of freedom	Some restrictions on freedoms of assembly and speech	Very limited freedom	Similar to socialism
Examples	Singapore	Sweden, Finland, Belgium	Cuba, North Korea, Vietnam	United States

resources is by free-market mechanisms, the leaders still call the system capitalism; if the dominant way of allocating resources is by the government, the leaders call it socialism. Figure 2.6 compares the various economic systems.

Like most other nations of the world, the United States has a mixed economy. The optimal degree of government involvement in the economy today is a matter of debate, as it has been at various times in the past. The U.S. government is the country's largest employer; in fact, more Americans work in the public sector (for government) than in the entire manufacturing sector.

There is much debate about how much the U.S. government should be involved in health care, education, business regulation, and other parts of the economy. According to *Forbes*, the best countries for business in 2009 include Denmark, the United States, Canada, Singapore, and New Zealand. At least 50 countries have recently passed or plan to pass laws that cut taxes on individuals and businesses in an effort to help entrepreneurship prosper.[37]

Should Americans care about the types of economic systems other countries employ? Yes, because the trend of globalization causes nations to depend on each other for products and services. It is in our best interest for other countries to prosper, too.

>> Economic Indicators

So far, we have discussed basic economic concepts, such as supply and demand, and several types of economies. This section will discuss some of the key economic indicators a government uses to figure out how well the economy is doing.

The major indicators of economic conditions are (1) gross domestic product (GDP), (2) unemployment rate, (3) price indexes and inflation, (4) interest rates, and (5) national debt. You'll see these terms used again and again in the media. Knowing and understanding these terms will greatly increase your ability to assess the nation's economy and become a stronger businessperson and consumer.

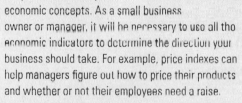

Career PERSPECTIVES

ECONOMICS AND YOU

Economics is an interesting field because it is a mix of business and research. No matter what your chosen career might be, you will definitely use economic concepts. As a small business owner or manager, it will be necessary to use all the economic indicators to determine the direction your business should take. For example, price indexes can help managers figure out how to price their products and whether or not their employees need a raise.

GDP is another important indicator to small business owners or managers. Knowing the overall health of the economy can help an entrepreneur determine if he should expand the business or hire more people. Following and understanding consumption figures are also crucial to being successful in business. Managers and business owners can determine where and how customers are spending money, allowing them to make better decisions about the types of products and services they offer. Supply and demand affect you on both a professional and a personal level. Think about buying gas for your car. The price goes up when supply is limited and demand is high.

Whether you use economic concepts in your workplace, personal life, or both, you will find this knowledge will help you stay one step ahead of your competition. What are some other ways that economic indicators will help you as you begin your career in business? How do you think they may affect you in your personal life?

[BUS] connections

1. What is the difference between socialism and communism? How are they the same? Which do you think is better, and why?

2. Compare free-market economies with socialism. What are the advantages and disadvantages of each?

3. What is a mixed economy? What would the United States have to do to move from a mixed economy to a pure free-market capitalism system? Explain. Why are so many countries moving toward mixed economies? Do you think that eventually countries will begin to move more toward pure systems (either free-market or command economies)? Why or why not?

GROSS DOMESTIC PRODUCT

Gross domestic product (GDP) is the total value of final goods and services produced in a country in a given year. Either a domestic or foreign-owned company may produce the goods and services included in the GDP, as long as the company is located within the measuring country's boundaries. For example, production values for a New Jersey factory owned by the Swiss food company Nestlé would be included in the U.S. GDP, because the production takes place within the country's borders. Likewise, revenue generated by an Australian factory owned by the U.S. food company Kraft would be included in Australia's GDP.

> **Gross domestic product (GDP)** The total value of final goods and services produced in a country in a given year.

Another way to measure GDP is per capita, which means per person. This measurement takes the total GDP and divides it by the number of people who live in the country. The United States had an estimated GDP per capita of $48,000 in 2009.[38] Countries with the lowest GDP per capita in 2008 include Nepal, Uganda, and the Comoros Islands.[39] The nations with the highest GDP per capita in the same year were Qatar, Luxembourg, and Kuwait.[40]

Gross national product (GNP), a similar term, refers to the value of goods and services produced by a country's factors of production—regardless of where these factors are based in the world. Production values from that Kraft factory in Australia would be included in Australia's GDP, but they wouldn't be included in the country's GNP. Because Kraft is a U.S. company, these revenues would be included in the U.S.'s GNP.

> **Gross national product (GNP)** The value of goods and services produced by a country's factors of production, regardless of where these factors are based.

Almost every discussion about a nation's economy is based on GDP. The total U.S. GDP in 2008 was about $14.33 trillion.[41] The level of U.S. economic activity is actually larger than the GDP figures show, because the figures don't consider illegal activities like sales of illegal drugs. A high GDP allows Americans to enjoy a high standard of living,[42] but during the last three months of 2008, the GDP of the United States fell to its lowest point in 26 years.[43]

In an economic boom, businesses do well. If GDP growth slows or declines, there are often negative effects on businesses. A major influence on the growth of GDP is how productive the workforce is—how much output workers create with a given amount of

input. A **recession** occurs when the GDP declines for two or more financial quarters (that is, three-month periods). During a recession, prices fall (a situation known as deflation, which will be covered later in this chapter), people purchase fewer products, and some businesses fail. A **depression** is a severe recession. A depression usually occurs during times of deflation and unemployment and is extremely serious. Eventually, a **recovery** will occur, and the economy will stabilize and begin to grow again.

> **Recession** A period during which the GDP of a nation declines for two or more quarters.
>
> **Depression** A severe recession.
>
> **Recovery** A period following a recession during which an economy stabilizes and begins to grow again.

So during a recession, do all businesses suffer? Not at all. Despite the fact that some businesses are losing money, others manage to prosper. For example, during tough economic times, many consumers repair used items instead of buying new ones; Roger Payne, an auto mechanic in Texas, had more customers during the depths of the 2008–2009 recession than ever before. During the same recession, some lawyers prospered as the number of bankruptcies increased, and for-profit universities and career schools benefited from an influx of students eager to train for a new career. Businesses that manufacture products enjoyed in the home, such as the Nintendo Wii, thrived

The Great Depression that began in the late 1920s in the United States lasted almost an entire decade. In this photo, a family impoverished by the Depression stands outside their shack.

because people tend to stay home more often when the economy slows.[44]

Some of today's top companies, such as Procter & Gamble, IBM, General Electric, United Technologies Corp., and FedEx, were founded at times when other companies were experiencing major losses.[45] It is possible to become a successful entrepreneur during a recession; you just have to manage the risk with the reward.

THE UNEMPLOYMENT RATE

The next economic indicator is the **unemployment rate**, which is the number of civilians 16 years of age and older who are unemployed and have tried to find a job within the prior four weeks. There are four types of unemployment: cyclical, seasonal, frictional, and structural; see Figure 2.7 to learn more about each.

> **Unemployment rate** The number of civilians 16 years of age and older who are unemployed and have tried to find a job within the prior four weeks.

In 2000, the U.S. unemployment rate reached its lowest point in recent history, falling as low as 3.9 percent, but the rate rose rapidly to over 6 percent as a result of the economic slowdown of 2002–2003. In May 2009, the unemployment rate in the United States reached 9.4 percent.[46]

Figure 2.8 shows trends in U.S. unemployment since 1948, and Figure 2.9 shows the period from 2008 to 2009, as the economy weakened and unemployment rose sharply. The U.S. government provides unemployment benefits to temporarily provide income for people who lose their jobs because of recessions, industry shifts, and other cyclical factors. However, people who are fired for certain reasons, such as failing a drug test, are often unable to collect unemployment benefits.[47]

Figure 2.8 The U.S. Unemployment Rate 1948–2009

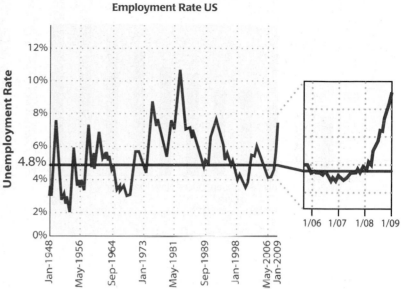

Employment Rate US

Source: http://www.therazor.org/images/unemployment_graph.jpg

Figure 2.7 The Four Types of Unemployment

Type	Description
Cyclical	Not enough jobs for the people who want them, usually as a result of political or economic forces.
Seasonal	Some work can only take place during certain months of the year (for example, construction workers who cannot work during harsh winters, or people who operate snowplows and thus have no work when it's too warm to snow), and seasonal unemployment affects these workers.
Frictional	A state wherein people are between jobs, such as a two-week period between ending one job and beginning another.
Structural	A major shift in an industry causes people to lose their jobs, like when telephone-based customer service jobs began to be outsourced to developing nations, such as India.

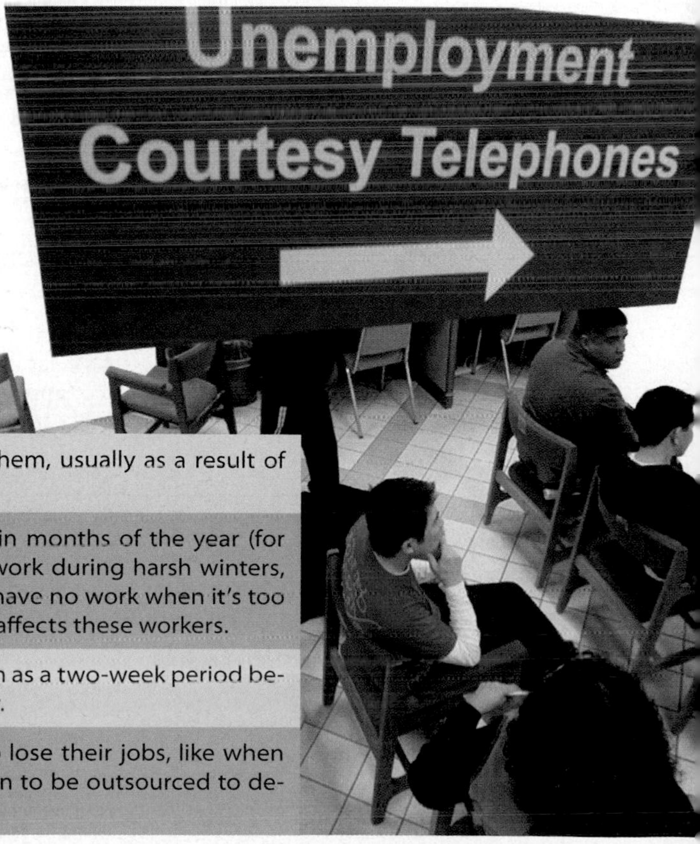

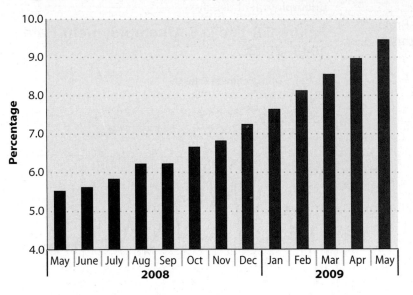

Figure 2.9 The U.S. Unemployment Rate 2008–2009

Source: http://stats.bls.gov/opub/ted/2009/jun/wk2/art02.htm

PRICE INDEXES

Another economic indicator is **inflation**, a general rise in the prices of goods and services over time.[48]

Inflation A general rise in the prices of goods and services over time.

Some amount of inflation—about 2 percent per year—is considered normal; goods are expected to get slightly more expensive to produce because of increases in wages and other manufacturing costs.

Figure 2.10 The U.S. CPI from January 1999 to January 2009

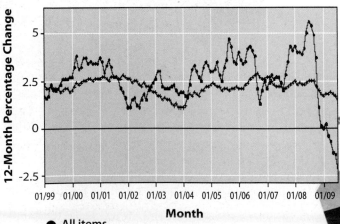

● All items
● All items less food and energy

Source: Bureau of Labor Statistics, Consumer Price Index, http://data.bls.gov/PDQ/servlet/SurveyOutputServlet?request_action=wh&graph_name=CU_cpibrief (accessed June 17, 2009).

Stagflation occurs when inflation and unemployment are simultaneously high. Many economists believe stagflation is a result of misguided fiscal and monetary policy by the federal government. Stagflation is harmful because it means that prices are rising while people are losing their jobs or do not have jobs.

Stagflation A situation where the economy is slowing but prices are rising.

Deflation, a situation in which prices are declining,[49] occurs when countries produce so many goods that people can't afford to buy them all. When there are too few dollars for too many goods, supply and demand are out of balance.

Deflation A general decline in the prices of goods and services over time.

Price indexes are economic indicators that reveal the effects of inflation. Two widely used measures of inflation are the consumer price index and the producer price index. The **consumer price index (CPI)** is a set of monthly statistics that measure the pace of inflation or deflation. The CPI measures costs of about 200 categories of goods and services—including housing, food, clothing, and medical care—to see if they are rising or falling.[50] In 2009, the CPI dropped to its lowest point in 59 years.[51] Figure 2.10 shows the U.S. CPI from 1999 to 2009.

Consumer price index (CPI) A set of monthly statistics that measures the pace of inflation or deflation.

You can access the CPI Inflation Calculator at http://www.bls.gov/data/inflation_calculator.htm to learn how much buying power a given amount of money had in any year from 1913 to today. For example, $5.00 in 1913 had the same buying power as $108.01 in 2009. The CPI is an important figure because certain wages and salaries, rents and leases, tax brackets, government benefits, and interest rates are based on it.

While the CPI measures prices at the consumer level, the **producer price index (PPI)** measures prices at the wholesale level. In other words, the PPI measures price change from the perspective of the seller, whereas the CPI measures the price change from the purchaser's perspective.[52] Figure 2.11 shows the PPI from 1999 to 2009.

Figure 2.11 PPI from 1999 to 2009

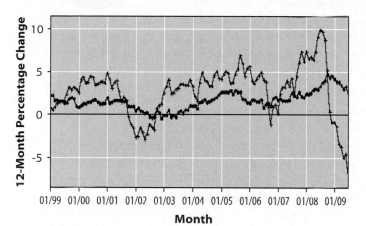

● **Finished goods less food and energy**
● **Finished goods**

Source: Bureau of Labor Statistics, Producer Price Index, http://data.bls.gov/PDQ/servlet/SurveyOutputServlet?request_action=wh&graph_name=WP_ppibrief (accessed June 17, 2009).

INTEREST RATES

Have you ever wondered how money gets added or subtracted from the economy? This process is managed by the Federal Reserve System (the Fed), a semi-public organization that is not under the direct control of the government but some of its administrators are appointed by the U.S. president.

Monetary policy is the management of the money supply and **interest rates** by the Federal Reserve Bank. This management helps control the growth or slowing of the economy. The Fed's most visible role is in the raising and lowering of interest rates. When the economy is booming, the Fed tends to raise interest rates, making money more expensive to borrow. Businesses borrow less, and the economy slows as businesspeople spend less money. When the Fed lowers interest rates, businesses borrow more, and the economy is expected to grow.

Raising and lowering interest rates should therefore help control the rapid ups and downs of the economy, but it doesn't always work. In 2008, the Fed

lowered interest rates to near zero, but the economy remained sluggish.[53]

The Fed also controls the money supply. A simple explanation of this function is that the more money the Fed makes available to businesspeople and others, the faster the economy is supposed to grow. To slow the economy (and prevent inflation), the Fed lowers the money supply. The Fed poured money into the economy early in 2008. What would you expect the result to be? Is that what happened?

To sum up, there are two major tools for managing the economy of the United States: fiscal policy (government taxes and spending) and monetary policy (the Fed's control over interest rates and the money supply). The goal is to keep the economy growing so that more people can move up the economic ladder and enjoy a higher standard of living and quality of life.

Many people wonder why the government doesn't simply print more money if it is needed. The main reason is fear of inflation. If the government printed more money, it would cost much more to buy the things we need simply because there is more money available. As you learned in the discussion about supply and demand, if there is more of something (in this case, money), it is worth less.

THE NATIONAL DEBT

Where do you think the government gets its money, and where is it spent? Mostly, government gets its revenue from taxes: individual income and corporate taxes; Social Security, Medicare, and payroll taxes; and other forms of taxation. It spends money on highways, social programs, education, defense, and so on.

The **national deficit** is the money the federal government spends over and above its revenue for a specific period of time. When a government spends more money than it collects, it raises enough money to pay its expenses by issuing government bonds. These bonds are basically IOUs on which it pays interest. These bonds can be bought by individuals, organizations, or other governments. The **national debt** is the sum of government deficits over time. As of June 2009, the U.S. national debt was over

Going GLOBAL

Is Offshoring Causing GDP and Productivity Growth to Be Overstated?

Economic statistics collected by the U.S. government are probably as honest and accurate as those collected anywhere in the world. Offshoring, GDP, and productivity growth are widely considered key indicators of national success—just what the doctor ordered, or are they? Measuring data about offshoring, the GDP, and why these factors relate to productivity growth is an endless challenge. Do you think the numbers are too positively or too negatively skewed? Does growth necessarily mean progress?

Question: Is offshoring causing GDP and productivity growth to be overstated?

Answer: A recent set of articles in *BusinessWeek* (see *BusinessWeek* Online June 8, 2007) suggests that the real cost of offshoring has been understated because there is a "flaw" in the way that price statistics treat offshoring and that, as a result, real GDP and productivity growth are actually less robust than official statistics indicate. However, analysts at [the U.S. Department of Commerce's Bureau of Economic Analysis (BEA)]—who are continuously updating the official estimates to reflect the impact of globalization—do not think that there is a significant bias on measured GDP or productivity growth.

The argument made in the articles hinges on the fact that the import price data—published by the Bureau of Labor Statistics and used by BEA to "deflate" or convert nominal imports to real imports—do not reflect the full cost saving when foreign suppliers are substituted for domestic suppliers. However, import price indexes are designed to measure the change over time in the prices paid by U.S. residents for imported goods and services; they do not directly compare the prices of imported goods (and services) to their counterparts produced in the United States.

This is a manifestation of an old and difficult problem in price measurement. The argument fails to recognize that an offset occurs when domestic goods and services are purchased in the United States. That is, if real imports are understated because shifts to foreign suppliers are not being adequately captured in the price data, it is also likely that domestic production is understated because of shifts to more efficient domestic suppliers. Furthermore, BEA uses chain-type measures that are designed to account for much of this substitution. Any remaining measurement errors should be offsetting because researchers have not demonstrated that errors in measuring imports are larger than offsetting errors in measuring domestic production.

There is no clear "fix" for the price measurement problem beyond the adoption of chained-dollar estimates to measure real GDP, which BEA adopted in 1996. Nominal, or current-dollar, GDP is not affected because the amount deducted from nominal GDP for imports represents the actual amount spent for imports. Further, there are no distortions in the nominal trade balance, or other nominal measures, such as corporate profits and wages and salaries.

Source: U.S. Department of Commerce Bureau of Economic Analysis Web site, http://faq.bea.gov/cgi-bin/bea.cfg/php/enduser/std_adp.php?p_faqid=447&p_created=1181595343 (accessed August 9, 2009).

Questions

1. Why do you think collecting data pertaining to the GDP and offshoring is difficult? How accurate do you think the currently collected data really are?

2. Which of the following factors do you think contribute to overstated productivity growth: government consumption spending, ethnic diversity, or educational quality? Explain your response.

Real World Apps

After attending his economics class for a few weeks, Jim realizes he had been in denial about the realities of the economy. In fact, the economy is affecting everything in his life—for example, the lender who had issued his school loan has closed its doors because so many other students defaulted on their loans.

Sure, right now might be a great time to buy a car, but getting credit is much harder now than it used to be. Regulatory changes in the banking industry in the 1980s and 1990s made banking and loans more competitive, but easy credit meant that many people who borrowed money for cars and homes weren't able to pay them back, particularly as the recession led to job losses.

All these seemingly distant events directly affect Jim. Armed with this newfound knowledge, Jim realizes that if he doesn't start paying attention to the economy now, he won't be able to someday fulfill his dream of successfully running his own business. Living in a country with a capitalist-based economy will allow him to achieve his dream someday if he works hard—but he must pay close attention to the fundamentals of economics.

Figure 2.12 The National Debt

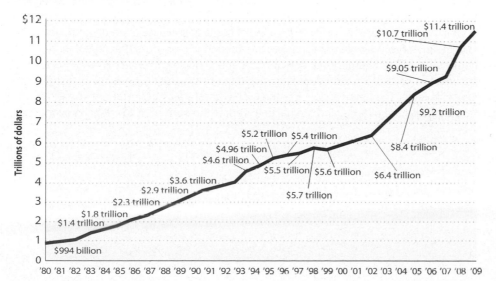

Monetary policy is the management of the money supply and interest rates by the Federal Reserve Bank. The Fed's most visible role is in the raising and lowering of interest rates. In good times, the Fed tends to raise interest rates to make it more expensive to borrow money. This slows down the economy. When the Fed lowers interest rates, businesses borrow more, and the economy usually grows.

[BUS] connections

1. Differentiate between GDP and GNP.
2. What are the four types of unemployment? Which type of unemployment have you heard of or seen the most in your own community?
3. Why is it important to understand inflation? How is it measured?

$11.4 trillion. That's close to $37,000 for every man, woman, and child in the United States.[54]

One way to lessen the deficit is to cut government spending. Many U.S. presidents have promised to make government smaller by lowering spending—but that doesn't happen very often. There always seems to be a need for more social programs or defense spending each year, and thus the deficits continue and add to the national debt. Some people believe government spending helps the economy grow. Others believe the money the government spends comes out of the pockets of consumers and businesspeople and thus slows growth.

The national debt in the United States is growing at a fast pace. It took the federal government 191 years to accumulate its first $1 trillion in debt, but since then, the debt's growth has taken off.[55] Figure 2.12 shows the growth of the U.S. national debt since 1980.

For REVIEW >>

1. Understand the basics of economics, including supply and demand.
   - Economics is the study of how society employs scarce resources to create and distribute products. This chapter introduced some basic economic concepts, such as opportunity cost, supply and demand, and the business cycle. Economist Adam Smith found that as individuals try to improve their own situations, their efforts serve as a guiding "invisible hand" that helps the larger economy grow and prosper. Supply is the availability of goods, and demand is the amount of goods consumers are willing to buy. If supply is higher than demand, the price of the good will normally decrease; if supply is lower than demand, the price will rise.

2. Describe free-market capitalism and degrees of competition.
   - Capitalism is an economic system in which all or most of the factors of production and distribution are privately owned and operated for profit. This system creates a free market, where decisions about what to produce and in what quantities are made by the market. Consumers in the United States and in other free-market countries send signals to producers about what to make, how many of an item to make, in what colors, and so on by choosing to buy (or not to buy) certain products and services. In socialism and communism, on the other hand, most means of production and distribution are owned by the government, which intends to distribute wealth more evenly than capitalism. Today, there is a trend toward mixed economies, where the government owns some factors of production, while private businesses own others. Perfect competition exists when there are many businesses in a market and no one business is large enough to dictate the price of a product. Monopolistic competition exists when a large number of businesses produce products that are very similar but are perceived by buyers as different (for example, hot dogs, candy, personal computers, or T-shirts). An oligopoly occurs when just a few businesses dominate a market, and a monopoly occurs when only one business controls the total supply of a product and its price.

3. Understand the differences between socialism and communism.
   - Communism and socialism are different concepts. Communism is an economic and political system in which the state (the government) makes almost all economic decisions and owns almost all the major factors of production, including housing for its people, and socialism is an economic system based on the premise that some, if not most, basic businesses should be owned by the government so profits can be evenly distributed among all people.

4. Discuss the major indicators of economic conditions.
   - Economists use various indicators to measure how well the economy is doing. The major indicators of economic conditions are (1) GDP, (2) unemployment rate, (3) price indexes and inflation, (4) interest rates, and (5) national debt. GDP measures the final goods and services produced in a country. The next economic indicator is the unemployment rate, which is the number of civilians 16 years of age and older who are unemployed and have tried to find a job within the prior four weeks. Price indexes are economic indicators that reveal the effects of inflation, which is a general rise in prices over time, or deflation, a general decline in prices. The CPI is a set of monthly statistics that measures the pace of inflation or deflation, and the PPI is a set of monthly statistics that measures prices at the wholesale level. The national deficit is the money the federal government spends over and above its revenue for a specific period of time, and the national debt is the sum of many deficits over time.

Key Terms

Brain drain	Economics	Macroeconomics	Perfect competition
Business cycle	Equilibrium point	Microeconomics	Producer price index (PPI)
Capitalism	Free market	Mixed economies	Product differentiation
Command economies	Free-market economies	Monetary policy	Recession
Communism	Gross domestic product (GDP)	Monopolistic competition	Recovery
Consumer price index (CPI)		Monopoly	Resource development
Deflation	Gross national product (GNP)	National debt	Socialism
Demand	Inflation	National deficit	Stagflation
Depression	Interest rates	Oligopoly	Supply
Deregulation	Invisible hand	Opportunity cost	Unemployment rate

<< Think AND DISCUSS

1. What are the advantages to capitalism? What are the disadvantages? Create a list of at least five for each. Discuss how each of the following events might affect the economy of the United States:

   a. An outbreak of the H1N1 (swine) flu.

   b. A passenger plane crashing into the Atlantic Ocean off the coast of Georgia.

   c. The increasing popularity of recycling and environmentalism in business.

   d. The election of a new U.S. president.

2. Do you agree with Adam Smith's theory that the "invisible hand" turns self-directed gain into benefit for all? Why or why not? Discuss in groups.

3. In groups, discuss examples of the following occasions:

   a. When demand has not met supply in consumer markets.

   b. When price strongly affects the demand of a product.

   c. When price does not affect the demand of a product.

INTERNET IN >> Action

1. Your boss, the owner of a local gas station, would like you to look up some data in order to predict future sales. Go to the CPI page of the Bureau of Labor Statistics at http://www.bls.gov/cpi/. In the database category, click on Average Price Data and Top Picks. Under Top Picks, select gasoline, all types, and review the data.
   - What was the average price for a gallon of gas last month?
   - What was its cost during the same month last year? Ten years ago?
   - How could you use these data to predict gas prices?

2. This chapter discussed inflation. Let's look at how inflation can affect the cost of things over time. Visit http://data.bls.gov/cgi-bin/cpicalc.pl and answer the following questions.
   - If you bought a pair of shoes for $25 in 1980, how much would those shoes cost you today?
   - If you spent $100 on two concert tickets today, how much would those tickets have cost in 1990?
   - You do some yard work for your neighbor and earn $50. How much would that $50 have been worth the year you were born?

Self-Assessment Exercises

BUSINESS CAREER QUIZ

Check Your Economics Knowledge Quiz!

Answer the following questions:

1. Which of these options best describes the U.S. Federal Reserve?
   a. Responsible for monetary policy and money supply
   b. Prints money
   c. Keeps the country out of debt
   d. Helps people in need

2. What is the basic purpose of profits in the U.S. market economy?
   a. To pay for wages and salaries of workers
   b. To lead businesses to produce what consumers want
   c. To transfer income to the wealthy
   d. All of the above

3. Who sets monetary policy in the United States?
   a. Congress
   b. The president
   c. U.S. Treasury
   d. Federal Reserve System

4. The prices of meat products in a competitive market are determined by:
   a. Government
   b. Business monopolies
   c. Supply and demand
   d. The CPI

5. The purchasing power of people's incomes is most affected by:
   a. The inflation rate
   b. The trade deficit
   c. The balance of payments

6. What was the current national rate of unemployment in 2009?
   a. 1 to 3 percent
   b. 4 to 6 percent
   c. 7 to 9 percent
   d. More than 10 percent

7. Which one of the following is the most widely used measure of inflation?
   a. The CPI
   b. The Index of Leading Economic Indicators
   c. The prime rate
   d. The federal funds rate

8. What was the current annual rate of inflation in 2009?
   a. 1 percent or less
   b. 2 to 3 percent
   c. 6 to 7 percent
   d. 10 to 12 percent

9. What economic policy would most likely be used to combat a recession when inflation is low?
   a. An increase in taxes
   b. An increase in the money supply
   c. An increase in stock market prices.

10. Economic growth is measured by a positive change in which of the following?
    a. The money supply
    b. The PPI
    c. The GDP
    d. The balance of payments

11. There is a deficit in the federal budget when:
    a. The government spends more than it collects in revenue.
    b. U.S. imports are greater than U.S. exports.
    c. The total demand for money is greater than the total supply of money.

Answers:

1. a	4. c	7. a	10. c
2. b	5. a	8. a	11. a
3. d	6. d	9. b	

If you got more than seven questions right, congratulations! You are comfortable with economics concepts. If you got fewer than seven right, consider rereading this chapter and reviewing the exercises to hone your economics knowledge. You can learn more by continuing to read periodicals and newspapers, watch the news, and think about how the concepts presented here relate to your daily life.

Source: Great Nebraska Economics Test, http://ecedweb.unomaha.edu/ecedweek/quiz.htm (accessed June 23, 2009). Reprinted with permission.

How Financially Literate Are You?

Take this financial literacy quiz to find out if you have the knowledge you need to build a sound financial future.

Choose the correct answers:

1. What is the highest recommended percentage of your after-tax income that should be spent on housing?
   a. 10 percent
   b. 25 percent
   c. 30 percent
   d. 45 percent

2. What is the maximum percentage of your budget that you should aim to spend on transportation?
   a. 20 percent
   b. 15 percent
   c. 10 percent
   d. 5 percent

3. When it comes to credit cards, it's better to have:
   a. No credit cards
   b. One credit card and carry a balance from month to month
   c. One or more credit cards, but pay off the balances every month
   d. One credit card that is never used

4. If you purchase a new sofa for $1,200 on a credit card with an 18 percent interest rate and only make the required minimum payment each month (2 percent of the balance), how long will it take to pay it off?
   a. Four years
   b. 10 years
   c. 25 years
   d. More than 40 years

5. How many months of expenses should you set aside in an emergency fund?
   a. One to two
   b. Three to six
   c. Six to eight
   d. Eight to twelve

Answers:

1. The answer is c. Unless you live in an area where accommodation is particularly expensive, such as New York City, 30 percent is a good percentage to aim for. Spending less than 30 percent is even better, especially if you are carrying a heavy debt load.

2. The answer is b. This should include car payments, insurance, gas, parking, and transit. Personal finance issues, such as budgets, will be discussed in the Bonus Chapter.

3. The answer is c. In order to build a strong credit score, which is a key component of your financial future, it is best to use a couple of select, low-interest credit cards and pay the balances in full every month.

4. The answer is d. In fact, it will take you just over 50 years to pay off the sofa. The total interest you'd pay would be almost $3,500, bringing the final cost of the sofa to nearly $4,700. It's best to avoid using high-interest cards to purchase items that you are unable to pay off quickly.

5. The answer is b. Three to six months of expenses is a good benchmark to aim for. Don't forget to account for any extra expenses that you may incur, such as tuition fees for your college-bound child.

Source: Lending Tree, "How Financially Literate Are You?" http://www.lendingtree.com/smartborrower/saving-money/financial-literacy-guide/financial-literacy-quiz/ (accessed June 23, 2009). Reprinted with permission.

- What does it take to be an entrepreneur?
- What are good reasons to incorporate a business?
- When starting a business, on what areas should you focus in order to succeed?

>> What Is Entrepreneurship?

Myth: To be an entrepreneur, you must be born that way.

Fact: Anyone can start a business.[1]

Entrepreneurship is a great way to apply the business skills you've learned and build a business out of a hobby, a passion, or some special ability or talent you possess. If you are committed to the idea, you may become very successful, but first, you must lay the groundwork for starting a business. Proper preparation is absolutely essential. This chapter will discuss the process to be carried out and the decisions that must be made before starting a business of your own.

ENTREPRENEURS AND ENTREPRENEURSHIP

The history of the United States is intertwined with the histories of its entrepreneurs. As mentioned in Chapter 1, an entrepreneur is any individual who owns and operates his or her own business. Let's say you are an adventure lover with a passion for rock climbing, mountain hiking, and whitewater raft-

ing. If you decided to put your interests to work for you by starting your own business leading groups on outdoor adventures, you're an entrepreneur. **Entrepreneurship** is accepting the risk of starting and running a business.

> **Entrepreneurship** Accepting the risk of starting and running a business.

One of the major challenges facing the United States today is the need to create more jobs. You can get some idea about the job-creating power of entrepreneurs by considering some of the great American entrepreneurs from the past and present. The following are a few of the many entrepreneurs who have helped shape the American economy:

- James Cash Penney opened the Golden Rule, a dry-goods and clothing store, in Wyoming in 1902.[2] The company is known today as JCPenney Corporation, Inc., which has 1,033 department stores throughout the United States and Puerto Rico. It is also the nation's largest catalog merchant of general merchandise.[3]

- Amazon.com got its financial start from investments by friends and family of founder Jeff Bezos. In fact, Bezos's parents personally invested $300,000—a huge portion of their retirement savings. Today, all of Bezos's initial investors—including his parents—are billionaires.[4]

- During one of his grueling workouts, it occurred to University of Maryland football player Kevin Plank that he could really use a shirt that could wick his perspiration away from his skin. He decided to create Under Armour Performance Apparel with $20,000 of his own money and $250,000 from

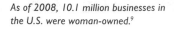

As of 2008, 10.1 million businesses in the U.S. were woman-owned.[9]

an SBA loan (he borrowed another $40,000 on his credit cards). When Plank first showed some of the clothing to his teammates, they ridiculed him.[5] But not for long—in fiscal year 2008, Under Armour's revenues were more than $725 million, with a net profit of more than $38 million.[6]

- In 1993, brothers David and Tom Gardner founded the Motley Fool, a financial company that provides news and other services to investors. The company began as a small investment newsletter titled *The Motley Fool*. The newsletter was pitched to 1,000 of the Gardners' friends and family members at $48 for an annual subscription. Only 37 of them subscribed. Today, the company is widely diversified, including best-selling books and video programming.[7]

There are countless more examples of small businesses that grew into large companies. Hundreds of people start new businesses in the United States every day. According to the U.S. Small Business Administration, in 2007 there were close to 27.2 million small businesses—an increase of more than 25 percent from 2000.[8]

Even kids and young adults dream about and have the passion to own their own business. According to a recent poll, 40 percent of people between the ages of 8 and 21 indicated that they would like to start their own business someday.[10] Many people start their own businesses, and many more aspire to, but what does it really take to become an entrepreneur?

Real World Apps

Sara Schmidtke has always dreamed of owning her own ice cream parlor. The town where she lives has two already, and she's visited both to find out what they do well—and what they don't do well. She has conducted extensive research about businesses that are designed to attract families with young children—her chosen demographic.

However, Sara isn't sure about the first steps she should take to get her business up and running. She has spoken to her family and friends about it, and their advice has not been very helpful (and has often been contradictory). Now, she's feeling overloaded with information and still doesn't know how to proceed. She decides to read the entrepreneurship chapter in her Business Now textbook to figure out what to do.

Larry Page and Sergey Brin, two college buddies, founded Google as graduate students in 1998. The company started with an initial investment of $100,000 from one of the founders of Sun Microsystems.[11] A lot has changed in only 11 years: Brin and Page were numbers 26 and 27, respectively, on Forbes's 2009 list of the world's billionaires.[12]

THE QUALITIES OF AN ENTREPRENEUR

The stories of most entrepreneurs are remarkably similar: Someone had a good idea or saw a need for a product or service; money was borrowed, and a business began. Successful entrepreneurs tend to have the following characteristics in common (see Figure 3.1):[13]

Figure 3.1 Entrepreneurial Characteristics

Self-directed
Self-nurturing
Action-oriented
Highly energetic
Tolerant of uncertainty
Drive to succeed
Perseverance

Figure 3.2 Why Do People Become Entrepreneurs?

Opportunity
Profit
Independence
Total business involvement
Challenge
Flexibility
The chance to make a difference

- *They are self-directed.* You should be thoroughly comfortable with your business and thoroughly self-disciplined, since you are your own boss. You will be responsible for your own success or failure.

- *They are self-nurturing.* You must believe in your idea, even when no one else does, and be able to replenish your own enthusiasm.

- *They are action-oriented.* Great business ideas are not enough. The most important thing is a burning desire to realize, actualize, and build your dream into reality.

- *They are very energetic.* It's your business, so you must be emotionally, mentally, and physically able to work long and hard.

- *They are tolerant of uncertainty.* Successful entrepreneurs take only calculated risks (if they can help it). Still, they must be able to take *some* risks.

- *They have a drive to succeed.* Businesses cannot prosper by themselves; they must be backed by committed people.

- *They persevere despite adversity.* In some cases, it takes many tries to get a business going. You must be able to effectively manage any setbacks.

It is important to know that most entrepreneurs

don't get the ideas for their products and services from some flash of inspiration. The source of innovation is more like a flash*light*. Imagine a search party walking around in the dark, shining flashlights, looking around, asking questions, and then looking some more.

You know starting a business can be risky, so why do people do it? People generally decide to risk becoming an entrepreneur for one or more of the reasons listed in Figure 3.2.[15]

- *Opportunity.* The opportunity to share in the American dream has tremendous allure. Many people, including those new to this country, may not have the skills necessary to work in today's complex organizations, but they do have the initiative and drive to work the long hours demanded by entrepreneurship. Others find that starting their own businesses offers them more opportunities than working for others. The same is true for many corporate managers who left the security of the corporate life (either by choice or as a result of downsizing) to run their own businesses. Royce Evans was laid off in December 2008 and decided to create Equinity Performance, a maker of shock-absorbing horse saddle pads.[16]

- *Profit.* Profit is another important reason to become an entrepreneur. The richest person in America is Bill Gates, the entrepreneur who founded Microsoft Corporation.

Tom Sternberg, founder of the office-supply chain Staples, is a "flashlight leader." He visits his own stores and those of his competitors at least once a week to figure out ways to improve his business.[14]

- *Independence.* Many entrepreneurs simply do not enjoy working for someone else. Many lawyers, for example, do not like the stress and demands of big law firms and prefer the satisfaction of starting their own businesses.

- *Total business involvement.* Entrepreneurs also prefer to be involved in the business's entire operation. Unlike working in a large business, people who own their own business are not confined to work in one area; entrepreneurs may be involved in sales, marketing, customer response, and so on.[17]

- *Challenge.* Some people believe that entrepreneurs are excitement junkies who flourish on taking risks. In their book *Running Your Own Business*, Nancy Flexman and Thomas Scanian contend that entrepreneurs take moderate, calculated risks, not gambles.[18] In general, entrepreneurs seek achievement more than power.

- *Flexibility.* Entrepreneurs can structure their businesses around their desired lifestyle. Cyndi Crews, who had worked as an IT manager at a large corporation, was laid off in 2002. She seized the opportunity and bought a franchise of Schooley Mitchell Telecom Consultants. Today, Crews works out of her home and plans her work schedule around her time with her family.[19]

- *The chance to make a difference.* Many individuals get into business wanting to make a difference.

Are you ready to become an entrepreneur? Start out by taking the entrepreneurship test at the end of this chapter. If you do plan to start a business someday, the next sections of this chapter will show you how to get started.

Julie Aigner Clark wanted to make a difference for children—including her own. Unable to find quality videos for her youngsters, Aigner-Clark founded Baby Einstein, a firm that makes videos and DVDs for babies and young children. Years later, she sold the business to the Walt Disney Company. Her newest venture, the Safe Side, manufactures products to keep kids out of harm's way.[20]

[BUS] connections

1. What characteristics are required to become an entrepreneur? Are there any not mentioned in the discussion that you think would be helpful?
2. What skills do you already have that would enable you to be successful in an entrepreneurial venture? Which do you think you need to develop further?
3. Why do people start new businesses? Do any of these reasons interest you? Explain.

← ETHICAL   DILEMMA →

If you were able to make a rather large sale and the customer wanted to pay you cash in order to avoid paying sales taxes, what would you do?

Career PERSPECTIVES

BECOMING AN ENTREPRENEUR

Are you an expert at something? Really good at something? Entrepreneurship is a way to utilize your skills and make money at it! As we discussed in this chapter, being an entrepreneur is more than having a good idea—it requires the personality traits we discussed plus careful planning to make sure the business works.

Many people decide to start a business around a hobby, which is a great idea, as long as you don't mind the hobby becoming your main source of income! For example, people who love scrapbooking may decide to open a scrapbooking store. Fashion fanatics may decide to open a clothing store. The more technically savvy may choose to open a computer repair business. The types of businesses that can be opened are countless; it depends on what you enjoy doing—and what you can make money doing.

What is your passion? In what areas do you excel? How can you build a business doing something you love?

>> Business Start-Up

How do you start or get into a business? If your family already owns and operates one, you may decide to learn the business by working for it and then purchase it when your family members are ready to retire. Otherwise, there are three alternatives: (1) starting a business from scratch, (2) buying an ongoing business, and (3) buying a franchise.

STARTING A BUSINESS FROM SCRATCH

Whether it starts as a part-time or full-time operation, a hobby, or a passionate dream to meet a **market** need or make a difference in the world, starting an entrepreneurial venture from scratch is probably the most common choice for budding entrepreneurs. It takes hard work, perseverance, a lot of sacrifices, and self-discipline, but you can create a profitable business venture—even if you begin with next to nothing.

> **Market** People with unsatisfied needs and wants who have both the resources and the willingness to buy.

Consider some of the following entrepreneurial success stories:[21]

- Josh Bezoni found the routine at his job boring, so he decided to quit and start his own business. After his first try, all he ended up with was huge credit-card debt. Realizing that he hadn't been passionate about the first business he'd started, he put his biology and nutrition degrees to use and founded SlimBodyCoach.com, a weight-loss coaching Web site. Today, he has a multimillion-dollar business. Bezoni's advice: "Think about something you're passionate about and that creates tremendous value for other people," he says. "If you can help people solve a problem they have, you can be successful in business."[22]

- After a divorce, Lucinda Yates found herself homeless. While living on the streets, she learned how to make jewelry from others who were in her situation. Afterward, she took her passion for making jewelry and turned it into a business. The company Designs by Lucinda raises millions of dollars for nonprofits.[23]

- Leslie Montie's two children have medical conditions that require them to maintain a certain diet. While still working full-time, Montie teamed with her parents to begin developing new ways to cook and flavor foods and still maintain the special diets her children needed. Eventually, Montie quit her job and devoted herself to her growing business. Her business, Wildtree, is now a success.[24]

The Advantages and Disadvantages of Starting from Scratch

Advantages. Starting a business from scratch offers several advantages. Entrepreneurs can be their own boss, be creative, and enjoy total independence. Since there are no rules or predetermined ways of doing things—as is the case with operating a franchise—entrepreneurs can operate their businesses in any way they see fit, freely choosing equipment, location, employees, and so on. The owner of a start-up business makes all the decisions about the operation of the business.[25]

Disadvantages. However, since there's no proven way of doing things, more cost and risk are involved. It may take some time for an entrepreneur to establish the product or service in the marketplace. Competitors may offer similar products or services that are already established in the market; in such a case, the newcomer would face tough competitive conditions.

Since the business has no track record, a detailed **business plan** must be developed—especially if financial help is needed to start the business. Even if financing is not a problem, it is critical that you develop a business plan to guide your journey.

> **Business plan** A detailed written statement that describes the nature of the business, the target market, the advantages the business will have in relation to competition, and the resources and qualifications of the owner(s).

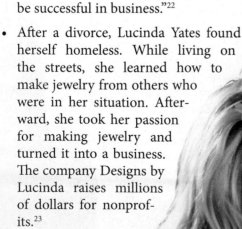

A babysitter with her two charges. When Adrienne Kallweit became frustrated in her attempts to find a trustworthy babysitter, she decided to launch a babysitter referral service, SeekingSitters, in 2004. In 2006, the company expanded through franchising and now has 23 locations in nine states. In 2008, the company recorded sales of $2.1 million.[74]

Finally, owning a business can be lonely—especially in the beginning—if you are a **sole proprietor**. Starting a business from scratch gives you flexibility, but at the same time it creates long working hours. Your personal and business lives will probably be more intertwined than ever before.[26] Figure 3.3 summarizes the advantages and disadvantages of starting a business from scratch.

Sole proprietor A business that is owned and typically managed by one person.

Figure 3.3 The Advantages and Disadvantages of Starting a Business from Scratch

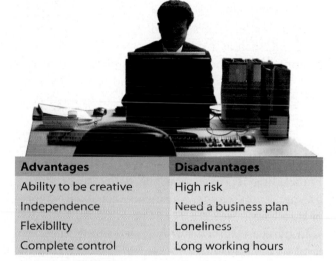

Advantages	Disadvantages
Ability to be creative	High risk
Independence	Need a business plan
Flexibility	Loneliness
Complete control	Long working hours

Keys to Getting Started

Let's say you have a passion or an interest and are wondering where to start. Always remember the following five keys to starting a business from scratch (see Figure 3.4):[27]

- *Find mentors.* Networking with others who have been through what you are going through is very valuable. **Mentors** can provide advice as well as support. You can find mentors by interviewing others in the same business you are interested in or on social networking sites, such as LinkedIn.

Mentor An adviser experienced in a particular job or type of business who acts as a guide for someone entering a field.

- *Do your research.* While it may not seem to be the most interesting activity, conducting background research about your industry, market need, financing, licenses, taxes, and insurance is absolutely necessary. Doing homework in the beginning will save you a lot of grief later on.

- *Know the industry.* There are many opportunities in many industries, and it can all be overwhelming. Pick an industry you have knowledge about and interest in. Otherwise, you may end up spending most of your time just learning the basics.

- *Market yourself.* Part of being an entrepreneur is learning how to make others believe in you and your ideas. You can take professional development classes, volunteer at a nonprofit organization, join industry committees, and blog about your entrepreneurial adventures to get your business's name out there.

- *Read.* There are probably lots of books and articles about the industry you're interested in. Reading about the experiences of others may help you avoid the mistakes they've made and can help you achieve their successes.

Figure 3.4 The Five Keys to Starting a Business from Scratch

Find mentors
Do your research
Know the industry
Market yourself
Read

BUYING AN EXISTING BUSINESS

A second option is purchasing an existing business. Like real estate agents, business brokers often connect sellers of businesses with buyers. For example, an art store owner who has decided to move to another state and must sell his business

Like real estate brokers, business brokers bring buyers and sellers together.

Figure 3.5 The Advantages and Disadvantages of Buying an Existing Business

Advantages	Disadvantages
Proven track record	Higher cost
Time and resource savings	May not be a preferred location
Training Ease of financing	Potential hidden problems

would likely contact a broker to help him find a buyer. Many other types of businesses, such as motels, convenience stores, and restaurants, are regularly sold through brokers. Those who prefer not to use a business broker can find many businesses for sale through ads found in newspapers and magazines and on the Internet. In either case, the most important thing is to determine the cost of the business you are considering versus its return (profit). Figure 3.5 summarizes the advantages and disadvantages of buying an existing business.

The Advantages and Disadvantages of Buying an Existing Business

Advantages. The biggest advantages of buying an existing business are its proven track record and the fact that you can save a significant amount of time, energy, and other resources by taking over an established business with a customer base, an inventory, and a physical structure and location. As a potential buyer, you can review important facts, such as sales numbers, to determine if the business will be profitable enough. Often, the previous owner is willing to stay on long enough to train the new owners. It's also possible that the sellers may be interested in financing the sale at a better rate than banks could offer.

Disadvantages. Of course, downsides exist as well. Since someone has already gone through the hard work and initial risk of operating the business and has documented profits and losses—exactly the reasons you'd be interested in buying an existing business—buying an existing business can be considerably more expensive than building one from the ground up. You may not like the location of the existing business. There could also be hidden problems the sellers failed to reveal, such as a declining customer base, uncollectible debts owed to the business by suppliers or customers, and so on. Performing extensive research about an existing business is essential before finalizing the purchase.

FRANCHISING

Franchising is a common alternative to starting a business from scratch. A franchise is not a legal form of business; instead, it is a type of business. People who purchase franchises must determine their own legal form of business, which will be covered in the next section. As you will learn in Chapter 11, franchising can also be a way to transform a business into a global enterprise. Franchising has penetrated every aspect of the global business world by offering consumers products and services that are reliable, convenient, and competitively priced. This type of business clearly has some advantages. See Figure 3.6 for a list of the top 10 franchises in 2009, according to *Entrepreneur.*

If you are considering buying an existing business, financing may be easier to secure. Bankers are often more comfortable lending to businesses with a record of success. [28]

Thinking Critically

>> ## Microloans Help Small Businesses Start, Grow, and Succeed

Many people dream of starting their own business but simply don't have the money. Those of you with an entrepreneurial spirit but limited resources will be interested in this loan program available through the Small Business Administration.

Wondering where to turn for a small loan to start a business or upgrade technology for your growing enterprise? Whether you need financing to start a one-person, home-based business such as child care, or you're feeling growing pains and need to upgrade your business infrastructure, an SBA microloan may be just the answer.

SBA's Microloan Program provides small loans of under $500 and up to $35,000 to start-up, newly established, or growing small businesses. The average microloan size is about $13,000. While the microloan program is open to all entrepreneurs, the program especially supports underserved markets, including borrowers with little to no credit history, low-income borrowers, and women and minority entrepreneurs in rural and urban areas who generally do not qualify for conventional loans or other, larger SBA guaranteed loans.

Small businesses are our nation's No. 1 private sector job creators. Helping a new business get off to the right start and assisting business owners as they grow successful enterprises is the ultimate goal of SBA's Microloan Program. To maximize chances for success, borrowers must participate in training, classroom or one-to-one counseling, and other forms of technical assistance.

One step to take before applying for a microloan is developing your business plan or updating your current business plan. SBA has many online resources to help you start, grow, and succeed in your business. The resources available to entrepreneurs and small business owners include an assessment tool to determine if you are ready to start a small business, a tutorial on developing your business plan, and training courses such as "How to Prepare a Loan Package." Go to www.sba.gov to discover what SBA has to offer.

Microloan applications are submitted to a community-based, nonprofit intermediary that serves as a microlender who then makes loans directly to entrepreneurs like you. All credit decisions are made by the microlender at the local level.

Increased funding under the American Recovery and Reinvestment Act allows SBA to finance up to $50 million in new lending and provides an added $24 million in technical assistance grants to microlenders through September 2010. Expanding SBA's Microloan Program helps ensure that entrepreneurs have loan options and are not left behind in the credit crunch.

Source: U.S. Small Business Administration Web site. http://www.sba.gov/idc/groups/public/documents/sba_homepage/recovery_act_microloans.pdf (accessed August 9, 2009)..

QUESTIONS

1. Why is it so important to have a well-developed business plan before applying for an SBA loan?

2. Visit SBA's Web site. Describe three resources the agency offers to help owners start, grow, and succeed in a small business.

Figure 3.6 The Top 10 Franchises in 2009

1. Subway (fast food)
2. McDonald's (fast food)
3. Liberty Tax Service (tax preparation services)
4. Sonic Drive-In Restaurants (fast food)
5. InterContinental Hotels Group (hospitality)
6. Ace Hardware Corp. (retail hardware sales)
7. Pizza Hut (pizza)
8. The UPS Store/Mail Boxes Etc. (postal and business services)
9. Circle K (convenience stores)
10. Papa John's International, Inc. (pizza)

Source: Top 50 Franchises, *Entrepreneur,* January 2009, p 141.

Which is the No. 1 franchise in the United States? For the past eight out of ten years, Subway has held on to the top spot.

According to the U.S. Department of Commerce, every eight minutes of every business day, a new franchise business opens.[29] Examples of franchises include McDonald's, Burger King, Subway, and Taco Bell in the fast-food industry; Jiffy Lube and AAMCO Transmission in the auto services industry; and Days Inn, Motel 6, and Hilton Hotels & Resorts in the hospitality industry.

Chain store A business location that is one of many stores, all of which have central management (meaning all stores are run by the same people) and share a brand name.

Company store A store owned and operated by a chain.

A franchise is different from a chain store. A **chain store** is a business location that is one of many stores, all of which have central management (meaning all stores are run by the same people) and share a brand name, such as Target or Macy's. A franchise, on the other hand, shares a brand name but does not have central management: the owner of each franchise store is responsible for his or her own business. The stores a chain owns are called **company stores**.

The Advantages and Disadvantages of Buying a Franchise

Perhaps one of the biggest advantages with franchising is the inherent marketing and management assistance you have at your disposal; it's quite like having full-time consultants available whenever you need them.[30] Figure 3.7 summarizes the advantages and disadvantages of buying a franchise.

Advantages. Compared with someone who starts a business from scratch, a **franchisee** (a person who buys a franchise) has a much greater chance of succeeding because the franchise has an established product (for example, Wendy's hamburgers or Domino's pizza) that has proven successful in the marketplace. The **franchisor** (a person or entity that owns the rights to the franchise) provides assistance with many facets of the business, such as choosing a location and promotional efforts.

Franchisee A person who buys a franchise.

Franchisor A person or entity that owns the rights to a franchise.

Many franchisors, such as Subway and McDonald's, engage in national-level promotional efforts, like television advertising, that benefit all franchisees, as well as company stores. Some franchisors help their franchisees succeed by helping with local marketing efforts as well.

Franchisors buy resources, such as parts, raw materials, and ingredients, in bulk at lower prices and pass these savings on to their franchisees. Since their costs are lower for these items, franchisees can then pass these savings on to their customers.[33] Franchi-

Sometimes, a chain owns some stores but franchises others, as McDonald's does.

Figure 3.7 The Advantages and Disadvantages of Buying a Franchise

Advantages	Disadvantages
Proven products/services	Start-up cost
Marketing assistance	Profit sharing
Training	Negative publicity by
Operations and purchase	association
assistance	Cannibalization
Ownership and low	Management restrictions
failure rate	

A franchise, which shares a brand name but does not have central management with other stores that have the same name, is different from a chain store, which is a business location that is one of many stores, all of which have central management and share a brand name.

Franchisors also provide intensive training. For example, in the United Kingdom, Starbucks offers its franchisees a training program that comprehensively trains their employees for their roles. Employees learn what it means to live and breathe the guiding principles of the company and make the distinctive Starbucks coffee, and managers participate in a parallel program.[31] At one point, Starbucks's U.S. operation even went so far as to shut down all of its 7,100 stores for one three-hour retraining program.[32]

sees also enjoy the benefits of being sole proprietors. If you buy a franchise operation, it's your store, and you'll enjoy many of the same incentives and profits as sole proprietors. You'll be your own boss, but you must follow the rules, regulations, and procedures set forth from your franchisor.

Many franchisors provide assistance in all phases of operation, including loans, to their franchisees. Furthermore, franchisees have a network of fellow franchisees who face similar problems and can share their experiences. For example, The UPS Store provides its 3,600 franchisees with a software program that helps them build data banks of customers' names and addresses. The company also provides one-on-one phone support and quick e-mail access through its help desk, which takes care to immediately address questions and concerns.

Another advantage to franchising is a lower failure rate, largely because of the support provided by the franchisor. Because a franchised business already has a locally or nationally recognized name, it also has established customers who trust its products. Figure 3.8 shows the process of buying a franchise.

Disadvantages. It almost sounds as

though franchising is too good to be true, but there are some potential pitfalls. The biggest disadvantage to franchising is the inherent start-up costs. It could cost as much as $1 million to open a McDonald's franchise, and a Hilton Garden Inn could cost more than $10 million.

Another disadvantage is that franchisees must share their profits. In addition to start-up fees, many franchisors demand either a large share of the franchise's profits or a percentage commission based on sales, not profit.[35] The share demanded by the franchisor is generally referred to as a royalty. For example, if a franchisor demands a 10 percent royalty on a franchise's net sales, 10 cents of every $1 collected at the franchise (before deducting taxes and other expenses) must be paid to the franchisor. For example, McDonald's requires a royalty of 12.5 percent; Hilton Garden Inn, 5 percent; and Soccer Shots, 7 percent.[36]

If a franchised business experiences bad publicity, it can be bad for individual franchisees as well. For example, an organization called the Center for Science in the Public Interest recently charged certain restaurants, including Ruby Tuesday, Uno Chicago Grill, and the Cheesecake Factory, with promoting "x-treme eating," its name for particularly high-volume, high-fat, and high-calorie menu items. As a result, several restaurants now have to label calorie content on menus and menu boards.[37] Some companies fight negative publicity at the corporate level. On its Web site, Starbucks offers a page called "Rumor Response" that ad-

Of course, not every franchise is prohibitively expensive. Soccer Shots, a program that teaches children how to play soccer, charges franchisees less than $15,000 to start their businesses.[34]

dresses and attempts to dispel any rumors about the company, its products, and its stores.[38]

Many McDonald's franchisees were angered by a 2008 national promotion in which the company's outlets gave away its new Southern-Style Chicken Sandwich with the purchase of a drink. Franchisees were expected to absorb the costs of the giveaway. A franchisee who owned 60 McDonald's outlets estimated that it cost him $600 per restaurant to participate in the giveaway.[39]

Also, **cannibalization**, or taking away customers from an existing franchise nearby, can be a problem. In the past, some TCBY franchisees have complained that too many new stores have opened and cannibalized their businesses. The Quiznos sandwich chain had a similar instance of this problem. The owners of one California franchise claimed that other Quiznos

> **Cannibalization** A situation in which a new franchise takes away customers from an existing franchise nearby.

To avoid the dilemma of cannibalization, many franchises, such as Cold Stone Creamery, tightly limit the number of franchises that can be opened in a particular area.

Figure 3.8 The Process of Buying a Franchise

Since buying a franchise is a major investment, be sure to check out a company's financial strength before you get involved. Watch out for scams too. Scams called *bust-outs* usually involve people coming to town, renting nice offices, taking out ads, and persuading people to invest. Then they disappear with the investors' money. For example, in San Francisco a company called T.B.S. Inc. sold distributorships for in-home AIDS tests. It promised an enormous market and potential profits of $3,000 for an investment of less than $200. The "test" turned out to be nothing more than a mail-order questionnaire about lifestyle.

A good source of information about evaluating a franchise deal is the handbook *Investigate before Investing*, available from International Franchise Association Publications.

Checklist for Evaluating a Franchise

The Franchise

Did your lawyer approve the franchise contract you're considering after he or she studied it paragraph by paragraph?

Does the franchise give you an exclusive territory for the length of the franchise?

Under what circumstances can you terminate the franchise contract and at what cost to you?

If you sell your franchise, will you be compensated for your goodwill (the value of your business's reputation and other intangibles)?

If the franchisor sells the company, will your investment be protected?

The Franchisor

How many years has the firm offering you a franchise been in operation?

Does it have a reputation for honesty and fair dealing among the local firms holding its franchise?

Has the franchisor shown you any certified figures indicating exact net profits of one or more going firms that you personally checked yourself with the franchisee?

Ask for the company's disclosure statement.

Will the firm assist you with:

- A management training program?

- An employee training program?
- A public relations program?
- Capital?
- Credit?
- Merchandising ideas?

Will the firm help you find a good location for your new business?

Has the franchisor investigated you carefully enough to assure itself that you can successfully operate one of its franchises at a profit both to itself and to you?

You, the Franchisee

How much equity capital will you need to purchase the franchise and operate it until your income equals your expenses?

Does the franchisor offer financing for a portion of the franchising fees? On what terms?

Are you prepared to give up some independence of action to secure the advantages offered by the franchise? Do you have your family's support?

Does the industry appeal to you? Are you ready to spend much or all of the remainder of your business life with this franchisor, offering its product or service to the public?

Your Market

Have you made any study to determine whether the product or service that you propose to sell under the franchise has a market in your territory at the prices you'll have to charge?

Will the population in the territory given to you increase, remain static, or decrease over the next five years?

Will demand for the product or service you're considering be greater, about the same, or less five years from now than it is today?

What competition already exists in your territory for the product or service you contemplate selling?

Sources: U.S. Department of Commerce, Franchise Opportunities Handbook; and Steve Adams, "Buying a Brand," *Patriot Ledger* (Quincy, MA), March 1, 2008.

Although corporations make up only 25 percent of the total number of businesses, they make 84 percent of the total revenues. Sole proprietorships are the most common form (71 percent), but they only earn 5 percent of the revenues.

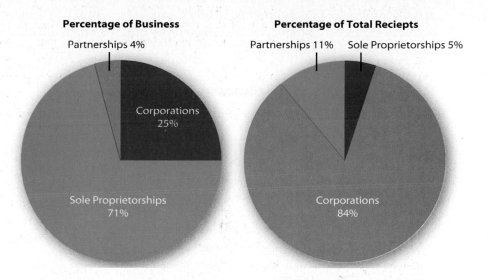

Figure 3.9 The Legal Forms of Business in the United States

Percentage of Business

Partnerships 4%

Corporations 25%

Sole Proprietorships 71%

Percentage of Total Reciepts

Partnerships 11% Sole Proprietorships 5%

Corporations 84%

franchises in the area were cutting into their business.[40]

Management assistance is an advantage, but it can also be a disadvantage. Because franchisors have an image to uphold, they have very tight restrictions on certain issues, such as signage, the products that can be sold, and even pricing, which allows little flexibility for the franchisee. If an owner decides to sell a franchise, he or she will probably face restrictions. In order to control the quality of their franchisees, franchisors often insist on approving new owners and ensuring that they meet the franchisor's standards.

If you consider opening a franchise, your first step should be to talk with present franchisees in your area to get an idea of their experiences. You should also discuss the idea with an attorney and an accountant to get their perspectives on the franchise agreement and its financial ramifications, respectively.

[BUS] connections

1. If a friend is interested in starting a business from scratch, what would you advise her to do first?

2. List the advantages of buying an existing business in the order of their attractiveness to you.

3. Why would someone want to open a franchise, as opposed to starting from scratch? How would you research a franchise before buying one?

>> The Legal Forms of Business Ownership

Once you have decided on a business type—starting from scratch, buying an existing business, or buying a franchise—you should explore the various legal forms of business ownership. Every year in the United States, more than 600,000 new businesses are

created—triple the number created in 1960—and the number of nonemployer firms (firms operated by their owners that do not employ any other people) in the United States has steadily risen throughout this decade.[41] Two-thirds of these new businesses survive at least two years; approximately 56 percent fail within their first four years of business.[42]

When a business fails, the entrepreneur may be personally responsible for whatever debts were incurred by the business while it was still in operation. The purpose of this section is to help you choose the correct form of business ownership for you. Choosing a form carefully can help you avoid losses if your business does not succeed.

The first task any entrepreneur must do is to decide the structure or legal form of the business. Figure 3.9 shows the total number of U.S. businesses classified by their legal forms.[43] Each form has advantages and disadvantages. First, we will describe the three primary legal forms for businesses, and then we will discuss other important factors in making a new business a success.

SOLE PROPRIETORSHIPS

A **sole proprietorship** is the easiest kind of business to start, and someone who starts a sole proprietorship is an entrepreneur. A sole proprietorship involves one person owning and running a business[44] on his or her own—a Web site development business run from home, a cabinet-building business, or any other type of business area in which the owner is an expert and wants to sell his

> **Sole proprietorship** A business operated by a sole proprietor.

or her skills. A sole proprietorship is a business operated by a sole proprietor. There are several advantages to a sole proprietorship, as opposed to other forms of business. Figure 3.10 summarizes the advantages and disadvantages of sole proprietorship.

The Advantages and Disadvantages of Sole Proprietorships

Advantages. All you have to do to start a sole proprietorship is to buy or lease the needed equipment (for example, a photographer's camera) and publish an announcement that you are in business. Of course, you may have to secure a business license or register your business's name as well. You may have to get a permit or license from the local government, but this is usually very easy to do. There's no one else to consult with about such decisions.[45] You get to be your own boss. You'll make all the decisions and receive the benefits of those decisions. You will take all the credit for (and assume the risks of) providing goods and services to your customers. You are the master of your own destiny: Whatever hours and efforts you put into the business go to create wealth for you, not someone else.

In addition to getting the emotional satisfaction of owning a business, you'll retain all the business's profits, another major advantage. Along the same lines, profits from a sole proprietorship are taxed as the personal income of the owner. And last, getting out of the business is just as easy as getting into it—you simply stop doing whatever it is that the business does.

Disadvantages. Despite these advantages, not everyone is equipped to own a business. It is challenging to save or borrow enough money to start a business and keep it going. The cost of supplies, inventory, rent, and other expenses can be too much to manage. Many would-be entrepreneurs have limited financial resources, and there are often limitations to how much one person can borrow from others.

Many sole proprietors find they have skill gaps that affect their ability to manage a business. For example, a person who is very good at building Web sites may lack skills in keeping tax and accounting records. An entrepreneur must be able to either handle all aspects of the business or find good people to manage those parts of the business where they lack strength.

Study Alert! Sole proprietors have independence and profit retention, but they are also liable for their business's debts.

Probably the biggest disadvantage of operating as a sole proprietor is that as the owner, you would have **unlimited liability**,[46] which means that from a financial perspective, there is no distinction between the business and the owner. If the business were to fail, you would be personally responsible for any of the debts the business incurred.

Unlimited liability The responsibility of business owners for all the debts of the business.

Most sole proprietors start businesses because of their interest in the product or service they are selling, but always remember that entrepreneurs typically work very long hours. Unlike a typical job where you get to leave at a specific time, an entrepreneur may find him- or herself working from 8:00 a.m. to 8:00 p.m., or even longer. Working hours like that over long periods of time can make it hard to stay interested in the business.

Another disadvantage is the lack of the fringe benefits one often receives when working for someone else. By definition, the owner of a sole proprietorship cannot be an employee; therefore, he or she is not permitted to participate in a company-funded employee benefit plan.[47] Finally, the fact that a sole proprietor has a limited life span is a disadvantage. If the entrepreneur dies or retires, the business no longer exists unless it is sold or taken over by heirs.

Sole proprietorships generally involve very little capital investment beyond the equipment needed to provide a product or service.

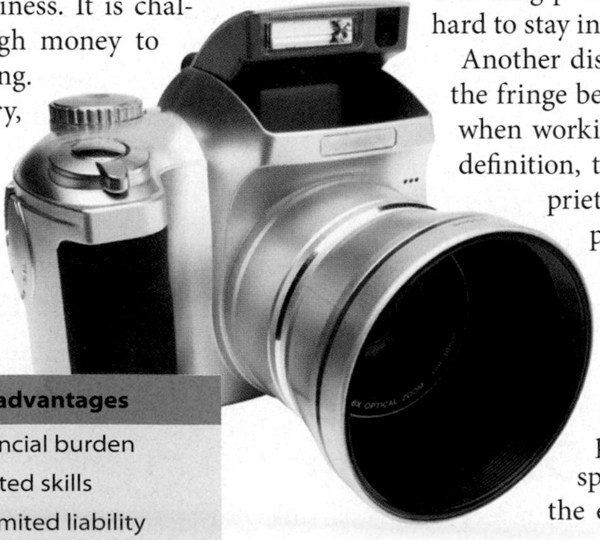

Figure 3.10 The Advantages and Disadvantages of Sole Proprietorships

Advantages	Disadvantages
Ease of entry and exit	Financial burden
Independence	Limited skills
Profit retention	Unlimited liability
Master of your own destiny	Long hours
	No fringe benefits
	Limited life span

Paying for your own sick leave, health insurance, and vacation time (after all, if you're not working, you're not earning) cuts into the profits of an entrepreneur.[48]

PARTNERSHIPS

The second legal form of business ownership is a **partnership**, which is a business with two or more owners. There are several types of partnerships: general, limited, master limited, and limited liability.[49] Figure 3.11 shows the key advantages and disadvantages of partnerships, and Figure 3.12 describes how to form a partnership.

> **Partnership** A legal form of business with two or more owners.

- A **general partnership** is a partnership in which all owners share business and financial obligations (debt, for example) of the business.

> **General partnership** A partnership in which all owners share in operating the business and in assuming liability for the business's debts.

TOUGH DECISIONS

While Melony Henshaw was in high school, her grandfather started a landscaping business, and Melony worked for him. During her college years, she helped her grandfather manage and expand the company. Unfortunately, her grandfather died shortly after she graduated from college, and his business was dissolved.

After graduating from college, Melony worked in the corporate world for nearly 10 years. She had a good career and was promoted into management. However, she longed to be more independent, so Melony began to consider owning her own business. After conducting some research, she decided a landscaping business made the most sense—after all, she knew a lot about plants and landscaping from the time she spent in her grandfather's business.

While attending a local chamber of commerce event, Melony learned of a successful landscaping contractor who was interested in selling his business within the next five years. She approached the owner with the idea of helping him manage the company for now; after she learned the business thoroughly, she would purchase the business.

It looked like Melony was in the right place at the right time. She had found a thriving business with a good reputation. Unfortunately, upon examining the books, she uncovered some disturbing issues. She discovered that several employees were being paid under the table, and some of the company's landscaping jobs were done as unrecorded cash sales in order to avoid paying taxes on the income. One day, Melony overheard two employees talking about how some of the managers allow workers to take long lunches or just sit around—all while still on the clock. Suddenly, Melony began to doubt her decision to purchase the business.

QUESTIONS

1. What are the ethical problems Melony is facing?
2. What policy changes should Melony make?
3. How would those changes change the business? Explain.

If you were able to make a rather large sale and the customer wanted to pay cash in order to avoid paying sales taxes, what would you do?

- A **limited partnership** is a partnership with one or more general partners and one or more limited partners. A **general partner** is an owner who has unlimited liability and is active in managing the firm. Every partnership must have at least one general partner. A **limited partner** is an owner who invests money in the business, but does not have any management responsibility or liability for losses beyond the initial investment. **Limited liability** means that limited partners are not responsible for the debts of the business beyond the amounts of their investment, and their personal assets are not at risk.

- A newer form of partnership, the **master limited partnership (MLP),** is somewhat like a corporation (to be discussed in the next section). It is traded on the stock exchanges like a corporation, but it is taxed like a partnership, and thus avoids corporate income tax.

- Another newer type of partnership was created to limit the disadvantages of unlimited liability. Many states now allow partners to form **limited liability partnerships (LLPs).** LLPs limit the risk of losing personal assets in that partners are only liable for mistakes they or people under their supervision make, and not the mistakes of their partners and those that the partners supervise. This is often a popular choice for doctors' practices, where a malpractice suit aimed at one doctor could endanger the business of other doctors in the practice.

  Always consult an attorney and a tax adviser before initiating a partnership. There are certain issues for which you need legal advice and others that require expert knowledge of taxation.

Limited partnership A partnership with one or more general partners and one or more limited partners.

General partner An owner (partner) who has unlimited liability and is active in managing the firm.

Limited partner An owner who invests money in the business but does not have any management responsibility or liability for losses beyond the investment.

Limited liability Means limited partners are not responsible for the debts of the business beyond the amount of their investment—their liability is limited to the amount they put into the company; their personal assets are not at risk.

Master limited partnership (MLP) Structured much like a corporation in that it acts like a corporation and is traded on a stock exchange like a corporation, but taxed like a partnership and thus avoids the corporate income tax.

Limited liability partnership (LLP) LLPs limit partners' risk of losing their personal assets to only their own acts and omissions and to the acts and omissions of people under their supervision.

Figure 3.11 The Advantages and Disadvantages of Partnerships

Partnerships can be stronger businesses than sole proprietorships because they have more resources.

Advantages	Disadvantages
More financial resources	Division of profits
Pooled knowledge	Unlimited liability
Risk distribution	Conflict among the partners
	Difficult to get out

The Advantages and Disadvantages of Partnerships

Advantages. There are several advantages to the partnership form of business ownership. As you know, two heads can be better than one, and when two or more people are involved, more financial resources are available to the business. Similarly, multiple partners can bring additional knowledge and a broader skill set than a sole proprietor. One partner might be good at architecture, while another partner might be very good at marketing an architecture firm. Partners can play off one another's strengths in order to make the business prosper. Last, partners share in the risks and losses, so they are not as great as they would be under a sole proprietorship.

Disadvantages. Unlike a sole proprietorship, where the owner keeps all of the profits, partnership profits must be divided among the partners. General partners are liable for the debts of the firm, no matter who actually incurred them. In

Figure 3.12 How to Form a Partnership

It's not hard to form a partnership, but it's wise for each prospective partner to get the counsel of a lawyer experienced with such agreements. Lawyers' services are usually expensive, so would-be partners should read all about partnerships and reach some basic agreements before calling a lawyer.

For your protection, be sure to put your partnership agreement in writing. The Model Business Corporation Act recommends including the following in a written partnership agreement:

1. The name of the business. Many states require the firm's name to be registered with state and/or county officials if the firm's name is different from the name of any of the partners.
2. The names and addresses of all partners.
3. The purpose and nature of the business, the location of the principal offices, and any other locations where business will be conducted.
4. The date the partnership will start and how long it will last. Will it exist for a specific length of time, or will it stop when one of the partners dies or when the partners agree to discontinue?
5. The contributions made by each partner. Will some partners contribute money, while others provide real estate, personal property, expertise, or labor? When are the contributions due?
6. The management responsibilities. Will all partners have equal voices in management, or will there be senior and junior partners?
7. The duties of each partner.
8. The salaries and drawing accounts of each partner.
9. Provision for sharing of profits or losses.
10. Provision for accounting procedures. Who'll keep the accounts? What bookkeeping and accounting methods will be used? Where will the books be kept?
11. The requirements for taking in new partners.
12. Any special restrictions, rights, or duties of any partner.
13. Provision for a retiring partner.
14. Provision for the purchase of a deceased or retiring partner's share of the business.
15. Provision for how grievances will be handled.
16. Provision for how to dissolve the partnership and distribute the assets to the partners.

a general partnership, partners are both jointly and individually responsible for the mistakes made in the business. Like a sole proprietor, a general partner could lose his or her personal possessions if the company goes bankrupt.

Once a partnership has been established, it can be difficult to leave it. Even in the event that all partners wish to terminate the business, arguments about who gets what and how the business's assets will be divided can cause further conflict and legal difficulties.

Critical business issues, such as how and where to spend money and how the business should be managed, can create conflicts if the partners disagree. Because of these conflicts, a partnership agreement should be contractually described in order to protect all parties.[50]

CORPORATIONS

In Chapter 1, Figure 1.7 (see page 10) lists the five largest corporations in 2008—companies like ExxonMobil, Wal-Mart, and General Electric. Although the word *corporation* makes people think of big businesses like these, it's not necessary to be big in order to incorporate. Many corporations are small, but despite their size they contribute mightily to the U.S. economy. Figure 3.13 shows the advantages and disadvantages of the corporate form of business ownership. Incorporation may be beneficial for small businesses as well. It is also important to point out that individuals can incorporate—a corporation isn't necessarily a business with many employees and lots of assets.

Before we discuss the types of corporations, it is important to address the concept of corporate governance, which refers to the processes, customs, policies, laws, and institutions that affect how a corporation is directed, administered, or controlled. When a person decides to form a corporation, she will put together a set of corporate governance guidelines, which is a written description of how the business will be run.

In many cases, board members do not actually work for the business; instead, they serve as an outside source to provide the business with guidance. For example, Build-A-Bear founder Maxine Clark and Kraft Foods chief marketing officer Mary Beth West both serve on the JCPenney board of directors.[51]

Figure 3.13 The Advantages and Disadvantages of Corporations

Advantages	Disadvantages
Limited liability	Double taxation
Shared ownership	More paperwork
Continuity	More regulations
Low tax rates	Owner's limited focus
Fringe benefits	

Corporate governance The processes, customs, policies, laws, and institutions that affect how a corporation is directed, administered, or controlled.

Board of directors The group ultimately responsible for the decisions of a business.

Conventional (C) corporation A form of business ownership that provides limited liability.

A major part of **corporate governance**—especially in a larger business—is the responsibility of a company's board of directors. A **board of directors** is a group of people who are ultimately responsible for decisions of a business.

Most corporations are **conventional (C) corporations**, which are state-chartered legal entities with the authority to act and have liability independent of their owners, which are the corporation's stockholders.[52] Besides the traditional C corporation, two new forms of corporations have been developed over the years: S corporations and limited liability corporations (LLCs).

Figure 3.13 summarizes the advantages and disadvantages of corporations, Figure 3.14 discusses the process of incorporation, and Figure 3.15 compares all the other ownership forms with corporations.

The Advantages and Disadvantages of Corporations

Advantages. A key advantage of incorporating a business is that it limits the owners' liability. Owners are not personally liable for the debts or any other problems of the corporation beyond the money they personally invest in it. They do not have to worry about losing personal belongings because of a business problem, which is a significant benefit.

A corporation can also allow many people to share in the ownership (and profits) of a business without actually working there or having other commitments to it. Corporations can choose whether to sell shares of ownership to outside investors or to remain privately held (which means that the immediate owners hold all the company's shares). Corporations have the ability to attract additional investors (sell more shares) when capital is needed[53] and can therefore raise additional funds without having to borrow from banks or other financial institutions.

Given that corporations have their own identity,[54] they are separate from their owners and can continue to exist if owners leave the company or die. Another benefit is that the first $75,000 of a C corporation's annual income is taxed at a low rate.[55] Last, unlike sole proprietorships, owner–employees can have fringe benefits, such as health care or company-funded retirement plans.

Figure 3.14 The Process of Incorporation

The process of forming a corporation varies somewhat from state to state. The articles of incorporation are usually filed with the secretary of state's office in the state in which the company incorporates.

The articles contain:

- The corporation's name
- The names of the people who incorporated it
- Its purposes
- Its duration (usually perpetual)
- The number of shares that can be issued, shareholders' voting rights, and any other rights the shareholders have
- The minimum amount of capital
- The address of the corporation's office
- The name and address of the person responsible for the corporation's legal service
- The names and addresses of the first directors
- Any other public information the incorporators wish to include

Before a business can so much as open a bank account or hire employees, it needs a federal tax identification number. To apply for one, get an SS-4 form from the IRS.

In addition to the articles of incorporation listed, a corporation has bylaws. These describe how the firm is to be operated from both legal and managerial points of view. The bylaws include:

- How, when, and where shareholders' and directors' meetings are held, and how long directors are to serve
- Directors' authority
- Duties and responsibilities of officers, and the length of their service
- How stock is issued
- Other matters, including employment contracts

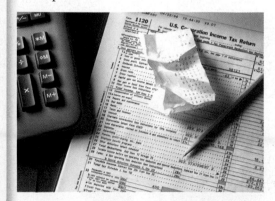

Corporations are sometimes subject to double taxation.

Figure 3.15 A Comparison of Business Ownership Forms

	Sole Proprietorship	PARTNERSHIPS		CORPORATIONS		
		General Partnership	Limited Partnership	Conventional Corporation	S Corporation	Limited Liability Company
Documents Needed to Start Business	None; may need permit or license	Partnership agreement (oral or written)	Written agreement; must file certificate of limited partnership	Articles of incorporation, bylaws	Articles of incorporation, bylaws, must meet criteria	Articles of organization and operating agreement; no eligibility requirements
Ease of Termination	Easy to terminate: just pay debts and quit	May be hard to terminate, depending on the partnership agreement	Same as general partnership	Hard and expensive to terminate	Same as conventional corporation	May be difficult, depending upon operating agreement
Length of Life	Terminates on the death of owner	Terminates on the death or withdrawal of partner	Same as general partnership	Perpetual life	Same as conventional corporation	Varies according to dissolution dates in articles of organization
Transfer of Ownership	Business can be sold to qualified buyer	Must have other partner(s)' agreement	Same as general partnership	Easy to change owners; just sell stock	Can sell stock, but with restrictions	Can't sell stock
Financial Resources	Limited to owner's capital and loans	Limited to partners' capital and loans	Same as general partnership	More money to start and operate; may sell stocks and bonds	Same as conventional corporation	Same as partnership
Risk of Losses	Unlimited liability	Unlimited liability	Limited liability	Limited liability	Limited liability	Limited liability
Taxes	Taxed as personal income	Taxed as personal income	Same as general partnership	Corporate, double taxation	Taxed as personal income	Varies
Management Responsibilities	Owner manages all areas of the business	Partners share management	Can't participate in management	Separate management from ownership	Same as conventional corporation	Varies
Employee Benefits	Usually fewer benefits and lower wages	Often fewer benefits and lower wages; promising employee could become a partner	Same as general partnership	Usually better benefits and wages, advancement opportunities	Same as conventional corporation	Varies, but are not tax deductible

Disadvantages. A key disadvantage of corporations is the **double taxation** factor.[56] Once corporations have paid their federal, state, and local taxes, whatever profits remain are distributed to the corporation's owners in the form of **dividends**. These dividends are also taxed at the owner's tax rate—hence the double taxation. There is also more time and additional regulations that need to be managed with corporations when compared with the other forms of ownerships. Finally, owners may become myopic with their limited focus on profits. If there are owners brought in to raise the capital who do not necessarily work at the company, they may have the limited interest of getting profits and not the long-term growth and competitive advantage of the firm.

Double taxation Occurs when the owners of a corporation are taxed twice—once when the corporation is taxed and then again when the dividends are taxed.

Dividends Part of a firm's profits that may be distributed to stockholders as cash payments or additional shares of stock.

S Corporations
Another form of corporation is an **S corporation**. This type of corporation

S corporation A legal form of corporation for which the biggest advantage is its tax status, which is the same as a sole proprietorship.

is sanctioned by the government and taxed liked a sole proprietorship and partnership. Paperwork must be filed to create an S corporation, and there are also restrictions on which businesses qualify to be an S corporation. Those restrictions are as follows:[57]

1. The company must have 100 or fewer shareholders.

2. Its shareholders can only be individuals or estates, and they must be citizens or permanent residents of the United States.

3. The company can have only one class of stock.

4. The company can derive no more than 25 percent of its income from passive sources, such as rent or interest.

Limited Liability Companies (LLCs)

Limited liability companies (LLCs) are similar to S corporations, but without the special restrictions. A relatively new form of business ownership, LLCs began in Wyoming in 1977. Hawaii was the last state to enact an LLC statute.[58]

LLCs enjoy limited liability (hence their name), and can choose the form of taxation they want. In addition, ownership rules are flexible, as are distributions of profits and losses. LLCs have more operational flexibility than other types of corporations; for example, they do not have to hold annual meetings. They are legal business entities that survive beyond the deaths or illnesses of their owners.[59] The corporation is not necessarily taxed directly, so it is possible that the only tax they incur is that of their dividends—thus avoiding double taxation.

Of course, there are also disadvantages to LLCs.

They cannot sell shares of stock, and they require more paperwork to start—although not as much as a traditional corporation.

>> Getting Started in Your Own Business

There are five main areas of focus when starting a small business:

- Planning the business
- Financing the business
- Knowing your customers (marketing)
- Managing employees
- Keeping records (accounting)

This section will address each of these areas and provide insight into how you can begin your own business. Many new businesses do fail, but proper focus on each of these five areas will help ensure that your business isn't one of them.

PLANNING THE BUSINESS

Many people are eager to start a small business, but have only a vague notion of what they want to do. Eventually, they come up with a more fleshed-out idea for a business and begin discussing the idea with instructors, friends, and other businesspeople. At this stage, the entrepreneur needs a business plan, which was described earlier in the chapter. A business plan also includes market research, which can help a business owner target his or her products to meet customer needs. (Market research will be discussed further in Chapter 4.)

Putting together a carefully considered business plan can save you a lot of grief later on down the road.
....

Going GLOBAL

A Bull Market in Social Entrepreneurs

Social entrepreneurs and the enterprises they create are gaining momentum in the market-place. The notion of starting a business for reasons other than profit maximization might sound surprising, but many people are finding that it's possible to turn good works into good business.

For graduating students at Stanford University, it's all too clear that the economy's in the tank. Ask Josh Nesbit. The lean 22-year-old graduating senior spent spring break in Uganda and Mozambique, where his start-up, Frontline SMS:Medic, is putting in place communications systems aimed at promoting health in rural areas. "The downturn is good for us," Nesbit says. It frees up talented student brainpower. And it focuses donors and philanthropic agencies on start-ups that can get quick results on minuscule budgets. "Our credentials matter less than the product," he adds. That means that if his start-up delivers results, "people pay attention."

While Stanford is famous for minting billionaires, including the founders of Google and Yahoo!, it's heating up as a hotbed for social entrepreneurs. A record 112 teams submitted business plans for a social entrepreneurship competition, Social E-Challenge, during the spring semester.

Nesbit's idea seems made for these spartan times. It operates on free open-source software, loads of volunteer labor, and discarded remnants of First World consumer culture—specifically, used cell phones. A year ago, Nesbit took 100 reconditioned cell phones and a laptop computer to St. Gabriel's Hospital in rural Malawi. There, two doctors were attempting to care for a dispersed population of 250,000 people, many of them infected with HIV. To help physicians get more frequent status updates at a lower cost, Nesbit and his coworkers distributed cell phones loaded with an open-source software, Frontline SMS, which enables phones to broadcast 160-character text messages to a network. After handing out the phones and training 75 community health volunteers in the area to use the tool, updates poured into the laptop at St. Gabriel's. Doctors there were able to respond to emergencies, get health updates, and follow the medicine regimens of patients suffering from AIDS and tuberculosis. According to Nesbit, the cost for the first six months was $250—and the system saved $4,000 in motorbike fuel alone.

Nesbit's company is run entirely by volunteers and students, six of them at Stanford. Nesbit says that he and the others graduating have landed fellowships and small grants to support themselves over the coming year. But the burn rate is low. "I could run this out of my parents' basement (in suburban Washington, D.C.) if I had to," he says.

Much like the famed Stanford Internet alums, Nesbit and his colleagues are launching a start-up with global ambitions. The only thing small about Frontline SMS:Medic is its operating budget. It seems to be in step with the times.

Source: Stephen Baker, "A Bull Market in Social Entrepreneurs," *BusinessWeek*, June 10, 2009 http://www.businessweek.com/technology/content/jun2009/tc20090610_144013.htm (accessed August 9, 2009). Reprinted with permission.

Questions

1. Think about the challenges involved in starting any business. What additional challenges would a social entrepreneur face?

2. Would Nesbit's business be more or less likely to attract investors than the average business? If you were starting a business like Nesbit's, where would you go first to find investors?

A business plan forces potential owners of small businesses to be quite specific about the products or services they intend to offer, which helps them get their feet on the ground in a realistic way. They must analyze the competition, calculate how much money they need to start, and cover other details of operation.

What goes into a business plan? Figure 3.16 provides an outline of a business plan, including its executive sum-

You must put together a business plan before approaching bankers or other investors for financing.

mary, supporting documents, and financial projections. Although there is no single formula for developing a business plan, some elements are common to all business plans. As you know, often one of the most difficult tasks in undertaking complex projects, such as writing a business plan, is knowing where to start. There are many computer software programs on the market now to help you get organized. If you would like to see sample business plans that successfully secured funding, go to Bplans. com (www.bplans.com). You can also learn more about writing business plans on the Small Business Administration Web site at www.sba.gov/starting.

If you do it well, it should take you a long time to write the business plan (usually about six months), but you must be able to convince your readers (such as bankers and investors) within five minutes that your plan is solid. Although there's no such thing as a perfect business plan, prospective entrepreneurs do think out the smallest details. Jerrold Carrington of Inroads Capital Partners advises that one of the most important parts of the business plan is the *executive summary* at the beginning of the plan. The executive summary, an overview of the business in the first few pages of the plan, must catch the reader's interest, as it is usually all potential investors ever look at. Many bankers receive several business plans every day. "You better grab me up front," says Carrington.

Figure 3.16 Outline of a Comprehensive Business Plan

OUTLINE OF A COMPREHENSIVE BUSINESS PLAN

A good business plan is between 25 and 50 pages long and takes at least six months to write.

Cover Letter

Your cover letter should summarize the most attractive points of your project in as few words as possible. Be sure to address the letter to the potential investor by name. "To whom it may concern" or "Dear Sir" is not the best way to win an investor's support.

Section 1—Executive Summary

Begin with a two-page or three-page management summary of the proposed venture. Include a short description of the business, and discuss major goals and objectives.

Section 2—Company Background

Describe company operations to date (if any), potential legal considerations, and areas of risk and opportunity. Summarize the firm's financial condition, and include past and current balance sheets, income and cash flow statements, and other relevant financial records.

Section 3—Management Team

Include an organization chart, job descriptions of listed positions, and detailed résumés of the current and proposed executives. A mediocre idea with a proven management team is funded more often than a great idea with an inexperienced team.

Section 4—Financial Plan

Provide five-year projections for income, expenses, and funding sources. Don't assume the business will grow in a straight line. Adjust your planning to allow for funding at various stages of the company's growth. Explain the rationale and assumptions used to determine the estimates. Assumptions should be reasonable and based on industry/historical trends. Avoid excessively ambitious sales projections; rather, offer best-case, expected, and worst-case scenarios.

Section 5—Capital Required

Indicate the amount of capital needed to commence or continue operations, and describe how these funds are to be used. Make sure the totals are the same as the ones on the cash-flow statement.

Section 6—Marketing Plan

Don't underestimate the competition. Review industry size, trends, and the target market segment. Discuss strengths and weaknesses of the product or service. The most important things investors want to know are what makes the product more desirable than what's already available and whether the product can be patented. Compare pricing to the competition. Forecast sales in dollars and units. Outline sales, advertising, promotion, and public relations programs.

Section 7—Location Analysis

In retailing and certain other industries, the location of the business is one of the most important factors. Provide a comprehensive demographic analysis of consumers in the area of the proposed business as well as a traffic-pattern analysis and vehicular and pedestrian counts.

Section 8—Manufacturing Plan

Describe minimum plant size, machinery required, production capacity, inventory and inventory-control methods, quality control, plant personnel requirements, and so on. Estimates of product costs should be based on primary research.

Section 9—Appendix

Include all marketing research on the product or service (off-the-shelf reports, article reprints, etc.) and other information about the product concept or market size. Provide a bibliography of all the reference materials you consulted.

Of course, finding money to finance your business is a critical step, too. Getting your completed business plan into the right hands—someone willing to invest in your idea—is almost as important as getting the right information into the plan. Finding funding requires research. The next section discusses the various sources of money available to new business ventures.

FINANCING THE BUSINESS

An entrepreneur has several potential sources of capital: personal savings, relatives, former employers, banks, finance companies, **venture capitalists** (a person or investment company that loans money to businesses), and government agencies such as the SBA, the Farmers Home Administration, and the Economic Development Authority. Isabella Capital, LLC, is a venture capital firm that focuses on woman-owned businesses.[60]

Venture capitalists People or companies that invest money in businesses in return for a stake in them.

There are also **angel investors**, usually wealthy people who invest their own money in a business in return for a share of the company. Angel investors are different from venture capitalists, in that venture capitalists usually invest other people's money, while angel investors invest their own funds. The Angel Capital Association operates in North America and works to bring together angel investors and entrepreneurs.[61]

Angel investors People (usually wealthy) who invest their own funds in a business in exchange for a stake in the company.

You might consider borrowing from a potential supplier to your future business. Helping you get started could be in the supplier's best interest, if there's a chance you'll become a big customer later. Be careful about how you approach this, however: it's usually not a good idea to ask such an investor for money at the outset. Begin by asking her for advice; if the supplier likes your plan, she may be willing to help you with funding.

The **Small Business Administration (SBA)** is a U.S. government agency that advises and assists small businesses by providing management training, financial advice, and loans. The SBA started a microloan demonstration program in 1991. The program provides small loans (up to $35,000) and technical assistance to entrepreneurs. Entrepreneurs targeted by the program include women, minorities, and low-income individuals, all of whom have historically found it more challenging to obtain loans because they were considered risky borrowers.[63] Rather than basing its loans on collateral, credit history, or previous business success, these programs decide worthiness on the basis of belief in the borrowers' integrity and the soundness of their business ideas.

Small Business Administration (SBA) A U.S. government agency that advises and assists small businesses by providing management training, financial advice, and loans.

This program helped Lowell Gray of Lynn, Massachusetts, who obtained a $25,000 microloan from the SBA to found Shore.net, an Internet service provider with 85 employees. Gray's company continued to grow until he eventually sold to

Christopher Kimball, the entrepreneur who started Cook's Illustrated magazine, and, subsequently, a wildly successful cooking-related publishing and media empire, raised $100,000 from angel investors among his friends and family to start his business.[62]

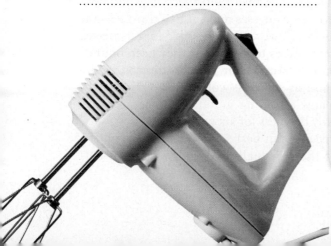

Figure 3.17 Types of Loans Offered by SBA

The SBA may provide the following types of financial assistance:

- *Guaranteed loans*—loans made by a financial institution that the government will repay if the borrower stops making payments. The maximum individual loan guarantee is capped at $1 million.
- *Microloans*—amounts ranging from $100 to $35,000 (average $10,500) to people such as single mothers and public housing tenants.
- *Export Express*—loans made to small businesses wishing to export. The maximum guaranteed loan amount is $250,000.
- *Community Adjustment and Investment Program (CAIP)*—loans to businesses to create new, sustainable jobs or to preserve existing jobs in eligible communities that have lost jobs due to changing trade patterns with Mexico and Canada following the adoption of NAFTA.
- *Pollution control loans*—loans to eligible small businesses for the financing of the planning, design, or installation of a pollution control facility. This facility must prevent, reduce, abate, or control any form of pollution, including recycling. The maximum guaranteed loan amount is $1 million.
- *504 certified development company (CDC) loans*—loans for purchasing major fixed assets, such as land and buildings, for businesses in eligible communities, typically rural communities or urban areas needing revitalization. The program's goal is to expand business ownership by minorities, women, and veterans. The maximum guaranteed loan amount is $1.3 million.

Most families are willing to take a Caribbean cruise or some sort of lavish vacation. However, not all of them have the means to do so. As a result, this market probably would not be a good market to pursue for a travel agency that sets up lavish vacations.

Primus Communications for an astonishing $43 million (today, Gray has reacquired control of the company).[64] Figure 3.17 shows a partial list of types of financial assistance offered by SBA.

KNOWING YOUR CUSTOMER

One of the most important elements of small-business success is *knowing the market*. As you learned earlier in the chapter, a market consists of people with unsatisfied wants and needs who have both the resources and the willingness to buy.

Once you've identified a market and its needs, you must set out to fulfill those needs. The way to do it is to offer top quality, at a fair price, with great service. Remember, it isn't enough to get customers—you have to keep them. Customer experience management (CEM) is a strategy where emphasis is placed upon customers and what they want. According to Bob Thompson, founder of CRMGuru, a site dedicated to helping companies keep customers happy, "A company has to consider not only how to get more customers, but also think about the customer's perspective. That's the only way to give customers more value so they won't stray to the competition."[65] Everything in your business must be geared toward bringing customers the satisfaction they deserve.

One of the greatest advantages small businesses have over larger ones is the ability to know their customers better, and to quickly adapt to their ever-changing needs. Next, let's consider the importance of effectively managing the employees who will help you serve your market.

MANAGING YOUR EMPLOYEES

As a business grows, it becomes impossible for an entrepreneur to oversee every detail of it, even if he or she is putting in 60 hours or more per week. This means that hiring, training, and motivating employees are critical responsibilities. (More detail on the management of human resources will be presented in Chapter 5.) It is not easy to find good, qualified help when you offer less money, skimpier benefits, and less room for advancement than larger firms. That's why employee relations are such an important part of small-business management.

Employees of small companies are often more satisfied with their jobs than are their counterparts in big business. Why? Quite often, they find their jobs more challenging, their ideas more accepted, and their bosses more respectful. Even the most fiercely independent entrepreneurs must eventually face the reality that to keep growing, they must delegate authority to others. Nagging questions like "Whom should I delegate authority to?" and "How much control should they have?" can be particularly touchy in small businesses with long-term employees or in family businesses.

As you might expect, entrepreneurs who build their companies from scratch often feel compelled to promote employees who have been with them from the start—even when those employees aren't qualified to serve as managers. Common sense probably tells you this sort of decision could be detrimental to the business. The same can be true of family-run businesses. Attitudes such as "You can't fire family" or the tendency to promote certain workers because "they're family" can hinder growth.

For example, Accent Administrative Staffing in Phoenix, Arizona, is operated by a brother, sister, and mother team. When they began to experience family problems, they went to counseling, and when that didn't work, the mother decided to leave the business. Luckily, the family is still close, but according to *Entrepreneur* magazine, that's not always the case.[66]

The odds are stacked against businesses that are family owned and operated: only about a third of family-run businesses make it to a second generation, a third of those businesses make it to a third generation, and so on. However, it is possible for businesses operated by families to succeed if they keep boundaries in place between their relationships as family members and as business colleagues. C.F. Martin and Company, a leading guitar manufacturer, has been a family business for six generations.[67]

Entrepreneurs can best serve themselves and the business if they gradually recruit and groom employees for management positions. Doing so helps entrepreneurs enhance trust and support of the manager among other employees—and themselves. When Heida Thurlow of Chantal Cookware suffered an extended illness, she let her employees handle the work she once had insisted on doing herself. The experience transformed her company from an entrepreneurial company into a managerial one. According to Thurlow, "Over the long run, that makes us stronger than we were."[68] Promoting employees from within a company has several advantages, such as reducing the time needed to train them and increased morale.[69]

RECORD KEEPING

Many small-business owners say the most important assistance they received in starting and managing their business involved accounting. A businessperson who ensures that an effective accounting system is in place early on will save herself much grief later on. We strongly recommend that you don't set up your own accounting system (unless you're an accountant, of course), because it's usually best to leave business financials to the experts.

However, even if an entrepreneur hires an accountant, he will still be responsible for some record-keeping activities. (More on record keeping will be covered in Chapter 8.) Computers simplify record keeping and enable a small-business owner to

Imagine a new business owner who is really good at his craft—for example, baking and decorating wedding cakes. Although he understands wedding cakes very well, he may not know a lot about accounting. Instead, he hires someone to set up an accounting system for him and to keep records on a monthly basis. This solution allows him more time to focus on making wedding cakes and not be bothered by worries about the books. This concept is referred to as focusing on one's core competency.

follow the progress of the business, such as sales, expenses, and profits, on a daily basis. An inexpensive computer system can also help owners with other record-keeping chores, such as inventory control, customer records, and payroll. A good accountant is invaluable in creating such systems and showing you how to keep them operating smoothly.

Many businesses fail because of poor accounting practices. A good accountant can help you make decisions, such as whether to buy or lease equipment and whether to own or rent the building. Accountants can also provide counseling for tax planning, financial forecasting, choosing sources of financing, and writing requests for funds.[70] Ask other small-business owners about their accountants. It pays to shop around for advice.

[BUS] connections

1. Explain each of the five areas of running a small business. Which do you think you would enjoy the most? Which would you find the most challenging?

2. What are the advantages of understanding some accounting practices, even if you don't do the accounting for your small business yourself?

3. Why is record keeping so important to a small business?

>> Small Business Failures versus Successes

At the outset, we must again debunk the most commonly heard small business failure myth:

Myth: Nine out of 10 businesses (90 percent) fail and close in the first year of operation.

Fact: According to the Census Bureau, two-thirds (66 percent) of new businesses survive their first two years, and about 50 percent survive four. Forty percent survive six years or more.[71] Furthermore, the businesses of entrepreneurs who seek help and obtain additional education and training survive and thrive at even higher rates. In this section, you'll learn why small businesses fail and how you can help ensure your own success.

WHY DO BUSINESSES FAIL?

Businesses usually fail due to one or more of the following reasons:[72]

1. *A lack of planning and overall poor management.* Entrepreneurs often are so engrossed in what they want to do with their product or service that many other aspects of the business get neglected, such as marketing, hiring the right people and providing training, satisfying customer needs, keeping good records, managing inventory, meeting proper licenses and regulatory requirements, and so on. A lack of business savvy when it comes to managing operations can lead to failure. That's where having a detailed business plan can be of immense help!

2. *A lack of marketing.* The basic essence of marketing is meeting the customer's needs. Often, entrepreneurs are so overconfident about their product or service that they believe it sells itself. Word of mouth is the best free form of advertising, but if an entrepreneur doesn't pay attention to all of the four Ps of marketing (discussed in Chapter 4), the business is less likely to survive and thrive. Marketing doesn't have to be expensive: appropriate use of promotions; having a Web site; and having a presence on social networking sites like Facebook, Twitter, MySpace, and LinkedIn can all provide a cost-effective virtual presence, promotional opportunities, and an effective way to reach target markets.

3. *A lack of financial understanding.* This is probably the fastest way a business can enter a downward spiral. Many business owners don't understand the actual costs of their product or service (including fixed costs like rent, utilities, and so on). Some don't realize how much money they lose by wasting raw materials, permitting employees to waste time on the clock, and using their own time unproductively. Some start their businesses without first getting sufficient capital to run them smoothly. Others don't keep careful records. And many entrepreneurs start their businesses with completely unrealistic expectations: "If this business isn't profitable within six months, it's not worth the effort."

4. *The wrong business partner.* A business partnership in which the partners are constantly going in different, and not complementary, directions can be extremely problematic. Such relationships are much more stressful and often result in conflict.

5. *No knack for sales.* Many people who are great at a particular skill, such as repairing cars or making quilts, lack a key ingredient of running a business: they don't know how to sell. If you can't sell your product, your business isn't moving forward as your expenses pile up.

6. *A bad location.* A bad location can result in the demise of even the best-managed businesses. If it is difficult for your customers to reach you, if your business has inadequate parking, or if the neighborhood is unsafe, it can be much harder for your business to succeed.

7. *Competition.* Entrepreneurs often underestimate their competition. There may be too many competitors in a particular market, or firms that aren't competing directly when you start your business may jump into it once you enter the field. Failure to incorporate the competitive actions and reactions is a certain move toward a short life span. Consider the decision of McDonald's management to compete directly with Starbucks by selling gourmet coffee at a significantly cheaper price. Starbucks' profits have declined since McDonald's entry into the market, and its stock price has suffered as well.

WHAT CAN ENTREPRENEURS DO TO SUCCEED?

Some businesses do fail, but it's possible for almost any business to succeed. Proper focus on each of the seven areas mentioned previously can help you steer your business in the right direction, toward success. Entrepreneurs can succeed if they:[73]

Always remember to seek help when you need it. There are many resources available to aid entrepreneurs.

Real World Apps

Now that she has read her textbook's chapter on entrepreneurship, Sara better understands the process of starting a business. Of the five areas of focus for starting a business, she had previously only focused on marketing; now she can spread her attention to other critical areas. After reading information about the different types of businesses, Sara weighed pros and cons of each and decided that a sole proprietorship would best meet her needs at this time, because she likes the independence a start-up offers.

Her next step will be obtaining financing for her ice cream shop. She will put together a business plan that defines her needs as a necessary step before obtaining a loan or any available grants. Before opening her business's doors, she will also come up with plans for managing any employees she might need to add as the business grows.

Sara has taken accounting courses, so she will keep her own books and track expenses. She is now aware that as the business grows, she will need to decide how best to use her skills—whether she should focus on management, marketing, or accounting and get help from others for the rest.

Who knew the ice cream business could be so complex? Sara is glad she took the time to read and research her options. She's confident that knowledge is the special ingredient that will ensure her success.

3. *Monitor and understand your cash flow.* The amount of capital small business owners have to work with is usually limited. Therefore, it must be closely monitored. Owners must make sure they have enough money to keep the business running until it generates money on its own.

4. *Focus on sales.* Although other aspects of a business cannot be neglected either, you must always keep a keen eye on sales. Sales keep your business moving and help mitigate cash-flow problems.

5. *Watch for changes in your business.* Don't get too comfortable with your business and the business's environment. You need to keep an eye on the changing trends, customer needs, competitive actions and reactions, emerging regulations, and so on. Recognizing these changes and effectively responding to or incorporating them helps ensure that your business will prosper.

6. *Seek help.* Businesses that seek help when they need it tend to succeed and last much longer than those that don't. There are plenty of resources available to entrepreneurs, such as the Small Business Administration, SCORE chapters, small business development centers, accountants, lawyers, and economic development centers at local universities.

7. *Have fun.* The most basic ingredients you need to succeed are passion and fun. If you're passionate about your work and truly enjoy doing what you do—and you take care of the other items mentioned earlier—success is right around the corner.

1. *Have a business plan.* Having as business plan allows you to think things through ahead of time. It's hard work and may not be exciting, but it will force you to focus on details while keeping an eye on the big picture.

2. *Learn to control your emotions and have realistic expectations.* Understand that you will have to work very long hours, will have to make sacrifices, and will not make millions of dollars immediately. Having realistic expectations and managing your emotions can help you develop the stamina to deal with the uncertainties that come with owning your own business.

BUS connections

1. Why do you believe businesses fail? Think of a business that recently failed in your area. Why do you think it failed?

2. Identify four factors that can help an entrepreneur succeed. What other factors do you believe can help an entrepreneur succeed?

3. Which of the four factors would be most challenging for you personally? Explain your response.

For REVIEW >>

1. Explain the traits of a successful entrepreneur.
   - This chapter covered the basics of entrepreneurship. People who are successful entrepreneurs are self-directed, self-nurturing, action-oriented, highly energetic, tolerant of uncertainty, have an innate drive to succeed and the ability to persevere despite adversity. Entrepreneurs take on the risk of starting their own business because of a variety of factors, including opportunity, the potential for profit, a desire for independence, the ability to be completely involved in the business, the challenge of business ownership, the flexibility it affords, and the idea that they can make a difference in the world.

2. Describe the alternatives to starting a business from scratch.
   - There are many opportunities and challenges involved with starting a business from scratch—such as going it alone and working long, lonely hours. Keys to starting a business from scratch include finding mentors, doing research, knowing the industry, learning how to market yourself and your ideas, and reading up on the industry you're looking to join. The first alternative, buying an existing business, is considerably safer than starting from scratch, but it can be expensive to do so. There may be hidden problems in the business as well. The second alternative, buying a franchise, has some major built-in advantages, like the fact that the company's products are already established in the market, and training and support are usually available from the franchisor. However, new franchises of the same business in the area could cannibalize an existing location's business, and negative publicity for the brand affects individual franchisees as well. Franchises can also be very expensive.

3. Discuss the legal forms of business ownership, and the advantages and disadvantages of each.
   - A sole proprietorship, which involves one individual owner, is the easiest kind of business to start. Advantages of sole proprietorships include ease of entry and exit into the business, independence, the ability to retain all the profits, and the ability to be the master of one's own destiny. Its disadvantages include the inherent financial burden, the fact that most entrepreneurs have limitations in terms of skills in some areas of the business, the fact that sole proprietors have unlimited liability, the long hours, the lack of fringe benefits, and the fact that the company literally can't go on without the proprietor's involvement.
   - Partnerships, which include general partnerships, limited partnerships, master limited partnerships, and limited liability partnerships, involve two or more owners. Partnerships benefit from greater financial resources, a larger pool of knowledge, and a better distribution of risk, but there are negatives as well: some partners still face unlimited liability, the possibility of conflict among the partners is strong, the business's profits must be divided, and it can be difficult to exit a partnership.
   - Corporations can be large or small. The types of corporation include conventional (C) corporations, S corporations, and limited liability corporations. Advantages of corporations include limited liability, shared ownership, ease of continuity if one or more owners exit the company, lower tax rates, and fringe benefits for owners, but disadvantages include the possibility of double taxation, additional paperwork to set up the business, greater regulations from government and other entities, and the danger of owners becoming focused on achieving profits over all else.

4. Describe the five main areas of focus when starting a small business.
   - There are five initial areas of concern for an entrepreneur, including putting together a carefully written and researched business plan; obtaining proper financing through such options as banks, friends and family, the Small Business Administration, or venture capitalists; defining and understanding the business's customers; determining how employees will be hired and managed; and hiring professional financial advisers to set up accounting practices for the business.

5. Explain why businesses fail and how they succeed.
   - Seven potential reasons were presented: a lack of planning and overall poor management, a lack of marketing, a lack of financial understanding, the wrong business partner, no innate ability for sales, a bad business location, and inappropriate attention to competition. Entrepreneurs can better ensure success by addressing these factors, having a solid business plan, learning to control their emotions and have realistic expectations, monitoring and understanding their cash flow, focusing on sales, watching for changes in their business, seeking help when it is needed, and having fun while doing it all.

Key Terms

Angel investors

Board of directors

Business plan

Cannibalization

Chain store

Company store

Conventional (C) corporations

Corporate governance

Dividends

Double taxation

Entrepreneurship

Franchisee

Franchisor

General partner

General partnership

Limited liability

Limited liability partnership (LLP)

Limited partner

Limited partnership

Market

Master limited partnership (MLP)

Mentor

Partnership

S corporation

Small Business Administration (SBA)

Sole proprietor

Sole proprietorship

Unlimited liability

Venture capitalists

1. Brainstorm a list of things you enjoy doing and are good at. These might include scrapbooking, sports, or public speaking. What possible businesses could you start that would utilize these skills and interests?

2. Make a list of several franchised businesses in your area. Would you be interested in starting a franchise? What are the advantages to a franchise? The disadvantages?

3. What are some considerations before choosing a partner for your business? Name at least five. Is there anyone you might consider partnering with? Why? Why not?

4. In groups, discuss the advantages and disadvantages of starting your own business. Next, have each person in the group discuss whether or not he or she would ever consider starting a business.

5. In groups, make a list of 10 personality traits an entrepreneur should have. Once the list is finished, rank them in order, from the most important to least important, and discuss why you ranked them as you did.

6. In groups, complete the matrix on the right. Think about the implications of unlimited and limited liability, ease to start, and other considerations we discussed in this chapter.

Business	Best legal form of business	Why did you choose this form?
A paper shop		
An Italian restaurant		
An accounting firm		
Consulting services		
Day spa		
Financial investment firm		
Construction company		

1. As discussed in this chapter, the Small Business Administration can be a valuable tool in starting a business. Visit its Web site, and after you have reviewed it thoroughly, answer the following questions:
   - According to the SBA, what elements should every business plan address?
   - Describe in detail two of the services the SBA provides.
   - Where is your local SBA office located?
   - What "special audiences" are addressed in the Web site's services section? How does this relate to diversity?

2. Visit Google or Bing.com to search for "sample business plans." Review at least two different business plans and answer the following questions.
   - What components did both business plans have?
   - Were any parts missing?
   - Did you think the business plans had enough detail to start a business and make it successful? Why or why not?
   - Did the business plan discuss not only the plans, but also how the plans would be executed and a timeline to do so? What are the advantages of including this information in a business plan?

Self-Assessment Exercises

BUSINESS CAREER QUIZ

Personality Profile for Entrepreneurs

Answer Yes or No to each question.

1. I am comfortable taking risks.	____Yes	____No
2. I think it is fun to take unfamiliar routes when driving.	____Yes	____No
3. I am outgoing.	____Yes	____No
4. I don't mind asking others for help when I need it.	____Yes	____No
5. People have told me I have a high energy level.	____Yes	____No
6. I don't wait for people to tell me what to do; I dig in and do it.	____Yes	____No
7. I don't mind working long hours.	____Yes	____No
8. I enjoy and embrace new experiences.	____Yes	____No
9. I am a good planner.	____Yes	____No
10. I like to be a leader and direct others.	____Yes	____No
11. If I want something, I go out and get it rather than waiting for it to be given to me	____Yes	____No

The more *Yes* answers you have, the more likely you are to succeed at being an entrepreneur. Our personalities can change over time, so even if you marked *No* for many answers, it just means you may not be ready to start a business right now—but who knows what the future may hold?

Self-Assessment

Entrepreneurship Quotient Quiz

In the following quiz, answer the questions according to how you think you might if you owned your own business. Then add up the points below to find your entrepreneurship quotient.

1. What's the key to business success?
   a. Business knowledge
   b. Market awareness
   c. Hands-on management
   d. Sufficient capital
   e. Hard work

2. I trust *(select all that apply)*
   a. nobody
   b. myself
   c. my partner
   d. a few key employees
   e. my customers

3. I am unhappy when my employees are
   a. late
   b. unhappy
   c. abrupt with customers
   d. resigning
   e. less dedicated than me

4. My customers are *(select all that apply)*
   a. always right
   b. too fussy
   c. demanding
   d. worth listening to
   e. dumb

5. The real key to business success is:
   a. hard work and perseverance
   b. fine products and service
   c. advertising
   d. knowing the fundamentals of business
   e. employees

6. The best competitive advantage is:
   a. experience
   b. understanding what the market wants
   c. confidence
   d. conducting a business ethically
   e. a detailed business plan

TOTAL: _____

Answers

1. a = 5, b = 4, c = 3, d = 2, e = 1
2. b = 5, e = 4, d = 3, c = 2, a = 1
3. b = 5, d = 4, c = 3, a = 2, e = 1

4. d = 5, c = 4, a = 3, b = 2, e = 1
5. e = 5, d = 4, a = 3, b = 2, c = 1
6. a = 5, b = 4, c = 3, e = 2, d = 1

Score Assessment

30–50   You are a successful entrepreneur whose operations reflect tried and true business practices.

20–29   Your business is probably headed for long-term success, but success will come sooner if you sharpen your awareness of solid management skills and marketing techniques.

10–19   While you may be enjoying customer loyalty and repeat business, never forget that savvy competition is always looking for ways to take the lead. Don't let comfort lull you into false security. Be creatively assertive!

0–9   You may well have the right product, but to sell it successfully, you need to increase your market awareness and improve your operating philosophy. Reach out for practical classes, seminars and advice from people who have good business track records. Keep persevering. It's the key ingredient to winning!

Source: Make Decisions Quiz (2009). Small Business Administration, http://www.sba.gov/smallbusinessplanner/manage/makedecisions/serv_manage_qures.html (accessed October 26, 2009).

4

THE FOUR Ps OF MARKETING: PRODUCT, PRICE, PLAC AND PROMOTION

After reading this chapter, you will be able to:

1 Define marketing and name the types of market segmentations.

2 Describe the various aspects of marketing's focus on developing a product.

3 Describe the different types of pricing that should be considered when marketing products.

4 Explain the concept of place and how it pertains to marketing.

5 Understand the different types of promotion and how they can be put together to create a unified image.

OPENING CASE: JONATHAN FIELDS AND SONIC YOGA

Shortly after Jonathan Fields opened Sonic Yoga in 2001, he teamed with researchers at Adelphi University to conduct a first-of-its-kind study of how efficiently the body burns calories while doing yoga. Fields considered how to take advantage of this situation and increase his company's exposure. Of course, a study on the effectiveness of yoga as an aid to losing weight would be of interest to countless Americans outside of the target market (people already interested in yoga) he served. He saw a golden opportunity to capitalize on the marketing potential of the study and contacted a number of fitness magazines about it, offering each exclusive rights if it agreed to do a story on the collaboration.

One of the magazines, *Self*, agreed to Fields's offer. After the article was written, an editor at *Self* followed up with Fields and mentioned that it would have been a nice feature of the article to mention that Sonic Yoga offered a workout video. Quickly, Fields replied that the studio did, in fact, have a video in production, and that it would be out by the date the magazine article hit the newsstands. He told the editor the name of the video and its price, and the editor agreed to mention it in the article.

This was an ambitious move for Fields, particularly since the video didn't exist. He'd made up the video's name and price on the spot. He and his partner quickly hustled a video into production, and it did indeed sell out after the article's publication. Despite its speed to market, the video was well reviewed. Since then, Sonic Yoga has made four additional videos.

The strongest message of this story is best told in Fields's own words: "If you want to be in the news, make news. You don't need connections, you don't need a publicist, but you do need to think way outside the box."[1]

Fields boldly developed a new product, its name, and its price in a few seconds. He gained national exposure for his business and illuminated his brand in the process. Fields lent credibility to his business through collaboration with an established brand (Adelphi University) and expanded his target audience in a flash by attracting novices interested in weight loss to the practice of yoga. He maintained his business's integrity by delivering a high-quality product—the video—just in time to take advantage of the free publicity the article provided. Quick thinking like this has helped Fields build a strong business; Sonic Yoga has served 15,000 students and has trained hundreds of teachers from around the world. It was rated New York City's No. 1 yoga studio by Citisearch in 2005, 2006, and 2007.

Questions

1 Visit www.sonicyoga.com. What type of person is the studio trying to market its products and services to?

2 Why was the collaboration with the university so important to Sonic Yoga?

Source: Adapted from Geoff Williams, "Top 10 Successful Marketing Stunts," *Entrepreneur*, July 2006, http://www.entrepreneur.com/marketing/marketingideas/article159484.html#ixzz0LEiaxpJa&D (accessed August 5, 2009), and Sonic Yoga's Web site, http://www.sonicyoga.com/2006/about.htm (accessed August 5, 2009).

- Why do marketers separate people in different groups?
- What is most important: product, pricing, distribution, or promotion?
- How do businesses figure out which promotional strategy is the right one for them?

>> Introduction to Marketing

Marketing is a fun business topic, because even if you don't intend to major in marketing, knowing a little about it can help you become a more informed and savvy consumer. **Marketing** goes beyond simply selling or advertising—it is the process of planning and executing the conception, pricing, promotion, and distribution of goods and services to facilitate exchanges that satisfy individual and organizational needs. Before exploring the mechanics of marketing through its four Ps (product, price, place, and promotion), you should understand two critical aspects of need satisfaction: market segmentation and consumer behavior.

Marketing The process of planning and executing the conception, pricing, promotion, and distribution of goods and services to facilitate exchanges that satisfy individual and organizational needs.

MARKET SEGMENTATION

According to the Selig Center for Economic Growth in Athens, Georgia, U.S. buying power in 2008 was estimated at $10.7 trillion. By 2013, that figure is expected to jump to $14 trillion.[2] Because consumer groups differ greatly in age, education level, income, and taste, a single business can't fill the needs of every group. Therefore, it must first decide which groups to serve and then develop products and services specially tailored to their needs.

Consider Mar-riott International, a leading hospitality company that owns more than 3,200 lodging properties in 66 countries. Marriott has developed different brands to serve the needs of different target groups, including:[3]

- JW Marriott Hotel & Resorts and Ritz-Carlton (luxury)
- Residence Inn and TownePlace Suites (extended short-term stays)
- Courtyard by Marriott (business)
- Fairfield Inn (economy)
- Marriott Conference Centers (business, with a particular need for meeting space)
- Marriott Vacation Club (time-share)
- Marriott ExecuStay and Marriott Executive Apartments (furnished apartments for long-term stays)

Marriott is just one of countless companies that have found success with studying the consumer market, breaking it down into categories, and then developing brands for each of those categories of consumers. The process of dividing the total market into several groups whose members have similar characteristics is called **market segmentation**.[4] Selecting which groups (market segments) an organization can profitably serve is called **target marketing**. The challenge is finding the right target market (the segment that would be most profitable to serve) for the new venture.

Market segmentation The process of dividing the total market into several groups whose members have similar characteristics.

Target marketing Selecting which market segments an organization can profitably serve.

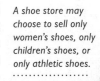
A shoe store may choose to sell only women's shoes, only children's shoes, or only athletic shoes.

tation. Marketers might even segment according to religion, race, and profession. Demographics are the most used segmentation variable, but not necessarily the best.

Perhaps you want to ensure that your product's advertising accurately portrays a target group's lifestyle. To do so, you'd practice **psychographic segmentation** and study the group's lifestyle, values, attitudes, and interests. Determining which benefits of a product are preferred among customers and using those benefits to promote the product is called **benefit segmentation**. Separating a market by usage (volume of product use) is called **volume (usage) segmentation**.

The best segmentation strategy is to use all the variables possible to come up with a consumer profile (a target market) that is sizable, reachable, and profitable. In some cases, that may mean not segmenting the market at all and instead going after the total market (everyone). In other cases, that may mean going after a much smaller segment or various segments of the whole. Targeting small but profitable market segments and creating products and services for them is called **niche marketing**.

> **Demographic segmentation** Dividing a market into demographic categories, such as age, income, or education level.

> **Psychographic segmentation** Dividing a market using the group's values, attitudes, and interests.

> **Benefit segmentation** Dividing a market by determining which benefits of the product to promote.

> **Volume segmentation** Dividing a market by usage (volume of use).

> **Niche marketing** The process of finding small but profitable market segments and creating products for them.

Segmenting the Consumer Market

There are several ways a firm can segment its consumer market (see Figure 4.1). For example, rather than trying to sell a product nationwide, you could focus on only one region of the country—perhaps in western states, such as California and Nevada. Dividing a market by geographic area (cities, counties, states, regions, and so on) is called **geographic segmentation**.

> **Geographic segmentation** Dividing a market into geographic regions.

Another option for market segmentation would be to target people in certain age groups. For example, the clothing company Aeropostale targets primarily young men and women ages 14 to 17.[5] Segmentation of a market by age, income, education level, or similar characteristics is called **demographic segmen-**

Mountain City Coffeehouse & Creamery in Frostburg, Maryland, is aware of a growing need among customers in its area for more health-conscious meals that are freshly prepared and taste delicious. To respond to this need, the business offers daily specials of fresh and healthy ethnic vegetarian dishes. The coffeehouse also determines who its best customers are—the people most interested in ethnic vegetarian food—and targets them with its marketing about these daily specials; that's a great example of benefit segmentation at work. Because the coffeehouse is near a university, during some parts of the day it attracts more faculty, and during others it attracts more students. Because of its awareness of these trends, it practices volume segmentation and provides special offers, such as offering discounts for students during times when students are less likely to visit.

Figure 4.1 Some Methods Marketers Use to Segment a Market

Main Dimension	Sample Variables	Typical Segments
Geographic segmentation	Region	Northeast, Midwest, South, West
	City or county size	Under 5,000; 5,000–10,999; 20,000–49,000; 50,000–99,999
	Density	Urban, suburban, rural
Demographic segmentation	Gender	Male, female
	Age	Younger than 5; 5–10; 11–18; 19–34; 35–49; 50–64; 65 and over
	Education	Some high school or less, high school graduate, some college, college graduate, postgraduate
	Race	Caucasian, African American, Indian, Asian, Hispanic
	Nationality	American, Asian, Eastern European, Japanese
	Life stage	Infant, preschooler, child, teenager, college age, adult, senior
	Income	Less than $15,000; $15,000–$24,999; $25,000–$44,999; $45,000–$74,999; $75,000 and over
	Household size	1; 2; 3–4; 5 or more
	Occupation	Professional, technical, clerical, sales supervisors, farmers, students, home-based business owners, retired, unemployed
Psychographic segmentation	Personalities	Gregarious, compulsive, extroverted, aggressive, ambitious
	Values	Actualizers, fulfillers, achievers, experiencers, believers, strivers, makers, strugglers
	Lifestyle	Upscale, moderate
Benefit segmentation	Comfort	Benefit segmentation divides an already established market into smaller, more homogeneous segments. Those people who desire economy in a car would be an example. The benefit desired varies by product.
	Convenience	
	Durability	
	Economy	
	Health	
	Luxury	
	Safety	
	Status	
Volume segmentation	Usage	Heavy users, light users, nonusers
	Loyalty status	None, medium, strong

For example, Dan Wiesel's business, Pet Airways, attracts customers who own large pets or people who fear for their pets' safety when their pets travel by air the usual way (as cargo in a plane's belly). His company's planes allow pets to travel in the main cabin and be monitored by a flight attendant; the pets' owners fly on "human" airlines and then meet their pets at their destination.[6]

As the world moves away from mass production and more toward customized goods and services, marketers often focus on **relationship marketing**. The goal of relationship marketing is to maintain customers over time by offering them new products that exactly meet their requirements. Today, technology enables sellers to work with individual buyers to determine their wants and needs and develop goods and services specifically designed for them (for example, hand-tailored shirts or customized vacations).

Relationship marketing A marketing strategy with the goal of keeping individual customers over time by offering them products that exactly meet their requirements.

Airlines, rental car companies, and hotels offer frequent-customer programs to their most loyal customers. These customers earn special services and awards. M&T Bank offers its customers a rewards program. Each time customers use their bank cards, they earn points that can be redeemed for merchandise, gift cards, and cash rewards.[7]

There are several resources for

Study Alert!

Niche marketing is marketing to a very special and narrow segment, but also a profitable, sustainable one. Relationship marketing helps companies establish and maintain customers over time by offering them new products that exactly meet their requirements.

specific information about target markets; for example, the U.S. Census Bureau (www.census.gov) offers countless statistics about the nation's citizens, and the Small Business Administration's home page (www.sba.gov) offers links to tools that can help entrepreneurs with marketing, such as statistics and research, success stories, monthly chat events, and e-newsletters.

CONSUMER BEHAVIOR

The study of consumer behavior is critical because before companies can sell effectively to a market, they must understand their customers' motivations and reasons for purchasing a product or service in the first place. Some consumers derive pleasure from buying high-status products, such as a Harvard education, a BMW, or an iPhone, because of an unconscious belief that these products give them desirable personal attributes, such as intelligence. For example, some people might buy Starbucks coffee because they want to show others they are conscientious about labor practices in developing countries and support Starbucks's use of "fair trade" coffee.[8]

Of course, a mental process goes on each time a consumer contemplates a purchase. The five steps in the consumer decision making process are *problem recognition, information search, alternative evaluation, purchase decision,* and *postpurchase evaluation.* Figure 4.2 illustrates some of the outside factors that influence the consumer decision-making process.

For example, you may become aware of a problem (a broken computer) that leads to an information search (finding out how much it will cost to have your computer fixed and then comparing that to how much it would cost to buy a new one). You might then arrive at a purchase deci-

Figure 4.2 Outside Influences on the Consumer Decision-Making Process

Marketing mix influences
- Product
- Price
- Place
- Promotion

Sociocultural influences
- Reference groups
- Family
- Social class
- Culture
- Subculture

Psychological influences
- Perception
- Attitudes
- Learning
- Motivation

Situational influences
- Type of purchase
- Social surroundings
- Physical surroundings
- Previous experience

Decision-making process
1. Problem recognition
2. Information search
3. Alternative evaluation
4. Purchase decision/or no purchase
5. Postpurchase evaluation (cognitive dissonance)

If you knew you wouldn't get caught, would you consider lying to a customer in order to get a sale?

sion (buying a new computer instead of fixing your old one) and then make a postpurchase evaluation (at first doubting whether you made the right choice and doing a little more research to reinforce your initial decision).

Marketing researchers investigate consumer thought processes and behavior at each stage to determine the best way to reach consumers. Consumer behavior researchers also study the various influences that affect consumer behavior. Figure 4.2 shows several influences that affect consumer buying behavior: the four Ps of marketing (discussed in the next section); psychological influences, such as perceptions and attitudes; situational influences, such as the physical surroundings; and sociocultural influences, such as culture.

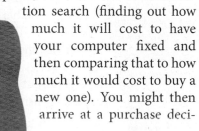

An airline's frequent-flyer program allows customers to earn "miles" that can be redeemed for free flights.

Every customer goes through the five steps of the consumer decision-making process when purchasing products.

Figure 4.3 Buying Habits by Race

Race	Where They Spend More, in Order of Importance
Hispanic Americans	Groceries, phone services, furniture, gasoline, clothing, and footwear
African Americans	Phone services, utilities, apparel, footwear, and groceries
Asian Americans	Food, housing, major appliances, telecommunications, education, and personal insurance

Table compiled from report at: http://www.terry.uga.edu/selig/docs/buying_power_2008.pdf, accessed July 7, 2009.

Figure 4.3 illustrates how market segmentation and consumer behavior can be used to understand the buying habits of consumers by race. Armed with this type of information, companies in certain industries, such as phone services, can focus their messages to target markets more effectively.

Business-to-Business Markets

So far, this discussion has focused on consumer markets, but business-to-business (B2B) markets account for a significant number of sales as well. B2B marketers include manufacturers; intermediaries, such as retailers; institutions, such as hospitals and schools; and the government.[9]

The B2B market is larger than the consumer market because items are often sold and resold several times in the B2B process before they are sold to the final consumer. A manufacturing firm purchases tools and component parts for the products it manufactures from other businesses as well. B2B marketing strategies often differ from consumer marketing because business buyers have a different decision-making process. Figure 4.4 compares B2B markets with the traditional consumer markets.

If a business purchases a copier and other office supplies from another business, a B2B market transaction has occurred.

>> The Four Ps of Marketing: Product

If customers aren't pleased by a business, the business won't be around for long. **Marketing management** refers to the process of overseeing all the aspects of marketing a particular product or service for the purpose of attracting and retaining customers. The activities of marketing are often referred to as the **marketing mix**, because they blend together in a well-designed marketing program. They are also known as the four Ps, which are:[10]

1. Product (what satisfies the market need)

2. Price (how much that product will cost)

3. Place (getting the product in a place where people can buy it)

4. Promotion (making sure people find out about the product)

> **Marketing management** The process of overseeing all the aspects of marketing a particular product or service for the purpose of attracting and retaining customers.

> **Marketing mix (the four Ps)** Product, price, place, and promotion, the four ingredients of a marketing program.

TOTAL PRODUCT OFFER

From a marketing perspective, a total product offer is more than just the good or service itself. It's the first, and perhaps most important, way to look at a product. A total product offer implies that a customer is not only buying a product or a service, but purchasing everything that goes along with it, such as service after the sale, the cachet of the brand name, and so on. In other words, **total product offer** consists of everything consumers evaluate when deciding whether to purchase a good or service. Thus, the basic product or service may be a laptop, a health-care service, or a brand of laundry detergent, but the total product offer may also consist of the value enhancers listed in Figure 4.5. Before consumers buy a product, they will probably evaluate and compare total product offers for the product and the products of its competitors.

> **Total product offer** Everything consumers evaluate when deciding whether to purchase a good or service.

Figure 4.4 Comparing B2B and Consumer Market Buying Behavior

	BUSINESS-TO-BUSINESS MARKET	CONSUMER MARKET
Market Structure	Relatively few potential customers Larger purchases Geographically concentrated	Many potential customers Smaller purchases Geographically dispersed
Products	Require technical, complex products Frequently require customization Frequently require technical advice, delivery, and after-sale service	Require less technical products Sometimes require customization Sometimes require technical advice, delivery, and after-sale service
Buying Procedures	Buyers are trained Negotiate details of most purchases Follow objective standards Formal process involving specific employees Closer relationships between marketers and buyers Often buy from multiple sources	Accept standard terms for most purchases Use personal judgment Informal process involving household members Impersonal relationships between marketers and consumers Rarely buy from multiple sources

Note that some of the attributes of total product offer are tangible (the product itself and its package) and others are intangible (the reputation of the producer and the image created by its advertising). In order to be successful, a marketer must think like a consumer: that is, evaluate the total product offer as a collection of impressions and consider what parts of it are important to the consumer. But how can a marketer know what benefits customers are looking for? This discovery process is known as market research.

MARKET RESEARCH

If a marketer knows what a customer wants, she and her team can develop the product and its advertising to meet the exact needs of that customer. This is usually done through **marketing research**, which is the analysis of markets to determine opportunities and challenges and find

Marketing research The analysis of markets to determine opportunities and challenges and to find the information needed to make good marketing decisions.

the information needed to make good marketing decisions. Marketing research helps determine what customers have purchased in the past, and what they might purchase in the future.[11]

For example, marketers conduct research on business trends, the viability of new products, global trends, and more.

Quantitative and Qualitative Research

When you first think of research, you might think of a group of doctors testing a drug or graduate students studying psychological behaviors in a group of subjects. That's quantitative research; in marketing, a

Service after the sale is part of Apple's total product offer. Customers can make an appointment with an Apple Genius who will help them learn how to use their computers or iPods.

Figure 4.5 Potential Components of a Total Product Offer

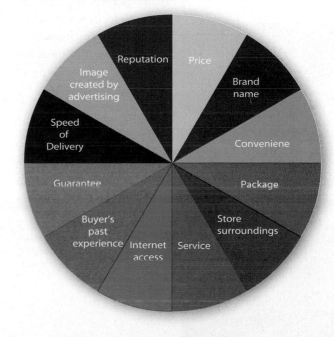

quantitative research study might be a statistical study of 3,000 people and their purchase choices according to their gender or income.

Much of marketing research involves quantitative research, which targets harder-to-measure concepts, such as attitudes and opinions. In most cases, a small group of people are interviewed about their attitudes and opinions about a product, and data about those concepts are gathered for further study.

This data collection can occur in several ways. **Primary research** is research collected firsthand by a marketer. The goal of primary research might be to answer a question, such as "Do consumers like this new flavor?" Primary research can be quite time-consuming and expensive, and it is usually conducted in the form of surveys or focus groups. A **focus group** is a small group of people who meet under the direction of a discussion leader who tries to understand their opinions about a product.

Secondary research, on the other hand, seeks data already available to the marketer, such as journal articles or other published findings. The disadvantage of secondary research is that the data were not specifically developed for the marketer's purpose, so they may not meet her need. However, secondary research has two powerful advantages: It is much less expensive and faster than using primary research.

Once researchers gather data, they review them in order to form some sort of conclusion, which could be as simple as adding more

Primary research Research collected firsthand by a marketer.

Focus group A small group of people who meet under the direction of a discussion leader who tries to understand their opinions about a product

Secondary research Research collected by a marketer that has already been compiled by others and published in print or online.

At focus groups, consumers give their opinions about products and services.

color options for a particular model of car, or more complex, such as making a subtle change to the car's design that could improve fuel economy.

PRODUCT DIFFERENTIATION

Product differentiation is the creation of real or perceived product differences. Actual product differences can be very subtle, so marketers must be creative in order to make their product seem special and distinct from the competition. The battle between Coca-Cola and Pepsi is a well-known example of competition by product differentiation. Although to most people, relatively little difference exists between the two, brand name, advertising, and other total product offer characteristics that encourage consumers to favor one soda over another.

Product differentiation The creation of real or perceived product differences.

Consumers tend to develop strong loyalties over perceived differences in taste and other product characteristics. For example, Starbucks and McDonald's are currently competing to convince consumers that theirs is the best coffee. Starbucks' CEO, Howard Schultz, has promoted a philosophy that the Starbucks brand means much more than coffee (such as its fair trade practices mentioned earlier in the chapter); accordingly, the company has rolled out a marketing campaign called "It's not just coffee" to compete directly with McDonald's "gourmet coffee on a budget" product line.[14]

Some classifications of consumer goods and services are listed in Figure 4.6. Once marketers establish the right class for a particular good, it's easier to find that good's market and reach the market's consumers. One classification system, based on consumer purchasing behavior, has four general categories—convenience, shopping, specialty, and unsought.

The president of Disney–ABC Television Group, Anne Sweeney, found that market research can occur at surprising times. While visiting college campuses with her daughter, Sweeney noted how acutely technology figured in lives of younger generations and went on to formulate "thousands of ideas" for firsthand market research from the trip.[12] In order to compete effectively, businesses need information, and marketing research gathers that information.[13]

Some bottled water brands, for example, have successfully differentiated their products. Although most bottled water is just that—water—some marketers have succeeded in making consumers think their bottled water is different from others.

Thinking Critically

>> Primary and Secondary Research

As a consumer, what factors influence your buying decisions? What goes on inside your head as you contemplate making a purchase is exactly what market researchers want to know. Research can reveal a wealth of information that's critical to designing an effective business marketing strategy.

A personal interview is one way of collecting primary research data about customers' needs, wants, and buying habits.

Primary research can be as simple as asking customers or suppliers how they feel about a business or as complex as surveys conducted by professional marketing research firms. Direct-mail questionnaires, telephone surveys, experiments, panel studies, test marketing, and behavior observation are all examples of primary research. Primary research is often divided into reactive and nonreactive research. Nonreactive primary research observes how real people behave in real market situations without influencing that behavior even accidentally. Reactive research, including surveys, interviews, and questionnaires, is best left to marketing professionals, as they can usually get more objective and sophisticated results. Those who can't afford high-priced marketing research services should consider asking nearby college or university business schools for help.

Secondary research exploits published sources like surveys, books, and magazines and applying or rearranging the information in them to bear on the problem or opportunity at hand. A tire sales business owner might guess that present retail sales of tires is strongly correlated with sales of new cars three years ago. To test this idea, it's easy to compare new car sales records with replacement tire sales three years later. Done over a range of recent years, this should prove or disprove the hypothesis and help marketing efforts tremendously. Localized figures tend to provide better information as local conditions might buck national trends. Newspapers and other local media are often quite helpful. There are many sources of secondary research material. It can be found in libraries, colleges, trade and general business publications, and newspapers. Trade associations and government agencies are rich sources of information.

Source: U.S. Small Business Administration Web site, "Market and Price," http://www.sba.gov/smallbusinessplanner/manage/marketandprice/SERV-MARKET-RESEARCH.html?cm_sp=ExternalLink-_-Federal-_-SBA (accessed August 11, 2009).

QUESTIONS

1. Describe a time you were involved in primary research as a customer. What business asked you to give your opinions about a product or service, and what form did the research take?

2. Did the research you participated in address the four Ps of marketing? Describe how it did or did not address the four Ps.

1. *Convenience goods and services* (sometimes called consumer products) are products the consumer wants to purchase frequently and easily, such as milk, ice cream, lottery tickets, soft drinks, bread, or magazines.

2. *Shopping goods and services* are products a consumer buys only after comparing value, quality, price, and style from a variety of sellers. Shopping goods and services are sold largely through shopping centers where consumers can make comparisons. Sears and Macy's are stores that sell mostly shopping goods. Examples include clothes, shoes, appliances, and auto repair services.

3. *Specialty goods and services* are consumer products with unique characteristics and brand identity. Because these products are perceived as having no reasonable substitute, the consumer puts forth special effort to purchase them. Examples include Rolex watches, expensive wine, jewelry, expensive cigars, and Coach and Louis Vuitton handbags, as well as services provided by medical specialists or business consultants.

4. *Unsought goods and services* are products that consumers are not aware of, or have not necessarily thought of buying, but suddenly find that they need them to solve an unexpected problem. Some examples of unsought products are car towing services, burial services, and dental work.

Another type of product is an **industrial good**, which could be a good or service. Raw materials, major equipment, accessory equipment, components, process materials, maintenance items, and business services are industrial goods. For example, Mueller Industries produces aluminum, copper, and plastic parts used in the plumbing, refrigeration, and air conditioning industries.[15] Industrial products are generally sold in the B2B market and not directly to consumers.

Industrial good A product used in the production of other products.

Chains that sell mostly convenience goods include 7-Eleven, Sheetz, and WaWa.

PACKAGING

Another important aspect of marketing is packaging. Because there are so many choices, packaging is extremely important in order to get a customer's attention. The goals of packaging include the following:

1. Protect the goods inside, stand up to rough handling and storage, be tamper-proof, deter theft, and yet be easy to open and use.

2. Attract the buyer's attention.

3. Describe the contents and give information about the contents.

4. Explain the benefits of the product inside.

5. Provide information on warranties, warnings, and other consumer matters.

6. Give some indication of price, value, and uses.

7. Provide the dimensions and weight of the actual package.

A marketer who can design a package with all of these components will likely see an increase in sales. The packaging of children's products is a particular

Marketing for unsought goods and services takes ingenuity. If a tornado damaged your home, you'd want the quickest service possible, and price wouldn't be as much of a factor as with the other classifications of products we have discussed. You may end up grabbing a phone book and calling the first contractor you'd find there—possibly the one with the largest advertisement or the one whose business name started with AAAA.

Figure 4.6 Various Categories of Consumer and Industrial Goods and Services

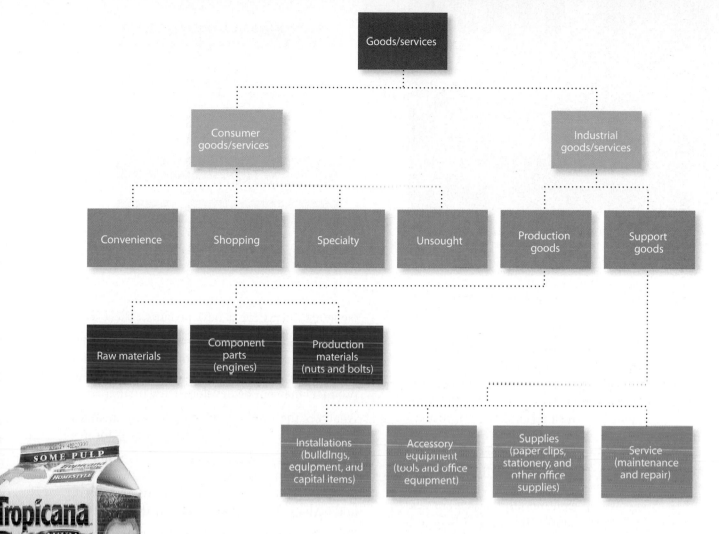

Packaging can make a huge difference. Do you prefer the orange with the straw?

challenge because many young children cannot read, marketers must get messages to children using visuals instead of words. If you've ever gone grocery shopping with a child, you know the power of packaging.

Consumers often develop an emotional attachment to certain products and their packaging. Altering that packaging can affect customer loyalty. For example, PepsiCo recently spent $35 million to redesign the carton of its Tropicana Pure Premium brand juice. The revised carton showed a picture of a glass of juice instead of an orange with a straw sticking out of it. Many customers complained that the new carton didn't stand out on the shelf and in fact looked more like that of a generic brand. Eventually, PepsiCo ended up switching the carton's design back

to its original form. Neil Campbell, the president of the Tropicana brand's North American division, remarked that the company had underestimated its customers' attachment to the packaging.[16]

BRANDING

A product's **brand** is the name and symbol that identifies it and positions it over similar products. **Brand equity** refers to the combination of factors people associate with a given brand name, including its reputation, image, and perceived quality. Companies work hard to maintain brand equity.

Brand is much more than a product. When entrepreneur Sir Richard Branson was once asked what

Brand A name, symbol, or design (or combination thereof) that identifies the goods or services of one seller or group of sellers and distinguishes them from those of others.

Brand equity The combination of factors, such as awareness, loyalty, perceived quality, images, and emotions, that people associate with a given brand name.

In 2001, Federal Express's managers realized that opinions were formed about the brand with every delivery, so it decided to make an effort to reinforce its brand identity—speediness—at every turn. The company even went so far as to shorten the company's name to FedEx, capitalizing on the fact that people often referred to any kind of overnight shipping as "FedExing"—an example of brand equity.[17]

his Virgin brand "stood for," instead of answering that it represented a music store or airline, he replied that it stood for fun. Refusing to limit his brand to a single business is one factor that has allowed him to expand it into an empire that today includes more than 350 companies.[18] The total experience a customer has builds brand equity and leads to **brand loyalty**, which is the extent to which a customer will choose one product over another on a continuous basis. For example, if a person is brand-loyal to a particular brand of shampoo, it probably won't matter to him if a new shampoo debuts on the market.

Brand loyalty The degree to which customers are satisfied, like a brand, and are committed to future purchases.

NEW-PRODUCT DEVELOPMENT PROCESS

During the new-product development process, which is outlined in Figure 4.7, a company:

Figure 4.7 The New-Product Development Process

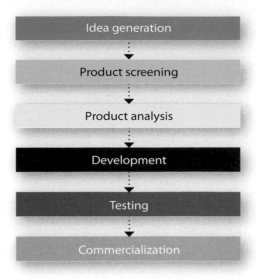

1. Generates ideas for a new product. These new ideas can come from employees or even suppliers.

2. Screens the product in terms of its profit potential and marketability. After this phase, some products may not be developed any further.

3. Analyzes the product, which generally includes making cost estimates and sales forecasts for it.

4. Develops the product. If the product's numbers look good (that is, its costs don't outweigh the projected revenues), it will be fully developed, and perhaps a prototype will be made.

5. Tests the product, which could include sharing the prototype with customers and getting feedback from them about it.

6. Commercializes the product, which includes promoting it to distributors and retailers and developing strong advertising and sales campaigns to generate and maintain interest in it.

Study Alert

Packaging must protect the goods inside; attract the buyer's attention; describe its contents and give information about it; explain the benefits of the product; provide information about warranties, warnings, and other consumer matters; give some indication of price, value and uses; and provide the dimensions and weight of the package.

[BUS] connections

1. What are the four Ps? Which of the four Ps do you think is most important? Why?
2. What are the different components of total product?
3. Describe the difference between the two types of market research.

>> The Four Ps of Marketing: Price

As you can imagine, price setting is among the most difficult challenges of marketing. A product's price needs to reflect its quality, brand, and image, and it must be high enough to ensure profits but not so high that people are unwilling to pay it. A firm generally keeps some of the following long-run objectives in mind when setting a pricing strategy:

1. *Achieving a targeted ROI or profit.* Ultimately, the goal of marketing is to make a profit by providing goods and services to others. Naturally, a long-run pricing objective of almost all firms is to optimize profit.[19]

2. *Building traffic.* Supermarkets often advertise certain products, such as diapers or paper towels, at or below cost to attract people to the store. These products are called **loss leaders**. The long-run objective of this strategy is to make profits by building a customer base that comes in to buy loss leaders and ends up buying more. Yahoo! once took on eBay's seller-paid auction service by offering its own auction service for free to both buyers and sellers. The strategy was intended to increase advertising revenue on the Yahoo! Web site and attract more people to Yahoo!'s other services.

   Loss leaders When a store advertises certain products at or below cost to attract people to the store.

3. *Achieving greater market share.* Companies compete fiercely for increased market share. Market share can be defined as the proportion of sales made by a company versus the total number of sales for that particular product. For example, many companies, including Best Buy, Home Depot, Sears, and Lowe's, are constantly jockeying to increase their respective shares of the home appliance market. The strategies these companies use to do so include offering attractive financing rates (in some cases, zero percent), free delivery, or rebates. In November 2008, for example, the market share of Microsoft's Windows product dipped below 90 percent for the first time in history as Apple's Macintosh operating systems surged in popularity.[20]

4. *Creating an image.* Particular brands of watches, perfumes, and other products are expensive in order to convey an image of exclusivity and status.

5. *Furthering social objectives.* A firm may intentionally price a product low so people with little money can afford it. Sometimes, the government intervenes in pricing certain agricultural products so everyone can get necessities like milk and bread at a low price.

A firm may have short-run objectives that differ greatly from its long-run objectives (such as a book publisher who distributes 1,000 copies of a new book for free in order to generate interest in it—obviously, free distribution is not a sustainable long-term strategy). All of these objectives should be clearly understood at the beginning of the marketing process and included in a strategic marketing plan. Pricing objectives should be influenced by other interrelated marketing decisions, including those about product design, packaging, branding, distribution, and promotion.

Image and pricing are closely tied. Consider a $1,700 Prada jacket. If the jacket cost less, it might not seem as desirable.

PRODUCT LIFE CYCLE

Besides meeting the pricing goals of the organization, prices are also based on the **product life cycle**, a theoretical model of what happens to sales and profits (the amount of money earned after expenses are paid) for a product class (for example, all dishwasher detergents) over time. Most products go through this life cycle, which consists of four stages: introduction, growth, maturity, and decline (see Figure 4.8). However, not all do, and particular brands may behave differently. For example, although frozen foods as a generic class may go through the entire cycle, one brand may never get beyond the introduction stage. In addition, some products become classics and never experience much decline.

Product life cycle A theoretical model of what happens to sales and profits for a product class over time.

Analyzing a product's life cycle may help provide some basis for anticipating future market developments and planning marketing strategies. It can also help reveal whether it may become popular or die sooner rather than later.

The life cycle affects pricing because the longer a product stays in a particular phase of the life cycle,

Figure 4.8 Sample Strategies Followed during the Product Life Cycle

The Hershey's chocolate bar is one example of a classic product. Introduced in 1900, it is still enjoyed by many today.[21]

LIFE CYCLE STAGE	MARKETING MIX ELEMENTS			
	PRODUCT	PRICE	PLACE	PROMOTION
Introduction	Offer market-tested product; keep mix small	Go after innovators with high introductory price (skimming strategy) or use penetration pricing	Use wholesalers, selective distribution	Dealer promotion and heavy investment in primary demand advertising and sales promotion to get stores to carry the product and consumers to try it
Growth	Improve product; keep product mix limited	Adjust price to meet competition	Increase distribution	Heavy competitive advertising
Maturity	Differentiate product to satisfy different market segments	Further reduce price	Take over wholesaling function and intensify distribution	Emphasize brand name as well as product benefits and differences
Decline	Cut product mix; develop new product ideas	Consider price increase	Consolidate distribution; drop some outlets	Reduce advertising to loyal customers only

Figure 4.9 Sales and Profits during the Product Life Cycle

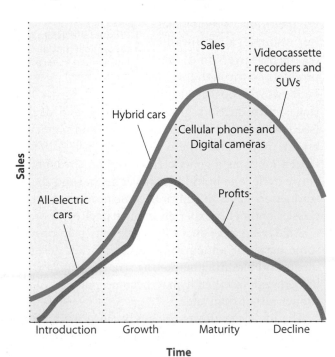

the more profit will be made. Remember, this success is also connected to the product's supply and demand issues, as discussed in Chapter 2. The higher the demand for a product, the higher its price can be. For example, airlines charge more for airline tickets during peak times, such as the holidays. Likewise, a product made popular by a fad, such as Crocs shoes, usually races through the life cycle much more quickly. Fad products must be priced to meet customers' expectations and with the knowledge that the product will have a short sales cycle and, thus, fewer sales over time. See Figure 4.9.

> **Study Alert**
>
> When pricing, firms must also keep in mind a product's stage in its life cycle—is it in its introduction, growth, maturity, or decline phase?

Target costing Designing a product so it satisfies customers and meets the profit margins desired by the firm.

Price leadership The procedure by which one or more firms that dominate a market set pricing standards that all the others follow.

Break-even analysis strategy Pricing a product based on how many you need to sell in order to make a profit.

Skimming price strategy Pricing a new product high to make optimum profit while there's little competition.

Penetration strategy Pricing a product low to attract many customers and discourage competition.

Everyday low pricing (EDLP) strategy Setting prices lower than competitors and then not offering any special sales.

High-low pricing strategy Setting prices that are higher than EDLP, but offering many special sales where prices are lower than those of competitors.

Bundling strategy Grouping two or more products together and pricing them as a unit.

Psychological pricing (odd pricing) strategy Pricing goods and services at price points that make the product appear less expensive than it is.

PRICING STRATEGIES

Managers use several different pricing strategies to ensure that objectives are met. These objectives may be designed to increase market share or profits, or they may be intended to build or burnish an image. These strategies include cost-based pricing, demand-based pricing (**target costing**), competition-based pricing (**price leadership**), **break-even analysis** pricing, **skimming**, **penetration**, **everyday low pricing (EDLP)**, **high-low pricing**, **bundling strategy**, and **psychological pricing**. See Figure 4.10 for descriptions and examples of each.

Many factors—the cost of production, competitors' prices, the product's phase in its life cycle, the product's image, and so on—affect pricing, and it can be very challenging to set prices. However, if the correct mix of factors is kept in mind while making a pricing decision, a marketer may find just the right price—one that will meet customers' expectations and result in profits.

Agents and brokers are a familiar type of intermediary. Real estate brokers are marketing intermediaries that typically don't take possession of the goods they sell.

>> The Four Ps of Marketing: Place

Place refers to the process of getting products to the places where they will be sold, or *distribution*, and the process of determining where the products will be sold. This section will also discuss the various intermediaries that can be used to facilitate this process. Finally, we will discuss retail outlets, which are usually the final destination of products (other than in consumers' hands, of course).

Place In marketing, the process of getting products to the places where they will be sold.

Hundreds of thousands of marketing intermediaries exist to help that process along, moving goods from their raw-material state to production facilities, warehouses, distributors, and then on to consumers. All of these steps in the process are "places" in the distribution chain. Place also refers to the marketing of services, in that the services must be accessible to the people who want them.[22] From a product perspective, there are several players in "place":

Marketing intermediaries are organizations that assist in moving goods and services from producers to their business and consumer users. They are called intermediaries because they are in the middle of a series of organizations that join together to help distribute goods. A wholesaler is a marketing intermediary.

A **channel of distribution** is the whole set of marketing intermediaries, including agents, brokers, wholesalers, and retailers, that join together to transport and store goods in their path (or channel) from producers to consumers. B2B products

Marketing intermediary An organization that assists in moving goods and services from producers to industrial and consumer users.

Channel of distribution A set of marketing intermediaries, such as wholesalers and retailers that join together to transport and store goods in their path (or channel) from producers to consumers.

[BUS] connections

1. What are three objectives that might be used when setting pricing strategies?
2. Discuss any four types of pricing strategies that might be used in marketing.
3. Which pricing strategy do you think is the most effective with you as a consumer?

Consider a box of Nestlé hot chocolate mix. Imagine how challenging it must be to get all the raw materials that make that hot chocolate together. Think of the effort involved in making millions of boxes of mix, as Nestlé does, and then distributing those packages to stores around the world. That hurdle is what thousands of manufacturing firms—companies that make everything from automobiles to toys—have to deal with every day.

have much shorter channels of distribution than consumer products.

Agents/brokers are marketing intermediaries who bring buyers and sellers together and assist in negotiating an exchange, but do not own the goods at any point in the process. Examples of such agents include travel agents, real estate agents, and stockbrokers.

> **Agents/brokers** Marketing intermediaries who bring buyers and sellers together and assist in negotiating an exchange but don't take title to the goods.

Figure 4.10 Pricing Strategies

Strategy	Definition	Example
Cost-based	Developing a product's price based on what it will cost to produce it and still maintain a profit. This strategy is inherently flawed because in the long run, the market, and not the manufacturer, will ultimately decide what the product's price will be.	A toy company prices a new doll at $15 because it is made of a costly new plastic that makes it more durable than competing dolls, which are priced in the $8–$10 range.
Demand-based (target costing)	Designing a product so it satisfies customers and meets the profit margins desired by the firm, with price being an input of the product development process (not an output).	Early in a new family sedan's product development process, a car company establishes a need to price the car for less than $15,000 in order to sell the desired quantity in the United States.
Competition-based (price leadership)	Pricing a product based on how competitors price their products—either at or below their prices. Price leadership is the procedure by which one or more firms that dominate the market set pricing standards that all the others follow.	Generally, if one airline reduces or raises its price for a particular destination, its competitors will soon follow.
Break-even analysis pricing	Pricing a product based on how many you need to sell in order to make a profit, according to the following formula: $$\text{Break-even point (BEP)} = \frac{\text{Total fixed cost}}{\text{Price of 1 unit} - \text{Variable cost of 1 unit}}$$	If a candle shop priced its candles at $4 each and had fixed monthly rent and electricity costs of $500 and variable per-candle production costs of $2, it could conduct a break-even analysis by subtracting the price ($4) from the per-candle costs ($2) and dividing that number ($2) into $500, its fixed monthly costs. The total would be 250, and that's how many candles the candle shop would have to sell each month to break even.
Skimming	Pricing a new product high to make optimum profit while there's little competition.	High-definition televisions were initially very expensive, which attracted many other manufacturers to the business. As competition increased, prices dropped.
Penetration	Pricing a product low to attract many customers and discourage competition.	In April 2008, Starbucks launched a new product, Pike Place Roast coffee, by giving it away free each Tuesday for a limited time.
Everyday low pricing (EDLP)	Setting prices lower than competitors and then not offering any special sales	Walmart is a prime example—the company even built a slogan around its everyday low pricing strategy: "Always."
High–low pricing	Setting ordinary prices higher than they would be under an EDLP strategy, but offering special sales that sell the goods at lower prices than competitors; this often trains customers to wait for sales.	A department store might price a dress at $150 but offer a 50 percent off sale on all dresses.
Bundling	Grouping together two or more products and pricing them as a unit, usually used to encourage people to purchase more (generally by discounting).	A clothing store might price the same polo shirt at $19 for one and $15 each if two or more are purchased.
Psychological pricing	Pricing goods and services at price points that make them appear less expensive	Gas stations almost always use psychological pricing; $2.99 per gallon sounds less than $3.

Wholesaler A marketing intermediary that sells to other organizations.

A **wholesaler** is a marketing intermediary that sells to other organizations, such as retailers, manufacturers, and hospitals. Wholesalers are part of the B2B system. Usually, consumers cannot buy directly from wholesalers. RetailPets.com, located in Westchester, Pennsylvania, provides retail pet stores, veterinarians, and nonprofit organizations with pet goods.[23]

Channels of distribution keep communication, money, and ownership of the goods flowing openly among the parties. These channels also help ensure that the right quantity and assortment of goods will be available when and

This distribution warehouse, a part of a channel of distribution, stores goods until they are needed.

A retailer is an organization that sells to consumers. Target and Old Navy are examples of retail organizations.

where they are needed.[24] Figure 4.11 depicts selected channels of distribution for both consumer and industrial (or B2B) goods. Next, we'll discuss specific intermediaries that assist in marketing distribution, including merchant wholesalers, agents and brokers, and retail intermediaries.

STRETCHING THE TRUTH

Adam Rooke is no stranger to the challenging field of marketing. Adam is the CEO and vice president of sales and marketing for Wallaby Promotions, a company that provides promotional products, printing, and graphics services. Although Adam has only been with Wallaby for seven years, he first became involved in direct selling and marketing more than thirty years ago. Adam is meeting with a client, Joanmarie Conaty, to talk about the nature of marketing and advertising, and what Wallaby can do for her company.

Adam says, "This is a tough economy. It's really competitive out there, and if you want people to know about your products, you're going to have to advertise. We supply quality products and have a solid reputation for good service. But when it comes to advertising and personal selling, some of my competitors paint too rosy a picture. In the end, they don't always deliver what they promise."

Concerned, Joanmarie responds, "What do you mean?"

If you knew you wouldn't get caught, would you consider lying to a customer in order to get a sale?

Adam lowered his voice and replied, "Just to land a sale, one of my competitors made several promises to do things the company simply couldn't do. The rep told the client that he would guarantee that the promotional products she was buying would deliver a 30 percent response from customers. That's just completely unrealistic. I think he just made it up to get the sale. In the end, he got the sale—and a very unhappy and disappointed client who didn't get her 30 percent response."

Speaking from years of experience, Adam adds, "Sales and marketing are all about building customer relationships. So when it comes to both advertising and direct selling, it's important to be honest with customers from the very beginning. Joanmarie, that's my promise to you, and it's a promise you can believe in."

QUESTIONS

1. Would you lie to an important customer in order to keep his or her business?
2. How can you keep your ethics in place and still effectively sell to customers if your competitor(s) offer similar products at a lower price?

MERCHANT WHOLESALERS

Merchant wholesalers are independently owned firms that assume ownership of the goods they handle (that is, they buy the goods). About 80 percent of wholesalers fall into this category. In April 2009, the sales of merchant wholesalers were $309.4 billion.[25] Figure 4.12 shows some facts about the wholesale trade industry. There are two types of merchant wholesalers: full-service wholesalers and limited-function wholesalers. *Full-service wholesalers* perform all the distribution functions.

> **Merchant wholesalers** Independently owned firms that own the goods they handle.

Limited-function wholesalers perform only selected functions, but they try to do those functions especially well. Three common types of limited-function wholesalers are rack jobbers, cash-and-carry wholesalers, and drop shippers.

Rack jobbers furnish racks or shelves full of merchandise to retailers, including display products, and sell them on *consignment.* That means they keep title to the goods until they are sold to customers, and then they share the profits with the retailer. Mer-

> **Rack jobbers** Wholesalers that furnish racks or shelves full of merchandise to retailers, display products, and sell on consignment.

Figure 4.11 Examples of Distribution Channels for Consumer and Industrial Goods

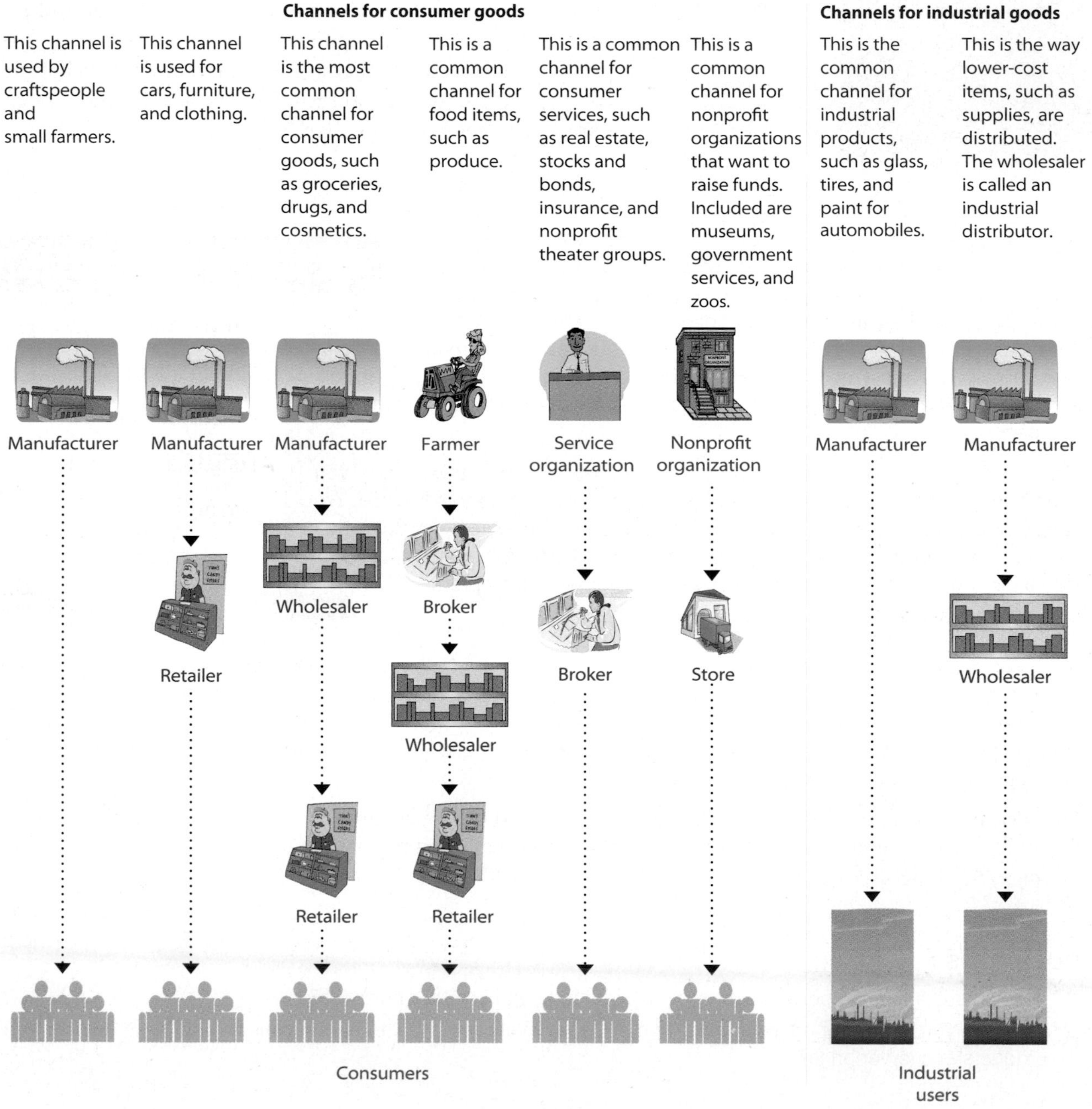

Channels for consumer goods

This channel is used by craftspeople and small farmers.

This channel is used for cars, furniture, and clothing.

This channel is the most common channel for consumer goods, such as groceries, drugs, and cosmetics.

This is a common channel for food items, such as produce.

This is a common channel for consumer services, such as real estate, stocks and bonds, insurance, and nonprofit theater groups.

This is a common channel for nonprofit organizations that want to raise funds. Included are museums, government services, and zoos.

Channels for industrial goods

This is the common channel for industrial products, such as glass, tires, and paint for automobiles.

This is the way lower-cost items, such as supplies, are distributed. The wholesaler is called an industrial distributor.

Manufacturer → Consumers

Manufacturer → Retailer → Consumers

Manufacturer → Wholesaler → Retailer → Consumers

Farmer → Broker → Wholesaler → Retailer → Consumers

Service organization → Broker → Consumers

Nonprofit organization → Store → Consumers

Manufacturer → Industrial users

Manufacturer → Wholesaler → Industrial users

Today, cash-and-carry wholesalers, such as Costco and Sam's Club (they're retailers, too), allow retailers and others to also use credit cards for wholesale purchases.

chandise like music, toys, hosiery, and health and beauty aids are sold by rack jobbers.

Cash-and-carry wholesalers supply mostly small retailers with a limited assortment of products. Traditionally, retailers visited the warehouses of such wholesalers, paid cash for goods there, and carried the goods back to their stores—thus, the term *cash-and-carry*.

Drop shippers solicit orders from retailers and other wholesalers and have the merchandise shipped directly from a producer to a buyer.

Cash-and-carry wholesalers Wholesalers that serve mostly smaller retailers with a limited assortment of products.

Drop shippers Wholesalers that solicit orders from retailers and other wholesalers and have the merchandise shipped directly from a producer to a buyer.

They own the merchandise but do not handle, stock, or deliver anything. That task is done by the producer.

AGENTS AND BROKERS

Agents and brokers bring buyers and sellers together and assist in negotiating an exchange. However, unlike merchant wholesalers, agents and brokers never own the products they distribute. As a rule, they do not carry inventory, provide credit, or assume risks. While merchant wholesalers earn a profit from the sale of goods, agents and brokers earn commissions or fees based on a percentage of revenue. Agents and

Figure 4.12 Facts about the Wholesale Trade Industry

Most wholesale trade businesses are small, employing fewer than 20 workers.
Wholesale trade firms can sell practically any type of product.
Wholesalers are vital to our nation's economy.
Radio frequency identification technology allows those in the wholesale industry to keep track of goods using a satellite and receiver system.
Work in the wholesale trade is relatively safe.
Merchant wholesalers are the largest group in the industry.

Source: "Wholesale Trade," Bureau of Labor Statistics, http://www.bls.gov/oco/cg/cgs026.htm (accessed July 5, 2009).

brokers differ in that *agents* maintain long-term relationships with the people they represent, whereas *brokers* are usually hired on a temporary basis.

Agents who represent producers are known as *manufacturer's agents* or *sales agents*. As long as they do not represent competing products, manufacturer's agents may represent multiple manufacturers in a specific territory. Manufacturer's agents are often used in the automotive supply, footwear, and fabricated steel industries. Sales agents represent single producers, usually in a larger territory. Sales agents are often used by small producers in the textile and home furnishing industries.

Brokers have no continuous relationship with buyers or sellers. Once they negotiate a contract between a buyer and seller, the relationship ends. Brokers are used by the producers of seasonal products (for example, fruits and vegetables) and in the real estate industry.

RETAIL INTERMEDIARIES AND RETAILING

Perhaps the most useful marketing intermediaries, as far as final consumers are concerned, are *retailers*. They bring goods and services to our neighborhoods and make them available to us. Next time you go to the supermarket to buy groceries, stop for a minute

Merchant wholesalers, agents and brokers, and retailers are market intermediaries. There are two types of merchant wholesalers: full-service and limited-function wholesalers. Three types of limited-function wholesalers are rack jobbers, cash-and-carry wholesalers, and drop shippers.

Study Alert

Drop shippers tend to handle bulky products, such as coal, lumber, and chemicals.

and consider the tremendous variety of products in the store. Think of how many marketing exchanges were involved to bring you the 47,000 items you'll find in the average U.S. grocery store.[26] Some products, such as spices, may have been imported from halfway around the world. Other products have been processed and frozen so that you can eat them out of season (for example, corn and green beans).

Retailing

The United States boasts approximately 2.3 million retail stores—not including retail Web sites. The U.S. retail industry generates $3.8 trillion in retail nonfood sales annually, and in 2005, retail organizations employed more than 15.3 million people. Retailing accounts for around 10 percent of the U.S. gross national product.[27]

Retailers compete on different aspects of business. Some compete on price, and others choose product variety or location as a differentiation tool. There are five major ways in which retailers compete for the consumer's dollar: price, service, location, selection, and entertainment. Because of this, retail is not just a form of distribution; it's also a form of competition.

- *Price*. Discount stores, such as Target and TJMaxx, and Internet discounters succeed by offering low prices. It's hard to compete with these price discounters over time, especially if they offer good service as well. Service organizations also compete on price. Southwest Airlines is a classic example of a business renowned for both excellent service and competitive pricing. The same is true for Motel 6.

- *Service*. A second competitive strategy for retailers is service. Retail service involves putting customers first, which requires all frontline people to be courteous and accommodating, and follow-up services, such as on-time delivery, guarantees, and fast installation. Consumers are frequently willing to pay more for goods and services if a retailer offers outstanding service—consider the example of Nordstrom.

- *Location*. Many services—especially convenience services, like banks and dry cleaners—compete effectively by having good locations. That's why automated teller machines are often located in convenient places where cash is needed, such as supermarkets or train stations. Many fast-food restaurants, such as Burger King and Pizza Hut, have locations on college campuses so students can reach them easily. Some dry cleaners pick up and deliver laundry to a home or business.

- *Selection*. A fourth competitive strategy for retailers is selection, the offering of a wide variety of items in the same product category. **Category killer** stores offer a wide selection of products at competitive prices. Their name derives from the fact that they are so competitive in their category that they usually overpower smaller competitors that don't offer comparable selection or price and drive them out of business.

> **Category killer** A store that offers a wide selection of goods in a specific category at competitive prices.

Toys"R"Us stores carry around 8,000 to 10,000 distinct toys and other items, and the company has more than 1,500 stores around the world.[28] Many independent toy stores closed their doors because they simply couldn't compete with the low prices and wide selection at Toys"R"Us.

- *Entertainment.* Many retailers use entertainment competition, an attempt to add value to the shopping experience of their customers. The New England–based furniture chain Jordan's offers live music every weekend.[29] Some malls offer "shoppertainment," an attempt to make shopping there fun.

>> The Four Ps of Marketing: Promotion

Promotion mix The combination of promotional tools an organization uses.

The last of the four Ps of marketing is *promotion,* an effort by marketers to inform and remind people in a target market about their products and persuade those people to purchase them.

As shown in Figure 4.13, those tools include advertising, personal selling, public relations, and sales promotion. The combination of promotional tools an organization uses is called its **promotion mix**.

One of promotion's greatest challenges is the communication process. A marketer must define a target audience, select methods to reach it, design the right message, and make sure the audience gets the message. Because these tasks are so challenging, many companies choose to hire advertising or promotion agencies.

An advertising agency can develop the target market, create advertisements and promotional plans, and implement those plans. Many companies find hiring such firms to be a time and money saver because they can leave promotion to experts in the field. In particular, small businesses can benefit from hiring an agency because agencies can help them compete with larger firms. Profits derived from an effective marketing strategy can more than pay for the expense of hiring an ad agency.[31]

Figure 4.13 The Promotion Mix

The Promotion Mix

- Advertising
- Personal selling
- Public relations
- Sales promotion

ADVERTISING

Advertising is paid, nonpersonal communication through various media by organizations and individuals who are in some way identified in the advertising message. Figure 4.14 lists various forms of media and their advantages and disadvantages.

Advertising Paid, nonpersonal communication through various media by organizations and individuals who are in some way identified in the advertising message.

The importance of advertising in the United States is easy to document. According to the Television Bureau of Advertising Online, the total ad volume in 2007 for all media including television, radio, newspaper, and so forth exceeded $279.6 billion.[32] Of those various forms of media, there's no doubt that for now, television is number one. Figure 4.15 lists the expenditures on various types of media.

The public benefits greatly from advertising expenditures. Advertis-

Many retailers compete in several of the areas just discussed. REI, a sporting goods retailer, offers a large selection of outdoor gear. REI is able to compete on selection because it offers all the items needed to go on a skiing trip or climb a mountain.[30] REI stores offer service competition, because its salespeople are trained regarding the products they sell and can provide information about every product. The chain's stores offer entertainment competition as well; a store in Seattle, Washington, has a climbing wall, waterfalls to test waterproof gear, and various terrains to test hiking boots.

ing allows us to learn about products, including prices, features, benefits, and so on, but it also often provides us with free entertainment. Additionally, the money advertisers spend for commercial time, for example, pays for the production costs of much of the television or radio programming we enjoy. Advertising also covers the major costs of producing newspapers and magazines. Consider a cable subscription for HBO. Because HBO does not advertise products on its channels, customers must pay for the programming on a subscription basis. Without advertising, consumers would no doubt pay more for many of the luxuries we currently enjoy.

Newspapers, radio, and business-listing phone books are especially attractive to local advertisers, because they are reasonably affordable. Television offers many advantages to national advertisers, but it is expensive. For example, 30 seconds of advertising during the Super Bowl cost an average of $3 million in 2009.[33] Think back to the break-even analysis discussed earlier in the chapter—how many cases of soda or bags of dog food must a company sell to pay for such commercials? The answer may seem to be "a lot," but few other media can allow advertisers to reach as many people and with such an impact.

Boston University professor John Verret remarked to CNN, "You have a better chance of reaching people with the Super Bowl than with any other media buy that's available."[34] Approximately 97.5 million people watched the game in 2009—comparatively few (29.1 million) watched the Academy Awards telecast in the same year.[35] The amount charged for television air time is directly related to the size of the potential audience.

Television advertising is not limited to traditional commercials that interrupt our favorite programs; sometimes the products *themselves* appear in the programs. Advertisers often pay to have their products appear in television programming, a practice called **product placement**. Have you noticed products being featured in movies and TV shows?

> **Product placement** Putting products in TV shows and movies, where they will be seen.

One of the characters in the Disney–Pixar movie *Toy Story* was based on the classic toy Slinky. The toy had been out of production for 10 years, but it made a comeback after the movie's release—to the tune of 20,000 orders. A new flavor of Crest toothpaste, vanilla, was once featured on an episode of NBC's

Figure 4.14 Advantages and Disadvantages of Various Forms of Media

MEDIUM	ADVANTAGES	DISADVANTAGES
Newspapers	Good coverage of local markets; ads can be placed quickly; high consumer acceptance; ads can be clipped and saved.	Ads compete with other features in paper; poor color; ads get thrown away with the paper (short life span).
Television	Uses sight, sound, and motion; reaches all audiences; high attention with no competition from other material.	High cost; short exposure time; takes time to prepare ads; digital video recorders skip over ads.
Radio	Low cost; can target specific audiences; very flexible; good for local marketing.	People may not listen to ads; depends on one sense (hearing); short exposure time; audience can't keep ads.
Magazines	Can target specific audiences; good use of color; long life of ads; ads can be clipped and saved.	Inflexible; ads must often be placed weeks before publication; cost is relatively high.
Outdoor	High visibility and repeat exposures; low cost; local market focus.	Limited message; low selectivity of audience.
Direct mail	Best for targeting specific markets; very flexible; ads can be saved.	High cost; consumers may reject ads as junk mail; must conform to post office regulations.
Yellow pages–type advertising	Great coverage of local markets; widely used by consumers; available at point of purchase.	Competition with other ads; cost may be too high for very small businesses.
Internet	Inexpensive global coverage; available at any time; interactive.	Relatively low readership in the short term (but growing rapidly).

Figure 4.15 2008 Expenditures in Various Types of Media

Media Type	TNS: Measured Media Spending
Magazine	**Totals (in millions)**
Consumer magazine	$23,722
Sunday magazine	1,904
B-to-B magazine	2,728
Local magazine	226
Newspaper	
National newspaper	2,962
Local newspaper	20,266
FSI	1,831
TV	
Network TV	26,710
Spot TV	15,154
Syndicated TV	4,445
Cable TV networks	18,828
Radio	
Network radio	975
National spot radio	2,223
Local radio	6,303
Other Media	
Outdoor	3,964
Internet	9,727
Totals	
Measured Media	141,969

Source: "Total U.S. Advertising Spending by Medium," *Advertising Age*, June 22, 2009, http://adage.com/datacenter/article?article_id=137427 (accessed July 20, 2009).

The Apprentice. Within hours of the episode's airing, Crest's Web site received 4.7 million hits from customers ready to try the new flavor.[36]

PERSONAL SELLING

Personal selling, the face-to-face presentation and promotion of goods and services, can occur on either a B2B or consumer level. Either way, the steps are the same. Effective selling is not simply a matter of persuading others to buy. In fact, it is more accurately described as helping others satisfy their wants and needs. Given that perspective, it's easy to see why salespeople are putting the Internet, portable computers, Blackberries, and other technology to use. This technology can help customers search the Internet, provide specifications for custom-made products, review prices, and generally do everything necessary to complete an order.

> **Personal selling** The face-to-face presentation and promotion of goods and services.

Of course, one of the greatest benefits of personal selling is that an actual person helps you complete a transaction. That salesperson should listen to your needs, help you reach a solution, and then make accomplishing that solution smoother and easier. Let's take a closer look at the process of selling.

PUBLIC RELATIONS

Public relations (PR) is a marketing function that evaluates public attitudes, changes policies and procedures accordingly, and executes a program of action and information to earn public understanding and acceptance. A good public relations program has three steps:

> **Public relations (PR)** The management function that evaluates public attitudes, changes policies and procedures accordingly, and executes a program of action and information to earn public understanding and acceptance.

Product placement is often subtle. You can see it in the carefully chosen car an actor drives in a film or even in the drinks provided to television hosts.

Going GLOBAL

Why Business Schools Should Focus on Emerging Markets

Clearly, marketing to emerging markets differs from marketing to domestic and other established markets. What will happen if business schools don't educate their students about emerging markets and train them to compete in these emerging markets?

Many business students study or work in another country as part of their overall academic programs. Yet too few of our students take advantage of opportunities to experience the emerging markets of the world, markets that are already important components of the global economy and whose role and influence will continue to grow in the decades to come.

As we near the second decade of the 21st century, the balance of global economic power is shifting toward the developing and emerging regions of the world. By one measure, the developing and emerging world is already producing nearly 50 percent of global economic output.

The BRIC countries—Brazil, Russia, India, and China—along with the rapidly growing economies of Mexico, Malaysia, Indonesia, and others, are now driving global growth. China is predicted to become the largest economy in the world by 2040, if not sooner. India's economy will soon eclipse that of Japan's. Brazil is a global leader in commodities but also a major contributor in more advanced industries, including regional passenger aircraft (Embraer). Even African countries are becoming more attractive locations for trade and investment, despite continued underdevelopment and social challenges.

Interestingly, the global economic crisis has not slowed this trend; if anything, it may accelerate it. To be sure, some regions, such as Central and Eastern Europe, are suffering particularly badly from the crisis. But the large emerging markets, notably China and India, continue to experience rapid growth, albeit at a slower pace than in previous years.

We have a long way to go. But, by putting a stake in the ground and committing ourselves to emerging markets, we believe we are preparing our students for this—and not the previous—century.

Source: Jonathan Doh, "Why Business Schools Should Focus on Emerging Markets," *BusinessWeek*, July 27, 2009, http://www.businessweek.com/bschools/content/jul2009/bs20090727_552599.htm (accessed August 11, 2009).

Questions

1. Name and discuss some challenges of marketing products to emerging markets.

2. Why do you think the global economic crisis has not slowed the trend of emerging markets becoming more attractive to investors?

---

1. *Listen to the public.* PR starts with good marketing research, including discovering and evaluating public attitudes. The best way to learn what the public wants is to listen to people often and in different forums, including the Internet.

2. *Change policies and procedures.* Businesses do not earn understanding by bombarding the public with propaganda; they earn understanding by having programs and practices in the public interest.

3. *Let people know you're being responsive to their needs.* It's not enough to simply have programs in the public interest. Businesses must tell the public about those programs.

According to the U.S. Bureau of Labor Statistics, PR is one of the three fastest-growing industries in the country.[36] Demand for PR specialists is expected to grow faster than the average for all occupations, estimated at 18 percent from 2006 to 2016.[37] It is the responsibility of a PR department to maintain close ties with the media, community leaders, government officials, and other corporate stakeholders. Its objective is to establish and maintain a dialogue with all stakeholders so the company can quickly respond to inquiries, complaints, and suggestions.

Publicity is the talking arm of PR. Here's how publicity works: Suppose a bakery's owners want consumers to know they're

> **Publicity** Any information about an individual, product, or organization that's distributed to the public through the media and that's not paid for or controlled by the seller.

Public relations work includes representing the company to the media.

Figure 4.16 Examples of B2B and Consumer Sales Promotion Techniques

B2B	Consumer
Trade shows	Coupons
Portfolios for salespeople	Cents-off promotions
Deals (price reductions)	Sampling
Catalogs	Premiums
Conventions	Sweepstakes
	Contests
	Bonuses (buy one, get one free)
	Catalogs
	Demonstrations
	Special events
	Lotteries
	In-store displays

about to open a new location, but they have very little money for promotions. One effective way to reach the public is through publicity. Publicity is any information about an individual, product, or organization that is distributed to the public through the media and that's not paid for, or controlled by, the seller. To get publicity, the bakery could prepare a press release that describes the new location and grand-opening events and send it to various local media outlets, such as radio stations or newspapers. These releases must be written with great care, so the media will want to publish or broadcast them.[38] In fact, different releases may need to be written for different forms of media.

Publicity has several advantages over other promotional tools, such as advertising: (1) publicity can reach people who don't normally read print advertisements, (2) the information may appear on the front page of a newspaper or in some other prominent position, or it could be given air time on a television news show, and (3) it is more believable than an advertisement, which is perhaps its greatest advantage. When a newspaper or magazine publishes a story as news, the reader treats that story as news—and news is more believable than advertising. That's why Gardenburger and other companies that sell soybean-based food products consistently send out press releases about the health benefits of their products.

There is good publicity (a product being featured in a news story as gaining in popularity) and bad publicity (tires being blamed for accidents).

There are several disadvantages to publicity as well. Marketers have no control over how, when, or if the media will use the story. The media are not obligated to use a publicity release, and most are thrown away. The story could be altered in such a way that it comes across as negative. Once a story has run, it's not likely to be repeated; in contrast, advertising can be repeated as often as needed. One way companies can help ensure that publicity is handled well by the media is to establish a friendly relationship with media representatives and answer their questions promptly when asked. Later, when businesses want their support, the media will be more likely to cooperate.

SALES PROMOTION

Sales promotion stimulates consumer purchasing and dealer interest by means of short-term activities. These activities include displays, trade shows and exhibitions, event sponsorships, and contests. Figure 4.16 lists some sales promotion techniques.

> **Sales promotion** A promotional tool that stimulates consumer purchasing and dealer interest by means of short-term activities.

Consider the free samples of products you get in the mail, the coupons you clip from newspapers, the contests sponsored by retail stores, and the prizes in cereal boxes. Consumer-oriented sales promotion programs like these are designed to supplement personal selling, advertising, and public relations efforts by creating enthusiasm for the overall promotional program. Sales promotion can take place both internally (within the company) and externally (outside the company).

After the company's employees and intermediaries have been motivated with sales promotion efforts, the next step is to promote to consumers through such strategies as distributing samples or coupons,

Sampling Letting consumers have a small sample of a product for no charge.

displays, store demonstrations, premiums, contests, rebates, and so on. Sales promotion is an ongoing effort to maintain customer enthusiasm, so different strategies must be used over time to keep the ideas fresh. One popular sales promotion tool is **sampling**—letting consumers have a small sample of the product for no charge.

Because many consumers won't buy a new product unless they've had a chance to see it or try it, many grocery stores often have people standing in the aisles handing out small portions of food and beverage products. Sampling is a quick, effective way to demonstrate a product's superiority at the time when consumers are making a purchase decision. Pepsi introduced its FruitWorks product line with a combination of sampling, event marketing, and a new Web site. It is even possible to sample articles of clothing. American Eagle Outfitters once ran a promotion offering a free T-shirt to customers who tried on a pair of jeans.[39]

Another effective method of sales promotion, **event marketing**, occurs when companies sponsor events, such as concerts or sporting events, to promote their products. Some companies partner with

Event marketing Sponsoring events such as rock concerts or being at various events to promote your products.

charitable organizations in order to give back to their communities while marketing a positive image. For example, Tutor.com sponsored the annual conference of the American Library Association. Connections made from that sponsorship allowed the company to land projects totaling more than $3 million per year in revenue.[40]

OTHER TYPES OF PROMOTION

Creating a buzz about a product can pay off. Two related concepts and means of promotion that try to do this are *viral marketing* and *word-of-mouth promotion*. **Viral marketing** (so called because the campaigns spread like a virus) is the term now used to describe everything from paying people

Viral marketing The term used to describe everything from paying people to say positive things on the Internet to setting up multilevel selling schemes whereby consumers get commissions for directing friends to specific Web sites.

to say positive things about a product on the Internet to paying consumers commissions for directing friends to specific Web sites. Here's how

Barnes & Noble does it: You send your friends an e-mail that tells them how much you enjoyed reading a certain book and provide a link to the book on the Barnes & Noble Web site. If they follow the link and buy a book, you'll get a 5 percent commission.

Today, **word-of-mouth promotion** can be one of the most effective promotional tools out there because the Internet allows one voice to easily reach many people.[41] In word-of-mouth promotion, people tell other people about products that they've purchased. Anything that encourages people to talk favorably about an event, product, or organization may be effective word-of-mouth promotion. Clever commercials can do the same.

Word-of-mouth promotion A promotional tool that involves people telling other people about products that they've purchased.

The idea is the same behind every sort of promotion—getting more and more people talking about products and brand names so customers remember them when they're ready to purchase.

INTEGRATED MARKETING COMMUNICATION: PUTTING PROMOTIONS TOGETHER

Ensuring that each target market has its own distinct promotion mix is very important. Because customers in each market are different, the promotions should be different, too. For example, one target market for a small restaurant located in a downtown area might be businesspeople looking for a good place for lunch, while another market could be people who bring their families for dinner. The promotions will be different for each group simply because each market has a different need and a different motivation for eating at the restaurant, *yet these various promotions are part of a concerted effort.*

Integrated marketing communication (IMC) is a way of thinking about promotion that combines all promotional tools into one comprehensive and unified promotional strategy. The idea is to use promotional tools and company resources to create a

Integrated marketing communication (IMC) Combines all the promotional tools into one comprehensive and unified promotional strategy.

Everyone likes a free sample. Sampling is a promotional strategy that lets people try a new product, often in a situation when they can buy it right away if they like it.

Real World Apps

After reviewing his Business Now textbook, Cedric realizes that marketing is much more complex than he'd previously assumed. In order to help his friend, he now knows the first step should be to define the shop's target market through market segmentation. He will help his friend dig up information about the area and sort through it to determine what subgroups of area residents might be potential customers.

Next, Cedric will break down the 4 Ps—product, price, place, and promotion—of the business to figure out where marketing mistakes have been inadvertently made. Cedric has already figured out that one error was opening the restaurant without establishing a brand name, making it harder to establish an identity.

Initially, Cedric had thought that promotion, the last piece of the marketing puzzle, was what marketing was all about. Now he realizes that if a business owner fails to do a lot of work before thinking about advertising and other forms of promotion, the business will suffer the consequences. Cedric is now ready to help his friend regroup and make the business a success—one marketing step at a time.

positive brand image and meet the firm's strategic marketing and promotional goals.[43] For example, IMC includes the promotion mix, logo, music in commercials, packaging, and branding of a prod-

Cape Cod Potato Chip Company in Hyannis, Massachusetts, relied on word-of-mouth advertising in order to get its business going in the 1980s, when it had no advertising budget. The town where the business is located is a booming tourist area, and travelers from around the United States would stop by the company's retail shop while they vacationed nearby. These people would then return home and mention Cape Cod Potato Chips to friends and family.[42]

uct. This concept goes well beyond traditional promotion, unifying all aspects of the product and its marketing and also the broader company goals. Good IMC should provide the customer with the same compelling message about a product, regardless of the media mix or the way the product comes to consumers' attention in one situation or another. The result is a unified image of the company in the public consciousness.

For some firms, advertising is outsourced to ad agencies, PR work is outsourced to PR firms, and selling is done in-house, and there is little coordination across promotional efforts. As a result, consumers often receive conflicting messages about a company and its products. For example, a company's TV ads may emphasize quality while its sales promotion team pushes coupons and employs discounting strategies. Such conflicting images are not as effective as creating a unified image via multiple promotional methods working in the same direction.

Small businesses that may not be able to use advertising agencies can nevertheless use IMC. Any signage, letterheads, and phone-book ads should all carry the same message, right down to the same colors and logos. Doing so helps consumers identify the brand in a unified manner.

The U.S. Department of Agriculture's (USDA) organic logo is particularly strong and has a positive image in the public consciousness.

[BUS] connections

1. List each type of promotion discussed. What are the advantages and disadvantages of each?
2. Which method of promotion do you think is most effective in selling to you? Which is the least effective?
3. Explain why IMC is beneficial to businesses.

For REVIEW >>

1. **Define marketing and name the types of market segmentations.**
   - Marketing goes beyond simply selling or advertising—it is the process of planning and executing the conception, pricing, promotion, and distribution of goods and services to facilitate exchanges that satisfy individual and organizational needs. Marketers usually find it necessary to segment markets, or break them into smaller groups, so they can better develop products for and market products to targeted groups. For example, a marketer can segment potential markets based on geographic, demographic, benefit, volume, or psychographic parameters, among others.
   - Marketers must understand consumer buying behavior, which starts with consumers recognizing a need or a problem and progresses through their own search for product information and evaluation of alternative products. Marketers must understand how to intervene in this process and influence the customer to select their product. The habits and processes of buyers in B2B markets, a huge share of sales in the United States, are very different from consumer behaviors.

2. **Describe the various aspects of marketing's focus on developing a product.**
   - The next section of the chapter introduced the marketing mix, which is also known as the four Ps of marketing—product, price, place, and promotion. A product's total product offer is everything consumers evaluate when deciding whether to purchase a good or service. Marketers conduct marketing research, which is a process of gathering primary or secondary data about consumers. Marketers are also responsible for product differentiation, which means creating real or perceived differences between a product and its competition. Packaging is also a concern for marketers, as they must be sure it protects the goods inside; attracts the buyer's attention; describes its contents; explains the benefits; provides information; gives some indication of price, value, and uses; and provides the dimensions and weight of the package. Branding, another important concept, involves the name and symbol of a product that identifies it and positions it over similar products.

3. **Describe the different types of pricing that should be considered when marketing products.**
   - Pricing a product is a strategic decision of crucial importance in marketing. Firms keep the following objectives in mind when determining price: achieving a targeted ROI or profit, building traffic, achieving greater market share, creating an image, and furthering social objectives. When pricing, firms must also keep in mind a product's stage in its life cycle—is it in its introduction, growth, maturity, or decline phase? Pricing strategies include cost-based pricing, demand-based pricing, competition-based pricing, break-even analysis, skimming, penetration, EDLP, high–low pricing, bundling, and psychological pricing.

4. **Explain the concept of place and how it pertains to marketing.**
   - Place refers to the process of getting products to the places where they will be sold, or their distribution, and to the process of determining where the products will be sold. Hundreds of thousands of marketing intermediaries exist to help that process along a channel of distribution, moving goods from their raw-material state to production facilities, warehouses, distributors, and then on to consumers. All of these steps in the process are "places" in the distribution chain. These marketing intermediaries include merchant wholesalers, agents and brokers, and retailers. Retailers compete with one another on price, service, product variety, location, or entertainment (or any combination of the five).

5. **Understand the different types of promotion and how they can be put together to create a unified image.**
   - One of promotion's greatest challenges is the communication process. A marketer must define a target audience, select methods to reach it, design the right message, and make sure the audience gets the message. Because these tasks are so challenging, many companies choose to hire advertising or promotion agencies. Promotion has four primary areas—advertising, personal selling, public relations, and sales promotion. There are a few other areas of promotion, such as viral marketing and word-of-mouth marketing, that are gaining prominence as the Internet becomes more popular on the marketing landscape. IMC combines all the tools of promotion into one comprehensive and unified promotional strategy.

Key Terms

Advertising

Agents/brokers

Benefit segmentation

Brand

Brand equity

Brand loyalty

Break-even analysis strategy

Bundling strategy

Cash-and-carry wholesalers

Category killer

Channel of distribution

Demographic segmentation

Drop shippers

Event marketing

Everyday low pricing (EDLP) strategy

Focus group

Geographic segmentation

High–low pricing strategy

Industrial good

Integrated marketing communication (IMC)

Loss leaders

Market segmentation

Marketing

Marketing intermediary

Marketing management

Marketing mix (the four Ps)

Marketing research

Merchant wholesalers

Niche marketing

Penetration strategy

Personal selling

Place

Price leadership

Primary research

Product differentiation

Product life cycle

Product placement

Promotion mix

Psychographic segmentation

Psychological pricing (odd pricing) strategy

Public relations (PR)

Publicity

Rack jobbers

Relationship marketing

Sales promotion

Sampling

Secondary research

Skimming price strategy

Target costing

Target marketing

Total product offer

Viral marketing

Volume segmentation

Wholesaler

Word-of-mouth promotion

1. This chapter discussed the consumer buying process. Consider the last item you bought and discuss how you went through that process when purchasing the item. Did you experience buyer's remorse?

2. Where might you place each of the following items in the product life cycle, and why?
   a. Electric car
   b. Videocassette recorder (VCR)
   c. 100-Calorie Snack Packs of chips and cookies
   d. Levi's jeans
   e. Red Bull energy drink
   f. Hanes T-shirts
   g. Coca-Cola

3. Do you think advertising promotes materialism in our society? Why or why not?

4. How might the promotion for a service product versus a consumer product be different? How might it be the same?

5. In groups, discuss how much of an impact pricing has on your purchase decisions? What other factors do you consider when purchasing items? Discuss for each of the following items:
   a. A car
   b. A candy bar
   c. Mustard
   d. Toothpaste
   e. Shampoo
   f. Cellular phone
   g. Soft drink
   h. Haircut
   i. Jeans

6. Pricing strategies were discussed in this chapter. In groups, discuss what pricing strategy you might use for each of the following products and why:
   a. A vacation package
   b. A luxury handbag
   c. A new brand of toothpaste
   d. The latest version of the iPhone

INTERNET IN >> Action

1. As discussed in this chapter, marketers use many tools to determine their target markets. Values, Attitudes, and Lifestyles (VALS) is one such tool. Visit http://www.sric-bi.com/VALS/presurvey.shtml and take the VALS survey.
   a. Read about your preferred consumer style.
   b. Click on each of the eight categories and read about each one.
   c. Do you agree or disagree with your category? Do you think it is reflective of your consumer style?
   d. If you had a secondary style, which one do you think it would be and why?
   e. What other tools besides VALS can marketers use to determine their target market?

2. Social networking sites, such as Facebook and MySpace, are popular tools for marketers. Using demographic data (such as location or age) a user has provided, marketers can show targeted advertisements to that particular person. If you have one of these accounts, log into it and view the advertisements. If you do not have an account, visit www.myspace.com and www.facebook.com. Answer the following questions:
   a. What advertisements do you see listed?
   b. Do you think these advertisements are specifically targeted toward you? Why or why not?

Self-Assessment Exercises

BUSINESS CAREER QUIZ

So which Lifestyle Do You Have?

In this chapter, you learned how marketers classify consumers into different categories in order to make it easier to market to them. Premium Knowledge Group[44] has developed classifications of consumers based on lifestyle factors, such as preferred television channels, media preference, demographics, and brand preferences. Based on these classifications, marketers can better sell to consumers. Take the quiz and see which category you are most like!

1. Your clothes are made by . . .
   a. Ralph Lauren   d. Target
   b. Old Navy   e. Marc Jacobs
   c. Ann Taylor

2. The car that most closely resembles the car you drive is:
   a. Land Rover   d. Honda
   b. Toyota   e. Volkswagen
   c. Rolls Royce

3. Your beauty product of choice is made by . . .
   a. MAC   d. Cover Girl
   b. Neutrogena   e. Calvin Klein
   c. Clinique

4. When making a beauty product purchase, you're most influenced by . . .
   a. convenience
   b. price
   c. quality
   d. organic and natural properties
   e. you don't buy many beauty products

5. When you planning a vacation, you would pick . . .
   a. a golf resort   d. A cruise
   b. Hawaii   e. the Caribbean
   c. Europe

6. You describe your ideal vacation as . . .
   a. exclusive   d. cheap
   b. relaxing   e. simple
   c. exotic

7. Out of this list, your favorite reading material is . . .
   A. *Forbes*
   B. *Time* magazine
   C. *Entertainment Weekly* magazine
   D. *The New York Times*
   E. *USA Today*

8. When shopping, you prefer . . .
   A. constant attention from clerks
   B. to be left alone to browse
   C. knowing service is readily available if needed
   D. a moderate level of assistance
   E. your own personal sales assistant

Key:

If you selected mostly As, you're trendy and prefer what's in demand; you stay away from controversy.

If you selected mostly Bs, you're traditional, and function and practicality matter to you.

If you selected mostly Cs, you're unique and possess a sense of pride over ownership.

If you selected mostly Ds, you're economical and like to feel good and make shopping decisions that fit your personality.

If you selected mostly Es, you're precise and seek balance and proportion.

Source: Megan Winslow, "Take the Lifestyle Quiz. Find Out what Consumer You Are," *Palm Beach Daily News*, http://www.palmbeachdailynews.com/biz/content/business/2009/05/06/QUIZ0507.html (accessed August 18, 2009).

MATERIALISM SELF-ASSESSMENT

One of the ways marketers can better sell to consumers is by understanding the level of materialism of a specific target market. Read each of the following statements, then indicate your agreement or disagreement with each statement by putting a number next to the question. The numbers correspond to the following responses (1 = strongly disagree; 2 = disagree; 3 = don't agree or disagree; 4 = agree; and 5 = strongly agree):

_____ I admire people who own expensive homes, cars, and clothes.

_____ My life would be better if I owned certain things I don't have.

_____ Some of the most important achievements in life include acquiring material possessions.

_____ I place a lot of emphasis on the amount of material objects people own as a sign of success.

_____ I'd be happier if I could afford to buy more things.

_____ I enjoy spending money on things that aren't practical.

_____ The things I own say a lot about how well I am doing in life.

_____ It sometimes bothers me quite a bit that I can't afford to buy all the things that I'd like.

_____ Buying things gives me a lot of pleasure.

_____ I like to own things that impress people.

_____ I like a lot of luxury in my life.

Now, add up your scores. The higher the score, the higher your inclination toward materialism.[45] How do you think marketers might use this information to define target markets? How might they use it in advertising?

Source: Richins and Dawson, " Materialism Quiz," *Journal of Consumer Research*, Vol. 19, p. 303–316. Copyright © University of Chicago Press. Reprinted with permission.

5

HUMAN RESOURCE MANAGEMENT

After reading this chapter, you will be able to:

1 Describe the human resource management (HRM) process.

2 Understand how human resource (HR) managers determine needs and recruit and select employees.

3 Illustrate the various types of employee training and development methods.

4 Describe different types of pay systems and how to evaluate employees.

5 Understand important laws affecting the workplace.

6 Describe the key challenges facing HR managers today.

ADRIENNE KALLWEIT AND SEEKINGSITTERS.COM

At first, Adrienne Kallweit figured it would be perfectly safe to hire her son's preschool teacher to babysit for him, but she later reconsidered and decided to be safe rather than sorry. Kallweit, a licensed private investigator by profession, decided to run a routine background check on the teacher. She was shocked by what she found—numerous character issues that indicated hiring the teacher as a babysitter would be putting her son at risk.

Like parents, organizations want to hire reliable, conscientious people to work for them. Human resource departments screen, select, train, and supervise employees to better ensure the growth and safety of the organization. After all, selecting the wrong employee can have serious consequences, including placing the company at risk for losing customers and other employees.

Kallweit decided to offer parents just this sort of human resource function. In 2004, she started SeekingSitters.com, a babysitter referral service that provides families with peace of mind about the sitters they hire to care for their children. Just like HR departments at large organizations, SeekingSitters.com subjects potential sitters to background screenings, personal character evaluations, reference checks, and in-person interviews—and for the protection of its sitters, it also performs personal identity verifications and criminal and sex-offender background checks on the families interested in hiring sitters. This creates a culture of safety, trust, and professionalism throughout all aspects of the organization. Kallweit remarked, "The fact that we provide a safe and reliable service really keeps us thriving, even in tough economic times. Our service is really needed."

Kallweit's idea has grown into a very successful business, with 23 locations in nine different states—some of which are franchises. The hiring process and customer selection process are mandatory for all franchise owners. All franchise owners are parents, too, so they understand what SeekingSitters.com's clients are looking for in a potential sitter. In 2008, the company had total sales of more than $2.1 million, and it hopes to expand by 10 more franchises in the coming year.

Kallweit knows that one bad employee could destroy her company. The issues facing SeekingSitters.com are similar to those that all organizations face. The hiring processes, training, and supervision of employees are the lifeblood of organizational success, and all three are the responsibility of an organization's HR department.

Questions

1. Why should SeekingSitters.com care about employees' personal histories if they're capable of excelling at their job? Why should the company care about a customer's history?

2. List and discuss the steps you would take to check someone out before hiring him or her.

3. What type of training do you think sitters working for SeekingSitters.com would need to be highly effective in their job? How would you evaluate an employee of SeekingSitters.com?

Sources: Adapted from Kevin Manahan, "Baby-Sitter Referral Service Born of Necessity," *Entrepreneur*, May 2009, http://www.entrepreneur.com/magazine/entrepreneur/2009/may/201166.html (accessed August 9, 2009); and http://workathomefranchise.com/aboutus.asp (accessed August 18, 2009).

- How do businesses find the right people for the right jobs?
- How can a business ensure that it is fairly evaluating and compensating its employees?
- As an HR manager, what laws should you pay attention to?

People, who are literally an organization's *human resources*, are the most valuable assets any company has. This chapter discusses the key functions of managing those human resources. Key human resource (HR) functions include determining how many people are needed and for how long and executing the hiring and training process. Once employees are hired and trained, determining how to compensate them correctly and motivating and evaluating their performance are important parts of the HR process. HR managers are charged with ensuring that employees are treated fairly and consistently.

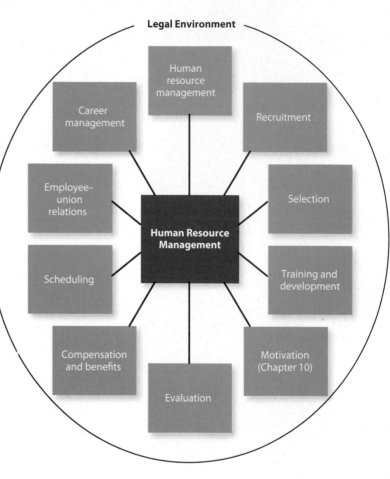

Figure 5.1 HR Management

>> The HR Management Process

HR management (HRM) is the process of determining HR needs and then recruiting, selecting, training and developing, compensating, evaluating, and scheduling employees to achieve organizational goals (see Figure 5.1). Known for years as the "personnel department," HRM was traditionally responsible for clerical functions like record keeping, finding employees when needed, and processing paperwork.

Human resource management (HRM) The process of determining HR needs and then recruiting, selecting, training and developing, compensating, appraising, and scheduling employees to achieve organizational goals.

Today, HRM is considered to be a vital strategic partner in the long-term survival and growth of an organization, and HR departments have broad responsibilities. They are involved in the legal aspects of employment, such as monitoring for illegal immigrants, and are also responsible for motivating people (see Chapter 10). HRM tasks require individuals who can think strategically and work closely with others. If you are interested in the HR field, take note: careers in HRM are expected to grow faster than the average for all occupations between 2006 and 2016.[1]

In addition, as a result of the rise of outsourcing—including outsourcing overseas, which is also known as offshoring (see Chapter 11 for more information

Real World Apps

After being laid off from her job as a manager in Fulbright Packaging's personnel department, Laurie Lambrecht-Silva has returned to college to obtain a business degree. Laurie had worked in the department for 22 years and lost her job when the department was eliminated.

Laurie has been surprised at how many of the concepts covered in her Introduction to Business course have been completely foreign to her, despite her years of work in the business world. She's looking forward to this week, during which the class will study HRM.

"Finally! A week where I don't have to study so hard," Laurie thinks. "I've been a manager in a personnel department for years, and HR is just a fancy new name for an old department!" For once, Laurie leaves for class sure of herself and excited about participating in the discussion.

Once class begins and the concepts of HRM are discussed, Laurie begins to realize why her department had been eliminated. Nothing she did there was remotely related to what the class was discussing.

"Wow, times sure have changed!" Laurie thinks, and decides to carefully read her textbook's chapter on HRM that evening.

>> HRM: Determining Needs, Recruiting, and Selecting

As Figure 5.1 suggests, the first three key functions of HRM are determining an organization's HR needs, recruiting from a diverse population, and selecting employees. Of course, all management, including HRM, begins with planning; in this case, that means determining HR needs.

DETERMINING HR NEEDS

There are five steps in the HR planning process (see Figure 5.2), which starts with understanding and describing what assets an organization has and ends with developing a strategic plan for HR.

1. *Prepare an HR inventory of the organization's employees.* This inventory should list each employee's name, education level, capabilities, training, specialized skills, and other information pertinent to the organization, such as languages spoken. This inventory will help reveal whether the organization's labor force is technically savvy and thoroughly trained.

2. *Prepare a job analysis.* A **job analysis** is a study of what employees do who hold various job titles. Such analyses are necessary in order to recruit employees with the skills to do the job and to determine what supplemental training is needed. The results of a job analysis are two written statements: job descriptions and job specifications. A **job description** specifies

> **Job analysis** A study of what employees do who hold various job titles.
>
> **Job description** Specifies the objectives of the job, the type of work to be done, the responsibilities and duties, the working conditions, and the relationship of the job to other functions.

about these topics)—many HR managers have to make difficult decisions about which, if any, jobs can be performed by other companies, including those overseas, and who may have to be laid off as a result.

[BUS] connections

1. What is HRM?
2. Identify the key functions of HRM.
3. How do you think HRM evolved over the years?

as the interns get invaluable experience and an advantage when competing for full-time compensated work with the company, and the employers get low- or no-cost workers for a set period of time. In addition to getting work experience, interns also get an opportunity to develop networks at the company and its affiliates. Both sides get an opportunity to explore the fit of the job and the person within the organization.

Figure 5.5 shows a list of the companies that hired the most interns in 2009; Walgreens led the pack, hiring 5,650 interns that year.

Recruiting qualified workers may be particularly difficult for small businesses, because they do not necessarily have enough staff to serve as internal sources and may not be able to offer compensation or benefits at a level that attracts external candidates. Some small businesses use other incentives, such as flexible schedules or work-from-home arrangements, to attract potential employees.

SELECTING EMPLOYEES

Selection The process of gathering information and deciding who should be hired, under legal guidelines, to serve the best interests of the individual and the organization.

Selection is the process of gathering information and deciding who should be hired, under legal guidelines, to serve the best interests of the individual and the organization. Selecting and training employees are extremely expensive processes in some firms. Just think what's involved: advertising or recruiting agency fees, interview time, medical exams, training costs, unproductive time spent learning the job, possible travel and moving expenses, and more. It can cost one and a half times the employee's annual salary to recruit, process, and train an entry-level worker.[8] A typical selection process involves six steps (see Figure 5.6):

Figure 5.5 Ten U.S. Companies that Hire the Most Interns

1. Walgreens (drugstores)
2. Southwestern (publishing and direct sales)
3. General Electric (energy and infrastructure)
4. Deloitte (professional services/accounting)
5. PricewaterhouseCoopers (professional services/accounting)
6. KPMG (professional services/accounting)
7. Northwestern Mutual Financial Network (insurance)
8. Lockheed Martin (aerospace/defense)
9. Ernst & Young (professional services/accounting)
10. Enterprise Rent-A-Car (car rental)

Source: Joyce Lee, "U.S. Companies that Hire the Most Interns," Forbes.com, July 7, 2009, http://www.forbes.com/2009/07/07/biggest-intern-companies-leadership-careers-jobs.html (accessed July 8, 2009).

1. *Obtain complete application forms.* Today, legal guidelines limit the kinds of questions that may appear on an application form. Nonetheless,

Like large businesses, many small businesses use Web sites like CareerBuilder, Monster, and LinkedIn to post opportunities or help them sift through the resumes of potential employees.

Figure 5.6 The Six Steps of the Selection Process

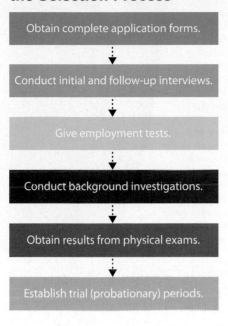

- Obtain complete application forms.
- Conduct initial and follow-up interviews.
- Give employment tests.
- Conduct background investigations.
- Obtain results from physical exams.
- Establish trial (probationary) periods.

such forms help the employer discover the applicant's educational background, past work experience, career objectives, and other qualifications directly related to the job's requirements. Large retail employers like Winn-Dixie and Finish Line make the application process more efficient by using an automated program called Workforce Acquisition.[9]

2. *Conduct initial and follow-up interviews.* A staff member from the HR department often screens applicants in a first interview. If the interviewer considers the applicant a potential hire, the manager who will supervise the new employee usually interviews the applicant as well. It is important that managers prepare adequately for the interview to avoid selection decisions they may regret.[10] Mistakes, such as not asking the right questions or speeding through an interview in order to fill the position quickly, can be very costly. Asking interviewees about their family situation, no matter how innocent the intention, could later be used as evidence if an applicant files discrimination charges.[11] For example, Ford Motor Company was forced to pay $10 million for allegedly using race as a basis for admittance to its apprenticeship program.[12] Initial interviews are often done over the phone to save time and money. If a department manager is interviewing a potential candidate, an HR representative may sit in on the interview to ensure that nothing illegal is asked, which helps protect the company in case of any future lawsuits.

3. *Give employment tests.* Organizations sometimes use tests to measure basic competencies in specific

job skills (for example, welding or typing) and to help evaluate applicants' personalities and interests.[13] The assessments should always be directly related to the job. Background checks can also help an employer identify which candidates are most likely to succeed in a given position. Certain Web sites, such as PeopleWise, allow prospective employers to conduct speedy background checks of applicants' criminal records, driving records, and credit histories and verify work experience and professional and educational credentials.

4. *Conduct background investigations.* Most organizations investigate a candidate's work record, school record, credit history, and references more carefully today than they did in the past.[14] Background checks help an employer identify which candidates are more likely to succeed in a given position.

5. *Obtain results from physical exams.* There are obvious benefits to hiring physically and mentally healthy people, but medical tests can't be given simply to screen out certain people. In some states, physical exams can be given only after an offer of employment has been accepted. In states that allow pre-employment physical exams, the exams must be given to everyone applying for the same position. There has been some controversy about pre-employment testing for drug or alcohol abuse, but today some 70 percent of U.S. firms test both current and prospective employees for drug use.

6. *Establish trial (probationary) periods.* Sometimes organizations hire employees conditionally, which allows them to prove their worth on the job. After a specified probationary period (perhaps six months or a year), the firm may either permanently hire or discharge that employee on the basis of supervisors' evaluations. Although such systems make it easier to fire inefficient or problem employees, they do not eliminate the high cost of turnover.[15]

The selection process is often long and difficult, but it is worth the effort to select new employees carefully because of the high cost of replacing them.[17] The process helps ensure that new employees meet the requirements in all relevant areas, including communication skills, education, technical skills, experience, and personality.

◄ ETHICAL   **DILEMMA ►**

If a minority employee is being denied a promotion she deserves, what other options does she have to move up the company ladder?

Firms whose employment needs vary sometimes hire contingent workers, rather than full-time employees, to save costs. **Contingent workers** are defined as workers who do not have the expectation of regular, full-time employment. Such workers include part-time workers, temporary workers, independent contractors, and interns. Companies may hire contingent workers when demand is high, during maternity leaves, or when quick service is important to satisfy customers.

Although exact numbers are difficult to gather, the Bureau of Labor Statistics estimates that there are approximately 5.7 million contingent workers in the United States, with the majority younger than 25.[18] Experts say temps are filling openings in an increasingly broad range of jobs, from unskilled manufacturing and distribution positions to middle management. Increasing numbers of contingent workers are educated professionals such as accountants, attorneys, and engineers. One explanation for the rapid growth of this employment category is an increased desire for creativity and independence in the workplace.[19]

*Providing a self-serve, electronic system for employment applications helps employers determine the best candidates **before** the interview process begins. An applicant sits down at a kiosk like the one pictured and spends approximately half an hour answering questions about job experience, time available to work, and personality. Afterward, a report is e-mailed to a hiring manager that recommends whether or not the applicant should be interviewed. If an interview is recommended, the report suggests questions the manager can ask to find the best-fitting position for the applicant. According to managers at movie rental giant Blockbuster, such a system has helped the company cut the hiring process's length from two weeks to three days and has reduced the employee turnover rate by 30 percent.[16]*

they must offer sophisticated training programs. Employers find that spending money on training is usually money well spent. **Training and development** include all attempts to improve productivity by increasing an employee's ability to perform.

Training and development All attempts to improve productivity by increasing an employee's ability to perform. Training focuses on short-term skills, development on long-term abilities.

Training focuses on short-term skills, whereas development focuses on long-term abilities. Both include three steps: (1) assessing organization needs and employee skills to determine training needs, (2) designing training activities to meet identified needs, and (3) evaluating the training's effectiveness.

EMPLOYEE TRAINING

When companies take the time and resources to invest in employees, payoffs result in many different forms—including increased shareholder returns.[21] Common training and development activities include employee orientation, on-the-job training,

Managers at Ruth's Chris Steak House, a Louisiana-based chain, have found that thoroughly training employees—including being clear about what it takes to move up in the company—has helped the company retain employees. Among other strategies, the chain gives its employees flash cards containing the most important information they need to know. Since the cards have been in use, employee turnover has decreased by 6 percent.[20]

[BUS] connections

1. Briefly describe the five steps of the HR planning process.
2. Differentiate between internal and external candidates.
3. Explain the six steps of the selection process.

>> HRM: Training and Development

Because employees need to learn how to work with equipment—such as computers and other job-related technology or equipment—companies often find that apprenticeship, off-the-job training, online training, vestibule training, job simulation, and management training.

Employee Orientation

Employee orientations introduce new employees into an organization; to fellow employees; to their immediate supervisors; and to the policies, practices, and objectives of the firm. Orientation programs range from informal talks to more formal activities that last a day or more and can include visits to various departments and reading employee handbooks.[22]

> **Employee orientation** The activity that introduces new employees to the organization; to fellow employees; to their immediate supervisors; and to the policies, practices, and objectives of the firm.

On-the-Job Training

On-the-job training, often the most fundamental and valuable type of training, involves immediately beginning job tasks and learning by doing or by watching and then imitating others. On-the-job training is the easiest kind of training to implement for relatively simple (clerking in a store) jobs or repetitive jobs (collecting refuse, cleaning carpets, or mowing lawns), but demanding or intricate jobs require a more intense training effort. For example, physical therapists are required to pass certain courses in science and then obtain three years of specialized training in the field.[24] Intranets and other new forms of technology can provide cost-effective, on-the-job training programs available 24 hours a day, all year long. Computer systems can monitor workers' input and give them instructions if they become confused about what to do next or report concerns to supervisors.

> **On-the-job training** Training at the workplace that lets the employee learn by doing or by watching others for a while and then imitating them.

Apprentice Programs

In an apprentice program, a learner works alongside an experienced employee in order to master the skills and procedures of a craft. Apprentices have the opportunity to work in as many as 850 occupations.[25] Some

For example, at Aflac, one of the nation's largest insurance companies, new employees are schooled about the company's history, values, and product integrity. They also learn about industry certifications that can be earned through on-site courses offered at the company during business hours.[23]

apprenticeship programs also involve classroom training. Many skilled crafts, such as bricklaying and plumbing, require a new worker to serve as an apprentice for several years. Trade unions often require new workers to serve in apprenticeships to ensure excellence among their members, as well as to limit entry to the union. Workers who successfully complete an apprenticeship earn the classification of *journeyman*. Apprenticeship programs may be shortened to prepare people for skilled jobs in changing industries, such as auto repair and aircraft maintenance, that require increased knowledge of computer technology. About 450,000 apprentices are registered with the U.S. Department of Labor.[26]

As baby boomers retire from skilled trades such as pipefitting, welding, and carpentry, shortages of trained workers will result.[27]

Off-the-Job Training

Off-the-job training occurs away from the workplace and consists of internal or external programs to develop skills or foster personal development. Training is becoming more sophisticated as jobs become more sophisticated. Furthermore, training is expanding to include education (through higher level courses) and personal development; subjects include time management, stress management, health and wellness, physical education, nutrition, and even art and languages.

> **Off-the-job training** Internal or external training programs away from the workplace that develop any of a variety of skills or foster personal development.

Online Training

Online training offers an example of how technology is improving the efficiency of many off-the-job training programs. You may have already enrolled in an online course. In such training programs, employees "attend" classes via the Internet. Another option is Web conferencing, which allows for inexpensive and easy teleconferencing and other forms of online meetings. Many col-

> **Online training** Training programs in which employees complete classes via the Internet.

leges and universities now offer a wide variety of Internet courses; these courses are sometimes called *distance learning* because the students are separated by distance from the instructor or content source.[29] One community college in Kentucky offers an online course called "Army 101" that gives applicants an inside look at life in the military.[30]

MANAGEMENT TRAINING

Managers need special training. To be good communicators, they especially need to learn listening skills and empathy. They also need time management, planning, and human relations skills.

Management development is the process of training and educating employees to become good managers, and then monitoring the progress of their managerial skills over time. Management development programs have sprung up everywhere, especially at colleges, universities, and private management development firms and corporations. Management training programs generally include several of the following:

Vestibule Training

Vestibule training (near-the-job training) is done in classrooms where employees are taught on equipment similar to that used on the job. Such classrooms enable employees to learn proper methods and safety procedures before assuming a specific job assignment in an organization. For example, X-ray technicians are responsible for not only prepping patients but also adjusting, facilitating, and operating X-ray equipment. They must be knowledgeable and comfortable with the equipment and the technology. X-ray technicians are certified only after they complete significant training on the equipment, and as the technology advances, their training continues.

Vestibule training Training done in schools where employees are taught on equipment similar to that used on the job.

Management development The process of training and educating employees to become good managers and then monitoring the progress of their managerial skills over time.

1. *On-the-job coaching.* A senior manager assists a lower-level manager by teaching needed skills and providing direction, advice, and helpful feedback. E-coaching is being developed to coach

Job Simulation

Job simulation is the use of equipment that duplicates job conditions and tasks so trainees can learn skills before attempting them on the job. Job simulation differs from vestibule training in that the simulation attempts to duplicate the *exact* combination of conditions that occur on the job. This training is given to astronauts, airline pilots, army tank operators, ship captains, and others who must learn difficult procedures off the job.

Job simulation The use of equipment that duplicates job conditions and tasks so trainees can learn skills before attempting them on the job.

This job simulator at the Federal Aviation Administration Academy in Oklahoma City, Oklahoma, helps air traffic controllers learn how to manage aircraft departures and arrivals. Experts see a coming shortage of trained controllers, who face mandatory retirement at age 56. Do you think simulation training is effective for jobs like this? Why or why not?

Thinking Critically

>> **What Other Factors besides a Company's Size Affect Its Likelihood of Providing Formal Training?**

A survey conducted by the Bureau of Labor Statistics suggests that there may be a direct link between a company's commitment to providing meaningful benefits and training for an employee and that employee's commitment to the company. Consider your personal workplace experience(s). Has this been true for you?

While size seems to be a very important factor, other characteristics of a company are also associated with formal training even after controlling for the influence of size. Firms that offer benefits like employee assistance programs, pension plans, employee wellness programs, and profit sharing are more likely to provide training than other businesses. This finding supports the idea that firms that foster a long-term commitment between themselves and their employees have a greater incentive to train workers.

Companies that use a number of work practices, such as just-in-time inventories, worker teams, total quality management, quality circles, peer review of employee performance, pay for knowledge, employee involvement in technology and purchase decisions, and job rotation, are more likely to provide formal training than are similar establishments that do not use as many of these practices.

The strong association between work practices and the provision of formal training supports the idea that "high-performance" workplaces—those that use many of the practices listed—are more likely to provide training to their employees.

Source: Bureau of Labor Statistics Survey of Employer-Provided Training Frequently Asked Questions, http://www.bls.gov/ept/eptfaq.htm (accessed September 1, 2009)

QUESTIONS

1. Do you find formal employee training to be valuable? What about training that isn't directly related to job duties—for example, teamwork or diversity training for employees who don't have frequent contact with coworkers, customers, and vendors? Describe your rationale.

2. Describe the types of formal training you have received in the past. Did the training support the organization's work practices and performance objectives? Why or why not?

managers electronically, though it will take time and experimentation before firms figure out how to make coaches come to life online.[31]

2. *Understudy positions.* Job titles such as *undersecretary* and *assistant* are part of a relatively successful way of developing managers. Selected employees work as assistants to higher-level managers and participate in planning and other managerial functions until they are ready to assume such positions themselves.

3. *Job rotation.* So they can learn about different functions of the organization, managers are often given assignments in a variety of departments. Such job rotation gives them the broad picture of the organization they need to succeed.[32]

4. *Off-the-job courses and training.* Managers periodically go to classes or seminars for a week or more to hone technical and human relations skills. Major universities like the University of Michigan, MIT, and the University of Chicago offer specialized short courses to assist managers

Figure 5.8 Top Five Companies to Work for in 2009

Company	What Makes It So Great
1. NetApp	Employee enthusiasm; five paid days off each year for volunteer work; $11,390 available each year in adoption aid; autism coverage.
2. Edward Jones	No plans for layoffs; hired 698 new financial advisers in 2009; building an addition to its headquarters to accommodate 500 new employees.
3. Boston Consulting Group	Aggressive recruitment of minorities; first-class health insurance, including $5 copays for doctor visits and 100 percent coverage of fertility treatments.
4. Google	On-site child care and fitness centers; subsidizes gym memberships; permits telecommuting.
5. Wegmans Food Markets	Employees can buy gift cards at a 10 percent discount; free yoga classes.

Source: "100 Best Companies to Work for 2009," *CNNMoney.com,* http://money.cnn.com/magazines/fortune/bestcompanies/2009/snapshots/1.html (accessed July 10, 2009).

Fringe Benefits and Retirement Plans

Perhaps the best known fringe benefits are sick-leave pay, vacation pay, pension plans, and health plans that provide additional compensation to employees beyond base wages. In recent years, benefits have grown faster than wages; thus, they cannot really be considered fringe anymore. In 1929, such benefits accounted for less than 2 percent of payroll; today, as you saw in Figure 5.7, they account for about 30 percent of total compensation.

Although the cost of health benefits has increased dramatically in recent years, many organizations offer health benefits to employees and their spouses,

> **Cafeteria-style fringe benefits** Fringe benefits plan that allows employees to choose the benefits they want up to a certain dollar amount.

domestic partners, and children. These benefits cover some or all of the cost of health insurance. Given the diverse needs of different employees, many large firms offer **cafeteria-style fringe benefits**, in which employees can choose the benefits they want up to a certain dollar amount. Such plans allow the organizations to meet equitably the diverse needs of their employees—anything from child-care benefits to pension plans.

Many companies partner with financial companies and set up investment plans to help employees save for their retirement. In most for-profit businesses, these funds are called 401(k) plans. In addition to setting up these funds, some companies even contribute tax-free

Figure 5.9 Pay Systems

Some of the different pay systems are as follows:

- *Salary:* Fixed compensation computed on weekly, biweekly, or monthly pay periods (e.g., $1,600 per month or $400 per week). Salaried employees do not receive additional pay for any extra hours worked.

- *Hourly wage or daywork:* Wage based on number of hours or days worked, used for most blue-collar and clerical workers. Often employees must punch a time clock when they arrive at work and when they leave. Hourly wages vary greatly. The federal minimum wage is $7.25, and top wages go as high as $40 per hour for skilled craftspeople. This does not include benefits, such as retirement systems, which may add 30 percent or more to the total package.

- *Piecework system:* Wage based on the number of items produced rather than by the hour or day. This type of system creates powerful incentives to work efficiently and productively.

- *Commission plans:* Pay based on some percentage of sales. Often used to compensate salespeople, commission plans resemble piecework systems.

- *Bonus plans:* Extra pay for accomplishing or surpassing certain objectives. There are two types of bonuses: monetary and cashless. Money is always a welcome bonus. Cashless rewards include written thank-you notes, appreciation notes sent to the employee's family, movie tickets, flowers, time off, gift certificates, shopping sprees, and other types of recognition.

- *Profit-sharing plans:* Annual bonuses paid to employees based on the company's profits. The amount paid to each employee is based on a predetermined percentage. Profit sharing is one of the most common forms of performance-based pay.

- *Gain-sharing plans:* Annual bonuses paid to employees based on achieving specific goals such as quality measures, customer satisfaction measures, and production targets.

- *Stock options:* The right to purchase stock in the company at a specific price over a specific period. Often this gives employees the right to buy stock cheaply despite huge increases in the price of the stock. For example, if over the course of his employment a worker received options to buy 10,000 shares of the company stock at $10 each and the price of the stock eventually grows to $100, he can use those options to buy the 10,000 shares (now worth $1 million) for $100,000.

Figure 5.10 Flextime

Flexible hours

Core time   Core time

Lunch period

6:30 7:00 7:30 8:00 8:30 9:00 9:30 10:00 10:30 11:00 11:30 12:00 12:30 1:00 1:30 2:00 2:30 3:00 3:30 4:00 4:30 5:00 5:30 6:00 6:30

Sarah's starting time   Sarah's lunch period   Sarah's finish time

money into employees' accounts. Suppose your employer matches your 401(k) contributions. If you contribute $100 to your account, your employer will put in an additional $100. You'll find more about the advantages of contributing to a 401(k) in the Bonus Chapter.

ALTERNATIVES TO TRADITIONAL SCHEDULING

Workplace trends and the increasing costs of transportation have led employees to look for scheduling flexibility. Flextime, in-home employment, and job sharing are becoming important benefits employees seek.

Flextime

A **flextime plan** gives employees some freedom to choose when to work, as long as they work the required number of hours. The most popular plans allow employees to come to work between 7:00 a.m. and 9:00 a.m. and leave between 4:00 p.m. and 6:00 p.m. Usually, flextime plans incorporate **core time**, the period when all employees are expected to be at their job stations. For example, an organization may designate core time as 9:00 a.m. to 11:00 a.m. and 2:00 p.m. to 4:00 p.m. During these hours, all employees are required to be at work, but otherwise they can set their own hours (see Figure 5.10). Flextime plans are designed to allow employees to adjust to work/life demands; dual-career families find them especially helpful.[39]

Flextime plan Work schedule that gives employees some freedom to choose when to work, as long as they work the required number of hours.

Core time In a flextime plan, the period when all employees are expected to be at their job stations.

However, flextime has some real disadvantages, and it may not be a good fit for every organization. For example, flextime cannot be offered for shift work like fast-food or assembly-line processes where everyone works at the same time. Another disadvantage to flextime is that managers often have to work longer days in order to assist and supervise employees. Flextime

Flextime schedules allow employees to set their hours around child-care schedules and other concerns.

also makes communication more difficult; certain employees may not be there when others need to talk to them. Furthermore, if not carefully supervised, some employees could abuse the system, causing resentment among others.

Another popular option, in use by approximately 33 percent of all U.S. companies, is the **compressed workweek**.[40] With compressed workweeks, employees work the full hours of a workweek in fewer than the standard number of days. For example, an employee may work four 10-hour days and then enjoy a three-day weekend instead of working five 8-hour days.[41] There are the obvious advantages of working only four days each week, but some employees get tired of working such long hours, and productivity sometimes declines. Many employees are

Compressed workweek Work schedule that allows an employee to work a full number of hours per week but in fewer days.

enthusiastic about this option and find such a system extremely beneficial. Whole Foods Market, American Fidelity Assurance, Mattel, and eBay are just a few businesses that offer this option.[42]

Telecommuting

Another popular option for scheduling workers and work arrangements is working from home, which also called **telecommuting**. Nearly 10 million U.S. workers now work at least several days per month at home.[43] Some companies that offer employees the option of telecommuting include Google, NuStar Energy, and Quicken Loans.[44] Home-based workers can choose their own hours, interrupt work for child care and other tasks, and take time out for various personal reasons. Working at home is not for everyone, of course. To be successful, a home-based worker must have the self-discipline to stay focused on work and not be easily distracted.

Telecommuting The practice of working from home.

Telecommuting can be a cost saver for employers. For example, a small or medium-sized business may save money on the number of desks it must buy and the amount of office space it must lease. By the end of 2009, it is expected that more than 27 percent of all U.S. workers will be telecommuting.[45]

Job Sharing

Job sharing An arrangement whereby two part-time employees share one full-time job.

Job sharing is an arrangement whereby two part-time employees share one full-time job. Benefits to job sharing include:

- Employment opportunities for those who cannot, or prefer not to, work full time
- An enthusiastic and productive workforce
- Reduced absenteeism and tardiness
  - Ability to schedule more part-time staff for peak demand periods (for example, banks on paydays)
  - Retention of experienced employees who might otherwise have retired

Figure 5.11 The Six Steps of a Performance Appraisal

However, as you might suspect, the disadvantages of job sharing include having to hire, train, motivate, and supervise twice as many people and to prorate some fringe benefits. Nonetheless, many firms that were reluctant to try job sharing have found that the benefits outweigh the disadvantages.[46] Because job sharing can create a better balance of work and life for employees, they are often motivated to give their best efforts to their companies.

APPRAISING EMPLOYEES

Managers must be able to determine whether or not their workers are performing effectively and efficiently with a minimum of errors and disruptions. They do so by using performance appraisals. A **performance appraisal** is an evaluation in which the performance level of employees is measured against established standards to make decisions about promotions, compensation, additional training, or firing. Performance appraisals consist of these six steps (see Figure 5.11):

Performance appraisal An evaluation that measures employee performance against established standards in order to make decisions about promotions, compensation, training, or termination.

1. *Establish performance standards.* This step is crucial. Standards must be understandable, measurable, and reasonable. Both manager and subordinate must accept them.

2. *Communicate those standards.* Managers often assume that employees know what is expected of them, but such assump-

tions are dangerous and usually unwarranted. Employees must be told clearly and precisely what the standards and expectations are and how they are to be met. Managers must also work with employees to establish goals over the next performance appraisal period. If employees have some say in their goals, they will feel more comfortable about meeting them.

3. *Evaluate performance.* If the first two steps are done correctly, performance evaluation is relatively easy. It is a matter of evaluating the employee's behavior to see if it matches the standards.

4. *Discuss results with employees.* Employees often make mistakes and fail to meet expectations at first. It takes time to learn a job and do it well. Discussing an employee's successes and areas that need improvement can provide managers an opportunity to be understanding and helpful and guide the employee to better performance. The performance appraisal can also allow employees to suggest how a task could be done better.

5. *Take corrective action.* As part of the performance appraisal, a manager can take corrective action or provide corrective feedback to help the employee improve his or her job performance. The key word is *performance.* One way to help employees improve is by working with them to develop a **performance improvement plan (PIP)**, a detailed document that explains what the employee needs to change and detailed steps on how to accomplish the change.

Performance improvement plan (PIP) A detailed document explaining what the employee needs to change and detailed steps on how to accomplish the change.

6. *Use the results to make decisions.* Decisions about promotions, compensation, additional training, and firing are all based on performance evaluations. An effective performance appraisal system is a way of satisfying certain legal conditions concerning such decisions.

Effective management helps employees achieve their goals and results in top performance, which is what performance appraisals are for—at all levels of the organization. In the *360-degree review*, management gathers opinions from all around the employee, including those under, above, and on the same level, to get an accurate, comprehensive idea of the worker's abilities.[47]

[BUS] connections

1. Explain the different pay systems. Which of these would you prefer to work under? Why?
2. Describe the six steps of the performance appraisal process.
3. Differentiate between the concepts of flextime and compressed workweek.

>> Laws Affecting HRM

The HR department is responsible for knowing the laws related to the workplace and being sure they are followed in all areas of the HRM process just discussed, as well as throughout the organization. This section will describe some major laws as they apply to employment. Figure 5.12 outlines the major laws affecting HR.

LAWS AND GOVERNMENT PROGRAMS PROTECTING EQUAL OPPORTUNITY

Legislation has complicated hiring, promoting, firing, and managing employee relations in general. Let's see how changes in the law have expanded the role and the challenge of HRM.

Until the 1930s, the U.S. government had little to do with HR decisions. Since then, legislation and legal decisions have greatly affected all areas of HRM, from hiring to training to monitoring working conditions. These laws were passed because many businesses did not exercise fair labor practices voluntarily.

One of the more important pieces of social legislation passed by Congress was the Civil Rights Act of 1964. This act generated much debate and was amended 97 times before final passage. Title VII of that act brought the government directly into the operations of

Title VII prohibits discrimination in hiring, firing, compensation, apprenticeships, training, terms, conditions, or privileges of employment based on race, religion, creed, sex, or national origin. The EEOA, an amendment to Title VII, permitted the EEOC to issue guidelines for acceptable employer conduct in administering equal employment opportunity. Subsequently, the EEOC became a formidable regulatory force in the administration of HRM.

Study Alert !

>> Challenges in HR

In most companies, the HR department is responsible for maintaining good employee relations. Smaller companies may not have an HR department, so many of these challenges will fall to the business owner. Challenges facing HR personnel include issues as controversial as executive compensation and problems as serious as sexual harassment.

WORKING WITH UNIONS

Like other managerial challenges, employee–management relations must be worked out through open discussion, goodwill, and compromise. It is important to know both sides of an issue in order to make reasoned decisions.

Labor unions are a key part of any discussion about employee–management relations in the United States. A **union** is an employee organization that has the main goal of representing members in employee–management bargaining over job-related issues. Workers originally formed unions to protect themselves from intolerable work conditions and unfair treatment. Workers also united in unions to secure some say in the operations of their jobs. Some observers say that the downsides to unions today are their cost to members and a

> **Union** An employee organization that has the main goal of representing members in employee–management bargaining over job-related issues.

LAWS PROTECTING AGING EMPLOYEES

Older employees are also guaranteed protection against discrimination in the workplace. In 2008, the EEOC received 24,415 claims of age discrimination, and $82.8 million was awarded in monetary benefits to charging parties during the same year.[54] Courts have ruled against firms in unlawful-discharge suits where age appeared to be the major factor in a dismissal.

The Age Discrimination in Employment Act of 1967 (ADEA) protects individuals aged 40 or older from employment and workplace discrimination in hiring, firing, promotion, layoff, compensation, benefits, job assignments, and training. The ADEA is enforced by the EEOC, applies to employers with 20 or more employees, and protects both employees and job applicants.[55] It also outlaws mandatory retirement in most organizations. It does, however, allow age restrictions for certain job categories, like airline pilot or bus driver, if evidence shows that the ability to perform significantly diminishes with age.

perceived lack of benefit relative to that cost among members.

Historically, employees turned to unions for help in gaining specific workplace rights and benefits. La-

[BUS] connections

1. Explain the purpose of affirmative action. Do you agree or disagree with this program? Explain your response.
2. What does reasonable accommodation under ADA mean?
3. What does ADEA protect?

Going GLOBAL

Live Abroad and Love It

Modern managers are challenged to operate in an increasingly intricate, interdependent, and dynamic global environment. Those involved in global business have to balance a complicated set of issues related to culture, politics, technology, business practices and global competition. In many cases, relocation is a fact of life. In general, companies must recognize the potential concerns and needs of their employees—particularly when international relocation is a factor—and they must figure out ways to satisfy those needs in order to make the transfer go smoothly.

Herman van Barneveld always wanted to travel. In fact, the 44-year-old vice president of finance at GlaxoSmithKline eagerly told HR at Glaxo's Netherlands office that he would be more than willing to relocate.

The explosion of the global economy means companies are sending more execs abroad for longer periods, rather than merely finding and training new execs within those countries. With this surge of exec expatriates (a GMAC Global Relocation Trends survey reported that 68 percent of multinational companies expected an increased expat population in 2008) comes increased pressure on companies to help employees adjust to new countries. The challenges range from figuring out how to help execs acclimate themselves to vastly different cultures to ensuring stable productivity levels.

Another Glaxo expat, Steve Nechelput, a vice president for finance, relocated from Britain to Mexico in 1996. The company paid for language classes for Nechelput and his wife. After five years in Mexico, Glaxo then set up Nechelput and his family in Philadelphia for a six-year stint.

Glaxo put van Barneveld and his family through a counseling program both before and after the move, with advice on transitioning from one market to another and a daylong workshop prepping the family for the cultural differences and similarities.

Nechelput says the most helpful action the company took was not in the pre-move stages, but rather in providing home leave (which allows the family to return to Britain once a year) and with educational support during these extended tours.

Source. "Live Abroad and Love It," *BusinessWeek*, August 26, 2008, http://www.businessweek.com/managing/content/aug2008/ca20080826_264779.htm (accessed August 10, 2009).

Questions

1. On a scale of one to ten (one being least prepared and ten being most prepared), how prepared do you think you are for a move to another country? List the pluses and minuses of working in a totally different environment and culture, and what sorts of support you'd seek from your employer if such a move were necessary.

2. Do you think an international move would be easier if you made it alone, or with your family? What sorts of support would your family members need from your employer if such a move were necessary?

---

bor unions were largely responsible for the establishment of minimum-wage laws, overtime rules, workers' compensation, severance pay, child-labor laws, job safety regulations, and more.[56] As a consequence, union membership soared in the early and middle part of the past century. Recently, however, union strength has waned.[57] Figure 5.13 shows union membership by state.[58]

Union members from TWU Local 100 picket outside the Jackie Gleason Bus Depot located in the Sunset section of Brooklyn during their strike. What impact does a union strike have on the public?

Figure 5.13 Union Membership by State

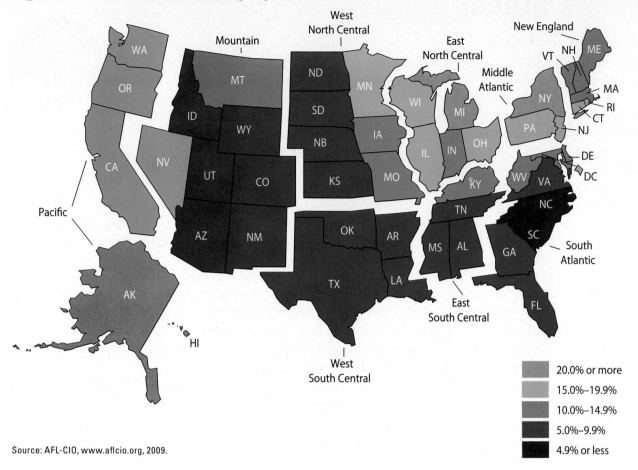

	20.0% or more
	15.0%–19.9%
	10.0%–14.9%
	5.0%–9.9%
	4.9% or less

Source: AFL-CIO, www.aflcio.org, 2009.

Throughout the 1990s and early 2000s, unions continued to lose the power they once had and membership continued to decline, but recently a slight turnaround has occurred. In 2008, 12.4 percent of employed wage and salary workers belonged to unions. This translates into an increase of about 428,000 people since 2007.[59] Business observers suggest that global competition, shifts from manufacturing to service and high-tech industries, growth in part-time work, and changes in management philosophies are among the reasons for labor's decline. Others contend that the decline is related to labor's success in seeing the issues it championed become law.[60]

Negotiation Tactics Used by Unions

Of course, there are some basic HR issues in relation to unions. First, HR departments are generally responsible for overseeing and carrying out the **negotiated labor–management agreement**, more informally referred to as the *labor contract*. This overarching contract sets the tone and clarifies the terms and conditions under which the management and the union will function over a specific period. Negotiations for these contracts cover a wide range of topics and often

take a long time to resolve. Figure 5.14 provides a list of topics commonly negotiated by management and labor during contract talks. Usually, HR departments are involved in these negotiations.

> **Negotiated labor–management agreement** Agreement that sets the tone and clarifies the terms under which management and labor agree to function over a period of time.

A **strike** occurs when workers collectively refuse to go to work. Strikes have been the most potent union tactic. They attract public attention to a labor dispute and can cause operations in a company to slow down or totally cease. Besides refusing to work, strikers may also picket the company, walking around the outside of the location carrying signs and talking with the public

> **Strike** Occurs when workers collectively refuse to go to work.

and the media about the issues in the dispute. Unions also often use picketing as an informational tool before going on strike. The purpose is to alert the public to an issue stirring labor unrest, even though no strike has been voted.

For example, in May 2009, teachers in California's Los Angeles County threatened to go on strike in an effort to get the Los Angeles Unified School District

Figure 5.14 Issues in a Negotiated Labor–Management Agreement

1. **Management rights**
2. **Union recognition**
3. **Union security clause**
4. **Strikes and lockouts**
5. **Union activities and responsibilities**
   a. Dues checkoff
   b. Union bulletin boards
   c. Work slowdowns
6. **Wages**
   a. Wage structure
   b. Shift differentials
   c. Wage incentives
   d. Bonuses
   e. Piecework conditions
   f. Tiered wage structures
7. **Hours of work and time-off policies**
   a. Regular hours of work
   b. Holidays
   c. Vacation policies

   d. Overtime regulations
   e. Leaves of absence
   f. Break periods
   g. Flextime
   h. Mealtime allotments
8. **Job rights and seniority principles**
   a. Seniority regulations
   b. Transfer policies and bumping
   c. Promotions
   d. Layoffs and recall procedures
   e. Job bidding and posting
9. **Discharge and discipline**
   a. Suspension
   b. Conditions for discharge
10. **Grievance procedures**
    a. Arbitration agreement
    b. Mediation procedures
11. **Employee benefits, health, and welfare**

to use economic stimulus money to prevent teacher layoffs during the 2009–2010 school year. However, a judge in the same county prohibited the teachers from doing so on the grounds that the strike violated the terms of the teachers' contract.[61] This ruling didn't stop some of the teachers—several began a hunger strike.[62] The strike lasted a total of 24 days, and the union claims that it prevented more than 500 layoffs.[63]

Unions also use boycotts as a means to obtain their objectives.[64] When a union mounts a **boycott**, it encourages both its members and the general public not to buy the products of a firm involved in a labor dispute. Strikes and boycotts are a last resort when negotiations break down. Management and unions usually agree on labor contracts without such drastic actions being necessary.

When union–management negotiations become difficult, mediation may help. **Mediation** is the use of a third party, called a *mediator,*

> **Boycott** When a union encourages both its members and the general public not to buy the products of a firm involved in a labor dispute.

These members of the International Association of Machinists and Aerospace Workers were among the 27,000 workers who voted to reject a new contract and go on strike against airplane manufacturer Boeing.

Mediation The use of a third party, called a mediator, who encourages both sides in a dispute to continue negotiating and often makes suggestions for resolving the dispute.

who encourages both sides in a dispute to continue negotiating and often makes suggestions for resolving the matter. Keep in mind that mediators evaluate facts in the dispute and then make suggestions, not decisions.[65] Elected officials (current and past), attorneys, and college professors often serve as mediators in labor disputes. The National Mediation Board provides federal mediators when requested in a dispute.[66]

Arbitration, a more extreme option than media-

Arbitration An agreement to bring in an impartial third party (a single arbitrator or a panel of arbitrators) to render a binding decision in a labor dispute.

tion, is used to solve intractable labor disputes.[67] Under arbitration, both parties agree to allow an unbiased third party to make a decision about the disagreement. There are two types of arbitration, binding and nonbinding. In binding arbitration, an impartial third party hears the complaints of both sides and makes a decision that cannot be appealed. In nonbinding arbitration, parties present their case and the arbitrator offers an opinion, but the parties are not required to agree with or follow the opinion.

Negotiation Tactics Used by Management

Like labor, management also uses specific tactics to achieve its goals. A **lockout** is an attempt by managers to put pressure on union workers by temporarily closing the business. When workers don't work, they don't get paid. Today, management rarely uses lockouts to achieve its objectives. However, the high-profile lockout of National Hockey League players that caused the cancellation of the entire 2004–2005 season reminds us this tactic is still viable.[68] Still, management today most often uses injunctions and strikebreakers to counter labor demands it sees as excessive.

An **injunction** is a court order directing someone

Lockout An attempt by managers to put pressure on union workers by temporarily closing the business.

Injunction A court order directing someone to do something or to refrain from doing something.

Strikebreakers Workers hired to do the jobs of striking employees until the labor dispute is resolved.

to do something or to refrain from doing something. Management has sought injunctions to order striking workers back to work, limit the number of pickets during a strike, or otherwise deal with actions that could be detrimental to the public welfare. **Strikebreakers** (called scabs by unions) are workers hired to do the jobs of striking employees

until the labor dispute is resolved. This tactic can help management by continuing production during strikes, but strikebreakers are generally not as well trained as the people they replace, and as a result quality levels can suffer.

EXECUTIVE COMPENSATION

According to *Forbes* magazine, Oracle CEO Larry Ellison was the highest-paid CEO in 2008—to the tune of $556 million.[69] Chapter 2 explained that the U.S. free market system is built on incentives; top executives have a lot of responsibility, and most get a lot of incentive-based compensation in exchange for that responsibility. Today, however, the government, boards of directors, stockholders, unions, and employees are challenging this principle and arguing that executive compensation has gotten out of line.[70] In fact, way out of line. In 2007, CEOs at the 500 largest U.S. firms actually took a pay cut. Still, the average total CEO compensation (salary, bonuses, and incentives) at a major company was $12.8 million, compared to just a bit over $35,000 for the aver-

age worker.[71] Even after adjusting for inflation, this represents an enormous increase from the $160,000 average CEO compensation in 1960. An average worker labors a full year to earn what a highly paid CEO earns in one day. Let's consider why executive compensation can be so high.

In the past, executive compensation and bonuses were generally determined by the firm's profitability or an increase in its stock price.[72] The assumption in using such incentives was that the CEO will improve the performance of the company and raise the price of the firm's stock. Today, however, executives generally receive stock options (the ability to buy company stock at a set price at a later date) and restricted stock (stock issued directly to the CEO that can't be sold usually for three or four years) as part of their compensation. In fact, stock options now account for over 50 percent of a CEO's compensation, and restricted stock makes up almost 25 percent— even when the company does not meet expectations.[73]

CNN reported that Google founders Larry Page and Sergey Brin were paid only $1 per year in 2005 and 2006—something they were easily able to do because much of their compensation comes from stock options.[74] A smaller salary can signal to shareholders and employees that the CEO is committed to the organization, which, in turn, can help motivate employees. The problem with executive compensation is exacerbated and highlighted when highly rewarded

CEOs may not be doing a good job running the company.

Today, government and shareholder pressure for full disclosure of executive compensation puts U.S. boards of directors on notice that they are not there simply to enrich CEOs.[75] The financial crisis of 2008–2009 strengthened shareholders' intentions to propose an overhaul of executive compensation.[76] President Obama and Congress put limits on executive compensation of firms receiving money under the federal government bailout programs.

Most U.S. executives are responsible for multibillion-dollar corporations, work 70-plus hours a week, and often travel. Many have made decisions that turned potential problems into successes and reaped huge compensation for employees and stockholders as well as themselves. Furthermore, there are few seasoned, skilled professionals who can manage large companies, especially troubled companies looking for the right CEO to accomplish a turnaround. There's no easy answer to the question of what is fair compensation for executives, but it's a safe bet the controversy will not go away.[77]

WORK–LIFE BALANCE

One of the recent concerns of HR managers is the need for a good work–life balance. Many workers, particularly those from Generation Y, are looking to effectively manage their professional and personal lives. This new generation favors teamwork and fears boredom.[78] Expectations are high in most companies, and many individuals feel they must work many hours in order to meet these expectations. Of course, long hours interrupt employees' personal lives, create more stress, and lower the quality of work.

HR professionals are constantly trying to find ways to help employees balance their lives in terms of work requirements and home responsibilities while still maintaining high performance levels in both areas. A good balance of work and personal life raises performance on the job.

COMPARABLE WORTH

A recent controversial HR issue is that of pay equity, or *comparable worth*, between women and men. **Comparable worth** is the concept that people in jobs that require similar levels of education, training, or skills should receive equal pay. This somewhat thorny issue is more important now than ever before, as today women

> **Comparable worth** The idea that people in jobs requiring similar levels of education, training, or skills should receive equal pay.

are a sizable and permanent part of the labor force. In 1890, for example, women made up only 15 percent of the labor force; as of November 2008, this percentage had increased to 49.1 percent. Because a disproportionate number of the jobs lost in the 2008–2009 recession belonged to men, many believe women will soon outnumber men in the labor force.[79]

Comparable worth goes beyond the concept of equal pay for equal work. Federal and state equal-pay laws have been in effect for many years. For example, the Equal Pay Act of 1963 requires companies to give equal pay to men and women who do the same job. Put simply, it's against the law to pay a female nurse less than a male nurse, unless factors such as seniority, merit pay, or performance incentives are involved.

The issue of comparable worth, however, really centers on comparing the value of different jobs; for instance, bank tellers or librarians (traditionally women's jobs) compared with truck drivers or plumbers (traditionally men's jobs). Such a comparison shows that "women's" jobs tend to pay less—sometimes much less.

In the United States in 2007, women earned approximately 81 percent of what men earned, though

the disparity varied considerably by profession, job experience and tenure, and level of education.[80] In the past, the primary explanation for this disparity was that women worked only 50 to 60 percent of their available years once they left school (experience and tenure), whereas men, on the whole, worked all of those years. This explanation is much less valid today because fewer women leave the workforce for an extended time. Other explanations suggest that many women devote more time to their families than men do and thus accept lower-paying jobs with more flexible hours.

Today women appear to be competing financially with men in fields such as health care, biotechnology, knowledge technology, and other knowledge-based jobs. Studies at the University of Michigan found that earnings of women with baccalaureate degrees were 96 percent of men's. Still, Heather Boushey, an economist at the Economic Policy Institute, and other critics claim women—especially women with children—still earn less, are less likely to go into business, and are more likely to live in poverty than men.[81] There is no question that pay equity promises to remain a challenging employee–management issue, and HR managers must be aware of the issues involved.

SEXUAL HARASSMENT

Sexual harassment refers to unwelcome sexual advances, requests for sexual favors, and other conduct (verbal or physical) of a sexual nature that creates a hostile work environment. Conduct on the job can be considered illegal under specific conditions:[82]

> **Sexual harassment** Unwelcome sexual advances, requests for sexual favors, and other verbal or physical conduct of a sexual nature that creates a hostile work environment.

- The employee's submission to such conduct is explicitly or implicitly made a term or condition of employment, or an employee's submission to or re-

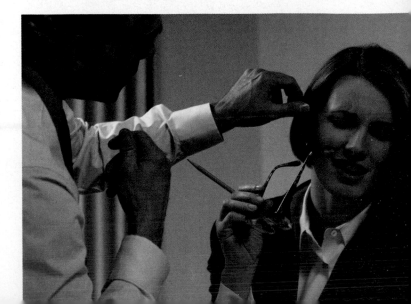

Real World Apps

Reading her textbook helped Laurie better understand the intricacies of modern HRM. Now, she knows that in order to be competitive, a company must integrate the strategic planning of an HR department into its overall objectives.

"In Fulbright's personnel department, we hired them and fired them, and that was pretty much it!" Laurie remembers. Modern HR departments are much more sophisticated; their work includes developing pay and benefit systems and training employees in order to increase retention of knowledgeable employees—thus making everyone more productive.

Because the legal landscape of employment practices has changed so dramatically, HR departments are now responsible for strictly overseeing compliance issues and developing and enforcing policies. The growing diversity of the labor pool has also added to the challenge. Recruiting and retaining the most qualified employees are ongoing struggles for many companies in an increasingly competitive marketplace.

After reading her text and discussing the material with her class, Laurie is happy she chose to further her education. She now understands that the skills she sharpened while working in Fulbright's personnel department were not the same as those necessary in a modern HR department. She's now on the path to starting a new career in HR.

Study Alert

Challenges facing HR personnel include working with unions (including understanding the negotiation tactics used by unions and management alike when creating labor contracts), addressing the controversial issue of executive compensation fairly for all parties, helping employees maintain a good work–life balance, ensuring that pay equity exists between men and women in the workforce, and preventing sexual harassment.

jection of such conduct is used as the basis for employment decisions affecting the worker's status. A threat like "Go out with me or you're fired" or "Go out with me or you'll never be promoted here" constitutes quid pro quo sexual harassment.

- The conduct unreasonably interferes with a worker's job performance or creates an intimidating, hostile, or offensive work environment. This type of harassment is hostile work environment sexual harassment.

The Civil Rights Act of 1991 governs sexual harassment of both men and women.[83] This fact was reinforced in 1997, when the Supreme Court said same-sex harassment also falls within the purview of sexual harassment law. The number of sexual harassment complaints filed annually with the EEOC grew from 6,000 in 1990 to over 16,000 in 2000. The number of charges seems to be declining since 2000, dropping to about 14,000 charges in 2008.[84] Sexual harassment cases cost a "typical Fortune 500 company $6.7 million per year in absenteeism, low productivity, and employee turnover."[85]

Companies have found that the courts mean business if they violate sexual harassment laws. Madison Square Garden lost a judgment of $11.6 million to a former executive who sued New York Knicks' basketball coach Isiah Thomas for sexual harassment.[86]

Some HR managers hold mandatory sexual harassment seminars for employees to bring awareness about this workplace issue. Many HR departments have set up rapid, effective grievance procedures and react promptly to allegations of harassment. Such efforts may save businesses millions of dollars in lawsuits and make the workplace more productive and harmonious.

[BUS] connections

1. Do you think unions are useful? Do you agree with their purpose?
2. Discuss two of the other HR challenges presented in this section. If you were an HR manager, which do you think would be most interesting to you? Which would be the most challenging? Explain your responses.
3. If you witnessed what you believed was an incident of sexual harassment involving two of your coworkers on the job, would you report the incident to HR? If not, what would you do? Detail the steps you would take.

For REVIEW >>

1. Describe the human resource management (HRM) process.
   - HRM is the process of determining HR needs and then recruiting, selecting, training and developing, compensating, evaluating, and scheduling employees to achieve organizational goals. Today, HRM is considered to be a vital strategic partner in the long-term survival and growth of an organization, and HR departments have broad responsibilities.

2. Understand how human resource (HR) managers determine needs and recruit and select employees.
   - The HR planning process is broken down into five steps: (1) Prepare an HR inventory of the organization's employees; (2) prepare a job analysis for each of the jobs in the organization; (3) assess future HR demand; (4) assess future HR supply; and (5) establish an HR strategic plan. Recruitment is the set of activities used to obtain a sufficient number of the right people at the right time; its purpose is to select those who best meet the needs of the organization. Recruiting sources are classified as either internal or external. The selection process is broken down into six steps: (1) Obtain complete application forms, (2) conduct initial and follow-up interviews, (3) give employment tests, (4) conduct background investigations, (5) obtain results from physical exams, and (6) establish trial (probationary) periods.

3. Illustrate the various types of employee training and development methods.
   - Training and development include all attempts to improve productivity by increasing an employee's ability to perform. *Training* focuses on short-term skills, whereas *development* focuses on long-term abilities. Both include three steps: (1) assessing organization needs and employee skills to determine training needs, (2) designing training activities to meet identified needs, and (3) evaluating the training's effectiveness. Training activities include employee orientation, on- and off-the-job training, apprentice programs, online training, vestibule training, and job simulation. Management development is the process of training and educating employees to become good managers, and then monitoring the progress of their managerial skills over time. Management development programs have sprung up everywhere, especially at colleges, universities, and private management development firms and corporations.

4. Describe different types of pay systems and how to evaluate employees.
   - Compensation is the combination of salary, vacation time, paid health care, and other benefits. A carefully managed compensation and benefit program can accomplish several objectives: (1) Attract the people the organization needs in sufficient numbers, (2) provide employees with an incentive to work efficiently and productively, (3) keep valued employees from going to competitors or starting competing firms, (4) maintain a competitive position in the marketplace and keeping costs low via high productivity from a satisfied workforce, and (5) provide employees with a sense of financial security via insurance and retirement benefits. Salary, hourly wage or daywork, piecework, commission plans, bonus plans, profit-sharing plans, gain-sharing plans, and stock options are all forms of pay systems. Many employees find scheduling flexibility options, such as flextime, in-home employment, and job sharing, as desirable as more traditional benefit options. A performance appraisal is an evaluation in which the performance level of employees is measured against established standards to make decisions about promotions, compensation, additional training, or firing.

5. Understand important laws affecting the workplace.
   - The HR department is responsible for knowing the laws related to the workplace and being sure they are followed in all areas of the HRM process. Title VII prohibits discrimination in hiring, firing, compensation, apprenticeships, training, terms, conditions, or privileges of employment based on race, religion, creed, sex, or national origin. The EEOA, an amendment to Title VII, permitted the EEOC to issue guidelines for acceptable employer conduct in administering equal employment opportunity. Subsequently, the EEOC became a formidable regulatory force in the administration of HRM. The ADA requires employers to give applicants with physical or mental disabilities the same consideration for employment as people without disabilities, and it requires them to make reasonable accommodations for the disabled as well. The Age Discrimination in Employment Act of 1967 (ADEA) protects individuals aged 40 or older from employment and workplace discrimination in hiring, firing, promotion, layoff, compensation, benefits, job assignments, and training.

6. Describe the key challenges facing HR managers today.
   - Challenges facing HR personnel include working with unions (including understanding the negotiation tactics used by unions and management alike when creating labor contracts), addressing the controversial issue of executive compensation fairly for all parties, helping employees maintain a good work–life balance, ensuring that pay equity exists between men and women in the workforce, and preventing sexual harassment.

Key Terms

Affirmative action

Arbitration

Boycott

Cafeteria-style fringe benefits

Comparable worth

Compensation

Compressed workweek

Congress of Industrial Organizations (CIO)

Contingent workers

Core time

Employee orientation

External candidates

Flextime plan

Human resource management (HRM)

Injunction

Internal candidates

Job analysis

Job description

Job sharing

Job simulation

Job specifications

Labor intensive

Lockout

Management development

Mediation

Negotiated labor–management agreement

Off-the-job training

Online training

On-the-job training

Performance appraisal

Performance improvement plan (PIP)

Reasonable accommodations

Recruitment

Reverse discrimination

Selection

Sexual harassment

Strike

Strikebreakers

Telecommuting

Title VII

Training and development

Union

Vestibule training

1. What might be the best types of training for the following jobs, and why?

   a. Cashier at 7-11

   b. Retail shoe store salesperson

   c. Office manager

   d. Electrician

   e. Airline pilot

   f. Ultrasound technician

   g. Management trainee for Walgreens

2. Are the following situations considered sexual harassment? Why or why not? Discuss what you might do in each situation.

   a. Your boss says to you, "I want to give you a raise, but only if you will go out with me."

   b. Your coworker has a calendar featuring suggestive photos of men hanging up in her cubicle.

   c. Your coworker keeps asking you out despite the fact that you've said you weren't interested a number of times.

   d. During lunch in your company break room, you overhear a group of your coworkers telling inappropriate jokes that you find offensive.

   e. A coworker tells you she likes your new haircut.

   f. You're frequently asked out by customers at the coffee shop where you work.

3. In groups, come up with three questions that would be appropriate to ask in a job interview. Next, come up with answers for each question.

4. What do you think is the most important part of the human resource process? Why?

5. Have you ever received a performance appraisal? Was it formal or informal? What components were included in the appraisal? Were you satisfied by the results? Was a performance plan part of the process?

6. What are the advantages and disadvantages of unions? In small groups, discuss at least five for each. Next, compile and discuss your lists with other groups.

1. Visit http://www.1st-writer.com/interview-questions-1.htm and take the site's interviewing quiz.
   a. What was your score?
   b. What are some strategies you could use to improve your interviewing ability?
2. Visit http://www.opm.gov/oca/fmla/ and read about the Family and Medical Leave Act (FMLA) of 1993.
   a. Discuss some of the revisions that have been made in FMLA in recent years.
   b. What are some benefits, above and beyond FMLA, that a company might offer to employees?
3. Visit http://www.affirmativeaction.org/about.html and read about affirmative action.
   a. What is the mission of this organization?
   b. What is the purpose of affirmative action?
   c. Do you agree or disagree with the concept of affirmative action? Why or why not?

Self-Assessment Exercises

BUSINESS CAREER QUIZ

Which Business Emphasis Should You Choose?

This chapter discussed how HR is responsible for interviewing and selecting employees. Test your interviewing skills with this short quiz:

1. Which of the following is *not* one of the suggested strategies for preparing for a job interview:
   a. Research the company/industry
   b. Prepare answers to possible interview questions
   c. Gather key resources (extra résumés, reference list) to take with you
   d. Plan to ask about salary and benefits at the beginning of the interview

2. True or false: Wearing a formal suit is always the safest "dress-for-success" attire.
   a. True   b. False

3. True or false: Being the most qualified candidate for the position just about guarantees you will get the job.
   a. True   b. False

4. True or false: Greeting the receptionist/assistant when you arrive and treating him or her with respect is an important key to success.
   a. True   b. False

5. Which is the most important part of the interview?
   a. The first minute
   b. Your answers to the toughest questions
   c. The final minute
   d. The entire interview

6. What are the **most** important keys to success in interviews?
   a. Good cologne and a nice smile
   b. Making eye contact, showing enthusiasm, and speaking clearly
   c. Fresh breath, a nice smile, and making eye contact
   d. Developing a rapport, good posture, and fresh breath

7. How early should you arrive for an interview?
   a. 1 hour   c. 10 minutes
   b. 30 minutes   d. 1 minute

8. True or false: You should use only examples from your actual work experience to answer a question during a job interview.
   a. True   b. False

9. The best thing to do in an interview when you get a question that temporarily stumps you is:
   a. Stare at the interviewer.
   b. Keep saying, "Good question, good question."
   c. Respond with, "I just really can't answer that."
   d. Paraphrase the question while giving yourself time to think.

10. True or false: Taking detailed notes in an interview is an accepted practice.
   a. True   b. False

Answers:
1. D. Discussing salary at a first interview is not recommended.
2. B. You should research what the employees wear, and dress one step up from that.
3. B. There are other factors, such as company fit and culture, that may determine whether you get hired.
4. A. Treating everyone with respect is an important key to success.
5. D. It is important to stay focused during the entire length of the interview.
6. B. While of course you want to have fresh (or neutral) breath, showing enthusiasm goes a long way in getting a job.
7. C. Always leave lots of time to get to an interview. Even if you have to wait outside the building for a little while, being early is always better than being late!
8. B. You can use work examples from school, clubs, and organizations, too.

9. D. You may feel temporarily stumped, but paraphrasing the question allows most people to come up with a good answer.
10. A. Taking notes is a good idea in an interview. They may be helpful to you later, and they show that you're interested in the job.

Scoring:
Number of questions you answered correctly:
9-10: You're in great shape and should do well in job interviews.
7-8: You're in good shape, but you need to polish some of your interviewing tactics.
5-6: You really need to work on your interviewing skills and better understand the job interviewing process.
4 or less: You need to spend a lot of time learning about the interviewing process. Don't worry, because there are many resources to help you. Do a Google search for "job interviewing tips" to access the most up-to-date information.

Source: Randall Hansen, "Quintessential Job Interviewing Quiz," www.randallhansen.com, accessed June 25, 2009.

Your Preferred Work Style

When considering job opportunities, it's important to find a company and a job that matches your preferred work style. This chapter discussed work–life balance and flexible work hours. Take the following quiz to determine your preferred work style in terms of the jobs' work-hour flexibility.

Rank each item on a scale of 1 to 5, where 1 = Strongly Disagree and 5 = Strongly Agree.

Strongly Agree	Somewhat Agree		Strongly Disagree	
5	4	3	2	1

1. _____ I like having flexibility in having lunches earlier or later.
2. _____ I prefer to not work a set schedule.
3. _____ I'm not a morning person, so I would prefer to start work later in the morning.
4. _____ I don't care about having "face time" at work.
5. _____ I don't want to worry about my job outside of work.
6. _____ I want to feel like my boss trusts me to get the job done, even if he or she doesn't see me in the office.
7. _____ I prefer to be at work earlier so I can leave earlier in the afternoon.
8. _____ I can be productive when working from home.
9. _____ Giving me additional vacation time or days off are a good way to motivate me.
10. _____ My mantra is, "if it doesn't get done today, it will still be there tomorrow."

Your scores:
50-40   You would be happiest in a job that allows flexible work hours. Work–life balance is important to you.
39-30   While you lean toward a flexible work style, you would be fine having a job with a more rigid schedule.
29-20   You lean toward preferring a set schedule of working hours.
19-0   You don't care much about flexibility at all. In fact, your preferred work style is a more rigid approach.

- Why is operations management important?
- How can businesses improve productivity, and what can these improvements do for them?
- What can a world-class standard do for a business?

>> Production, Production Management, and Operations Management

PRODUCTION AND PRODUCTION MANAGEMENT

Production is the creation of *goods* using land, labor, capital, entrepreneurship, and knowledge, which are called the factors of production. Production has historically meant *manufacturing*, and the term **production management** has described the management activities that helped firms create goods. But, as you learned in Chapter 1, the nature of business has changed significantly in the last 20 years. During this period of time, the service sector, including Internet services, has grown dramatically. *The United States has become a service economy—that is, one dominated by the service sector.*

> **Production** The creation of finished goods and services using the factors of production: land, labor, capital, entrepreneurship, and knowledge.

> **Production management** The term used to describe all the activities managers do to help their firms create goods.

Operations management in a hospital assembles inputs including doctors, nurses, specialized medical equipment, patients, and computers to create services to treat the sick and injured through a process called health care.

OPERATIONS MANAGEMENT

Operations management is a specialized area in management that converts or transforms resources, including human resources like technical skills and innovation, into goods *and* services. It includes inventory management, quality control, production scheduling, follow-up services, and more. In a clothing factory, operations management transforms raw materials, human resources, fabric, supplies, thread, and other resources into pants, shirts, skirts, and dresses. It does this through the processes of fabrication and assembly.

> **Operations management** A specialized area in management that converts or transforms resources (including human resources) into goods and services.

In a college or university, operations management takes inputs such as information, professors, supplies, buildings, offices, and computer systems and creates services that transform students into educated people. It does this through a process called education.

Some organizations—such as factories, farms, and mines—produce mostly goods. Others—such as schools, consulting firms, and government agencies—produce mostly services. Still others produce a combination of goods and services.[1] For example, some automobile manufacturers not only make cars but also provide services, such as repairs, financing, and insurance. At Dunkin' Donuts, you get goods like doughnuts and coffee, but you also get services, such as order taking, order filling, food preparation, and cleanup.

OPERATIONS MANAGEMENT IN THE SERVICE SECTOR

Operations management in the service industry is all about creating a good experience for those who use the service.[2] In a Ritz-Carlton hotel, for example, operations management includes restaurants that offer the finest in service, elevators that run smoothly, and a front desk that processes guests quickly. It may include fresh-cut flowers in the lobbies and dishes of fruit in every room. More important, it may mean spending thousands of dollars to provide training in quality management for every new employee.[3]

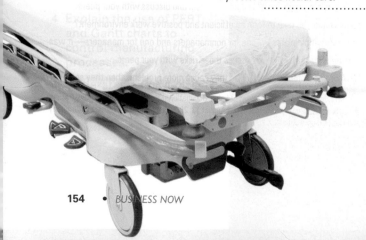

Operations management for services is all about enriching the customer experience. Hotels, for instance, have responded to the needs of business travelers with in-room Internet access and other kinds of office-style support, as well as stored information about the preferences of frequent guests.

Ritz-Carlton's commitment to quality is apparent in the many innovations and changes that were initiated over the years. These innovations included installation of a sophisticated, computerized guest-recognition program and a quality management program designed to ensure that all employees are "certified" in their positions.

Hotel customers today want in-room Internet access and a help center with toll-free telephone service. Executives traveling on business may need video equipment and a host of computer hardware and other aids. Foreign visitors would like multilingual customer support services. Hotel shops need to carry more than souvenirs, newspapers, and some drug store and food items to serve today's high-tech travelers. The shops may also carry laptop computer supplies, electrical adapters, and the like. Operations management is responsible for locating and providing such amenities to make customers happy. Ritz-Carlton uses an internal measurement system to assess the performance results of its service delivery system.

In short, delighting customers by anticipating their needs has become the quality standard for luxury hotels, as it has for most other service businesses. But knowing customer needs and satisfying them are two different things.[4]

ETHICAL DILEMMA

If you have too much to do and too little training, what are your options for keeping customers happy?

[BUS] connections

1. What have U.S. manufacturers done to regain a competitive edge?
2. How is operations management in the service sector different from operations management in the manufacturing sector?
3. What led companies to focus on operations management rather than production?

That's why operations management is so important: It is the implementation phase of management. Can you see the need for better operations management in airports, hospitals, government agencies, schools, and nonprofits like the Red Cross? The opportunities seem almost unlimited. Much of the future of U.S. growth is in these service areas, but growth is also needed in manufacturing. Next we'll explore production processes and what companies are doing to keep the United States competitive in that area.

>> Advances in Production Techniques

PRODUCTION PROCESSES

Common sense and some experience have already taught you much of what you need to know about production processes. You know what it takes to write a term paper or prepare a dinner. You need money to buy the materials, you need a place to work, and you need to be organized to get the task done. The same is true of the production process in industry. It uses basic inputs to produce outputs (see Figure 6.1). *Production* adds value, or utility, to materials or processes.

The production process consists of taking the factors of production (such

Figure 6.1 The Production Process

INPUTS	PRODUCTION CONTROL	OUTPUTS
Land	Planning	Goods
Labor	Routing	Services
Capital	Scheduling	Ideas
Entrepreneurship	Dispatching	
Knowledge	Follow-up	

as land) and using those inputs to produce goods, services, and ideas. Planning, routing, scheduling, and other activities are the means to accomplish the objective—output.

Form utility is the value producers add to materials in the creation of finished goods and services, such as transforming silicon into computer chips or putting services together to create a vacation package. Form utility can exist at the retail level as well. For example, a butcher can produce a specific cut of beef from a whole cow, or a baker can make a specific type of cake from basic ingredients.

> **Form utility** The value producers add to materials in the creation of finished goods and services.

Manufacturers use several different processes to produce goods. Andrew S. Grove, the former chairman of computer chip manufacturer Intel, uses this analogy to explain production:

> Imagine you're a chef . . . and your task is to serve a breakfast consisting of a three-minute soft-boiled egg, buttered toast, and coffee. Your job is to prepare and deliver the three items simultaneously, each of them fresh and hot.

Grove says this task encompasses the three basic requirements of production: (1) to build and deliver products in response to the demands of the customer at a scheduled delivery time, (2) to provide an acceptable quality level, and (3) to provide everything at the lowest possible cost.

Let's use the breakfast example to understand process and assembly. **Process manufacturing** physically or chemically changes materials. For example, boiling physically changes the egg. Similarly, process manufacturing turns sand into glass or computer chips. The **assembly process** puts together components (eggs, toast, and coffee) to make a product (breakfast). Cars are made through an assembly process that puts together the frame, engine, and other parts.

> **Process manufacturing** The part of the production process that physically or chemically changes materials.
>
> **Assembly process** The part of the production process that puts together components.

Production processes are either continuous or intermittent. A **continuous process** is one in which long production runs turn out finished goods over time. As a chef, you could have a conveyor belt that continuously lowers eggs into boiling water for three minutes and then lifts them out on a continuous basis. A three-minute egg would be available whenever you wanted one. (A chemical plant, for example, runs on a continuous process.)

> **Continuous process** A production process in which long production runs turn out finished goods over time.

It usually makes more sense when responding to specific customer orders to use an **intermittent process**. Here the production run is short (for example, one or two eggs) and the producer adjusts machines frequently to make different products (like the oven in a bakery or the toaster in the diner). (Manufacturers of custom-designed furniture would use intermittent processes.)

> **Intermittent process** A production process in which the production run is short and the machines are changed frequently to make different products.

Today many manufacturers use intermittent processes. Computers, robots, and flexible manufacturing processes allow firms to turn out custom-made goods almost as fast as mass-produced goods were once produced. We'll discuss how they do that in more detail in the next few sections as we explore advanced production techniques and technology.

The ultimate goal of operations management is to provide high-quality goods and services instantaneously in response to customer demand. Traditionally, organizations were not designed to be this responsive to customer needs. Rather, they were designed to make goods efficiently and inexpensively.

Today's major automobile assembly plants are set up as continuous-process operations to mass-produce goods. How many cars do you think a major auto plant is likely to produce each month?

The idea behind mass production was to make a large number of a limited variety of products at very low cost.

Over the years, low cost often came at the expense of quality and flexibility. Suppliers didn't always deliver when they said they would, so manufacturers had to carry large inventories of raw materials and components to keep producing. Such inefficiencies made U.S. companies vulnerable to foreign competitors who were using more advanced production techniques.

As a result of new global competition, companies have had to make a wide variety of high-quality,

Production lines allow for the efficient and speedy production of goods that are consistent in size, weight, color, and other measures of quality.

custom-designed products at very low cost. Clearly, things on the production floor had to change in order to make that possible.

The Japanese electronics maker Sharp has plans to build factories in China, Southeast Asia, Europe, and North America. This effort is an attempt to cut costs and compete with others in its industry. Sharp prides itself on its means of production; its president, Mikio Katayama, remarked, "Our core technology isn't making LCD [liquid crystal display] panels and it isn't making LCD TVs. It's production technology."[5]

Several major developments have made companies more competitive: (1) computer-aided design and manufacturing, (2) flexible manufacturing, (3) lean manufacturing, and (4) mass customization.

COMPUTER-AIDED DESIGN AND MANUFACTURING

The one development that has changed production techniques more than any other is the integration of computers into the design and manufacturing of products. The first thing computers did was help in the design of products, in a process called **computer-aided design (CAD)**. Today CAD systems allow designers to work in three dimensions.

Computer-aided design (CAD) The use of computers in the design of products.

The next step was to bring computers directly into the production process with **computer-aided manufacturing (CAM).** CAD/CAM, the use of both computer-aided design and computer-aided manufacturing, makes it possible to custom-design products to

Computer-aided manufacturing (CAM) The use of computers in the manufacturing of products.

meet the needs of small markets with very little increase in cost. A manufacturer programs the comput-

Real World Apps

STAYING COMPETITIVE

Jerry Sui, who owns a small manufacturing company, is concerned about staying competitive in today's global marketplace. In order to do so, he decided to return to college to earn a degree in business 25 years after graduating from high school. Jerry's Introduction to Business class is about to tackle the topic of production and operations management.

Jerry thinks, "Now there's something I'm really interested in." Jerry has many questions about what he can do to streamline his company's operations; in fact, the machinery and processes at his company are the same that he's been using for more than two decades. In the past, Jerry always believed that if something isn't broken, it shouldn't be fixed, but he can't help but notice that his competitors have been consistently outperforming him.

Jerry settles in for his reading assignment from his Business Now textbook before class. He thinks, "Maybe I can learn something new—something that will help me compete with the youngsters!"

er to make a simple design change, and that change is readily incorporated into production. In the clothing industry, a computer program establishes a pattern and cuts the cloth automatically, even adjusting to a specific person's dimensions to create custom-cut clothing at little additional cost. In food service, CAM supports on-site, small-scale, semiautomated, sensor-controlled baking in fresh-baked cookie shops to make consistent quality easy to achieve.

Bob Montgomery, a former professional surfer and construction foreman, had the groundbreaking idea of creating a motorized surfboard. While designing his product, he encountered a few bumps in the road; eventually, he turned to CAM to help him smooth out the problems. The software allowed Montgomery and his team of engineers to design everything on the "jet boards," as he calls them. Since he integrated CAD technology into his production process, Montgomery's surfboard has been introduced in the United States and 35 other countries.[6]

CAD has doubled productivity in many firms. But in the past, CAD machines couldn't communicate with CAM machines directly. Today, however, software programs unite CAD and CAM: the result is **computer-integrated manufacturing (CIM)**. The software is expensive, but it cuts as much as 80 percent of the time needed to program machines to make parts. Johns-Byrne, a printing company, uses CIM in its plant in Niles, Illinois. The company has noticed decreased overhead, reduced outlay of resources, and fewer errors. IBM also uses CIM in a semiconductor facility.

> **Computer-integrated manufacturing (CIM)** The uniting of computer-aided design with computer-aided manufacturing.

FLEXIBLE MANUFACTURING

Flexible manufacturing means designing machines to do multiple tasks so they can produce a variety of products. Allen-Bradley, part of Rockwell Automation, uses flexible manufacturing to build motor starters. Orders come in daily, and within 24 hours, the company's 26 machines and robots manufacture, test, and package the starters—which are untouched by human hands. Allen-Bradley's machines are so flexible that managers can include a special order, even a single item, in the assembly without slowing down the process. Did you notice that these products were made without any labor? One way to compete

> **Flexible manufacturing** Designing machines to do multiple tasks so that they can produce a variety of products.

with cheap overseas labor is to have as few workers as possible.

When you decide to purchase a car, there are many options to think about. For example, you can choose the car's interior and exterior color, audio equipment, or upholstery fabric. BMW realizes that its customers often change their minds, so the company uses a flexible manufacturing system to ensure that customer preferences specified when the car was ordered can be easily changed—as late as only six days before production begins.[7]

3-D CAD tools allow designers to create cloth prototypes without a pattern's traditional stages—seaming, trying on, alterations, and so on.

LEAN MANUFACTURING

Lean manufacturing is the production of goods using less of everything than is used in mass production: less human effort, less manufacturing space, less investment in tools, and less engineering time to develop a new product. A company becomes lean by continuously increasing its capacity to produce high-quality goods while decreasing its need for resources.[8] Here are some characteristics of lean companies:[9]

> **Lean manufacturing** The production of goods using less of everything compared to mass production.

- They take half the human effort.[10]
- They have half the defects in the finished product or service.
- They require one-third of the engineering effort.
- They use half the floor space for the same output.
- They carry 90 percent less inventory.

Technological improvements are largely responsible for the increase in productivity and efficiency of U.S. plants. That technology made labor more productive and made it possible to pay higher wages. On the other hand, employees can get frustrated by innovations (e.g., they must learn new processes), and companies must constantly train and retrain employees to stay competitive.[11] The need for more productivity and efficiency has never been greater. The solution to the economic crisis depends on such innovations. One step in the process is to make products more individualistic. The next section discusses how that happens.

MASS CUSTOMIZATION

To *customize* means to make a unique product or provide a specific service to specific individuals.[12]

> **Mass customization**
> Tailoring products to meet the needs of individual customers.

Although it once may have seemed impossible, **mass customization**, which means tailoring products to meet the needs of a large number of individual customers, is now practiced widely.[13] See Figure 6.2 for some examples of mass customization at work.

More and more manufacturers are learning to customize their products. Some colleges are developing products for individual students.[14] Some General Nutrition Center (GNC) stores feature machines that enable shoppers to custom-design their own vitamins, shampoo, and lotions. The Custom Foot stores use infrared scanners to precisely measure each foot so shoes can be made to fit perfectly. Adidas can make each shoe fit perfectly for each customer. InterActive Custom Clothes offers a wide variety of options in custom-made jeans, including four different rivet colors. You can even buy custom-made M&Ms in your choice of colors.

Nike offers customized shoes, and Kleenex customers can create their own tissue boxes. Joe Pine, a management adviser and author of the book *Mass Customization*, has remarked, "We're training people to getting used to getting ex-

actly what they want. That creates a snowball effect and they're going to start demanding it from other companies."[15]

Mass customization exists in the service sector as well. Capital Protective Insurance uses the latest

Figure 6.2 Mass Customization at Work

Company	Mass Customization Approach
Dell Computer (computer manufacturer)	Dell Computer was an early leader in providing build-your-own computers to customers, but in April 2008, the company announced it would cut back on its customization options, expand its line of prepackaged models, and have other companies build more of its products.
ChemStation (soap manufacturer)	ChemStation customizes liquid soap products to customers' exact specifications. Its system analyzes customers' use patterns and ships new batches of soap automatically when it determines the customer needs more—removing the need for the customer to order the soap.

Sources: "Dell to Cut Back Customizing of Its PCs," *Los Angeles Times*, April 3, 2008, http://articles. latimes.com/2008/apr/03/business/fi-dell3 (accessed August 12, 2009); and Connie Mok, Alan Stutts, and Lillian Wong, "Mass Customization in the Hospitality Industry: Concepts and Applications," Hotel-Online.com, http://www.hotel-online.com/Trends/ChiangMaiJun00/CustomizationHospitality.html (accessed August 3, 2009).

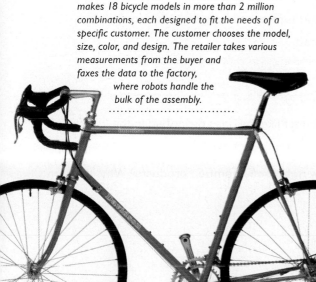

The National Bicycle Industrial Company in Japan makes 18 bicycle models in more than 2 million combinations, each designed to fit the needs of a specific customer. The customer chooses the model, size, color, and design. The retailer takes various measurements from the buyer and faxes the data to the factory, where robots handle the bulk of the assembly.

Thinking Critically

In the 1990s, a few companies offered custom-fitted clothing, where jeans or footwear were tailored to fit consumers via a mass-customization process. Interest in these products was limited at the time, but recent innovations in mass-customization technology and flexible manufacturing have made the processes more affordable, and today's more individualistic consumer base is more interested in customized clothing, jewelry, and other products.

In the early 1990s, an entrepreneur named Sung Park started a company called Custom Clothing Technology Corp. to sell software that would enable apparel companies to take your measurements and crank out a perfectly fitting bathing suit, bra, pair of pants, or shoes. It seemed like the concept of mass customization, long touted by consultants and academics, was ready for its moment in the spotlight.

But while Levi Strauss for a time used the technology to sell "Personal Pair" jeans in its retail stores, the mass customization wave never seemed to reach the shore. Today, most Americans still buy mass-produced, off-the-shelf products. A growing group of Boston area start-ups, however, are taking another crack at customized apparel and accessories. Offering business suits, engagement rings, or a pair of stiletto heels, these entrepreneurs believe that consumers have become more comfortable with e-commerce over the past decade and a half, and more desirous of unique products. Offshore factories have also developed the flexibility necessary to produce one-of-a-kind items.

"All of the planets are starting to align," says Park. Some of the executives running local customization companies say they hope to benefit from a cultural shift. "When I grew up, in the 1970s, we all wore our hair the same way and we wore the same clothes," says Deb Bessemer, chief executive of Lexington-based Paragon Lake Inc., which works with jewelry stores to let customers design their own baubles. "But the new generation of people in their 20s is more individualistic. They don't want the same ring or pair of earrings that their friends also have."

Many of the big companies that were part of the first wave of mass customization in the 1990s, like Nike and Levi Strauss, are inherently more comfortable with the scale, costs, and logistics of mass production. It could be that this new cluster of start-ups—companies that will either live or die based on whether they can profitably do mass customization, and turn consumers on to it—could have a much bigger impact on the way we buy over the years ahead.

Source: Adapted from Scott Kirsner, "The Custom Touch," *Boston Globe*, August 2, 2009, http://www.boston.com/business/articles/2009/08/02/mass_start_ups_take_another_run_at_custom_made_apparel/ (accessed August 12, 2009).

QUESTIONS

1. As a consumer, would you consider buying a customized product like the ones described in the article? Why or why not?

2. Do you agree with Sung Park's assertion that the time is now right for customized products? Why or why not?

computer software and hardware to sell customized risk-management plans to companies. Health clubs offer unique fitness programs for individuals, travel agencies provide vacation packages that vary according to individual choices, and some colleges allow students to design their own majors. It is much easier to custom-design service programs than to custom-make goods, because there is no fixed tangible good to adapt. Each customer can specify what he or she wants, within the limits of the service organization—limits that seem to be ever-widening.

[BUS] connections

1. Define and differentiate the following: process manufacturing, assembly process, continuous process, and intermittent process.
2. What do you call the integration of CAD and CAM?
3. What is form utility?

ENSURING QUALITY

Steve Phillips is the CEO of Phillips Manufacturing. Recently, the company's sales have suffered, and Steve is feeling pressure from competitors around the world. He needs to find new ways to increase company efficiency and effectiveness in order to accomplish his firm's strategic goals and mission. He attended a national conference of manufacturers in order to have an opportunity to discuss the issues of global competition with his peers.

Steve returned to the office full of ideas. He arranged a two-day meeting with his management team to develop new operations strategies. There, he laid out his goals for the firm's managers—they were to establish world-class quality standards, improve customer service satisfaction, bolster the company's operations planning (including using resources more effectively, improving scheduling and work methods, and maintaining more control over activities), and implement reasonable strategies to meet the company's goals. One by one, the managers spoke up as Steve described his new vision for the company.

Jack Lamborn, the customer service manager, described his frustration. As business had dropped off, cuts had been made in the customer service workforce. "How can we be expected to perform at a high level with five fewer people in the department?"

If you are facing tough economic conditions and have laid people off, what are your options for keeping customers happy?

Theresa Taggart, the sales manager, scoffed at this remark, saying, "We owe our customers good customer service. The inconsistent service your department is providing is hurting my department's sales. That hurts the company overall."

Michelle Lopane, the plant manager, piped up. "I've been talking with my shift managers and the line employees, and all I hear is complaining—there's tremendous pressure on them, and I think that's what's causing the absenteeism problem we've been seeing. I just don't think our employees are as committed as they used to be."

Many of the other managers agreed with Michelle, who added that she believed Jack's staff needed more training and development to provide good customer service and that her own staff needed more training and development to accomplish the production and quality goals they found so overwhelming.

After Steve left the meeting, the managers stayed behind to further discuss their mutual concern about employee morale.

Jack remarked, "I doubt Steve's commitment to actually accomplishing this vision of his. Of course, I'd like to participate in achieving these objectives, but considering how little time I have, and how much pressure I'm under to meet my short-term budget, I really don't see how this is going to be possible. How on earth are we going to find the time or the money for the training our staff needs?"

QUESTIONS

1. Are there any ethical issues in this situation? How can the managers and employees satisfy Steve's desire to move the company forward and still meet all their short-term company goals?
2. How can the managers improve customer service inexpensively and effectively?

>> Critical Issues in Operations Management Planning

Operations management planning helps solve many of the problems in the service and manufacturing sectors. These include facility location, facility layout, materials requirement planning, purchasing, inventory control, and quality control. The resources used may be different, but the management issues are similar.

FACILITY LOCATION

Facility location is the process of selecting a geographic location for a company's operations. In keeping with the need to focus on customers, one strategy is to find a site that makes it easy for consumers to use the company's services and to communicate their needs. Flower shops and banks are putting facilities in supermarkets so their products and services are more accessible than in freestanding facilities.

Facility location The process of selecting a geographic location for a company's operations.

You can find fast-food restaurants inside some gas stations. Customers order and pay for their meals at the pumps, and by the time they've filled their tanks, it's time to pick up their food.

The ultimate in convenience is never having to leave home to get services. That's why there is so much interest in Internet banking, Internet shopping, online education, and other services.[16] For brick-and-mortar retailers to beat such competition, they have to choose good locations and offer outstanding service. Study the location of service-sector businesses—such as hotels, banks, athletic clubs, and supermarkets—and you'll see that the most successful are conveniently located.

Facility Location for Manufacturers

Volkswagen's factory in Bratislava, Slovakia, turns out 250,000 cars a year, including Audi's Q7 SUV, which used to be made in different European plants. Geographic shifts in production sometimes result in pockets of unemployment in some geographic areas and tremendous growth in others. We are witnessing such changes in the United States, as automobile production shifted from Detroit to more southern cities.

Why would companies spend millions of dollars to move their facilities from one location to another? In their decisions, they consider labor costs; availability of resources, including labor; access to transportation that can reduce time to market; proximity to suppliers; proximity to customers; crime rates; quality of life for employees; cost of living; and the need to train or retrain the local workforce.

In 2008, Whirlpool closed a dishwasher manufacturing plant in Jackson, Tennessee, blaming "the global recession, decreased demand, increased costs, and falling profits" for the move. In all, 500 employees lost their jobs.[17] Carlisle Tire and Wheel bought the defunct Whirlpool plant and retooled it to manufacture tires, wheels, and inner tubes. The company's move created 440 new jobs in the community.[18]

Even though labor is becoming a smaller percentage of total cost in highly automated industries, low-cost labor or the right kind of skilled labor are key reasons many producers move their plants to Malaysia, China, India, Mexico, and other countries. In general, however, U.S. manufacturing firms tend to pay more and offer more benefits than local firms elsewhere in the world. One result of the financial crisis is that U.S. workers may be forced to take less pay and receive fewer benefits in order to stay competitive.

Inexpensive resources are another major reason for moving production facilities. Companies usually need water, electricity, wood, coal, and other basic resources. By moving to areas where these are inexpensive and plentiful, firms can significantly lower not only the cost of buying such resources but also the cost of shipping finished products. Often the most important resource is people, so companies tend to cluster where smart and talented people are.

Witness Silicon Valley in California and similar areas in Colorado, Massachusetts, Virginia, Texas, Maryland, and other states.

Time-to-market is another decision-making factor. As manufacturers attempt to compete globally, they need sites that allow products to move quickly, at the lowest costs, so they can be delivered to customers fast. Access to highways, rail lines, waterways, and airports is thus critical. Information technology (IT) is also important to quicken response time, so many firms are seeking countries with the most advanced information systems.

Another way to work closely with suppliers to satisfy customers' needs is to locate production facilities near supplier facilities. That cuts the cost of distribution and makes communication easier.

Many businesses are building factories in foreign countries to get closer to their international customers.[19] That's a major reason the Japanese automaker Honda builds cars in Ohio and the German company Daimler AG builds certain models of its Mercedes brand in Alabama. When U.S. firms select foreign sites, they consider whether they are near airports, waterways, and highways so raw and finished goods can move quickly and easily.

Taking Operations Management to the Internet

Many rapidly growing companies do very little production themselves. Instead, they outsource engineering, design, manufacturing, and other tasks to companies that specialize in those functions, such as Solectron, Flextronics, and SCI Systems. They create new relationships with suppliers over the Internet, making operations management an *interfirm* process in which companies work closely together to design, produce, and ship products to customers.

Manufacturing companies are developing Internet-focused strategies that will enable them and others to compete more effectively in the future. These changes are having a dramatic effect on operations managers, as they adjust from a one-firm system to an interfirm

Businesses also study the quality of life for workers and managers. Are good schools nearby? Is the weather nice? Is the crime rate low? Does the local community welcome new businesses?[20] Do the chief executive and other key managers want to live there? Sometimes a region with a high quality of life is also an expensive one, which complicates the decision. In short, facility location has become a critical issue in operations management.

environment and from a relatively stable environment to one that is constantly changing and evolving.

FACILITY LAYOUT

Facility layout is the physical arrangement of resources, including people, to most efficiently produce goods and provide services for customers. Facility layout depends greatly on the processes that are to be performed. For services, the layout is usually designed to help the consumer find and buy things, including on the Internet. Some stores have kiosks that enable customers to search for goods online and place orders or make returns and credit payments in the store. In short, the facilities and Internet capabilities of service organizations are becoming more customer-oriented.

> **Facility layout** The physical arrangement of resources, including people, to most efficiently produce goods and provide services for customers.

Some service-oriented organizations, such as hospitals, use layouts that improve efficiency, just as manufacturers do. For manufacturing plants, facilities layout has become critical because cost savings of efficient layouts are enormous.

Many companies are moving from an *assembly line layout*, in which workers do only a few tasks at a time, to a *modular* layout, in which teams of workers combine to produce more complex units of the final product. There may have been a dozen or more workstations on an assembly line to complete an automobile engine in the past, but all that work might be done in one module today.

When working on a major project, such as a bridge or an airplane, companies use a *fixed-position* layout that allows workers to congregate around the product to be completed.

A *process* layout is one in which similar equipment and functions are grouped together. The order in which the product visits a function depends on the design of the item. This allows for flexibility.

Several factors should be kept in mind when considering which layout is right for a small business, including:

1. *Maximizing space.* This factor includes everything from ensuring that warehouse corridors are wide enough to accommodate forklifts going in opposite directions to having enough office space for the people who need it

2. *Expansion plans.* It's vital to plan for future growth when setting up a layout for a small business, including being able to scale up production if necessary.

At Cisco Systems, work spaces in some offices are fluid and unassigned, so employees with laptops and mobile phones can choose where to sit when they arrive each day.

needs a fast-moving employee base to achieve maximum productivity. Figure 6.3 illustrates typical layout designs.

MATERIALS REQUIREMENT PLANNING

Materials requirement planning (MRP) is a computer-based operations management system that uses sales forecasts to make sure needed parts and materials are available at the right time and place. **Enterprise resource planning (ERP),** a newer version of MRP, combines the computerized functions of all the divisions and subsidiaries of the firm—such as finance, MRP, human resources, and order fulfillment—into a single, integrated software program that uses a single database. The result is shorter time between orders and payment, less staff needed to do ordering and order processing, reduced inventories, and better customer service. For example, the customer can place an order, either through a customer service representative or online, and immediately see when the order will

> **Materials requirement planning (MRP)** A computer-based operations management system that uses sales forecasts to make sure that needed parts and materials are available at the right time and place.
>
> **Enterprise resource planning (ERP)** A newer version of materials requirement planning that combines the computerized functions of all the divisions and subsidiaries of the firm—such as finance, human resources, and order fulfillment—into a single integrated software program that uses a single database.

3. *Safety.* The business facility layout must comply with Occupational Safety and Health Association (OSHA) guidelines and any other safety regulations.

4. *Ease of movement.* The layout must accommodate easy flow of traffic for both people and materials.

5. *Handling materials.* The design should permit simple and efficient movement of raw materials and finished inventory.

6. *Shipping/receiving constraints.* This often-forgotten factor can become a big problem. If there is not enough space for shipments to come in and go out, the business may suffer.

7. *Employee morale.* Effective ways to heighten employee morale through facility layout include attractive design, keeping work areas light and open, placing workers near windows, including recreational/lunch areas in the design, and so on.

8. *Facilitation of communication.* The layout should allow communication to move freely among various areas of the business (finance, production, shipping, and so on) as well as the business's vendors and customers.

9. *Attractiveness.* Any facility that receives visitors—customers, vendors, or any other type of stakeholders other than employees—should be attractive, clean, and inviting.[21]

The Igus manufacturing plant in Cologne, Germany, can shrink or expand in a flash. Its flexible design keeps it competitive in a fast-changing market. Because the layout of the plant changes so often, some employees use scooters in order to more efficiently provide needed skills, supplies, and services to multiple workstations. A fast-changing plant

Facility layout is the physical arrangement of resources, including people, to most efficiently produce goods and provide services for customers. Many companies are moving from an assembly line layout, in which workers do only a few tasks at a time, to a modular layout, in which teams of workers combine to produce more complex units of the final product.

Study Alert

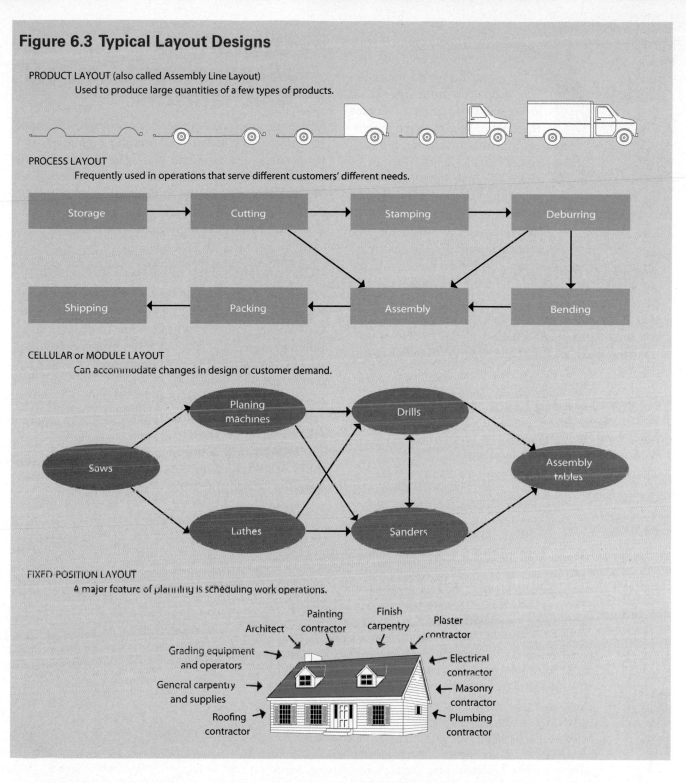

Figure 6.3 Typical Layout Designs

PRODUCT LAYOUT (also called Assembly Line Layout)
Used to produce large quantities of a few types of products.

PROCESS LAYOUT
Frequently used in operations that serve different customers' different needs.

Storage → Cutting → Stamping → Deburring

Shipping ← Packing ← Assembly ← Bending

CELLULAR or MODULE LAYOUT
Can accommodate changes in design or customer demand.

Saws
Planing machines
Lathes
Drills
Sanders
Assembly tables

FIXED-POSITION LAYOUT
A major feature of planning is scheduling work operations.

Architect
Painting contractor
Finish carpentry
Plaster contractor
Grading equipment and operators
General carpentry and supplies
Roofing contractor
Electrical contractor
Masonry contractor
Plumbing contractor

be filled and how much it will cost. The representative can instantly see the customer's credit rating and order history, the company's inventory, and the shipping schedule. Everyone else in the company can see the order, so when one department finishes its portion of the order, the ERP system automatically routes the project to the next department. The customer can see exactly where the order is at any point by logging into the ERP system.[22]

PURCHASING

Purchasing is the function that searches for high-quality material resources, finds the best suppliers, and negotiates the best price for quality goods and services.[23] In the past, manufacturers dealt with many suppliers so that if one couldn't deliver, the

> **Purchasing** The function in a firm that searches for high-quality material resources, finds the best suppliers, and negotiates prices for goods and services.

firm could get materials from someone else. Today, however, manufacturers rely more heavily on just one or two suppliers, because the relationship between suppliers and manufacturers is much closer than before. Producers share so much information that they don't want too many suppliers knowing their business.

The Internet has transformed the purchasing function. A business looking for supplies can contact an Internet-based purchasing service and find the best items at the best price. Similarly, a company wishing to sell supplies can use the Internet to find all the companies looking for such supplies. The time and dollar cost of purchasing items has thus been reduced tremendously.

[BUS] connections

1. What are the major criteria for facility location?
2. What is the difference between MRP and ERP?
3. How have purchasing positions changed since the advent of the Internet?

>> Operations Management Control Mechanisms

Operations managers must ensure that products are manufactured and delivered on time, on budget, and to specifications. How can managers be sure all will go smoothly and be completed by the required time? This section will explore three control mechanisms: just-in-time inventory control, the Program Evaluation and Review Technique, and Gantt charts.

JUST-IN-TIME INVENTORY CONTROL

One major cost of production is the expense of holding parts, motors, and other items in storage for later use. Storage not only subjects items to obsolescence, pilferage, and damage but also requires construction and maintenance of costly warehouses. To cut such costs, many companies have implemented a concept called **just-in-time (JIT) inventory control**. JIT systems keep a minimum of inventory on the premises—and deliver parts, supplies, and other

> **Just-in-time (JIT) inventory control** A production process in which a minimum of inventory is kept on the premises and parts, supplies, and other needs are delivered just in time to go on the assembly line.

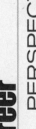

needs just in time for them to go on the assembly line. To work effectively, however, the process requires an accurate production schedule (using ERP) and excellent coordination with carefully selected suppliers, who are usually connected electronically so they know what will be needed and when. Sometimes the suppliers build new facilities close to the main producer to minimize distribution time. JIT runs into problems when suppliers are farther away. Weather may delay shipments, for example.

JIT systems make sure the right materials are at the right place at the right time at the cheapest cost to meet both customer and production needs. That's a key step in modern production innovation.

PROGRAM EVALUATION AND REVIEW TECHNIQUE (PERT)

One popular technique for monitoring the progress of production was developed in the 1950s for constructing nuclear submarines: the **program evaluation and review technique (PERT)**. PERT users analyze the tasks to complete a given project, estimate the time needed to complete each task, and compute the minimum time needed to complete the whole project.

> **Program evaluation and review technique (PERT)** A method for analyzing the tasks involved in completing a given project, estimating the time needed to complete each task, and identifying the minimum time needed to complete the total project.

The steps used in PERT are (1) analyzing and sequencing tasks that need to be done, (2) estimating the time needed to complete each task, (3) drawing a PERT network illustrating the information from steps 1 and 2, and (4) identifying the **critical path**. The critical path is the sequence of tasks that takes the longest time to complete. We use the word "critical" because a delay anywhere along this path will cause the project or production run to be late.

> **Critical path** In a PERT network, the sequence of tasks that takes the longest time to complete.

Figure 6.4 illustrates a PERT chart for producing a music video. The boxes indicate completed tasks, and the arrows indicate the time needed to complete each. The path from one completed task to another illustrates the relationships among tasks; the arrow from "set designed" to "set materials purchased" indicates that we must design the set before we can purchase the materials. The critical path, indicated by the bold black arrows, shows that producing the

DePuy Inc., a subsidiary of Johnson and Johnson, uses a JIT system to provide doctors and hospitals with medical supplies, such as the titanium prosthetic hip joints shown above, as they are needed. Hospitals are open around the clock and often deal with life-threatening situations, so materials must be available when doctors need them. DePuy takes advantage of an automated system that ensures quality products are shipped on time.[24]

Figure 6.4 PERT Chart for a Music Video

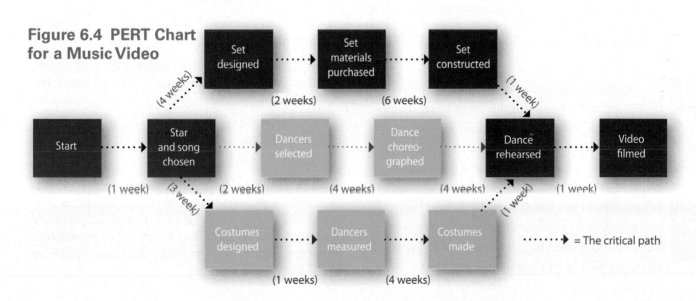

Figure 6.5 Gantt Chart for a Doll Manufacturer

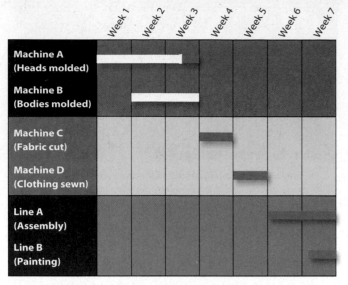

	Week 1	Week 2	Week 3	Week 4	Week 5	Week 6	Week 7
Machine A (Heads molded)							
Machine B (Bodies molded)							
Machine C (Fabric cut)							
Machine D (Clothing sewn)							
Line A (Assembly)							
Line B (Painting)							

set takes more time than auditioning dancers, choreographing dances, or designing and making costumes. The project manager now knows it's critical that set construction remain on schedule if the project is to be completed on time, but short delays in dance and costume preparation are unlikely to delay it.

GANTT CHARTS

A PERT network can be made up of thousands of events over many months. Today, this complex procedure is done by computer. Another more basic strategy manufacturers use for measuring production progress is a Gantt chart. A **Gantt chart** (named for its developer, Henry L. Gantt) is a bar graph, now also prepared by computer, that clearly shows what projects are being worked on and how much has been completed at any

Gantt chart Bar graph showing production managers what projects are being worked on and what stage they are in at any given time.

given time. Figure 6.5, a Gantt chart for a doll manufacturer, shows that the dolls' heads and bodies should be completed before the clothing is sewn. It also shows that at the end of week 3, the dolls' bodies are ready, but the heads are about half a week behind. Using a Gantt-like computer program, a manager can trace the production process minute by minute to determine which tasks are on time and which are behind, so that adjustments can be made to allow the company to stay on schedule.

>> Quality Control and Standards

Maintaining **quality** means consistently producing what the customer wants while reducing errors before and after delivery to the customer. In the past, firms often conducted quality control at the end of the production line. Products were completed first and then tested for quality. This resulted in several problems:

Quality A never-ending process of continually improving what a company produces.

1. The need to inspect work required extra people and resources.

2. If an error was found, someone had to correct the mistake or scrap the product. This, of course, was costly.

3. If the customer found the mistake, he or she might be dissatisfied and might even buy from someone else thereafter.

Such problems led to the realization that quality is not an outcome; it is a never-ending process of continually improving what a company produces. Quality control should thus be part of the operations management planning process rather than simply an end-of-the-line inspection.[25]

Six Sigma quality A quality measure that allows only 3.4 defects per million opportunities.

Statistical quality control (SQC) The process some managers use to continually monitor all phases of the production process to ensure that quality is being built into the product from the beginning.

Statistical process control (SPC) The process of testing statistical samples of product components at each stage of the production process and plotting those results on a graph. Any variances from quality standards are recognized and can be corrected if beyond the set standards.

Companies have turned to the use of modern quality-control standards such as Six Sigma.[26] **Six Sigma quality,** which sets a benchmark of just 3.4 defects per million opportunities, detects potential problems to prevent their occurrence. That's important to a company that makes 4 million transactions a day, like some banks.

Statistical quality control (SQC) is the process some managers use to continually monitor all phases of the production process and ensure that quality is being built into the product from the beginning. **Statistical process control (SPC)** is the process of testing statistical samples of product components at each stage of production and plotting the test results on a graph. Managers can thus see and correct any deviation from quality standards. Making sure products meet standards all along the production process reduces the need for a quality-control inspection at the end because mistakes are caught much earlier in the process. SQC and SPC thus save companies much time and money.

Some companies use a quality-control approach called the Deming cycle (after the late W. Edwards Deming, the father of the movement toward quality). Its steps are Plan, Do, Check, Act (PDCA). Again, the idea is to find potential errors before they happen.

U.S. businesses are getting serious about providing top customer service, and many are already doing it. Service organizations are finding it difficult to provide outstanding service every time because the process is so labor intensive.

For example, the employees of Alaska Air Cargo are required to complete a rigorous training program because the company specializes in transporting perishable items—in particular, Alaskan seafood. The program has been designed in an effort to improve quality control for the seafood and prevent spoilage.[27]

As the popularity of quality-control systems has grown, recognition programs that celebrate the achievements of high-performing firms and standards for quality control have become more common. In the next section, we highlight the Malcolm Baldrige National Quality Awards. The International Organization for Standardization has pioneered several quality-control standards that are widely accepted.

THE BALDRIGE AWARDS

In 1987, a standard was set for overall company quality in the United States with the introduction of the Malcolm Baldrige National Quality Awards, which were named in honor of the late U.S. secretary of commerce. Companies can apply for these awards in each of the following areas: manufacturing, services, small businesses, education, and health care.

To qualify, an organization has to show quality in seven key areas: leadership, strategic planning, customer and market focus, information and analysis, human resources focus, process management, and business results. Major criteria for earning the award include whether customer wants and needs are being met and whether customer satisfaction ratings are better than those of competitors. As you can see, the focus is shifting away from just making quality goods and services to providing top-quality customer service in all respects.

One Baldrige Award winner was Sunny Fresh Foods, a small company that makes more than 200 different egg products. Sunny Fresh was the first food company to win the award and one of only a few small-company winners. The company used the Baldrige criteria to drive business systems development and business systems redesign.

The Bama Company of Tulsa, Oklahoma, makes pies, biscuits, and pizza crusts. Using Baldrige criteria, the company increased overall customer satisfaction from 75 percent to almost 100 percent. Richland College, in Dallas, Texas, was the first community college to receive a Baldrige Award. With over 20,000 students, Richland reduced its operational costs while improving services and implemented stakeholder listening services to measure satisfaction.

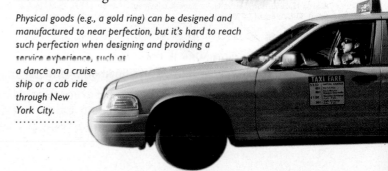

Physical goods (e.g., a gold ring) can be designed and manufactured to near perfection, but it's hard to reach such perfection when designing and providing a service experience, such as a dance on a cruise ship or a cab ride through New York City.

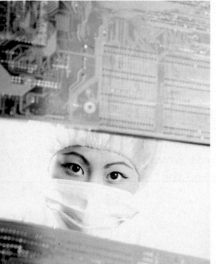

Going GLOBAL

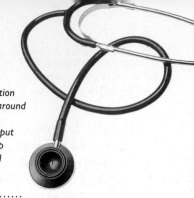

Six Sigma Is Out, Extreme Lean Manufacturing Is In

Striving for superior efficiency is a part of lean manufacturing, but the concept as a whole is far more comprehensive. The following article suggests that "extreme" lean manufacturing could help U.S. manufacturers better compete with "globalized" companies that offshore their operations.

When surgical device maker Conmed decided in 2007 to streamline production, executives explored the usual options. The Utica (N.Y.) company could ship more manufacturing to China. Or it could invest in automation. Conmed chose a third path: It completely overhauled its production. Long assembly lines at its 600-worker Utica plant have given way to compact U-shaped workstations. Piles of plastic boxes stuffed with enough parts to last weeks have been replaced by just a few bins containing the exact number of parts needed.

No longer do workers furiously crank out products that languish in warehouses. Instead they build only as many as customers need at the time. Conmed calculates that every 90 seconds hospitals worldwide use one of its disposable devices. So that's precisely how long it takes for a new one to roll off its assembly line.

Lean manufacturing—producing goods with minimal waste of time, materials, and money—was pioneered by Japanese companies decades ago. Now a growing number of U.S. businesses are trying a more extreme form of lean. Besides making factories superefficient, they are gearing output to current demand rather than three- to six-month forecasts. In capital-starved times, companies can ill afford to tie up cash by letting parts and finished goods lie idle in inventory. Even if companies place orders, there's no guarantee they'll get the financing to complete the purchase.

Do the improvements yield savings superior to what could be had in China? Wages there, though vastly lower, are largely offset by the costs of long lead times, inventory pileup, quality problems, and unforeseen delays. "If more U.S. companies deploy these production methods," says Johnson, "we can compete with anybody."

Source: Pete Engardio, "Six Sigma Is Out. Extreme Lean Manufacturing Is In," *BusinessWeek*, March 12, 2009, http://www.businessweek.com/magazine/content/09_12/b4124060294724.htm (accessed August 12, 2009).

Questions

1. In your opinion, why is it so expensive for companies to warehouse raw materials and finished products?

2. Do you agree with the article's assertion that "extreme lean" manufacturing processes could be the answer to competing with offshore manufacturers? Why or why not?

Mercy Health System, a recent recipient of the prestigious Baldrige National Quality Award, consists of 3 hospitals and 64 other facilities in Wisconsin and Illinois. The organization has built its "culture of excellence" around the four criteria of top quality in patient care, service standards that put patients first, committed partnership with its nearly 4,000 employees and physicians, and cost management for long-term financial success.

The 2008 Baldrige Award recipients included Cargill Corn Milling North America of Wayzata, Minnesota (manufacturing category); Poudre Valley Health System of Fort Collins, Colorado (health care category); and Iredell-Statesville Schools, Statesville, North Carolina (education category).[28]

ISO 9000 AND ISO 14000 STANDARDS

The International Organization for Standardization (ISO) is a worldwide federation of national standards bodies from more than 140 countries that set global measures for the quality of individual products. ISO is a nongovernmental organization established in 1947 to promote the development of world standards to facilitate the international exchange of goods and services. (ISO is not only an acronym. It also comes from the Greek word *isos*, meaning "oneness.") **ISO 9000** is the common name given to quality management and assurance standards. Some of the latest standards are called ISO 9000: 2008. You will find more changes in the ISO 9001 standards.[29]

> **ISO 9000** The common name given to quality management and assurance standards.

The standards require that a company determine what customer needs are, including regulatory and legal requirements, and make communication arrangements to handle issues such as complaints.[30] Other standards cover process control, product testing, storage, and delivery.

What makes ISO 9000 so important is that the European Union (EU) is demanding that companies that want to do business with the EU be certified by ISO standards. Some major U.S. companies are also demanding that suppliers meet these standards. Several accreditation agencies in Europe and the United States will certify that a company meets the standards for all phases of its operations, from product development through production and testing to installation.

ISO 14000 is a collection of the best practices for managing an organization's impact on the environment. As an environmental management system, it does not prescribe a performance level. Requirements for certification include having an environmental policy, having specific improvement targets, conducting audits of environmental programs, and maintaining top management review of the processes.

> **ISO 14000** A collection of the best practices for managing an organization's impact on the environment.

Certification in both ISO 9000 and ISO 14000 would show that a firm has a world-class management system in both quality and environmental standards. In the past, firms assigned employees separately to meet each set of standards. Today, ISO 9000 and ISO 14000 standards have been blended so an organization can work on both at once.[31] ISO is now compiling social responsibility guidelines to go with the other standards.

Today, foreign producers are streaming to the United States to take advantage of its labor force and opportunities. The United States is still the leader in nanotechnology, biotechnology, and other areas.[32] Its workforce is creative and dynamic. Nonetheless, U.S. business cannot stand still; it must keep up with the latest production techniques and processes.

As the U.S. service sector becomes a larger part of the overall economy, managers will be more occupied with service productivity, and with blending services and manufacturing through the Internet.[33] How can U.S. manufacturers and service organizations maintain a competitive edge? Most of them are:

- Focusing more on customers.

- Maintaining closer relationships with suppliers and other companies to satisfy customer needs.

- Practicing continuous improvement.

- Focusing on quality.

- Saving on costs through site selection.

- Relying on the Internet to unite companies that work together.

- Adopting such production techniques as ERP, CIM, flexible manufacturing, and lean manufacturing.

STAYING COMPETITIVE

Real World Apps

After reading the chapter, Jerry understands why and how his business operations must change in order to succeed in a constantly changing marketplace. Implementing lean manufacturing techniques will enable him to cut the fat out of his production processes. It seems so simple that he's astounded he didn't think of it on his own.

"I'm going to get all my managers on board and discuss what steps we will take next," Jerry thinks. "First, we'll consider the physical layout of the facility. Are we using our space efficiently? When the production floor was originally designed, it was based on convenience not on efficiency. Who knows how many man-hours have been wasted on inefficient workflow?"

Next on Jerry's list is revamping materials management. He's going to move beyond his old-fashioned tool and supply sheds. He also has lots of inventory just sitting around depreciating—JIT inventory processes will make sure his supplies are on hand when they're needed, and no sooner. Jerry realizes that his old-fashioned notion of having supplies always on hand has hurt his company's bottom line.

Full of information and ideas, Jerry is anxious to implement some new procedures. He can't wait to get started leading his company into a new era of productivity and efficiency using the concepts he's learned.

[BUS] connections

1. What is Six Sigma quality?

2. What does a company have to do to win the Baldrige Award?

3. Describe the ISO 9000 and ISO 14000 standards.

For REVIEW >>

1. Describe production and operations management.
   - Production management is all the activities managers do to help their firms create goods. To reflect the change in importance from manufacturing to services, the term "production" is often replaced by the term "operations." Operations management is the specialized area in management that converts or transforms resources, including human resources, into goods and services. Firms in both the manufacturing and service sectors use operations managers.

2. Identify and describe techniques that improve productivity.
   - The production process consists of taking the factors of production (such as land) and using those inputs to produce goods, services, and ideas. Planning, routing, scheduling, and other activities are the means to accomplish the objective—output. Form utility is the value producers add to materials in the creation of finished goods and services. Process manufacturing is the part of the production process that physically or chemically changes materials, and the assembly process is the part of the production process that puts together components. In a continuous process, long production runs turn out finished goods over time, and in an intermittent process, the production runs are short and machines are changed frequently to make different products. Design changes made in CAD, or computer-aided design, are instantly incorporated into the CAM, or computer-aided manufacturing, process. The linking of CAD and CAM is computer-integrated manufacturing (CIM). Flexible manufacturing means designing machines to produce a variety of products, and lean manufacturing is the production of goods using less of everything than in mass production: less human effort, less manufacturing space, less investment in tools, and less engineering time to develop a new product.

3. Describe various operations management planning issues.
   - Operations management planning helps solve many of the problems in the service and manufacturing sectors, including facility location, facility layout, materials requirement planning (MRP), purchasing, inventory control, and quality control. Facility location is the process of selecting a geographic location for a company's operations. Facility layout is the physical arrangement of resources, including people, to most efficiently produce goods and provide services for customers. Many companies are moving from an assembly line layout, in which workers do only a few tasks at a time, to a modular layout, in which teams of workers combine to produce more complex units of the final product. MRP is a computer-based operations management system that uses sales forecasts to make sure that needed parts and materials are available at the right time and place, and enterprise resource planning (ERP) is a newer version of MRP that combines the computerized functions of all the divisions and subsidiaries of the firm—such as finance, human resources, and order fulfillment—into a single, integrated software program that uses a single database.

4. Explain the use of PERT and Gantt charts to control manufacturing processes.
   - One major cost of production is the expense of holding parts, motors, and other items in storage for later use. To cut such costs, many companies have implemented a concept called just-in-time (JIT) inventory control. JIT systems keep a minimum of inventory on the premises and deliver parts, supplies, and other needs just in time to go on the assembly line. The program evaluation and review technique (PERT) is used to analyze the tasks to complete a given project, estimate the time needed to complete each task, and compute the minimum time needed to complete the whole project. A Gantt chart (named for its developer, Henry L. Gantt) is a bar graph that clearly shows what projects are being worked on and how much has been completed at any given time. PERT is a tool used for planning, and a Gantt chart is a tool used to measure progress.

5. Understand world-class quality standards.
   - Six Sigma quality, which sets a benchmark of just 3.4 defects per million opportunities, detects potential problems to prevent their occurrence. Statistical quality control (SQC) is the process some managers use to continually monitor all phases of the production process and ensure that quality is being built into the product from the beginning, and statistical process control (SPC) is the process of testing statistical samples of product components at each stage of production and plotting the test results on a graph. The Malcolm Baldrige National Quality Awards are given out each year for excellence in overall company quality in each of the following areas: manufacturing, services, small businesses, education, and health care. To qualify, a company must demonstrate quality in seven key areas: leadership, strategic planning, customer and market focus, information and analysis, human resources focus, process management, and business results. International standards that U.S. firms strive to meet include ISO 9000: 2008 (ISO 9001) and ISO 14000.

Key Terms

Assembly process

Computer-aided design (CAD)

Computer-aided manufacturing (CAM)

Computer-integrated manufacturing (CIM)

Continuous process

Critical path

Enterprise resource planning (ERP)

Facility location

Flexible manufacturing

Form utility

Gantt chart

Intermittent process

ISO 9000

ISO 14000

Just-in-time (JIT) inventory control

Lean manufacturing

Mass customization

Materials requirement planning (MRP)

Operations management

Process manufacturing

Production

Production management

Program evaluation and review technique (PERT)

Purchasing

Quality

Six Sigma quality

Statistical process control (SPC)

Statistical quality control (SQC)

1. What does operations management include? Which area do you think is most important, and why?

2. Think of a project you need to finish over the next few months—perhaps painting a room in your home or apartment or getting ready for a final exam. Develop a PERT chart for this project.

3. How does operations management vary from the service sector to the manufacturing one? What skills are needed for each? Which skills are the same for both, and which are different?

4. What is the difference between an intermittent process and a continuous one? In which situations would it be best to use intermittent versus continuous, and vice versa?

5. In groups, discuss what the form utility might be for each of the following industries:

   a. Coffee shop
   b. Airplane manufacturer
   c. Lawn care services
   d. An online retail clothing store
   e. A shoe manufacturer
   f. A river-rafting guide company

6. Discuss the following questions in groups: Are there any disadvantages to computer-aided manufacturing? If so, what are they? What are some of the downsides to using technology in the manufacturing process? How can companies mitigate these disadvantages?

7. Define just-in-time inventory. What are the advantages to this kind of system? What are the disadvantages?

INTERNET IN >> Action

1. Visit the Web site http://www.sixsigmaonline.org/index.html.
   a. What is Six Sigma?
   b. What must a company do in order to become Six Sigma certified?
   c. What are the advantages to using Six Sigma?

2. Visit the Web site www.nike.com. Click "Shop," and then click "Customize." Chose any of the available products to customize. After customizing your product, answer the following questions:
   a. Which product did you choose to customize?
   b. Are you willing to pay more for a customized product?
   c. From the manufacturing perspective, how are companies able to make custom products and still keep costs low?

Self-Assessment Exercises

BUSINESS CAREER QUIZ

Test Your ISO 14000 Knowledge

As discussed in this chapter, ISO 14000 helps companies review their environmental awareness and responsibility. Test your knowledge of ISO 14000 in the following exercise. Answer each question as either true or false.

1. ISO 14000 aims to set specific environmental standards for businesses.
2. ISO stands for Interoperated Standard Organization.
3. One of the benefits of ISO 14000 can be reduced costs to the company.
4. ISO 14000 is only for companies based in the United States.
5. Only manufacturing companies can benefit from ISO 14000.
6. ISO 14000 provides detailed information on how to monitor and report greenhouse gas emissions.
7. ISO 14000 standards are monitored by the same organization that monitors ISO 9000 standards.
8. ISO provides a model of how to set up and operate a system that meets ISO 14000 standards.
9. ISO 14000 provides information on how to make sure a company's suppliers are also meeting ISO 14000 standards.
10. ISO 14000 suggests standards for companies, but it does not help companies monitor how they are actually complying with the standards.

Answers

1. **False.** ISO 14000 does not set specific standards, because they would be different for various industries. Rather, the goal is to set a framework for companies' policies, plans, and actions.
2. **False.** ISO, the International Organization for Standardization.
3. **True.** Companies can save money when they reduce waste and consumption of energy, and when they are better able to manage their distribution systems.
4. **False.** ISO 14000 can be used by companies operating in any country.
5. **False.** In 2007, 29 percent of ISO 14000 certifications went to companies in the service sector.
6. **True.** Several sections in the ISO document discuss how to report and minimize greenhouse gas emissions.
7. **True.** Members of the organization bring forth sets of standards for many different goals. ISO does not exclusively deal with environmental issues; it helps companies set standards for a wide variety of sectors of business.
8. **True.** ISO uses a "Plan, Do, Check, Act" system that requires companies to establish objectives (plan), implement these plans (do), measure results (check), and correct and improve (act).
9. **True.** A key part of ISO 14000 is its requirement for companies to not only review their own environmental policies, but also the policies of their suppliers.
10. **False.** ISO 14000 suggests using a continuous improvement approach, so companies can constantly monitor their compliance and improve upon it.

Source: Information from ISO Web site, http://www.iso.org/iso/iso_catalogue/management_standards/iso_9000_iso_14000/iso_14000_essentials.htm (accessed August 18, 2009).

Would You Be Good at Operations Management?

Take this quiz to see if you have the skills to be successful in the field of operations management.

1. Do you consider yourself to be a jack-of-all-trades (that is, are you good at many different things)?
2. Are you organized?
3. Do you have good people skills?
4. Can you work with tight deadlines?
5. Do you like to solve problems?
6. Do you write to-do lists?
7. Can you adapt easily to change?
8. Are you comfortable not always knowing what your job might entail on a day-to-day basis?
9. Are you a team player? Are you willing to help others if needed?

Answers

Operations management roles differ from company to company and industry to industry, but there are a few constants. An operations manager needs to be detail oriented and a fast learner, and he or she should be able to work effectively with other people. If you answered "yes" to most of these questions, you just might be well suited to a career in operations management.

Source: Information compiled from various career Web sites, including www.monster.com, www.salary.com, and www.careerplanner.com.

- How has technology changed the way we do business?
- What software do you use in your daily life, and how it has improved your productivity?
- How can you protect yourself from hackers, viruses, and spyware?

>> The Role of Information Technology in Business

How can technology help businesses around the world? Remember: Change is the only constant. Business owners and managers who rely on outdated ways of operating can't compete with those who know how to use the latest technology.

Think about the technology that exists today that didn't exist when you were 10 years old. Now take a moment to imagine what the next 10 years will bring. Would you feel confident about going on a job interview tomorrow if you only understood the technology that existed when you were a child?

Consider the typewriter. Whether manual or electric, it dominated office technology for years. After the rise of the personal computer, the typewriter became obsolete. Some typewriter manufacturers, such as IBM, made a move into computers; other leaders in the industry, such as Smith Corona, were driven into bankruptcy.[4]

The importance of business knowledge is nothing new—what *is* new is a recognition of the need to manage it like any other asset. To manage knowledge, a company must learn how to share information throughout the organization and implement systems for creating new knowledge. This need is creating new technologies that support the exchange of information among staff, suppliers, and customers. In order to be successful, firms must figure out how to harness technology and provide a pipeline of interaction and information between themselves and their stakeholders. This chapter will discuss software and hardware in technology, how technology helps manage information in businesses, and challenges in information technology today.

Figure 7.1 shows some of the worst technology predictions of all time. Have you ever thought that a technology would fail, and then later it became a big success?

Would you want to create your assignments using this?

Figure 7.1 The Worst Tech Predictions of All Time

1. "I think there is a world market for maybe five computers."
   —Thomas Watson, president of IBM, 1943
2. "Television won't be able to hold on to any market it captures after the first six months. People will soon get tired of staring at a plywood box every night."
   —Darryl Zanuck, executive at 20th Century Fox, 1946
3. "Nuclear-powered vacuum cleaners will probably be a reality within 10 years."
   —Alex Lewyt, president of vacuum maker Lewyt Corporation, 1955
4. "There is no reason anyone would want a computer in their home."
   —Ken Olsen, founder of Digital Equipment Corporation, 1977
5. "Almost all of the many predictions now being made about 1996 hinge on the Internet's continuing exponential growth. But I predict the Internet will soon go spectacularly supernova and in 1996 catastrophically collapse."
   —Robert Metcalfe, founder of 3Com, 1995
6. "Apple is already dead."
   —Nathan Myhrvold, former Microsoft chief technology officer, 1997
7. "Two years from now, spam will be solved."
   —Bill Gates, founder of Microsoft, 2004

Source: Robert Strohmeyer, "The 7 Worst Tech Predictions of All Time," http://tech.msn.com/news/articlepcw.aspx?cp-documentid=16829041 (accessed February 11, 2009).

Real World Apps

Tom DiPietropolo has worked as a bank teller since he graduated from high school 15 years ago. In the years he has worked in the financial industry, he's seen many changes and innovations alter the way business is done on a daily basis.

Many of these changes have been technology based. When he first started working at the bank, he had to manually count the money in his cash drawer at the beginning and end of each day. Now, electronic change and bill counters make those mundane and time consuming responsibilities a snap—but they also make Tom think that maybe his work isn't as important or necessary as it used to be.

Tom's branch of the bank has undergone several layoffs, and several branches in the area have closed altogether. He believes that, in many ways, technology has taken the "personal touch" out of banking.

"Technology is a huge pain in my neck," Tom muses. He can't possibly imagine the positives of technology outweighing the negatives in his role at the bank. However, after giving the matter a great deal of thought, he decides to enroll in an Introduction to Business course at a local college in order to catch up with technology.

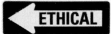 

If you discovered that a coworker was viewing inappropriate Web sites and sending personal e-mails on his work computer, what would you do?

A BRIEF HISTORY OF INFORMATION TECHNOLOGY

To understand why technology matters today, you should first have a basic understanding of technology's past. In the 1970s, business technology was known as **data processing (DP)**. Although many people use the words *data* and *information* interchangeably, they are different. **Data** are raw, unanalyzed, and unorganized facts and figures. **Information** is the processed and organized data that can be used for managerial decision making. DP supported existing business, and people who worked in DP were support staff who rarely came in contact with customers. DP's primary purpose was to improve the flow of financial information.

> **Data processing (DP)** The name given to business technology in the 1970s. Its primary purpose was to improve the flow of financial information.
>
> **Data** Raw, unanalyzed, and unorganized facts and figures.
>
> **Information** The processed and organized data that can be used for managerial decision making.

In the 1980s, business technology became known as **information systems (IS)**. While DP was a behind the-scenes activity, IS soon moved into the center of the business. Its role changed from *supporting* the business to *doing* business. Customers began to interact with a wide array of technological tools, from automated teller machines (ATMs) to voice mail. As businesses increased the use of IS, they became more dependent on them. Until the late 1980s, business technology was just an addition to the existing way of doing business. Keeping up to date was a matter of using new technology to improve old methods (such as using a fax machine to send a message instead of mailing it). As the 1990s approached, change began to accelerate. Businesses shifted to using new technology based on new methods. Business technology then became known as **information**

> **Information systems (IS)** The name given to business technology in the 1980s. Its role changed from supporting the business to doing business.

technology (IT), and its role became to *change* business.

Obviously, the roles of IT staff members have changed as technology itself has improved and evolved. The chief information officer (CIO) has moved out of the back room and into the boardroom and now spends less time worrying about keeping systems running and more time finding ways to boost business by applying technology to purchasing decisions, operational strategy, marketing, and sales. Today, the role of the CIO is to help the business use technology to communicate more efficiently with others while offering better service and reducing costs.[5]

IT CHANGES TWO CRITICAL ELEMENTS: TIME AND PLACE

Time and place have always been at the center of business. Customers had to wait for a business to be open in order to make a transaction, and they had to go to the place of business to make that transaction. They went to stores to buy clothes. They went to banks to arrange for loans. *Businesses* decided when and where customers did business with them.

Consider how IT has changed the entertainment industry. If you wanted to see a movie 40 years ago, you had to go to a movie theater. Twenty-five years ago, you could wait for it to be on television. Twenty years ago, you could wait for it to be on cable television or go to a video store and rent it. Ten years ago, you could go to a store and rent or buy a DVD. Today, you can order a movie on demand by satellite or cable. You can download it to your Xbox Live, rent a DVD copy of it online, or download it to your computer using the Internet. In addition, you can go to a grocery store or other business with a Redbox kiosk and rent a movie for a dollar a day.[6]

At work, Internet and intranet communication allows contributors to collaborate using shared documents and avoid time-consuming (and often expensive, when travel is involved) face-to-face meetings. E-mail and other electronic means of communication reduce costs and time spent.

IT allows businesses to sell goods and services at the customer's convenience. Time is no longer a factor. Today, you can shop, arrange a home mortgage loan, or buy a car on the Internet any time you like.

THE EFFECT OF IT ON LOCATION

As IT breaks down time and location barriers, it creates organizations and services that are independent of location. For example, the NASDAQ (USA) and the Eurex (Europe) are electronic stock exchanges without trading floors. Buyers and sellers make trades by computer.

Since location is not as much of a factor as it used to be, IT allows work to go to people, rather than people going to work. Data and information can flow across continents in seconds, allowing businesses to conduct work around the globe continuously. Physical location is much less important. Regardless of a business's size, effective use of technology frees it from the constraints of physical location. Rather, team members and clients can communicate in several ways using a process called *virtualization*.

Virtualization permits accessibility through technology; as a result, business may be conducted anywhere, at any time.[7] Virtualization is a process that allows networked computers to run multiple operating systems and programs through one central computer at the same time.[8] For example, you can carry around a virtual office in your briefcase, pocket, or purse, using such tools as Blackberries or wireless-enabled laptop computers. The centralized storage systems of virtualization give companies ready access to update system software and fix problems, a practice as cost-effective as it is convenient.

Big companies are big believers in virtualization. VMware, based in Palo Alto, California, is the current leader in virtualization software and systems. However, competitors like Citrix, Sun Microsystems, and Microsoft are threatening to steal some of the 85 percent market share VMware currently has.

Police have benefited greatly from virtualization, which allows them to access a tremendous amount of data in real time while they are on the streets.

Instant messaging allows businesspeople to communicate in real time, making e-mail seem as slow as sending a message in a bottle.

According to VMware, virtualization technology saves clients, on average, 50 percent of their previous hardware and operating costs and 80 percent of their previous energy costs. Ninety-seven percent of companies on the *Fortune 500* list are VMware clients.[9]

The way people do business drastically changes when companies increase their technological capabilities. Electronic communications can provide substantial time savings, whether you work in an office, at home, or on the road. E-mail ends the tedious game of telephone tag and is far faster than paper-based correspondence.

Instant messaging (IM) is now a favorite real-time business communication tool. For example, the first thing many businesspeople do after they turn on their computers is check to see if any of their colleagues are logged into IM. Using IM, busi-

> **Instant messaging (IM)** A computer application that allows business professionals to communicate in real time.

ness professionals can participate in multiple conversations at once. Its other advantage, of course, is that it is immediate—even more so than e-mail—and has no additional incremental cost.

IM also allows businesses to improve customer service. Many companies' Web sites feature chat functions that allow users to communicate with a customer service representative in real time and then save the communication, if needed. This can be particularly helpful when customers receive technical support or other information that will need to be referred to in the future.

Being present with customers in the moment allows for more efficient service. Some wireless devices and cell phones have an IM feature that makes it possible to communicate at times when a phone conversation would not be possible and avoids the incremental cost (if any) of text messages.[10] Businesses that use IM may find that employees report fewer interruptions during their workdays, as questions can be resolved more quickly through short messages.[11] See Figure 7.2 for other examples of ways in which IT is changing business.

Figure 7.2
How IT Is Changing Business

Organization	Technology is breaking down corporate barriers, allowing functional departments or product groups (even factory workers) to share critical information instantly.
Operations	Technology shrinks cycle times, reduces defects, and cuts waste. Service companies use technology to streamline ordering and communication with suppliers and customers.
Staffing	Technology eliminates layers of management and cuts the number of employees. Companies use computers and telecommunication equipment to create "virtual offices" with employees in various locations.
New products	IT cuts development cycles by feeding customer and marketing comments to product development teams quickly so they can revive products and target specific customers.
Customer relations	Customer service representatives can solve customers' problems instantly by using company-wide databases to complete tasks from changing addresses to adjusting bills. Information gathered from customer service interactions can further strengthen customer relationships.
New markets	Since it is no longer necessary for customers to walk down the street to get to stores, online businesses can attract customers to whom they wouldn't otherwise have access.

Study Alert

Today, time is no longer a factor. Customers decide when they will interact with businesses, thanks to technological innovations like virtualization, a process that allows networked computers to run multiple operating systems and programs through one central computer at the same time.

E-BUSINESS AND E-COMMERCE

E-business, or electronic business, is any electronic business data exchange using any electronic device.

> **E-business** Any electronic business data exchange using any electronic device.

That includes selling products online,[12] which is called e-commerce. E-business is much more than just selling—it includes visiting a Web site to check availability of a particular product, checking your bank balance online, or visiting a Web site to research a purchase. So, unlike e-commerce, which always results in a transaction or exchange, e-business is often simply the sharing of information.

It's important to understand the difference between these terms; many people use them interchangeably, but they are actually quite different. Any

> **E-commerce** Selling products or services online through e-business.

business that participates in e-commerce is engaging in e-business as well, but a business may engage in e-business without necessarily offering **e-commerce**. In 2007, retail e-commerce sales increased by 18.4 percent.[13] During the first three months of 2009, U.S. retail e-commerce sales were estimated at $31.7 billion.[14]

For example, you might decide to buy a new iPod, but you may at first be unsure about which model is the right choice—perhaps capacity is more important to you than the iPod's physical size. You'd visit the Apple site to learn more about the various models' memory capacity and dimensions and then visit several retail sites, such as Costco.com, to check the iPod model's price. Until an actual transaction takes place at one of these sites, you're conducting e-business. Once that transaction is made, e-commerce has occurred.

U.S. President Barack Obama has made improving and expanding broadband technology a priority of his administration.[15]

BROADBAND TECHNOLOGY

The more traffic on the Internet, the slower connections become. Tools to unlock these traffic jams include **broadband technology**, a continuous connection to the Internet that allows users to send and receive mammoth video, voice, and data files faster than ever before. Even though broadband in the United States is dramatically faster than dial-up connections, its average

> **Broadband technology** Technology that offers users a continuous connection to the Internet and allows them to send and receive mammoth files that include voice, video, and data much faster than ever before.

speed of 2.3 megabits per second is snail-like compared to Japan's 63 megabits per second.

Broadband is fast, but scientists and other scholars who access, transmit, and manipulate complex mathematical models, data sets, and other digital elements need an even faster solution. To meet this need, they've created a private Internet for research purposes only. **Internet2** is more than 22,000 times faster than today's public infrastruc-

> **Internet2** The private Internet system that links government supercomputer centers and a select group of universities; it runs more than 22,000 times faster than today's public infrastructure and supports heavy-duty applications.

ture and supports countless heavy-duty applications, such as videoconferencing, collaborative research, distance education, digital libraries, and full-body simulations known as *teleimmersion*.

A key element of Internet2 is a network called very-high-speed backbone network service, which was set up in 1995 as a way to link government supercomputer centers and a select group of universities. Internet2 makes it possible for a remote medical specialist to assist in a medical operation over the Internet without having the connection deteriorate as, say, home users check sports scores.[16]

Today, more than 325 member universities participate in Internet2.[17] Whereas the public Internet divides bandwidth equally among users (if there are 100 users, they each get to use 1 percent of the available bandwidth), Internet2 is more capitalistic. Users who are willing to pay more can use more bandwidth.

Some fear Internet2 may soon be overrun by undergrads engaged in music swapping and other resource-hogging pursuits, but the designers of Internet2 are thinking ahead. They're confident that history will indeed repeat itself, so they're planning

YouTube and the micro-blogging site Twitter are among the largest Web 2.0 businesses, where ordinary people create all the content. But despite their enormous popularity and, for some, new corporate ownership (NewsCorp now owns MySpace, and Google bought YouTube in 2006), most Web 2.0 companies have made little or no profit; almost all rely on advertising to generate revenue.[21]

to filter Internet2 technology so there will be plenty of room on the road for all of us—at a price, of course.

SOCIAL NETWORKING AND WEB 2.0

Every day, millions of people worldwide develop their own online identities on social networking sites like Facebook and MySpace. They use the sites to share pictures and videos, or just send a quick hello to an old friend. While sites focused on non-work related socializing are the most popular, there are hundreds of other social networking sites for nearly any purpose.

LinkedIn.com encourages professionals to post résumés and develop business relationships, while PatientsLikeMe.com lets members share experiences of their illnesses and network with people affected by the same ailments. Ning.com allows users to create their own social networking sites—on whatever subject they choose.

For businesses, social networking provides an array of opportunities and challenges. It's an inexpensive way to gain exposure. Most importantly, it gives businesses tools to collaborate with consumers on product development, service enhancement, and promotion.

In a recent survey, 93 percent of social media users felt companies should have a social media presence.[18] However, despite the fact that increasing numbers of companies use these sites to help them woo customers, many ban employees from using social networking sites at work.[19] The reason? Employee productivity may suffer as a result of social media's time-wasting allure. There's another risk as well. Because companies are unable to completely control their identities on social networking sites—after all, they are collaborative spaces that permit their customers and stakeholders to interact with them—there's always the possibility that negative comments can appear in a very public space. A single disparaging remark on a social networking forum can have devastating effects on a company's reputation.

For all its strengths and weaknesses, social networking is the best example of what tech publisher Tim O'Reilly in 2004 dubbed "Web 2.0." **Web 2.0** is the set of tools that allow people to build social and business connections, share information, and collaborate on projects online with user-generated sites like blogs, wikis, social networks and other online communities, and virtual worlds.[20] (Web 1.0 referred to corporate-generated sites like Google and Amazon.)

Today's Web 2.0 companies may be transformed by yet another generation of innovators that expand the utility of the Web, create location-based services, and tie financial payment systems to existing sites (translation: they make money). Figure 7.3 shows the innovations of several Web 2.0 businesses.

Location-based services are tied to devices that can track a user's whereabouts and suggest places, like restaurants or shops, in the area. If you happen to have a global positioning system in your car, this location-based technology is not new to you, but now that same location tracking power can be put in a portable device, such as a cell phone. Someday, you might get a text message from McDonald's offering you a discount on a latte as you walk by a franchise's door. Experts predict that portable location-based services will become a $13 billion industry by 2013.[22] It looks like the start of Web 3.0.

> **Web 2.0** The set of tools that allow people to build social and business connections, share information, and collaborate on projects online (including blogs, wikis, social networking sites and other online communities, and virtual worlds).

In many ways, conducting business has become easier with the help of technology, but sometimes it can all be too much. Imagine that you're reading a menu in a restaurant, and you feel completely overwhelmed by the choices available. As a result, you can't figure out what you want to eat. It's the same with information in today's world. One of the challenges of both e-business and e-commerce is that both can cause *information overload* to the consumer, which will be addressed in the next section.

[BUS] connections

1. What is data processing? How has technology changed from data processing to IT?
2. How has instant messaging changed the way people do business? How has this technology affected you directly?
3. How do you use technology as a consumer?

Career PERSPECTIVES

A CAREER IN IT

According to the U.S. Department of Labor, careers in IS are expected to grow at a faster rate than other professions through 2014.[23] Job opportunities in this area should remain plentiful. Examples of entry-level jobs in computer information systems (CIS) include junior database administrators and technical support specialists.

Experienced IT professionals have the option of becoming an IS manager. These management positions sometimes earn more than $100,000 per year. IS managers often oversee security for intranets and extranets, and they might also administer and manage complex database systems for a company. There is also work in systems integration, which means combining two or more existing systems into a single, more efficient system. Computer systems analysts, computer programmers, and customer support representatives are also positions in this field.

Many companies employ specialists in CIS. Manufacturing, government, insurance, retail, and financial firms are all examples of possible employers of CIS employees.

Although many programming jobs are outsourced, companies are still going to have a need for locally based people to run and manage their information systems. What areas of IT appeal to you most? Would you enjoy running a computer network for a company, or possibly coming to coworkers' rescue as a help desk representative?

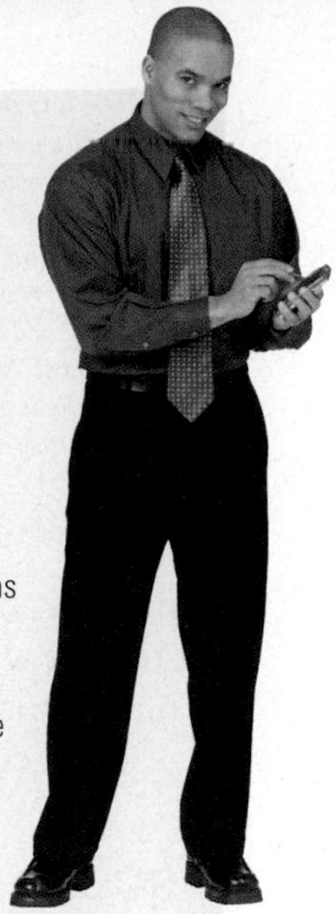

Figure 7.3 Web 2.0 Businesses Revolutionize the Internet

Company	The Change
ThinkFree	ThinkFree offers an office productivity suite that combines the best features of the Internet and the desktop; users collaborate with others and interact in ways desktop applications won't permit.
WidgetBox	WidgetBox creates Web widgets (small programs that can be embedded into a Web page) for use with blogs, social networks, online auctions, and Web pages.
Hinchcliffe & Company	According to the company's founder, Hinchcliffe & Company is the first dedicated professional services firm to focus solely on using Web 2.0 to transform the way a company does business.
KickApps	KickApps puts a new twist on viral marketing by helping businesses take advantage of the human networking aspects of Web 2.0.
FeedBurner	FeedBurner allows users to syndicate their audio, video, or text content. The company also provides detailed analytics about popularity and viewership statistics.
Near-Time	Near-Time enables companies to use self-service Web 2.0 applications to create better partnerships with customers and suppliers.
Spymac	In its sixth redesign, the Web 2.0 site called Leapfrog allows users to upload, embed and store content, video chat, and post and find movies with no additional software required. The site adjusts to the needs of visitors from 150 countries in terms of page design, interface, and language.
Paltalk	Paltalk, the largest video chat community on the Internet, gives users complete control to build and shape online communities where a worldwide audience can hold multiperson video chats with as many as 1,000 people in each chat room.
37signals	The company offers a growing roster of lean online applications, including the project collaboration tool Basecamp.

Source: "The Faces of Web 2.0," Entrepreneur.com, http://www.entrepreneur.com/slideshow/173148.html (accessed July 15, 2009). Reprinted with permission.

Going GLOBAL

Bill Gates' Fix for India's Ills: Technology

Businesses in many developing nations desperately need incentives to innovate and invest in technology. Billionaire Bill Gates has set his sights on providing incentives to help businesses improve technology infrastructure in India in an effort to help the country and its citizens improve living conditions for all.

Bill Gates thinks he has solutions for India's biggest challenges. How can the country solve its healthcare problems, the nightmare of distributing vaccines, and the shortage of doctors? Alleviate poverty and streamline public distribution of food rations? How about providing the urban poor with jobs? You guessed it: technology.

"India is taking its self-confidence, [the realization] that it is very innovative, and now saying let's invest in ourselves," says Gates. "In spite of the tough times, this country hasn't said let's pull back on investing in the future."

To some extent, India has been a bit of a proving ground. Motorola tried producing a $14 cell phone. It flopped. Such missteps haven't discouraged Gates from pushing ahead. The Bill & Melinda Gates Foundation, the largest charitable trust in the world, handed out a $1 million grant in early June to Maryland's CHF International to set up a labor network for nearly 90 million urban workers. The idea is to provide some sort of a formal connection between those who hire unskilled laborers and the laborers themselves.

A Web site called Babajob.com, set up three years ago in Bangalore, India's IT capital, helps daily wage earners and domestic workers—easily the most exploited of India's labor force—find employers online. Internet access is a hurdle for most workers, [but] the group plans to overcome that by allowing urban poor to input data with more accessible cell phones.

With Web penetration still in the single digits in urban areas and far less in the countryside, people are looking more closely at mobile phones, which in India are cheaper to use than almost anywhere in the world. Farmers in Maharashtra, a western Indian state, use text messaging–based technology to track food prices in faraway markets.

The most ambitious effort is the Unique Identification project, which aims to provide 1.2 billion Indians with universally accepted proof of their identity. An ID card with a microchip or a verifiable numerical code could curb corruption, help with bank accounts, generate access to social services, and keep track of the administration of vaccines and health issues. Gates believes Microsoft would bid for contracts in implementing the program.

A slum in Mumbai, India.

Source: Mehul Srivastava, "Bill Gates' Fix for India's Ills: Technology," *BusinessWeek*, July 27, 2009, http://www.businessweek.com/globalbiz/content/jul2009/gb20090727_450174.htm, (accessed August 17, 2009). Reprinted with permission.

Questions

1. How could Gates's efforts in India affect the businesses operating there?
2. How could Gates's efforts in India benefit its workers and consumers?

All the information stored in this file cabinet would take up a tiny part of a compact flash drive..

>> Managing Information

New technologies available today bring us volumes of information that would have otherwise been very time consuming to gather, but this information can be useless or even oppressive if we don't know how to use and manage it. Voice mail, e-mail, the Internet, iPods, text messaging, and IM can make businesspeople can feel overwhelmed with information.[24] In fact, a recent study found that information overload can be so distracting that it causes intelligence to plummet.[25] This information overload is called **infoglut**.

The availability of digital information is growing at a rapid rate. In 2007, the digital universe was 10 percent bigger than previous estimates determined it would be. In that year, for the first time ever, the amount of data created exceeded the amount of storage space available for it. By 2011, permanent storage space won't be available for about half of all the digital information that has been created.[26] However, businesspeople can take a few preventive measures to ensure that they get the right amount of information when it's needed most.

When managing information, you must first distinguish between what is and what isn't useful. *Usefulness* is based on the following four characteristics (see Figure 7.4):

1. *Quality.* Quality means the information is accurate and reliable. When a retail store enters a sale into a cash register, it is automatically added to the day's total sales. If that information is wrong, it can have a domino effect on all other information such as revenue projections, and so on.

2. *Completeness.* There must be enough information to allow individuals to make a decision but not so much as to confuse the issue. Today, the problem is often too *much* information, rather than too little.

3. *Timeliness.* Information must reach business owners and managers quickly. Sales information from two years ago must be available when needed to accurately compile a sales forecast. If locating that information takes several weeks, it may be

Princess Cruises maintains a database with extensive personal information about its passengers. Each passenger completes a "cruiser information" form; in exchange for the data passengers provide, the company notifies them of special offers and last-minute deals.

virtually useless, because a decision may already have been made.

4. *Relevance.* Information systems often provide too much data. Managers need to learn to ask the right questions in order to get the relevant data they need.

The importance of information management cannot be overemphasized. For most companies, proper management of information is the core of their business. For example, Motorola uses a system called Compass to manage the information contained in the company's 4,400 blogs, its millions of documents, and countless sites maintained by the company and its partners.[27]

People must be able to access easy-to-use, organized data when they need it, which is where data storage comes in. A **data warehouse** stores data on a specific subject over a period of time. However, the warehouse is not very useful if the data are difficult to retrieve.

That's where data mining comes in. **Data mining** looks for hidden patterns in the data in a data warehouse and discovers relationships among the data. In Internet retail, data mining is called *shopping cart analysis*. Using shopping cart analysis, a manager can see what items people buy to-

Figure 7.4 Characteristics of Information Usefulness

1. Quality
2. Completeness
3. Timeliness
4. Relevance

Data warehousing comes in many different shapes and sizes. Las Vegas casinos like the MGM Grand Hotel use several different software applications to keep updates on those in its customer loyalty club. Data used in these applications are only 12 hours behind real time; this allows the company to reward its customers with points that can be used toward purchases while still on vacation.[28]

Thinking Critically

>> Computer and Information Systems Managers: The Nature of the Work

An increasing level of dependency on businesses' information technology departments has brought about new challenges for their managers and staff. The Bureau of Labor Statistics's *Occupational Outlook Handbook, 2008–2009 Edition* explains the expanding roles of computer and information systems managers and the many challenges that confront them.

Computer and information systems managers play a vital role in the implementation of technology within their organizations. They do everything from helping to construct a business plan to overseeing network security to directing Internet operations, including:

- Planning, coordinating, and facilitating the computer-related activities of firms.
- Determining both technical and business goals in consultation with top management and making detailed plans.
- Directing the work of systems analysts, computer programmers, support specialists, and other computer-related workers.
- Planning and coordinating activities, such as installing and upgrading hardware and software, programming, designing systems, developing computer networks, and implementing Internet and intranet sites.
- Maintaining and securing networks.
- Analyzing the computer and information needs of their organizations from an operational and strategic perspective; determining immediate and long-range personnel and equipment requirements.
- Assigning and reviewing the work of their subordinates and staying abreast of the latest technology to ensure that the organization does not lag behind competitors.

Computer and information systems managers spend most of their time in offices. Most work at least 40 hours a week, and some may have to work evenings and weekends to meet deadlines or solve unexpected problems. Some computer and information systems managers may experience considerable pressure to meet technical goals with short deadlines or tight budgets. As networks continue to expand and more work is done remotely, computer and information systems managers have to communicate with and oversee offsite employees using modems, laptops, e-mail, and the Internet.

Like other workers who spend most of their time using computers, computer and information systems managers are susceptible to eyestrain, back discomfort, and hand and wrist problems, such as carpal tunnel syndrome.

Source: Adapted from the Bureau of Labor Statistics, *Occupational Outlook Handbook, 2008–2009 Edition*, Computer and Information Systems Managers, http://www. bls.gov/oco/ocos258.htm#nature (accessed August 17, 2009).

QUESTIONS

1. Are the challenges and demands placed on computer and information systems managers and their staffs unique, or are they part of a growing trend of expectations about technology in the workplace?

2. Have you ever interacted with a computer or information systems manager in a workplace setting? Did you observe the manager participating in some of the responsibilities described?

>> IT Challenges

Technology has many advantages, but there are some challenges as well. According to the Javelin Strategy and Research Center, the identities of 10 million people were stolen in 2008. Much of the identity theft is perpetrated by hackers who break into computer networks to steal credit card and Social Security numbers and other private data.

Globally, businesses lose $221 billion per year to identity theft, according to the Aberdeen Group. Victims lose an average of $851 to $1,378 in out-of-pocket expenses to resolve identity theft. [50] Figure 7.5 lists several types of tax-related identity theft that were identified by the U.S. Internal Revenue Service in 2009. As the costs of identity theft continue to escalate, people are continually developing ways to prevent it.

Intrusion by hackers, viruses, government information security, privacy issues, phishing, computer and network stability, and reliability of data are all of concern to computer users today. What might seem like a little "glitch" could cost a business or industry millions of dollars, as we'll discuss in the upcoming sections.

HACKERS AND VIRUSES

One ongoing problem with computer technology that's likely to persist in the future is that computers are susceptible to hackers. For example, according to *Information Week*, hackers broke into computers of TJX, the owners of TJMaxx, and allegedly stole customer credit card numbers. This kind of security breach can cause millions of dollars worth of damage—directly to a company's bottom line, and indirectly to its reputation. [51]

A hacker broke into a Twitter employee's personal e-mail account and obtained information to access the employee's Google Apps account—where the hacker located valuable notes and financial information about Twitter. The incident has evoked concerns regarding the storing of private information on the internet and the interconnectedness of social Web sites. [52]

Computer security is more complicated today than ever before. When information was processed on mainframes (a single computer that ran all of the computers in a company) the single data center was easier to control because access to it was limited. Today, computers and their information are accessible not only within a company, but also outside the company via extranets, the Internet, and other portals.

One ongoing security issue involves the spread of computer viruses over the Internet. A **virus** is a piece of programming code intentionally inserted into other programming to cause an unexpected and usually undesirable event. Viruses are spread by downloading infected programming over the Internet or by sharing an infected file. The user is usually unaware of the source of the file containing the virus. The virus lies dormant until circumstances cause its code to be executed by the computer. Some viruses are playful, but some can be quite harmful, erasing data or causing your hard drive to crash. In 2009, a computer worm known as Conficker made its way to at least 9 million personal computers across the globe. The worm's ability to wreak havoc has been said to be the digital version of Pearl Harbor. [53]

> **Virus** A piece of programming code inserted into other programming to cause an unexpected and usually undesirable event.

Some hackers use "zombie computers" called botnets to launch *denial-of-service* (DOS) attacks on the Web sites of companies and government agencies. The botnets are machines that have been infected with viruses that allow the hackers who created the viruses to control them. Then the hackers who infected them rent them out to anyone who is interested in causing harm to a government agency or business, ordering them to constantly attempt to access a particular Web site. Eventually, the site is so besieged with access requests that it cannot function. According to *BusinessWeek*, 1,300 DOS attacks were reported on August 10, 2009, nearly double the number on the same day two years before. [54]

Certain programs can "inoculate" your computer so it does not "catch" a known virus. New viruses are being developed constantly, and consequently, antivirus programs have only limited success. Computer users should be sure to keep their antivirus protection programs up to date. More importantly, they should also follow safe computing practices, including not downloading files from unknown sources, and scanning file storage devices, such as CDs and USB flash drives, before accessing files on them. Even businesses protected by firewalls can be unwittingly

Figure 7.6 Ways to Protect Computers from Viruses

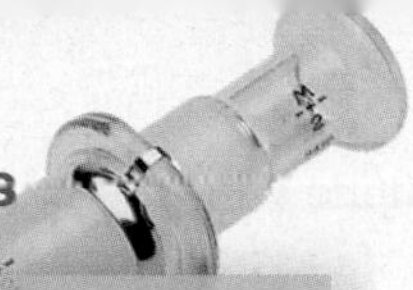

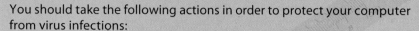

You should take the following actions in order to protect your computer from virus infections:

- **Use a high-quality antivirus program.** Scan your computer and all files using the virus check program regularly and install the updates.

- **If you get public domain software,** (1) ensure that the source is reliable and (2) scan the software using the antivirus program.

- **Before using a disk that has been in another computer,** scan it for viruses.

- **Practice "safe computing."** (1) Do not download files from unknown sources, and (2) if and when you do have to download, always scan all Internet downloads and e-mail attachments with an antivirus program.

affected by computer viruses that have been accidentally downloaded by employees. Figure 7.6 offers steps you should take to minimize the threat of virus infection to your computer. Following these steps, however, does not guarantee you won't get a virus.

SecureWorks, an Internet security service provider, reported that the United States had the highest number of computers infected with viruses worldwide in 2008. Often, the infected computers' viruses remain dormant for a period of time, while the computer continues to spread the virus to other machines.[55] Figure 7.7 lists some common types of viruses. Have you ever been affected by one of these types of viruses?

GOVERNMENT INFORMATION SECURITY

Before September 11, 2001, corporate and government security officials worried mostly about online theft, credit card fraud, and hackers. Today, they are also concerned about cyberterrorism.[56] In one instance, which occurred on July 4, 2009, government and company Web sites in the United States and South Korea came under attack. The virus used in this scenario attempted to block users' access to data; in some cases, the assault was successful.

In the United States, the U.S. Departments of Transportation and State, the Treasury Department, the White House, the New York Stock Exchange, Yahoo!, and the Federal Trade Commission have been targeted by cyberterrorism.[57] According to Mike McConnell, former director of the National Security Agency, if 30 terrorists armed with hacker skills and $10 million attacked the United States today, they could be able to shut down entire communications systems; the movement of money through banks, businesses, and other institutions; electricity transmission; and transportation networks.

In order to prevent such a disaster from happening, government agencies need cooperation from businesses, because 85 percent of systems are in the private sector. Many technology workers are reluctant to give information about security breaches to the gov

Some businesses fear that public awareness of security breaches will be embarrassing and costly.

Figure 7.7 Most Common Types of Viruses

Viruses. A virus is a small piece of software that piggybacks on real programs. For example, a virus might attach itself to a program such as a spreadsheet program. Each time the spreadsheet program runs, the virus runs, too, and it has the chance to reproduce (by attaching to other programs) or wreak havoc.

E-mail viruses. An e-mail virus travels as an attachment to e-mail messages; it usually replicates itself by automatically mailing itself to dozens of people in the victim's e-mail address book. Some e-mail viruses can be activated without actually clicking on the message; instead, they're launched when the message is previewed.

Trojan horses. A Trojan horse is simply a computer program. The program claims to do one thing (for example, it may claim to be a game) but instead does damage when you run it (for example, it may erase your hard disk). Trojan horses have no way to replicate automatically.

Worms. A worm is a small piece of software that uses computer networks and security holes to replicate itself. A copy of the worm scans the network for another machine that has a specific security hole. It copies itself to the new machine using the security hole, and then starts replicating from there, as well.

Source: Marshall Brain, "How Computer Viruses Work," Howstuffworks.com, http://computer.howstuffworks.com/virus.htm (accessed August 17, 2009). Reprinted with permission.

ernment for fear that the public will lose faith in the company's ability to protect its assets and reputation. In addition, some believe providing this kind of information is a violation of their privacy, and the government should not be told. The Critical Infrastructure Information Act, which was enacted in 2002, assures businesses that any information they provide to the government regarding critical infrastructure (such as water supply, electrical systems, or telecommunications data) is exempt from disclosure by the Freedom of Information Act.

PRIVACY AND PHISHING

The increasing use of technology creates major concerns about privacy. E-mail is no more private than a postcard—you should always assume that anyone can read what you write in an e-mail, no matter how private you may consider the communication to be. You do not need to be the target of a criminal investigation to have your e-mail reviewed by someone in your company or in your personal life.

More than 25 percent of U.S. companies review employee e-mail regularly—and doing so is completely legal. Just as employers can listen to their employees' telephone conversations, they can track e-mail to detect trade secrets being passed, non–work-related traffic, harassment, and conflicts of interest. According to an American Management Association study, 30 percent of the companies surveyed had fired workers for misusing the Internet, and 28 percent had terminated employees for inappropriate use of e-mail.[58]

Most e-mail travels over the Internet as **unencrypted** plain text, meaning that the information being sent is not in a secret code, and therefore anyone can view it. Some e-mail systems have the ability to en-

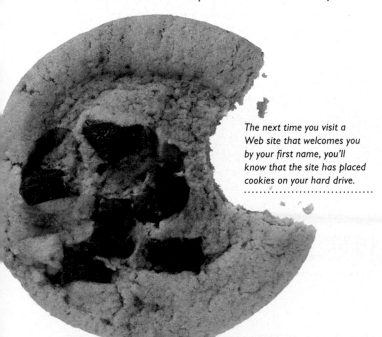

The next time you visit a Web site that welcomes you by your first name, you'll know that the site has placed cookies on your hard drive.

One year, candy maker Hershey couldn't get its treats to the stores on time during the busy Halloween season. Its new $115 million computer system failed; as a result, shipments were disrupted and retailers were forced to order Halloween treats from other companies. Consequently, Hershey suffered a 12 percent decrease in sales that quarter.[62]

crypt messages to ensure that corporate messages are kept private. People who use browser-based e-mail services, such as Google's Gmail, can obtain encryption services from companies like VeriSign for a low cost—perhaps as little as $10 a year. The downside is that legitimate recipients of your messages must get a "key" to open and read them.

The Internet presents increasing threats to your privacy, as more personal information is stored in computers and more people are able to access that data—both legally *and* illegally. The Internet allows Web surfers to access all sorts of information about businesses and individuals. Social networking sites, such as Myspace.com, allow people to post personal information about themselves—sometimes a little *too* personal. Always keep in mind that anything you post to the Internet or send via e-mail or other digital transmission could potentially come back to haunt you.

Some employers even check the Internet to see how employees or prospective employees are portraying themselves. A survey conducted by CareerBuilder.com found that 33 percent of the employers surveyed chose not to hire a candidate based on information they found about the candidate on social networking sites.[60] Need more proof? Think about the scandals related to beauty pageant contestants who have lost their titles because of racy photos of them found on the Internet. A picture can be worth a thousand words.

Some computer users are concerned that Web sites have gotten downright nosy. In fact, many Web servers track users' movements online. Web surfers are often willing to swap personal details for free access to online information—but you should always remember that sometimes companies and people who acquire that personal information then share it with others without your permission.

Web sites often send **cookies** to your computer that stay on your hard drive. These pieces of infor-

> **Unencrypted** An encryption is a secret code given to information when it is passing through the Internet. An unencrypted piece of data can be seen by anyone; it is less secure.

Real World Apps

After learning about the importance of IT to the world of business in his Introduction to Business class, Tom decided to find out all he could about the effects of technology in his own workplace.

Tom found that over the years, the financial industry has been greatly enhanced by the introduction of e-business and e-commerce. What Tom once thought were negative and impersonal changes were actually great strides forward—like the ability of people to check their bank balances any time of the day or night, and not having to wait until the bank was open for business. True, his bank's workforce had shrunk because advances in technology required fewer personnel, but these advances also enabled decision making to be faster and more efficient. Without e-mail, IM, and virtual meetings, even Tom had to admit that his job would be considerably harder and more boring. He also couldn't deny that customers were more satisfied, rather than less so—after all, decisions about loans and other consumer products were often made much more quickly by data analysis systems.

While it might be true that the personal touch is somewhat diminished, the average consumer rarely has to enter a bank these days. Online banking is a common practice, and ATMs handle much of the responsibilities that tellers once managed. Today, business moves at a fast pace and technology allows that pace to be maintained. Old fears about Internet security issues have been diminished due to the availability of stronger encryption programs and more up-to-date virus software applications.

Tom now realizes that computers, the Internet, and technological advancements are here to stay, but they will never remain the same. Thanks to these advances, he's a more productive and versatile employee today.

mation, such as registration data or user preferences, are sent over the Internet by a Web site to a Web browser. The browser saves and sends back the information to the server whenever the user returns to that site. These little tidbits sometimes contain little more than your name and a password, which the Web site recognizes the next time you visit the site, so you don't have to reenter the information every time you visit. The cookies used by Amazon.com also remember the items you've browsed before on the site. Other cookies track your movements around the Web and then blend that information with a database so a company can tailor the ads to your preferences.

Cookies Pieces of information, such as registration data or user preferences, sent by a Web site over the Internet to a Web browser that the browser is expected to save and return to the server whenever the user returns to that Web site.

You should think carefully about how much personal information you are willing to give away. Remember, we are living in an information economy, and information is a commodity—an economic good with a measurable value. Once that information is out there, it's very hard—if not impossible—to remove it.

Phishing is another type of online security threat. A scammer will embellish an e-mail message with a stolen logo for a well-recognized brand—such as eBay, PayPal, or Citibank—that makes the message look authentic. Phishing messages often state something like "Account activation required" or "Your account will be canceled if you do not verify." When victims click the link contained in the message, they are sent to a phony Web site that uses their personal information to commit fraud.

Goodmail Systems Inc. has developed a way to fight phishing by verifying e-mails that are legitimate. Clients route their e-mail to consumers through Goodmail, which marks each message with a blue-ribbon icon to prove it is safe.[61] That sounds fine, but how long will it be before scammers add fake blue ribbon icons to their messages? The best way to avoid a phishing scam is to never access a Web site through a link in an e-mail message. Instead, always open a new window and visit the page you're looking to access directly.

As more people log on to the Internet, the number of legal issues surrounding its use will likely increase. Today, copyright and pornography laws are crashing into the virtual world. Other legal questions relate to intellectual property and contract disputes, online sexual and racial harassment, and the use of electronic communication to promote crooked sales schemes. Cybercrimes cost businesses in the United States billions of dollars a year.

STABILITY

Technology can provide significant increases in productivity and efficiency, but instability in technology also has a significant impact on business. In 2008, the delays of hundreds of flights were attributed to a possible computer failure at the Federal Aviation Administration (FAA). The FAA and its systems have been under ongoing scrutiny for persistent flight delays across the nation.[63] These pervasive problems could negatively affect the airline industry as a whole as consumers become frustrated by constant delays and decide to seek other ways of reaching their destinations.

We have all experienced computer glitches that caused delays or garbled data. What's to blame? Sometimes problems are caused by human error, such as not thoroughly testing a new computer application before distributing it. Other problems that cause instability are computer viruses, problems with servers, and incompatible hardware and software. These problems could affect you personally: for example, if your co-workers' computers were newer than yours and new software applications were introduced that your computer couldn't run, you wouldn't be able to do your job as effectively as your colleagues could. The various permutations of computer error; human error; malfunctioning software; and overly complex marriages of software, hardware, and networking equipment present never-ending challenges for IT administrators and users alike.

RELIABILITY OF DATA

Of course, not all information found online is reliable. Many people consider the information they find on the Internet to be true: When asked what data source they trusted most, a whopping 37 percent of people chose the Internet. Television came in second, at 17 percent; newspapers, 16 percent; and radio, 13 percent.[64] When evaluating data on the Internet, always consider the following factors:

- *Accuracy.* How reliable and error free is the information? Has it been edited and fact checked?

- *Authority.* What is the authority or expertise of the individual or group that created this site? How knowledgeable is the person or group that contributed it? Is the site sponsored or cosponsored by an individual or group that has created other Web sites? Is contact information for the author or producer included in the document?

- *Objectivity.* Is the information presented with a minimum of bias? To what extent is the information trying to sway the opinion of the audience?

[BUS] connections

1. What are some of the challenges facing IT today and in the future?
2. What risks might one face when using the Internet?
3. What should you consider when evaluating data on the Internet?

- *Currency.* Is the content of the work up to date? When was the information produced? When was the Web site last revised? How up to date are the links? How reliable are the links?

- *Coverage.* Are the topics explored in depth? What is the overall value of the content? What does it contribute to the literature in its field? Given the ease of self-publishing on the Web, this issue is much more relevant than it would be if you were auditing conventionally published resources.

If you first consider that all the data you see on the Internet might not be reliable, you can make better decisions when determining what data to use in your research. You'll be able to quickly eliminate any data that may be biased or out of date.

For REVIEW >>

1. Explain information technology's role in business.

   • Business technology is now known as information technology (IT), and its role is to become the way of doing business, rather than just using technology to help with business functions. Time and place have always been at the center of business. In the past, businesses decided when and where customers did business with them. Today, customers decide when they will interact with businesses, thanks to technological innovations like virtualization, a process that allows networked computers to run multiple operating systems and programs through one central computer at the same time. E-business and e-commerce are related concepts, but unlike e-commerce, which always results in a transaction or exchange, e-business is often simply the sharing of information. Broadband technology, a continuous connection to the Internet that allows users to send and receive mammoth video, voice, and data files faster than ever before, has enabled e-business and e-commerce sites to flourish. The next innovation is the Internet2 system, which is far faster than broadband and supports countless heavy-duty applications. Social networking Web sites, which are among the companies known as Web 2.0 firms, are a vital way in which businesses reach and interact with their customers.

2. Understand how information is managed.

   • To manage knowledge, a company must learn how to share information throughout the organization and implement systems for creating new knowledge. This need is creating new technologies that support the exchange of information among staff, suppliers, and customers. In order to be successful, firms must figure out how to harness technology and provide a pipeline of interaction and information between themselves and their stakeholders. Infoglut is a common problem, as the vast amounts of information that are available can be very hard to filter out and store. Data warehouses are used to store data on a specific subject over a period of time, and data mining is a technique used to look for hidden patterns in the data in a data warehouse and discover relationships among the data.

3. Describe various types of hardware and software.

   • The term *hardware* refers to many varieties of computing devices: computers, pagers, cellular phones, printers, scanners, fax machines, personal digital assistants (PDAs), iPods, and much more. Some experts think we have entered the post-PC era and are moving toward an array of Internet appliance options instead. These include PDAs (such as Blackberries), smartphones, netbooks, and computers built into car dashboards. Wi-Fi networks allow users to connect to the Internet—and thus to their work and their lives—anywhere at any time. Firewalls, which may be either hardware- or software-based, can protect intranets and other computer networks from intrusion from unwanted visitors, such as hackers. Virtual private networks use shared public resources, but they are much safer and more secure forms of data transfer than the Internet. The term *software* refers to a set of programs and procedures used to operate a computer and perform specific tasks with the computer. Businesspeople most frequently need and use software for (1) writing, (2) calculating or manipulating numbers, (3) filing and retrieving data, (4) presenting information visually, (5) communicating, (6) accounting, and (7) browsing the Internet or intranets. Shareware is software that is copyrighted but distributed to potential customers free of charge. It is different from public domain software (freeware), which is free for the taking.

4. Discuss challenges in information technology.

   • Identity theft is a massive challenge in the world of IT; the identities of 10 million people were stolen in 2008 alone. IT professionals must also combat attempts by hackers to steal data and spread computer viruses on company equipment. Government Web sites have also become vulnerable to these attacks and, in their case, national security is at risk. There are growing concerns about violations of consumers' and businesses' privacy on the Internet, particularly as businesses and individuals use the technology to compile increasing amounts of data about them. E-mail is particularly at risk because it is unencrypted and thus is readable by virtually anyone who knows how to obtain it. Social networking sites also present a problem because so many users post extremely personal information there, where anyone—including potential employers—can see it. Commercial Web sites often send cookies to users' computers that collect personal data about them; they use these data to more appropriately target their marketing to the consumers. Phishing, a type of online security threat, is used to trick consumers into divulging personal data by sending them e-mail messages warning them that they must visit a particular Web site and update their information (or a similar enticement). Sites and systems are also susceptible to stability problems, which can negatively affect a business when these issues compound to such a degree that customers' trust is eroded.

Key Terms

Broadband technology	Hackers	Shareware
Cookies	Infoglut	Software
Data	Information	Unencrypted
Data mining	Information systems (IS)	Virtual private network (VPN)
Data processing	Information technology (IT)	Virtualization
Data warehouse	Instant messaging (IM)	Virus
E-business	Internet2	Web 2.0
E-commerce	Intranet	Wireless fidelity (Wi-Fi)
Extranet	Portal	Wireless networking
Firewall	Public domain software (freeware)	

<< Think AND DISCUSS

1. Develop a list of computer programs you would use if you owned a retail clothing business. Which do you think would be the most necessary? What kinds of things could you do with each program? If you were to open a restaurant, which programs would be the same? Which might be different?

2. What was the last technology purchase you made? What kinds of things did you evaluate before making the purchase decision? What would you do differently next time if making a similar purchase?

3. Computer glitches are a normal part of daily life—and business life, too. Discuss a computer glitch you have experienced, and discuss how the glitch affected you.

4. Discuss in groups: How has technology changed since you were in kindergarten? How do you think it will be different 10 years from now?

5. Discuss in groups: With technology comes the ability to have quick and easy electronic communication. What are the differences between communicating electronically—say via e-mail—versus in person? Discuss at least five differences. Do you have any pet peeves about electronic communication, such as e-mail?

INTERNET IN >> Action

1. This chapter discussed the fact that there is an almost endless supply of information available on the Web, but not all of it is from reliable sources.
   - Perform a Google or Bing search of the terms "employee intranet." View at least three intranet sites and write down the names. What information does each one provide? How is this useful to the company's employees?

2. Visit a favorite Web site. What components of this Web site make you inclined to use it? Are there any features it doesn't have that you wish it did? Write your thoughts in a one-page paper.

Self-Assessment Exercises

BUSINESS CAREER QUIZ

Is Distance Learning Right for You?

Many schools and universities are moving toward offering more online classes. Take this quiz to see if online classes are for you.

1. My technology access is best described as:
   a. I have a computer at home with Internet access, and I have an e-mail account.
   b. I have regular access to the Internet, and I have an e-mail account.
   c. I don't have a computer or Internet access, nor do I have an e-mail account.
2. My technology skills are:
   a. very good; I can use e-mail, Web browsers, and word-processing software and can download files and create attachments. I like trying to solve technology problems on my own and don't get frustrated easily.
   b. average; I can use e-mail, Web browsers, and word-processing software. I don't feel comfortable solving technology problems on my own.
   c. below average; I have used e-mail, Web browsers, and word-processing software, but I get frustrated when things don't work the way they should.
3. Face-to-face communication is:
   a. not essential to me; I understand that quality learning can take place without face-to-face interaction.
   b. important to me; I wonder about my ability to learn without being able to see the instructor or other students.
   c. Essential; I can't learn unless I can interact in person with the instructor and other students.
4. When I need help in a class.
   a. I feel comfortable asking questions and asking for help when I need it.
   b. I hesitate to ask questions of the instructor, but I will ask for help if I need it.
   c. I don't like to ask questions or ask for help.
5. The amount of uninterrupted time I have to devote to an online class is:
   a. 15 hours or more per week.
   b. 10 to 15 hours, and only at restricted times (e.g., only at night).
   c. less than 10 hours per week.
6. I would describe my personal style as:
   a. self-motivated, self-disciplined, and organized.
   b. motivated, but I need help remembering assignments and due dates.
   c. disorganized; I need someone to motivate me and help me stay on top of my coursework.
7. When it comes to procrastination:
   a. I rarely procrastinate
   b. I sometimes procrastinate
   c. I always procrastinate; I prefer to work under pressure.

Self-Assessment Exercises

BUSINESS CAREER QUIZ (CONTINUED)

8. My reading and writing abilities are:
    a. above average; I have confidence in my abilities.
    b. just okay; I read well but prefer not to express myself in writing.
    c. below average; I don't like reading and look for classes without a lot of writing.
9. My critical-thinking skills are:
    a. very good; I can analyze class materials and formulate opinions on what I have learned.
    b. fair; I often struggle to read something and formulate an option on it.
    c. poor; analyzing material is not something I do well.
10. Class discussions are:
    a. important to me and useful to help me learn the information; I often participate in class discussions.
    b. somewhat important to my learning.
    c. not very useful to me; I don't usually participate.
11. When it comes to learning:
    a. I welcome opportunities to learn new things and master new technology.
    b. I get nervous around new technology but like to learn.
    c. I get very nervous and would rather not try it.
12. My reason for taking an online class would be:
    a. I've taken one before and enjoyed it.
    b. I'm curious about online classes and have room in my schedule.
    c. I need the class for graduation, and I can't fit the class into my regular schedule.

Your score: Give yourself 3 points for every A answer, 2 points for every B answer, and 1 point for every C answer.

36–29: You are a great candidate for online classes. You are comfortable with new technology and might learn well this way.

28–19: You might be a good candidate for online classes, but you should adjust your study schedule or get more comfortable with technology before taking an online class.

18–12: Online learning is not always the best option for every person. You might consider taking most of your classes in a traditional classroom, and if you do take an online class, make sure it is one you are really interested in and think you will enjoy.

Source: "Is Online Learning Right for Me?" *Washington Online,* http://www.waol.org/prospective_students/isonline4me_n.asp (accessed July 1, 2009).

How Tech Savvy Are You?

Do you own:

_____ A PDA
_____ A DVR
_____ A satellite radio subscription
_____ An MP3 player
_____ A high-definition television
_____ A VOIP telephone

In the past 30 days, have you used:

_____ Online banking or bill-paying services
_____ Read or contributed to blogs
_____ Internet gaming
_____ Podcasts
_____ Downloaded audio
_____ Downloaded video
_____ Instant messaging

Have you ever used your cell phone to:

_____ Download ringtones or play video games
_____ Send e-mail
_____ Text or multimedia messaging
_____ Stream video
_____ Access the Internet

How many questions did you check off? If you checked off eight or more, you're tech savvy! If you checked off less than eight, consider trying harder to embrace technology; you will find it's easy to use and very useful.

Source: Lane, Carol. "Are You Tech Savvy?" The San Diego Traveler. http://www.thesandiegotraveler.com/are-you-tech-savvy (accessed July 1, 2009).

- Aside from borrowing from friends or family members, how can businesses owners raise capital?
- Why are accounting and finance important?
- How can a ratio analysis from financial statements help you make informed decisions?

SWITCHING GEARS

Real World Apps

Wedding planning is a passion for Mei Lynn D'Alessandro. Since girlhood, she's been fascinated with the entire wedding process—the planning, preparation, and execution. After graduating from high school, Mei Lynn started a wedding-planning business. For many years, she ran the business as a sole proprietor. Mei Lynn gradually built a clientele that referred her to others, and she earned a reputation for being the best wedding planner in the area. She added a few employees, including a bookkeeper and an assistant, and the business continued to flourish.

The recent economic downturn has caused many engaged couples to scale back their wedding plans, and Mei Lynn's business has slowed dramatically. At the same time, a few newlywed couples failed to pay Mei Lynn for her services. To her horror, Mei Lynn realizes she cannot to pay her employees for their work and can't run her business on a cash basis anymore.

Mei Lynn needs a crash course in finance and accounting to figure out how to run her business—particularly through these hard times. She's managed to get by with the help of Rick Fritzinger, her bookkeeper, but she's on her own now. In fact, she had become so reliant on Rick for financial matters that he had even handled her personal retirement accounts and stock purchases. Mei Lynn knows she needs to be more aware of the world of finance and accounting for her own good, so she enrolls in an Introduction to Business course at her local community college.

>> Money and Financial Instruments

Although you may not have plans to become a financial manager or an accountant, learning about finance and accounting is extremely important. As a businessperson, you will be constantly dealing with numbers. You'll need to know about accounting when it comes time to file your personal and business tax returns, and you'll also need to know a little about the legal ramifications of accounting practices.[1]

If you are thinking about buying a business, you'll have to examine the business's bookkeeping records in order to figure out if it's a worthwhile investment. Once you own the business, you'll constantly monitor its earnings and expenses to determine how well your company is doing[2] and whether you have enough funds to operate it or need to raise additional capital. This chapter will cover some basic information on how people use finance and accounting to better understand and control their businesses.

THE IMPORTANCE OF MONEY

The U.S. economy depends heavily on **money**—its availability and its value relative to other currencies. Economic growth and the creation of jobs depend on money. Money is so important to the economy that many institutions have been cre-

> **Money** Anything that people generally accept as payment for goods and services.

ated to manage it and make it available when you need it. You can easily get cash from an automated teller machine almost anywhere in the world, but cash is only one form of payment you can use to buy things. Many businesses accept credit cards, debit cards, or checks. For example, Visa, the largest retail electronic payment network in the world,[3] processed 10.3 billion transactions during the third quarter of 2009 alone.[4] Behind the scenes of this free flow of money is a complex banking system that makes the transactions possible.

Barter is the direct trade of goods and services for other goods and services.[6] Though barter may sound like something from the past, many people have discovered the benefits of bartering online. Others barter goods and services the old-fashioned way—face to face. In Siberia, people have bought movie tickets with eggs, and in Ukraine, people have paid their energy bills with sausages and milk. Today, you can visit a *barter exchange*, where you can put goods or services into the system and get trade credits for other goods and services you need. The barter exchange makes it easier to barter because you don't have to find bartering partners—the exchange does it for you.[7]

Tough economic times have led to an increase in bartering online. Miriam Brown of New Orleans, Louisiana, turned to the online community Craigslist to find a place to stay for her vacation on Cape Cod, Massachusetts. To make her vacation a reality, Brown traded her accounting skills and her husband's talent for home repair for room and board.[8] Between January 2008 and January 2009, the number of postings in Craigslist's bartering area increased by 100 percent. U-exchange.com, a similar site that offers swapping and trading services, received 1.1 million hits between mid-Jan-

> **Barter** The direct trade of goods and services for other goods and services.

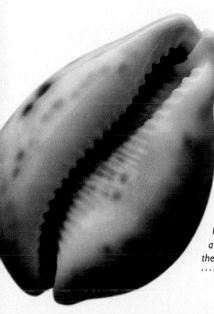

Until the 1880s, the shells of cowries, a type of marine animal, were among the world's most popular currencies.[5]

◀ **ETHICAL**   **DILEMMA** ▶

If you suspected that a longtime friend and coworker of yours who was having personal problems was also behaving unethically at work, how would you handle the situation?

uary and mid-February 2009; the site had about 362,000 hits during the same time period in 2008.[9]

Unfortunately, eggs and milk are hard to carry around. Money must be portable, divisible, durable, and stable, so people can trade goods and services without carrying the actual goods around with them. Money is anything people generally accept as payment for goods and services. In the past, objects as diverse as salt, feathers, fur pelts, stones, rare shells, tea, and horses served as money.[10]

Using coins and paper money as units of value simplifies the exchange of goods. Eventually, coins became a standard form of money because they met the following five critical standards:

- *Portability.* Coins are a lot easier to take to market than pigs or other heavy products.

- *Divisibility.* Different-sized coins could be made to represent different values. For example, prior to 1963, a U.S. dollar coin contained four times the amount of silver in a quarter. Silver is now too expensive to use in coins, so today's coins are made of other metals.

- *Stability.* When everybody agrees on the worth of a particular coin, the value of money is relatively stable.

- *Durability.* Coins can last for thousands of years; archaeologists have found many coins from ancient Rome, among other past civilizations.

- *Uniqueness.* It is difficult to counterfeit, or copy, elaborately designed and minted coins.

Soon, paper money joined coins as a monetary standard, but advances in technology have made it increasingly easy to counterfeit paper money. As a result, the government has gone to great lengths to make it easy to differentiate the real thing from a forgery. That's why today's dollars have certain unique characteristics: slightly off-center portraits, a variety of colors in each bill (including blue, peach, and green in the $20 bill) and "invisible" lines that show up when held up to the light.[11]

Business owners take extra precautions to prevent counterfeit money from ending up in their cash registers. Nicolas Ostergaard owns the Jukebox, a deli and pub in North Carolina. After a teenage customer paid his check with a counterfeit $100 bill, Ostergaard decided to stop accepting bills larger than $50.

According to the Federal Reserve, about $2.6 billion in counterfeit bills were in circulation in the United States as of June 2008.[12]

Electronic cash (e-cash) is another form of money. Today, you can make online bill payments using your bank's Web site or certain software applications, and you can send e-cash safely to anyone using the PayPal service. Recipients can choose automatic deposit to their bank, e-dollars for spending online, or a traditional check in the mail. Engine Room Digital Marketing, a Web site design firm from Portland, Oregon, uses a billing service called Billing Orchard to send invoices and collect payments over the Web. Engine Room's owner, James Faulknor, remarked, "If we had to bill each client each month, we'd be in the billing industry, not the Web industry."[13]

THE FUNCTION OF SECURITIES MARKETS

In addition to providing personal funds or borrowing money from family, friends, or banks, businesses can raise funds or capital by selling stock of their company or issuing bonds. Before discussing stocks and bonds, however, it's important to understand the securities markets where these stocks and bonds are traded. First, **securities** are stocks and bonds that are traded, and the **securities market** is a financial marketplace where stocks and bonds are traded. The **New York Stock Exchange (NYSE)** and the **NASDAQ** (a completely electronic exchange) are examples of securities markets. Figure 8.1 shows the companies represented in the Dow Jones Industrial Index (Dow), the most widely used indicator of the stock market.

Securities Stocks and bonds that are traded.

Securities market A place where stocks and bonds are traded.

New York Stock Exchange (NYSE) A securities market.

NASDAQ A completely electronic securities market.

These institutions serve two major functions: First, they help businesses find long-term funding to finance capital needs, such as starting up the company, expanding the business, or buying major goods and services. Second, they provide private investors a place to buy and sell the securities (investments), such as stocks and bonds, that can help them build their financial future.

Securities markets are divided into primary and secondary markets. *Primary markets* handle the sale of new securities. Corporations

Figure 8.1 The Original Dow and the Dow Today

THE ORIGINAL DOW 12	THE 30 CURRENT DOW COMPANIES	
American Cotton Oil	Alcoa	Intel
American Sugar Refining Co.	American Express	Johnson & Johnson
American Tobacco	AT&T	JPMorgan Chase
Chicago Gas	Bank of America	Kraft
Distilling & Cattle Feeding Co.	Boeing	McDonald's
General Electric Co.	Caterpillar	Merck
Laclede Gas Light Co.	Chevron	Microsoft
National Lead	Cisco	Pfizer
North American Co.	Coca-Cola	Procter & Gamble
Tennessee Coal, Iron & Railroad Co.	DuPont	3M
U.S. Leather	ExxonMobil	Travelers
U.S. Rubber Co.	General Electric	United Technologies
	Hewlett-Packard	Verizon
	Home Depot	Walmart Stores
	IBM	Walt Disney

make money on the sale of their securities only once—when they are first sold on the primary market. The first public offering of a corporation's stock is called an **initial public offering (IPO)**. In the economic downturn that prevailed during 2008, there were only 43 IPOs in the United States—a remarkable drop from 2007's 272 IPOs. It was the slowest year for IPOs since 1979.[14]

After the first public offering, the *secondary market* handles the trading of securities among investors, with the proceeds of a sale going to the investor selling the stock, not to the corporation whose stock is sold. For an example, imagine a vegetarian restaurant chain called Healthy Hearts that's just held an IPO. The company offered 2 million shares of stock in the company at $15 a share; after the initial offering was complete, the company had raised $30 million.

One of Healthy Hearts's original shareholders, Raj, then sells 100 shares of the stock to another investor, José. Healthy Hearts collects nothing from this transaction, because José is buying the stock from Raj, not from Healthy Hearts. However, it is possible for companies like Healthy Hearts to offer additional shares of stock in order to raise additional capital.

Purchasing shares isn't just for the general public. Many people who work for a company—executives and workers alike—may own shares in that company. When demand for shares is high, executives or workers can sell their shares and make money from the transaction, just like everyone else who owns the shares. In May 2006, the second-largest credit card issuer, MasterCard, offered 61.5 million shares at an IPO price of $39 per share.[15] By November 2007, shares of MasterCard were trading on the NYSE at

Following MasterCard's lead, the world's largest credit card company, Visa, filed plans in November 2007 for a $10 billion IPO.[19] When Visa finally did go public in March 2008, the credit card company became the largest IPO in history; buyers paid $17.9 billion, or $44 per share.[20]

$195 per share.[16] In October of that same year, three officers of the company collectively sold 35,500 shares at prices ranging from $162 to $178 per share.[17] In late August 2009, MasterCard shares were selling at $201 per share.[18]

Issuing stock, or "going public," is one way companies can gain new funding. Unfortunately, new companies often start without sufficient capital, and many established firms fail to do adequate long-term financial planning. Businesses normally prefer to meet long-term financial needs by using retained earnings (past profits) or by borrowing from a lending institution (a bank, pension fund, or insurance company, for example). However, if such long-term funding is not available, a company may be able to raise funds by issuing corporate bonds (taking on debt) or selling stock (shares of ownership). Issuing corporate bonds is a form of *debt financing*, and selling stock in the corporation is a form of *equity financing*. These forms of debt or equity financing are not available to all companies, especially small businesses. However, many firms use such financing options to meet long-term financial needs.

Investment bankers can help companies meet these financial needs. These people are specialists who assist in the issuance and sale of new securities, understanding as they do the surrounding regulations and the necessity of gaining the **Securities and Exchange Commission's (SEC)** permission for stock or bond issuances. An investment bank also underwrites new issues of stocks or bonds.[21] In other words, an investment bank buys all of the stocks or bonds (or signs a good-faith intent to do so), and then sells all (or most) of them.

RAISING FUNDS BY ISSUING BONDS

A **bond** is a corporate certificate indicating that a person has lent money to a firm. A company that issues bonds has a legal obligation to make regular interest payments to investors and to repay the entire bond *principal* amount (the face value of the bond) at a prescribed time, which is called the **maturity date**.

The interest rate paid on a bond varies according to certain factors, such as the state of the economy, the reputation of the company issuing the bond, and the going interest rate for government bonds or bonds of similar companies. Once an interest rate is set for a corporate bond issue, except in the case of floating-rate bonds, it cannot be changed. The interest rate being paid by U.S. government bonds clearly affects the interest rate a firm must agree to pay, because government bonds are considered safe investments. Bonds offer the following long-term financing advantages to an organization:

- Bondholders are creditors, and not owners, of the firm, and they seldom have a vote on corporate matters. Thus, management maintains control over the firm's operations.

- Interest paid on bonds is tax deductible to the firm issuing the bond.

- Bonds are a temporary source of funding for a firm. They are eventually repaid, and the debt obligation is eliminated.

- Bonds can be repaid before the maturity date if they contain a call provision, and they may also be convertible to shares in the company.

Figure 8.2 Types of Government Securities that Compete with Corporate Bonds

U.S. government bond	Issued by the federal government; considered the safest type of bond investment
Treasury bill (T-bill)	Matures in less than a year; issued with a minimum denomination of $1,000
Treasury note	Matures in 10 years or less; sold in denominations of $1,000 and $5,000
Treasury bond	Matures in 25 years or more; sold in denominations of $1,000 and $5,000
Municipal bond	Issued by states, cities, counties, and other state and local government agencies; usually exempt from federal taxes
Yankee bond	Issued by a foreign government; payable in U.S. dollars

However, bonds also have several drawbacks:

- Bonds increase debt (long-term liabilities) and may adversely affect the market's perception of the firm.

- Paying interest on bonds is a legal obligation. If interest is not paid, bondholders can take legal action to force payment.

- The face value (denomination) of bonds must be repaid on the maturity date. Without careful planning, this repayment can cause cash-flow problems when the bonds come due.

The government can issue bonds as well. Figure 8.2 shows some different types of bonds that can be issued by governments. Independent rating firms, such as Standard & Poor's and Moody's Investors Service, rate both government and corporate bonds according to their degree of risk, and they provide investors with risk analysis information and research.[22] Bonds can range from the highest quality to junk bonds.[23] Figure 8.3 describes the range of ratings.

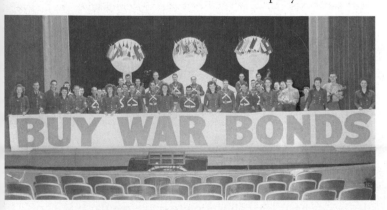

During World War II, the U.S. government sold bonds to raise money to fight the war.

RAISING FUNDS BY SELLING STOCKS

Stocks can be another way for companies to gain financing. **Stocks** are shares of ownership in a company. A *stock certificate* is evidence of stock ownership that

Thinking Critically

>> Small Businesses Recover with the SBA's ARC Loan Program

America's small businesses are the backbone of its economy. The U.S. Small Business Administration (SBA) has provided countless valuable services to small-business owners for many years, and it has now developed a program to respond to the needs of small businesses during the recession of 2008–2009: a deferred-payment loan program.

Lenders play a critical role in the health of the American economy, and they are especially vital to small businesses. The U.S. SBA is implementing a temporary loan program to help struggling American small businesses while reducing risk during the tough economic conditions associated with the 2008–2009 recession.

SBA has designed a deferred-payment loan program to help small businesses make payments on existing debt. Section 506 of the American Reinvestment and Recovery Act authorized SBA to help viable small businesses make payments on existing small business debt. The America's Recovery Capital, or ARC, Loan Program, is designed to give viable small businesses facing immediate financial hardship some temporary financial relief so they can keep their doors open, refocus, and get their cash flow back on track. ARC loans are available through SBA-approved small business lenders and have been authorized through September 30, 2010, or until the appropriated funds run out, whichever comes first.

Small business owners benefit from these loans, of course. For example:

- ARC loans are interest-free to the borrower, have deferred payments for 12 months, and have no SBA fees associated with them.

- ARC loans allow borrowers to redirect cash flow from making loan payments to investing in their businesses.

Lenders benefit from ARC loans, too. For example:

- They carry reduced risk. The SBA guarantees them 100 percent, which provides greater security and confidence to lend.

- SBA will pay monthly interest to lenders at reasonable rates throughout the term of the loan.

- Existing SBA lenders are eligible to make ARC loans, and delegated lenders may make ARC loans on a delegated basis.

Source: U.S. Small Business Administration Participant Lender Fact Sheet. "Lenders Can Help America's Small Businesses Recover with SBA's ARC Loans," http://www.sba.gov/idc/groups/public/documents/sba_homepage/sba_rcvry_act_arc_lnderloans.pdf (accessed August 19, 2009).

QUESTIONS

1. Do you think this loan program will be a tool for long-term success or a quick fix for companies in a short-term cash crunch? Explain your response.

2. Who benefits most from the implementation of this program: the government, lenders, or businesses? How do each of these entities benefit from the loans the program facilitates?

Figure 8.3 Bond Ratings: Moody's Investors Service and Standard & Poor's Investor Service

Rating		
MOODY'S	**STANDARD & POOR'S**	**DESCRIPTIONS**
Aaa	AAA	Highest quality (lowest default risk)
Aa	AA	High quality
A	A	Upper medium grade
Baa	BBB	Medium grade
Ba	BB	Lower medium grade
B	B	Speculative
Caa	CCC,CC	Poor (high default risk)
Ca	C	Highly speculative
C	D	Lowest grade

Stock Shares of ownership in a company.

Par value The dollar amount assigned to each stock certificate on the corporation's charter.

specifies the name of the company, the number of shares it represents, and the type of stock being issued (see Figure 8.4). Today, stock certificates are generally held electronically for the owners of the stock. Certificates sometimes indicate a stock's **par value**, which is a dollar amount assigned to each share of stock by the corporation's charter. Some states use par value as a basis for calculating the state's incorporation charges and fees. Because par values do not reflect the market value of the stock, most companies issue *no-par* stock.

Dividends are part of a firm's profits that may be distributed to stockholders as cash payments or additional shares of stock. Dividends are declared by a corporation's board of directors and are gen-

Dividend Part of a firm's profits that may be distributed to stockholders as cash payments or additional shares of stock.

erally paid quarterly.[24] Although companies that issue bonds are legally obligated to pay interest to the bondholders, companies that issue stock are not required to pay dividends.[25] Many companies that are growing instead choose to reinvest those funds that would have gone to dividends to continue their growth, which satisfies shareholders. For example, consider the technology companies Microsoft and Apple. Microsoft pays a dividend to its shareholders. In the second quarter of 2009, it paid $0.13 per share. If you owned 100 shares of Microsoft, you received $13 in dividends from the company at the end of that quarter. On the other hand, Apple does not pay dividends to its shareholders; instead, it chooses to reinvest the money it earns into the company's growth.[26]

The following are some advantages to the firm that is issuing stock:

- As owners of the business, stockholders never have to be repaid.

- There is no legal obligation to pay dividends to stockholders. Therefore, income (retained earnings) can be reinvested in the firm for future financing needs.

- Selling stock can improve the condition of a firm's balance sheet, because issuing stock creates no debt.

A corporation can buy back its stock to improve its balance sheet and make the company appear stronger financially. When the stock price of the company is low, the board of the company can authorize a stock repurchase program. When fewer shares are available for purchase to outsiders, share prices rise—that's simple supply and demand economics, which you learned about in Chapter 2.

Disadvantages of issuing stock include the following:

- As owners, stockholders (usually only common stockholders) have the right to vote for the company's board of directors. Typically, one vote is granted for each share of stock. Hence, the firm's direction and control can be altered by the sale of additional shares of stock.

Figure 8.4 Stock Certificate for Pet Inc.

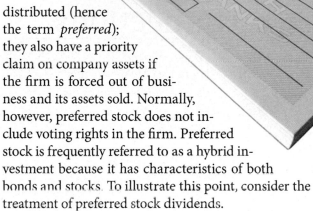

- Dividends are paid from profit after taxes and are not tax deductible.

- Management decisions can be affected by the need to keep stockholders happy.

Companies can issue two classes of stock: preferred and common. Let's see how these two forms of equity financing differ.

Common Stock

Common stock is the most basic form of ownership in a firm. In fact, if a company issues only one type of stock, it must be common. Holders of common stock have the right (1) to vote for company board directors and on important issues that affect the company, and (2) to share in the firm's profits through dividends, if approved by the firm's board of directors. Having voting rights in a corporation allows common stockholders to influence corporate policy, because the elected board chooses the firm's top management and makes major policy decisions. Common stockholders also have a *preemptive right*, which is the first right to purchase any new shares of common stock the firm decides to issue. This right allows common stockholders to maintain a proportional share of ownership in the company. Companies can issue common stock as a strategy to raise additional funds to purchase another company. For example, Amazon.com bought Zappos.com in exchange for 10 million shares of Amazon common stock, which had a value at the time of the purchase of about $847 million.[27]

> **Common stock** The most basic form of ownership in a firm.

Preferred Stock

> **Preferred stock** Stocks that offer investors a preference (hence the term "preferred") in the payment of dividends.

Owners of **preferred stock** are given preference in the payment of company dividends and must be paid their dividends in full before any common stock dividends can be distributed (hence the term *preferred*); they also have a priority claim on company assets if the firm is forced out of business and its assets sold. Normally, however, preferred stock does not include voting rights in the firm. Preferred stock is frequently referred to as a hybrid investment because it has characteristics of both bonds and stocks. To illustrate this point, consider the treatment of preferred stock dividends.

Preferred stock dividends differ from common stock dividends in several ways. Preferred stock is generally issued with a par value that becomes the base for the dividend the firm is willing to pay. For example, if the par value of a preferred stock is $25 a share and its dividend rate is 4 percent, the firm is committing to a $1 dividend for each share of preferred stock the investor owns (4 percent of $25 = $1). In this example, someone who owned 100 shares of this preferred stock would receive a fixed yearly dividend of $100. In addition, a preferred stockholder is also assured that this dividend must be paid in full before any common stock dividends can be distributed.

In this respect, preferred stocks are quite similar to bonds: both have a face (or par) value and both have a fixed rate of return.[28] Also like bonds, preferred stocks are rated by Standard & Poor's and Moody's Investors Service according to risk.

So how do bonds and preferred stocks differ? Remember that companies are legally bound to pay bond interest and repay the face value (denomination) of the bond on its maturity date. In contrast, even though preferred stock dividends are generally fixed, they do not legally have to be paid. Also, stock (preferred or common) never has to be repurchased. Although both bonds and stocks can increase in market value, the prices of stocks generally increase at a higher percentage than bonds. Of course, the market value of both could also go down.

Preferred stock can have special features that don't apply to common stock. For example, like bonds, preferred stock can be callable, which means that preferred

stockholders could be required to sell their shares back to the corporation. In some situations, preferred stock can also be convertible to shares of common stock. Preferred stock may also be cumulative, which means that if one or more dividends are not paid when promised, the missed dividends must be accumulated and paid later. All dividends, including any back dividends, must be paid in full before any common stock dividends can be distributed.

[BUS] connections

1. What is money, and what are its five characteristics?
2. What is the difference between common stock and preferred stock?
3. Why are bonds considered a form of debt financing? Identify its advantages and drawbacks.

IS HE REALLY A FRIEND?

Johnnie Phelps, the owner of Phelps Electronics, is devastated. He has just learned some very disconcerting information about Nick Drabotsky, who has served as his office manager and accountant for more than 30 years.

Johnnie had first become concerned three months earlier, when Nick suddenly announced that he and his wife were divorcing. Johnnie was friendly with Nick's wife, Rachel, so he talked to her about the divorce. Rachel explained that Nick's spending had gotten out of control, and she had found out that he had gambled away much of their life savings.

Worried about how Nick's erratic behavior might be affecting his own business, Johnnie hired Rita Sanchez, a certified public accountant, to review Phelps Electronics's books. Rita performed an initial review of the books and then met with Johnnie to discuss her findings and recommendations.

If you suspected that a longtime friend and coworker of yours who was having personal problems was also behaving unethically at work, how would you handle the situation?

Rita began the discussion. "First of all, Johnnie, I think you should immediately set up greater internal controls and regular audits of your books. Internal controls are designed to ensure accurate and honest accounting procedures and compliance with laws and regulations."

Johnnie thought a moment and responded, "Nick has many responsibilities, and given what's going on in his personal life, I'm sure he doesn't have time to do internal audits regularly. I trust him—I'm just concerned that he might be missing things because he's so distracted. Nick's always been a dear friend to me, and he's been with me for many years."

Rita said, "Are there procedures to prevent or detect duplicate payments to vendors, determine if a vendor actually exists, or follow up payments for goods not received? I found a stack of invoices from one of your suppliers—let's see, I think the company is named Wellco—but found no evidence that any of the parts listed on the invoices were ever delivered to Phelps."

Johnnie looked down, stunned. He knew that Wellco was the name of a company owned by Nick's best friend, and that there would be no reason for Phelps to buy equipment from Wellco. Johnnie wondered what to do.

QUESTIONS

1. What are the ethical issues in this situation?
2. If you were Johnnie, what would you do?

>> Introduction to Accounting

The goal of this section is not to show you everything there is to know about accounting; rather, its purpose is to expose you to some basics of accounting, as well as to some career opportunities in the accounting field. Anyone can benefit personally and professionally by having a basic working knowledge of accounting.

As you read this section, keep in mind that many terms are used here that a person who has never been exposed to accounting may understand to have a different meaning. Consider accounting an entirely new language, and the terms in this chapter will be much easier to comprehend. Let's start by defining accounting, discussing the types of accounting found in business, and then covering the six-step accounting cycle.

WHAT IS ACCOUNTING?

Financial information is primarily based on information generated from accounting. **Accounting** is the recording, classifying, summarizing, and interpreting of financial events and transactions in an organization to provide management and other interested parties with the financial information they need to make good decisions about its operation. Financial transactions can include such specifics as buying and selling goods and services, acquiring insurance, paying employees, and using supplies. Once business transactions have been recorded, they are usually classified into groups that have common characteristics. For example, all purchases are grouped together, as are all sales transactions. The method used to record and summarize accounting data into reports is called an *accounting system*, which illustrates the operating performance of the firm.

Another major purpose of accounting is to report financial information to people outside the firm, such as owners, creditors, suppliers, investors, and

Accounting Recording, classifying, summarizing, and interpreting financial events and transactions to provide management and other interested parties with the information they need to make good decisions.

the government (for tax purposes). The SEC recently charged General Electric with allegedly misreporting financial information. The company did not deny the accusation or admit responsibility, but it agreed to pay a $50 million fine.[29]

In sum, accounting is the measurement and reporting of financial information to various stakeholders regarding the economic activities of the firm. Accounting work is divided into several major areas, which are discussed in the next section.

AREAS OF ACCOUNTING

The accounting profession is divided into five key areas: managerial and financial, auditing, tax, governmental, and not-for-profit. All five areas are important, and all create career opportunities for those interested in accounting.[30]

Managerial and Financial Accounting

Managerial accounting is used to provide information and analysis to managers *within* an organization to assist them in decision making. **Financial accounting**, on the other hand, generates information for use *outside* an organization.

Managerial accounting is concerned with measuring and reporting costs of production, marketing, and other functions, preparing budgets (planning); checking whether or not units are staying within their budgets (controlling); and designing strategies to minimize taxes.[31]

Managerial accounting Provides information and analysis to managers within the organization to assist them in decision making.

Financial accounting Generates information for use outside the organization.

The information and analyses prepared by financial accountants go not only to a company's owners, managers, and employees, but also to creditors, lenders, employee unions, customers, suppliers, government agencies, and the general public. These external stakeholders are interested in important financial questions such as: Is the organization profitable? Is it able to pay its bills? How much debt does the organization hold? Financial accountants also have the important responsibility of preparing **annual reports**, which are yearly statements of the financial condition, progress, and expectations of an organization.

Annual report Yearly statement of the financial condition, progress, and expectations of an organization.

People who want to work in the accounting field are required to take courses in both managerial and financial accounting. Some elect to pursue a career

Certified management accountant (CMA) A professional accountant who has met certain educational and experience requirements, passed a qualifying exam in the field, and been certified by the Institute of Certified Management Accountants.

Certified public accountant (CPA) An accountant who has passed a series of examinations established by the American Institute of Certified Public Accountants (AICPA) and does accounting work for no one particular firm.

as a certified management accountant or a certified public accountant. A **certified management accountant (CMA)** is a professional accountant who has met certain educational and experience requirements, passed a qualifying exam in the field, and been certified by the Institute of Certified Management Accountants. An accountant who passes a series of examinations established by the American Institute of Certified Public Accountants and meets the state's requirement for education and experience earns recognition as a **certified public accountant (CPA)**. CPAs find careers as private accountants or public accountants and are often sought to fill other financial positions within organizations.[32]

Private accountant An accountant who works for a single firm, government agency, or nonprofit organization on the payroll of the company or organization.

Public accountant An accountant who does not work for a specific company.

Private accountants work for a single firm, government agency, or nonprofit organization and are on the payroll of the company or organization. However, not all firms or nonprofit organizations want or need a full-time accountant. Accountants who do not work for a specific company are called **public accountants**. Public accountants can be hired to help businesses with payroll, taxes, and other projects, but they need not be employees of the company. That's useful to know in case you're interested in starting your own business. You can find public accountants in your community, and many public accountants work for large accounting firms. Figure 8.5 shows the top five public accounting firms in the United States.

Figure 8.5 The Top Five Public Accounting Firms in the United States

Deloitte and Touche

Ernst & Young

PricewaterhouseCoopers

KPMG

Grant Thornton

Source: "Top 100 Accounting Firms in the U.S.," http://www.accountingmajors.com/accountingmajors/articles/top100.html (accessed August 16, 2009).

Users of financial information must be confident that the information provided to them is accurate, especially in light of the many corporate accounting scandals that have occurred in recent years. The independent **Financial Accounting Standards Board (FASB)** defines the set of **generally accepted accounting principles (GAAP)** accountants must follow. If financial reports are prepared in accordance with GAAP, users can expect the information to meet standards that accounting professionals have agreed on.[33]

Financial Accounting Standards Board (FASB) The group that oversees accounting practices.

Generally accepted accounting principles (GAAP) A set of principles followed by accountants in preparing reports.

Auditing

The job of reviewing and evaluating the records used to prepare a company's financial statements is referred to as **auditing**. Accountants within an organization often perform internal audits to ensure that proper accounting procedures and financial reporting are being followed. According to the Bureau of Labor Statistics, employment for accountants and auditors is expected to grow by 18 percent from 2006 to 2016, much faster than the average for all occupations.[34]

Public accountants also conduct **independent audits** of account-

Auditing The job of reviewing and evaluating the records used to prepare a company's financial statements.

ing and related records. An independent audit is an unbiased evaluation of the accuracy of a company's financial statements. An accountant who meets certain educational requirements can be considered for a professional accreditation in auditing known as *certified internal auditor* (CIA).

Tax Accounting

Taxes are the price we pay for roads, parks, schools, police protection, the military, and other functions provided by government. Federal, state, and local governments require individuals and organizations to file tax returns at specific times and in a precise format. Of course, for personal taxes, the deadline to file for most Americans is April 15 of each year. Businesses, however, generally have to file and pay taxes on a quarterly basis, and tax accountants ensure that company taxes are filed correctly.

A tax accountant is trained in tax law and is responsible for preparing tax returns or developing tax strategies to save the company money. Since governments often change tax policies according to specific needs or objectives, the job of the tax accountant is always challenging.[35] Also, as the burden of taxes grows in the economy, the role of the tax accountant becomes increasingly important to the organization or entrepreneur.

Government and Not-for-Profit Accounting

Government and *not-for-profit* accounting meet the needs of organizations whose purpose is not generating a profit, but serving ratepayers, taxpayers, or others according to an approved budget. All governments—federal, state, and local—must have an accounting system that helps taxpayers, special interest groups, legislative bodies, and creditors ensure that government is fulfilling its obligations and making proper use of taxpayers' money. Government accounting standards are set by an organization called the **Governmental Accounting Standards Board (GASB).**[36] Various national, state,

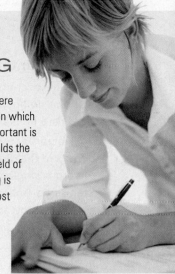

THE WORLD OF ACCOUNTING

As you'll learn in this chapter, there are several types of accounting in which you can be involved. What's important is that you choose the area that holds the most interest for you. Like the field of information systems, accounting is expected to grow faster than most industries well into the next decade. That's great news for those of you who may choose accounting as a future career!

A relatively new accounting field called *forensic accounting* entails investigating possible securities fraud, contract disputes, and other complex and possibly criminal financial transactions, such as money laundering. Forensic accountants have an accounting background but also have experience in law.

One salary survey concluded that accountants and auditors with less than a year of experience earn between $28,250 and $45,000 a year. Those with one to three years of experience earn between $33,000 and $52,000. Senior accountants and auditors earn between $40,750 and $69,750; managers, between $48,000 and $90,000; and directors of accounting and auditing, between $64,750 and $200,750. This wide range of salaries reflects differences in size of firm, location, level of education, and professional credentials.

If you want to succeed in business, you need to know about accounting. It's almost impossible to run any business, regardless of size, or understand business operations without being able to read, understand, and analyze accounting reports and financial statements. Accounting reports and financial statements reveal as much about a business's health as pulse rate and blood pressure readings describe a person's health.

Do you think accounting might be right for you? Does the idea of forensic accounting intrigue your inner detective? Would you rather work as a private accountant and focus on a single business? Perhaps you're interested in becoming a public accountant—either running your own business or working for a large accounting firm. Accounting provides countless options for anyone embarking on a new career.

Going GLOBAL

Global Accounting Standards? Not So Fast

For years now, countries around the world have been hoping to create a single set of international financial reporting standards, but the following article predicts that such standards are unlikely to occur in the near future.

The uproar over fair value accounting practices, which some critics have blamed for the depths of the global financial crisis, threatens to sink a long-sought move by countries around the world toward a single set of international financial reporting standards (IFRS). The U.S. Financial Accounting Standards Board has been working with London's International Accounting Standards Board (IASB) since 2002 toward what accounting professionals call convergence.

With finance ministers from the 20 wealthiest nations set to discuss ways to reform the global financial system, the time seems ripe for a move to harmonize accounting standards across borders, making it easier for investors to compare companies operating in different geographic regions. The major stumbling blocks, critics say, include the IASB's lack of independent funding and its tendency to cave in to political pressure.

The key difference between U.S. generally accepted accounting principles (GAAP) and IFRS is that U.S. standards are based on explicit rules, while the international standards' reliance on principles gives companies more room to use their judgment in deciding how to recognize revenue and other key metrics. Adoption of IFRS would also probably trigger a big tax hike for U.S. companies, which would no longer be able to use the last-in-first-out (LIFO) inventory accounting method, which doesn't exist under the international standards. The LIFO method assumes that goods purchased most recently are sold first and that the remaining items have been purchased at earlier periods, yielding a lower gross profit during high-inflation periods than the first-in-first-out accounting method.

The most strident critics of migration to IFRS argue that the primary goal of the SEC and the U.S. Treasury Department is attracting capital to U.S. markets, rather than ensuring that the highest-quality accounting standards prevail. While attracting more capital to the U.S. "is a valid business objective, it's not clear we can do that by going to international financial reporting standards," says Ashwinpaul Sondhi, president of A.C. Sondhi Associates in Maplewood, New Jersey, who has served on CFA Institute committees.

Another concern is whether the SEC would continue to have regulatory oversight if U.S. companies adopt IFRS.

Source: David Bogoslaw, "Global Accounting Standards? Not So Fast," *BusinessWeek*, November 13, 2008, http://www.businessweek.com/investor/content/nov2008/pi20081112_143039.htm (accessed August 18, 2009).

Questions

1. If global accounting standards are adopted, do you think the SEC will continue to have the regulatory oversight it currently has? Explain your response.

2. How did the recession of 2008–2009 change the U.S. Financial Accounting Standards Board's priorities?

and local agencies provide opportunities for accounting professionals, including the Federal Bureau of Investigation, the Internal Revenue Service, state departments of natural resources, or county departments of revenue.

Nonprofit organizations also require accounting professionals. In fact, nonprofit organizations have a growing need for trained accountants because contributors to nonprofits want to see exactly how and where the funds they contribute are being spent.

Charities—such as the United Way or the Red Cross, for example—state universities and colleges, hospitals, and labor unions all hire accountants to learn and account for how the funds they raise are being spent.

Maher-Duessel, an accounting firm in the Pittsburgh, Pennsylvania, area, specializes in government and not-for-profit accounting. The firm was founded with a mission to make a difference in the lives of others and to create a work environment that offers flex-

ibility and fun for all employees. One of the firm's five partners, Robert Lent, remarked, "The people that we serve are the people who need help. They can't afford the high-level CPAs. They need us to come in and hold their hand." Maher-Duessel's employees rated the firm the best place to work among companies with fewer than 50 employees in a survey conducted by the *Pittsburgh Post-Gazette*.[37]

THE SIX-STEP ACCOUNTING CYCLE

The accounting cycle is a six-step procedure (see Figure 8.6) that results in the preparation and analysis of the major financial statements. The accounting cycle generally involves the work of both a bookkeeper and an accountant. It is important to note that accounting is different from bookkeeping. **Bookkeeping** is simply the recording of business transactions; accounting goes much further. Rather than simply recording transactions, accountants classify and summarize financial data according to formal standards and principles.

Bookkeeping The recording of business transactions.

The first three steps of the six-step accounting cycle are the continual operations discussed previously: (1) analyzing and categorizing documents, (2) putting the information into journals, and (3) posting that information into ledgers. The next step is (4) preparing a **trial balance**. A trial balance is a summary of all the financial data in a firm's account ledgers. It is used to check whether the figures are correct and balanced, much

Trial balance A summary of all the financial data in the account ledgers that is used to check whether the figures are correct and balanced.

the same way that you balance your checkbook and compare it to your bank statement.

If the information in the account ledgers is not accurate, it must be corrected before the firm's financial statements are prepared and analyzed in the final two steps of the accounting cycle: (5) preparing the financial statements, including a *balance sheet*, *income statement*, and *statement of cash flows*; and (6) analyzing the financial statements and evaluating the overall financial condition of the firm. As you can imagine, computers and accounting software have simplified this process considerably.

Keep in mind that the financial statements are a result of the ongoing work of bookkeepers and managerial accountants and their recording of daily transactions. This chapter's next section discusses preparation of financial statements.

BUS connections

1. Define accounting.
2. Identify and describe the five areas of accounting.
3. Describe the six steps of the accounting cycle.

Figure 8.6 Steps in the Accounting Cycle

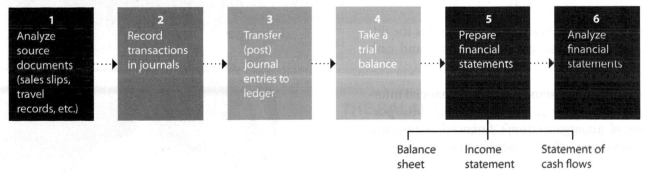

1	2	3	4	5	6
Analyze source documents (sales slips, travel records, etc.)	Record transactions in journals	Transfer (post) journal entries to ledger	Take a trial balance	Prepare financial statements	Analyze financial statements

Balance sheet   Income statement   Statement of cash flows

For REVIEW >>

1. **Understand the importance of money and explain the differences between stocks and bonds.**

   - The U.S. economy depends heavily on money—its availability and its value relative to other currencies. Money is anything people generally accept as payment for goods and services. Economic growth and the creation of jobs depend on money. Stocks are shares of ownership in a company. Common stock is the most basic form of ownership in a firm. Holders of common stock have the right (1) to vote for company board directors and on important issues that affect the company, and (2) to share in the firm's profits through dividends, if approved by the firm's board of directors. Preferred stocks offer investors a preference (hence the term *preferred*) in the payment of dividends. A bond is a corporate certificate indicating that a person has lent money to a firm. Preferred stocks are similar to bonds: both have a face (or par) value, both have a fixed rate of return, and both are rated according to risk. They differ in that companies are legally bound to pay bond interest and repay the face value of the bond on its maturity date. Although both bonds and stocks can increase in market value, the prices of stocks generally increase at a higher percentage than bonds. Securities are stocks and bonds that are traded, and the securities market is a financial marketplace where stocks and bonds are traded.

2. **Describe the steps in the accounting cycle and explain the different areas of accounting.**

   - The six-step accounting cycle is: (1) analyzing and categorizing documents; (2) putting the information into journals; (3) posting that information into ledgers; (4) preparing a trial balance; (5) preparing the financial statements, including a balance sheet, income statement, and statement of cash flows; and (6) analyzing the financial statements and evaluating the overall financial condition of the firm. Managerial accounting is used to provide information and analysis to managers within an organization to assist them in decision making. Financial accounting, on the other hand, generates information for use outside an organization. It is important to note that accounting is different from bookkeeping. Bookkeeping is simply the recording of business transactions; accounting goes much further.

3. **Explain how the major financial statements differ.**

   - A financial statement is a summary of all the transactions (for example, all the expenses and revenues) that have occurred over a particular period of time. Financial statements indicate a firm's financial health and stability. The balance sheet details what a company owns and owes on a certain day. Assets are the things a company owns outright, including equipment, cash, and property. The sum of the value of the assets minus liabilities is owners' equity. The income statement shows what a firm sells its products for and what its selling costs are over a specific period; it reports a firm's financial operations over a particular period of time, usually a year, a quarter of a year, or a month. It reveals whether the business is actually earning a profit or losing money. The statement of cash flows highlights the difference between cash coming into and cash going out of a business. It reports cash receipts and disbursements related to the three major activities of a firm: operations, investments, and financing.

4. **Explain the importance of ratio analysis in reporting financial information.**

   - Ratio analysis is the assessment of a firm's financial condition, using calculations and financial ratios developed from the firm's financial statements. Financial ratios provide key insights into how a firm compares to other firms in its industry in the important areas of liquidity, debt, profitability, and business activity. The current ratio is the ratio of a firm's current assets to current liabilities. Leverage (debt) ratios measure the degree to which a firm relies on borrowed funds in its operations. The debt to owners' equity ratio measures the degree to which the company is financed by borrowed funds that must be repaid. Profitability (performance) ratios measure how effectively a firm is using its various resources to achieve profits. The basic EPS ratio helps determine the amount of profit earned by a company for each share of outstanding common stock. The diluted EPS ratio measures the amount of profit earned by a company for each share of outstanding common stock, but this ratio also takes into consideration stock options, warrants, preferred stock, and convertible debt securities the firm can convert into common stock. The return on sales ratio measures how much profit a company earns for every dollar in revenue. The return on equity ratio measures how much was earned for each dollar invested. Activity ratios show how effectively management turns over inventory. The inventory turnover ratio measures the speed with which inventory moves through a firm and gets converted into sales.

Key Terms

Account receivable

Accounting

Annual report

Assets

Auditing

Balance sheet

Barter

Bond

Bookkeeping

Certified management accountant (CMA)

Certified public accountant (CPA)

Common stock

Cost of goods sold (cost of goods manufactured)

Dividend

Financial accounting

Financial Accounting Standards Board (FASB)

Financial statement

Generally accepted accounting principles (GAAP)

Governmental Accounting Standards Board (GASB)

Gross profit (gross margin)

Gross sales

Income statement

Independent audit

Initial public offering (IPO)

Liabilities

Liquidity

Managerial accounting

Maturity date

Money

NASDAQ

Net sales

New York Stock Exchange (NYSE)

Operating expenses

Owners' equity

Par value

Preferred stock

Private accountant

Public accountant

Ratio analysis

Revenue

Securities

Securities and Exchange Commission (SEC)

Securities market

Statement of cash flows

Stock

Trial balance

1. Suppose you don't plan to major in accounting, but in another area of business instead. Name five ways understanding accounting can help you as a business owner or manager.

2. What's the difference between managerial and financial accounting? In what ways are they the same?

3. In groups, respond to the following question: Assuming you're an investor, how might you use at least three of the ratios discussed in this chapter to determine whether to invest in a company?

4. In groups, respond to the following scenario: Discuss the purpose of an income statement, a balance sheet, and a cash flow statement. As a manager, how might you use this information to make better strategic decisions?

1. Visit Google or Bing and do a search for "company reports." When you find one for a company that is interesting to you, view the company report and answer the following questions:

    a. What was the company's net sales for the year?

    b. What were the three largest expenses the company had during the year?

    c. What was the stockholders' equity for the company?

    d. What was the net income and percent of net income for the company?

2. Visit the Web site http://www.bankrate.com/brm/news/biz/bizcalcs/ratiocalcs.asp. Once there, choose two ratios to calculate using the company report you found for Question 1.

    a. Discuss the numbers you used for each ratio.

    b. What would the ratios mean to you as an investor? As a manager of the company?

Self-Assessment Exercises

How Much Do You Know about the Sarbanes-Oxley Act?

Take this quiz to find out more about the Sarbanes-Oxley Act and its effect on accounting practices in all companies. Indicate whether each statement is true or false:

1. **T F** The Sarbanes-Oxley Act is also known as the Public Company Accounting Reform and Investor Protection Act of 2002.

2. **T F** The act applies to both public and private companies.[61]

3. **T F** The Public Company Accounting Board is the semipublic group that oversees, regulates, and disciplines accounting firms who do not comply with the Sarbanes-Oxley Act.

4. **T F** Some people think that the Sarbanes-Oxley Act overregulates companies.[62]

5. **T F** The Sarbanes-Oxley Act holds a company's board of directors more accountable for fraud that occurs within their organization

6. **T F** The Sarbanes-Oxley Act was signed by U.S. president Bill Clinton.

7. **T F** The Sarbanes-Oxley Act includes a provision for protecting whistleblowers.[63]

8. **T F** A company that does not follow the Sarbanes-Oxley Act could face fines.

9. **T F** A company's financial officer or CEO does not have to sign off on a certification that states that all information contained in a financial report is true.

10. **T F** The number of companies that went private increased threefold in the year after the Sarbanes-Oxley Act was passed.

Answers:

1. **True.** The act was passed in light of major scandals that occurred in such companies as Enron and WorldCom.

2. **False.** It applies only to publicly traded companies. Privately held companies do not have to comply with the Sarbanes-Oxley Act.

3. **True.** This board only regulates accounting firms that act as auditors, not actually companies themselves.

4. **True.** As with any piece of legislation, there are people who believe the government is too involved, and people who believe the government needs to be more involved.

5. **True.** Before, these individuals were not held personally accountable; today, they may face criminal charges if wrongdoing is uncovered.

6. **False.** The act was signed by George W. Bush in 2002.

7. **True.** Whistleblowers are people who publicly accuse others in their company of misconduct. The Sarbanes-Oxley Act gave whistleblowers increased protection.

8. **False.** Actually, part of the Sarbanes-Oxley Act (section 906) states that officers of companies who fail to comply with the act's requirements could face criminal penalties.[64]

9. **False.** Actually, they do. This is per the act's section 302, which requires company officers to sign off.

10. **True.** Many companies did not want to deal with the expense of implementing the Sarbanes-Oxley Act, so they chose to become private companies instead.[65]

How many did you get right? Knowing about the Sarbanes-Oxley Act, and other important pieces of legislation that affect a company's financial matters, is important not only to accountants but also anyone who plans to own, manage, or run a business.

BUSINESS CAREER QUIZ

Is Accounting the Right Career for You?

Take this short quiz to see your aptitude toward a career in accounting. Mark yes or no for each question.

_____1. Do you work well with others?

_____2. Do you like to learn new skills?

_____3. Do you consider yourself to be honest and ethical?

_____4. Do you enjoy challenging situations?

_____5. Do you tend to follow the rules?

_____6. Do you enjoy a good mystery?

_____7. Are you detail oriented?

_____8. Are you good at reading between the lines?

_____9. Do you consider yourself an analytical person?

If you answered yes to more than five of these questions, a career in accounting might be a good choice for you. Accounting involves more than just numbers—it is about analyzing businesses based on their financials and making recommendations to management about how to increase profits! Accountants are key players in business successs, and they work for companies large and small in all industries.

9

MANAGEMENT
FUNCTIONS AND STYLE

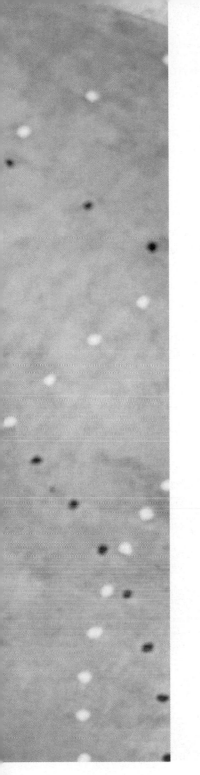

After reading this chapter, you will be able to:

1 Describe the changes occurring in management today.

2 Explain the four functions of management.

3 Describe various management styles and know when they are appropriate.

4 Explain future challenges for management.

THE DWORSKY BROTHERS AND CONSOLIDATED CONTAINER COMPANY

By 2004, the company that began its existence as Consolidated Container Company—which specializes in recycling, cleaning, and reconditioning steel and plastic drums for clients in the petroleum, chemical, and coating industries—found itself in trouble: it was losing more than $100,000 a month. Its revenue had fallen for six years in a row, from $19.1 million in 1998 to $10.5 million in 2004. Its owners put it up for sale.

Prior to 1990, Consolidated Container, founded in 1905, had been a family owned company. William and Phillip Dworsky's father and uncle had sold the company in that year, and the new owners changed the company's name and raised prices in an attempt to widen profit margins. These changes and others damaged relationships with customers and employees, and productivity dropped. Clearly, an absence of leadership at the top of the organization was causing the business to suffer.

William and Phillip Dworsky had been watching the company's value fall since the sale, and the brothers saw an opportunity to buy back the company at a quarter of its 1998 value. The brothers had worked at the company for most of their lives, and since the sale, they'd been operating their own container businesses. They jumped at the opportunity. "We saw the opportunity to succeed in the business that we both knew," Phillip Dworsky remarked.[1] Despite the obvious problems of the business, the brothers decided it was a worthwhile endeavor.

First, they reinstated the firm's original name, Consolidated Container, and organized a plan to repair the company's many fractured elements. One element of the plan was to establish a participative leadership approach with the company's employees. "We asked for the opportunity to restore that lost trust, and that effort was embraced," Phillip Dworsky remarked.[2] "It's been a great relationship ever since." Within the first year, productivity increased by 20 percent, and it went on to double during the next three years. The company erased its losses from previous years, and profit margins began to match industry averages.

By the end of 2008, the Dworskys had raised annual revenue to $16.3 million, and the company was comfortably profitable.[3] Consolidated Container's new management planted the seeds necessary for success: the tools of planning, organizing, and controlling operations were put to use to change the company's fortune. The brothers' close oversight of the business and their choice of a participative leadership also improved the company's chances of success. The vision at Consolidated Container is to be in business for the next 100 years as well.

Questions

1 Do you think managers have to form relationships with employees in order to maximize production, or is it better for them to just tell employees what to do? Explain your response.

2 Why do you think the participative management style worked well for Consolidated Container?

3 Think about a manager you've had in the past who you liked and admired. List five things you liked about that manager. Next, list five things you didn't like about that manager. Discuss your responses with your peers.

Sources: Phil Bolsta, "Consolidated Container Company: Back in the Family," *TwinCities Business*, December 2008, http://www.tcbmag.com/superstars/smallbusinesssuccessstories/106536p1.aspx (accessed August 5, 2009); and Consolidated Container Company Web site, http://www.containerexperts.com/aboutus.cfm and http://www.containerexperts.com/PressDetail.cfm?PressID=5139&REFURL=news.cfm (accessed August 5, 2009).

- What work functions do all managers perform?
- What managerial style suits you best and allows you to work most effectively?
- Is a management career worth exploring, especially considering the challenges faced by today's managers?

>> Management and Today's Managers

Effective management and leadership are the foundation of a flourishing business. Without good management, a company can offer the best product at a good price and still not succeed. It takes an excellent manager to plan, organize, control, and lead a business not just to sell but also to inspire others to want to work hard for the benefit of the company. Leadership, which is discussed further in Chapter 10, is different from management. Management is an appointed position with a title, while leadership tends to have a broader scope.

A manager plans, organizes, leads, and controls various functions within an organization. A leader has vision and inspires others to grasp that vision and transform it into action. Leaders establish values and emphasize corporate ethics. They motivate people to do things willingly that they would not do otherwise. To be effective, all managers must be leaders; however, all leaders do not necessarily have to be managers.

At one time, managers were called bosses, and their job consisted of telling people what to do, watching over them to be sure they did it, and reprimanding those who didn't. Many managers still behave that way. Perhaps you've witnessed such behavior; many basketball coaches have adopted this style.

‹ ETHICAL DILEMMA ›

If you discovered that one of your longtime employees, a person you truly trusted, was receiving bribes while conducting company business, what would you do?

Today, however, some managers tend to be more progressive. For example, they emphasize teams and team building; they create drop-in centers, team spaces, and open work areas. They may change the definition of *work* from a task you do for a specified period in a specific place to something you do anywhere, any time.[4] They tend to guide, train, support, motivate, and coach employees rather than tell them what to do.[5] Managers of high-tech firms, for instance, realize that many workers often know more about technology than they do.[6] Thus, most modern managers emphasize teamwork and cooperation rather than discipline and order giving.

Rather than telling employees exactly what to do, managers today tend to give their employees enough independence to make their own informed decisions about how best to please customers. How do you think most employees respond to this new empowerment on the job?

The people entering management today are different from those who entered in the past. Leaders of *Fortune 100* companies tend to be younger; more of them are female, and fewer of them were educated at elite universities.[7] Managers in the future are more likely to be working in teams and assuming complete-

1. What are some of the changes happening in management today?
2. How are managers different from leaders?
3. Define management.

ly new roles in the firm. For one thing, they will be taking a leadership role in adapting to climate change. Furthermore, they'll be more involved in expanding their businesses' operations overseas and into emerging markets.[8]

What these changes mean for you is that managerial work will require you to build new skills. You'll need to be a skilled communicator, a team player, a planner, an organizer, a motivator, and a leader. In this chapter and future chapters, you'll learn more about these aspects of management, and you'll be better able to decide whether you want a career in management.

Management is the process of planning, organizing, leading, and controlling people and other available resources to accomplish organizational goals and objectives. Without management, organizations would be able to accomplish very little. Management is a position of power, a position that is granted to individuals because they are capable. Managers are expected to make decisions and make sure organizational tasks are accomplished. All managers are charged with four key functions: planning, organizing, leading, and controlling people and other organizational resources. To be a good manager, you must perform all four of these functions well.

> **Management** The process of planning, organizing, leading, and controlling people and other available resources to accomplish organizational goals and objectives.

>> The Functions of Management

A manager's job is to ensure that goals are met and tasks are completed. As mentioned in the preceding section, the four main functions of management are planning, organizing, leading, and controlling (see Figure 9.1).

Planning includes anticipating trends and determining the best strategies and tactics to achieve organizational goals and objectives. One managerial objective is to please customers. To do so, companies develop planning teams to help monitor the business environment, find opportunities, and watch for challenges. **Planning** is a key management function because the other functions depend heavily on having a good plan, no matter what the size of the business. For example, a restaurant owner needs to be constantly aware of the surrounding competition and base her goals and objectives on anticipated challenges.

Organizing includes designing the structure of an organization and creating conditions and systems in which everyone and everything work together to achieve the organization's goals and objectives.[10] Many of today's organizations are designed around the customer. Managers organize their businesses in order to ensure that everyone is working to satisfy customer needs and maximize profit. Organizations must remain flexible and adaptable because customer needs change, and organizations must either change along with them or risk losing business.

In a recession, companies must work harder than ever before to adapt to customer needs. During the

> **Planning** A management function that includes anticipating trends and determining the best strategies and tactics to achieve organizational goals and objectives.
>
> **Organizing** A management function that includes designing the structure of the organization and creating conditions and systems in which everyone and everything works together to achieve the organization's goals and objectives.

Figure 9.1 What Managers Do

Planning
- Setting organizational goals.
- Developing strategies to reach those goals.
- Determining resources needed.
- Setting precise standards.

Organizing
- Allocating resources, assigning tasks, and establishing procedures for accomplishing goals.
- Preparing a structure (organization chart) showing lines of authority and responsibility.
- Recruiting, selecting, training, and developing employees.
- Placing employees where they'll be most effective.

Leading
- Guiding and motivating employees to work effectively to accomplish organizational goals and objectives.
- Giving assignments.
- Explaining routines.
- Clarifying policies.
- Providing feedback on performance.

Controlling
- Measuring results against corporate objectives.
- Monitoring performance relative to standards.
- Rewarding outstanding performance.
- Taking corrective action when necessary.

Some modern managers perform all of these tasks with the full cooperation and participation of workers. Empowering employees means allowing them to participate more fully in decision making.

recession of 2008–2009, the *Wall Street Journal* highlighted the efforts of one communications company, Sprint, to change its organizational focus in order to maintain more existing customers. Sprint changed its previous customer service focus from keeping customer service calls short to making sure issues were resolved during the first customer call. Likewise, the leadership of the restaurant chain Cheesecake Factory shifted its business goals from opening more restaurants to improving customer service.[12]

Leading Creating a vision for an organization and guiding, training, coaching, and motivating others to work effectively to achieve the organization's goals and objectives.

Empowerment Giving frontline workers the responsibility, authority, freedom, training, and equipment they need to respond quickly to customer requests.

Leading means creating a vision for an organization and communicating, guiding, training, coaching, and motivating others to work effectively to achieve the organization's goals and objectives. The trend is to **empower** employees and give them as much freedom as possible so they become self-directed and self-motivated. In other words, empowering employees means giving employees the authority (the right to make a decision without consulting a manager) and responsibility (the requirement to accept the consequences of one's actions) to respond quickly to customer requests.

Leading was once known as directing, or telling employees exactly what to do. In many smaller firms and in certain industries (such as fast-food restaurants), managers still do exactly that. In most large modern firms, however, managers no longer tell people exactly what to do because workers often know how to do their jobs better than their manager does. Nonetheless, leadership is necessary to keep employees focused on the right priorities and timelines. Leaders are also responsible for training, coaching, and motivating employees, and for performing other leadership tasks.[13]

Controlling involves establishing clear standards to determine whether an organization is progressing toward its goals and objectives, rewarding people for doing a good job, and taking corrective action if they are not. In short, controlling means measuring whether what actually occurs is in line with the organization's goals.

Controlling A management function that involves establishing clear standards to determine whether or not an organization is progressing toward its goals and objectives, rewarding people for doing a good job and taking corrective action if they are not.

The four functions just addressed—planning, organizing, leading, and controlling—are the heart of management. Let's explore these functions in more detail, beginning with planning.

Planning is what helps managers understand the environment in which their business must operate. When people's tastes and preferences for restaurant meals change, food service managers need to be ready to respond with menu alternatives. What changes have occurred in your own preferences?

PLANNING

Planning, the first managerial function, involves setting an organizational vision, mission, goals, and

Real World Apps

Denny Spisak is graduating from college in three months with a degree in business administration. He's weighing his options for future career paths and is not sure where his skills and abilities will fit into an organization. In order to figure out which path he should choose, Denny decides to make a list of his strengths and weaknesses to better understand where his interests and talents lie. In particular, he's thinking hard about whether or not he has a future in management.

Management positions scare Denny. He's not sure if he is management material. He wonders, "Are management skills learned, or are you born with them?" Denny is a shy, quiet person, and he's not comfortable bossing other people around.

Denny thinks, "A boss has to be in charge, be confident, and know everything about his job and the jobs of people who work for his. Or does he?"

Since Denny really loves research, he decides to find out as much as he can about management functions and styles by reading his Business Now textbook's chapter on management. He decides that perhaps if he has a better understanding of management, it won't scare his as much. Denny is interested in travel, international business, and globalization, so he thinks he might be able to find a career path that involves both management and business in an international setting. Who wouldn't love to work in a foreign country?

jectives. Most successful companies employ several strategies to ensure that their plans are realistic and achievable.

Creating a corporate **vision** and a **mission statement** can be very challenging. The *vision*, a forward-looking statement, provides a broad explanation of why the organization exists and where it's headed in the future. The *mission statement* is an outline of the organization's fundamental purpose. In its mission statement, an organization describes "what business we are in."[14] Figure 9.2 shows the mission statement and the vision of ABC Supply Co., a roofing, siding, and windows distributor.

> **Vision** An encompassing explanation of why the organization exists and the direction it's trying to go.
>
> **Mission statement** An outline of the fundamental purposes of an organization.

Writing a Mission Statement

A meaningful mission statement should include the following components:

- Customer needs
- Company philosophy and goals
- The organization's self-concept
- Long-term survival
- The nature of the company's products or services
- Social responsibility
- Care for employees

Mission statements can vary in length and content; however, effective mission statements include each of the above components. It should identify your company, what it stands for, what it does, and why it does what it does. It's best to have the input of all members of an organization when developing a mission statement. Figure 9.3 shows sample mission statements of two different organizations. How well do they address each of the components mentioned previously?

A firm's mission statement becomes its foundation for setting specific goals. **Goals** are the broad, long-term accomplishments an organization wishes to attain. In order to be achievable, goals must be mutually agreed upon by workers and management. Thus, goal setting is often a team process.

One element of controlling is rewarding employees for doing a good job.

Figure 9.2 Mission and Vision of ABC Supply Co., a Roofing, Siding, and Window Distributor

Our Mission and Vision: ABC Supply Co.
Since our founding in 1982, our mission has remained unchanged—make it easy for our customers. From the services we provide to the products we sell, we're committed to helping contractors succeed and grow their business.

We Fulfill That Mission By:
- Stocking the brands and products contractors want and need at a competitive price.
- Maintaining a state-of-the-art delivery system that ensures orders are delivered to the job site when and where they are needed.
- Actively listening to our customers to find out what they want and need, what we're doing well and how we can improve—and then implementing many of their suggestions.
- Providing ongoing training for every ABC Supply associate, ensuring they have the knowledge and expertise they need to provide world-class customer service.
- Training every ABC employee so they can provide contractors with the information and techniques they need to remain competitive.
- Challenging our associates to set goals for themselves and creating an environment that helps them realize those dreams.
- Judging our own success by the success of our customers. We know that we will only be successful when our customers are successful.

By staying true to this mission, we will realize our vision of being the supplier of choice for our contractor customers and being known as the greatest place to work in the United States.

Source: www.abcsupply.com/About.aspx?id=460, accessed September 4, 2007.

Objectives are specific statements that detail how to achieve an organization's goals in the short term. One of your goals for reading this chapter, for example, is to learn basic concepts of management. An objective you could use to achieve this goal is to correctly answer the questions in the [BUS] connections boxes located throughout the chapter. To make goals and objectives most effective, you can use a framework called SMART objectives, which is illustrated in Figure 9.4.

Goals The broad, long-term accomplishments an organization wishes to attain.

Objectives Specific statements that detail how to achieve an organization's goals in the short term.

SWOT and PEST Analyses

When planning and setting goals for a company, managers must also determine how well the company is doing at any given point in time. Using a **SWOT analysis**, which is an analysis of an organization's strengths, weaknesses, opportunities, and threats, is a good way to approach this task.

SWOT analysis A planning tool used to analyze an organization's strengths, weaknesses, opportunities, and threats.

To begin a SWOT analysis, managers must first scrutinize the business in general, including asking a few key questions. What does the company do well? What does the company do poorly? Next, managers must perform an external environmental

analysis to determine what external factors could affect the business. For example, a small retailer might consider recent advances in technology and the growing popularity of online shopping to be an excellent opportunity to develop an e-commerce Web site or to sell some of its products on an online auction site, such as eBay.[15]

Of course, not all the external factors present opportunities. The analysis of the external factors includes identifying any threats to the business—anything that could negatively affect the business. For example, the rapid increase in oil prices that occurred during 2007 and 2008 negatively affected most businesses, because it caused gasoline and energy expenses to rise across the board.[16] Once a SWOT analysis is performed, a company is in a better position to

Figure 9.3 Sample Mission Statements

Mission statement for HemCon Medical Technologies, Inc., an Oregon-based medical supply firm.
HemCon Medical Technologies, Inc., through the use of breakthrough technology and proprietary manufacturing processes, will provide the U.S. Armed Services and its allies with superior products for severe hemorrhage control while in parallel developing high value added products and applications to serve civilian markets within hospitals, first responders, emergency/trauma, and over-the-counter [applications].

Mission statement for Higher One, a Connecticut-based financial services and payment company enabling institutions of higher education to streamline business processes while improving student services.
When Higher One was founded, we agreed that as long as we still believed that there is a way to succeed, then the business still had a chance at success. No matter what happened, how dreary the outlook, we committed to our belief that there is a way to succeed, and we would keep working together to find innovative ways to get there.

"There is a way" is more than just a belief that everything is possible. It epitomizes what Higher One means to everyone who works at Higher One, works with Higher One, is a Higher One customer, or is a potential customer.

When serving customers, working with partners, or going about the everyday business that makes Higher One run, remember, "There is a way" means:

1. Focus: We strive for excellence in execution. This means that we channel a great amount of effort toward a small list of value-oriented objectives.

2. Integrity: We are honest and straightforward about our goals and objectives; and we have the courage to pursue them. We demonstrate honest and ethical behavior in all dealings with customers, clients, colleagues, suppliers, partners, investors, and governments.

3. Creative thinking: We are both thoughtful and creative in our approach to problem-solving. We are steadfast in our belief that "there is a way."

4. Teamwork: We believe that the achievements of any organization are the result of the combined effort of each individual. The combined effort of a team produces results greater than the sum of individual efforts.

5. Open communication: We value all thoughtful opinions, suggestions, solutions and questions. Within Higher One, we give candid, constructive and direct feedback.

6. Stellar service: We strive to balance the human and business needs in every internal and external customer interaction. We recognize that exceptional internal service is a necessary foundation for exceptional external service.

Every day we use this principle to work toward our mission!

Sources: "Our History," http://www.hemcon.com/AboutUs/HistoryMission.aspx, accessed August 5, 2009, and "The Higher One Philosophy—There Is a Way," http://www.higherone.com/about/higherone_Philosophy.shtml, accessed August 6, 2009.

develop goals and objectives because managers can see the entire spectrum of their business—both internally and externally. Figure 9.5 lists some of the potential issues companies consider when conducting a SWOT analysis.

An organization's external environment can be divided into two parts: the microenvironment, which is very specific, and the macroenvironment, which is the general business environment. A firm's microenvironment includes its customers, distributors, suppliers, and competitors. These specific environmental factors are particularly important because they directly affect the firm's performance. Macroenvironmental factors affect an organization indirectly; these factors include political, economic, sociocultural, and technological changes.

A **PEST analysis**—which is an analysis of the **p**olitical, **e**conomic, **s**ocial, and **t**echnological factors at work in a firm's macroenvironment—can help a firm understand its position and find opportunities for growth. As with the SWOT analysis, a company exam-

PEST analysis An analysis of outside factors that could affect a business: political, economic, social, and technological.

Thinking Critically

The World of Sales Management

Every company is in business to make a profit, and managing a company's sales force is certainly a high priority. As you read the information below from the U.S. Bureau of Labor Statistics's *Occupational Outlook Handbook 2008–2009*, think about this role. Do you think it might be the right career path for you?

In small firms, the owner or chief executive officer might assume all sales management responsibilities. In large firms, which may offer numerous products and services nationally or even worldwide, an executive vice president directs overall sales policies. But there are many opportunities for sales managers in almost every industry and at many different levels within a business.

Sales managers direct a firm's sales program. They assign sales territories, set goals, and establish training programs for the sales representatives. Sales managers advise sales representatives on ways to improve their performance. In large, multiproduct firms, they oversee regional and local sales managers and their staffs. Sales managers maintain contact with dealers and distributors. They analyze sales statistics gathered by their staffs to determine sales potential and inventory requirements and to monitor customers' preferences. Such information is vital in the development of products and the maximization of profits. The following are a few key points about sales management jobs:

- Keen competition is expected for these highly coveted jobs.
- College graduates with related experience, a high level of creativity, strong communication skills, and computer skills should have the best job opportunities.
- High earnings, substantial travel, and long hours, including evenings and weekends, are common.
- Because of the importance and high visibility of their jobs, these managers often are prime candidates for advancement to the highest ranks.

Sales managers work in offices close to those of top managers. Working under pressure is unavoidable when schedules change and problems arise, but deadlines and goals must still be met.

Most sales management positions are filled by promoting experienced staff or related professional personnel. For example, many managers are former sales representatives, purchasing agents, or buyers. In small firms, where the number of positions is limited, advancement to a management position usually comes slowly. In large firms, promotion may occur more quickly.

As a sales manager, your earnings could reach as high as six figures, but salary levels vary substantially, depending upon the level of managerial responsibility, length of service, education, size of firm, location, and industry. Size of a manager's sales territory is another important determinant of salary. Many managers earn bonuses equal to 10 percent or more of their salaries.

Source: U.S. Bureau of Labor Statistics, *Occupational Outlook Handbook, 2008–09 Edition,* http://www.bls.gov/oco/ocos020.htm (accessed August 25, 2009).

QUESTIONS

1. What elements of a sales management role appeal to you? Which would not be right for you?

2. In your opinion, what is the most important responsibility a sales manager has?

Figure 9.4 Guidelines for Setting SMART Objectives

1. **Specific** — Make sure the objective is specific. Rather than saying "increase sales" say "Increase sales by 10%."

2. **Measurable** — A company should be able to easily see if a goal is met. "Better customer service" is a hard goal to measure, but "increase customer service survey by 1 point in six months" is very measurable.

3. **Achievable** — Are the objectives achievable and attainable? Increasing company size by $1 million might not be achievable; however, increasing by $100,000 might be just difficult enough to be challenging, but not impossible.

4. **Realistic** — Can the company achieve the goal with the resources available? If a company does not have enough sales staff to increase sales, then increasing sales may not be the right goal. Hiring more people might be the better goal.

5. **Time** — What is the deadline for achieving goals? Is it six months, one year? Make sure it is realistic.

In his classic article, Doran explains the SMART way to write goals and objectives. Over time, a few of the terms, such as A = "agreed to" or R = "resource based," have been modified by other authors.

Source: George T. Doran, "There's a S.M.A.R.T. Way to Write Management Goals and Objectives," *Management Review* (AMA Forum), November 1981, pp. 35–36.

ines these four external areas to determine what elements of them could affect its business in the future. With the combined tools of SWOT and PEST analyses, any business, big or small, can plan more efficiently and effectively.

Political factors could include legal and regulatory issues, such as new laws being passed that could affect the way a company does business. In 2007, Congress passed laws that incrementally raised the federal minimum wage from $5.15 per hour to $7.25 per hour over a two-year period. Obviously, this change affected any business with employees.

A manager performing a PEST analysis would also examine economic factors—such as interest rates, unemployment rates, availability of credit, inflation rates, and so on—to determine how these might affect his or her business. Higher unemployment rates lower a community's disposable income, which in turn lowers consumer spending.

Sociocultural factors, including birth and death rates, marriage trends, divorce rates, immigration and emigration rates, and

Figure 9.5 SWOT Matrix

If Domino's Pizza opened a store next to a family-owned pizza parlor, the family-owned pizza business would suffer as a result—at least temporarily.

Potential Internal STRENGTHS
- Core competencies in key areas
- An acknowledged market leader
- Well-conceived functional area strategies
- Proven management
- Cost advantages
- Better advertising campaigns

Potential Internal WEAKNESSES
- No clear strategic direction
- Obsolete facilities
- Subpar profitability
- Lack of managerial depth and talent
- Weak market image
- Too narrow a product line

Potential External OPPORTUNITIES
- Ability to serve additional customer groups
- Expand product lines
- Ability to transfer skills/technology to new products
- Falling trade barriers in attractive foreign markets
- Complacency among rival firms
- Ability to grow due to increases in market demand

Potential External THREATS
- Entry of lower-cost foreign competitors
- Rising sales of substitute products
- Slower market growth
- Costly regulatory requirements
- Vulnerability to recession and business cycles
- Changing buyer needs and tastes

so on, also change the business landscape. For example, in the United States, life expectancy has grown from 47.3 years in the 1900s to a record 77.9 years in 2004.[17] By 2010, it is expected to reach 78.3 years, and 79.5 years in 2020.[18] Businesses must respond to the needs of these older consumers, and the fact that people live longer means a business has more consumers to respond to overall.

Technology changes affect businesses, too. The Internet has changed the way people communicate and do business. An effective Web site distributes information and helps create new revenue streams for a business.

Forms of Planning

Next, we'll consider the four forms of planning: strategic planning, tactical planning, operational planning, and contingency planning (see Figure 9.6).

Strategic planning is the process of setting major long-term goals for a company. Often, these goals concern the growth of the company or potential new products. It

> **Strategic planning** The process of determining the major long-term goals of the organization and the policies and strategies for obtaining and using resources to achieve those goals.

provides a foundation for the policies, procedures, and strategies for obtaining and using resources to achieve those goals. For example, the strategic plan for Mountain City Coffeehouse & Creamery in Frostburg, Maryland, includes long-term goals of opening new locations and kiosks, establishing the coffeehouse as an art venue, and expanding its catering menu selections.

Tactical planning is the process of developing detailed, short-term statements about what is to be done, who is to do it, and how it is to be done. These statements are a series of short-term goals that must be achieved in order to meet the long-term strategic plans and goals. To continue the example of the Mountain City Coffeehouse & Creamery, tactical plans for expanding the restaurant's catering menu could include developing a new list of special entrees and tactical plans for achieving the strategic goal of establishing the coffeehouse as an art venue could include collecting local artists' information and organizing art displays that change monthly.

> **Tactical planning** The process of developing detailed, short-term statements about what is to be done, who is to do it, and how it is to be done.

Sea-Land Service, Inc., a shipping company based in Charlotte, North Carolina, uses the tactical plan of allowing its best customers to visit its company headquarters in order to achieve its strategic goals of creating new ideas and reinforcing relationships. During these customer visits, employees from Sea-Land's various departments, including operations and finance, meet with customers to assess and describe what's going on with the business in the present and where it's headed in the future.[20]

Figure 9.6 Planning Functions
FORMS OF PLANNING

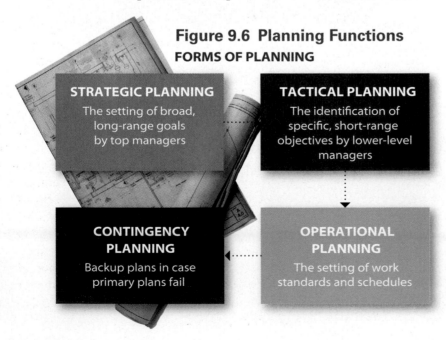

STRATEGIC PLANNING
The setting of broad, long-range goals by top managers

TACTICAL PLANNING
The identification of specific, short-range objectives by lower-level managers

CONTINGENCY PLANNING
Backup plans in case primary plans fail

OPERATIONAL PLANNING
The setting of work standards and schedules

Very few firms bother to make contingency plans. If something changes the market, such companies may be slow to respond. Most organizations do strategic, tactical, and operational planning.

Operational planning The process of setting work standards and schedules necessary to implement the company's tactical objectives.

Operational planning is the process of setting work standards and schedules necessary to implement the company's tactical objectives. A manager uses an operational plan to set up the business's daily and weekly operations. Mountain City Coffeehouse & Creamery's operational plans include its weekly orders of ingredients from different vendors, its employee work schedules, and its daily opening and closing routines.

Contingency planning The process of preparing alternative courses of action that may be used if the primary plans don't achieve the organization's objectives.

Contingency planning is the process of preparing alternative courses of action that may be used if a business's primary plans do not achieve its objectives. For example, contingency plans for meeting the sales goals for Mountain City Coffeehouse & Creamery include using more direct forms of advertising to attract students at a nearby college, increasing the frequency of advertisements on local radio stations, and offering regular customers special discounts tied to frequency and volume.

Contingency planning is particularly important for companies that conduct business operations in other countries. In recent years, foreign franchises of certain U.S.-owned businesses, including McDonald's, were attacked as an expression of anti-American sentiment. McDonald's has responded by developing new menu items that are better suited to the tastes of the nations in which they do business and shifting the focus away from traditional "American" menu items, like the Big Mac, in those areas.[21]

Crisis planning is the part of contingency planning that involves reacting to sudden changes in the environment. According to the Creative Group, 33 percent of the average executive's time is spent responding to crises or problems.[22] In 2009, Agility Recovery Solutions and Hughes Marketing Group

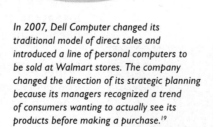

In 2007, Dell Computer changed its traditional model of direct sales and introduced a line of personal computers to be sold at Walmart stores. The company changed the direction of its strategic planning because its managers recognized a trend of consumers wanting to actually see its products before making a purchase.[19]

surveyed more than 700 business owners and executives throughout North America about their disaster recovery and business continuity plans. The study found that 94 percent of companies have formal data backup plans, and 75 percent of companies believe they can have their employees back at work within days of a disaster. However, the following findings call some of that optimism into question:

- Only 28 percent have access to alternative office space.
- Only 41 percent have access to mobile office space.
- Only 54 percent are able to acquire temporary office equipment.
- Only 57 percent have access to generators.[23]

ORGANIZING

After managers have planned a course of action, they must organize the firm to accomplish their goals. Operationally, organizing means allocating resources (such as funds for various

Organization chart A visual device that shows relationships among people and divides the organization's work; it shows who reports to whom.

Span of control The optimal number of subordinates (employees) a manager supervises.

functions within departments), assigning tasks, and establishing procedures for accomplishing the organizational objectives. An **organization chart** is a visual diagram that shows relationships among people who work in a business. The chart also divides the organization's work; it shows who is accountable for the completion of specific duties, and who reports to whom. An organization chart includes top, middle, and first-line or supervisory managers (see Figure 9.7). In addition, it shows the **span of control**, which is the number of subordinates a manager supervises. The optimum span of control depends greatly on the type of company and experience of employees.

Levels of Management

Top management, the highest level of management, consists of a company's president and the other key executives who participate in the development of strategic plans. Top managers generally include a company's CEO, chief operating officer (COO), chief financial officer (CFO), and chief information officer (CIO). In some companies, the CIO is called the chief knowledge officer (CKO).

Top management The highest level of management, consisting of the president and other key company executives who develop strategic plans.

Sometimes, a business's CEO is also its president. The CEO is generally responsible for all top-level decisions in the firm and for introducing change into the organization. The COO is responsible for putting those changes into effect. His or her tasks include structuring work, controlling operations, and rewarding employees in order to ensure that all strive to carry out the leader's vision. The CFO is responsible for obtaining funds, planning budgets, collecting funds from people or organizations who owe the company money, and so on. The CIO or CKO is responsible for getting the right information to other managers so they can make good decisions.

Middle management The level of management that includes general managers, division managers, and branch and plant managers who are responsible for tactical planning and controlling.

Middle management includes the general managers, division managers, district managers, and plant managers who are responsible for tactical planning and controlling. Many firms have eliminated some of their middle managers through downsizing (see more about downsizing at the end of this chapter); as a result, the managers who remain have more employees to supervise. To some degree, middle management jobs have fallen out of favor with employees. Some view middle management as a job that requires more work, presents little opportunity to move up in the company, and provides fewer benefits. Therefore, companies like IBM have created incentives to get employees excited about middle-management positions. For example, IBM allows middle managers the opportunity to work on international assignments in an effort to develop new skills. The company also offers telecommuting and other programs that make middle-level management more attractive to employees.[25]

Supervisory (first-line) managers are directly responsible for conducting operational planning, supervising workers, and evaluating their daily performance. They're often known as first-line managers (or supervisors) because they're the first level above workers. This is the first management position you're likely to attain after college.

Supervisory (first-line) management Managers who are directly responsible for supervising workers and evaluating their daily performance.

Skills at Different Levels of Management

Few people are trained to be good managers. Usually a person is selected to become a manager because he or she excels at a particular skill, such as providing excellent customer service in a medical office. Such managers tend to become deeply involved in showing others how to do things, helping them, supervising them, and generally being very active in operations-related tasks. The further up the managerial ladder a person moves, the less important his or her original job skills become. Figure 9.8 shows that a manager must have three categories of skills:

Organizations of all kinds need contingency plans for unexpected events. Amtrak and the Transportation Security Administration recently conducted drills at 150 train stations to help officers prepare to work together in case of an emergency.

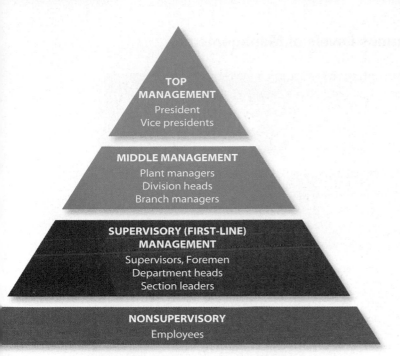

Figure 9.7 Levels of Management

1. **Technical skills** involve the ability to perform tasks in a specific discipline (such as selling a product or developing software) or department (such as marketing or information systems). These skills are especially important for supervisory managers, because they work closely with employees. Top-level managers may not need to use technical skills as much, as they are more focused on using their conceptual skills.

2. **Human relations skills** involve communication and motivation; they enable managers to work with and through people. These skills also include leadership, coaching, morale building, delegating, training and development, and supportiveness. Human relations skills are critical in all three levels of management.

3. **Conceptual skills** involve the ability to picture the organization as a whole and the relationships among its various parts. Conceptual skills are needed in planning, organizing, controlling, developing systems, analyzing problems, decision making, coordinating, and delegating. Generally speaking, this skill set is needed for top-level managers and may not be as important for first-line supervisors.

Technical skills Skills that involve the ability to perform tasks in a specific discipline or department.

Human relations skills Skills that involve communication and motivation; they enable managers to work through and with people.

Conceptual skills Skills that involve the ability to picture the organization as a whole and the relationship among its various parts.

Types of Organizational Structures

Earlier in the chapter, you learned about organization charts. A major part of the organizing function is defining the parameters within which managers work. A firm's *organizational structure* describes the way in which the company is organized and how its employees fit into the bigger picture of the company. A manager must thoroughly understand what kind of structure his or her company has. There are several types of organizational structures a company can have, as noted in Figures 9.9a and 9.9b.

In a *line-and-staff* structure, the staff personnel advise and assist the line personnel in meeting the goals of the organization. Line personnel are responsible for directly achieving organizational goals; they include production, distribution, and marketing employees. Staff personnel include employees in marketing research, legal departments, information technology, and human resource management.

In a *matrix* organization, on the other hand, people from various departments are teamed up to accomplish a common goal, such as getting a project done for a client. Specialists from different parts of the organization work together temporarily on specific projects but still remain part of a line-and-staff structure.

The process of setting up individual departments to do specialized tasks is called *departmentalization*. The traditional way to departmentalize organizations is by function, such as production or finance. It is prob-

When Robert Polet was appointed CEO of Gucci, many observers were skeptical. Much of the ridicule aimed his way centered on his previous job—president of the global ice cream and frozen-foods division at Unilever, the makers of Popsicle brand treats. Not everyone was sure Polet could make the transition from food to fashion. Polet proved them wrong; his hands-off management approach led the company to booming sales and profit growth.[24]

Figure 9.8 Skills Needed at Various Levels of Management

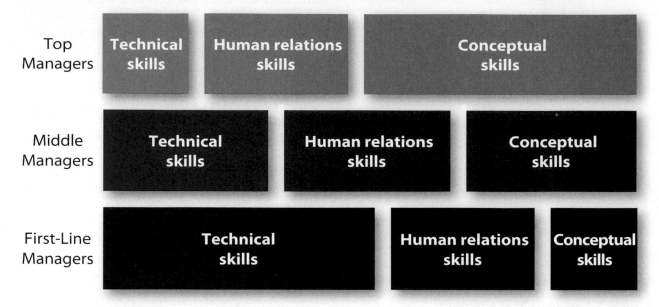

Top Managers	Technical skills	Human relations skills	Conceptual skills
Middle Managers	Technical skills	Human relations skills	Conceptual skills
First-Line Managers	Technical skills	Human relations skills	Conceptual skills

ably the most common form of departmentalization in small to medium-sized businesses. A functional structure groups workers into departments because they perform similar tasks, have similar expertise, or use the same resources. The major manufacturer 3M makes a wide variety of products, and it organizes its various product lines according to customer depart-

In a company that manufactures custom closets, a salesperson, production person, and installer may all work together to design a product for a customer—a good example of a matrix organization.

mentalization. Some of its departments include displays and graphics, electronics, health care, safety and security, transportation, manufacturing, office, and home and leisure.[26] Figure 9.10 shows five ways a firm can departmentalize.

When a firm groups individuals and tasks around its major product lines, it is organized by product departmentalization. For example, a book publisher might have textbook, trade book, and technical book departments. In some organizations, it makes more sense to group activities around the major customers they serve. For example, a stock trading or brokerage firm may group its activities into a division that serves individual clients and another that serves institutional clients.

Certain organizations group their tasks and processes in order to meet the different needs of customers in different geographic regions. For example, a restaurant company may create northeastern, southeastern, northwestern, and southwestern regional units. Other firms find it more efficient to separate their activities by process. For example, a small clothing manufacturing firm might group activities into separate departments that size and cut the garments, dye the garments, stitch the garments together, and finish the garments with accessories, respectively.

Firms often use a combination of these departmentalization techniques. These are called hybrid forms. For example, a restaurant chain may be organized by both functional areas (sales, marketing, and purchasing) and geographic areas (northeast, southeast, northwest, and southwest stores). Figure 9.11 shows an example of a combination of a geographic departmentalization with a matrix-style organization.

Figure 9.9a Line-and-Staff versus Matrix Organization

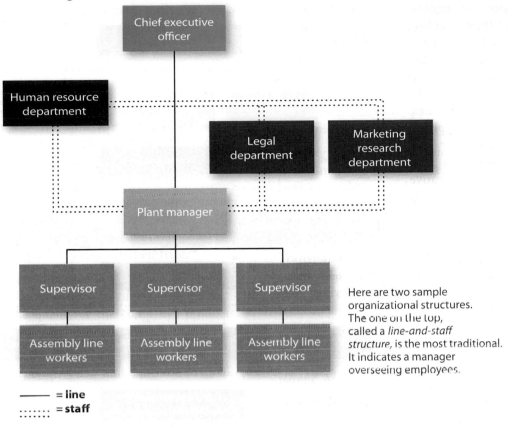

Here are two sample organizational structures. The one on the top, called a *line-and-staff structure,* is the most traditional. It indicates a manager overseeing employees.

——— = line
······· = staff

Figure 9.9b Line-and-Staff versus Matrix Organization

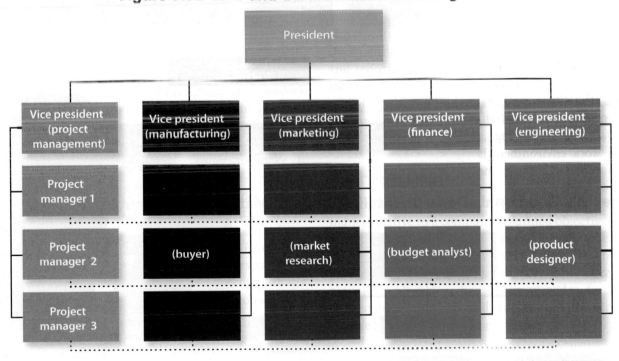

The second structure, called a *matrix organization*, utilizes a more nontraditional form, with work teams made up of people from several departments. This kind of structure can be an advantage in many types of industries where several experts might be needed to complete one project.

Figure 9.12 The Control Process

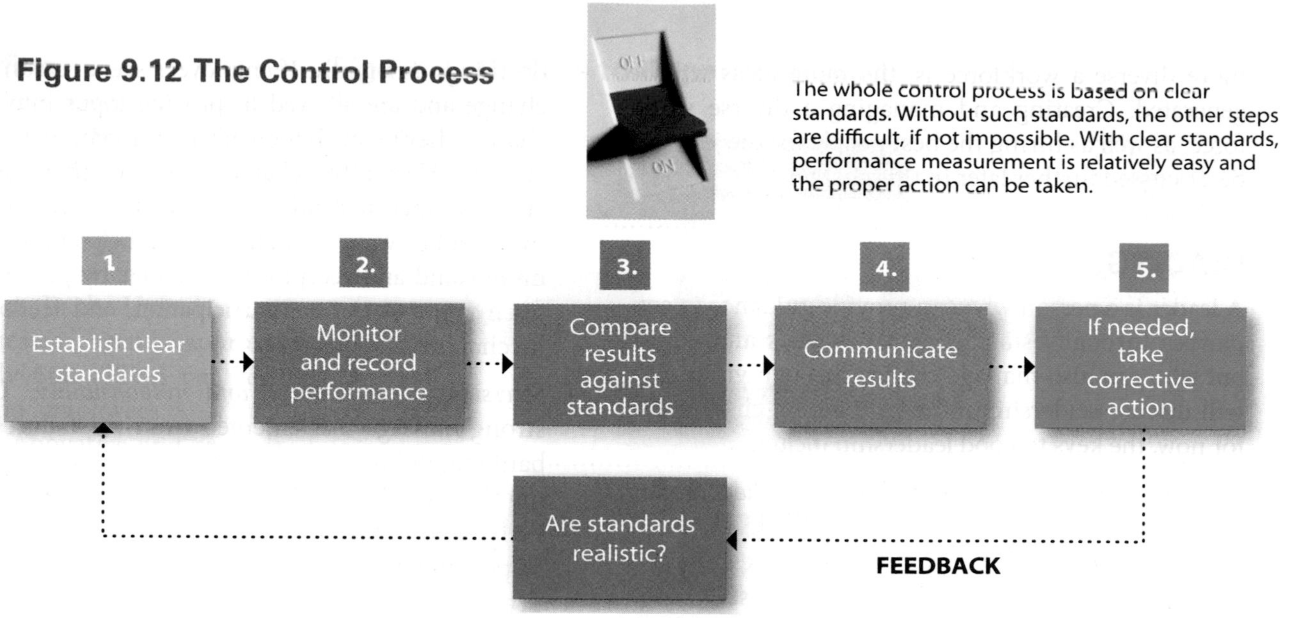

The whole control process is based on clear standards. Without such standards, the other steps are difficult, if not impossible. With clear standards, performance measurement is relatively easy and the proper action can be taken.

1	2.	3.	4.	5.
Establish clear standards	Monitor and record performance	Compare results against standards	Communicate results	If needed, take corrective action

Are standards realistic?

FEEDBACK

2. *Monitoring and recording actual performance.* A manager observes and records employee performance against the standards that have been set.

3. *Comparing results against plans and standards.* After performance standards have been put into place and actual performance has been measured, the manager must compare the two.

4. *Communicating results and deviations to the employees involved.* If performance standards have not been met, or if they have been met or exceeded, the manager must communicate this information to the employees.

5. *Taking corrective action when needed and providing positive feedback.* For example, if certain employees don't have the necessary training to run new machines, their manager would suggest the corrective action of offering the needed training so the employees can meet the desired standard.

WHAT ELSE DO MANAGERS DO?

Obviously, the kinds of tasks managers do vary greatly in each industry. Some managers may work directly with employees to get a task done, such as a supermarket manager who takes over at the cash register when the lines get too long. But generally speaking, managers are also responsible for setting an ethical standard, creating an environment for a good work–life balance, and making sure high-quality products are being produced.

As we will explore in Chapter 12, managers establish a company's ethical framework. Employees look to managers for guidance and consider them an example; therefore, if a manager acts unethically, there is

a good chance his or her employees will do the same. For example, if a manager takes longer lunches than the company generally allows, employees who work for the manager may start to do the same. If a manager is regularly late for work, the employees may think it's acceptable to be late.

Besides setting the tone for ethics, managers also need to do what they can to ensure a good work–life balance for employees. **Work–life balance** is a person's control over the interactions between his or her work life and family and personal life. A positive work–life balance can be achieved when people feel satisfied about their personal life and fulfilled by their work life.

Work–life balance A person's control over the interactions between his or her work life and family and personal life.

Managers can sometimes create work–life balance issues when their expectations exceed what a person can accomplish within a regular workweek. Once a situation reaches that point, the person in question is probably working too much and generally does not have a good balance between work and life.

Consider a manager who comes to your desk on Friday at 4 p.m. and asks you to complete a 30-page report by Monday morning at 9 a.m. Not only is this unrealistic, but it would also create a stressful situation for you. While you're furiously working on the report all weekend, you won't have a good work–life balance, since to finish the report, almost every minute will need to be focused on work.

There will always be circumstances where deadlines take precedence over a good work–life balance, but when these circumstances happen too often, employees can end up unhappy and burned out. Eastwick Communications, a public relations firm based in California, and Scalent Systems Inc., a software company located in California's Silicon Valley, try to instill a healthy work–life balance in their employees. Both companies hold holiday parties to help employees unwind. They also offer flexible scheduling and telecommuting options. Recruitment and retention are valid reasons for managers to take work–life balance issues seriously, and companies that are able to effectively manage them ultimately have happier, more productive employees.[30]

Managers are also responsible for ensuring the quality of their company's products or services. In a sense, this overall goal embodies and results from all other managerial functions.

> **Total quality management (TQM)** A management strategy whereby quality goods are ensured at every phase of the production process.

Total quality management (TQM) is a management strategy whereby quality goods are ensured at every phase of the production process; TQM also applies to service organizations.

According to the principles of TQM, a manager must inspire employees to be concerned at every stage of production about providing excellent quality. The basis for TQM rests on attention to satisfying customer needs and continuous improvement in everything the organization does.

For example, if a table manufacturer were to employ a TQM philosophy, all of its employees would be carefully trained to look for defects in materials or flaws in procedure at every point in the manufacturing process. Everyone in the company would be responsible for ensuring high quality from start to finish; therefore, TQM helps ensure that customer needs will be satisfied at the highest level possible.

Career PERSPECTIVES

BECOMING A MANAGER

If management sounds like something you might be interested in for a future career, the possibilities are endless. There are management jobs in every industry and career track. For example, if you are studying nursing, you may choose to pursue a job at a hospital or a nursing home. Either type of business will have administrative positions that oversee and manage the nursing staff, and eventually, you'll have the experience and knowledge to take on that challenge. Likewise, if you plan to have a career in accounting, you may want to pursue a position where you'll oversee and manage a team in a business's finance department.

If you are planning to become an entrepreneur, management skills will be necessary to handle the day-to-day operations in your business, particularly where your employees are concerned. Effective management is the key to a successful start-up, because you will be dependent on others—at least to some degree—to make things happen for your business. Even people who do not work for you directly—vendors, suppliers, and customers, for example—require some level of management.

The best way to break into management is to earn a degree or certificate in a field of interest. The next step is to get established in a nonmanagement position at a company and make sure your supervisor knows you're interested in a management position someday. Take initiative. Engage in extra projects—especially those that put you in a leadership role. Your supervisor will notice, and your career in management will blossom!

What areas of management interest you most? Do you like to plan, organize, lead, and control operations? Do you see yourself as an autocratic, participative, or free-rein manager? Why?

[BUS] connections

1. What are the four functions of management? Which do you think is the most important? Why?

2. Can you apply the different forms of planning to your own career or your progress toward your degree? Explain.

3. Describe the different skills needed at different levels of management.

>> MANAGEMENT STYLES

Now that you've learned what a manager does, it's important to know that there are several management or leadership styles that managers can follow in order to achieve their goals. No one style is better than another, as it depends on the situation, and certain styles are better suited to certain situations.[31] Figure 9.13 summarizes the autocratic, participative, and free-rein styles.

Going GLOBAL

The Needs of the Global Economy Workforce

In the coming years, further global expansion among companies is contingent on hiring and training the best possible workforce. Talent management is becoming one of the most important roles of a manager, and globalization is a leading reason why. This *BusinessWeek* article by an employee of the consulting firm Accenture attempts to explain the needs of the global economy workforce.

Right now, the issues of gender, a high-performing workforce, the skills gap, demographics, and the growing confidence of emerging-market multinationals are all converging at a time of great uncertainty. This translates into increased opportunity for emerging markets—and increased pressure for established ones.

To achieve both long-term success and high performance, management must anticipate the motivations and concerns of every sector of tomorrow's workforce and plan accordingly. Accenture conducted a study, *One Step Ahead of 2011: A New Horizon for Working Women.* Interviews with 4,000 women and men in 17 countries produced a surprising conclusion: 68 percent of businesswomen in India, 63 percent in South Africa, 61 percent in China, and 52 percent in Brazil feel confident about their ability to succeed in a global business world. By contrast, only 46 percent of U.S. women—and men—feel that they're ready to compete in the larger international talent pool.

Employers in traditional economies will have to address significant gaps in skills so their employees can match the confident outlook of those in up-and-coming economies. Additionally, a willingness to use technology, such as blogs and social networks, will be critical to business success in the next four years.

Accenture offer[s] arrangements such as flex-time, "future leave," and telecommuting that make it possible for employees to balance work–life demands—and we encourage clients to do likewise. We counsel our employees to develop successful talent strategies in the same way they build marketing or financial strategies.

Baby boomers (born between 1940 and 1964), Generation X (born between 1964 and 1979), and Generation Y (born between 1979 and 2000) all have distinct values, expectations, and attitudes toward work—and motivational factors also differ significantly. In Accenture's study, baby boomers in India, China, and Brazil were as confident about succeeding in a global economy as their younger peers. In the U.S., however, while Generations X and Y were confident, baby boomers were particularly pessimistic. Only 34 percent of the boomers were confident about their ability to compete in the global economy of the future. In the European Union countries, boomers and Generation X were both gloomy, and only the youngest—Generation Y—respondents viewed the future with confidence.

Women—particularly Western women—must strive to develop the critical skills necessary for career success in the globalized marketplace. At the same time, they must stretch out of their comfort zones and learn to speak up. Companies that recognize the training, coaching, and opportunities that women need—and act accordingly—will have a competitive advantage. So, too, will those companies that welcome a diverse workforce, creating global networks of expert resources that include people, knowledge, and tools.

Talent management—attracting, developing, and retaining the right women (and yes, men, too) for today's business imperatives and meeting or anticipating their cultural, career, and life needs—has truly become a global issue.

Source: Armelle Carminati, "The Needs of the Global Economy Workforce," *BusinessWeek*, November 25, 2008, http://www.businessweek.com/managing/content/nov2008/ca20081125_850677_page_2.htm (accessed August 25, 2009).

Questions

1. Why do you think a majority of Americans are unsure that they can compete in a global talent pool?

2. Do you agree with the author's assertion that generational influences—specifically, the outlook among people of certain generations—affect the global economy? Discuss your response.

AUTOCRATIC LEADERSHIP

Autocratic leadership involves making managerial decisions without consulting others.[32] A manager can make autocratic decisions without being an autocratic leader in general. For example, a manager might make a decision to change the bonus structure of his or her sales force. In this type of situation, it's probably a good idea not to consult the employees, because it's unlikely that they will have an unbiased view about their own salary.

Autocratic leadership A leadership style that involves making managerial decisions without consulting others.

Phil Jackson, the coach of the Los Angeles Lakers, led his team to an NBA championship—his tenth—in 2009 by using an autocratic leadership approach. An autocratic approach is best when working with sports teams. A coach should determine positioning and strategy, since he or she tends to see the bigger picture.

The New York Times is managed by autocratic leadership. In a newsroom environment, where deadlines approach quickly, autocratic leadership can be advantageous since there is no time for debate. However, this management approach can become disadvantageous when employees are afraid to make a decision or think they must consult their boss before acting.[33] At one time, the autocratic management style of the United States Postal Service was blamed for the organization's general inefficiency and reports of angry employees. Later efforts to improve the organization's efficiency were hampered by poor labor relations that stemmed from the long-term effects of the management style.[34]

PARTICIPATIVE LEADERSHIP

In organizations that are run with **participative (democratic) leadership**, managers and employees work together to make decisions. Research has found that employee participation in decisions may not always increase effectiveness, but it usually increases job satisfaction. Many progressive organizations are highly successful at using a democratic style of leadership that values such traits as flexibility, good listening skills, and empathy.

Participative (democratic) leadership A leadership style that consists of managers and employees working together to make decisions.

Many small to medium-size firms successfully use this leadership style. Even large firms have effectively implemented this democratic style of management in their workplaces. For example, Cisco, IBM, and FedEx all recognize the importance of a more participative management style. In small firms, employees discuss management issues and resolve those issues together in a democratic manner, with everyone having at least some opportunity to contribute to decisions.

Figure 9.13 Various Leadership Styles

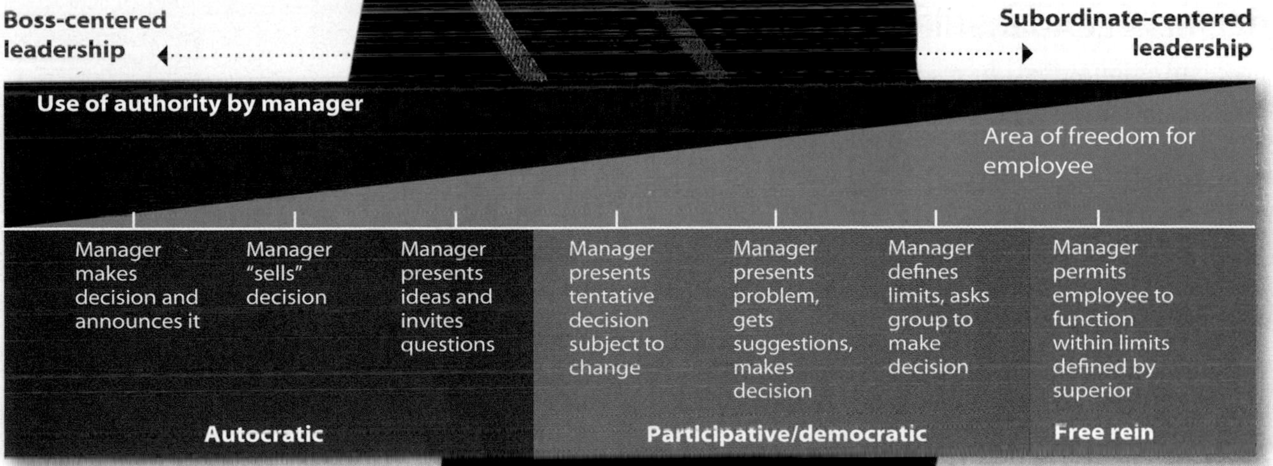

Boss-centered leadership
Subordinate-centered leadership
Use of authority by manager
Area of freedom for employee
Manager makes decision and announces it
Manager "sells" decision
Manager presents ideas and invites questions
Manager presents tentative decision subject to change
Manager presents problem, gets suggestions, makes decision
Manager defines limits, asks group to make decision
Manager permits employee to function within limits defined by superior
Autocratic
Participative/democratic
Free rein

Source: Reprinted by permission of the *Harvard Business Review*. An exhibit from "How to Choose a Leadership Pattern" by Robert Tannenbaum and Warren Schmidt (May/June 1973). Copyright © 1973 by the Harvard Business School Publishing Corporation, all rights reserved.

New Mexico State University management professor Jon Howell asserts that former U.S. Army general and president Dwight Eisenhower was a prime example of a participative leader. Eisenhower treated others with patience, listened to their point of view, and remained objective when making decisions. These traits helped him manage millions of soldiers as the supreme commander of the Allied forces during World War II.[35]

Baseball managers are usually autocratic leaders. That makes sense, since you don't want baseball players deciding whether or not to play as a team. On the other hand, can you see why it is not so good to use autocratic leadership with a team of doctors? What kind of leadership would you expect to succeed in a nonprofit agency full of volunteers?

FREE-REIN LEADERSHIP

In organizations that have **free-rein leadership**, which is also called *laissez-faire leadership*, managers set objectives and employees are relatively free to do whatever it takes to accomplish those objectives. This style might be used when employees know their jobs very well and trust exists among management and employees.

Free-rein leadership A leadership style that involves managers setting objectives and employees being relatively free to do whatever it takes to accomplish those objectives.

For example, managers who work for technology companies may not know how to develop new software; free rein may be the best style for those organizations. Free-rein managers' personal traits include warmth, friendliness, and understanding. One way in which a manager can create warmth is to introduce a healthy dose of laughter into the workplace. FUN-

sulting, etc., which is based in Washington, D.C., is a company that helps organizations bring laughter into the workplace, making employees healthier and happier. Laughter can help to prevent burnout and increase productivity and creative thinking.[36] More and more firms are adopting this style of leadership at least to some degree.

THEORY X

Management theorist Douglas McGregor observed that managers' attitudes about their employees usually fall into one of two categories, Theory X or Theory Y.[37] **Theory X managers** tend to believe:

Theory X managers Managers who believe the average person dislikes work, has relatively little ambition, and wishes to avoid responsibility, so workers must be forcefully directed or threatened with punishment.

An administrator of a hospital may use the free-rein method because doctors often know better than the administrator what is best for the patients.

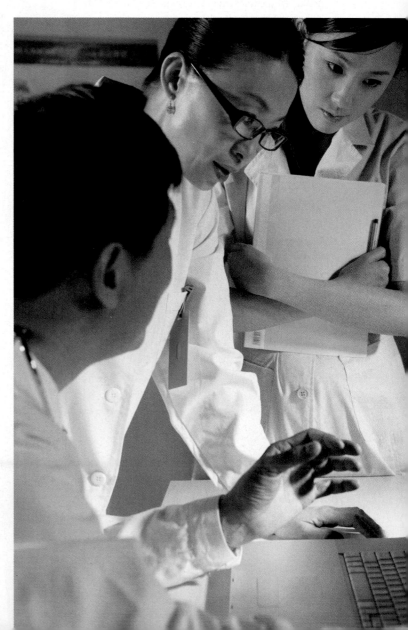

- The average person dislikes work and will avoid it if possible.

- Because of this dislike, workers must be forced, controlled, directed, or threatened with punishment to make them put forth the effort necessary to achieve the company's goals.

- The average worker prefers to be directed, wishes to avoid responsibility, has relatively little ambition, and wants security.

- The average employee's primary motivators are fear and money.

The natural consequence of these attitudes, beliefs, and assumptions is that a Theory X manager will be very involved in the work of his or her employees and will watch them closely, telling them what to do and how to do it. Motivation is more likely to take the form of punishment for bad work rather than reward for good work. Theory X managers give workers little responsibility, authority, or flexibility. Employees with a Theory X manager tend to be motivated by fear of "getting in trouble" rather than doing what is best for the company. This type of motivation may work in the short term, but it is unlikely that this approach will work in the long term. This type of approach does not take into account the idea that everyone can be a leader.

Theory X managers do not come in one-size-fits-all packages. Take Salina Lo of Ruckus Wireless, for example. She doesn't match the typical Theory X stereotype, but on the job, this graduate of the University of California at Berkeley is a tough and exacting Theory X manager. Her in-your-face style has earned her a reputation as one of the industry's toughest managers.

THEORY Y

Theory Y managers Managers who believe most people like work and naturally work toward goals to which they are committed. People are capable of using imagination and creativity to solve problems. Each worker is stimulated by rewards unique to that worker.

McGregor's Theory Y describes a very different type of manager. A **Theory Y manager** has the following beliefs and attitudes about employees:

- Most people like work; it's as natural as play or rest.

- Most people naturally work toward goals to which they are committed.

- The depth of a person's commitment to goals depends on the perceived rewards for achieving them.

- Under certain conditions, most people not only accept but also seek responsibility.

- People are capable of using a relatively high degree of imagination, creativity, and cleverness to solve problems.

- In industry, the average person's intellectual potential is only partially realized.

- People are motivated by a variety of rewards. Each worker is stimulated by rewards unique to that worker (time off, money, recognition, and so on).

Rather than emphasize authority, direction, and close supervision, Theory Y emphasizes a relaxed managerial atmosphere in which workers are free to set objectives, be creative, be flexible, and go beyond the goals set by management. The trend in many U.S. businesses is toward Theory Y management; one reason why is that many service industries, including restaurants, find that Theory Y helps motivate employees. Motivated employees usually mean happy customers, which can improve a business's bottom line. Under Armour founder Kevin Plank believes that one of the keys to motivating employees, particularly in small business, is possessing and spreading a positive attitude.[39]

THEORY Z

One reason many U.S. companies choose a more flexible managerial style is to meet competition from firms in Japan, China, and the European Union. In the 1980s, Japanese companies seemed to be outperforming U.S. businesses. William Ouchi, management professor at the University of California–Los Angeles, wondered whether the reason was the way Japanese companies managed their workers. Ouchi developed **Theory Z**, a hybrid style of management that combines characteristics of Japanese and American management styles and includes a focus on trust and intimacy in the workplace. Theory Z managers treat their employees like family. Theory Z blends a Japanese management style approach favoring consensus with appreciation of the values placed on individual rights and individual achievements by American approaches.

Theory Z A management theory that focuses on trust and intimacy within the work group.

Figure 9.14 A Comparison of Theories X, Y, and Z

THEORY X	THEORY Y	THEORY Z
1. Employees dislike work and will try to avoid it.	1. Employees view work as a natural part of life.	1. Employee involvement is the key to increased productivity.
2. Employees prefer to be controlled and directed.	2. Employees prefer limited control and direction.	2. Employee control is implied and informal.
3. Employees seek security, not responsibility.	3. Employees will seek responsibility under proper work conditions.	3. Employees prefer to share responsibility and decision making.
4. Employees must be intimidated by managers to perform.	4. Employees perform better in work environments that are nonintimidating.	4. Employees perform better in environments that foster trust and cooperation.
5. Employees are motivated by financial rewards.	5. Employees are motivated by many different needs.	5. Employees need guaranteed employment and will accept slow evaluations and promotions.

Eikoh Harada, a Japanese-born manager who now runs the McDonald's restaurant chain's operations in Japan, is a great example of the blending of American and Japanese management styles. Previously, operations of Japanese McDonald's restaurants were completely localized—McDonald's employees in Tokyo weren't allowed to e-mail colleagues in the United States. However, things changed at McDonald's Japan once Harada took over, bringing with him knowledge gained while working for U.S.-based companies like Apple Computer. Only four years after Harada took control of operations, net income for McDonald's Japan jumped 59 percent, to $124 million.[39]

Managers who implement Theory Z–style management tend to believe in:

- Long-term employment with a single company.
- Collective decision making. In these organizations, the entire group helps make decisions.

- Individual responsibility. All employees have an important role to play, and if they don't fulfill their roles, they're disappointing the entire team.

- Slow evaluation and promotion. Employees are not promoted quickly, nor are their evaluations performed quickly. Ouchi believed that this slow progression was the best way to nurture management skills.

- A specialized career path. All employees are given a clear path for their careers with the company.

- Holistic concern for employees and their families. Managers are concerned about their employees' performance at work as well as their home life.

Figure 9.14 compares Theories X, Y, and Z. Individual managers rarely fit neatly into just one of these categories. Most companies—and people—blend a variety of different managing styles, with varying amounts of employee participation.

Which management style is best? Research reveals that successful management depends largely on the goals and values of

Great Lakes Industry employee Gary Lykins works out on company fitness equipment during his shift. His employer provides paid health coaches and reduces health insurance premiums and copayments for employees who participate in its wellness programs. Can you think of any other examples of the kind of holistic concern for employees suggested by William Ouchi's Theory Z style of management?

the firm, the employees who are being led, and the situations in which they are working. For example, autocratic leadership might be the best choice in a situation where things need to be done quickly, or when employees are new and not yet familiar with the specifics of their job. Free-rein leadership might be best in a situation where experienced employees are working on a long-term project. Any management style from autocratic to free rein can be successful depending on the people and the situation involved. In fact, each manager should consider creating his or her own hybrid style of management and varying it depending on the circumstances faced.

[BUS] connections

1. Do you think you would work well under free-rein leadership? Why or why not?
2. Have you ever had a Theory X, Y, or Z manager? If yes, describe your experience working for that person.
3. Which leadership style do you think would work best for you? Which leadership style do you think you already have?

Study Alert

A Theory X manager believes the average person dislikes work, has relatively little ambition, and wishes to avoid responsibility. A Theory Y manager believes most people like work and naturally work toward goals to which they are committed.

IF I COULD DO IT AGAIN

In this morning's managers' meeting, Juanita Navarette, the sales manager at Phelps Electronics, discovered that Nick Drabolsky, the company's office manager and accountant, had been fired late Friday evening. Juanita had worked with Nick for more than 10 years, and because of her position, she had met with him almost daily regarding inventory and delivery issues.

Juanita knew that Johnnie Phelps, the company's owner, had been under great pressure to reduce costs. She also knew that because one of Nick's responsibilities was to oversee company purchasing, Nick had been pushing aggressively for the best deals out there. At the meeting, little was revealed about the details of Nick's dismissal, but unlike the others, Juanita wasn't that surprised about the news.

In recent years, Juanita had become friendly with Gianna Cathay, a sales representative for one of Phelps Electronics' largest parts suppliers. Over dinner one evening, Gianna had revealed some disturbing news about Nick to Juanita.

◄ ETHICAL | **DILEMMA ►**

If you discovered that one of your longtime employees, a person you truly trusted, was receiving bribes while conducting company business, what would you do?

Gianna whispered, "With the tight economy and so many of my customers cutting back or folding, I had to go to great lengths to keep your account. After all, you're one of my larger customers. Even though I was giving you a great deal in the first place, Nick still expected something in return for the business!"

Juanita, taken aback, responded, "What do you mean?"

Gianna replied, "You know Nick's new Lexus? How do you think he could afford that? He made us lease the car for him! I've talked to some other vendors too, so I know I'm not the only one who had to 'take care' of Nick."

Juanita recalled that conversation with Gianna, which had taken place more than a year ago. She thought, "Maybe I should have said something to Johnnie then. Perhaps he could have intervened and helped Nick before he got out of control."

QUESTIONS

1. Who has acted unethically in this situation? How so?
2. If you were Juanita, what would you have done after the conversation with Gianna? Would you have told Johnnie about it?
3. If you were Johnnie, and you found out that Juanita had known about Nick's arrangement with Gianna for some time, what would you do?

Most modern managers emphasize teamwork and cooperation rather than discipline and giving orders.

managers and lower-level workers. In a single day in January 2009, top companies in the United States cut 70,000 jobs![48] Eventually, some Dutch, Japanese, and Indian firms made similar cuts.[49] Furthermore, it became more difficult to get financing for new ventures or to modernize older plants. Managers tended to be more cautious in starting new ventures as they waited to see what the economy would do in the future.

Managers practice the art of getting things done through organizational resources that are available (e.g., workers, financial resources, information, and equipment). At one time, managers were commonly referred to as bosses, and their job consisted of telling people what to do and then watch-

ing over them to make sure they did it. Some managers still behave that way, but today, management is becoming more progressive. Many managers are being educated to guide, train, support, motivate, and coach employees, rather than simply telling them what to do. In other words, managers are focused on leadership as much as they are on managing.

Thus, most modern managers emphasize teamwork and cooperation rather than discipline and giving orders. Today's managers face challenges like global competition, downsized and diverse workforces, technological changes, increased accountability, and intensified scrutiny. To accomplish their organizational goals and objectives effectively and efficiently in today's challenging environment, managers must rely on building appropriate leadership skills and learning key motivational techniques. These skills and techniques are discussed in the next chapter.

[BUS] connections

1. Why are managers facing intense scrutiny?

2. How is diversity affecting today's work environment?

3. Define downsizing. Is downsizing the same thing as rightsizing? Explain your response.

Notification of Termination

For REVIEW >>

1. Describe the changes occurring in management today.
   - A manager plans, organizes, and controls functions within an organization. A leader has vision and inspires others to grasp that vision, establishes corporate values, emphasizes corporate ethics, and doesn't fear change. Rather than telling employees exactly what to do, managers today tend to give their employees enough independence to make their own informed decisions about how best to please customers. They emphasize teams and team building, and they may change the definition of *work* from a task you do for a specified period in a specific place, to something you do anywhere, any time. Today, managers tend to be younger, more of them are female, and fewer of them were educated at elite universities. Managerial work will require you to build new skills. You'll need to be a skilled communicator, a team player, a planner, an organizer, a motivator, and a leader.

2. Explain the four functions of management.
   - Planning includes anticipating trends and determining the best strategies and tactics to achieve organizational goals and objectives. Goals are different from objectives. Goals are the broad, long-term accomplishments an organization wishes to attain, and objectives are specific statements that detail how to achieve an organization's goals in the short term. A company's vision, a forward-looking statement, provides a broad explanation of why the organization exists and where it's headed in the future. Its mission statement is an outline of the organization's fundamental purpose. A SWOT analysis is a planning tool used to analyze an organization's strengths, weaknesses, opportunities, and threats. A PEST analysis measures the political, economic, social, and technological factors that could affect a business. Strategic planning is the process of determining the major goals of the organization and the policies and strategies for obtaining and using resources to achieve those goals; tactical planning is the process of developing detailed statements about what is to be done in the short term, who is to do it, and how it is to be done; operational planning is the process of setting work standards and schedules necessary to implement the company's tactical objectives; and contingency planning is the process of preparing alternative courses of action that may be used if the primary plans don't achieve the organization's objectives. Organizing includes designing the structure of an organization and creating conditions and systems in which everyone and everything works together to achieve the organization's goals and objectives. Top management, the highest level of management, consists of a company's president and other key company executives who develop strategic plans. Middle management is the level of management that includes general managers, division managers, and branch and plant managers who are responsible for tactical planning and controlling. Supervisory (first-line) managers are directly responsible for supervising workers and evaluating their daily performance. Leading involves creating a vision for the organization and guiding, training, coaching, and motivating others to work effectively to achieve the organization's goals and objectives. Controlling involves establishing clear standards to determine whether or not an organization is progressing toward its goals and objectives, rewarding people for doing a good job, and taking corrective action if they are not. Good managers also consider the work–life balance of their employees. Total quality management (TQM) is a management strategy where quality is reviewed at every phase of the production process, even in service organizations.

3. Describe various management styles and know when they are appropriate.
   - Autocratic leadership involves making managerial decisions without consulting others. Participative (democratic) leadership involves managers and employees working together to make decisions. In organizations that have free-rein leadership, which is also called laissez-faire leadership, managers set objectives and employees are relatively free to do whatever it takes to accomplish those objectives. A Theory X manager believes the average person dislikes work, has relatively little ambition, and wishes to avoid responsibility. A Theory Y manager believes most people like work and naturally work toward goals to which they are committed. A Theory Z manager focuses on trust among managers and employees and treats employees like family.

4. Explain future challenges for management.
   - The business scandals that plagued the 2000s have placed business managers under intense scrutiny. Outsourcing to India and other countries has caused major debates about lost jobs in the United States,

but new twists in globalization have created a sort of reverse outsourcing. Companies need workers who are able to self-manage and cope with change. At the same time, these new workers demand more freedom of operation and different managerial styles. Because of this new type of worker, managers need to use effective leadership skills in the workplace. Currently, there are four generations with different values and goals working side by side—the baby boomers, Generation X, Generation Y, and the Millennials. Each generation has a different expectation of management, which can create misunderstandings that managers must acknowledge and handle. Besides generational challenges, immigration and diverse national backgrounds in the workplace can also cause challenges for managers. Downsizing refers to shrinking the organization by reducing the workforce. Rightsizing is often used synonymously with downsizing; however, rightsizing suggests matching resources to needs.

Key Terms

Autocratic leadership

Conceptual skills

Contingency planning

Controlling

Downsizing

Empowerment

Free-rein leadership

Goals

Human relations skills

Leading

Management

Middle management

Mission statement

Objectives

Operational planning

Organization chart

Organizing

Participative (democratic) leadership

PEST analysis

Planning

Rightsizing

Span of control

Staffing

Strategic planning

Supervisory (first-line) management

SWOT analysis

Tactical planning

Technical skills

Theory X managers

Theory Y managers

Theory Z managers

Top management

Total quality management (TQM)

Transparency

Vision

Work–life balance

1. Which management style would be the best in the following situations, and why?

   a. The FBI is about to enter a home where people are making drugs.
   b. An employee has been doing the same job for 20 years and is really good at what she does.
   c. An employee is new to the job.
   d. A manager is new to the job, but she is working with very experienced employees.
   e. A salesperson lives in a different state from his manager and has the highest sales in the region.

2. Which of the four management functions do you think are important to a business? Why?

3. What is the difference between a vision and a mission statement?

4. What is the difference between a goal and an objective? Name one of your goals and one of your objectives.

5. In groups, discuss the following: Why is a SWOT analysis used? How might it be used to determine a company's goals and objectives? Perform a SWOT analysis for the company of your choice.

INTERNET IN >> Action

1. Job seekers can sometimes get an idea of a company's culture by reviewing its mission statement. Visit: http://www.missionstatements.com/company_mission_statements.html and review three company mission statements. Then answer the questions below.

   a. For each company, list the company focus.
   b. Is each company's focus made clear in its mission statement?
   c. Can you guess what management style each company might use simply by reviewing its mission statement?
   d. By reviewing the mission statement, do you see clear company goals?
   e. Judging by the mission statement, what is the company culture?

2. Visit the company Web site of your choice. Based on the location of the company's offices and what you read on the Web site, perform a PEST analysis for that company.

3. Perform a Google or Bing search to find news articles about one of the management challenges listed in this chapter. Write a one-paragraph summary of the article, adding your thoughts as to how this challenge can be remedied.

Self-Assessment Exercises

BUSINESS CAREER QUIZ

Is Your Boss a Theory X or a Theory Y Manager?

Score these statements as follows:
5 = always, 4 = mostly, 3 = often, 2 = occasionally, 1 = rarely, 0 = never.

1. My boss asks me politely to do things, gives me reasons why, and invites my suggestions.
2. I am encouraged to learn skills outside of my immediate area of responsibility.
3. I am left to work without interference from my boss, but help is available if I want it.
4. I am given credit and praise when I do good work or put in extra effort.
5. People leaving the company are given an exit interview to hear their views on the organization.
6. I am incentivized to work hard and well.
7. If I want extra responsibility my boss will find a way to give it to me.
8. If I want extra training my boss will help me find how to get it or will arrange it.
9. I call my boss and my boss's boss by their first names.
10. My boss is available for me to discuss my concerns or worries or suggestions.
11. I know what the company's aims and targets are.

As You READ >>

- How are managers and leaders different?
- What makes a good leader?
- What are the most effective ways to motivate employees?

Leadership and employee motivation are key factors in an organization's success. At Curves, Gary and Diane Heavin implemented many of the leadership and motivation techniques we will discuss in this chapter: allowing and encouraging employees' decision-making abilities; tying their pay to performance; and making their fitness centers fun, competitive places to work. We will also cover how leadership and motivation can make a business successful, the techniques used to become a leader, and how leaders can make a business a great place to work. Which companies are the best in the world for nurturing their people and developing top leaders? Figure 10.1 shows five companies that were recognized for their excellence in leadership development in 2008.[1]

Figure 10.1 Top Companies for Leadership Development

Company	Notable Products/Industry
3M	Post-It Notes, Scotch tape
Procter & Gamble	Pampers diapers, Charmin and Bounty paper products, Tide detergent
General Electric	Home appliances, NBC Universal entertainment, generators,
Coca-Cola	Beverages
Southwest Airlines	Airline

Source: J.P. Donlon, "Best Companies for Leaders: 3M Shoots to the Top of the Current Ranking," *Entrepreneur,* from *Chief Executive,* January–February 2009, http://www.entrepreneur.com/tradejournals/article/194323583.html (accessed August 6, 2009).

Real World Apps

Tony Hodge loves being in charge. His 20 years of experience in the Army taught him everything he needs to know about leadership. Now, the military is paying for him to attend college, and he's currently working toward a degree in accounting. His Introduction to Business class will be covering the topic of leadership tomorrow morning, and Tony is confident he'll be well ahead of his classmates. As a noncommissioned officer in the military, he acquired valuable leadership skills the average person doesn't have.

Of course, the civilian world views leadership a little differently than the military does. Tony knows that in order to work in the civilian workforce, he needs to translate his military-based leadership skills into skills better suited for leading in the modern workplace—but what exactly are those skills? In Tony's opinion, the civilian world of business kept changing while the traditional formal structure of Army leadership remained pretty much the same. Modern, informal leadership styles are foreign to Tony, but he knows that he needs to adapt. Soldiers do as they're told, but the same isn't always true for workers in a company.

"What motivates today's employees?" wonders Tony. "Are camaraderie and teamwork even possible in today's workplace?"

>> Management and Leadership

What's the difference between management and leadership? **Leadership** is creating a vision for others to follow, establishing corporate values and ethics, and transforming the way the organization does business in order to improve its effectiveness and efficiency.[2] As discussed in the last chapter, management is the process of planning, organizing, leading, and controlling people and other available resources to accomplish organizational goals and objectives. In other words, a leader provides guidance in the broadest sense, while a manager actively oversees and manages the specific activities that must be accomplished in order to reach company goals.

> **Leadership** Creating a vision for others to follow, establishing corporate values and ethics, and transforming the way the organization does business in order to improve its effectiveness and efficiency.

In order to offer that guidance, a leader must also be able to *motivate* others to want to do the things he or she believes need to be done. A leader can make things happen despite the fact that he or she may or may not have the responsibility and authority to make managerial decisions. Many believe that a person can't be a leader unless he or she has power in an organization, but that's not always the case. Leadership is everywhere—for example, an employee who shows a coworker how to complete a task is exhibiting leadership skills. Almost everyone has the ability to be a leader; he or she just has to be willing to provide guidance and motivate others.

Imagine for a moment that you are a server in a restaurant. The restaurant's *manager* is responsible for setting the daily schedule, setting goals for the month and the year, and monitoring the business's progress on a weekly and monthly basis—remember, in Chapter 9, you learned that planning, organizing, leading, and controlling are management functions. Unfortunately, the manager is also a pretty unpleasant person—she isn't very helpful to you and doesn't listen to what you have to say. Now imagine that one of your fellow servers, a person who doesn't have any real power and authority, motivates you to work

harder and better because she is always upbeat, listens to her peers, and provides great service to her customers. This person is a *leader*. While your fellow server may not have the authority or power to give you a pay raise or schedule you for more hours, she makes the whole operation run more smoothly and satisfactorily. The leadership she exhibits in providing great customer service motivates you to excel, too.

Consider the same scenario again, but this time, your manager also happens to be very charismatic, caring, and enthusiastic. Your manager in this case is also a leader. Because of her leadership characteristics, you may work harder for her than you would for the first manager, and you're more likely to want to stay in the job. This manager exhibits qualities of both a leader and a manager at the same time.

So can you be a manager without being a leader, and vice versa? Not every manager is a leader, and not every leader is a manager. But it's hard to be an *effective* manager without also being a leader. Leadership goes with the territory.

Leaders are found in every walk of life and at every level. As discussed in Chapter 9, to be an effective manager, a person must be a good leader, since leading is a key function of management. However, to be an effective leader, a person doesn't have to be a manager; leadership is a quality found among people in every level of an organization. Figure 10.2 shows the overlapping roles of management and leadership, and Figure 10.3 addresses typical characteristics associated with management and leadership.

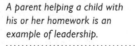

A parent helping a child with his or her homework is an example of leadership.

[BUS] connections

1. Define leadership.
2. What are some differences between managers and leaders? What are some similarities?
3. Can you be a good manager without being a leader? Explain.

Figure 10.2 Not Every Manager Is a Leader—Separate and Overlapping Roles

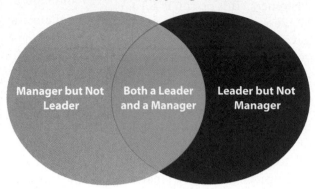

Manager but Not Leader | Both a Leader and a Manager | Leader but Not Manager

Figure 10.3 Characteristics Associated with Management and Leadership

Leaders	Managers
Innovate	Administer
Develop	Maintain
Inspire	Control
Hold a long-term view	Hold a short-term view
Ask what and why	Ask how and when
Originate	Initiate
Challenge the status quo	Accept the status quo
Do the right things	Do things right

Source: Distinctions were taken from W. G. Bennis, *On Becoming a Leader* (Reading, MA: Addison-Wesley, 1989).

>> Leadership Qualities and Styles

Nothing has challenged researchers in the area of management more than the endless quest for the very "best" leadership traits, behaviors, or styles. Many studies have been performed to determine what characteristics make leaders different from other people.[3] Intuitively, one would draw the same conclusion as many of these researchers: It's hard to pinpoint a single set of distinct qualities that all leaders have, or a single set of leadership qualities that guarantees success as a leader. In fact, most studies on leadership have been neither statistically significant nor reliable.

Some leaders are well groomed and tactful, while others are messy and abrasive. But the latter may be just as effective as the former, and vice versa. Even so, some tentative conclusions have been drawn about what may make for good leadership. In this section, we explore a few of the leadership qualities that have been identified by researchers and authors as being present in most good leaders. Figure 10.4 shows the seven qualities that tend to help leaders achieve effective results, which are explained in the following sections.[4]

Figure 10.4 Qualities that Help Leaders Achieve Effective Results

1. Exhibiting integrity, ethics, responsibility, and self-knowledge
2. Having vision, understanding the business, and understanding the tasks
3. Listening willingly, accepting constructive criticism, and communicating effectively
4. Exhibiting an openness to change
5. Being decisive and committed
6. Having a positive attitude and enthusiasm
7. Taking care of people and inspiring them

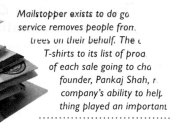

Mailstopper exists to do go
service removes people fron.
trees on their behalf. The c
T-shirts to its list of proa
of each sale going to cha
founder, Pankaj Shah, r
company's ability to helf.
thing played an important

Despite Chouinard's unconventiona
practices—or perhaps because of them—Pa
gross sales have reached $280 million.[5] Patago
set a trend that even retailing giants like Walma
following. Matt Kistler, a senior vice president at ﹐
Club, a division of Walmart, says, "The one thing ﹐
impresses me is the power of the people who work
Patagonia. I was very impressed to see how involve
in sustainability their employees are. They're tremendously knowledgeable and want to do the right thing."[6]

1. Exhibiting Integrity, Ethics, Responsibility, and Self-Knowledge

Effective leaders tend to be, and are often perceived
as being, highly ethical, trustworthy, and reliable. Effective leaders do the right thing, time after time, and
they take responsibility for their actions. These leaders
also know the importance of self-knowledge—they
know what their strengths and limitations are, and
what their principles, beliefs, and values are. Self-
knowledge (sometimes called self-awareness) is critical in developing self-confidence. If leaders are aware
of their limitations, they can surround themselves
with people who have comple-
mentary skills and fill the gaps
of their leadership.

For example, Yvon Chouinard,
founder and owner of the outdoor gear
company Patagonia, has defied much of
the conventional wisdom and traditional
corporate-style ideas of doing business.
Patagonia strives for environmental sustainability through reducing waste during the production process, stressing
the use of recycled materials (Patagonia fleece is made from used soda
bottles) and organic raw materials
like cotton (despite the fact that
organic cotton can be twice as expensive), and advis-
ing customers to receive their Patagonia products via
ground service because air freight consumes much
more energy. Patagonia was also an early adopter of
such employee-first practices as onsite day care and
maternity *and* paternity leave. Chouinard also supports his employees' outdoor interests by offering
them flextime—if the surf's up, his employees take off.

◀ ETHICAL

DILEMMA ▶

If a coworker of yours
was being sexually
harassed and she
believed her manager
would do nothing
about it, what could
she do to combat
the problem?

2. Having Vision, Understanding the Business, and Understanding the Tasks

Great leaders know what basic tasks are necessary to
run their businesses, and they also have a deep un
derstanding of their business. More importantly, they
have a forward-looking "big picture" of the organization. Successful leaders can visualize and articulate
where they see their organization in five to ten years.
Leaders don't need to know every detail of every job,
but they should have a good grasp of the business.

Ken Hendricks, the found-
er of ABC Supply, spent
the first few years of his career learning the business
of roofing and siding from his father.
Inspired, Hendricks started his own
roofing company. In 1982, along with
his wife, Diane, he took a risk and acquired three supply centers. ABC Supply was formed with a simple dream—
to take better care of contractors than
any other company. Today, the company has more than 350 stores
in 45 states. Hendricks learned
the business hands-on and has a
deep understanding of his business. He describes his
vision for ABC Supply: "We will realize our vision of
being the supplier of choice for our contractor customers and being known as the greatest place to work
in the United States." Is Hendricks's vision succeeding? In 2006, he received *Inc.* magazine's Entrepreneur of the Year Award, and in 2007 and 2008, ABC
Supply received the Gallup Great Workplace Award.[8]

t. Using a variety of incentives and showing [em]pathy and flexibility in regard to his em[plo]yees' needs, he has enabled his employees to [tra]nscend their self-interest and achieve a greater [or]ganizational and environmental good. He sets [th]e example himself by sacrificing personal fi[n]ancial gains to help the environment through [w]aste-reducing and other efforts. As a result, for every job Patagonia has to offer, it receives 900 applications, and the turnover rate at Patagonia is less than 4 percent.[16]

Another example is that of former Xerox CEO Ann Mulcahy. When Mulcahy took over the company, it was $17.1 billion in debt. Advisers tried to coax Mulcahy into filing bankruptcy, but she wouldn't consider it: Mulcahy had a vision that she and her employees would turn the company back into a profitable, viable business. Her intelligence, combined with her energy, drive, dedication to hard work, and ability to work alongside her subordinates, helped her accomplish that goal.[24]

Transactional Leadership

Unlike the transformational leader, the **transactional leader** works by providing a clear structure and guidelines for employees. As the term "transaction" suggests, this leadership style is based on the exchange process. Employees are given performance standards and are rewarded or punished for the level at which those standards are met or missed.

> **Transactional leader** A leader who gets people to do things by providing structure and guidelines based on the exchange process.

Most managers follow the transactional leadership style, and few build upon the transactions and take their employees to the transformational level. Figure 10.6 shows the differences between transactional and transformational leaders.

Transactional leadership is often practiced by sports coaches. Good coaches clearly state what must be done in order to defeat opponents, and players are either rewarded or punished based on their performance. A winning team might be treated to pizza after the game, and a losing team might be punished with extra exercise at the next practice. Some players have such a high commitment to winning that they'll even play when injured. At his coach's request, quarterback Otto Graham of the Cleveland Browns once played with a cracked rib.[25]

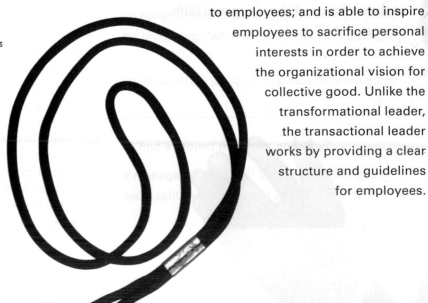

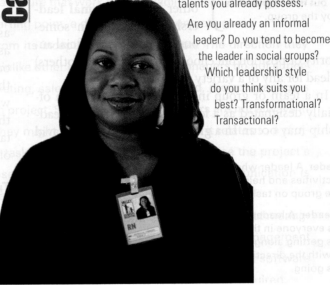

Figure 10.6 Characteristics of Transactional and Transformational Leaders

Transactional Leader	Transformational Leader
Contingent reward. Contracts exchange of rewards for effort, promises rewards for good performance, recognizes accomplishments	**Charisma.** Provides vision and a sense of mission
Management by exception (active). Watches and searches for deviations from rules and standards, takes corrective action	**Inspiration.** Communicates high expectations
Management by exception (passive). Intervenes only if standards are not met	**Intellectual stimulation.** Promotes intelligence
Laissez-faire. Abdicates responsibilities, avoids making decisions	**Individualized consideration.** Gives personal attention

Source: B. M. Bass et al., "Transactional to Transformational Leadership: Learning to Share the Vision," *Organizational Dynamics*, Winter 1990, p. 22. Copyright © 1990. Used with permission of Elsevier, Inc.

[BUS] connections

1. What are the seven qualities of a good leader? Which do you have already, and which do you plan to develop?
2. What are the key differences between transformational and transactional leaders? Which aspects of these leadership characteristics do you want to develop? Explain.
3. What style of leader would you prefer to work for? What leadership style do you think you have?

Going GLOBAL

Samsung Electronics: Same CEO, New Leadership Team

This article from *BusinessWeek* discusses Samsung's attempt to replace key members of its executive team in order to move forward from a damaging scandal and improve the business's transparency.

Hoping to shake off a damaging financial scandal, Samsung Electronics has appointed several younger executives to a new leadership team. It will combine its handset, television, computer, and all other consumer businesses into one group. Choi Gee Sung, who had been running the company's mobile phone business, will head the newly formed Digital Media & Communications unit.

The bigger role for Choi improves his chances of succeeding Chief Executive Lee Yoon Woo. Lee is seen as only a stopgap leader, mainly playing a coordinating role for Samsung's various groups. Though he remains CEO for now, his operational responsibilities will now be limited to the struggling electronics parts businesses. The reorganization is the first major change at Samsung since it was tainted by a tax evasion scandal. The scandal led to a suspended three-year jail sentence for former Chairman Lee Kun Hee.

Samsung execs say the company will soon follow up with more organizational shuffling deeper within the company. More divisional changes, such as streamlining manufacturing units, are expected to follow in the coming weeks. "There has been a sense of crisis in the company for more than a year," says one senior manager who asked not to be identified. "Radical change is in store." Analysts say the rise of Choi and other nonengineers shows that Samsung, having established its technological credentials, wants to listen more carefully to customers when developing future products. "Samsung's benchmark is shifting from Japanese companies to innovators like Apple," says Kang Shin Woo, chief investment officer at fund manager Korea Investment Trust Management.

A new generation of leaders at Samsung also raises hopes among shareholder activists that it will embrace international business practices. After last year's tax scandal, Samsung disbanded its powerful Strategic Planning Office, which Korean prosecutors alleged arranged illegal business deals to benefit the Lee family at the expense of other shareholders. "The younger leaders open the way for Samsung to improve transparency," says Kim Sun Woong, head of the Center for Good Corporate Governance.

Source: Moon Ihlwan, "Samsung Electronics: Same CEO, New Leadership Team," *BusinessWeek*, January 16, 2009, http://www.businessweek.com/globalbiz/content/jan2009/gb20090116_469350.htm (accessed August 26, 2009).

Questions

1. Do you believe that replacing managers will help Samsung regain trust among its stakeholders? Discuss your response.

2. In your opinion, what type of leader was Chairman Lee Kun Hee? Explain your response.

>> The Importance of Motivation

People are willing to work—and work hard—if they think their work makes a difference and is appreciated. Companies that work to maintain strong employee morale will reap the benefits. Consider the following statistic: Within firms with low employee morale, every $1 spent is worth about 25 cents; however, firms whose employees have high morale earn $3 for every $1 they spend.[26]

People gain **motivation** in a variety of ways, such as recognition, accomplishments, personal goals, money, and status.[27] While motivation—the drive to satisfy a need—ultimately comes from within, there are ways to inspire people to do a good job. An **intrinsic reward** is the personal satisfaction you feel when you do a good job and achieve your goals. The belief that your work makes a significant contribution to an organization or society is a form of intrinsic reward. An **extrinsic reward** is something given to you by someone else in recognition of good work. Pay raises, bonuses, promotions, and public recognition are examples of extrinsic rewards. Figure 10.7 shows examples of extrinsic and intrinsic rewards.

To help you understand the concepts, theories, and practices of motivation, we'll discuss some traditional theories on motivation, as well as modern applications of these theories and managerial procedures for implementing them.

Motivation The drive to satisfy a need.

Intrinsic reward The personal satisfaction you feel when you perform well and achieve goals.

Extrinsic reward A reward given to an employee, such as a promotion or pay raise.

Figure 10.7 Extrinsic and Intrinsic Rewards

Intrinsic	Extrinsic
Personal satisfaction	Compensation
Being told you did a good job	Raise
Finishing something/ accomplishment	Promotion
Interpersonal relations	Benefits

TAYLOR'S PRINCIPLES OF SCIENTIFIC MANAGEMENT

Many books have been written about how to effectively motivate people, but employee motivation in the workplace was rarely discussed before early in the 20th century. In 1911, Frederick Taylor published one of the most well-known books on employee motivation, *The Principles of Scientific Management*. Taylor performed **time and motion studies**, in which someone observed the tasks performed to complete a job and recorded the time needed to do each task. The goal of the studies was to reduce the number of motions required to perform a task, thereby increasing efficiency and productivity.

Time and motion studies Studies of the tasks performed to complete a job and the time needed to do each task.

By performing time and motion studies, Taylor found that an average person could shovel more dirt, coal, or any other substance (in fact, *25 to 35 tons more each day*) if he or she was trained to use the most efficient motions and the proper shovel. Therefore, Taylor determined that if workers were armed with the right training and the right tools, productivity could increase exponentially.

The success of these findings led businesses to perform time and motion studies for virtually every factory job. As researchers determined the most efficient ways of doing things, efficiency became the standard for goal setting. In 2009, productivity of U.S. workers during the second quarter grew at an annual 6.4 percent pace, the fastest it has in almost six years.[28]

Figure 10.8 presents Taylor's four principles of **scientific management**. Scientific management had a profound impact on American industries and productivity. However, despite his contributions, Taylor's philosophy and teachings had shortcomings; for example, his studies viewed people largely as machines

Scientific management Studying workers to find the most efficient processes and then teaching people those techniques.

Figure 10.8 Taylor's Scientific Management Principles

1. Scientifically study each part of a task and develop the best method of performing the task.

2. Carefully select workers and train them to perform the task by using the scientifically developed method.

3. Cooperate fully with workers to ensure that they use the proper method.

4. Divide work and responsibility so that management is responsible for planning work methods using scientific principles and workers are responsible for executing the work accordingly.

Source: F. W. Taylor, *The Principles of Scientific Management* (New York: Harper, 1911).

that needed to be properly programmed.[29] There was little concern for the psychological or the human aspect of their work. Taylor simply believed that workers would perform at a high level if they received enough pay, and his philosophy left no room for employee initiative.

Taylor developed his principles early in the 20th century. Do they still apply today? Are organizations using any of them now? The answer is a definite yes—in fact, you see Taylor's ideas at work every time you visit a fast-food restaurant, where workers have specialized equipment and training to help them make the exact same meal, time after time, as quickly as possible. Car and computer manufacturing facilities and hospitals also function more efficiently due to the application of scientific management principles.[30]

Others followed Taylor's lead in researching employee efficiency. Frank and Lillian Gilbreth put

United Parcel Service (UPS) teaches its drivers how fast to walk (three feet per second), how many packages to pick up and deliver per day (an average of 100), and how to hold their keys (teeth up, third finger).[31] UPS's efficiency, productivity, technology improvement, and service delivery earned the company a place in Fortune's list of most admired companies in 2009.[32]

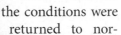

Taylor's ideas to use in a three-year study of bricklaying. As a result of the study, they developed the **principle of motion economy**, which showed that every job could be broken down into a series of elementary motions called a "therblig." From that point, each motion was analyzed to improve its effectiveness.

> **Principle of motion economy** A theory developed by Frank and Lillian Gilbreth that every job can be broken down into a series of elementary motions.

MAYO'S HAWTHORNE STUDIES

Taylor's research also led to a study conducted between 1927 and 1933 at Western Electric Company's Hawthorne plant in Cicero, Illinois. Elton Mayo and his colleagues from Harvard University conducted the study to determine the impact of physical conditions, such as lighting, temperature, humidity, and other factors, on worker productivity. Mayo found that with every change in environmental factors, including either brightening or dimming the lighting, productivity went up. In fact, after a series of 13 experimental periods, Mayo found that productivity went up *each time*. Even when all the conditions were returned to normal, and Mayo expected that productivity levels would revert to the pre-experiment level, worker productivity increased yet again. Upon interviewing the workers, the team made astounding discoveries.[33]

The workers in the study thought of themselves as a social group. The atmosphere of the study was informal, so they felt they could speak freely with their supervisors, the researchers, and each other. They felt "special"

Little did Elton Mayo and his research team from Harvard University know that they would forever change managers' beliefs about employee motivation. Their research at the Hawthorne plant of Western Electric (pictured here) in Cicero, Illinois, gave birth to the concept of human-based motivation by showing that employees behaved differently simply because they were involved in planning and executing the experiments.

and worked hard to remain in the group; thus, they were extremely motivated to perform well.

In addition, the workers were more motivated because they were involved in planning the experiments. For example, at one point in the study, the researchers planned to change the workers' pay schedule; after being notified of the change, the workers rejected the pay schedule that was proposed and recommended another, which was eventually used. Thus, the workers believed that their ideas were respected and that they were involved in managerial decision making. No matter what the physical conditions were, the workers enjoyed the atmosphere of their special room and the additional pay they got for more productivity. Job satisfaction increased dramatically.

Researchers now use the term **Hawthorne effect** to refer to the tendency for people to behave differently when they know they are being studied.[34] Because of the findings of the Hawthorne studies, the emphasis of research shifted from Taylor's scientific management toward Mayo's human-based management.

Hawthorne effect The tendency of people to behave differently when they know they are being studied.

For example, Delphi Automotive Systems Corp. in Oak Creek, Wisconsin, has moved from a scientific management style to a more human-centered approach. The plant, a former division of General Motors, manufactures catalytic converters for automobiles. Delphi employees previously produced these parts by working along an assembly line, with each person completing an assigned task as the catalytic converters moved along a conveyor belt. Today, the plant in Oak Creek has about 10 ice-hockey rinks worth of free floor space. Employees now work in "work cells," where they have more involvement in and responsibility for the product. They can determine their own schedules and are offered stock options. Workers are encouraged to submit new ideas for improvement, and those who submit ideas get to participate in raffles for desirable prizes, such as lawn mowers or televisions. As a result, motivation among employees at Delphi has increased, which has led to an increase in productivity. In the past, deliveries took approximately 21 days to complete; today, the company can ship an order on a Friday that had been placed the previous Monday.[35]

Many theories about the human side of motivation emerged in the years that followed the Hawthorne studies; Abraham Maslow's theory of the hierarchy of needs is one of the best known.

MASLOW'S HIERARCHY OF NEEDS

Psychologist Abraham Maslow believed that in order to understand motivation at work, one must understand human motivation in general. He believed that motivation arises from need—that people are motivated to satisfy their unmet needs. Once those needs have been satisfied, they no longer provide motivation. Furthermore, Maslow believed that needs could be placed in a hierarchy of importance. Figure 10.9 shows **Maslow's hierarchy of needs**, which is broken into the following levels:[36]

Maslow's hierarchy of needs Theory of motivation based on unmet human needs from basic physiological needs to safety, social, esteem, and self-actualization needs.

- *Physiological needs*: Basic survival needs, such as the needs for food, water, and shelter.

- *Safety needs*: The need to feel secure at work and at home.

- *Social needs*: The need to feel loved, accepted, and part of a group.

- *Esteem needs*: The need for recognition and acknowledgment from others, as well as self-respect and a sense of status or importance.

- *Self-actualization needs*: The need to develop to one's fullest potential.

Figure 10.9 Maslow's Hierarchy of Needs

Most of the world's workers struggle all day long to obtain their basic physiological and safety needs.

Self-actualization needs

Esteem needs

Social needs

Safety needs

Physiological needs

When one need is satisfied, another higher-level need emerges and motivates the person to do something to satisfy it, and the satisfied need is no longer a motivator. For example, if you eat a four-course dinner, hunger would cease to be a motivator (at least for several hours), so your attention might turn to your surroundings (safety needs) or family (social needs). Of course, lower-level needs (e.g., thirst) may emerge at any time, and if they are not met, they'll probably distract you from your higher-level needs, such as the need for recognition or status.

In developed countries, such as the United States, lower-level needs no longer dominate, so workers seek to satisfy growth needs, such as social, esteem, and self-actualization needs. Knowing this is very important to management and leadership, because if managers and leaders can recognize where their employees are on the hierarchy of needs, they can tailor training and programs to satisfy those needs.

WHAT CAN I DO?

← ETHICAL   DILEMMA →

If a coworker of yours was being sexually harassed and she believed her manager would do nothing about it, what could she do to combat the problem?

Ana Romanowski, a department manager at a location of Kelly's Grocery, is consoling her friend Madison Raphael, who is also a manager at Kelly's.

Madison, who has been crying, says, "I miss Natalie."

Natalie, their previous store manager, had always treated employees fairly and respectfully. She had an open-door policy, and she listened to employees and used many of their suggestions. She was a hands-on manager who got to know her employees. They knew that she cared about them as well as the store's success. Unfortunately, Natalie's husband was recently transferred for work, so she resigned and moved with him.

Ana replies, "She was a great manager."

Talking about their new manager, Pat Curl, Madison says, "Pat's a joke. Natalie never would have allowed this to go on."

Madison says, "People don't enjoy working here anymore. Amir, the new produce manager, is fed up; he put in his notice today."

Ana exclaims, "Others are talking about quitting. Pat doesn't listen and just sits in his office."

Madison is upset because the new assistant manager, Micah, has asked her out twice. She's refused both times, but Micah is now angry and still pushes her to go out with him. She pleads, "Ana, what can I do? I'm a single mom—I need this job! I can't just quit. I'm sure Pat knows all about this but won't do anything about it. Micah is his friend."

Ana considers Madison's dilemma for a moment. "Maybe you should report Micah's behavior to the corporate office."

Madison scoffs. "I can't believe that you of all people would suggest that. Remember what happened to you when you fell in the back of the store and filed a workman's compensation claim? You almost didn't get promoted to manager because corporate didn't believe you'd really hurt yourself. If it weren't for Natalie, there's no way you would have gotten this promotion."

Ana replies, "How could I forget? If Natalie hadn't gone to bat for me, I probably would have been fired, not promoted."

Madison asks, "How can I say anything? If I report Micah, corporate will hold this against me, too. They'll all just say I'm a single mom who's husband hunting or that I'm trying to file a lawsuit to make a bunch of money."

QUESTIONS

1. What are the ethical issues in this situation?
2. What should Madison do?

HERZBERG'S TWO-FACTOR THEORY

So far, our exploration of motivation has been focused on extrinsic rewards or human needs. Frederick Herzberg's theory explored what managers can do to help employees become motivated by their *jobs*. Of all the factors that managers could control, Herzberg wondered, which are most effective in generating an enthusiastic work effort?

In the 1960s, Herzberg conducted a study in which he asked workers to rank various job-related factors in order of their importance, relative to motivation.[37] Herzberg wanted to know what factors made workers enthusiastic about their work and willing to work to their full potential. Herzberg's subjects reported that their motivating factors were, in order of importance:

1. Sense of achievement

2. Earned recognition

3. Interest in the work itself

4. Opportunity for growth

5. Opportunity for advancement

6. Importance of responsibility

7. Peer and group relationships

8. Pay

9. Supervisor fairness

10. Company policies and rule

11. Status

12. Job security

13. Supervisor friendliness

14. Working conditions

Note that the highest-ranking factors were all related to job contentment. Workers like to think they are contributing to their companies (a sense of achievement was rated first). They want to earn recognition (number 2) and believe that their jobs are important (number 6). They want responsibility, which is why continued training and learning are so important to them, and they want to be acknowledged for that responsibility by being promoted or financially re-

warded (numbers 4 and 5). Of course, workers also want their jobs to be interesting (number 3).

Herzberg noted that workers did not consider most factors related to their job's environment as motivators. He was also surprised to see that workers rated pay as low as they did (number 8), indicating that employee motivation is driven by much more than salary. Workers felt that the absence of good pay, job security, friendly supervisors, and the like would cause dissatisfaction, but the presence of those factors did not motivate them to work harder.

Herzberg concluded that certain factors, called **motivators**, cause employees to be productive while giving them a great deal of satisfaction. Other elements of the job, which he called **hygiene factors** (or maintenance factors), could cause dissatisfaction if they were not present (or not present in sufficient amounts), but enhancing these factors does not necessarily motivate employees. Figure 10.10 shows a list of motivators and hygiene factors.

> **Motivators** Job factors that cause employees to be productive and give them satisfaction.
>
> **Hygiene factors** Job factors that can cause dissatisfaction if missing but do not necessarily motivate employees if increased.

Herzberg's motivating factors suggest that the best way to motivate employees is to make their jobs more interesting, assist them as they try to achieve their objectives, and recognize those achievements through advancement and added responsibility. Figure 10.11 compares Maslow's hierarchy of needs theory and Herzberg's theory of factors.

As a leader and manager, you can implement these theorists' ideas in several ways. For example, you've learned that just a pay raise won't make workers work harder; instead, managers must ensure that employees have a path for promotion, are challenged by their jobs, and are recognized for good performance. Herzberg's work has shown that the type of work an employee does is directly related to motivation. So what can managers do to *enrich* employees' work? They can explore the concepts of job rotation, job enlargement, and job enrichment.

Job rotation involves occasionally moving employees from one job to another to give them a little variety and to enable them to cross-train in different areas. The casino operator ResortsWorld has its floor staff rotate jobs so they learn how to staff each game on the casino floor—one week, an employee might be a blackjack dealer, and the next, she might be working as a croupier.[38] American Express allows employees who have worked at the company for 12 to 24 months the opportunity to apply for a new position.[39] **Job enlargement** combines a series of tasks into a single challenging assignment, and **job enrichment** is a motivational strategy that involves making the job more interesting in order to motivate employees.

Researchers and managers who believe in the power of job enrichment suggest that the following five characteristics of work are important factors in individual motivation and performance:[40]

1. *Skill variety.* The extent to which a job demands different skills.

2. *Task identity.* The degree to which a job requires doing tasks with visible outcomes from beginning to end.

3. *Task significance.* The degree to which a job has a substantial effect on the lives or work of others in the company.

4. *Autonomy.* The degree of freedom, independence, and discretion in scheduling work and determining procedures.

5. *Feedback.* The amount of direct and clear information that is received about job performance.

Job rotation A motivational technique that involves moving employees from one job to another.

Job enlargement A motivational technique that involves combining a series of tasks into one challenging assignment.

Job enrichment A motivational strategy that involves making the job more interesting.

Figure 10.10 Herzberg's Motivators and Hygiene Factors

Motivators	Hygiene (Maintenance) Factors
(These factors can be used to motivate workers.)	*(These factors can cause dissatisfaction, if missing, but changing them will have little motivational effect.)*
Work itself	Company policy and administration
Achievement	Supervision
Recognition	Working conditions
Responsibility	Interpersonal relations (coworkers)
Growth and advancement	Salary, status, and job security

Variety, identity, and significance contribute to the meaningfulness of a job. Autonomy gives people a feeling of responsibility, and feedback contributes to a feeling of achievement and recognition. Job enrichment makes work fun.

Elizabeth Smith left her position as Kraft Foods' group vice president of the company's U.S. beverage and grocery businesses to become a brand president at the beauty company Avon. Some said Smith was committing "career suicide" by switching to a less prestigious job, but she viewed the move as an opportunity to learn new things, gain global experience, and have some fun along the way.

Figure 10.11 Comparison of Maslow's Hierarchy of Needs and Herzberg's Theory of Factors

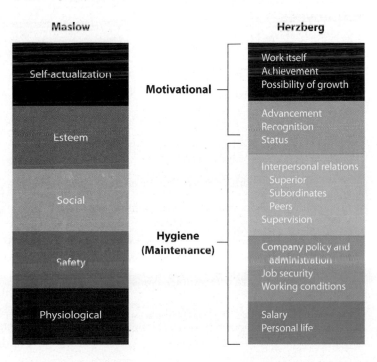

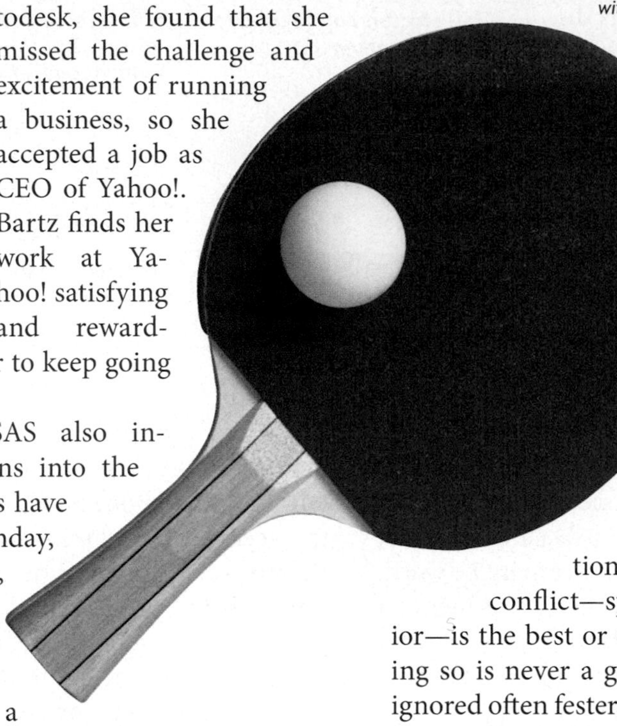

Carol Bartz also enjoys her work. After retiring from her position as CEO of software manufacturer Autodesk, she found that she missed the challenge and excitement of running a business, so she accepted a job as CEO of Yahoo!. Bartz finds her work at Yahoo! satisfying and rewarding, which motivates her to keep going day after day.[41]

Software supplier SAS also incorporates fun traditions into the workplace; its employees have fresh fruit every Monday, M&Ms on Wednesdays, and breakfast treats on Fridays.[43] Would you want to leave work if your workplace were a fun place where you really felt at home? Figure 10.12 lists 10 quick ways to motivate employees.

Some myths persist about motivation in the workplace, as well. Of course, many believe that money is the primary motivator for employees. However, re-

Fun at work can be a little misleading. It's not all parties all the time—although at Google, ranked the number four best place to work on Fortune's 2009 list, it really does seem like employees are having fun all the time. Employees enjoy their jobs because they can be themselves. They are fully engaged in working toward accomplishing Google's mission with all the amenities they can imagine, such as free gourmet meals, an on-premises gym for workouts, ping-pong and pool tables, and swimming pools. Google employees come to work to get energized by their coworkers, and they often report feeling sad about leaving at the end of the day.[42]

search has shown that any delight at receiving a pay raise or bonus is short-lived. Status and recognition are much more important in terms of motivation. Some also believe that ignoring conflict—specifically bad employee behavior—is the best or easiest course of action, but doing so is never a good idea. Conflicts that remain ignored often fester, and bad employee behavior that goes unchecked harms everyone's morale.[44]

Figure 10.12 Ten Quick Ways to Motivate Employees

1.	Praise employees.
2.	Discuss possibilities of promotions.
3.	Be clear about expectations.
4.	Involve the employee in a variety of tasks.
5.	Ensure that the employee sees how his or her work contributes to the big picture.
6.	Make sure that the employee's work is meaningful.
7.	Provide both positive and negative feedback.
8.	Allow for autonomy.
9.	Increase the depth of employee tasks.
10.	Provide adequate opportunities for success.

Source: David Javitch, "5 Employee Motivation Myths Debunked," Entrepreneur.com, June 19, 2009, http://www.entrepreneur.com/humanresources/employeemanagementcolumnistdavidjavitch/article202352.html (accessed August 24, 2009).

[BUS] connections

1. How did scientific management set the stage for further research on employee motivation?
2. Where would you place yourself on Maslow's hierarchy of needs? At this very moment, what is your most dominant need?
3. Which strategy do you believe is a better motivator—job rotation, job enlargement, or job enrichment? Which would motivate you? Why?

>> Employee Improvement and Empowerment

Next, we'll discuss several methods and theories used to help employees improve their performance and feel empowered in their jobs. Empowerment is a critical part of making these methods and theories work—after all, what is the point of having employees engage in company decision making if their managers don't empower them make decisions? The topics covered in this section include goal-setting theory, management by objectives, reinforcement theory, and equity theory.

GOAL-SETTING THEORY AND MANAGEMENT BY OBJECTIVES

Goal-setting theory The idea that setting ambitious but attainable goals can motivate workers and improve performance.

Goal-setting theory is based on the idea that setting ambitious, but attainable, goals can motivate workers and improve performance. In order for the theory to work, the goals must be realistic, accepted by the employees, accompanied by feedback, and supported by organizational conditions.

All members of an organization should basically agree about the organization's overall goals and the specific objectives each department and individual must meet. If employees don't have a say in setting the company's goals, they're much less likely to accept them. On the other hand, if employees help choose the company's goals, they're more likely to be committed and motivated to achieve them. Research from Watson Wyatt, a global consulting company, shows that employees who are highly engaged in the goal-setting process are more than twice as likely to become top performers as those who have less of a say in the company.[45] One employee of the Swiss food company Nestlé remarked that he believed that much of his success at the company was due to the fact that he clearly understood the goals of the organization and how they translated to his day-to-day activities on the job.[46]

In the 1960s, management expert Peter Drucker developed such a system to involve everyone in the organization in goal setting and implementation.[47] Called **management by objectives (MBO)**, it is a system of goal setting and implementation that involves a cycle of discussion, review, and evaluation of objectives among top and mid-level managers, supervisors, and employees.

Management by objectives (MBO) A system of goal setting and implementation that involves a cycle of discussion, review, and evaluation of objectives among top and mid-level managers, supervisors, and employees.

Figure 10.13 describes the circular flow of MBO. The process begins when managers and employees establish a set of mutually agreed-upon goals for a specific period of time. Then, the criteria for assessing work performance are determined. Once these criteria are established, employees develop action plans to achieve their goals. Managers provide the employees with intermittent feedback, which serves both as a motivational tool and a control mechanism. At the end of the period, the employee performance is measured and compared to the established goals. Appropriate rewards are tied to goal accomplishment, and the cycle continues.[48]

Figure 10.13 The Cycle of Management by Objectives

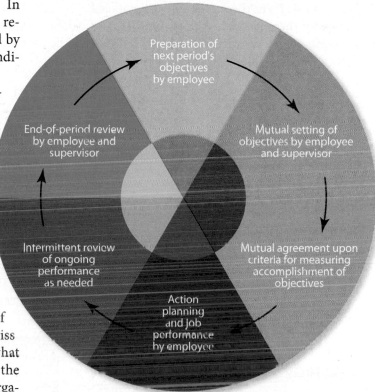

Source: K. Davis and J. Newstrom. *Human Behavior at Work: Organizational Behavior* (New York: McGraw-Hill, 1989), p. 209.

Problems can arise when upper-level managers use MBO as a strategy for forcing other managers and workers to commit to goals they haven't agreed to fulfill. Employee involvement is the key to using MBO as a motivational tool. The more an employee is involved in the process, the better the chance that he or she will work harder to achieve the goals.

REINFORCEMENT AND EQUITY THEORY

Reinforcement theory is based on the idea that positive and negative reinforcement motivate a person to behave in certain ways. According to this theory, motivation is the result of the carrot-and-stick

Reinforcement theory The idea that positive and negative reinforcement motivate a person to behave in certain ways.

approach, which means that it is dependent on a system of rewards and punishment. People act in order to receive rewards (positive reinforcement) and avoid punishment (negative reinforcement). Positive reinforcements include praise, recognition, or pay raises. Negative reinforcements include reprimands, reduced pay, and layoffs or firings. A manager might also try to stop undesirable behavior by not responding to it, which is called *extinction*. Figure 10.14 illustrates how a manager can use reinforcement theory to motivate workers.

Equity theory addresses questions like, "If I do a good job, will it be worth it?" and "What's fair?" The theory is based on perceptions of fairness and how those perceptions affect an employee's willingness to perform. Employees try to maintain equity of their inputs and outputs as they compare them with the inputs and outputs of others in similar positions. Equity comparisons are compiled from the information that is available to them through personal relationships, professional organizations, and other environments in their lives.[49]

Equity theory The idea that employees try to maintain equity between inputs and outputs compared to others in similar positions.

IBM offers rewards based on worker performance. The company's pay system offers bonuses of up to 30 percent of annual salary to its most productive work-

ers. Like most of his coworkers, IBM employee Steven Cohn believes that his compensation at the company should be based on his merit and market value.[50]

When workers perceive *inequities*, they try to reestablish equitable exchanges in a number of ways. For example, if three coworkers received a 5 percent pay raise and a fourth received only 2 percent after all put in roughly the same effort, the latter employee would probably react in one of the following ways:

1. Reduce efforts in future work.

2. Ask the supervisor for a larger raise or an explanation.

3. Rationalize the situation by thinking, "I guess I wasn't working that hard after all," or "The others must have put in more work than I did."

Remember that equity judgments are based on perceptions and are therefore subject to perception errors. It's the manager's job to minimize misperceptions whenever possible through clear and frequent communication.

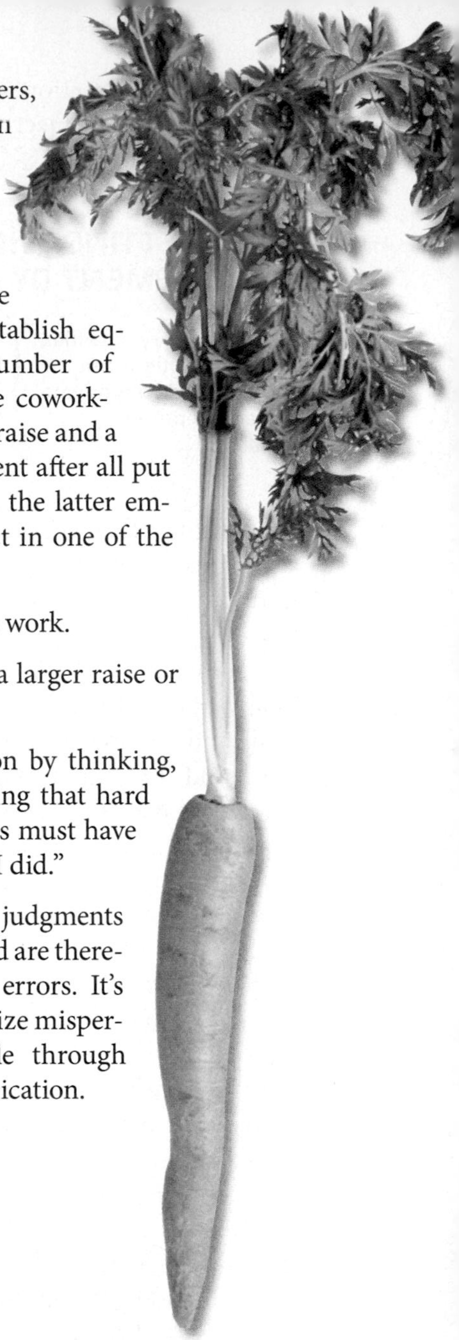

Figure 10.14 Reinforcement Theory

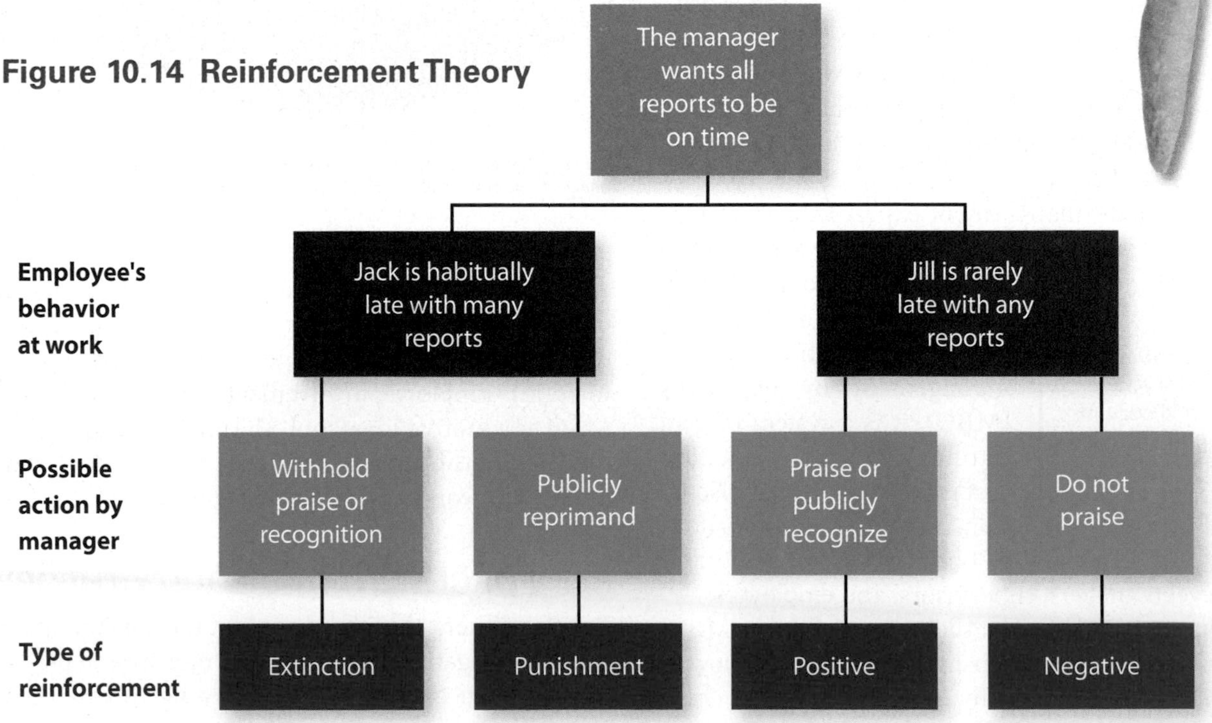

		The manager wants all reports to be on time		
Employee's behavior at work	Jack is habitually late with many reports		Jill is rarely late with any reports	
Possible action by manager	Withhold praise or recognition	Publicly reprimand	Praise or publicly recognize	Do not praise
Type of reinforcement	Extinction	Punishment	Positive	Negative

Real World Apps

Tony's ideas about leadership in the civilian world have been confirmed. Unlike the military, varied leadership qualities and styles are encouraged and nurtured in modern organizational structures. Of course, many of the challenges leaders face today are the same as those faced by past generations—the differences lie in the diversity and complexity of the business environment. Tony now understands that the key to successful leadership is not one single thing but a multitude of ideas and theories that have gradually been adapted to modern times.

Good leaders and managers are developed and nurtured by an organization through training and experience, but not everyone can lead. Tony has learned that leadership skills are both inherent and learned, not one or the other. Most employees will follow an honest person who is not afraid to lead by example and encourages participation and involvement.

Motivating employees is a constant organizational challenge. One device is to use traditional theories, such as Maslow's hierarchy of needs, to categorize and understand employee needs. If a leader can ensure that employee needs are met, those employees will be more motivated to work. Tony was also intrigued by the idea of using management by objectives as a way to align goals and objectives. What Tony previously thought were just theories unconnected to reality in fact make a great deal of sense. In the civilian world, employees are empowered and are now a part of the strategic planning of an organization.

The challenges of business today require forward-thinking leaders. Change is constant. Tony thinks of an old military adage: "Adapt or die." He chuckles as it occurs to him that military and civilian leaders can learn a lot from each other.

EMPLOYEE EMPOWERMENT

Empowerment can be a powerful motivator. **Empowerment** of employees means trusting them to make the right decisions. In order to make empowerment work, employees' decisions should not be second-guessed. If an employee makes a mistake, it should be accepted and corrected, but not punished. Punishing employees for taking a risk or making a judgment call sends the wrong message—it tells them to avoid risks and aim for mediocrity. Empowerment allows employees to feel a sense of ownership in the company.

Motivation doesn't have to be difficult. It begins with acknowledging a job well done. You can motivate others simply by telling them you appreciate their efforts—especially in front of other people. Remember: Always praise in public and punish in private. It's a simple concept, but it goes a long way to build trust and self-esteem in employees.

> **Empowerment** To give power or authority; to grant employees the ability and trust to make decisions.

The Pampered Chef, a direct seller of kitchen products, believes in the concept of employee empowerment. The company's representatives, who are called consultants, perform demonstrations of the products in their own homes and in the homes of their friends. Consultants are allowed to set their own goals and are given the option of working either full or part time. Such flexibility has given many consultants an opportunity to empower themselves.[51]

[BUS] connections

1. Explain the steps in the cycle of management by objectives.
2. Compare and contrast reinforcement and equity theories.
3. Define empowerment. Discuss a job you had in which you did not feel empowered, and a job in which you did feel empowered. Was your motivation level different at the two jobs?

1.   Understand the difference between management and leadership.

    •   Leaders offer guidance or direction, and managers plan, organize, lead, and control their employees and other available resources. A leader provides guidance in the broadest sense, while a manager actively oversees and manages the specific activities that must be accomplished in order to reach company goals. Leaders must also be able to motivate others to want to do the things they believe need to be done. Many believe that a person can't be a leader unless he or she has power in an organization, but that's not always the case. Almost everyone has the ability to be a leader; the person just has to be willing to provide guidance and motivate others.

2.   Describe the qualities of a leader and the differing leadership styles.

    •   Most people agree that good leaders exhibit integrity, ethics, responsibility, and self-knowledge; have vision, understand their business, and understand the tasks that are required; listen willingly, accept constructive criticism, and communicate effectively; exhibit an openness to change; are decisive and committed; have a positive attitude and enthusiasm for their work; and take care of people and inspire them. In formal leadership, someone has been given authority to make decisions or lead a group. On the other hand, informal leadership occurs when someone may not have official authority or position but chooses (or is chosen by others) to lead for any of a variety of reasons. A transformational leader has a clear vision of the direction in which he or she wants the company to go; has lots of energy, charisma, and enthusiasm that can be easily transferred to employees; and is able to inspire employees to sacrifice personal interests in order to achieve the organizational vision for collective good.

3.   Understand the importance of motivation.

    •   While motivation—the drive to satisfy a need—ultimately comes from within, there are ways to inspire people to do a good job. An intrinsic reward is the personal satisfaction you feel when you do a good job and achieve your goals. The belief that your work makes a significant contribution to an organization or society is a form of intrinsic reward. An extrinsic reward is something given to you by someone else in recognition of good work. Frederick Taylor's time and motion studies observed the tasks performed to complete a job and recorded the time needed to do each task. Taylor determined that if workers were armed with the right training and the right tools, productivity could increase exponentially. Taylor's four principles of scientific management were to scientifically study each part of a task and develop the best method of performing the task; carefully select workers and train them to perform the task by using the scientifically developed method; cooperate fully with workers to ensure that they use the proper method; and divide work and responsibility so that management is responsible for planning work methods using scientific principles and workers are responsible for executing the work accordingly. Abraham Maslow believed that motivation arises from need—that people are motivated to satisfy their unmet needs, and that these needs could be placed in a hierarchy of importance, in the following order: physiological, safety, social, esteem, and self-actualization needs. Frederick Herzberg conducted a study in which he asked workers to rank various job-related factors in order of their importance, relative to motivation. Herzberg concluded that certain factors, called motivators, cause employees to be productive while giving them a great deal of satisfaction. Other elements of the job, which he called hygiene factors, could cause dissatisfaction if they were not present (or not present in sufficient amounts), but enhancing these factors does not necessarily motivate employees.

4.   Describe the key principles of employee improvement theories.

    •   Goal-setting theory is based on the idea that setting ambitious, but attainable, goals can motivate workers and improve performance. In order for the theory to work, the goals must be realistic, accepted by the employees, accompanied by feedback, and supported by organizational conditions. All members of an organization should basically agree about the organization's overall goals and the specific objectives each department and individual must meet. MBO is a system of goal setting and implementation that involves a cycle of discussion, review, and evaluation of objectives among top and mid-level managers, supervisors, and employees. Problems can arise when upper-level managers use MBO as a strategy for forcing other managers and workers to commit to goals they haven't agreed to fulfill. Reinforcement theory is based on the idea that positive reinforcement, like praise and pay raises, and negative reinforcement, like reprimands and reduced pay, motivate a person to behave in certain ways. Equity theory suggests that employees try to maintain equity between inputs and outputs compared to others in similar positions. Empowerment can be a powerful motivator; it means trusting employees to make the right decisions. If an employee makes a mistake, it should be accepted and corrected, but not punished.

Key Terms

Empowerment	Job enlargement	Reinforcement theory
Equity theory	Job enrichment	Scientific management
Extrinsic reward	Job rotation	Social leader
Formal leadership	Leadership	Task leader
Goal-setting theory	Management by objectives (MBO)	Time and motion studies
Hawthorne effect	Maslow's hierarchy of needs	Transactional leader
Hygiene factors	Motivation	Transformational leader
Informal leadership	Motivators	
Intrinsic reward	Principle of motion economy	

1. What are the three most important qualities of a leader? Why are these qualities so important?

2. Is management the same as leadership? Why or why not? How are they the same? How are they different?

3. In groups, discuss what specific action a manager might take to motivate employees based on each level of Maslow's hierarchy (for example, in order to meet his employees' physiological needs, a manager could host a pizza party).

4. In groups, discuss some ways that managers, either now or in the past, have tried to motivate you. Were their attempts successful? If not, what would have worked better?

INTERNET IN >> Action

1. Visit your favorite search engine. Type in "great leaders of all time" and review the results. Which leaders are listed? What qualities do they have in common? What qualities are different?

2. Visit your favorite search engine and perform a search for "Herzberg hygiene factors." Review the results and then answer the following questions.
   a. What Web sites did your search lead you to?
   b. What is the difference between hygiene factors and motivational factors?
   c. List five hygiene factors and five motivational factors.
   d. Do you agree with the motivational factors listed in the last question? Why or why not?

3. Visit www.colorcode.com and take the site's free personality test. After you receive the results via e-mail, answer the following questions.
   a. What color is your personality?
   b. Do you feel your color is an accurate depiction of you? Why or why not?
   c. What leadership traits does your color have?

11

BUSINESS
IN GLOBAL MARKETS

LEARNING OUTCOMES

After reading this chapter, you will be able to:

1 Understand the importance of global trade.

2 Discuss the roles of comparative and absolute advantage in global trade.

3 Discuss the two indicators for measuring global trade.

4 Explain different types of trade protections and trade agreements.

5 Discuss the different strategies for reaching global markets.

6 Explain the forces affecting trade in the global market.

BOB HAGUE AND HAGUE QUALITY WATER INTERNATIONAL

The recession that plagued the United States and the rest of the world in 2008 and 2009 forced many small businesses to shift their focus to the global market. That was certainly true for Hague Quality Water International, an Ohio-based manufacturer of water conditioning equipment for new homes. In fact, Hague Quality Water's exporting strategy into international markets proved to be largely responsible for the company's survival during difficult economic times. "We've had no layoffs, and I partially credit international sales for helping me to prevent that," said the company's president, Bob Hague.[1]

As lending standards tightened in the United States, rates of new-home construction steadily decreased. Hague was forced to enlarge his consumer base, and he turned to the global stage to make that happen. After all, more than 95 percent of the world's population and more than 70 percent of its purchasing power exist outside the U.S.'s boundaries. As Deborah Scherer, director of the global markets division at the Ohio Department of Development, remarked, "If you are considering entering into any market outside the U.S., and you have not done so yet, now is the time to start building those relationships. When the market turns around, you'll be ready."[2]

Shifting Hague Quality Water's focus to international sales and relationship building led to an 87 percent increase in sales. Today, exports account for 20 percent of the company's annual sales—about $30 million—and the segment is growing fast. Overseas, Bob Hague found that the new-home construction market was more stable, and his business had less competition in foreign markets. In 2009, Hague Quality Water received the Small Business Environmental Exporter of the Year from the Export–Import Bank of the United States, a government agency that helps U.S. companies sell goods in other nations.

Conducting business in other nations isn't easy. Exporters must consider trade agreements, trade practices, and many other detailed aspects of the countries in which they seek to do business. Hague remarked, "We try to anticipate requirements we will have in the international markets, such as different plumbing requirements, different languages, and different regulations."[3] Having a thorough understanding of the differing factors in foreign markets allows a business in Groveport, Ohio, to know whether its operations in a country halfway around the world can become profitable.

Globalization has allowed the 100 people who work for Hague Quality Water International to keep their jobs and prosper through difficult economic times. It has also allowed Hague Quality Water to remain competitive in the domestic market.

Questions

1. What type of issues or challenges might Hague Quality Water International encounter while doing business in Russia? What about in Ukraine? Japan? China?

2. Do you think it's a good idea to expand operations to a global level? Why or why not? What are the disadvantages and advantages of such a move?

3. What types of businesses are best to expand globally? Discuss with your peers why these particular kinds of businesses would be effective on a global scale.

Source: Lori Murray, "Firm Finds Growth in Overseas Arena," *Dayton Business Journal*, May 29, 2009, http://www.bizjournals.com/dayton/stories/2009/06/01/smallb1.html (accessed September 2, 2009).

As You READ >>

- Why should a business engage in global trade?
- What strategies can a business use to reach global markets?
- What external factors affect a business that's involved in global trade?

What is global business, and why should people who don't buy or sell goods globally care about it? Why should small business owners care about it?

Global business refers to any activity that seeks to provide goods and services to others across national borders while operating at a profit. Many people think that if they don't buy and sell goods on a global scale, global business doesn't affect them—but that's simply not true. Global business plays a role in the daily lives of almost all people, and it affects consumers and business owners alike. Like Bob Hague of Hague Quality Water International, the owners of businesses large and small are finding globalization to be profitable. Businesses can find entirely new markets in which to sell their products, and they can save on the costs of labor by moving parts of their operations—manufacturing, for example—overseas. Of course, companies also face new cultural challenges when they engage in international business.

Global business Any activity that seeks to provide goods and services to others across national borders while operating at a profit.

>> The Global Market

Have you ever thought about traveling to exotic cities like Paris, Tokyo, Rio de Janeiro, or Cairo? For many decades, travel to global destinations was out of reach for most Americans, but today the situation has changed. It's now commonplace for people to travel internationally for business and pleasure alike.

It's hard to find a major U.S. company that does not cite global expansion as a link to its future growth. Today, more than 90 percent of the companies that do business on a global scale consider job candidates with experience working in other countries to have an edge over candidates without it.[4] Knowing about global business can lead you to exciting new career paths.

The United States market has more than 307 million potential consumers, but there are more than 6.7 billion potential consumers in the 193 countries that make up the global marketplace.[5] About 70 percent of the purchasing power in the world exists beyond U.S. borders.[6] It's easy to see why the global market is attractive to large and small businesses alike. (See Figure 11.1 for a map of the world and important statistics about world population.)

At the same time, 75 percent of the world's population lives in developing nations. In many of these areas, technology, education, and per-capita income standards still lag behind those of developed (or industrialized) nations, such as the United States. About half of the world's population gets by on less than $2 per day.[7] These developing areas are home to 90 percent of the world's 1.2 billion people between the ages of 16 and 24, most of whom live in African and Asian nations. As these young people get older, many will be looking to move to urban areas in order to access better employment, education, and healthcare opportunities.[8] Over time, these nations will develop the wealth and resources needed to purchase goods from other countries, and that's where global business gets interesting.

Today, Americans buy billions of dollars' worth of goods made in faraway countries, such as India, Vietnam, and China. McDonald's is a popular dining option in Germany, Saudi Arabia, and countless other global markets.[9] Walmart International has 3,760 stores in 15 markets outside the continental United States.[10] American stars, such as Harrison Ford and Angelina Jolie, continuously draw crowds to movie theaters around the globe. As advances in technology, travel, and communication continue over the next few years, it will be interesting to see how the world continues to evolve and develop. The world of importing and exporting, which we will discuss in the next section, is certain to expand.

Figure 11.1 World Population by Region

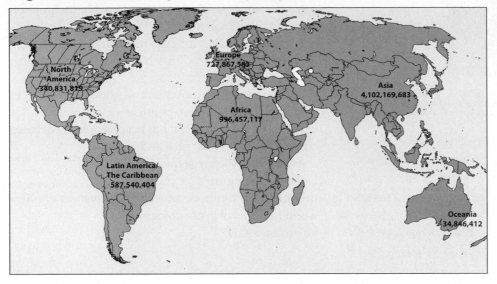

Source: U.S. Central Intelligence Agency, *Central Intelligence Agency World Factbook*, https://www.cia.gov/library/publications/the-world-factbook/fields/print_2119.html (accessed September 2, 2009).

More than 60 percent of the world's population lives in Asia.

Exporting Selling products to another country.

Importing Buying products from another country.

The United States imports more products than any other country in the world,[11] and it is the third largest exporting nation, lagging behind Germany and China.[12] Large corporations and small businesses alike contribute to this statistic. Consider this statistic: Every $1 billion that is spent on exporting goods and services creates 14,000 high-paying jobs in the U.S.[13]

So what are exporting and importing all about? **Exporting** is sell-

Teams from Major League Baseball, the National Basketball Association, and the National Football League play games in Mexico, Italy, Japan, and elsewhere.

ing products to another country. **Importing** is buying products from another country. As you might expect, given the size of the potential markets, competition among exporting nations and companies is very intense. U.S. companies face aggressive competition from exporters in such countries as Germany, Japan, and China.[14] Today in the United States, small and medium-sized businesses account for 97 percent of exporters and 99 percent of exporting firm growth.[15]

WHY TRADE GLOBALLY?

In an economic sense, there are several reasons why countries trade with other countries. First, no nation—not even a technologically advanced one—can produce all of the products its people want and need. Second, even if a country did become self-sufficient, other nations would seek to trade with that country in order to meet the needs of their own people. Third, some nations (for instance, Venezuela) have an abundance of natural resources but lack technological know-how, while others, such as Japan, Taiwan, and

Figure 11.2 The Pros and Cons of Free Trade

Pros	Cons
The global market contains over 6 billion potential customers for goods and services.	Domestic workers (particularly in manufacturing-based jobs) can lose their jobs due to increased imports or production shifts to low-wage global markets.
Productivity grows when countries produce goods and services in which they have a comparative advantage.	Workers may be forced to accept pay cuts from employers, who can threaten to move their jobs to lower-cost global markets.
Global competition and less-costly imports keep prices down, so inflation does not curtail economic growth.	Moving operations overseas because of intense competitive pressure often means the loss of service jobs and growing numbers of white-collar jobs.
Free trade inspires innovation for new products and keeps firms competitively challenged.	Domestic companies can lose their comparative advantage when competitors build advanced production operations in low-wage countries.
Uninterrupted flow of capital gives countries access to foreign investments, which help keep interest rates low.	

Real World Apps

Samantha Ortiz long dreamed of running her own business, and five years ago, she finally made the leap. Samantha's Custom Interior Decorations has flourished since then. She's built a strong local clientele, and a more widespread distribution is the next step in Samantha's business plan. Everyone tells her she should consider doing business overseas, as she could dramatically reduce her production costs and possibly expand her sales as well.

Running her own business has taught Samantha many lessons about entrepreneurship, distribution, and inventory—the hard way. Now, she's wondering about globalization, which she's read a lot about. "What the heck is globalization, anyway, and what does it mean to me and my business?" Samantha wonders.

Samantha understands that the world is changing, but she isn't sure how these changes will affect her plans for her business.

Before going further, Samantha needs to gather information. She's learned a little about globalization, but what she's learned has only raised more questions. If she adapts to the current economic trends of outsourcing and working overseas, will she really make more money? Should she try to set up franchises for her products? What are the legal restrictions in other markets, and how will she learn about tariffs and fees? It's time Samantha found some answers. She decides to enroll in an Introduction to Business course in order to learn more about taking her business to the next level—the worldwide stage.

[BUS] connections

1. Define global business.
2. Why must countries export and import goods?
3. Why do companies decide to engage in global business?

Switzerland, have sophisticated technology but few natural resources. Trade relations enable each nation to produce and sell what it is most capable of producing and to buy what it needs in a mutually beneficial exchange relationship. This happens through a process called free trade.[16]

Free trade is the movement of goods and services among nations without political or economic trade barriers. Over the years, it has become a hotly debated concept.[17] Some of the pros and cons of free trade are shown in Figure 11.2. Figure 11.3 shows the top 10 countries in the world in terms of gross domestic product (GDP).

> **Free trade** The movement of goods and services among nations without political or economic trade barriers.

Figure 11.3 The 10 Highest GDP Countries in the World

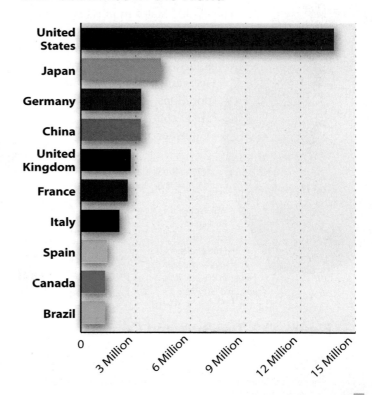

>> Comparative Advantage and Absolute Advantage

Wine has been exported from European nations, such as France and Italy, for centuries, but in recent years, Australia and Chile have also begun to export wine on a massive scale.

Global trade is the exchange of goods and services across national borders, but exchanges between and among countries involve more than goods and services. Countries also exchange art, sports, cultural events, medical advances, space exploration, and labor—just to name a few items. According to the **comparative advantage theory**, which was suggested in the early 19th century by the English economist David Ricardo, a country should sell to other countries the products it produces most effectively and efficiently and buy from other countries the products it cannot produce as effectively or efficiently. Every country has a comparative advantage in something. Comparative advantage theory is the guiding principle that supports the idea of free economic exchange.[18]

Global trade The exchange of goods and services across national borders.

Comparative advantage theory A theory that states that a country should sell to other countries those products that it produces most effectively and efficiently and buy from other countries those products that it cannot produce as effectively or efficiently.

For example, the United Kingdom sells its wool, and France sells its wine. Brazil has a comparative advantage when it comes to the production of ethanol, a biofuel. Brazilian ethanol is primarily made from sugar cane, but in the U.S. ethanol is made from corn. About U.S. production of ethanol, Matt Hartwig, a spokesman for the Renewable Fuels Association, remarked, "The reason we use corn and grains in this country to make ethanol is that's what we produce best. It's the easier thing for us to do at the moment."[19]

Spain enjoys a comparative advantage when it comes to saffron, the world's most expensive spice.[20] Saffron is actually the styles and stigmas of a saffron crocus flower, and it is notoriously hard to cultivate. In fact, it takes about 12 days for an experienced saffron cultivator to pick enough of the plant to equal one pound of saffron. The spice is cultivated in many countries, but Spain's saffron is highly prized. Saffron from Spain costs around $600 to $2,000 per pound by the time it arrives at retail stores.[21]

A country has an **absolute advantage** if it has a monopoly on producing a specific product or is able to produce it more efficiently than all other countries. For instance, South Africa once had an absolute advantage in diamond production. Most absolute advantage situations involve natural resources that one country has and others do not have. Absolute advantage can also be difficult to sustain if conditions change or if resources are discovered elsewhere.

Absolute advantage The advantage that exists when a country has a monopoly on producing a specific product or is able to produce it more efficiently than all other countries.

For thousands of years, China had an absolute advantage in silk production. The technique of silk-making was considered so sacred to the Chinese culture that anyone who revealed its secrets would be sentenced to death.[22] Demand for the fiber became so high that several different routes, which were collectively known as the Silk Road, were created in order to facilitate the trade of silk and other commodities between Europe and China.[23] The rare gemstone tanzanite is exclusively found within the borders of the African nation of Tanzania, which gives Tanzania an absolute advantage.

Because countries are interested in knowing how their trade output compares with that of other countries, there are several ways in which trade can be measured. We'll discuss those methods of measurement in the next section.

Tulips, which the country exports worldwide, are a hallmark of the small nation known as The Netherlands.

>> Measuring Global Trade

In measuring global trade, nations rely on two key indicators: balance of trade and balance of payments.

BALANCE OF TRADE, BALANCE OF PAYMENTS, AND TRADE DEFICITS AND SURPLUSES

The **balance of trade** is a nation's ratio of exports to imports. A *favorable* balance of trade, or **trade surplus**, occurs when the value of the country's exports exceeds that of its imports. An *unfavorable* balance of trade, or **trade deficit**, occurs when the value of a country's imports exceeds that of its exports. It's easy to understand why countries prefer to export more than they import. If you sell $500 worth of goods and buy only $300 worth, you'll have an extra $200. However, if you buy $500 worth of goods and sell only $300 worth, you'll find yourself in debt.

The **balance of payments** is the difference between money coming into a country (from exports) and money leaving the country (for imports), plus or minus any money flows coming into or leaving a country from other factors, such as tourism, foreign aid, military expenditures, and foreign investment. The goal is always to have more money flowing into the country than flowing out of the country—in other words, a *favorable* balance of payments. Conversely, an *unfavorable* balance of payments exists when more money is flowing out of a country than coming in.

For many years, the United States exported more goods and services to other countries than it imported. In every year since 1976, however, the United States has bought more goods from other nations than it has sold to other nations, resulting in a trade deficit.[24] For example, in 2008, the United States exported $71.5 billion worth of goods to China, while it imported an astonishing $337.8 billion worth of goods from the same nation—that adds up to a trade deficit of $266.3 billion.[25]

Balance of trade The total value of a nation's exports compared to its imports measured over a particular period.

Trade surplus A favorable balance of trade; occurs when the value of a country's exports exceeds that of its imports.

Trade deficit An unfavorable balance of trade; occurs when the value of a country's imports exceeds that of its exports.

Balance of payments The difference between money coming into a country (from exports) and money leaving the country (for imports) plus money flows from other factors, such as tourism, foreign aid, military expenditures, and foreign investment.

Wisconsin-based Trek Bicycle Corporation started with small roots in 1976 and quickly moved to a broader market. In 1988, it made its first step into globalization with a research trip to Europe. Trek quickly became the largest bike manufacturer in the world, with locations in more than 15 countries.

The United States exports a much lower percentage of its products than many other countries do.[26] Figure 11.4 lists the major trading partners of the United States, and Figure 11.5 lists the 10 largest exporters worldwide. In the early 1980s, for example, no more than 10 percent of American businesses exported products. However, since the late 1980s, slow economic growth in the United States and other economic factors lured more businesses to global markets.[27] Today, most large businesses are involved in global trade, and growing numbers of small and me-

◄ ETHICAL   DILEMMA ►

If your manager told you to give a gift to a prospective customer in a foreign country in order to make a sale, how would you handle the situation?

Figure 11.4 Top 10 Countries with which the U.S. Trades

Country	Total U.S. Imports and Exports as of June 2009 (in Billions)
Canada	$35.11
China	$29.53
Mexico	$24.56
Japan	$11.71
Federal Republic of Germany	$8.66
United Kingdom	$7.95
South Korea	$5.66
France	$5.50
Netherlands	$3.98
Brazil	$3.88

"Top 10 Countries with which the U.S. Trades," U.S. Census Bureau, http://www.census.gov/foreign-trade/top/dst/current/balance.html (accessed August 25, 2009).

dium-size businesses are going global as well. Nevertheless, the total percentage of U.S. products that are exported is still low.

Figure 11.5 Top 10 Largest Exporters Worldwide

Rank	Country	Exports	Date Of Information
1	European Union	$ 1,952,000,000,000	2007
2	Germany	$ 1,498,000,000,000	2008 est.
3	China	$ 1,435,000,000,000	2008 est.
4	United States	$ 1,291,000,000,000	2008 est.
5	Japan	$ 746,500,000,000	2008 est.
6	France	$ 601,900,000,000	2008 est.
7	Italy	$ 546,900,000,000	2008 est.
8	Netherlands	$ 533,200,000,000	2008 est.
9	Russia	$ 471,600,000,000	2008 est.
10	United Kingdom	$ 464,900,000,000	2008 est.

U.S. Central Intelligence Agency, *Central Intelligence Agency World Factbook*, https://www.cia.gov/library/publications/the-world-factbook/rankorder/2078rank.html (accessed September 2, 2009).

UNFAIR TRADE PRACTICES

In supporting free trade, nations seek to make certain that global trade is conducted fairly. Many countries enforce laws to prohibit unfair trade practices. One such practice is called **dumping**.[28] Dumping is the practice of selling products in a foreign country at lower prices than those charged in the producing country. Dumping can also include selling products in a country below the actual cost of producing the product. This tactic is sometimes used to reduce surplus products in foreign markets or to gain a foothold in a new market. Some governments may offer financial incentives to certain industries to sell goods in global markets for less than they sell them at home. Japan and Russia, for example, have been accused of dumping steel in the United States, and Canada has been accused of dumping softwood lumber.[29]

> **Dumping** Selling products in a foreign country at lower prices than those charged in the producing country.

Because of the global economic recession of 2008 and 2009, some countries dumped products in an effort to save money. India filed 42 antidumping suits—a new record—in the second half of 2008; 17 of these cases were against China, its northeastern neighbor.[30] From the period between 1995 and 2008, steel and similar products have been the subject of 414 antidumping suits filed with the World Trade Organization.[31]

U.S. laws against dumping are specific: they require that foreign firms price their products to include 10 percent overhead costs plus an 8 percent profit margin.[32] However, it can take time to prove accusations of dumping. Dumping promises to remain a difficult trade issue in the coming years because it can hinder a country from selling its own products domestically at a fair price. Dumping can affect and skew trade measurement data as well.

Selling items on the **gray market** is also an unfair trade practice. The gray market refers to the flow of goods in a distribution channel or chan-

> **Gray market** The flow of goods in a distribution channel or channels other than those intended by the manufacturer or licensor.

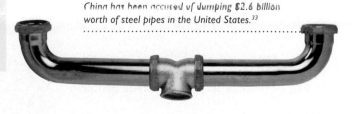

China has been accused of dumping $2.6 billion worth of steel pipes in the United States.[33]

nels other than those intended by the manufacturer or licensor. Despite the fact that selling on the gray market is highly unethical, the practice is widespread. (You'll learn more about ethics in Chapter 12.)

For example, suppose a Chinese business owner is manufacturing designer suits in his factory that normally sell for $1,000 each. If the factory owner were to make more suits than the designer had ordered and sell the extras on an auction Web site at a reduced cost, he'd be selling on the gray market. Apple's iPhone is distributed exclusively through authorized channels in the United States, Britain, France, and Germany, but unauthorized distributors in China, Eastern Europe, Australia, and other locations have been selling the phones on the gray market. By early 2008, between 800,000 and 1 million iPhones were distributed through unauthorized channels.[34] More than half a million cars that were originally sold in other countries have been imported to the United States by way of the gray market during the last 25 years.[35]

Now that we've discussed some basics about global business, we'll next explore how and why countries enact policies in order to protect their local markets.

[BUS] connections

1. What are two indicators used to measure the effectiveness of global trade?
2. What role do unfair trade practices play in global trade?
3. Who are the top three trading partners of United States?

>> Trade Protection and Agreements

Trade protectionism The use of government regulations to limit the import of goods and services.

As discussed in Chapter 1, economic, legal, technological, competitive, and social forces are all challenges of global trade, but the *political* atmosphere among nations can be a much greater barrier than any of these other factors. **Trade protec-**

tionism is the use of government regulations to limit the import of goods and services. Advocates of trade protectionism believe it allows domestic producers to survive and grow, thus producing more jobs. Countries often use protectionist measures to guard against unfair trade practices, such as dumping; many countries are wary of foreign competition in general.[36]

Naturally, nations want to sell more goods to other nations than they buy, because it's desirable to have a favorable balance of trade. Doing so also helps them protect and support their domestic industries. This philosophy has led governments to implement **tariffs**, which are taxes on imports. Tariffs make imported goods more expensive to buy.

Tariff A tax on imports.

Generally, there are two different kinds of tariffs: protective and revenue. *Protective tariffs* (import taxes) are designed to raise the retail price of imported products so domestic goods will be more competitively priced. These tariffs are meant to save jobs for domestic workers and to keep industries (especially new ones in the early stages of growth) from closing down entirely because of foreign competition. *Revenue tariffs* are designed to raise money for a government. Revenue tariffs are also commonly used by developing countries to help young businesses and industries compete in global markets.

Today, there is still considerable debate about the degree of protectionism a government should practice. The United States publishes the **Harmonized Tariff Schedule**, which includes tariff costs for every product from every country, so business owners who import goods into the United States will know the tariffs they face, and business owners in the United States will know what tariffs their foreign competitors will face in the U.S. market.

Harmonized Tariff Schedule A schedule of tariff costs for every product from every country that is published by the U.S. government.

An **import quota**, which is another type of protectionist policy, limits the number of products in certain categories that a nation can import. The goal of a quota is to prevent other countries from flooding a market with products and thereby driving down the price according to the laws of supply and demand, which were discussed in Chapter 2.

Import quota A protectionist policy that limits the number of products in certain categories that a nation can import.

The United States has import quotas on a number of products, including shrimp and sugar.

An **embargo** is a complete ban on the import or export of a certain product or the stopping of all trade with a particular country. Political disagreements have caused

Embargo A complete ban on the import or export of a certain product or the stopping of all trade with a particular country.

The United States's embargo against Cuba's government has existed since 1960.

many countries, including the United States, to establish embargoes against Cuba's communist regime.[37] The United States and Israel have discussed the possibility of imposing an oil embargo on Iran until the country agrees to disclose more information about its uranium enrichment program. Uranium is used to produce nuclear power, but it's also used to produce nuclear weapons.[38] In addition, the United States also prohibits the export of specific products globally. The Export Administration Act of 1979 prohibits the exporting of goods (e.g., high-tech weapons) that would endanger national security.

Nontariff barriers are not as specific or formal as tariffs, import quotas, and embargoes, but they can be quite detrimental to free trade. Countries often set restrictive standards that detail exactly how a product must be sold in a country. For example, Denmark requires butter to be sold in cubes, not tubs. This policy makes it more difficult for foreign companies to sell butter in Denmark, so it is considered to be a kind of protectionist policy.

Nontariff barriers Restrictive standards that detail exactly how a product must be sold in a country.

Another good example of a nontariff barrier is Japan's tradition of *keiretsu* (pronounced "kay-RET-soo"). For years, Japan steadfastly argued that it had some of the lowest tariffs in the world and welcomed foreign exporters, but some American businesses found it very difficult to establish trade relationships in Japan. Many believed *keiretsu* was the root of the problem. Under *keiretsu*, major Japanese companies built "corporate families" that forged semipermanent ties with suppliers, customers, and distributors, with the full support of the Japanese government. They believed that these huge corporate alliances would provide economic payoffs by nurturing long-term strategic thinking and mutually beneficial cooperation.[39] As the Japanese economy has faltered, so has *keiretsu*, and U.S. businesses are now finding Japan to be a friendlier destination for exports.

Australia's government has created nontariff barriers for its free broadcast programming. Of all television shows broadcast between 6 a.m. and midnight, at least 55 percent must be of Australian origin, and 25 percent of all music broadcast on the radio during the same hours must be from Australian groups or musicians.[40] India has asked the World Trade Organization to build a database of all nontariff barriers worldwide so they'll be easier to monitor. Such a database would help prevent countries from quickly changing trade barriers in an effort to block a particular nation's access.[41]

Barriers to trade are a reality around the world, but there are also many policies and organizations in place that are designed to limit, if not eliminate, barriers to trade. We'll explore those in the next section.

The key tools of trade protectionism are tariffs, import quotas, and embargoes.

Study Alert

Common markets reflect a desire among nations to become an economic union using the same currency and to help focus efforts on free trade.

a trading bloc.[48] Like the EU, its economic goals include a single currency. Recently, a proposal was revived to combine Mercosur and the Andean Pact (an alliance among Venezuela, Colombia, Peru, and Ecuador) into a Union of South American Nations that would pave the way for an economic free-trade zone that spans South America.[49]

ORGANIZATION OF THE PETROLEUM EXPORTING COUNTRIES (OPEC)

The Organization of the Petroleum Exporting Countries (OPEC), which was founded in 1960, is a major force in worldwide trade. Because petroleum products are used in every market worldwide, OPEC becomes more important to the world economy ev-

ery day. Today, the following nations are OPEC members: Algeria, Angola, Ecuador,[50] Iran, Iraq, Kuwait, Libya, Nigeria, Qatar, Saudi Arabia, United Arab Emirates, and Venezuela. The organization's mission includes the following:

1. To coordinate and unify the petroleum policies of the member countries and determine the best means for safeguarding their individual and collective interests.

2. To seek ways and means of ensuring the stabilization of prices in international oil markets, with a view to eliminating harmful and unnecessary fluctuations.

3. To provide an efficient, economic, and regular supply of petroleum to consuming nations and a fair return on capital to those investing in the petroleum industry.[51]

The Organization of the Petroleum Exporting Countries (OPEC) An organization of 13 oil-producing nations that work together to protect their interests.

Figure 11.7 Members of the European Union

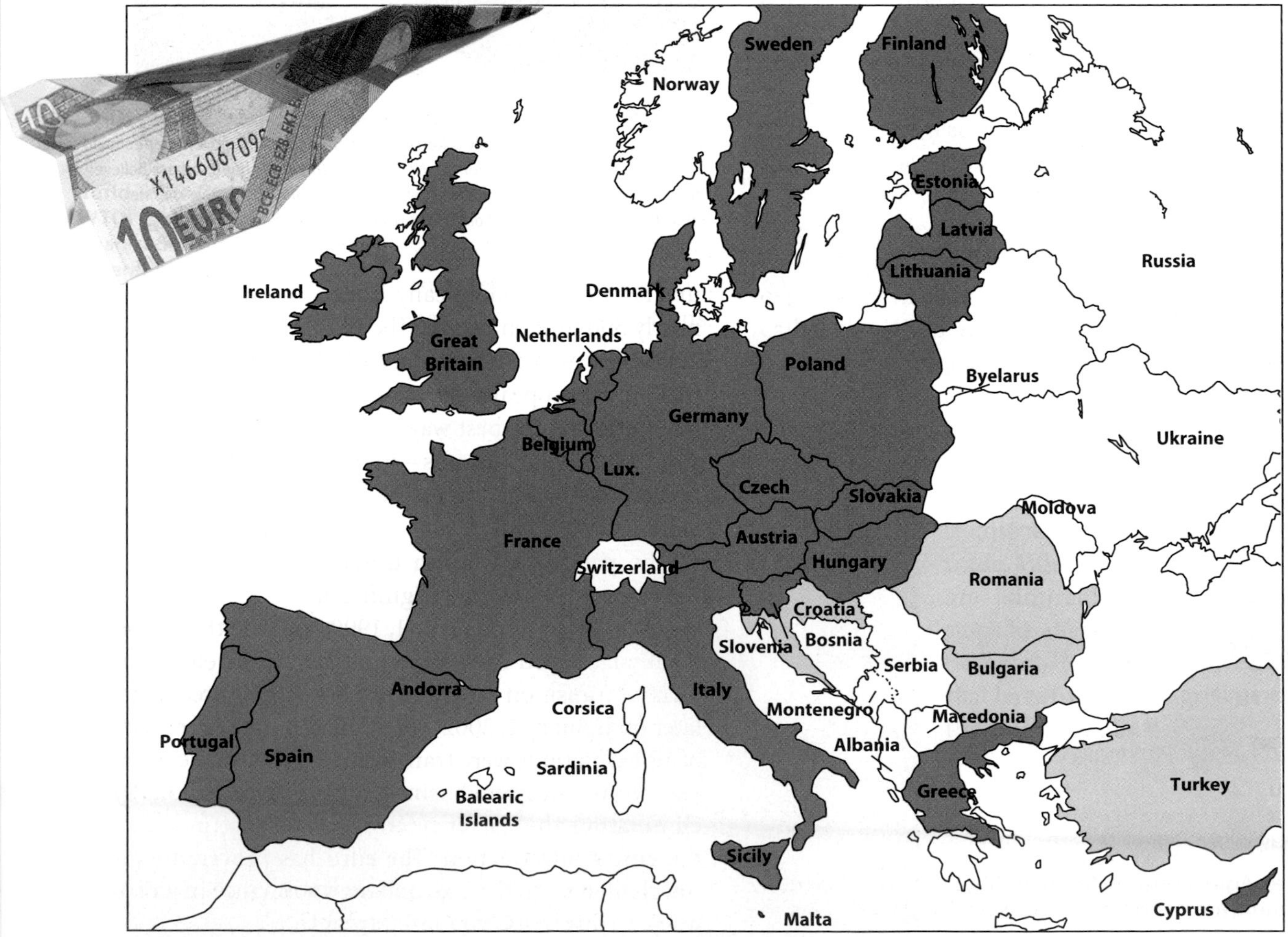

Current EU members are highlighted in dark blue. Countries that have applied for membership are in light blue.

Going GLOBAL

U.S. Free Trade Agreements

Free trade is typically the best way to deepen and improve relations between countries, but recessions can make trade considerably more difficult. As unemployment rises, governments become more focused on protecting their own interests and businesses and less interested in trade. However, the United States remains very interested in maintaining positive trade relations with other nations, and this article from the U.S. Department of Commerce details a few trade agreements the U.S. has forged.

Trade agreements help open markets and expand opportunities for American workers and businesses. They can help any company enter and compete more easily in the global marketplace. Trade agreements are also a tool for promoting fair competition and encouraging foreign governments to adopt open and transparent rulemaking procedures, as well as nondiscriminatory laws and regulations. Trade agreements can strengthen the business climate by including commitments on issues of concern along with the reduction and elimination of tariffs. These agreements may include commitments on such topics as:

- Improving intellectual property rights protections
- Enhancing labor rights
- Government procurement
- Opening service sectors to competition
- Enhancing rules on foreign investment
- Environmental standards
- Improving customs facilitation

The United States is party to many bilateral (between two countries) and multilateral (between multiple countries) trade agreements. Countries with which the United States has active bilateral trade agreements include Australia, Bahrain, Chile, Israel, Jordan, Morocco, Peru, Oman, and Singapore. The active multilateral trade agreements that the United States has signed include the North American Free Trade Agreement and the Central America–Dominican Republic Free Trade Agreement (CAFTA–DR).

The United States is also party to the GATT, which is overseen by the WTO along with 152 other countries. U.S. trade agreements with Panama, Korea, and Colombia are pending congressional approval. The United States is also in negotiations on trade agreements with Malaysia, Thailand, the United Arab Emirates, and the Southern African Customs Union, which includes Botswana, Lesotho, Namibia, South Africa, and Swaziland.

Source: The U.S. Department of Commerce, "U.S. Free Trade Agreements," http://www.export.gov/fta/ (accessed September 3, 2009).

Questions

1. Do you believe free trade with other nations is a threat to the United States's manufacturing base? Explain your response.

2. Why do you believe creating and upholding trade agreements with other nations is such a high priority for the United States?

THE NORTH AMERICAN FREE TRADE AGREEMENT (NAFTA)

In the early 1990s, the ratification of the **North American Free Trade Agreement (NAFTA)**, which created a free trade zone among the United States, Canada, and Mexico, was hotly debated, and to this day the merits of the agreement continue to be a political issue. It is important to note that NAFTA is quite different from an economic union, such as the EU.

North American Free Trade Agreement (NAFTA) An agreement that created a free-trade area among the United States, Canada, and Mexico.

Common markets take free trade to a much higher level than NAFTA.

The objectives of NAFTA were to (1) eliminate trade barriers and facilitate cross-border movement of goods and services among the three countries; (2) promote conditions of fair competition in this free-trade area; (3) increase investment opportunities in the territories of the three nations; (4) provide effective protection and enforcement of intellectual property rights (patents, copyrights, etc.) in each nation's territory; (5) establish a framework for further

Figure 11.8 The Growing U.S. Trade Deficit with Mexico

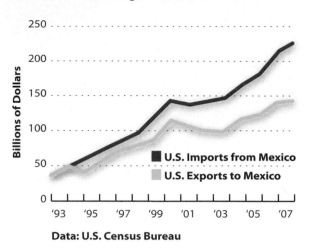

Growing Deficit With Mexico

- ■ U.S. Imports from Mexico
- ■ U.S. Exports to Mexico

Data: U.S. Census Bureau

Source: http://www.businessweek.com/magazine/content/08_13/b4077000640600.htm (accessed August 29, 2009).

Warner Bros. has licensed hundreds of companies to make products related to its series of hit films based on the best-selling Harry Potter books, which have been translated into dozens of languages.

regional trade cooperation; and (6) improve working conditions in North America.[52] Today, the three NAFTA countries have a combined population of over 444 million people and a GDP of $17 trillion.[53] Figure 11.8 illustrates the rising trade gap between the U.S. and Mexico.

NAFTA remains controversial.[54] On the positive side, the value of U.S. exports to NAFTA partners has increased since its signing. Trade volume among the three partners has expanded from $289 billion in 1994 to $930 billion today.[55] On the downside, the U.S. Department of Labor estimates that the United States has lost 500,000 jobs to Mexico since enacting NAFTA; some labor economists believe the actual number is much higher. Annual per-capita income in Mexico still lags considerably behind that of the United States, causing illegal immigration to remain a major problem. Some critics also argue that working conditions in Mexico are less safe than they were before NAFTA, especially in southern Mexico.

Here are the realities of NAFTA. The United States traded $967 billion in goods with Canada and Mexico during 2008—of that, goods exports totaled $412 billion, and goods imports totaled $555 billion. The U.S. goods trade deficit with the two nations was $143 billion in 2008.[56] On the positive side, Mexico has reformed its trade laws, and that's helped the country entice foreign investors, stabilize its economy, and increase its exports. In the United States, manufacturing has increased by 58 percent since its passage, and agricultural exports have flourished. On the negative side, the fact that operations can be easily moved to either Canada or Mexico has resulted in lower wages in the U.S. in certain businesses and industries. Hundreds of thousands of U.S. jobs have been lost to the other NAFTA nations as well.

The controversies surrounding NAFTA have not changed the United States's commitment to free-trade agreements. In 2005, Congress passed the Central American Free Trade Agreement (CAFTA), creating a free-trade zone with Costa Rica, the Dominican Republic, El Salvador, Guatemala, Honduras, and Nicaragua.[57] CAFTA supporters claimed the agreement would open new markets, lower tariffs, and ease regulations among the member nations. Its critics countered that the measure would hurt U.S. jobs, especially in the sugar and textile industries. Free traders hope CAFTA is a stepping stone to the creation of a Free Trade Area of the Americas

Figure 11.9 Strategies for Reaching Global Markets

Licensing | Exporting | Franchising | Contract manufacturing | International joint ventures and strategic alliances | Foreign direct investment

LEAST ← Amount of commitment, control, risk, and profit potential → **MOST**

(FTAA), which would encompass the 800 million
people living in all the nations between the Patagonia
region at the southernmost point of South America
and Alaska. The FTAA agreement remains stalled
due to political and trade differences among the potential member nations.

>> Strategies for Reaching Global Markets

A business can use several strategies to enter the global
market (see Figure 11.9), including licensing, exporting, franchising, contract manufacturing, international joint ventures and strategic alliances, and foreign direct investment. A company can be involved in global
business in varying degrees. Many smaller companies

China now produces and exports 80 percent
of the toys manufactured worldwide.

first "try out" the market by licensing or exporting
goods, and as their success grows, they consider becoming more involved in global business.

LICENSING

A firm (the licensor) may decide to compete in a global
market by **licensing** to a foreign company (the licensee)
the right to manufacture its
product or use its trademark
for a fee (a royalty). A company with an interest in licens-

> **Licensing** A global strategy
> in which a firm (the licensor)
> allows a foreign company
> (the licensee) to produce its
> product in exchange for a
> fee (a royalty).

ing generally needs to send company representatives
to the foreign producer to help set up the production
process. The licensor may also assist or work with a
licensee in such areas as distribution, promotion, and
consulting. A licensing agreement is simply one where
a company allows another company to produce goods
under its name. Of course, these arrangements have
both benefits and challenges.

A licensing agreement can be beneficial to a firm
in several different ways. Through licensing, an organization can gain revenues beyond what it could have
generated in its home market. In addition, foreign li-
censees often purchase start-up supplies, component
materials, and consulting services from the licensing
firm.

Such agreements have been very profitable for companies like Disney, Coca-Cola, and PepsiCo. These
firms often enter foreign markets through licensing
agreements that typically extend into long-term service contracts. Godiva Chocolatier, which began as a

The sun never sets on Mickey and the gang, which is making Disney
very happy. The firm has had great success licensing the famous
mouse and his cast of characters in Europe and Asia. Here, Mickey
welcomes visitors to Tokyo Disneyland. Oriental Land Company and
the Hong Kong government have licensing agreements with Walt
Disney Company.[59] Oriental Land Company owns and operates Tokyo
Disneyland and Tokyo Disney Sea Park under a licensing agreement.

censing company's technology or product secrets, it could be tempted to break the agreement and begin to produce a similar product on its own. If legal remedies are not available, the licensing firm could lose its trade secrets—not to mention the agreed-upon royalties.

EXPORTING

As global competition has intensified, the U.S. government has created export assistance centers (EACs)[60] to provide hands-on exporting assistance and trade-finance support for small and medium-sized businesses that choose to directly export goods and services. A nationwide network of EACs now exists in over 126 U.S. cities and 80 countries worldwide.[61]

Tired of studying and want a quick snack? How about a piping hot Domino's pizza with squid and sweet mayonnaise to satisfy your craving? Domino's serves pizzas around the globe that appeal to different tastes.

small shop in Brussels, Belgium, now operates more than 450 boutiques and shops worldwide. The company has been licensing its brand since 1992. One recent licensing arrangement involved teaming up with the restaurant chain the Cheesecake Factory to produce Godiva Double Chocolate Cheesecake.[58]

Licensing can also be a good option for small companies with an idea for a new product that would better serve a foreign market. A licensing agreement would allow a licensee company to produce and sell the new product in the other market, and very little investment on the part of the licensor would be required. In addition to paying the costs, the licensee would work hard to make such an agreement succeed because it would be responsible for sales in the new market.

However, companies that enter into licensing agreements may experience some problems. For one thing, a firm must grant licensing rights to its product for an extended period—sometimes 20 years or longer. If a product experiences remarkable growth and success in the foreign market during that time, the bulk of the revenues earned belong to the licensee. In addition, a licensing firm could actually sell its newfound expertise in a product area. If a foreign licensee learns a li-

Still, even with help from these EACs, many U.S. firms are reluctant to go through the trouble of establishing foreign trading relationships. In such cases, specialists called export-trading companies (or export-management companies) can step in to negotiate and establish trading relationships. An export-trading company not only matches buyers and sellers from different countries but

Imagine that you have a really great idea for a new no-skid dog bowl. You spend lots of time and money building a model of this new product and decide to have it produced in China by a contract manufacturer. Unfortunately, China has lax copyright laws, which means that the manufacturer might copy your innovative design and sell its copycat product on the gray market.

also provides necessary services, such as dealing with foreign customs offices, documentation requirements, and even weights and measures, in order to ease the process of entering global markets. Export-trading companies also help exporters with a key risky element of doing business globally: getting paid.

Today, more than 230,000 small businesses are exporting goods into foreign countries. The U.S. Small Business Administration reports that small firms make up 97 percent of all U.S. exporters. Exports are found in unlikely places, too—for example, in 2007, American universities exported $18 billion in educational services to 730,000 foreign students.[62]

FRANCHISING

As you learned in Chapter 3, a franchising agreement is an arrangement whereby someone with a good idea for a business (the franchisor) sells the rights to use the business's name and sell its products and services (the franchise) to others (the franchisees) in a given territory. Popular both domestically and internationally, franchising differs from licensing in that where licensing might be used to sell a single product, franchising allows the use of an entire *business concept*, including packaging, how the good is manufactured, and the look and feel of the business.

U.S. franchisors, such as McDonald's, Dairy Queen, Arby's, and Days Inn, have units around the world that are operated by foreign franchisees, but global franchising is not limited to only the large franchisors. For example, Rocky Mountain Chocolate Factory, a Colorado-based producer of premium chocolate candies with 235 retail stores worldwide, recently entered into a franchising agreement with the Muhairy Group of the United Arab Emirates.[63] The Muhairy Group will open stores in Saudi Arabia, Oman, Kuwait, Bahrain, and Qatar, where chocolate is considered a gourmet luxury comparable to caviar.[64] Likewise, the athletic footwear chain Athlete's Foot, which began in Pittsburgh, Pennsylvania, opened its first international franchise in Adelaide, Australia. Today, the company has expanded into more than 40 countries.[65]

However, franchisors must be careful about adapting their products or services in the countries they serve. For example, KFC's first 11 Hong Kong outlets failed within two years because Hong Kong diners found its chicken too greasy and messy.[66] McDonald's erred during its original entry into the Netherlands market; it set up most of its franchises in the suburbs, as it does in the United States, but it soon learned that the Dutch mostly live—and dine—in the nation's cities.[67]

Pizza Hut originally approached the global market with a one-pie-fits-all strategy, but it found out the hard way that Germans like small, individual pizzas, and not the large pies preferred in the United States. Domino's Pizza has adapted its products to customers in India. Some followers of the Jain religion do not eat onions or garlic, so the company

created pizza options that don't use these common ingredients. Likewise, both Pizza Hut and Domino's franchises in many Muslim nations do not offer pepperoni, a pork-based sausage product.[68]

CONTRACT MANUFACTURING

Contract manufacturing involves a foreign company's production of private label goods to which a domestic company then attaches its own brand name or trademark. The practice is also known as *outsourcing*.[69] For example, Dell Computer contracts with Quanta Computer of Taiwan to make its notebook PCs. Many other well-known U.S. firms, such as Levi Strauss and Nike, practice contract manufacturing. Most of the clothing industry is involved in contract manufacturing, as is Cisco Systems, the world leader in Internet router gear. Cisco is heavily dependent on contract manufacturers, such as Solectron and Flextronics, to manufacture its products.[70] Electronics companies Sony and Sharp outsource the manufacture of their televisions; in fact, during the period between January and March 2009, one in four televisions sold globally were made by a contract manufacturer.[71]

Contract manufacturing enables a company to experiment in a new market without incurring heavy start-up costs. If they succeed, they've penetrated a new market with relatively low risk. A firm can also use contract manufacturing temporarily to meet an unexpected increase in orders. One of the major disadvantages of contract manufacturing is that intellectual property and copyright laws differ in every country. As global trade grows, worldwide standards for intellectual property laws are becoming increasingly necessary.

Contract manufacturing A foreign country's production of private-label goods to which a domestic company then attaches its brand name or trademark; part of the broad category of outsourcing.

INTERNATIONAL JOINT VENTURES AND STRATEGIC ALLIANCES

A **joint venture** is a partnership in which two or more companies (often from different countries) undertake a major project. According to Coopers & Lybrand, a New York–based international professional services firm, companies that engage in partnerships grow much faster than companies that do not.[72] Joint ventures can even be mandated by governments as a condition of doing business in their country.

For example, it's often hard to gain entry into the Chinese market, but agreeing to a joint venture with a Chinese firm can help matters tremendously. Volkswagen and General Motors entered into joint ventures with Shanghai Automotive Industrial Corporation, China's largest domestic car company, to build cars in China, the world's fastest-growing auto market.[73] General Motors has also formed a $293 million alliance with a Chinese auto manufacturer to create a new line of light-duty trucks and vans.[74]

Joint ventures are developed for other business reasons as well. Global Engine Manufacturing Alliance, a coalition formed by Chrysler, Mitsubishi Motors, and Hyundai Motor Company, is a joint venture that will develop aluminum engines used by all three companies. The Newman's Own food brand, which donates its profits to charity, partnered with McDonald's to offer its salad dressings with McDonald's salads. The alliance greatly expanded Newman's Own's charitable donations, and McDonald's became the only fast-food restaurant to offer an all-natural salad dressing option.[75] Joint ventures can also unite unusual partners. For example, a few years ago, the University of Pittsburgh and the Italian government entered a joint venture to build a new medical transplant center in Sicily.

The benefits of international joint ventures are clear:

Joint venture A partnership in which two or more companies (often from different countries) undertake a major project.

Campbell Soup Company formed joint ventures with Japan's Nakano Vinegar Company and Malaysia's Cheong Chan Company to expand its rather low share of the soup market in both countries.

The United States has been and remains a popular global spot for foreign direct investment. Global automobile manufacturers like Toyota, Honda, and Mercedes have spent millions of dollars building facilities in the United States, like the Honda plant in Marysville, Ohio, pictured here.

1. Shared technology.

2. Shared marketing and management expertise.

3. Entry into markets where foreign companies are often not allowed unless their goods are produced locally.

4. Shared risk.

The drawbacks are not so obvious. One partner can learn the other's technology and practices, and then go off on its own and use what it has learned. Also, over time, a shared technology may become obsolete, or the joint venture may become too large or inflexible.

In a **greenfield investment**, one alternative to a joint venture, a company builds its own factories and offices in a different country. One obvious disadvantage to a greenfield investment is a lack of knowledge about the country's ways of doing business. A greenfield investment is a form of foreign direct investment that will be discussed later in this section.

> **Greenfield investment** A form of foreign direct investment in which a company builds factories and offices in a foreign country on its own.

The vast potential of the global market is also fueling the growth of strategic alliances. A **strategic alliance** is a long-term partnership between two or more companies established to help each company build competitive market advantages. Such alliances can provide both companies with access to markets, capital, and technical expertise. Consider Procter & Gamble: The company increased its productivity levels by 60 percent by creating alliances outside the company for research and development purposes.[76]

> **Strategic alliance** A long-term partnership between two or more companies established to help each company build competitive market advantages.

Unlike joint ventures, strategic alliances do not typically involve sharing costs, risks, management, or even profits. Many executives and management consultants predict that few companies in the 21st century will succeed in the global market by going it alone,[77] and most will need to form strategic alliances. Small businesses involved in strategic alliances can derive a significant portion of their revenue as a direct result of the alliance.[78]

Strategic alliances can be flexible, and they can be effective between firms of vastly differing sizes. For example, Motorola, a large communications equipment manufacturer, once entered into a strategic alliance with a Canadian firm with only six employees. In light of the worldwide economic crisis of 2008–2009, financing firm Guidant Financial Group and the Entrepreneur's Source, a career and business coaching company, formed a strategic alliance to provide resources to small business owners and those wishing to become entrepreneurs.[79]

FOREIGN DIRECT INVESTMENT

Foreign direct investment (FDI) is the buying of permanent property and businesses in foreign nations. In 2008, FDI in the United States totaled $325.3 billion.[80] Figure 11.10 shows the countries with the most FDI in the U.S. in 2008. As the size of a foreign market expands, many firms increase FDI and establish a foreign subsidiary. A **foreign subsidiary** is a company that is owned in a foreign country by the home company, which is called the *parent company*. Such a subsidiary would operate much like a domestic firm in the foreign nation, with production, distribution, promotion, pricing, and other business functions under the control of the foreign subsidiary's management.

> **Foreign direct investment (FDI)** The buying of permanent property and businesses in foreign nations.
>
> **Foreign subsidiary** A company owned in a foreign country by another company, called the parent company.

The legal requirements of both the country where the parent firm is located (called the *home country*) and the foreign country where the subsidiary is located (called the *host country*) must be observed. The primary advantage of a foreign subsidiary is that the home company maintains complete control over any technology or expertise it may possess. The major shortcoming associated with creating a subsidiary is that the parent company must commit a large amount of funds and technology within foreign boundaries. Should relations with the host country falter, the firm's assets could be taken over by the foreign government.

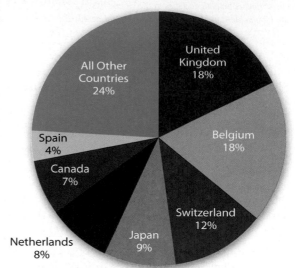

Study Alert

A multinational corporation manufactures and markets products in many different countries, and it has multinational stock ownership and multinational management.

Expropriation When a host government takes over a foreign subsidiary in a country.

Multinational corporation An organization that manufactures and markets products in many different countries and has multinational stock ownership and multinational management.

In addition to its U.S. stores, Build-A-Bear Workshops operate stores in Australia, Denmark, England, Japan, South Korea, France, and Taiwan.

Such a takeover is called an **expropriation**. Obviously, creating a subsidiary might not be the best course of action for a smaller business; however, as small companies grow, this option for global business could become more feasible.

The consumer products giant Nestlé is an example of a major firm with many foreign subsidiaries. The Swiss-based company bought the brands Ralston Purina, Chef America (maker of Hot Pockets), and Dreyer's Ice Cream in the United States, as well as Perrier in France.[81] The Dutch company Unilever spent millions of dollars to acquire the Ben & Jerry's brand of ice cream as a foreign subsidiary in the United States,[82] and it continues to look for similar opportunities around the globe.

Nestlé and Unilever are also examples of multinational corporations. A **multinational corporation** manufactures and markets products in many different countries, and it has multinational stock ownership and multinational management. Multinational corporations are typically extremely large corporations, but not all large firms involved in global business are multinationals. For example, even a business that literally exports everything it produces, thus deriving 100 percent of its sales and profits globally, isn't necessarily a multinational corporation. Only firms that have manufacturing capacity or some other physical presence in different nations can truly be called multinational.

Becoming involved in global business requires

Figure 11.10 The Countries with the Most FDI in the United States in 2008

United Kingdom 18%

Belgium 18%

Switzerland 12%

Japan 9%

Netherlands 8%

Canada 7%

Spain 4%

All Other Countries 24%

*2008 data preliminary
Source: Bureau of Economic Analysis, International Transactions Accounts

selecting a market-entry strategy that best fits the goals of the business. As you can see, the different strategies discussed here reflect the different levels of ownership, financial commitment, and risk a company can assume. Whatever operating strategy a particular business chooses, it's always important to remain aware of key market forces that will affect the business's ability to trade in global markets. That's the topic of the next section.

[BUS] connections

1. Why would a firm choose to export rather than become involved in a joint venture?
2. If you ran a small candy-manufacturing business, what would be the best way to get involved in global business?
3. What are the advantages and disadvantages of creating a subsidiary?

>> Forces Affecting Trade in Global Markets

Succeeding in any business takes work and effort because challenges exist in all markets. Understandably, the hurdles are higher and more complex in global markets than in domestic ones. Global businesses must deal with differences in sociocultural forces, economic and financial forces, legal and regulatory forces, and physical and environmental forces. These forces affect any business—big or small—that is entering foreign markets. Managers must be aware of these forces when making strategic decisions.

SOCIOCULTURAL FORCES

The term **culture** refers to the set of values, beliefs, rules, and institutions held by a specific group of people.[83] Primary components of a culture can include social structures, religion, manners and customs, values and attitudes, language, and personal communication. If you hope to get involved in global trade, you must be aware of the cultural differences among nations.

Culture The set of values, beliefs, rules, and institutions held by a specific group of people.

Ethnocentricity An attitude that one's own culture is superior to other cultures.

Different nations have very different ways of conducting business, and unfortunately, American businesses have often failed to adapt to those ways. In fact, American businesspeople are frequently accused of **ethnocentricity**, which is an attitude that one's own culture is superior to all others.

In contrast, many foreign businesses have adapted well to U.S. culture. Think of how effectively German and Japanese carmakers have adapted to Americans' wants and needs in the auto industry—today, the Japanese automaker Toyota attributes 70 percent to 80 percent of its sales revenues to the American market.[84] Business and economics students at China's Xiamen University are required to take golf lessons,[85] because many business transactions in the United States are completed on the golf course.

Religion

Religion is an important part of any society's culture, and it can have a significant impact on business operations. In fact, religion may be the most important of all the sociocultural forces. Consider the violent clashes that have occurred among religious communities in India, Pakistan, Northern Ireland, and the Middle East—clashes that have wounded these areas' economies. Unfortunately, sometimes companies fail to consider the religious implications of their business decisions. For example, both McDonald's and Coca-Cola offended Muslims in Saudi Arabia by putting the Saudi Arabian flag on their packaging. The flag's design contains a passage from the Koran, Islam's sacred scripture, and Muslims believe that its text should never be thrown away.[86]

In a classic story, a U.S. manager in Islamic Pakistan toured a new plant under his control. While the

Figure 11.11 Oops! Did We Say That?

A global marketing strategy can be very difficult to implement. Consider the problems these well-known companies encountered in global markets.

- PepsiCo attempted a Chinese translation of "Come alive; you're in the Pepsi generation" that read to Chinese customers as "Pepsi brings your ancestors back from the dead."

- Coors Brewing Company provided its slogan "Turn it loose" in Spanish and found that it translated as "Suffer from diarrhea."

- Perdue Chicken used the slogan "It takes a strong man to make a tender chicken," which was interpreted in Spanish as "It takes an aroused man to make a chicken affectionate."

- KFC's slogan "Finger-lickin' good" was understood in Japanese as "Bite your fingers off."

- On the other side of the translation glitch, Electrolux, a Scandinavian vacuum manufacturer, tried to sell its products in the U.S. market with the slogan "Nothing sucks like an Electrolux."

plant was in full operation, he went to his office to make some preliminary production forecasts. Suddenly all the machinery in the plant stopped. The manager rushed out, suspecting a power failure, only to find his production workers on their prayer rugs. Upon learning that Muslims are required to pray five times a day, he returned to his office and lowered his production estimates. Do you think the manager should have done the research in advance to know and understand such cultural aspects?

Human Resource Management

Understanding sociocultural differences is important when managing employees. In Latin American countries, workers believe managers are in positions of authority to make decisions about the well-being of the

Thinking Critically

>> India: A Growing Link in the Global Supply Chain

India is already a huge player in the global marketplace, and certain government initiatives, reduced bureaucratic constraints, and greener alternatives to fossil fuels could propel the nation to an even greater presence in global supply-chain partnerships. In this article, Samir Das discusses the current manufacturing and engineering capacity of India and the government's role in building a positive business environment.

With more than 500,000 new engineering graduates each year, India is in a strong position to be an engineering powerhouse. While India is one of the biggest players in the services and information technology sector, the same cannot be said of [its] supply chain and engineering capability. India's manufacturing exports still amount to less than 10 percent of GDP; more than one-third of China's GDP comes from manufacturing.

Bureaucratic hurdles and a tough approvals system for setting up new businesses are not as severe as in the past, but they continue to create bottlenecks. Land acquisition is a major hindrance to setting up new plants. Illiteracy and unskilled labor are disincentives to organizations that thrive on high productivity. So, too, are infrastructure problems such as clogged ports and roads, power failures, and water shortages. In spite of these many challenges, India is slowly but surely making a mark in the global supply chain.

India currently imports nearly two-thirds of its crude oil. With volatile oil and gas prices worldwide, self-sufficiency in energy is a national imperative. The Indian government has come up with a National Exploration Licensing Policy, or NELP, under which exploration and production companies have acquired exploration blocks. Oil refining companies in India have world-class capabilities, but the government's oil subsidy policy and differential pricing has [sic] been hurting their bottom line. Future growth in the oil and gas sector depends on new discoveries. To be more self-sufficient and globally competitive, India needs to shift from pricey crude imports to higher volumes of Indian crude.

India also is looking toward adapting cheaper, greener alternatives, such as liquefied natural gas, biofuels, and hydrogen energy. However, for this movement to pick up momentum, the government needs to offer more incentives for research and adoption of these fuels.

India is one of the world's leading iron ore exporters, but Indian steel manufacturers have had trouble obtaining it. Only a handful of manufacturers have their own captive iron ore mines; the rest depend on government-owned mines. To drive growth in the Indian steel industry, the government should encourage investment in fresh mining of iron ore, coal, and gas. The government should also formulate a policy to encourage investors to buy (or lease) iron ore and coking coal deposits abroad. In the short term, the government should narrow the supply gap by diverting some iron ore exports to domestic steel producers.

Source: Samir Das, "India: A Growing Link in the Global Supply Chain," *BusinessWeek*, April 10, 2009, http://www.businessweek.com/globalbiz/content/apr2009/gb20090410_901489.htm (accessed September 3, 2009).

QUESTIONS

1. How can India take better advantage of its successes in the services and information technology sector to improve its position in global supply-chain management?

2. How do you think the Indian government could further enhance the nation's business environment?

The euro officially became the common currency of most of the members of the EU on January 1, 2002, replacing the mark, franc, lira, peseta, and other former currencies.

while; according to research conducted by Foreign Currency Direct, 29 percent of small firms trading globally lose money due to exchange rates.[98]

The effects of currency valuation can be especially harsh for developing economies. Often, the only possibility for trade in many developing nations is through one of trade's oldest forms: *bartering*, the exchange of merchandise for other merchandise or service for service, with no money involved.[99] **Countertrading** is a complex form of bartering in which several countries may be involved, each trading goods for goods or services for services. It has been estimated that countertrading accounts for 25 percent of all global exchanges.[100]

Consider this example: The Jamaican government wants to buy vehicles from Ford Motor Company in exchange for Jamaican bauxite, a mineral compound that is a source of aluminum ore. Ford doesn't need bauxite, but it does need platinum, a precious metal used to make catalytic converters for its cars. In a countertrade agreement, Ford may trade the vehicles to Jamaica, which trades its bauxite to South Africa, a country that mines platinum. South Africa then trades its platinum to Ford. This countertrade is thus beneficial to all three parties. With many countries still in the developing stage, there is no question that countertrading will continue in global markets throughout this century. Trading products for products helps businesses avoid some of the financial problems and currency constraints that exist in global markets.

Having a thorough understanding of the economic conditions, currency fluctuations, and countertrade opportunities in global markets is vital to a company's

Countertrading A complex form of bartering in which several countries may be involved, each trading goods for goods or services for services.

success. In financing export operations in the United States, banks have traditionally been the best source of the capital needed for global investment. However, when U.S. banks are unwilling to provide export financing, exporters often turn to foreign banks and other sources for financing. This is especially true for small and medium-sized businesses, which sometimes must creatively scour the globe to secure financing.

LEGAL AND REGULATORY FORCES

In any economy, both the conduct and direction of business are firmly tied to the legal and regula-

Figure 11.12 Countries Where Bribery and Unethical Business Practices Are Commonplace

1. Somalia
2. Myanmar
3. Iraq
4. Haiti
5. Afghanistan
6. Sudan
7. Guinea
8. Chad
9. Equatorial Guinea
10. Congo, Democratic Republic

Source: "2008 Corruption Perceptions Index," Transparency International, http://www.transparency.org/news_room/in_focus/2008/cpi2008/cpi_2008_table (accessed September 1, 2009).

tory environment. In the United States, for example, federal, state, and local laws and other government regulations have a strong effect on business practices. In global markets, no central system of law exists, so several groups of laws and regulations may apply. This makes the task of conducting global business extremely difficult; the myriad laws and regulations in global markets are often inconsistent or completely different. Important legal questions related to antitrust rules, labor relations, patents, copyrights, trade practices, taxes, product liability, child labor, prison labor, and other issues are written and interpreted differently in each nation.[101]

American businesspeople are required to follow U.S. laws and regulations when conducting business

Real World Apps

After reading her Business Now textbook's chapter on business in global markets, Samantha has a better grasp on the concept of globalization. Trade is without boundaries, and countries and markets that were isolated in the past are now viable, even for small businesses like her own. Decreased transportation costs, coupled with lower labor costs and tax incentives, allow increased expansion possibilities.

Samantha can choose a few different paths to expand her business; for example, she may choose to export her products or services, license them to other companies, franchise her concept, or turn to contract manufacturers to create upholstery fabrics based on her designs. Based on what she's learned so far, she thinks that exporting her products might be her best first move. Later on, as her business grows, she will seek contract manufacturers to manufacture and sell her products in other countries. Before she decides which foreign locations to expand into, she'll do some further research into tariffs and trade agreements.

Understanding legal restrictions and opportunities is just part of the overall puzzle of international trade. Samantha will also research the various cultures and traditions in the markets she's thinking about entering to ensure that her products are acceptable to those potential consumers. After all, although globalization has made trade easier and opened or eliminated physical boundaries, cultural boundaries can be much harder to breach.

All the additional information Samantha has read about global business makes her realize that her business is ready for the next step. There's a big world waiting to be discovered, and Samantha feels like a pioneer!

globally. Sometimes U.S. laws, such as the Foreign Corrupt Practices Act of 1978, can create competitive disadvantages for American businesspeople when competing with foreign competitors.[102] This particular law specifically prohibits "questionable" or "dubious" payments to foreign officials in order to secure business contracts—which runs contrary to beliefs and practices in many countries, where corporate or government bribery is not only acceptable but also perhaps the only way to secure a lucrative contract.[103]

Figure 11.12 shows a partial list of countries where bribery or other unethical business practices are most common. Fortunately for U.S. companies, the Organization for Economic Cooperation and Development is leading a global effort to fight corruption and bribery in foreign markets.

PHYSICAL AND ENVIRONMENTAL FORCES

Certain physical and environmental forces can also have an important impact on a company's ability to

Kazahkstan extracts over 63 million tons of oil each year. Its oil field in the Caspian Sea is expected to extract 3 million barrels of oil per day by 2015.

conduct business in global markets. In fact, technological constraints may make it difficult—or perhaps impossible—to build a large presence in the global market. For example, the transportation and storage industries in some developing countries are so primitive that distribution in these nations is made extremely difficult, if not impossible. This is especially true with regard to food, which can spoil before reaching the market. Compound this challenge with a lack of clean, running water or effective sewer systems, and you can see how difficult it would be to operate a business in such a region.

American exporters must also be aware that certain technological differences affect the nature of exportable products. For example, residential electrical systems in most developing countries do not match those of U.S. homes, in kind or capacity. An American appliance manufacturer obviously would have to take this fact into consideration, and that adds cost to the development of a product. Computer and Internet use in many developing countries is thin or nonexistent. For example, the popularity of Web sites like Facebook and YouTube is growing quickly in developing nations like Turkey, Indonesia, India, and Brazil, but these businesses are finding it more costly to operate in these nations because of the unreliability of their infrastructure.[104] These facts make for a tough business environment in general, and for e-commerce in particular.

THE FUTURE OF GLOBAL TRADE

Global trade opportunities grow more interesting each day. New and expanding markets present great potential for trade and development. Changes in technology also have changed the landscape of global trade, as businesses find that many foreign markets are often no further than a click away. Let's look briefly at issues that are certain to influence global markets in the 21st century.

Advances in communication technology have made distant global markets instantly accessible. The lure of more than 6.7 billion consumers is hard to pass up. Nowhere is the lure of global markets keener than in the developing countries of Asia—particularly China, now that its fast-growing economy is shifting its economic philosophy from central planning to free markets.[105] During the period of turmoil in the U.S. stock markets in late 2008 and early

Russia is a prize coveted by global traders. Like China, Russia presents enormous opportunities. Philip Morris, Bristol-Myers Squibb, and Gillette are multinational firms with manufacturing facilities in Russia, and PepsiCo has been doing business in Russia for many years. Oil giants Chevron and ExxonMobil are hard at work in Russia's Caspian Sea in an effort to find new oil reserves. The United States was the eighth-largest investor in Russia during the first half of 2009.[108] However, severe political and social problems still persist in Russia and in many of the other nations that were formerly states in the Soviet Union. Even so, for many businesses, Russia's 142 million potential customers who crave American goods represent an opportunity that's too good to pass up.[109]

Like countless other industries, the health care industry is changing radically as a result of globalization. Today, many medical professionals train in the U.S. and "export" their educations back to their home countries. Others decide to work and live in the U.S.

2009, the Chinese stock market proved to be more stable. In fact, China's real estate, auto, and industrial industries witnessed growth between February and June 2009, while the same industries languished or worsened in the United States. As a result of these factors, WTO increased its GDP growth estimates for China in 2009 from 6.5 percent to 7.2 percent.[106]

Many multinational companies, including General Motors, Caterpillar, and Levi Strauss, have invested heavily in China's future. Not long ago, investments in China were considered to be very risky and not worth the effort, but today U.S. companies are flocking to China. Some economists suggest that soon, U.S. foreign direct investment could surpass exports as the primary means by which U.S. companies deliver goods to China.

The economic crisis of 2008 and 2009 caused foreign direct investment in China to slip—during the period from January to July 2009, China's FDI was 20.3 percent lower than it had been a year earlier. However, in the long term, the country's FDI is expected to grow.[107] With 338 million users, China passed the U.S. as the world's largest Internet market in 2008. Concerns remain about China's one-party political system, its human rights policies, its growing trade imbalance with the United States, and difficulties in its financial markets, but Congress granted China permanent normal trading rights in 2000, thus paving the way for China's 2001 acceptance into the WTO. Still, many analysts warn that it may take a long time for profits to materialize for companies doing business in China.

While China, Russia, and Japan attract most of the attention in Asia, U.S. businesses are also investing in India, Taiwan, Indonesia, Thailand, Singapore, the Philippines, South Korea, and Malaysia. Technology has continued to grow at an amazing rate—in many cases making markets around the world instantly accessible. The growth of the Internet and advances in e-commerce enable companies worldwide to bypass normal distribution channels and reach vast markets—quickly, efficiently, and cheaply.

[BUS] connections

1. What are some forces that must be considered in global business? Give an example of a business consideration for each.
2. Which force affecting trade would be most important for an Internet-based business to consider? What about a business that manufactures paper products?
3. Why is it so important for businesspeople to consider the cultural aspects of global business?

For REVIEW >>

1. Understand the importance of global trade.
   - Global business refers to any activity that seeks to provide goods and services to others across national borders while operating at a profit. Just about any kind of product can be imported or exported. Exporting is selling products to other countries. Importing is buying products from other countries. Free trade is the movement of goods and services among nations without political or economic trade barriers.

2. Discuss the roles of comparative and absolute advantage in global trade.
   - Global trade is the exchange of goods and services across national borders, but exchanges between and among countries involve more than goods and services. The comparative advantage theory states that a country should sell to other countries those products that it produces most effectively and efficiently and buy from other countries those products that it cannot produce as effectively or efficiently. Absolute advantage is the advantage that exists when a country has a monopoly on producing a specific product or is able to produce it more efficiently than all other countries.

3. Discuss the two indicators for measuring global trade.
   - The balance of trade is the relationship of exports to imports. The balance of payments is the balance of trade plus other money flows such as tourism and foreign aid. Global trade also sometimes involves some unfair trade practices, such as dumping and gray market activities. Dumping is selling products for less in a foreign country than in your own country. The gray market refers to the flow of goods in a distribution channel or channels other than those intended by the manufacturer or licensor.

4. Explain different types of trade protections and trade agreements.
   - Trade protectionism is the use of government regulations to limit the import of goods and services. The key tools of protectionism are tariffs, import quotas, and embargoes. Tariffs are taxes on foreign products. Protective tariffs raise the price of foreign products and protect domestic industries; revenue tariffs raise money for the government. Import quotas limit the number of products in certain categories that a nation can import. An embargo prohibits the importing or exporting of certain products. Nontariff barriers are restrictive standards that detail exactly how a product must be sold in a country. The GATT established an international forum for negotiating mutual reductions in trade restrictions. The WTO, which replaced the GATT, is an international organization that mediates trade disputes among nations. Common markets are regional groups of countries that have common external tariffs, no internal tariffs, and coordinated laws to facilitate exchange among member countries.

5. Discuss the different strategies for reaching global markets.
   - Ways of entering world trade include licensing, exporting, franchising, contract manufacturing, joint ventures and strategic alliances, and foreign direct investment. Licensing is a global strategy in which a firm (the licensor) allows a foreign company (the licensee) to produce its product in exchange for a fee (a royalty). Franchising differs from licensing in that where licensing might be used to sell a single product, franchising allows the use of an entire business concept, including packaging, how the good is manufactured, and the look and feel of the business. Contract manufacturing is a foreign country's production of private-label goods to which a domestic company then attaches its brand name or trademark. Joint ventures are partnerships in which two or more companies (often from different countries) undertake a major project. Strategic alliances are long-term partnerships between two or more companies established to help each company build competitive market advantages. Foreign direct investment is the buying of permanent property and businesses in foreign nations. A multinational corporation manufactures and markets products in many different countries, and it also has multinational stock ownership and multinational management.

6. Explain the forces affecting trade in the global market.
   - Potential stumbling blocks to world trade include sociocultural forces, economic and financial forces, legal and regulatory forces, and physical and environmental forces. Culture is the set of values, beliefs, rules, and institutions held by a specific group of people. Religion is an important part of any society's culture, and it can have a significant impact on business operations. Understanding sociocultural differences is important when managing employees. Sociocultural differences affect not only management behaviors, but also global marketing strategies. The exchange rate is the value of one nation's currency relative to the currencies of other countries. Changes in a nation's exchange rates can have important implications in global markets. In global markets, no central system of law exists, so several groups of laws and regulations may apply. The myriad laws and regulations in global markets are often inconsistent or completely different. Certain physical and environmental forces can also have an important impact on a company's ability to conduct business in global markets.

Key Terms

Absolute advantage

Balance of payments

Balance of trade

Common market

Comparative advantage
theory

Contract manufacturing

Countertrading

Culture

Dumping

Embargo

Ethnocentricity

European Union (EU)

Exchange rate

Exporting

Expropriation

Foreign direct investment
(FDI)

Foreign subsidiary

Free trade

General Agreement on
Tariffs and Trade (GATT)

Global business

Global trade

Gray market

Greenfield investment

Harmonized Tariff
Schedule

Import quota

Importing

Joint venture

Licensing

Multinational corporation

Nontariff barriers

North American Free Trade
Agreement (NAFTA)

Organization of the
Petroleum Exporting
Countries (OPEC)

Strategic alliance

Tariff

Trade deficit

Trade protectionism

Trade surplus

World Trade Organization
(WTO)

1. What are the primary components of culture discussed in this chapter? Rank order them from the most important to the least important, and discuss why you ranked them in that manner.

2. What are the advantages to having a free-trade zone, such as NAFTA? What are the disadvantages?

3. What are the sociocultural forces discussed in this chapter? Describe each in your own words. Why is it important to have an awareness of these forces before doing business in global markets?

4. In groups, discuss the following question: What are some of the dangers of ethnocentric thinking when doing business in global markets? Make a list of at least ten items.

5. In groups, discuss the following question: What are the advantages and disadvantages of trade protectionism? Name at least five of each. Based on your list, do you think protectionism is a good idea or a bad idea? Explain your response.

INTERNET IN >> Action

1. Visit http://www.worldbank.org/. Name two recent projects the World Bank has been involved in. How much funding did these projects receive? What is the purpose of the World Bank? Do you think the World Bank accomplishes its mission?

2. Visit http://hts.usitc.gov/ and view the list of categories of the Harmonized Tariff Schedule of the United States. Look up three products in the schedule and record the following information on each:
   a. Article description
   b. Unit of quantity
   c. General rate of duty
   d. Any special duty

larity among the values and standards of different groups for what is right and wrong. The Bible, Aristotle's *Ethics*, the Koran, and the *Analects* of Confucius, among many other texts, all include similar basic moral guidelines. These texts agree that integrity, respect for human life, self-control, honesty, courage, and self-sacrifice are "right," and cheating, cowardice, and cruelty are "wrong."

All of the world's major religions support a version of what's known as the Golden Rule: Do unto others as you would have them do unto you. You might think, then, that no matter where you live—anywhere in the world—ethics are the same. Practically speaking, this isn't always the case, because cultures intervene to cloud particular issues.

Keep in mind that ethics are not the same as the law. Generally, something that is **illegal** is also unethical, but the reverse is not always the case. *Illegal* means you could be fined or imprisoned by a court of law for engaging in a particular action, but unethical actions aren't always illegal. For example, stealing company funds is illegal, and if you're caught, you'd probably go to jail; such behavior is also obviously unethical. What about gossiping maliciously behind the backs of your coworkers? It's not illegal to gossip, but it might be considered unethical. Remember, ethical standards are right versus wrong behavior according to society. But each member of society is an individual with a different personal cultural background. That's why it's often difficult to understand what others perceive as being ethical or unethical.

> **Illegal** An act for which you could be fined or imprisoned.

In 1995, Michael Ovitz became president of the entertainment company Disney. After clashing with the company's chairman, Michael Eisner, Ovitz was fired 16 months later and walked away with a severance package that eventually reached $140 million. Disney based Ovitz's firing on its allegation that Ovitz used company money to buy luxuries and gifts for himself and his associates, an accusation Ovitz denied. Such

actions were not illegal but certainly could be considered unethical.[4]

APPROACHES TO ETHICAL DECISIONS

Ethics cannot always be based on law, nor is it sufficient to consider your own feelings, or "gut instinct," about what's right in every case. Rather, ethics must be based on some universally applied principles. The following discussion describes five approaches you can use when trying to make an ethical decision: the utilitarian approach, the rights approach, the fairness or justice approach, the common good approach, and the virtue approach.[5]

The giant accounting firm Arthur Andersen became famous for shredding Enron-related documents. While the Andersen employees shown here thought it was funny to give document shredding lessons at an Arthur Andersen Night before an Oregon baseball game in 2002, no one's laughing now. Andersen's 28,000 employees lost their jobs when the company was found guilty of obstructing the government's investigation of Enron. The verdict was later overturned.

The Utilitarian Approach

Some people believe ethical choices are ones that benefit the most people or those that harm the fewest people. In line with this thinking, ethical actions by corporations would benefit the most and harm the fewest stakeholders in that corporation—for example, its shareholders, its employees, its physical environment, its community, and its customers. This approach is focused on the consequences of actions, because it tries to do more good, and less harm.

The Rights Approach

Others believe that that the most ethical forms of behavior are those that pay the most attention to the moral rights of those affected by the behavior. Those who subscribe to this belief also believe that human beings have a fundamental right to dignity and to choose what they wish to do. Accordingly, their rights should be respected. These moral rights include the freedom to make personal choices, be treated honestly and fairly, be protected from harm, and be entitled to privacy, among others. It's also worth mentioning that the belief that people have these fundamental duties comes with a duty to respect the same rights among other people.

The Fairness or Justice Approach

Perhaps you believe that everyone should be treated the same, no matter what. Under this belief system, ethical actions would treat everyone the same, or at least in some sort of fair manner based on a standard. For example, if a group of people with the same title were paid the same salary unless one or more of the people reached a particular goal, in which case he or she would receive a bonus, they would receive equal treatment with an exception based on a fair standard.

The Common Good Approach

If you believe that everyone in a society is interconnected, and that betterment of the community should be the primary goal of ethical acts, you believe in the common good approach. People who subscribe to this belief place respect and compassion for others above other priorities when making ethical decisions. Of course, systems of laws, public services like police and fire departments, parks systems, health

care resources, and public education are all common good endeavors.

The Virtue Approach

One of the oldest approaches to ethical decision making is the idea that certain ideal virtues are inherent. These virtues, such as prudence, integrity, generosity, courage, self-control, fidelity, trust, and compassion, encourage people to be the very best people they can be—and that leads them to commit ethical acts. "Virtuous" people consider a decision by thinking about the kind of person they want to be, and deciding whether or not a particular decision is representative of that kind of person.

[BUS] connections

1. Think of a recent ethical decision you had to make. Reflect on your decision now. Do you still believe it was the right decision? Why or why not?

2. What are the challenges of ethical decision making?

3. Describe the five approaches to making ethical decisions.

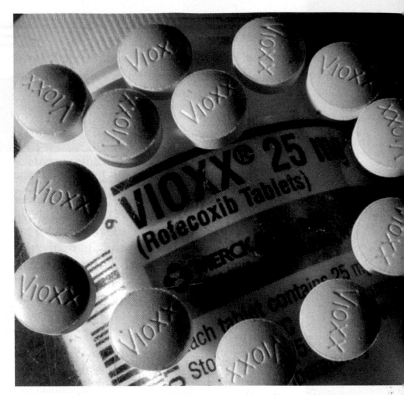

H. Dean Steinke blew the whistle on his former employer—drug company Merck, maker of Vioxx and Zocor—charging that it gave doctors excessive financial incentives to prescribe the drugs and discounts unavailable to government health programs. The case ended with a $671 million settlement and a $68 million reward to Steinke.

Figure 12.2 Strategies for Ethics Management

Features of Compliance-Based Ethics Codes	Features of Integrity-Based Ethics Codes
Ideal: Conform to outside standards (laws and regulations)	Ideal: Conform to outside standards (laws and regulations) and chosen internal standards
Objective: Avoid criminal misconduct	Objective: Enable responsible employee conduct
Leaders: Lawyers	Leaders: Managers with the aid of lawyers and others
Methods: Education, reduced employee discretion, controls, penalties	Methods: Education, leadership, accountability, decision processes, controls, and penalties

Integrity-based ethics codes move beyond legal compliance to create a "do-it-right" climate that emphasizes core values such as honesty, fair play, good service to customers, a commitment to diversity, and involvement in the community.

Trust and cooperation between workers and managers must be based on fairness, honesty, openness, and moral integrity. The same applies to relationships among businesses and between nations. A business should be managed ethically for many reasons: to maintain a good reputation; to keep existing customers and attract new ones; to avoid lawsuits; to reduce employee turnover; to avoid government intervention in the form of new laws and regulations controlling business activities; to please customers, employees, and society; and simply to do the right thing.[16]

Some managers think ethics is a personal matter—either individuals have ethical principles or they don't. These managers feel they are not responsible for an individual's misdeeds and that ethics has nothing to do with management. But a growing number of people think ethics has everything to do with management. Individuals do not usually act alone; they need the implied, if not the direct, cooperation of others to behave unethically in a corporation.

For example, there have been reports of cell phone service sales representatives who actually lie to get customers to extend their contracts—or some that even extend contracts without the customer's knowledge. Some phone reps intentionally hang up on callers to prevent them from canceling their contracts. Why do these sales reps sometimes resort to overly aggressive tactics? Because poorly designed incentive programs reward them for meeting certain goals, in some cases doubling or tripling their salaries with incentives. Do their managers explicitly tell them to deceive customers? No, but the message is clear. Overly ambitious goals and incentives create an environment in which mistakes like this can occur.[17]

Although ethics codes vary greatly, they can be classified into two major categories: *compliance-based ethics* and *integrity-based ethics*. See Figure 12.2.

Compliance-based ethics codes emphasize preventing unlawful behavior by increasing control and penalizing wrongdoers. Whereas compliance-based ethics codes are based on avoiding legal punishment, **integrity-based ethics codes** define an organization's guiding values, create an environment that supports ethically sound behavior, and stress a shared accountability among employees. In both codes of ethics, the company's leadership must set the pace for ethical standards. In other words, the leadership cannot act unethically and expect employees to act ethically.

Here are six steps many believe can improve a business's ethics:[18]

Compliance-based ethics codes Prevent unlawful behavior by increasing control and penalizing violations.

Integrity-based ethics codes Define the organization's guiding values and create an environment that supports ethically sound behavior.

1. Top management must adopt and unconditionally support an explicit corporate code of conduct.

2. Employees must understand that expectations for ethical behavior begin at the top and that senior management expects all employees to act accordingly.

3. Managers and others must be trained to consider the ethical implications of all business decisions.

4. An ethics office must be set up with which employees can communicate anonymously. **Whistleblowers**, insiders who report illegal or unethical behavior, must feel protected from retaliation. In 2002, President George W. Bush signed the Corporate and Criminal Fraud Accountability Act, also called the Sarbanes-Oxley Act, which is discussed in the next section.[19]

Whistleblowers Insiders who report illegal or unethical behavior.

5. Outsiders, such as suppliers, subcontractors, distributors, and customers, must be told about the ethics program. Pressure to put aside ethical considerations often comes from the outside, and it helps employees resist such pressure when everyone knows what the ethical standards are.

6. The ethics code must be enforced. It is important to back any ethics program with timely action if any rules are broken so all employees know that the code is serious. This last step is perhaps the most critical. No matter how well intended a company's ethics code is, it is worthless if it is not enforced. An ethics office must be set up. Phone lines to the office should also be established so that employees who don't necessarily want to be seen with an ethics officer can inquire about ethical matters anonymously.[20]

The Sarbanes-Oxley Act

The **Sarbanes-Oxley Act**, which is also called the Corporate and Criminal Fraud Accountability Act, passed in 2002. This piece of legislation has proven to be the most comprehensive act of its kind in regard to ethics. The bill passed into law with an overwhelming majority in Congress in response to the unethical behavior that occurred in the early part of the 2000s. Sarbanes-Oxley has been extremely important in requiring companies to act ethically.

Sarbanes-Oxley Act Legislation passed in 2002 that set new standards for ethical codes of conduct within organizations.

The act has several components. First, whistleblowers receive greater protection from retaliation. Second, the act set forth new penalties for boards of directors, accounting firms, and management if inaccurate or fraudulent financial reporting is found. In fact, CEOs must personally sign off on companies' financial statements, making them more accountable. Third, the act founded a new public agency that oversees, regulates, and inspects accounting firms.[21]

As vice president for corporate development at Enron, Sherron Watkins sensed something was wrong with the financial reporting. She "blew the whistle" on her bosses at Enron.

Although it would appear that the Sarbanes-Oxley Act affects only the leaders of a business, that's not true. Sarbanes-Oxley can affect people from all areas of a business.[22] For example, the act says that physical copies of certain paperwork must be kept for a minimum length of time. If a group of coworkers joined forces to clean out files and recycle old papers, they'd find the work a lot more challenging, because they'd have to weed out any papers that specifically applied to Sarbanes-Oxley. The bill can affect just about every profession, too. If an administrative assistant working for an executive caught the executive embezzling money from his company, the assistant would be protected as a whistleblower if he informed other managers about the behavior he'd witnessed.

Some observers feel Sarbanes-Oxley is flawed. For example, the act only applies to companies that are publicly traded on the stock market, which means that private companies, no matter how large, are not held to the same practices and standards as those that are publicly traded.[23] Another flaw is the financial and time cost to businesses to implement the act's provisions, especially the cost to small businesses. In fact, there are many companies that now specialize in selling software to help companies make the transition to this new law.

During the mid 1990s, TAP Pharmaceutical Products vice president Douglas Durand became suspicious that the company was colluding with doctors to make millions in profit from the Medicare program. He spent the next seven months compiling evidence against his employer and then quit his job, hoping that he'd get a large reward from the government for the information he provided. His plan worked; as a result of his whistleblowing, Durand received a $126 million reward.[24] See Figure 12.3 for more information about awards to whistleblowers.

As you can see, this law affects both big and small business and both investors and employees. It is one of the most far-reaching laws of its kind, and time will tell if it is effective in making the changes it was designed to make.

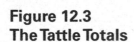

Figure 12.3
The Tattle Totals

Company	Government's Estimated Loss	Settlement Paid by Company	Whistle-blower Reward
AstraZeneca	$39 million	$355 million	$47 million
Schering-Plough	$293 million	$345 million	$32 million
Warner-Lambert	$150 million	$430 million	$25 million
TAP Pharmaceutical Products	$145 million	$885 million	$95 million

The feds have recouped billions from pharmaceutical fraud cases. The whistleblowers have done well, too.

....

Source: Neil Weinberg, "The Dark Side of Whistleblowing," *Forbes*, March 14, 2005, http://www.forbes.com/forbes/2005/0314/090.html (accessed September 1, 2009).

>> Corporate Social Responsibility

Corporate social responsibility is the concern businesses have for the welfare of society. It goes well beyond merely being ethical. Just as we all need to be good citizens and contribute what we can to society, corporations need to be good citizens as well. Of course, as can be said of many individuals, many corporations behave as good citizens only because they know it's good for business.

> **Corporate social responsibility** The level of concern a business has for the welfare of society.

There are three determinants or categories by which you can judge the social performance of a company. Those determinants are corporate philanthropy, corporate responsibility, and corporate policy.

CORPORATE PHILANTHROPY

Corporate philanthropy is one indicator of social responsibility. It includes charitable donations to nonprofit groups of

> **Corporate philanthropy** An indicator of social responsibility that includes charitable donations.

Figure 12.4 Corporate Charitable Donations in 2008

Andersen Corporation, a privately owned manufacturer of windows, patio doors, and storm doors, has partnered with Habitat for Humanity, making a commitment to build 100 homes during a five-year period throughout the United States and Canada.[27]

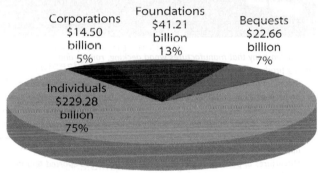

Corporations $14.50 billion 5%

Foundations $41.21 billion 13%

Bequests $22.66 billion 7%

Individuals $229.28 billion 75%

Source: American Association of Fundraising Counsel, Giving USA 2009 Report, www.aafrc.org (accessed September 5, 2009).

all kinds. Corporate charitable donations amount to billions of dollars every year (see Figure 12.4).[25] Strategic philanthropy involves companies making long-term commitments to one cause, such as McDonald's founding and support of Ronald McDonald Houses, which house families whose critically ill children require treatment away from home.[26] Philanthropy isn't limited to large corporations, as many small businesses also participate in corporate philanthropy.

CORPORATE RESPONSIBILITY

Corporate responsibility is all-encompassing, because it includes everything that has to do with acting responsibly within society, including hiring minority workers, making safe products, minimizing pollution, using energy wisely, and providing a safe work environment. Green Mountain

Corporate responsibility An indicator of social responsibility that includes the actions the company takes that could affect others.

Coffee Roasters is a perfect example of a company that behaves responsibly and has responsible methods. According to a 2007 survey in *Business Ethics* magazine, Green Mountain Coffee Roasters ranked as the top corporate citizen. The company takes a dozen employees a year on tour throughout the coffee-growing regions of South America, hoping the employees will come away with a sense of the hard work and risk taking that go into growing coffee.[28]

Small businesses also work for the welfare of society. While it's important to always manage customer relations, it is particularly important to do so during times of recession. Many small firms increase their charitable donations (particularly of time) and offer volunteer services when the economy is poor and business is slow. The owner of Divine Catering LLC, George Amorim, donated his catering services to several local charities during the summer of 2009 in hopes that his efforts would increase business in the fall of that year, when many people and organizations host holiday parties.[30]

McDonald's Corporation funds Ronald McDonald Houses, which allow families to stay near their hospitalized children for free for the duration of the child's care.

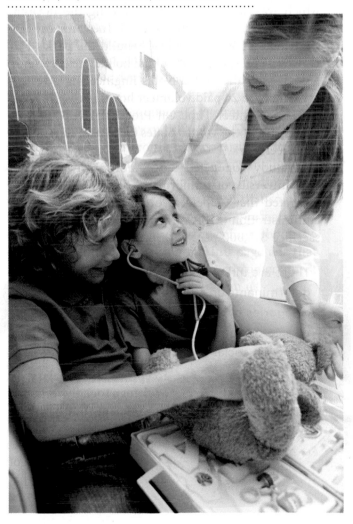

BREWING
a better world
GMCR

their family and friends. For example, let's suppose you run a publicly traded consulting firm. You know that your firm is about to lose its biggest client and that the loss will deeply affect your revenue. As a result, you decide to sell 20 percent of the stock you hold in your firm. This is an example of insider trading—you had inside knowledge others didn't have, and as a result, you benefited from it.

Insider trading isn't limited to company executives and their friends. Before it was publicly known that IBM was going to take over Lotus Development, an IBM secretary told her husband, who told two coworkers. Those coworkers told friends, relatives, and business associates—even a pizza delivery man. A total of 25 people ended up trading illegally on the insider tip within a six-hour period. When the deal was announced publicly, Lotus stock soared by 89 percent. One of the insider traders, a stockbroker who passed the information to a few customers, made $468,000 in profits. The U.S. Securities and Exchange Commission (SEC) filed charges against the secretary, her husband, and 23 others. Four defendants settled out of court by paying penalties that equaled twice their profits. Prosecutors are increasingly pursuing insider trading cases to ensure that the securities market remains fair and equally accessible to all.

Another form of social responsibility includes honest bookkeeping. World-Com, for example, admitted that intentional accounting "irregularities" made the company appear $4 billion more profitable than it actually was.[43]

EMPLOYEES

Businesses have several responsibilities to employees. First, they have a responsibility to create jobs if the businesses themselves want to grow. It has been said that the best social program in the world is a job. Once a company creates jobs, it has an obligation to see to it that hard work and talent are fairly rewarded. Employees also need to have realistic hope for a better future, which comes only through a chance for upward mobility. People need to see that integrity, hard work, goodwill, ingenuity, and talent will pay off. If a company treats employees with respect, employees usually will respect the company in return.

A **pension** is a promise of a steady income after retirement, assuming the employee has worked a minimum number of years with the company. Unfortunately, many companies are reneging on their promises to pay pensions to retirees. Struggling auto companies, such as Ford and General Motors, have had to make hard decisions about the millions of dollars they owe people through their pensions.

Pension A promise made by a company to pay a monthly dollar amount to employees who have worked a minimum number of years.

Given that replacing employees costs about 150 percent of their annual salaries, retaining workers is good for business as well as for morale.[44] When employees feel they have been treated unfairly, they often strike back. Getting even is one of the most powerful incentives for good people to do bad things. Not many disgruntled workers are desperate enough to resort to violence in the workplace, but a great number do relieve their frustrations in more subtle ways, such as blaming mistakes on others, not accepting responsibility for decision making, manipulating budgets and expenses, making commitments they in-

No more fabric spun by silkworms. Think recycled cola cans and fabric spun from corn. This picture shows Malden Mills, makers of Polartec Fabric, which is made with recycled plastic bottles.

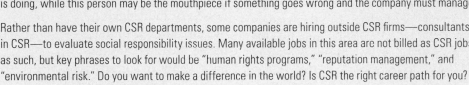
tend to ignore, doing the minimum needed to get by, and making results look better than they are. The loss of employee commitment, confidence, and trust in the company and its management can be very costly and entirely unnecessary.

In other words, social responsibility to employees means having a job at a company that pays fairly, keeps promises, and treats people with respect. Diversity is also part of a socially responsible company. According to the 2007 list of socially responsible companies in *Business Ethics* magazine, one of the reasons why Motorola was ranked in the top 10 was its diverse workforce.[45] On Motorola's Web site, the company breaks down the diversity of its workforce by gender and race, including a breakdown of its global senior management by gender.[46]

When the largest fire Massachusetts had seen in over 100 years broke out at Malden Mills, a textile company, its employees were devastated. Instead of taking the $300 million in insurance money and retiring, company owner Aaron Feuerstein decided to rebuild the business right where it had always been, in Lawrence, Massachusetts. He also paid employees their full salaries for 60 days after the fire.[47]

Sometimes downsizing is unavoidable, and companies must make cuts. There are some effective ways to ethically handle necessary reductions in the workforce. First, employers should be honest with their employees about the potential for future layoffs. Some fear that productivity will suffer or valued employees will resign if they are forewarned, but not being honest with employees generally results in the employees drawing much more dire conclusions than the actual truth. In general, employees should be informed of a layoff in person or, if they are out of town, on the phone. Firing an employee via e-mail is never a good idea. Employees should also be given considerable notice of a layoff well before their actual last day.[48]

Ethical companies often help their laid-off employees find new work as well. Some of these methods include contacting other potential employers in their networks to see if they have any openings, creating groups on social or professional networking sites like Facebook or LinkedIn to help former employees find work, providing excellent and honest references, helping former employees find service providers that can assist with résumé advice or other skills, and remaining in close contact with former employees.[49]

Not all environmental strategies are financially beneficial. In the early 1990s StarKist responded to consumer concerns about dolphins in the eastern Pacific dying in nets set out for yellowfin tuna. The company announced that it would sell only skipjack tuna, which don't swim near dolphins, from the western Pacific. Unfortunately, customers were unwilling to pay a premium for dolphin-safe tuna and considered the taste of skipjack inferior. Nor was there a clear environmental gain: For every dolphin saved in the eastern Pacific, thousands of immature tuna and dozens of sharks, turtles, and other marine animals died in the western Pacific fishing process.

SOCIETY AND THE ENVIRONMENT

One of business's major responsibilities to society is to create new wealth. More than a third of working Americans receive their salaries from nonprofit organizations that, in turn, receive their money from businesses. Foundations, universities, and other nonprofit organizations own billions of shares in publicly held companies. As those stock prices increase, more funds are available to benefit society.

Businesses are also partially responsible for promoting social justice. Business is perhaps the most crucial institution of civil society. Many companies believe they have a role in building communities that goes well beyond simply "giving back." To them, charity is not enough. Their social contributions include cleaning up the environment, building community centers, providing computer lessons, caring for the elderly, and supporting children from low-income families. For its own well-being, business depends on its employees being active in politics, law, churches and temples, the arts, charities, and so on.

ShoreBank, a Chicago-based banking and lending institution, was founded with a mission to invest "in people and their communities to create economic equity and a healthy environment."[50] Employees of the company volunteer in the communities served by the bank. Some employees who are active in the company's Working in the Schools Power Lunch program read to local third-grade students during their lunch hours.[51]

As concern about global warming has increased, the green movement has emerged in nearly every aspect of daily life. What makes a product green? Some believe a product's carbon footprint (the amount of carbon released during production, distribution, consumption, and disposal) defines how "green" it is. Many variables contribute to a product's carbon footprint. The carbon footprint of an ear of corn includes not only the carbon released by the fertilizer to grow the corn, but also the carbon in the fertilizer itself, the gas used to run the farm equipment and transport the corn to market, the electricity to make the plastic packages, and so on.

No specific guidelines define the carbon footprints of products, businesses, or individuals or outline how to communicate them to consumers. PepsiCo presents carbon information with a label on bags of cheese and onion potato chips, for example, that says "75 grams of CO_2." That's simple enough, but what does it really mean?[52]

The green movement has provided consumers with lots of product choices. However, making those choices means sorting through the many and confusing claims made by manufacturers. The noise in the marketplace challenges even the most dedicated green activists, but taking the easy route of buying what's most readily available violates the principles of the green movement.[53]

Businesses are also clearly taking responsibility for helping to make their own environment a better place. Environmental efforts may increase a company's costs, but they also may allow the company to charge higher prices, to increase market share, or both. For example, Ciba Specialty Chemicals, a Swiss textile dye manufacturer, developed dyes that require less salt than traditional dyes.[54] Since used dye solutions must be treated before they are released into rivers or streams, less salt and unfixed dye in the solution lowers the company's water-treatment costs. Patents protect Ciba's low-salt dyes, so the company can charge more for its dyes than other companies can charge for theirs. Ciba's experience illustrates that, just as a new machine enhances labor productivity, lowering environmental costs can add value to a business.

Seventh Generation, a company based in Burlington, Vermont, creates nothing but nontoxic and environmentally friendly products. Some of these products include nonchlorine bleach, chlorine-free baby diapers, phosphate-free cleaners, and 100 percent recycled paper towels and bathroom and facial tissue.[55] The company's products are more expensive than those of their less environmentally friendly com-

Green jobs "cannot be easily outsourced, say, to Asia," says the president of Green for All, an organization that promotes renewable energy. "If we are going to weatherize buildings, they have to be weatherized here. If you put up solar panels, you can't ship a building to Asia and have them put the solar panels on and ship it back. These jobs have to be done in the United States."

petitors, but Seventh Generation products are strong sellers nonetheless.[56]

The green movement has had a positive effect on the U.S. labor force. Emerging renewable-energy and energy-efficiency industries account for 8.5 million jobs; by 2030, these industries will create as many as 40 million more positions in engineering, manufacturing, construction, accounting, and management, according to a green-collar job report by the American Solar Energy Society.[57]

Environmental quality is a public good; that is, everyone gets to enjoy it regardless of who pays for it. The trick for companies is to find the right public good that will appeal to their target market. Figure 12.6 shows examples of socially responsible business activities. Many corporations are publishing reports that document their net social contribution. To do that, a company must measure its positive social contributions and subtract its negative social impacts, an interesting process that we will discuss in the next section.

Figure 12.6 Examples of Socially Responsible Business Activities

- Community-related activities such as participating in local fundraising campaigns, donating executive time to various nonprofit organizations (including local government), and participating in urban planning and development.

- Employee-related activities such as establishing equal opportunity programs, offering flextime and other benefits, promoting job enrichment, ensuring job safety, and conducting employee development programs.

- Political activities such as taking a position on nuclear safety, gun control, pollution control, consumer protection, and other social issues; and working more closely with local, state, and federal government officials.

- Support for higher education, the arts, and other nonprofit social agencies.

- Consumer activities such as ensuring product safety, creating truthful advertising, handling complaints promptly, setting fair prices, and conducting extensive consumer education programs.

Source: http://www.andersenwindows.com/servlet/Satellite/AW/Page/awGeneral-3/1104867941491 (accessed September 2, 2009).

Thinking Critically

>> **Corporate Social Responsibility in a Recession**

In challenging economic times, companies may need to reevaluate their social responsibility efforts. In the following article, Jack and Suzy Welch look at CSR in a recession, and how companies can and should adapt their plans depending on their financial circumstances.

In this enlightened day and age, whether times are good or bad, companies must be socially responsible. But tough economic conditions underscore a blunt reality. A company's foremost responsibility is to do well. That may sound politically incorrect, but the reason is inexorable. Winning companies create jobs, pay taxes, and strengthen the economy. Winning companies, in other words, enable social responsibility, not the other way around. And so, right now—as always—companies should be putting profitability first. It's the necessity that makes every other necessity possible.

We're not suggesting that companies abandon philanthropy and other charitable initiatives until the sky is blue again. We're only saying that corporate social responsibility—or CSR, as it has come to be known—needs to adapt to the circumstances. Companies can contribute to society with cash or products, giving away grants, goods, or their services to schools, homeless shelters, hospitals, and the like. Second, companies can focus their CSR on community involvement, by supporting employees who mentor students or volunteer for a myriad of causes. And third, companies can put CSR into their product and service strategies, focusing on green initiatives, for instance, or factoring environmental concerns into their manufacturing processes. When the tide is high, of course, many companies practice all three forms of CSR to some degree, or at least the first two. Not only is it the right thing to do but CSR can play a powerful part in recruiting talent, retaining talent, and keeping up morale. But how should companies think about CSR now, with margins narrowing, layoffs rampant, and consumers embracing the "new frugality"?

To start with, the contribution of cash and goods most likely has to decrease, if it hasn't already. In troubled times, cash flow is critical and delivering it often means survival. Moreover, when you're letting people go with one hand, doling out checks to "worthy causes" with the other is hard to rationalize. The decision for managers, then, is how to distribute a smaller pot.

Even in these uncertain times, CSR belongs in every company. But every company must face reality. You have to make money first to give it away.

Source: Jack and Suzy Welch, "Corporate Social Responsibility in a Recession," *BusinessWeek*, May 20, 2009, http://www.businessweek.com/magazine/content/09_22/b4133000801325.htm (accessed September 6, 2009).

QUESTIONS

1. Do you think companies should plan their social responsibility efforts around their intrinsic values? What about when times are tight? Discuss your response.

2. Describe an example of CSR that you're personally aware of. Does it make you more or less likely to purchase the company's products? Explain why or why not.

MEASURING SOCIAL RESPONSIBILITY

It's nice to talk about organizations becoming more socially responsible. It's also encouraging to see them make efforts toward creating safer products, cleaning up the environment, designing more honest advertising, and treating all people fairly. Keep in mind, however, that the majority of these efforts are made with the company's profit motive in mind. These companies know they will benefit by satisfying the demands of the customers.

A social audit is one measure of a company's social responsibility. A **social audit** is a systematic evaluation of a company's progress toward implementing programs that are socially responsible. Normally, a social audit is initiated by the company but handled by an outsider who specializes in this area. The idea is that positive actions (charitable donations, good hiring practices) will be subtracted from negative actions (layoffs, pollution), resulting in a net plus or minus. Another way to measure social responsibility would be to just record positive actions.

In addition to social audits conducted by companies themselves, there are four types of groups that serve as watchdogs regarding how well companies enforce their ethical and social responsibility policies:

> **Social audit** A systematic evaluation of a company's progress toward implementing programs that are socially responsible.

1. *Socially conscious investors* insist that a company extend its own high standards to its suppliers. Social responsibility investing (SRI) is on the rise, with approximately $2 trillion invested in SRI funds in the United States already.[59]

2. *Environmentalists* apply pressure by naming names of companies that don't abide by the environmentalists' standards. Here's an example: The Rainforest Action Network, Greenpeace International, Friends of the Earth, and the Center for Science in the Public Interest are all against the use of large-scale farmed palm oil, a type of vegetable oil made from palm trees. In order to keep up with the demand for this type of oil, farmers are burning forests to expand their plantations. Environmentalist groups are pushing companies, such as Nabisco, Kellogg's, and General Mills, to buy their palm oil from organic producers.[60]

3. *Union officials* hunt down labor law violations and force companies to comply in order to avoid negative publicity.

4. *Customers* make buying decisions based on their social conscience. Among people who responded to a recent survey, 55 percent make special efforts to buy from retailers with green reputations, 74 percent buy environmentally friendly products, and 60 percent are willing to pay more for them.[61]

Exactly what these groups are looking for changes as constantly as the worldview changes. For example, until September 11, 2001, no group formally screened publicly traded companies to determine potential links to terrorism or the spread of weapons of mass destruction. Now some groups have begun to look at companies that may be even peripherally linked to terrorist organizations. It isn't enough for a company to be ethical and socially responsible—it must also convince its customers of its efforts, as well.

Rhino Entertainment is a vintage music and video distributor that has a simple mission: "To put out some great stuff, have some fun, make some money, learn from each other, and make a difference wherever we can." Individual staff members are assigned to oversee community and environmental activities. The company has bins for can and paper recycling, as well as clothing donations, throughout its offices. Employees also receive an hour off for every hour they spend volunteering.[58] The company budgets a percentage of its revenues to go to charities that empower groups to help themselves. By promoting "doing the right thing" in its company, Rhino ensures that society benefits from its business as well as other social programs.

[BUS] connections

1. Identify the key stakeholders in a business, and name at least two social responsibility concerns for each of these stakeholders.
2. How can a company be responsible toward the environment and be profitable at the same time?
3. What are social audits? Do they motivate companies to act responsibly? Why or why not?

>> Ethics and Social Responsibility on a Global Scale

For many years, concern has grown about the ethics of purchasing diamonds mined in war zones. In fact, the proceeds from the sales of many of these diamonds are used to finance the war effort. These diamonds have been called "blood diamonds" or "conflict diamonds." In 2000, representatives from a group of diamond-producing African nations met in Kimberley, South Africa, to determine a way to stop the traffic of conflict diamonds. The result of that summit, the Kimberley Process, was approved by the United Nations in 2002.[62]

As discussed in the last section, it's in the best interest of companies to be socially responsible, as it creates more loyalty among customers, shareholders, and employees. Socially responsible behavior also benefits society, both at home and abroad.

Ethical problems and issues of social responsibility are not unique to the United States. Top business and government leaders in Japan were caught in a major "influence-peddling" (read: bribery) scheme in Japan.[63] Similar charges have been brought against top officials in South Korea, the People's Republic of China, Italy, Brazil, Pakistan, and Zaire. What's new about the moral and ethical standards by which these government leaders are being judged? They're much stricter than they've been in previous years, and top leaders are now being held to a higher standard. In fact, the United States is aggressively prosecuting bribes-for-business violations.[64]

Government leaders are not the only ones being held to higher standards. Many American businesses are demanding socially responsible behavior from their international suppliers by making sure they and *their* suppliers do not violate U.S. human rights and environmental standards.

For example, Sears will not import products made by Chinese prison labor. The clothing manufacturer Phillips–Van Heusen said it would cancel orders from suppliers that violate its ethical, environmental, and human rights codes. Dow Chemical expects its suppliers to conform to tougher American pollution and safety laws, rather than the local laws of the

---

YOUNG BLOOD

Miller's Cajun Foods, a New Orleans, Louisiana–based business that was founded in 1922, supplies specialty food products to restaurants and grocery stores nationwide. Chris Perlee, the grandson of the company's founder, started working for the company when he was only 16 years old. Twenty years later, his father retired, and Chris took over as CEO.

Because of its unique and tasty quality products, Miller's has earned a strong reputation, but its excellence stretches beyond just making good food. After Hurricane Katrina, the company quickly rebuilt its headquarters and extended its outreach to help surrounding communities as well. Miller's was selected by a leading business magazine as one of the best places to work in the region.

However, an economic downturn caused sales to fall and manufacturing costs to skyrocket. Board members pressured Chris to develop a plan to significantly reduce costs. They told Chris that stockholders were becoming impatient and believed drastic changes needed to be made in order to increase profits.

◄ ETHICAL   DILEMMA ►

If you could hire younger employees to replace older, more expensive employees, would you? Why or why not?

Chris had concerns about several of the board's proposals. He believed they could damage the company's reputation and hurt certain groups of stakeholders. For example, they considered using cheaper and lower-quality ingredients and not changing the products' prices. Chris believed suppliers and customers would notice the difference, which would eventually drive sales down even further. The board also proposed laying off some longtime employees, and instead hiring younger, less-experienced people to replace them, and cutting other employees' hours down to part-time so the company wouldn't have to pay for their health insurance.

Chris believed these proposals could hurt the company and its stakeholders, but speaking out against them could affect his future with the company. He began to think about how he could ethically deal with this situation.

QUESTIONS

1. What are the ethical dilemmas Chris faces? Are any or all of the suggestions by the board ethical?
2. What are Chris's alternatives? What would be the consequences of each alternative?

Real World Apps

Emanuel realizes the complexity of the current marketplace has changed not only the players but also the rules. Ethics are the standards of moral behavior, but everyone defines moral behavior differently. To create an ethical workplace, the code of conduct he is creating with his team must define acceptable behavior for their organization and its employees.

Emanuel now understands the importance of the company's code of conduct. The employees' individual actions define the overall ethical image that customers, vendors, and varied stakeholders will see. Top-down support will be necessary for successful implementation of the new code of conduct as well.

It will be necessary to get input from the other employees regarding what issues concern them, and what they believe the company's social responsibility to be. Emanuel knows that without the support of the employees, the change won't be successful. He also knows that the new code of conduct will have to be enforced.

The Sarbanes-Oxley Act set the standards for ethical codes in organizations and provided protection for those reporting unethical acts. Emanuel understands that his organization also needs to set rules for reporting infractions and protecting those who report them to comply with the rules of Sarbanes Oxley and other important legislation.

countries in which they operate. Despite the fact that McDonald's denied rumors that one of its suppliers allowed its cattle to graze on cleared rainforest land, the company banned the practice anyway.[65] High-end jewelers Cartier and Tiffany no longer purchase gems from suppliers in Myanmar because of its government's suppression of protests by monks and students.[66] Barrick Gold expects its suppliers to behave in a socially responsible manner, including reviewing Barrick's Supplier Code of Ethics policy, documenting that they agree to abide by the code, and completing a self-assessment scorecard.[67]

The justness of requiring international suppliers to adhere to U.S. ethical standards is not as clear-cut as you might think. Is it always ethical for companies to demand compliance with the standards of their own

countries? What about countries where child labor is an accepted part of society, and families depend on their children's salaries for survival? What about foreign companies doing business in the United States? Should they expect American companies to comply with their ethical standards? What about multinational corporations? Since they span different societies, do they not have to conform to any one society's standards? Why is Sears applauded for not importing goods made in Chinese prisons, when there are many enterprises in the United States that use prison labor? None of these questions is easy to answer, but they give you some idea of the complexity of social responsibility issues in international markets.

To identify some form of common global ethics and fight corruption in global markets, partners in the Organization of American States signed the Inter-American Convention against Corruption. The United Nations adopted a formal condemnation of corporate bribery, as did the European Union and the Organization for Economic Cooperation and Development. The International Organization for Standardization (ISO) plans to publish a standard on social responsibility called ISO 26000, with guidelines on product manufacturing, fair pay rates, appropriate employee treatment, and hiring practices.[68] These standards are advisory only and will not be used for certification purposes. The formation of a single set of international rules governing multinational corporations is unlikely in the near future. In many places, "fight corruption" remains just a slogan, but even a slogan is a start.

[BUS] connections

1. What are two ethical challenges businesses face when operating overseas?
2. What can consumers do to ensure that companies are acting socially responsibly, both at home and abroad?
3. Do you think it's right that American companies must apply the same ethical standards they use domestically when conducting business globally?

For REVIEW >>

1. Define ethics and understand the approaches to making ethical decisions.
   - Ethics are an understanding of the standards of moral behavior—behavior toward others that is accepted by society as right versus wrong. There are five approaches you can use when trying to make an ethical decision: the utilitarian approach, the rights approach, the fairness or justice approach, the common good approach, and the virtue approach. The utilitarian approach suggests that the most ethical choices are ones that benefit the most people or those that harm the fewest people. The rights approach suggests that the most ethical forms of behavior are those that pay the most attention to the moral rights of those affected by the behavior. The fairness or justice approach suggests that everyone should be treated the same, or at least in some sort of fair manner based on a standard. The common good approach suggests that everyone in a society is interconnected and that betterment of the community should be the primary goal of ethical acts. The virtue approach suggests that certain virtues, such as generosity, compassion, and honesty, are inherent and that these virtues lead people to think of the ethical repercussions of their acts.

2. Understand the questions to ask in personal ethical decision making and list the six steps in setting up a corporate ethics code.
   - When making ethical decisions, individuals should always consider the following three questions: (1) Is my proposed action legal? (2) Is it balanced? (3) How will it make me feel about myself? The six steps that should be followed when setting up a corporate ethics code are: (1) top management must adopt and unconditionally support an explicit corporate code of conduct; 2) employees must understand that expectations for ethical behavior begin at the top, and that senior management expects all employees to act accordingly; (3) managers and others must be trained to consider the ethical implications of all business decisions; (4) an ethics office, with which employees can communicate anonymously, must be set up; (5) outsiders, such as suppliers, subcontractors, distributors, and customers, must be told about the ethics program; and (6) the ethics code must be enforced.

3. Describe the indicators of corporate social responsibility.
   - There are three determinants or categories by which you can judge the social performance of a company: corporate philanthropy, corporate responsibility, and corporate policy. Corporate philanthropy includes charitable donations to nonprofit groups of all kinds. Corporate responsibility includes hiring minority workers, making safe products, minimizing pollution, using energy wisely, and providing a safe work environment. Corporate policy is the position a company takes on social and political, and sometimes internal, business ethics issues.

4. Examine corporate responsibility to various stakeholders and how social responsibility can be measured.
   - A business has many stakeholders, including its customers, investors, and employees, and society and the environment. Many believe consumers have four basic rights: (1) the right to safety, (2) the right to be informed, (3) the right to choose, and (4) the right to be heard. Customers prefer to do business with companies they trust and don't want to do business with companies they don't trust. Social responsibility to investors means (1) doing the right thing to make money for stockholders and (2) avoiding potential legal issues by trading stocks fairly and keeping accurate financial records. Businesses have a responsibility to create jobs if they wish to grow. If a company treats employees with respect, employees usually will respect the company in return. One of business's major responsibilities to society is to create new wealth. Businesses are also partially responsible for promoting social justice, and they are clearly taking responsibility for helping to make their own environment a better place.

5. Discuss ethics and social responsibility on a global level.
   - Ethical problems and issues of social responsibility are not unique to the United States. Government leaders are now being held to a higher standard, and they're not the only ones: Many U.S. businesses are demanding socially responsible behavior from their international suppliers by making sure they and *their* suppliers do not violate U.S. human rights and environmental standards. The justness of requiring international suppliers to adhere to American ethical standards is not clear-cut. The United Nations adopted a formal condemnation of corporate bribery, as did the European Union and the Organization for Economic Cooperation and Development. The International Organization for Standardization (ISO) plans to publish a standard on social responsibility called ISO 26000, with guidelines on product manufacturing, fair pay rates, appropriate employee treatment, and hiring practices. The formation of a single set of international rules governing multinational corporations is unlikely in the near future.

Key Terms

Compliance-based ethics codes

Corporate philanthropy

Corporate policy

Corporate responsibility

Corporate social responsibility

Ethics

Illegal

Insider trading

Integrity-based ethics codes

Pension

Sarbanes-Oxley Act

Social audit

Whistleblowers

1. What factors have shaped your personal ethics? Are ethics the same for everyone? Why or why not?

2. Do you think companies need to behave socially responsibly if they are earning profits? Why or why not?

3. Name at least three issues facing companies in the area of ethics and social responsibility today (hint: consider going to a search engine and reading newspaper articles). How would you expect companies to behave in these situations? Do you think the government needs to regulate business to ensure that they are more socially responsible?

4. In groups, discuss two companies you think are socially responsible. What actions make you feel this way? Next, discuss two companies you think are *not* socially responsible. What actions make you feel this way?

5. In groups, discuss the following situations to determine how you might behave if faced with these ethical dilemmas:

   a. A cashier hands you $5 extra in change at the grocery store

   b. You know a coworker is stealing products from your company, but she's also one of your best friends.

   c. You saw and heard your boss sexually harassing another employee.

   d. You received an extra $520 in your paycheck as a result of a mistake made by the accounting department.

1. Visit http://www.myfootprint.org. Follow the links to take the site's quiz.

   a. What is your carbon footprint?

   b. Was it smaller or bigger than expected?

   c. What changes can you make in your life to reduce your carbon footprint?

   d. What changes do you think businesses should make to reduce their carbon footprint? Name at least four.

2. Visit www.nike.com and review the site's "About Nike" page. What is the company doing to promote social responsibility? Do you think these efforts are effective?

Self-Assessment Exercises

BUSINESS CAREER QUIZ

Would You…?

Take this quiz by answering yes or no for each of the following questions:

1. ____ Y ____ N Speed if you are running late to an appointment?
2. ____ Y ____ N Pretend to be sick to get out of work when you really aren't?
3. ____ Y ____ N Download music or movies from the Internet without paying for them?
4. ____ Y ____ N Include false information on a résumé or application hoping it will get you a job?
5. ____ Y ____ N Copy a classmate's work to earn a better grade, or let someone copy your work?
6. ____ Y ____ N Use your work computer, which is only supposed to be used for work, to plan a vacation.
7. ____ Y ____ N Lie to a friend?
8. ____ Y ____ N Exaggerate your abilities in order to impress someone?
9. ____ Y ____ N Keep extra money handed to you by a bank teller or cashier?
10. ____ Y ____ N Fail to keep a promise?

Answers

The more questions you answer "no," the more ethical you are. For the questions you answered yes, consider why you answered the question that way. Do you think your reasons are justified?

Ethical Orientation Questionnaire

Please answer the following questions.

1. Which is worse?
   A Hurting someone's feelings by telling the truth
   B. Telling a lie and protecting someone's feelings

2. Which is the worse mistake?
   A. To make exceptions too freely
   B. To apply rules too rigidly

3. Which is it worse to be?
   A. Unmerciful
   B. Unfair

4. Which is worse?
   A. Stealing something valuable from someone for no good reason
   B. Breaking a promise to a friend for no good reason

5. Which is it better to be?
   A. Just and fair
   B. Sympathetic and feeling

6. Which is worse?

   A. Not helping someone in trouble.

   B. Being unfair to someone by playing favorites.

7. In making a decision, you rely more on

   A. Hard facts.

   B. Personal feelings and intuition.

8. Your boss orders you to do something that will hurt someone. If you carry out the order, have you actually done anything wrong?

   A. Yes.

   B. No.

9. Which is more important in determining whether an action is right or wrong?

   A. Whether anyone actually gets hurt.

   B. Whether a rule, law, commandment, or moral principle is broken.

Answers

To score: The answers fall in one of two categories, J or C. Count your number of J and C answers using this key:

1. A _ C; B _ J	4. A _ J; B _ C	7. A _ J; B _ C
2. A _ J; B _ C	5. A _ J; B _ C	8. A _ C; B _ J
3. A _ C; B _ J	6. A _ C; B _ J	9. A _ C; B _ J

What your score means: The higher your J score, the more you rely on an ethic of justice. The higher your C score, the more you prefer an ethic of care. Neither style is better than the other, but they are different. Because they appear so different, they may seem opposed to one another, but they're actually complementary. In fact, your score probably shows that you rely on each style to a greater or lesser degree. (Few people end up with a score of 9 to 0.) The more you can appreciate both approaches, the better you'll be able to resolve ethical dilemmas and to understand and communicate with people who prefer the other style.

An ethic of justice is based on principles like justice, fairness, equality, or authority. People who prefer this style see ethical dilemmas as conflicts of rights that can be solved by the impartial application of some general principle. The advantage of this approach is that it looks at a problem logically and impartially. People with this style try to be objective and fair, hoping to make a decision according to some standard that's higher than any specific individual's interests. The disadvantage of this approach is that people who rely on it might lose sight of the immediate interests of particular individuals. They may unintentionally ride roughshod over the people around them in favor of some abstract ideal or policy. This style is more common for men than women.

An ethic of care is based on a sense of responsibility to reduce actual harm or suffering. People who prefer this style see moral dilemmas as conflicts of duties or responsibilities. They believe that solutions must be tailored to the special details of individual circumstances. They tend to feel constrained by policies that are supposed to be enforced without exception. The advantage of this approach is that it is responsive to immediate suffering and harm. The disadvantage is that, when carried to an extreme, this style can produce decisions that seem not simply subjective, but arbitrary. This style is more common for women than men.

To learn more about these styles and how they might relate to gender, visit www.ethicsandbusiness.org/kg1.htm.

Source: Thomas I. White, Discovering Philosophy—Brief Edition, 1e, © Copyright 1996. Adapted with permission of Pearson Education, Inc., Upper Saddle River, NJ.

BONUS CHAPTER

MANAGING
YOUR FINANCES

After reading this chapter, you will be able to:

1 Describe the importance of education in making money and six steps to developing financial discipline.

2 Explain strategies for building a financial base.

3 Define the different types of insurance and how they can protect your financial base.

4 Describe strategies for effective retirement planning.

NANCY NELSON AND HUMANIX

At some point, most people have to create a personal budget. They do so by projecting expected income and expected expenses. If they're fortunate enough to have money left over, they'll probably put it into a savings account or a retirement fund or spend it on something special. But what happens when unexpected bills come up or when a financial crisis arises?

Like Nancy Nelson, president of the recruiting firm Humanix, the owners of some businesses offer direct loans to their employees. In October 2008, Nelson told her staff, "If you're finding yourself in a corner, where you can't see your way out of it, first look to us and see what we can do."

Since that October day, Humanix has extended more than $15,000 in loans to various employees. Each of the loans has been short term and interest free. One recruiter with the firm, Cindy McGinty, was forced to borrow $1,000 from Humanix to pay for car repairs after an accident; eight months later, she borrowed from the company again to finance expensive dental work. McGinty remarked, "They saved me."

Of course, people are individually responsible for their own finances, and employers like Humanix are unusual. You must keep careful track of your finances in order to keep your household financially secure. This bonus chapter will help you consider steps to reach a level of financial security. As you read through it, think about how you're currently managing your assets, and determine whether you can manage them more efficiently. Consider whether you have too much debt. Look for ways to save money.

Many financial advisers recommend that you should have a cushion of savings that equals approximately three to six months' worth of living expenses. You should make sure you have adequate insurance coverage for your life, home, health, and car, and you should be setting aside money for retirement. The younger you are when you begin to save for retirement, the more your money will grow—as you'll learn in this chapter.

Not everyone is lucky enough to work for a company like Humanix, which helps its employees out when life's inevitable financial crises come up. This bonus chapter will help you learn how to take care of yourself financially.

Questions

1. Create a budget for the next six months, including your anticipated income and expenses.

2. Do you usually use a credit card for your purchases? Discuss your answer with your peers.

3. When do you think you will retire? Are you already preparing for your retirement now? What steps are you taking toward saving for retirement? If you haven't yet begun to save, how and when do you plan to begin?

Source: John Tozzi, "Helping an Employee in a Personal Financial Crisis," *BusinessWeek*, July 28, 2009, http://www.businessweek.com/smallbiz/content/jul2009/sb20090728_320881.htm (accessed September 11, 2009).

- How can you become more financially disciplined?
- What types of investments should you consider?
- How can you protect your assets and plan for your retirement?

>> Financial Planning

In our capitalist society, money represents the means to an end. If that end goal is to take nice vacations, raise a family, invest in stocks and bonds, buy the goods and services you want, give generously to others, and retire with enough money to live out your years in comfort, you'll need to have some income. To get that, you'll need to get an education, work hard, save and invest your money wisely, and spend carefully. This chapter will give you insight about how to manage your finances. Are you ready to do the hard work it takes to become wealthy? To reach this ambitious goal, you must be committed and your attitude must always stay positive.

EDUCATION AND MAKING MONEY

The journey to financial success starts with education, and you're already well on your way! People who hold bachelor's degrees have an average salary of around $51,000 per year, compared with an average salary of $31,500 for high school graduates.[1] If you compound this difference over the course of a lifetime, a college grad makes $300,000 more than a high school grad![2] Therefore, you'll probably be repaid your investment in a college education many times over. See Figure A.1 for an idea of how much difference a college degree could make by the end of a 30-year career. That doesn't mean that good careers aren't available to non–college graduates. It just means those with an education are more likely to earn more during their lifetime.

The lifetime incomes of families headed by individuals with varied levels of education are estimated as

If you are financially secure, you'll be able to give generously to causes that matter to you.

Figure A.1 Salary Comparison of High School and College Graduates

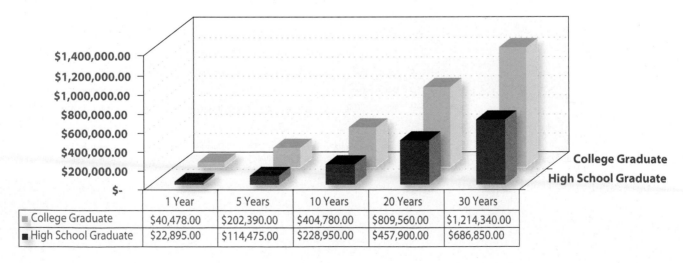

	1 Year	5 Years	10 Years	20 Years	30 Years
College Graduate	$40,478.00	$202,390.00	$404,780.00	$809,560.00	$1,214,340.00
High School Graduate	$22,895.00	$114,475.00	$228,950.00	$457,900.00	$686,850.00

Real World Apps

Shana McKeown is in her final semester of college. She and her friends are all interviewing for jobs and getting ready for the real world—but Shana is afraid.

Shana has had a checking account since she was 16 years old, but her mother controls it. Whenever she's gotten into trouble—financially speaking, of course—her mom has added money to the account. Shana never learned how to balance her checking account because she knew her mother would always take care of it.

Now Shana is looking for an apartment and thinking about the many expenses she'll have when she's on her own, and she's beginning to realize that there's a lot she doesn't understand about finances. For example, the manager of one apartment she's considering renting asked her about renters' insurance. She didn't even know such a thing existed! She has car insurance, of course—but she's on her parents' policy. Oh, no! She's going to have to get car insurance, too?

Shana thinks, "I need some information—quick." She dusts off her Business Now textbook from an earlier semester and turns to the Managing Your Finances chapter to brush up on the basics of financial knowledge.

follows: no high school degree, $630,000; high school degree, $994,080; associate degree, $1,269,850; and bachelor's degree, $1,667,700.[3] The College Board estimates that the typical bachelor's degree recipient earns 61 percent more than a high school graduate over a 40-year career. Higher levels of education lead to higher earnings and more tax revenue for governments, and these factors benefit society as well. By the time he or she reaches the age of 33, the average college graduate who enrolled in school at age 18 has earned enough in salary to offset the full tuition and fees spent over the four years of school, all student-loan interest, and lost earnings during the college years.[4]

THE NEED FOR FINANCIAL PLANNING

Many people find successful careers and earn a good living, but, at retirement, they find that they have little to show for their efforts. Making money is one thing; saving, investing, and spending it wisely is something else. Less than 10 percent of the U.S. population has accumulated enough money by retirement age to live comfortably.[5] For the first time in 10 years, a Gallup poll released in 2009 showed that more than 50 percent of nonretired Americans didn't think they would have enough money to live comfortably after retirement.[6] (See Figure A.2.) Only one out of every 10 U.S. adults has accumulated enough money by retirement age to live comfortably, and 36 percent of U.S. households don't have a retirement account.[7] If you follow the six steps listed in the next section, you'll be on your way to becoming one of the few with enough to live comfortably after retirement. These steps are useful whether you have $500 or $500,000 in your savings account.

Figure A.2 Will You Have Enough?

When you retire, do you think you will have enough money to live comfortably, or not? Based on non-retirees

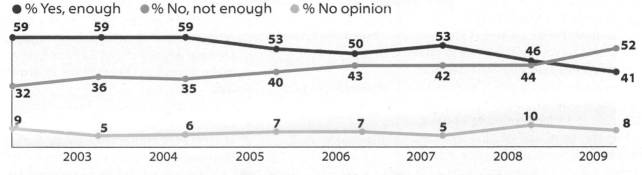

Source: Frank Newport, "Americans Increasingly Concerned About Retirement Income," Gallup, April 20, 2009, http://www.gallup.com/poll/117703/Americans-Increasingly-Concerned-Retirement-Income.aspx (accessed September 4, 2009).

This chapter provides information on becoming financially disciplined.

SIX STEPS TO FINANCIAL DISCIPLINE

The only way to save enough money to achieve your financial goals is to make more than you spend. A recent Nielsen survey revealed that one in four Americans has nothing left after funding basic expenses.[8] Saving money can be difficult, but it *is* possible, no matter what your income is. In fact, it's absolutely necessary to save in order to become financially secure in the future. You can save money for the future and still live comfortably, purchasing the goods and services you need.

Step 1: Take an Inventory of Your Financial Assets

To inventory your current assets, you must develop a balance sheet for yourself. In Chapter 8, you learned that a balance sheet starts with the fundamental accounting equation:

$$\text{Assets} = \text{Liabilities} + \text{Owners' equity}$$

You can develop your own balance sheet by listing your assets (for example, your savings account, checking account, investments, TV, DVDs, computer, bicycle, car, jewelry, and clothes) on one side, and your liabilities (for example, your rent, school loans, credit card debt, and auto loans) on the other. Assets include anything you own.

For the purposes of this exercise, evaluate your assets on the basis of their current value, not their purchase price, as is required for formal accounting statements. If you have no debts (liabilities), then your assets equal your net worth, or owner's equity. If you have debts, you must subtract them from your assets to figure out your net worth.

Next, create an income statement. At the top of your statement is your revenue (all the money you take in from your job[s], your investments, and so on). Subtract from the revenue all of your costs and expenses (your rent or mortgage, credit card and other loan payments, utilities, commuting costs, and so on) to figure out your net income, or profit. Software programs like Quicken and Web sites like Dinkytown.com have a variety of tools that can help you make these calculations.

If the value of your liabilities exceeds the value of your assets, you are not on the path to financial security. You may need more financial discipline in your life. Many students find that their liabilities *do* exceed their assets. If this is the case, you'll probably be able to change the situation after you finish your college education and get a good-paying job.

Now is a great time to think about how much money you'll need to accomplish all your goals. The more you visualize your goals, the easier it is to begin saving for them.

Step 2: Keep Track of All Your Expenses

Sometimes, you probably find yourself running out of cash (cash flow). In these circumstances, the only way to trace where the money is going is to keep track of every cent you spend. Keeping detailed records of your expenses can seem rather tedious, but it's a necessary chore if you want to be financially disciplined. In fact, tracking your expenses could turn out to be an enjoyable task—because you'll find that it will help you become completely in control of your own finances.

Actually keeping those records is very simple. Carry a notepad with you wherever you go, and record what you spend as you go through the day. Consider that notepad to be your financial journal. At the end of the week, record your journal entries into a record book or computerized accounting program. Develop certain categories (accounts) to make the task easier and more informative.

For example, you can have a category called "food" for all the food you bought at grocery or convenience stores during the week. Use a separate category for meals eaten away from home, be-

ETHICAL **DILEMMA**

How can your own unethical decisions affect your reputation and the reputations of the people you love?

ties, entertainment, donations to charity, and gifts. Most people like to have a category called "miscellaneous" for spontaneous purchases that don't fit into any of the other categories. After monitoring their expenses for a while, people are often surprised by how much money disappears into this miscellaneous category.

You should develop accounts based on what's most important to you or where you spend the most money. Once you've recorded all of your expenses, it is relatively easy to see where you're spending too much money and figure out what you need to do to save more money.

Study Alert!

Running a household is similar to running a small business. It takes the same careful record keeping, the same budget processes and forecasting, the same control procedures, and often the same need to periodically borrow funds.

cause you'll quickly see that meals eaten out cost a lot more than the ones you consume at home. According to the Bureau of Labor Statistics, in 2008, the average U.S. household spent $6,133 on eating out. If each of those meals had been prepared at home, they'd cost a fraction of that total.[9]

Other categories could include costs for an automobile (including car payments, insurance, gas, and maintenance), clothing, utili

Staying on a budget requires a lot of restraint.

Step 3: Prepare a Budget

Once you understand your current financial situation and your sources of revenue and expenses, you can prepare a personal budget. Remember, budgets are financial plans. Your household budget should include your mortgage or rent, utilities, food, clothing, vehicles, furniture, life insurance, car insurance, and medical care.

It's also important to make choices about how much you will allow yourself to spend on dining out, entertainment, and so on. Keep in mind that what you spend now reduces what you can save later. For example, spending $5 a day for cigarettes adds up to $35 a week, $140 a month, and almost $1,700 a year. If you can save $5 a day, you'll have a significant amount of money saved by the end of the year. If you can maintain that savings all the way through college, you'll have more than $7,000 saved by your graduation. And that's before adding any interest earned. Cost-saving choices you might

Figure A.3 Possible Cost-Saving Choices

FIRST CHOICE COST PER MONTH	ALTERNATE CHOICE COST PER MONTH	SAVINGS PER MONTH
Starbucks caffè latte $3.00 for 20 days = $60.00	Quick Trip cappuccino $0.60 for 20 days = $12.00	$48.00
Fast-food lunch of burgers, fries, and soft drink $4.00 for 20 days = $80.00	Lunch brought from home $2.00 for 20 days = $40.00	$40.00
Evian bottled water $1.50 for 20 days = $30.00	Generic bottled water $0.50 for 20 days = $10.00	$20.00
CD = $15.00	Listen to old CDs = $0.00	$12.00
Banana Republic T-shirt = $34.00	Old Navy T-shirt = $10.00	$24.00
		x 48 months
Total savings through 4 years of college		$7,056.00

The effect of the choices you make today can have a dramatic impact on your financial future. Compare the differences that these few choices you can make now would mean to your future net worth. If you would make the lower-cost choices every month during your four years of college, and invest the savings in a mutual fund earning 6 percent compounded annually, you would double your money every 12 years.

consider to reach this goal are listed in Figure A.3.

Running a household is similar to running a small business. It takes the same careful record keeping, the same budget processes and forecasting, the same control procedures, and often the same need to periodically borrow funds. Suddenly, concepts such as credit and interest rates become only too real, which is where some knowledge of finance, investments, and budgeting pays off. The time spent learning about budgeting techniques will ultimately benefit you for the rest of your life.

Step 4: Pay Off Your Debts

After paying your monthly bills, you should next use the remaining money to pay off your debts. Always start with the debts that carry the highest interest rates. You may be paying 18 percent—or more—in interest on your credit card debt. Here's a mind-boggling statistic: Americans carry more than $1 trillion in credit card balances from month to month.[10] A survey of students on 100 U.S. college campuses found that 26 percent of them had been charged a fee for a late payment on a credit card.[11]

Just the act of paying off these debts will set you on a path toward financial freedom. It's better to pay off a debt with an 18 percent interest rate than to put the money in a bank account that earns 2 percent or perhaps even less. Check your credit card statements and other mailings carefully, because many companies frequently raise interest rates. In some cases, interest rates have jumped from 7.99 percent to 26 percent in a single statement cycle.[12] You can always call your credit card company and ask for a lower interest rate, but this approach is not as effective as it was in the past.

Step 5: Start a Savings Plan

In 2007, the average U.S. consumer had a personal savings rate of less than 1 percent, but during the economic recession of 2008 and 2009, savings in the United States reached its highest level in decades. In 2009, the U.S. consumer had a personal savings

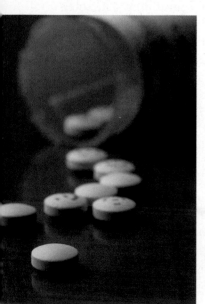

Expenses continue to escalate for the retired—particularly for prescription drugs. Save aggressively now so your future will be more secure.

rate of 5 percent.[13] Saving money every month in a separate account for large purchases will help you in the future, such as when you need to purchase a car or a house. When it comes time to make those purchases, you'll have more cash on hand to make a down payment—or, in some cases, to buy the item outright. Bigger down payments lead to lower finance charges, and they can even help you obtain lower interest rates. The best way to save money is to *pay yourself first.*

If you've created a budget that realistically identifies your expenses, you'll be able to put part of every paycheck into a savings account and then plan what to do with the rest.[14] Be sure to have a certain amount of every check deducted automatically and diverted to another account—that way, you'll never miss the money. You'll be pleasantly surprised when the money starts accumulating and earning interest over time. Figure A.4 shows how you can turn an investment of $5,000 into nearly $70,000 after 25 years. Figure A.5 shows how money grows with monthly deposits.

Figure A.4 How Money Grows

This chart illustrates how $5,000 would grow at various rates of return. Recent savings account interest rates were very low (less than 2 percent), but in earlier years they've been over 5 percent.

Annual Rate of Return			
Time	**2%**	**5%**	**8%**	**11%**
5 years	$5,520	$6,381	$7,347	$8,425
10 years	6,095	8,144	10,795	14,197
15 years	6,729	10,395	15,861	23,923
20 years	7,430	13,266	23,305	40,312
25 years	8,203	16,932	34,242	67,927

Figure A.5 How Money Grows with Monthly Deposits

This calculation is based on an initial deposit of $5,000 with monthly deposits of $60. How can you save $60 in a month?

Annual Rate of Return				
Time	**2%**	**5%**	**8%**	**11%**
5 years	$ 9,308	$10,487	$11,857	$ 13,414
10 years	14,069	17,551	22,075	27,965
15 years	19,330	26,605	37,296	53,121
20 years	25,144	38,225	59,975	96,613
25 years	31,569	53,137	93,762	171,807

Step 6: Borrow Money Only to Buy Assets That Have the Potential to Increase in Value or Generate Income

Never borrow money for ordinary expenses. It'll just get you deeper in debt. If you have budgeted for emergencies, such as car repairs and health care costs, you should be able to stay financially secure. Most financial experts recommend saving about six months of earnings for contingency purposes, which means keeping the money in highly liquid (easily accessible) accounts, such as a regular bank savings account or money-market fund.

You should only borrow for the most unexpected of expenses. It's hard to wait until you have enough money to buy what you want, but learning to wait is a critical part of self-discipline. Of course, you can always try to produce more income by working overtime or getting a second job.

Study Alert!

The six steps to financial discipline are: (1) take an inventory of your financial assets, (2) keep track of all your expenses, (3) prepare a budget, (4) pay off your debts, (5) start a savings plan, and (6) borrow money only to buy assets that have the potential to increase in value or generate income.

Keep in mind that borrowing money for education expenses or to purchase a home is a *good* kind of borrowing. In other words, these investments will likely grow in value over time. While it's sometimes necessary, borrowing money to buy a car is the sort of debt that doesn't pay you back in the long run, because cars depreciate in value. In almost all cases, a car will never be worth more than it is the day you make the purchase.

Charging items on a credit card is the same as borrowing money. A good rule of thumb is to never charge more on a credit card than you can pay off at the end of the month. The credit card company is giving you the money now, but you'll have to pay it back later—plus fees and interest. For example, suppose you paid $9.00 for a movie ticket with your credit card. If you don't pay off your credit card each month, you'll be paying interest on that $9.00. If your interest rate is 14 percent, the ticket will cost $10.26 at the end of the next month. Two months down the road, it'll be up to $11.70. After six months, the $9.00 ticket will cost $19.77—more than twice what you would have paid if you'd used cash.

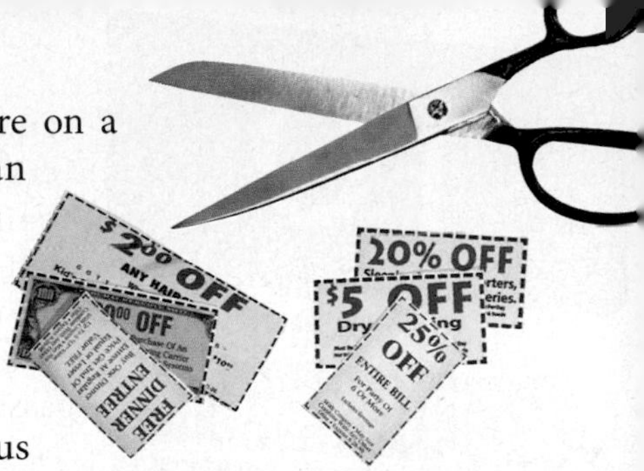

By following these six steps, you'll have enough money to cover your expenses, and you'll be able to set aside enough money to make you financially secure in the future. At first, you may find it hard to live within a budget, but the ultimate payoff is well worth the pain.

[BUS] connections

1. What role does education play in your lifetime income potential?
2. Write down the six steps to controlling your assets. Which are you good at? Which may need improvement?
3. Why do you think some people choose to not live on a budget?

>> Investing and Managing Credit: Building a Financial Base

As discussed in earlier chapters, one of the fastest way to build wealth is through entrepreneurship. Spending less and saving more allows you to have the capital necessary to venture into the entrepreneurial world. However, living *frugally* (spending only on what is absolutely necessary) is extremely difficult for the average person.[15] Most people are eager to spend their money on a new car, furniture, CDs, and clothes,[16] or they want a fancy apartment with all the

amenities. A capital generating strategy may require forgoing most—but not all—of these luxuries in order to accumulate investment money. It will mean passing up an expensive new car, purchasing a used car instead, and saving the difference.

Of course, this doesn't mean that you'll never be able to buy what you want. It does mean, however, that you must balance those "wants" purchases carefully and make sure that you are still saving aggressively in order to meet your goals. Many students think that they should have the same standard of living that their parents have immediately after graduating from college. You must keep in mind that it took your parents years to reach the standard of living they currently have.

You should plan your financial future with the same excitement and dedication you bring to other aspects of your life, and you should keep your finances in mind always. For ex-

If the value of your retirement account plunges, you may have to defer your dream of an early retirement.

ample, if you are considering making a commitment to a life partner, you must discuss financial issues. Conflicts over money are a major cause of separations and divorce—a study conducted by Citibank demonstrated that arguments over money contribute to 57 percent of divorces.[17]

Agreeing on a financial strategy before making a commitment is critical to maintaining a successful relationship. One strategy to consider is trying to live on one income and save the other. The longer you wait before assuming joint financial responsibilities, the more likely it is that you or your partner will be earning enough to make that savings plan work. If one person nets $30,000 in income per year after taxes, saving that income for five years can quickly add up to $150,000 (plus interest).

What should do you do with the money you accumulate? Your first investment might be a low-priced home. You should make this investment as early as possible. Doing so means locking in your costs for housing at a fixed amount, which isn't possible if you're renting. As for how much to spend on that home, a good rule of thumb is to never buy a home that costs more than two and one-half times your annual income. Buy for the long term and stay within your means. We'll discuss home buying further in the next section.

REAL ESTATE: A RELATIVELY SECURE INVESTMENT

In July 2009, 5.24 million existing homes were sold,[18] and in June 2009, the mean price of a home in the United States was $276,900.[19]

Homes provide several investment benefits. First, a home is the one investment you can actually live in. Second, once people buy a home, the payments are relatively fixed (of course, taxes and utilities go up). As incomes rise, house payments get easier and easier to make, but renters often find that rent tends to go up at least as fast as income. Paying for a home is a good way of forcing yourself to save, because every month, you must make the payments.

Those payments are an investment that proves very rewarding over time for most people. As capital accumulates and values rise, people can sell their first homes and buy different homes in better locations or homes that offer more living space. They may consider purchasing investment properties instead.

Furthermore, a home is a good asset to use when applying for a loan. Figure A.6 lists various types of home loans. When choosing a loan, it's important not to get sold on the most popular or lowest-cost mortgage. Instead, consider the options carefully and figure out what type of mortgage best suits your needs.

If you understand the benefits of home ownership versus renting, you'll be in a better position to decide whether those same principles will apply if you decide to start your own business. For example, can you purchase a work space, or should you rent it? Should you purchase or rent equipment, vehicles, and other capital investments for the business?

Figure A.7 will give you some idea of how expensive a house you can afford, given your income. You can find current mortgage interest rates and mortgage calculators at www.interest.com.

Another advantage to buying a home is that the interest paid on the mortgage is tax deductible and

Figure A.7 How Much House Can You Afford?

Income	Monthly Payment	Interest Rates			
		5%	6%	7%	15%
$30,000	$ 700	$106,263	$ 98,303	$ 91,252	$ 56,870
50,000	1,167	180,291	167,081	155,376	98,606
80,000	1,867	287,213	266,056	247,308	155,916
100,000	2,333	361,240	334,832	311,433	198,013

Your mortgage payments shouldn't amount to more than 28 percent of your net income.
Source: Federal Housing Finance Board.

Figure A.6 Types of Home Mortgages

Fixed rate	The interest rate is fixed and payment is the same throughout the life of the loan.
Adjustable rate mortgage (ARM)	The interest rate changes; therefore, the payment will change throughout the life of the loan.
Interest-only mortgage	The interest is not charged for a certain period of time. When that period ends, the payment will change once interest is added.
80/20 loan	If a buyer does not have a down payment, he or she takes out two loans, one for 80 percent of the value of the home and one for 20 percent for the down payment.

so are the property taxes (if you live in a state with property taxes). During the first few years of a standard mortgage, virtually all the payments go toward paying down the interest on the loan, so almost all of your early payments will be tax deductible. That's a tremendous benefit for home owners and investors. For example, if your payments are $1,000 a month in a new mortgage, most of that $1,000 is made up of interest payments and property taxes. At the end of the year, a large percentage of the $12,000 you paid throughout the year can be deducted from your income, and you won't have to pay income taxes on that $12,000.

WHERE TO PUT YOUR SAVINGS

So now you know that one place to invest the money you have saved is in a home. Where are some other good places to invest your savings? For a young person, one of the worst places to keep long-term investments is in a bank savings account. As noted earlier, it's important to keep about six months' worth of earnings stashed in the bank for emergencies, but the bank is not the best place to put your investments. According to the 2008 National Foundation for Credit Counseling Financial Literacy Survey, the majority of Americans do not have an emergency fund; in fact, more

Investing in Bonds

Investors looking for guaranteed income and limited risk often turn to U.S. government bonds for a more secure investment. These bonds have the financial backing and full faith and credit of the federal government. Municipal bonds, which are also secure choices, are offered by local governments. Many have advantages beyond security—such as the benefit of tax-free interest.[24] Some are even insured. Corporate bonds are a bit riskier and more challenging.

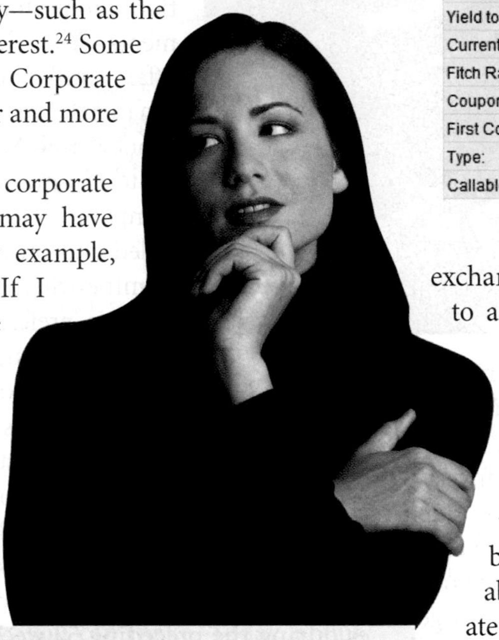

As a first-time corporate bond investor, you may have some questions. For example, you may wonder, "If I purchase a corporate bond, do I have to hold it until the maturity date?" The answer is no: Bonds are bought and sold every day on major securities exchanges. However, if you decide to sell your bond to another investor before its maturity date, you may not get its face value. If your bond does not have features that make it attractive to other investors—such as a high interest rate or early maturity—you may have to sell at a *discount*, which is a price below the bond's face value. But if other investors do value it, you may be able to sell your bond at a *premium*, a price above its face value. Bond prices generally fluctuate inversely with current market interest rates. *As interest rates go up, bond prices fall, and vice versa.* Like all investments, bonds have a degree of risk.

Your second question might be, "How can I assess the investment risk of a particular bond issue?" Rating services like Standard & Poor's and Moody's Investors Service rate the risk of many corporate and government bonds. You should always keep in mind the risk–return tradeoff: The higher a bond's risk might be, the higher the interest rate the issuer must offer.[25] Investors will invest in a bond considered risky only if the potential return is high enough. In fact, some will invest in bonds considered "junk" because they promise such high returns.

Understanding bond quotations. Bond prices are quoted as a percentage of $1,000, and their interest rate is often followed by an *s* for easier pronunciation. For example, 9 percent bonds due in 2020 are called "9s of '20." Figure A.9 is an example of a bond quote for Goldman Sachs from Yahoo! Finance. The quote highlights the bond's interest rate (coupon rate), maturity date, rating, current price, and whether it's a callable bond.

The more you know about bonds, the better prepared you will be to talk intelligently with investment counselors and brokers. Always be sure their advice is consistent with your best interests and investment objectives.

Figure A.9 Understanding Bond Quotations

GOLDMAN SACHS GROUP INC As of 4-May-2009

OVERVIEW	
Price:	104.32
Coupon (%):	7.350
Maturity Date:	1-Oct-2009
Yield to Maturity (%):	-3.289
Current Yield (%):	7.045
Fitch Ratings:	A
Coupon Payment Frequency:	Semi-Annual
First Coupon Date:	1-Apr-2000
Type:	Corporate
Callable:	No

Career PERSPECTIVES

BECOMING FINANCIALLY SECURE

The concepts discussed in this chapter, and throughout the text, have identified ways for you to become financially successful. The first step is finding a job you like and that pays enough to meet and exceed your expected expenses. As you consider job offers, it will be important for you to consider benefits beyond salary. Does the prospective employer have a 401(k) that matches part of your contributions? Does the company provide or subsidize health insurance for its employees? Can you purchase disability insurance through the company?

The second step is careful financial planning. By saving and investing your money and not spending beyond your means, you can substantially increase your ability to become financially secure through your retirement and beyond. Make sure you also protect yourself from unexpected losses by ensuring that you have appropriate auto, life, and health insurance.

We hope this chapter will give you some basic ideas and tools with which you can begin thinking about financial planning. Whether you use a financial adviser or do your own planning, now is the time to begin doing such planning for a successful financial future. What steps are you planning to take now to become more financially secure?

Figure A.10 Understanding Mutual Fund Quotations

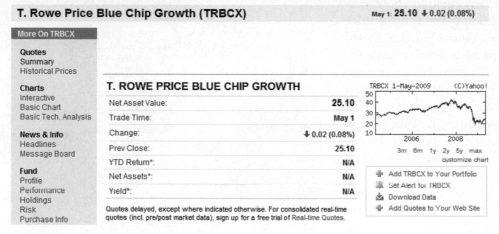

T. Rowe Price Blue Chip Growth (TRBCX)   May 1: **25.10** ↓0.02 (0.08%)

More On TRBCX

Quotes
Summary
Historical Prices

Charts
Interactive
Basic Chart
Basic Tech. Analysis

News & Info
Headlines
Message Board

Fund
Profile
Performance
Holdings
Risk
Purchase Info

T. ROWE PRICE BLUE CHIP GROWTH

Net Asset Value:	**25.10**
Trade Time:	**May 1**
Change:	↓0.02 (0.08%)
Prev Close:	25.10
YTD Return*:	N/A
Net Assets*:	N/A
Yield*:	N/A

Quotes delayed, except where indicated otherwise. For consolidated real-time quotes (incl. pre/post market data), sign up for a free trial of Real-time Quotes.

TRBCX 1-May-2009   (C)Yahoo!

⊕ Add TRBCX to Your Portfolio
🔔 Set Alert for TRBCX
⬇ Download Data
⊕ Add Quotes to Your Web Site

Investing in Mutual Funds and Exchange-Traded Funds

A **mutual fund** buys stocks and bonds and then sells shares in those securities to the public. A mutual fund is like an investment company that pools investors' money and then buys stocks or bonds in many companies in accordance with the fund's specific purpose. Mutual fund managers are specialists who pick what they consider to be the best stocks and bonds available.

> **Mutual fund** An organization that buys stocks and bonds and then sells shares in those securities to the public.

Investors can buy shares of the mutual fund and thus take part in the ownership of many different companies they could not afford to invest in individually. Funds range from very conservative funds that invest only in government securities to others that specialize in emerging high-tech firms, Internet companies, foreign companies, precious metals, and other investments with greater risk. Some mutual funds invest exclusively in socially responsible companies. Thus, for a fee, mutual funds provide professional investment management and help investors diversify. U.S. investors have invested $12 trillion in mutual funds.[26]

Young or new investors are often advised to buy shares in *index funds* that invest in a certain kind of stocks or bonds or in the market as a whole.[27] An index fund may focus on large companies, small companies, emerging countries, or real estate (real estate investment trusts, or REITs). One idea is to diversify your investments by investing in a variety of index funds. A stockbroker, CFP, or banker can help you find the option that best fits your investment objectives. The newsletter *Morningstar Investor* is an excellent resource for evaluating mutual funds, as are business publications such as *BusinessWeek, The Wall Street Journal, Money,* and *Investor's Business Daily.*

Exchange-traded funds (ETFs) resemble both stock and mutual funds. They are collections of stocks and bonds that are traded on securities exchanges but themselves are traded more like individual stocks than like mutual funds.[28] Mutual funds, for example, permit investors to buy and sell shares only at the close of the trading day. ETFs can be purchased or sold at any time during the trading day.

> **Exchange-traded funds** Collections of stocks that are traded on exchanges but are traded more like individual stocks than like mutual funds.

The key points to remember about mutual funds and ETFs is that they offer small investors a way to spread the risk of stock and bond ownership and have their investments managed by a financial specialist for a fee. Financial advisers put mutual funds and ETFs high on the list of recommended investments, particularly for beginning investors.

Understanding mutual fund quotations. You can investigate the specifics of various funds by contacting a broker or contacting the fund directly by phone

Figure A.11 Comparing Investments

Investment	Degree of risk	Expected income	Possible growth (capital gain)
Bonds	Low	Secure	Little
Preferred stock	Medium	Steady	Little
Common stock	High	Variable	Good
Mutual funds	Medium	Variable	Good
ETFS	Medium	Variable	Good

or through its Web site. Business publications and online sources also provide information about mutual funds. Consider the example of the T. Rowe Price Blue Chip Growth fund from Yahoo! Finance, shown in Figure A.10. The fund's name is listed in large letters. The net asset value (NAV) is the price per share of the mutual fund. The NAV is calculated by dividing the market value of the mutual fund's portfolio by the number of shares it has outstanding. The Yahoo! chart also shows the fund's YTD (year-to-date) return, the change in the NAV from the previous day's trading, and the fund's net assets.

Figure A.11 evaluates bonds, stocks, mutual funds, and ETFs according to risk, income, and possible investment growth (capital gain).

LEARNING TO MANAGE YOUR CREDIT

Credit companies are quite willing to give students credit cards. Credit card offers can be enticing, including free gifts for applying and low interest rates in the first year.

Companies like Visa, MasterCard, American Express, and Discover are well known to most people. They're not always well liked, of course, but having credit can be very helpful at times. Here's the downside, and it's a big one: Credit card purchases have finance charges that usually amount to anywhere from 12 percent to 25 percent, which means that if you finance a TV, home appliances, and other purchases with a credit card, you may end up spending much more than if you had paid with cash (remember that movie ticket example earlier in the chapter?). A good manager of personal finances, like a good businessperson, pays off debt on time and takes advantage of the savings made possible by paying early. Peo-

ple who have established a capital fund can tap that fund to make large purchases and then pay back the fund (with interest, if so desired) rather than paying finance charges to a credit card company.

Credit cards are an important part of a personal finance system, even if you rarely use them. First, some merchants request credit cards as a form of identification. It may be difficult to buy certain goods or services, such as renting a car, without having a credit card, because businesses use them for identification and ensured payment. Second, credit cards can be used to keep track of purchases. For example, a gasoline credit card provides records of purchases over time for income tax and financial planning purposes. Third, it's sometimes easier to write a single check at the end of the month for multiple purchases than to carry around cash. Besides, when cash is stolen or lost, it's gone forever; a stolen credit card can be canceled.

Finally, a credit card is simply more convenient than cash or checks. If you come upon a special sale and need more money than you have on you, paying by credit is quick and easy (but remember—it is borrowing money!). You can carry less cash and don't have to worry about keeping your checkbook balanced as often. As mentioned before, if you do use a credit card, always be sure to pay the balance in full during the period when no interest is charged.

Also, you may want to choose a card that pays you back in cash, such as the Discover card, or a card that offers paybacks, such as credit toward the purchase of a car, free long-distance minutes, reward points, or frequent-flier miles. The value of these givebacks can vary from 1 percent to 5 percent of the purchase totals.[29] According to credit giant Visa, rewards

Thinking Critically

>> Protect Your Money: Check Out Brokers and Investment Advisers

Most people are at least a little anxious about entrusting their finances to someone else, whether that person is a broker or an investment adviser. This article from the U.S. Securities and Exchange Commission provides information that can help you protect yourself from fraud and other forms of financial loss.

Federal or state securities laws require brokers, investment advisers, and their firms to be licensed or registered and to make important information public. It's up to you to protect your investment dollars.

Before you invest or pay for any investment advice, make sure your brokers, investment advisers, and investment adviser representatives haven't had run-ins with regulators or other investors. You also should check to see whether they are registered or licensed. This is very important, because if you do business with an unregistered securities broker or a firm that later goes out of business, there may be no way for you to recover your money—even if an arbitrator or court rules in your favor.

The Central Registration Depository (CRD) is a computerized database that contains information about most brokers, their representatives, and the firms they work for. For instance, you can find out if brokers are properly licensed in your state and if they have had run-ins with regulators or received serious complaints from investors. You'll also find information about the brokers' educational backgrounds and where they've worked before their current jobs.

You can ask either your state securities regulator or the Financial Industry Regulatory Authority (FINRA) to provide you with information from the CRD. Your state securities regulator may provide more information from the CRD than FINRA, especially when it comes to investor complaints, so you may want to check with that department first. You'll find contact information for your state securities regulator on the Web site of the North American Securities Administrators Association. Because some investment advisers and their representatives are also brokers, you may want to check both the CRD and Form ADV. If you plan to do business with a brokerage firm, you should find out whether the firm is a member of the Securities Investor Protection Corporation (SIPC). SIPC provides limited customer protection if a brokerage firm becomes insolvent—but it doesn't insure against losses attributable to a decline in the market value of your securities.

Here are a few questions to ask:

- What experience do you have, especially with people in my circumstances?
- Where did you go to school? What is your recent employment history?
- What licenses do you hold? Are you registered with the SEC, a state, or FINRA?
- Is your firm a member of SIPC?
- What products and services do you offer?
- Can you only recommend a limited number of products or services to me? If so, why?
- How are you paid for your services? What is your usual hourly rate, flat fee, or commission?
- Have you ever been disciplined for unethical or improper conduct or sued by a client?

Source: U.S. Securities and Exchange Commission Web site, "Protect Your Money: Check Out Brokers and Investment Advisers," June 16, 2008, http://www.sec.gov/investor/brokers.htm (accessed September 10, 2009).

QUESTIONS

1. Have you ever used, or considered using, a financial adviser or broker? Why or why not? If you have, what criteria did you use to select the adviser or broker?

2. What specific steps would you take to protect yourself and your finances from fraud?

cards now make up more than half of all credit cards, and about 80 percent of money spent on credit cards goes on rewards cards. Consumers say that rewards are the second-most important reason why they apply for a specific card, immediately behind a no-annual-fee policy and ahead of low interest rates.[30] With some rewards cards, you actually earn money back instead of paying 14 percent interest. That's quite a difference.

Going GLOBAL

Ways to Profit from the U.S. Savings Surge

It's no secret that economic turmoil dramatically affects consumer behavior. When consumers have little left to borrow against, and few lenders willing to give them credit, they must stop their spending sprees and live within their means. This article suggests some potential benefits of the savings revolution.

A growing sense of insecurity about jobs, future income, household debt, and falling home values is driving American consumers back to an activity that's rarely been seen over the past 20 years: saving money. Consumers are coming to grips with the realization that easy credit won't be available to pay for cars, homes, or any other big-ticket purchases in the years immediately ahead.

During the past two decades of credit expansion, Americans went from squirreling away more than 7.0 percent of their after-tax income to less than zero (–0.7 percent) in the third quarter of 2005, according to the Commerce Dept.'s Bureau of Economic Analysis. That means consumers were not only spending all of their after-tax income but drawing from prior savings or increasing their borrowing to fund their spending. After hitting that low, the personal saving rate remained at 1.0 percent or below from the fourth quarter of 2004 through the first quarter of 2008, before spiking to 2.6 percent in the second quarter of 2008 and climbing to 2.9 percent by the final quarter of the year.

The fear is that too quick a rise in the saving rate could push U.S. consumer spending off a cliff. That would not only be disastrous given that consumer spending accounts for more than two-thirds of U.S. gross domestic product, but would also undercut one of the major goals of the nearly $800 billion economic stimulus package the Senate approved on Feb. 10.

Before the recession, consumption had been growing at an average rate of 3.5 percent a year, when adjusted for inflation, says Ethan Harris, co-head of U.S. economics research at Barclays Capital. If the saving rate ratchets up quickly during the recession, a realistic scenario for consumption growth over the next five or six years could be around 2 percent, with spending growth trailing income growth by 1 percent, he adds. He expects discretionary items to be hit harder than other types of consumption.

Even after banks have wiped their balance sheets clean of toxic assets, expect to see a period of slower growth for the financial services sector. The product lines that drove profit margins, such as credit cards and home equity loans, will be constrained or will have to compete for better-quality customers.

While domestic stocks are the place to focus until the recession starts winding down, eventually equities in emerging markets will be a better bet, especially if depressed consumer spending slows GDP growth to the point that it lags growth in economies overseas. The sharp drop in investment returns in emerging markets over the past year has soured investors on those countries for the moment, but most people expect India and China to resume their hyper-charged expansion as soon as the global recession has passed.

A general savings glut around the world is likely to further fuel the development of emerging markets. Exchange-traded funds and mutual funds that provide diversified exposure to those markets will be the best way to play them, while investors wealthy enough to have separately managed accounts could choose individual stocks in those markets.

Source: David Bogoslaw, "Ways to Profit from the U.S. Savings Surge," *BusinessWeek*, February 12, 2009, http://www.businessweek.com/investor/content/feb2009/pi20090211_410557.htm (accessed September 10, 2009).

1. Do you believe that it's possible for American consumers to continue their trend of aggressive saving without undermining economic recovery? Explain your response.

2. Will consumers continue to save and live within their means after the economy fully recovers, or will they return to their old ways? Explain your response.

The flip side of credit cards' convenience is that they can be dangerously tempting. Too often, consumers buy goods and services they wouldn't normally buy if they had to pay cash or write a check. Using credit cards, consumers often pile up debts to the point where they are unable to pay. As of March 2009, most U.S. consumer debt was credit card debt—around $950 billion of it.[31] If you don't think you can stick to a financial plan or household budget, *it may be better not to have a credit card at all.*

Credit cards can be a helpful tool for the financially careful buyer, but they're also a financial disaster to people with little financial restraint and tastes beyond their income.[32] College students take note: Of the debtors seeking help at the National Consumer Counseling Service, more than half were between 18 and 32 years of age.

Knowing what is in your credit report can help you plan for future purchases and investments. Consumers are allowed access to their credit reports from all three major agencies once per year.

Credit Reports

Approximately 37 percent of Americans admit that they don't know their credit score.[33] You should access your credit report at least once a year in order to make sure that it is correct and up to date. You can obtain your credit report by contacting one, or all, of the three main credit reporting agencies: Equifax, Experian, and Trans Union. A recent amendment to the Fair Credit Reporting Act requires these companies to provide your credit report to you for free once each year.[34]

The primary reason to review your credit report is to monitor the activity reported on it. With certain critical personal information about you, like your Social Security number, people can open accounts in your name and make fraudulent charges. A check of your credit report would reveal any of this illegal activity.

Your credit report also includes the names of companies that have checked your credit score, as well as the companies that have already extended credit to you. The free report you can obtain once a year includes the credit score issued to you by each of the respective credit agencies, but it does not include your FICO score, which is based on several factors, such as on-time payments to creditors and amounts owed. **FICO** is an acronym for Fair Isaac Corporation, the company that provides the most well-known and widely used credit score model in the United States. You can purchase information about your FICO score from the credit reporting agencies or directly from Fair Isaac at myFICO.com.

The FICO score is the information that is used to determine the interest rate you should pay and whether or not you should get a loan. In other words, it predicts how likely you are to default on a loan. Obviously, your credit report can affect your ability to buy a car, buy a home, or obtain school loans, which is why it is so important to keep track of this information.

> **FICO** A credit score provided by the Fair Isaac Corporation that can be obtained from one of the three major credit bureaus.

[BUS] connections

1. Is real estate always a good investment? Explain your response.
2. What methods of investment appeal to you most? Why do you prefer these particular methods?
3. What are the advantages to staying out of credit card debt? What are the short-term payoffs?

>> Insurance: Protecting Your Financial Base

Most young people rarely ever think about getting sick, having an accident, or dying. But concerns about the future aren't only for the elderly—just consider this statistic: 1,700 college students between the ages of 18 and 24 die each year from unintentional alcohol-related injuries. Another 600,000 are unintentionally injured as a result of intoxication.[35]

These certainly aren't pleasant things to think about, but it's reality. Unfortunately, young people die every day as a result of accidents or other unexpected causes. You can only imagine the emotional and financial havoc such a loss can cause. To protect your loved ones from the loss of your income, you should consider buying life insurance. You should also have auto insurance to protect you and your car in the event of an accident, renters' or homeowners' insurance to protect your home and belongings, and health insurance to pay for your medical expenses—particularly any catastrophic ones. **Insurance** is a written contract between the party being insured and an insurer where the financial responsibility for losses transfers to the insurer up to a specified limit.

> **Insurance** A contract between the party being insured and an insurer where the financial responsibility for losses transfers to the insurer up to a specified limit.

AUTO INSURANCE

The first type of insurance we'll discuss is auto insurance. Most states require auto insurance, and if you owe money on your car, the lender will require insurance as well. *Liability insurance* guarantees that if you have an accident, your insurance company will pay to repair the damage to the other vehicle(s), but not your vehicle. *Full coverage* guarantees that the company will pay for the damage to all cars involved. *Uninsured motorist coverage* pays for damages to your car if you're hit by someone without insurance. One study of young singles revealed that 20 percent would let their auto insurance run out in order to save money.[36] Don't let that happen to you!

LIFE INSURANCE

These days, many households have two incomes coming in. If both spouses are working, the loss of one spouse can mean a sudden, significant drop in income. To provide protection from such risks, a couple—or a business—should buy life insurance.

The least expensive and simplest form of life insurance is **term insurance**.[37] It is pure insurance protection for a given number of years that typically costs less the younger you are when you buy it (see Figure A.12).

> **Term insurance** Pure insurance protection with no savings feature for a given number of years that typically costs less the younger you are when you buy it.

Typically, life insurance costs increase as your age does. With term life insurance, the price is fixed for the term of the policy (for example, with a 10-year-term policy, the price will not change for 10 years). If you choose to renew the policy, however, your premium will be based on your current age, and the premiums will be considerably higher. Check prices through a service like InsWeb.com or use one of Quicken's personal finance software packages.

How much insurance do you need? According to *Newsweek* magazine, a family with one baby should have policies that equal seven times their family income plus $100,000 for a college fund. The policies should be apportioned according to each spouse's income: A spouse who earns 60 percent of the income should have 60 percent of the insurance. Before buying life insurance, always check out the insurance company first by reviewing its rating with rating services like A.M. Best (www.ambest.com) or Moody's Investors Service (www.moodys.com).

Another type of life insurance, **whole life insurance**, is also called permanent life insurance—you pay the same premium for your entire life. However, part of the money you pay for whole life insurance goes toward pure insurance, and another part

> **Whole life insurance** Life insurance where some part of the money you pay goes toward pure insurance and another part goes toward savings, so you are buying both insurance and a savings plan.

Universal life insurance A permanent insurance plan that allows flexibility in your insurance and savings amounts.

goes toward savings, so you're buying both insurance and a savings plan. This option may be a good choice for people who have trouble saving money. A **universal life** policy lets you choose how much of your payment should go to insurance and how much to investments. The investments in such plans traditionally are very conservative but pay a steady interest rate.

Variable life insurance A form of whole life insurance that invests the cash value of the policy in stocks or other high-yielding securities.

Variable life insurance is a form of whole life insurance that invests the cash value of the policy in stocks or other high-yielding securities. Death benefits may thus vary, reflecting the performance of the investments. After watching the stock market go up for many years, many people switched their whole life policies to variable policies in order to get higher potential returns. When the stock market plunged, that choice suddenly didn't seem like such a good idea.

Figure A.12 Why Buy Term Insurance?

Insurance Needs in Early Years Are High	Insurance Needs Decline as You Age
1. Children are young and need money for education.	1. Children are grown.
2. Mortgage is high relative to income.	2. Mortgage is low or completely paid off.
3. Often there are auto payments and other bills to pay.	3. Debts are paid off.
4. Loss of income would be disastrous.	4. Insurance needs are low.
	5. Retirement income is needed.

Life insurance companies recognized a desire among consumers for higher returns on their insurance and for protecting themselves against running out of money before they died. To meet these needs, they began selling annuities. An **annuity** is a contract to make regular payments to a person for life or for a fixed period. With an annuity, you are guaranteed an income until you die. There are two kinds of annuities: fixed and variable. *Fixed annuities* are investments that pay the policyholder a specified interest rate. They are not as popular

Figure A.13 Ward's Five Top-Performing Life/Health Insurance Companies in 2009

1. Aetna Life Insurance Company
2. AFLAC
3. American Family Life Insurance Company
4. American Fidelity Assurance Company
5. American Republic Insurance Company

Source: "Ward Group Identifies 2009 Ward's 50 Top Performing Insurance Companies," Finance.Yahoo.com, July 9, 2009, http://finance.yahoo.com/news/Ward-Group-Identifies-2009-bw-1816529715.html?x=0&.v=1 (accessed September 6, 2009).

as variable *annuities*, which provide investment choices identical to mutual funds. Such annuities are gaining in popularity relative to term or whole life insurance.

Annuity A contract to make regular payments to a person for life or for a fixed period.

People often choose more risk in order to get greater returns. However, you must be very careful when selecting an insurance company and figuring out what type of policy is right for you. It may be wise to consult a financial adviser who is not an insurance agent before buying an insurance policy. He or she can help you make an informed decision about life insurance.

HEALTH INSURANCE

The most recent U.S. Census estimated that 46 million Americans, or 18 percent of the population, are without health insurance.[38] You may have health insurance coverage through your parents or an employer. If not, you can buy insurance from a health insurance provider (e.g., Blue Cross/Blue Shield), a health maintenance organization, or a preferred provider organization. For quick online help in picking a health insurance provider, eHealthInsurance.com can help you get affordable health insurance quotes and compare individual health insurance plans side by side so you can find the best medical insurance plans for your needs and budget.

Deductible The amount that must be spent on health care before insurance companies will cover the remaining expenses.

Copayment An amount paid by the insured party when medical services are rendered.

When buying insurance, keep in mind that deductibles sometimes have to be met. A **deductible** is an amount that must be spent on health care before insurance companies cover the remaining expenses. A copayment is sometimes required as well. A **copayment** is an amount paid when medical services are rendered. A copayment can be as little as $10, but in some cases (such as when you visit a specialist), it could be quite a bit more. Another important consideration is whether or not doctors will accept your health care plan. Since there are so many varieties, be sure to do a careful search to find the best program for you and your family.

It's dangerous not to have health insurance, both from a financial perspective and a health perspective. Hospital costs are simply too high to risk financial ruin by going without insurance. In fact, it's often a good idea to supplement health insurance policies with **disability insurance**, which pays part of your medical and living expenses in the event of a long-term illness or an accident. Your chances of becoming disabled at an early age are much higher than your chances of dying in an accident. Call an insurance agent or check the Internet for possible costs of disability insurance. The cost is relatively low to protect yourself from losing your income for an extended period of time.

The United States is the only industrialized nation in the world that doesn't ensure or provide every citizen with access to affordable health care. As a result, nearly 18,000 uninsured people die every year.[39] Whether or not health care should be universal in the United States is a hotly debated topic. Proponents of such a system argue that access to affordable health care is an economically feasible idea and a moral right

Disability insurance A type of insurance that pays part of the cost of a long-term sickness or an accident.

HONESTY MATTERS

Donna and Susan are walking through a grocery store. Donna's husband, Will, and Susan's husband, Bob, have been friends for more than 20 years. As Donna and Susan walk through the produce department, Susan pauses by the grapes and quickly eats a few. Donna says nothing.

How can your own unethical decisions affect your reputation and the reputations of the people you love?

Later, Susan swipes a few olives from the salad bar. Donna whispers, "What are you doing?"

Susan replies, "I'm just tasting them, so I know whether to buy them or not."

Donna picks up a few items, and they proceed to the checkout. After Donna finishes paying for her items and the two women leave, Donna continues to think about her friend's behavior at the store. Still bothered by the incident, Donna mentions, "I'm still wondering about the grapes and the olives. You tasted them, but you didn't pay for them."

Exasperated, Susan replies, "Are you still on that? It was just a handful of grapes. Come on. What's your problem? I had to taste them to know if they were any good."

Donna considers Susan's answer. "But why did you have to taste the olives? You know what olives taste like. And anyway, you didn't buy the grapes or the olives." She continues, "Some of the things you do are dishonest, Susan. I'm concerned."

Susan glares at Donna. "What do you mean?"

"Last weekend," Donna says, "you and Bob came over for dinner, and you talked about not reporting some of your income on your taxes. Last month, Bob mentioned to Will that you'd exaggerated the value of some of the items included in your homeowners' insurance policy. Susan, what if you get caught? More importantly," Donna pauses, "did it ever occur to you that if you get caught, it will affect your whole family—including your children and grandchildren?"

QUESTIONS

1. What are the ethical issues in this situation?
2. How do you think the moral decisions Susan makes will affect her children and grandchildren?

every American should have.[40] Those against such reform cite such arguments as reduced quality of care as a result of a lack of competition, government meddling in private health care matters, and the possibility of compromised patient confidentiality.[41]

HOMEOWNERS' OR RENTERS' INSURANCE

As you begin to accumulate possessions, consider getting insurance to protect against their loss. Homeowners' insurance is required by mortgage companies and is sometimes paid with your mortgage payment. You can also buy flood, hurricane, and earthquake insurance as separate policies.

Only 43 percent of those who rent have renters' insurance,[42] but you'd be surprised at how much it would cost to replace your belongings—clothes, furniture, pots, pans, appliances, sporting goods, electronic equipment, computers, and more—in the event

Cherie Froeba photographs the inside of her home in St. Bernard's Parish, Louisiana, for insurance purposes when she visits it for the first time after the floods following Hurricane Katrina. With her husband, Froeba returned to salvage any personal effects, including her grandmother's Bible. St. Bernard's Parish was one of the worst hit areas in Louisiana.

of a fire or burglary. Renters' or homeowners' insurance covers losses of your possessions, but you must be careful to specify that you want *guaranteed replacement cost*, which means that the insurance company will give you whatever it costs to buy all of those things *new*. Such insurance costs a little more than a policy without guaranteed replacement, but you'll get a lot more money if you have a loss.

The other option is to buy insurance that covers the depreciated cost of you items. For example, a sofa you bought five years ago for $600 may be worth only $150 now. The current value is what you would get from this type of insurance policy—not the $700 or more you may need to buy a brand-new sofa. The same is

Figure A.14 How Much Insurance Should You Have?

Value of a typical single-person household	
Furniture	$8,000
TV, DVD player, stereo, DVDs, and CDs	$2,000
Home computer	$1,500
Microwave	$120
Other appliances	$240
Clothing	$3,000
Paintings, prints, photos	$800
Glassware, china, and silverware	$600
Sports equipment	$600
Cameras and photographer's equipment	$800
Books	$700
Jewelry	$1,000
Other property	$4,000
Total	$23,360

Source: "The Basics of Renters Insurance," Insure.com, August 28, 2008 http://www.insure.com/articles/homeinsurance/renters.html (accessed September 6, 2009).

true for a computer that you paid $950 for a few years ago. If it were to be stolen, you would get only a few hundred dollars for it, rather than the replacement cost.

Most insurance policies do not cover expensive items, such as jewelry or sterling silverware. You can buy a **rider** (sometimes called supplemental insurance) to your insurance policy that will cover such items at a very reasonable cost. Ask your agent about such coverage.

Rider Supplemental insurance; also means an amendment to a contract.

BUS connections

1. What types of insurance should you consider purchasing now? What insurance might you need in the future?

2. What is the difference between a variable life insurance policy and a term policy?

3. Is it advisable to have a health insurance policy if you're healthy? Explain.

or older, you can make an additional $1,000 "catch-up" contribution.) Normally, you'd pay taxes on that $5,000 when you receive it as income—but because you put it into an IRA, you won't. If you're in the 25 percent tax bracket, that means you'll save $1,250 in taxes! Put another way, the $5,000 you save costs you only $3,750—a huge bargain.

The earlier you start saving, the better, because your money has a chance to double and double again.[47] If you save $5,000 a year for 35 years in an IRA and earn 10 percent each year, you'll accumulate savings of more than $1.5 million. If you start when you're just out of school, you'll be a millionaire by the time you're 55, simply by saving $5,000 a year and earning 10 percent interest.

By increasing the contribution to the maximum allowable each time it is raised, a person can reach his or her million-dollar goal even earlier. The actual rate of return depends on the type of investments you choose. It is important to remember that future rates of return cannot be predicted with certainty and that investments that pay higher rates of return also have higher risk and volatility. For example, the stock market boomed during the mid- to late 1990s and then plummeted for several years starting in 1999.

A second kind of IRA is the **Roth IRA**. People who invest in a Roth IRA don't get upfront deductions on their taxes, as they would with a traditional IRA, but the earnings grow tax-free and are also tax-free when they're withdrawn.

Therefore, there's a fundamental difference between a traditional IRA and a Roth: traditional IRAs offer tax savings when money

goes in, and Roth IRAs offer tax savings when money comes out. Financial planners highly recommend IRAs, but they differ as to which kind is best. Both have advantages and disadvantages, so it's best to consult a financial planner to help you figure out which one is right for you. You may even decide to have both kinds of accounts. See Figure A.16 for a comparison of Roth and traditional IRAs.

The actual rate of return on investments can vary widely over time, but the average rate for the S&P 500 between 1970 and 2003 was 11 percent per year. The S&P 500 was down 5.2 percent from 2004 to 2009 and 22.4 percent from 1999 to 2009. Nonetheless, some analysts predict that trend will reverse in the immediate future.[48] (See Figure A.17.)

Consider this: If you began contributing $5,000 to an IRA earning 10 percent when you were 22 years old and stopped contributing after only five years, you'd accumulate $33,000 by the time you're 27. *Even if you never added another penny to the IRA, by the time you reach the age of 65, you'd have almost $1.1 million. If you waited until you were 30 to start saving, you'd need to save $5,000 every year for 35 years to

> **Roth IRA** An investment that does not get upfront deductions on taxes, but the earnings grow tax-free and are tax-free when they are withdrawn.

Online financial calculators like this one from Leadfusion can help you determine how much money you will need for retirement.

Source: www.leadfusion.com

have the same nest egg. And what would you have if you started saving at 22 *and* continued nonstop every year until 65? More than $3 million![49] Can you see why investment advisers often say that an IRA is the best way to invest in your retirement?

In most cases, you can't withdraw money from either type of IRA until you're 59½ years old without paying a 10 percent penalty and taxes on the income. That's a benefit for you, because it can keep you from tapping into your IRA in an emergency or when you're tempted to make a large impulse purchase. But the money is there if a real need or emergency arises. The government now allows you to take out some funds to invest in an education or a first home. But check the rules; they change over time.

For example, Kip Tobin of Akron, Ohio, lost his job working for a rubber importer. Tobin decided to enter the world of entrepreneurship, but he had little cash on hand to do so. With the help of a broker who managed some complicated legal transactions, Tobin accessed his IRA funds without incurring a penalty. As a result, he and two partners were able to start a new business helping professionals in the Akron area. Tapping his IRA worked out for Tobin, but doing so is very risky and must be carefully planned.[50]

There are many types of IRAs, each with a wide range of investment choices. Banks, savings and loans, and credit unions all offer different types of IRAs. Insurance companies offer such plans as well. People who will consider more risk can put IRA funds into stocks, bonds, mutual funds, or precious metals. Investors can switch from fund to fund, or from investment to investment, with IRA funds and can even open several different IRAs, as long as the total amount invested does not exceed the government's limit. Consider contributing to an IRA through payroll deductions to ensure that the money is invested before you are tempted to spend it. Opening an IRA may be one of the wisest investments you make.

401(K) PLANS

A **401(k) plan** is an employer-sponsored savings plan that allows you to deposit a set amount of pretax dollars and collect compounded earnings tax-free until withdrawal, when the money is taxed at ordinary income tax rates. 401(k) plans now account for 49 percent of America's private pension savings. More than 220,000 companies now offer 401(k) retirement plans, covering some 55 million workers. For 28 percent of these employees, a 401(k) or similar defined-contribution plan is their only pension. Unfortunately, only about 70 percent of eligible employees make any contributions to the accounts.[51] That's a huge mistake, as you will see.

> **401(k) plan** An employer-sponsored savings plan that allows you to deposit a set amount of pretax dollars and collect compounded earnings tax-free until withdrawal, when the money is taxed at ordinary income tax rates.

These plans have three benefits: (1) the money put in reduces present taxable income, (2) tax is deferred on the earnings, and (3) employers often match part of the deposits made. More than 80 percent of 401(k) plans offer a match, sometimes 50 cents for every dollar. No investment will give you a better deal than an instant 50 percent return on your money. You should deposit at least as much as your employer matches, often up to 15

Figure A.17 S&P 500 Index Historic Calendar Year Returns 1926–2007[59]

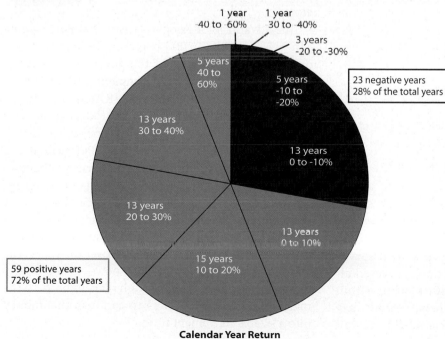

1 year
−40 to −60%

1 year
−30 to −40%

3 years
−20 to −30%

5 years
−10 to
−20%

23 negative years
28% of the total years

5 years
40 to
60%

13 years
30 to 40%

13 years
0 to −10%

13 years
20 to 30%

13 years
0 to 10%

15 years
10 to 20%

59 positive years
72% of the total years

Calendar Year Return

Real World Apps

percent of your salary. According to a 2008 survey of 531 companies, 72.7 percent of those surveyed allowed employees to participate in 401(k) plans within the first three months of employment.[52] Funds may not normally be withdrawn from a 401(k) account until individuals reach 59½, but fund owners may be able to *borrow* from the account. Usually people may select how the money in a 401(k) plan is invested—stocks, bonds, and, in some cases, real estate.

A simple 401(k) plan exists for firms that employ 100 or fewer employees. Employees are allowed to invest an amount (in 2009, a maximum of $16,500) that may be matched by the employer. This is a rather new program, but it should also prove popular among small businesses that are trying to attract good employees.

Be careful not to invest all your money in the company where you work. Although the company may be doing quite well, there is always a possibility that it could collapse and leave you with almost nothing. Employees at some companies, including Enron, have lost much—or, in some cases, all—of their 401(k) money. It's always best to diversify your funds among different companies and among stocks, bonds, and real estate investment trusts.

KEOGH PLANS

Millions of sole proprietors don't have the benefit of a corporate retirement system. They can contribute to IRAs, but the amount they can invest in these funds is limited. The alternative for all those doctors, lawyers, real estate agents, artists, writers, and other self-employed people is to establish their own Keogh plan. **Keogh plans** are like IRAs for entrepreneurs. You can also look into simplified employee pension plans, the best types of IRAs for sole proprietors.

> **Keogh plan** Similar to an IRA but designed for entrepreneurs with higher maximum contributions.

The advantage of Keogh plans is that participants can invest up to $40,000 per year. The amount was originally much lower, but the government decided to encourage self-employed people to build their retirement funds. Like traditional IRAs, Keogh funds aren't taxed until the funds are withdrawn, nor are the returns the funds earn. Thus, a person in the 25 percent tax bracket who invests $10,000 yearly in a Keogh saves $2,500 in taxes—which means the government is financing 25 percent of the person's retirement fund. As with an IRA, that's a great deal.

However, like the IRA, there's also a 10 percent penalty for early withdrawal, and funds may be withdrawn in a lump sum or spread out over the years. The key decision is the one you make now—to begin early to put funds into an IRA, a Keogh plan, or both, so the magic of compounding interest can turn that money into a sizable retirement fund.

FINANCIAL PLANNERS

If the idea of developing a comprehensive financial plan for yourself or your business seems overwhelming, relax. Help is available. The people who can help you develop a comprehensive program that covers investments, taxes, insurance, and other financial matters are called financial planners.

Certified financial planner (CFP) A licensed person who manages investments.

Be careful, though—anybody can claim to be a financial planner today. It's best to find a person who has earned the distinction of being a **certified financial planner (CFP).** A CFP must complete a curriculum on 106 financial topics and pass a 10-hour examination. In the United States today, there are more than 36,000 CFPs. Employment for financial analysts and advisers is expected to grow tremendously—by 37 percent, much faster than the average for all occupations—between the years of 2006 and 2016.[53] Businesspeople can also turn to their accountants or finance departments for legitimate financial planning help.

In the past few years, there has been an explosion in the number of companies offering other businesses financial services, sometimes called one-stop financial centers or financial supermarkets because they provide a variety of financial services, ranging from banking services to mutual funds, insurance, tax assistance, stocks, bonds, and real estate. It pays to shop around for financial advice. Ask friends and family for referrals. Find someone who understands your business and is willing to spend some time with you.

Good financial planners take time to understand their clients' needs before making suggestions. Most financial planners begin by selling life insurance, since they believe most working people should carry basic term insurance coverage. They'll also explore your health insurance plans, looking for both medical expense and disability coverage. They may also recommend major medical protection to cover catastrophic illnesses.

Financial planners can advise you on the proper mix of IRAs, stocks, bonds, real estate, and so on. Financial planning covers all aspects of investing, all the way to retirement and death. In the next section, you'll learn about estate planning.

ESTATE PLANNING

It's never too early to start thinking about estate planning and retirement. An important first step is to select a guardian for minor children, which can be a very difficult decision to make. That person should have a genuine concern for your children as well as a parental style and moral beliefs you endorse. You must also ensure that you leave sufficient resources to rear your children, not only for living expenses but also for medical bills, college, and other major expenses. Life insurance is often a good way to ensure such a fund. Be sure to discuss all these issues with the guardian, and choose a contingent guardian in case the first choice is unable to perform the functions.

Will A document that names a guardian for your children, states how you want your assets distributed, and names the executor for your estate.

Executor A person who assembles and values your estate, files income and other taxes, and distributes assets.

A second step is to prepare a will. A **will** is a document that names a guardian for children, states how assets are to be distributed, and names the executor of the estate. Fifty-eight percent of Americans don't have a will.[54] An **executor** assembles and values the estate, files income and other taxes, and assists with the distribution of assets. Often the executor will work closely with the deceased person's attorney to ensure that the terms of the will are properly administered.

Power of attorney A contract that gives signing power from one person to another to make decisions.

A third step is to prepare a durable **power of attorney**. This document gives an individual the power to take over your finances if you become incapacitated. Today, only 26 percent of Americans have a power of attorney for their finances.[55] A durable power of attorney for health care allows you to name a person you trust to make health decisions for you if you're unable to make decisions for yourself. A similar number—only 27 percent—of Americans have a power of attorney for health care.[56]

Many Americans suffer the effects of poor estate planning. Almost 20 percent of Americans have personally experienced problems after the death or incapacitation of a loved one due to a lack of a plan or an improperly prepared plan, including conflicts over asset distribution. In addition, it is less common for people of color to have estate plans in place—only 45 percent of African Americans and Hispanics have any type of estate planning, compared to 57 percent of white Americans. Only 28 percent of African-American adults and 20 percent of Hispanic adults have wills, compared to 46 percent of whites. Overall, death is a taboo topic for some Americans. Eight percent of those Americans without an estate plan say they don't have one because they don't want to think about dying or becoming incapacitated.[57]

There are other steps to follow that are beyond the scope of this text. You may need to contact a financial planner or attorney to help you prepare the paperwork and do the planning necessary to preserve and protect your investments for your children, spouse, and others. Estate planning is very complex, but good planning begins with a strong financial base.

As you've learned, accumulating enough funds to be financially secure is a complex and difficult matter. Investing that money and protecting it from loss make the process even more involved. It's never too early to start a saving and investment program. There are many millionaires in the United States and around the world. They have taken various paths to their wealth, but the most common ones are entrepreneurship and wise money management.[55] We hope this chapter helps you join their ranks.

For REVIEW >>

1. **Describe the importance of education in making money and six steps to developing financial discipline.**
   - People who hold bachelor's degrees have an average salary of around $51,000 per year, compared with an average salary of $31,500 for high school graduates. If you compound this difference over the course of a lifetime, a college grad makes $300,000 more than a high school graduate. Therefore, you'll probably be repaid your investment in a college education many times over. The six steps to financial discipline are (1) take an inventory of your financial assets, (2) keep track of all your expenses, (3) prepare a budget, (4) pay off your debts, (5) start a savings plan, and (6) borrow money only to buy assets that have the potential to increase in value or generate income.

2. **Explain strategies for building a financial base.**
   - In order to accumulate money, you should first find a job. Try to live as frugally as possible. Invest your savings to generate even more capital. A home is the one investment you can live in. Second, once you buy a home, the payments are relatively fixed (though taxes and utilities go up). As your income rises, the house payments get easier to make, while rents tend to go up at least as fast as income. The government allows you to deduct interest payments on the mortgage, which lets you buy more home for the money. It is best, in the long run, to invest in stock. Although stocks go up and down in value, in the long run they earn more than most other investments. Diversify among mutual funds and other investments. Credit cards can be very dangerous. You should pay off the balance in full during the period when no interest is charged. Not having to pay 16 percent interest is as good as earning 16 percent tax free.

3. **Define the different types of insurance and how they can protect your financial base.**
   - Insurance protects you from loss. If you were to die, your heirs would lose the income you would have earned. You can buy life insurance to make up for some or all of that loss. Term insurance is pure insurance protection for a given number of years. You can buy much more term insurance than whole life insurance for the same amount of money. It is important to have health insurance to protect against large medical bills. You also need car insurance (get a high deductible) and liability insurance in case you injure someone. You should also have homeowners' or renters' insurance.

4. **Describe strategies for effective retirement planning.**
   - Social Security depends on payments from current workers to cover the needs of retired people. Fewer workers are paying into the system, so you cannot rely on it to cover all your retirement expenses. Supplement Social Security with savings plans of your own. Everyone should have an IRA or some other retirement program. A Roth IRA is especially good for young people because your money grows tax free and is tax free when you withdraw it. For entrepreneurs, a Keogh plan is a wise choice. If you work for someone else, check out the 401(k) plan. Find a financial adviser who can recommend the best savings plan and help you make other investments. You need to choose a guardian for your children, prepare a will, and assign an executor for your estate. Sign a durable power of attorney to enable someone else to handle your finances if you are not capable. The same applies to a health durable power of attorney. Estate planning is complex and often calls for the aid of a financial planner/attorney, but the money is well spent to protect your assets.

Key Terms

Annuity	Diversification	Insurance	Stockbroker
Certified financial planner (CFP)	Exchange-traded funds	Keogh plan	Term insurance
Contrarian approach	Executor	Mutual fund	Universal life insurance
Copayment	FICO	Power of attorney	Variable life insurance
Deductible	401(k) plan	Rider	Whole life insurance
Disability insurance	Individual retirement account (IRA)	Roth IRA	Will
		Social Security	

1. What are some potential benefits and drawbacks of owning your own home? List at least five of each.

2. What are some differences between traditional IRAs and Roth IRAs? Name and describe at least three differences.

3. What are the steps for financial discipline discussed in this chapter? Have you personally taken these steps? Do you plan to? Describe why or why not. Are there things you could do to better manage your finances beyond the ideas explained in this chapter? Describe any that come to mind.

4. What is the purpose of a 401(k) plan? Why should you always invest in your company's 401(k) plan?

5. In groups, discuss why it is never too early to start thinking about saving for retirement. List the various ways you can save for retirement that were discussed in this chapter.

6. In groups, name and describe at least three different types of insurance. What are the advantages to each type of coverage? The drawbacks?

1. Visit and review http://www.kiplinger.com/tools/budget. Fill out the form and then answer the following questions.

   a. Are there any expenditures you can cut back on in order to save money?

   b. Do you think you can realistically stick to this budget? Why or why not?

   c. Suppose your car breaks down. It will cost $1,500 to fix it. How will this affect your budget?

   d. List some major items that you would like to purchase two years, five years, and ten years from now. What can you do to make sure these goals are met?

2. Visit http://www.bankrate.com/calculators/savings/simple-savings-calculator.aspx and answer the following questions.

   a. If you initially deposited $500 and added $20 per month, what would your investment be worth in 10 years, assuming an interest rate of 6.5 percent? In 20 years?

   b. What if you earned 10 percent interest? By how much would the total go up?

   c. What if you earned 1 percent interest? By how much would the total go up?

   d. Revisit the budget you made in Question 1. What would you consider giving up in order to ensure that you can save more aggressively?

   e. Are you willing to take on extra risk in order to have more after 10 or 20 years? Why or why not?

Self-Assessment Exercises

BUSINESS CAREER QUIZ

How Well Do You Know Stock Market Lingo?

1. Market capitalization is the total dollar value of a company's:
   a. stock
   b. assets
   c. annual sales
   d. bonds

2. Standard and Poor's 500 (S&P 500) does not include:
   a. foreign companies
   b. construction companies
   c. oil companies
   d. entertainment companies

3. The NASDAQ includes:
   a. 500 companies
   b. 1,500 companies
   c. 4,000 companies
   d. 10,000 companies

4. Most stocks are traded:
   a. by mail
   b. on Wall Street
   c. on exchanges
   d. By phone

5. The NYSE is located in:
   a. Los Angeles
   b. New York
   c. Boston
   d. Seattle

6. The Dow Jones Industrial Average is composed of:
   a. 500 large stocks
   b. 30 large stocks
   c. 30 small stocks
   d. 100 small stocks

7. Stocks that are less volatile and independent from the business cycle are called:
   a. blue chips
   b. growth stocks
   c. income stocks
   d. defensive stocks

8. Stocks that pay relatively high dividends are called:
   a. income stocks
   b. blue chips
   c. defensive stocks
   d. cyclical stocks

9. Dollar cost averaging:
   a. requires less paperwork periodically
   b. is the best way to beat the market value
   c. means to invest a fixed amount
   d. means to invest on a dollar

10. No-load mutual funds:
    a. cannot be bought via the Internet
    b. do not charge extra fees to buy or sell shares
    c. are FDIC insured
    d. do not perform as well as load funds

Answers:
1. A. Market capitalization is the total value of company stock.

2. A. The S&P 500 only includes companies based in the United States.
3. C. The NASDAQ includes 4,000 companies.
4. C. Stocks are traded on exchanges, such as the NASDAQ.
5   B. NYSE stands for the New York Stock Exchange, which is located in New York City.
6. B. The Dow Jones includes 30 large stocks.
7. D. Defensive stocks are less volatile.
8. A. Income stocks pay higher dividends than most stocks.
9. D. Dollar cost averaging is the concept of investing a set amount periodically, such as every quarter.
10. B. No load means that extra fees are not charged.

Source: Personal Finance Quizzes. (2002-2009). Stocks, Quiz 1 and 2 from http://www.quiz-tree.com/Personal-Finance_main.html (accessed September 11, 2009).

Impulse Spending Quiz

1. Do you ever go shopping and leave a store with nothing or just what you came in for, and nothing else?
    a. Almost never   c. Sometimes
    b. Rarely   d. All the time. I know exactly what I plan to buy before I walk in.

2. When you shop with friends, do you feel the need to buy more?
    a. Yes. I have more fun when I spend in groups.
    b. Sometimes, if my friend convinces me to buy something.
    c. Rarely, unless I see something on sale.
    d. Never. I know what I am looking for and never veer from my plan.

3. Do you ever spend money you don't have?
    a. Yes, all the time. I figure by the time my credit card bill comes, I'll be able to pay it somehow.
    b. Sometimes, if I really need something, I figure I'll borrow from friends or family if I have to.
    c. Rarely, unless it is a true emergency—meaning that I can't cover my basic expenses.
    d. Never. I have a budget I stick with and always have six months' salary saved for emergencies.

4. Do you ever make only the minimum payment on your credit card?
    a. Always   c. Rarely
    b. Sometimes   d. Never

5. Do you research an expensive purchase (more than $100) or buy the first thing you see?
    a. If something catches my eye, I buy it.
    b. I might glance at a review before I go to the store, but that's it.
    c. I research prices, but if something strikes me, I'll buy it without looking back.
    d. I research extensively by comparing prices at both online and bricks-and-mortar stores and
       checking for sales, rebates, and coupons. Once I'm ready to make a purchase, I first thoroughly
       examine the merchandise and read all the fine print before I buy.

Answers:

If you answered "d" for every question, congratulations! You're a savvy consumer. You know how to spend wisely and make every penny count.

If you answered "a" for every question, you need help! Find a professional to help you work out a budget and learn how to stick with it. You need to address your spending problem before it gets completely out of control.

If you answered "b" or "c" for four out of five questions, you may not be in too much trouble yet, but you should start watching every penny. Once you start tracking your expenses, you'll begin to realize how much money you're wasting without even knowing it.

Source: Dubuque, Marie. Impulse Spending Quiz, May 4, 2008. http://consumereducation.suite101.com/article.cfm/impulse_spending_quiz (accessed September 11, 2009).

The numbers following the definitions indicate the pages on which the terms were identified and defined. Consult the index for further page references to the topic.

A

Absolute advantage The advantage that exists when a country has a monopoly on producing a specific product or is able to produce it more efficiently than all other countries. **303**

Account receivable An amount of money owed to the firm that it expects to be paid within one year. **222**

Accounting Recording, classifying, summarizing, and interpreting financial events and transactions to provide management and other interested parties with the information they need to make good decisions. **215**

Advertising Paid, nonpersonal communication through various media by organizations and individuals who are in some way identified in the advertising message. **109**

Affirmative action Employment activities designed to "right past wrongs" by increasing opportunities for minorities and women. **139**

Agents/brokers Marketing intermediaries who bring buyers and sellers together and assist in negotiating an exchange but don't take title to the goods. **104**

Angel investors People (usually wealthy) who invest their own funds in a business in exchange for a stake in the company. **79**

Annual report Yearly statement of the financial condition, progress, and expectations of an organization. **215**

Annuity A contract to make regular payments to a person for life or for a fixed period. **379**

Arbitration An agreement to bring in an impartial third party (a single arbitrator or a panel of arbitrators) to render a binding decision in a labor dispute. **144**

Assembly process The part of the production process that puts together components. **156**

Assets Economic resources (things of value) owned by a firm. **222**

Auditing The job of reviewing and evaluating the records used to prepare a company's financial statements. **216**

Autocratic leadership A leadership style that involves making managerial decisions without consulting others. **257**

B

Balance of payments The difference between money coming into a country (from exports) and money leaving the country (for imports) plus money flows from other factors, such as tourism, foreign aid, military expenditures, and foreign investment. **304**

Balance of trade The total value of a nation's exports compared to its imports measured over a particular period. **304**

Balance sheet The financial statement that reports a firm's financial condition at a specific time. **222**

Bankruptcy The legal process by which an individual or business unable to meet financial obligations can seek court protection under these laws and can be relieved of those debts by a court. **12**

Barter The direct trade of goods and services for other goods and services. **207**

Benefit segmentation Dividing a market by determining which benefits of the product to promote. **91**

Board of directors The group ultimately responsible for the decisions of a business. **74**

Bond A corporate certificate indicating that a person has lent money to a firm. **210**

Bookkeeping The recording of business transactions. **219**

Boycott When a union encourages both its members and the general public not to buy the products of a firm involved in a labor dispute. **143**

Brain drain The loss of the best and brightest people to other countries. **42**

Brand A name, symbol, or design (or combination thereof) that identifies the goods or services of one seller or group of sellers and distinguishes them from those of others. **99**

Brand equity The combination of factors, such as awareness, loyalty, perceived quality, images, and emotions, that people associate with a given brand name. **99**

Brand loyalty The degree to which customers are satisfied, like a brand, and are committed to future purchases. **100**

Break-even analysis strategy Pricing a product based on how many you need to sell in order to make a profit. **103**

Broadband technology Technology that offers users a continuous connection to the Internet and allows them to send and receive mammoth files that include voice, video, and data much faster than ever before. **182**

Bundling strategy Grouping two or more products together and pricing them as a unit. **103**

Business A person, partnership, or corporation that seeks to provide goods and services to others at a profit. **2**

Business cycle A common pattern in which there is a period of rapid economic growth (recovery and prosperity) when supply and demand stimulate each other, alternating with a period of decline (contraction or recession) with diminishing demand and supply. **36**

Business plan A detailed written statement that describes the nature of

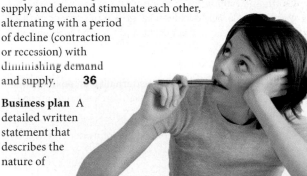

the business, the target market, the advantages the business will have in relation to competition, and the resources and qualifications of the owner(s). **62**

Business-to-business (B2B) A business that produces products to sell to another business. **15**

Business-to-consumer (B2C) A business that produces products to sell directly to the consumer. **15**

C

Cafeteria-style fringe benefits Fringe benefits plan that allows employees to choose the benefits they want up to a certain dollar amount. **134**

Cannibalization A situation in which a new franchise takes away customers from an existing franchise nearby. **68**

Capitalism An economic system in which all or most of the factors of production and distribution are privately owned and operated for profit. **37**

Capitalist system A system in which companies and businesses are owned by citizens instead of the government. **14**

Cash-and-carry wholesalers Wholesalers that serve mostly smaller retailers with a limited assortment of products. **107**

Category killer A store that offers a wide selection of goods in a specific category at competitive prices. **108**

Certified financial planner (CFP) A licensed person who manages investments. **387**

Certified management accountant (CMA) A professional accountant who has met certain educational and experience requirements, passed a qualifying exam in the field, and been certified by the Institute of Certified Management Accountants. **216**

Certified public accountant (CPA) An accountant who has passed a series of examinations established by the American Institute of Certified Public Accountants (AICPA) and does accounting work for no one particular firm. **216**

Chain store A business location that is one of many stores, all of which have central management (meaning all stores are run by the same people) and share a brand name. **66**

Channel of distribution A set of marketing intermediaries, such as wholesalers and retailers that join together to transport and store goods in their path (or channel) from producers to consumers. **103**

Command economies Economic systems in which the government largely decides what goods and services will be produced, who will get them, and how the economy will grow. **44**

Common market (trading bloc) A regional group of countries that have a common external tariff, no internal tariffs, and coordinated laws to facilitate exchange among member countries. **309**

Common stock The most basic form of ownership in a firm. **213**

Communism An economic and political system in which the state (the government) makes almost all economic decisions and owns almost all the major factors of production, including housing for its people. **42**

Company store A store owned and operated by a chain. **66**

Comparable worth The idea that people in jobs requiring similar levels of education, training, or skills should receive equal pay. **146**

Comparative advantage theory A theory that states that a country should sell to other countries those products that it produces most effectively and efficiently and buy from other countries those products that it cannot produce as effectively or efficiently. **303**

Compensation The combination of salary, vacation time, paid health care, and other benefits. **132**

Compliance-based ethics codes Rules that prevent unlawful behavior by increasing control and penalizing violations. **340**

Compressed workweek Work schedule that allows an employee to work a full number of hours per week but in fewer days. **135**

Computer-aided design (CAD) The use of computers in the design of products. **157**

Computer-aided manufacturing (CAM) The use of computers in the manufacturing of products. **157**

Computer-integrated manufacturing (CIM) The uniting of computer-aided design with computer-aided manufacturing. **158**

Conceptual skills Skills that involve the ability to picture the organization as a whole and the relationship among its various parts. **249**

Consumer price index (CPI) A set of monthly statistics that measures the pace of inflation or deflation. **48**

Contingency planning The process of preparing alternative courses of action that may be used if the primary plans don't achieve the organization's objectives. **247**

Contingent workers Employees that include part-time workers, temporary workers, seasonal workers, independent contractors, interns, and co-op students. **128**

Continuous process A production process in which long production runs turn out finished goods over time. **156**

Contract A legally enforceable agreement between two or more parties. **12**

Contract manufacturing A foreign country's production of private-label goods to which a domestic company then attaches its brand name or trademark; part of the broad category of outsourcing. **316**

Contrarian approach Purchasing stock when others are selling. **370**

Controlling A management function that involves establishing clear standards to determine whether or not an organization is progressing toward its goals and objectives, rewarding people for doing a good job, and taking corrective action if they are not. **240**

Conventional (C) corporation A form of business ownership that provides limited liability. **74**

Cookies Pieces of information, such as registration data or user preferences, sent by a Web site over the Internet to a Web browser that the browser software is expected to save and send back to the server whenever the user returns to that Web site. **197**

Copayment An amount paid by the insured party when medical services are rendered. **380**

Core time In a flextime plan, the period when all employees are expected to be at their job stations. **135**

Corporate governance The processes, customs, policies, laws, and institutions that affect how a corporation is directed, administered, or controlled. **74**

Corporate philanthropy An indicator of social responsibility that includes charitable donations. **342**

Corporate policy The position a firm takes on social and political issues. **344**

Corporate responsibility An indicator of social responsibility that includes the actions the company takes that could affect others. **343**

Corporate social responsibility The level of concern a business has for the welfare of society. **342**

Cost of goods sold (cost of goods manufactured) A measure of the cost of merchandise sold, or the cost of the raw materials and supplies used for producing items for sale. **225**

Countertrading A complex form of bartering in which several countries may be involved, each trading goods for goods or services for services. **323**

Critical path In a PERT network, the sequence of tasks that takes the longest time to complete. **167**

Culture The set of values, beliefs, rules, and institutions held by a specific group of people. **319**

D

Data Raw, unanalyzed, and unorganized facts and figures. **179**

Data mining Looking for hidden patterns in the data in a data warehouse and discovering relationships among the data. **186**

Data processing (DP) The name given to business technology in the 1970s. Its primary purpose was to improve the flow of financial information. **179**

Data warehouse An electronic storage place for data on a specific subject (such as sales) over a period of time. **186**

Database An electronic storage file for information. **15**

Deductible The amount that must be spent on health care before insurance companies will cover the remaining expenses. **380**

Deflation A general decline in the prices of goods and services over time. **48**

Demand The quantity of products people are willing and able to buy at different prices at a specific time. **35**

Demographic segmentation Dividing a market into demographic categories, such as age, income, or education level. **91**

Demographics Statistics about the human population with regard to its size, density, and other characteristics. **18**

Depression A severe recession. **46**

Deregulation The removal of government control and strict oversight in a market that thereby opens the market for others to enter. **40**

Disability insurance A type of insurance that pays part of the cost of a long-term sickness or an accident. **380**

Diversification Buying several different types of investments to spread the risk of investing. **371**

Diversity Broad differences among a group of people, including their ethnicity, sex, color, sexual orientation, body size, age, and so on. **17**

Dividends Part of a firm's profits that may be distributed to stockholders as cash payments or additional shares of stock. **75, 212**

Double taxation Occurs when the owners of a corporation are taxed twice—once when the corporation is taxed and then again when the dividends are taxed. **75**

Downsizing The elimination of many management jobs, and other types of jobs, by using cost-cutting methods and technology, such as computers. **263**

Drop shippers Wholesalers that solicit orders from retailers and other wholesalers and have the merchandise shipped directly from a producer to a buyer. **107**

Dumping Selling products in a foreign country at lower prices than those charged in the producing country. **305**

E

E-business Any electronic business data exchange using any electronic device. **182**

E-commerce The buying and selling of goods over the Internet. **15, 182**

Economics The study of how individuals and society choose to use scarce resources to produce goods and services and distribute them for consumption. **33**

Effectiveness Producing the desired results. **14**

Efficiency Producing goods using the least amount of resources. **14**

Embargo A complete ban on the import or export of a certain product or the stopping of all trade with a particular country. **307**

Employee orientation The activity that introduces new employees to the organization; to fellow employees; to their immediate supervisors; and to the policies, practices, and objectives of the firm. **129**

Empowerment Giving frontline workers the responsibility, authority, and freedom to respond quickly to customer requests. **17, 240, 293**

Enterprise resource planning (ERP) A newer version of materials requirement planning that combines the computerized functions of all the divisions and subsidiaries of the firm—such as finance, human resources, and order fulfillment—into a single integrated software program that uses a single database. **164**

Entrepreneur A person who risks time and money to start and manage a business. **2**

Entrepreneurship The process of accepting the risk of starting and running a business. **58**

Equilibrium point The point at which the amount of goods sought by buyers is equal to the amount of goods produced by suppliers. **36**

Equity theory The idea that employees try to maintain equity between inputs and outputs compared to others in similar positions. **292**

Ethics The standards of moral behavior; that is, behavior that is accepted by society as right versus wrong. **334**

Ethnocentricity An attitude that one's own culture is superior to other cultures. **319**

European Union (EU) An agreement among European member countries to eventually reduce all barriers to trade and become unified, both economically and politically. **309**

Event marketing Sponsoring events such as rock concerts or attending various events to promote your products. **114**

Everyday low pricing (EDLP) strategy Setting prices lower than competitors and then not offering any special sales. **103**

Exchange rate The value of one nation's currency relative to the currencies of other countries. **321**

Exchange-traded funds Collections of stocks that are traded on exchanges but are traded more like individual stocks than like mutual funds. **373**

Executor A person who assembles and values a person's estate, files income and other taxes, and distributes assets. **388**

Expenses The costs of purchasing the goods and services that are needed to operate a business. **3**

Exporting Selling products to another country. **301**

Expropriation When a host government takes over a foreign subsidiary in a country. **318**

External candidates Potential employees who do not already work for a firm. **125**

Extranet A semiprivate network that uses Internet technology and allows more than one company to access the same information or allows people on different servers to collaborate. **190**

Extrinsic reward A reward given to an employee, such as a promotion or pay raise. **284**

F

Facility layout The physical arrangement of resources, including people, to most efficiently produce goods and provide services for customers. **163**

Facility location The process of selecting a geographic location for a company's operations. **162**

Factors of production The resources used to create wealth: land, labor, capital, entrepreneurship, and knowledge. **24**

FICO A credit score assigned by the three major credit reporting bureaus. **377**

Financial accounting Generates information for use outside the organization. **215**

Financial Accounting Standards Board (FASB) The group that oversees accounting practices. **216**

Financial statement A summary of all the financial transactions that have occurred over a particular period. **220**

Firewall Hardware or software that prevents outsiders from accessing information a user does not want others to see. **189**

Flexible manufacturing Designing machines to do multiple tasks so that they can produce a variety of products. **158**

Flextime plan Work schedule that gives employees some freedom to choose when to work, as long as they work the required number of hours. **135**

Focus group A small group of people who meet under the direction of a discussion leader who tries to understand their opinions about a product or service. **96**

For-profit organizations Organizations that are motivated to earn profits. **10**

Foreign direct investment (FDI) The buying of permanent property and businesses in foreign nations. **317**

Foreign subsidiary A company owned in a foreign country by another company, called the parent company. **317**

Form utility The value producers add to materials in the creation of finished goods and services. **156**

Formal leadership Someone who has been given authority to make decisions or lead a group. **281**

401(k) plan An employer-sponsored savings plan that allows you to deposit a set amount of pretax dollars and collect compounded earnings tax free until withdrawal, when the money is taxed at ordinary income tax rates. **385**

Franchisee A person who buys a franchise. **66**

Franchisor A person or entity that owns the rights to a franchise. **66**

Free market A system in which decisions about what to produce and in what quantities are made by the market. **37**

Free-market economies Economic systems in which the market largely determines what goods and services get produced, who gets them, and how the economy grows. **44**

Free-rein leadership A leadership style that involves managers setting objectives and employees being relatively free to do whatever it takes to accomplish those objectives. **258**

Free trade The movement of goods and services among nations without political or economic barriers. **19, 302**

G

Gantt chart Bar graph showing production managers what projects are being worked on and what stage they are in at any given time. **168**

General Agreement on Tariffs and Trade (GATT) A 1948 agreement that established an international forum for negotiating mutual reductions in trade restrictions. **308**

General partner An owner (partner) who has unlimited liability and is active in managing the firm. **72**

General partnership A partnership in which all owners share in operating a business and in assuming liability for the business's debts. **71**

Generally accepted accounting principles (GAAP) A set of principles followed by accountants in preparing reports. **216**

Geographic segmentation Dividing a market into geographic regions. **91**

Global business Any activity that seeks to provide goods and services to others across national borders while operating at a profit. **300**

Global trade The exchange of goods and services across national borders. **303**

Globalization The worldwide integration of government policies, cultures, social movements, and financial markets through trade and the exchange of ideas. **21**

Goal-setting theory The idea that setting ambitious but attainable goals can motivate workers and improve performance. **291**

Goals The broad, long-term accomplishments an organization wishes to attain. **242**

Goods Tangible products, such as cameras, food, computers, clothing, and cars. **2**

Governmental Accounting Standards Board (GASB) This group sets standards for governmental agencies' accounting practices. **217**

Gray market The flow of goods in a distribution channel or channels other than those intended by the manufacturer or licensor. **305**

Greenfield investment A form of foreign direct investment in which a company builds factories and offices in a foreign country on its own. **317**

Gross domestic product (GDP) The total value of final goods and services produced in a country in a given year. **46**

Gross national product (GNP) The value of goods and services produced by a country's factors of production, regardless of where these factors are based. **46**

Gross profit (gross margin) How much a firm earned by buying (or making) and selling merchandise, without expenses. **225**

Gross sales Total of all sales the firm completed. **224**

H

Hackers People who unlawfully break into computer systems. **190**

Harmonized Tariff Schedule A schedule of tariff costs for every product from every country that is published by the U.S. government. **306**

Hawthorne effect The tendency of people to behave differently when they know they are being studied. **286**

High-low pricing strategy Setting prices that are higher than EDLP, but offering many special sales where prices are lower than those of competitors. **103**

Human relations skills Skills that involve communication and motivation; they enable managers to work through and with people. **249**

Human resource management (HRM) The process of determining HR needs and then recruiting, selecting, training and developing, compensating, appraising, and scheduling employees to achieve organizational goals. **122**

Hygiene factors Job factors that can cause dissatisfaction if missing but do not necessarily motivate employees if increased. **288**

I

Illegal An act for which a person could be fined or imprisoned. **336**

Import quota A protectionist policy that limits the number of products in certain categories that a nation can import. **306**

Importing Buying products from another country. **301**

Income statement A summary of all the resources, called revenue, that have come into the firm from operating activities; money resources the firm used up; expenses it incurred in doing business. **224**

Independent audit An evaluation and unbiased opinion about the accuracy of a company's financial statements. **217**

Individual retirement account (IRA) A tax-deferred investment plan that allows you (and your spouse, if married) to save part of your income for retirement. **383**

Industrial good A product used in the production of other products. **98**

Inflation A general rise in the prices of goods and services over time. **48**

Infoglut The phenomenon of information overload in business. **186**

Informal leadership Someone who does not have official authority but is recognized as a leader by the group. **281**

Information The processed and organized data that can be used for managerial decision making. **179**

Information systems (IS) The name given to business technology in the 1980s. Its role changed from supporting the business to doing business. **179**

Information technology (IT) The name given to business technology in the 1990s. Its role became the way of doing business, rather than just using technology to help with business functions. **180**

Initial public offering (IPO) The first public offering of a corporation's stock. **209**

Injunction A court order directing someone to do something or to refrain from doing something. **144**

Insider trading When insiders of a company (such as employees) using private company information to further their own financial situation. **346**

Instant messaging (IM) Allows business professionals to communicate in real time, for free, via computer. **181**

Insurance A written contract between the party being insured and an insurer where the financial responsibility for losses transfers to the insurer up to a specified limit. **378**

Integrated marketing communication (IMC) Combines all the promotional tools into one comprehensive and unified promotional strategy. **114**

Integrity-based ethics codes Define the organization's guiding values and create an environment that supports ethically sound behavior. **340**

Interest rate A rate charged for using money. **49**

Intermittent process A production process in which the production run is short and the machines are changed frequently to make different products. **156**

Internal candidates Employees who already work for a firm who may be transferred or promoted. **125**

Internet2 The private Internet system that links government supercomputer centers and a select group of universities; it runs more than 22,000 times faster than today's public infrastructure and supports heavy-duty applications. **182**

Intranet A companywide network, closed to public access, that uses Internet-type technology. **189**

Intrinsic reward The personal satisfaction you feel when you perform well and achieve goals. **284**

Invisible hand A phrase coined by Adam Smith to describe the process that turns self-directed gain into social and economic benefits for all. **35**

ISO 9000 The common name given to quality management and assurance standards. **170**

ISO 14000 A collection of the best practices for managing an organization's impact on the environment. **171**

J

Job analysis A study of what employees do who hold various job titles. **123**

Job description Specifies the objectives of the job, the type of work to be done, the responsibilities and duties, the working conditions, and the relationship of the job to other functions. **123**

Job enlargement A motivation technique that involves combining a series of tasks into one challenging assignment. **289**

Job enrichment A motivational strategy that involves making a job more interesting in order to motivate employees. **289**

Job rotation A motivation technique that involves moving employees from one job to another. **289**

Job sharing An arrangement whereby two part-time employees share one full-time job. **136**

Job simulation The use of equipment that duplicates job conditions and tasks so trainees can learn skills before attempting them on the job. **130**

Job specifications A written summary of the minimum qualifications (education, skills, etc.) required of workers to do a particular job. **124**

Joint venture A partnership in which two or more companies (often from different countries) undertake a major project. **316**

Just-in-time (JIT) inventory control A production process in which a minimum of inventory is kept on the premises and parts, supplies, and other needs are delivered just in time to go on the assembly line. **166**

K

Keogh plan A plan that is similar to an IRA but designed for entrepreneurs with higher maximum contributions. **386**

L

Labor intensive When a firm's primary cost of operations is the cost of its labor force. **133**

Leadership Creating a vision for others to follow, establishing corporate values and ethics, and transforming the way an organization does business in order to improve its effectiveness and efficiency. **273**

Leading Creating a vision for an organization and guiding, training, coaching, and motivating others to work effectively to achieve the organization's goals and objectives. **240**

Lean manufacturing The production of goods using less of everything compared to mass production. **158**

Liabilities What a business owes to others (debts). **223**

Licensing A global strategy in which a firm (the licensor) allows a foreign company (the licensee) to produce its product in exchange for a fee (a royalty). **313**

Limited liability Means limited partners are not responsible for the debts of the business beyond the amount of their investment—their liability is limited to the amount they put into the company; their personal assets are not at risk. **72**

Limited liability partnership (LLP) LLPs limit partners' risk of losing their personal assets to only their own acts and omissions and to the acts and omissions of people under their supervision. **72**

Limited partner An owner who invests money in the business but does not have any management responsibility or liability for losses beyond the investment. **72**

Limited partnership A partnership with one or more general partners and one or more limited partners. **72**

Liquidity Refers to how fast an asset can be converted into cash. **222**

Lockout An attempt by managers to put pressure on union workers by temporarily closing the business. **144**

Loss When a business's expenses are more than its revenues. **4**

Loss leaders When a store advertises certain products at or below cost to attract people to the store. **101**

M

Macroeconomics The study of the operation of a nation's economy as a whole. **33**

Management The process of planning, organizing, leading, and controlling people and other available resources to accomplish organizational goals and objectives. **239**

Management development The process of training and educating employees to become good managers and then monitoring the progress of their managerial skills over time. **130**

Management by objectives (MBO) A system of goal setting and implementation that involves a cycle of discussion, review, and evaluation of objectives among top and mid-level managers, supervisors, and employees. **291**

Managerial accounting Provides information and analysis to managers within the organization to assist them in decision making. **215**

Market People with unsatisfied needs and wants who have both the resources and the willingness to buy. **58**

Market segmentation The process of dividing the total market into several groups whose members have similar characteristics. **90**

Marketing The process of planning and executing the conception, pricing, promotion, and distribution of goods and services to facilitate exchanges that satisfy individual and organizational needs. **90**

Marketing intermediary An organization that assists in moving goods and services from producers to industrial and consumer users. **103**

Marketing management The process of overseeing all the aspects of marketing a particular product or service for the purpose of attracting and retaining customers. **94**

Marketing mix (the four Ps) Product, price, place, and promotion, the four ingredients of a marketing program. **94**

Marketing research The analysis of markets to determine opportunities and challenges and to find the information needed to make good marketing decisions. **95**

Maslow's hierarchy of needs Theory of motivation based on unmet human needs from basic physiological needs to safety, social, esteem, and self-actualization needs. **286**

Mass customization Tailoring products to meet the needs of individual customers. **159**

Master limited partnership (MLP) Structured much like a corporation in that it acts like a corporation and is traded on a stock exchange like a corporation, but taxed like a partnership and thus avoids the corporate income tax. **72**

Materials requirement planning (MRP) A computer-based operations management system that uses sales forecasts to make sure that needed parts and materials are available at the right time and place. **164**

Maturity date The date a bond can be cashed in. **210**

Mediation The use of a third party, called a mediator, who encourages both sides in a dispute to continue negotiating and often makes suggestions for resolving the dispute. **144**

Mentor An adviser experienced in a particular job or type of business who acts as a guide for someone entering a field. **59**

Merchant wholesalers Independently owned firms that own the goods they handle. **106**

Microeconomics The study of the behavior of people and organizations in particular markets. **33**

Middle management The level of management that includes general managers, division managers, and branch and plant managers who are responsible for tactical planning and control. **248**

Mission statement An outline of the fundamental purposes of an organization. **241**

Mixed economies Economic systems in which some allocation of resources is made by the market and some by the government. **45**

Monetary policy The management of the money supply and interest rates by the Federal Reserve Bank. **49**

Money Anything that people generally accept as payment for goods and services. **206**

Monopolistic competition A market condition in which a large number of businesses produce products that are very similar but are perceived by buyers as different. **39**

Monopoly A form of competition in which only one business controls the total supply of a product and its price. **40**

Motivation The drive to satisfy a need. **284**

Motivators Job factors that cause employees to be productive and give them satisfaction. **288**

Multinational corporation An organization that manufactures and markets products in many different countries and has multinational stock ownership and multinational management. **318**

Mutual fund An organization that buys stocks and bonds and then sells shares in those securities to the public. **373**

N

NASDAQ A completely electronic securities market. **208**

National debt The sum of government deficits over time. **49**

National deficit The money the federal government spends over and above its revenue for a specific period of time. **49**

Negotiated labor–management agreement Agreement that sets the tone and clarifies the terms under which management and labor agree to function over time. **142**

Net sales Gross sales minus returns, discounts, and allowances. **224**

New York Stock Exchange (NYSE) A securities market. **208**

Niche marketing The process of finding small but profitable market segments and creating products for them. **91**

Nonprofit organizations Organizations that are not driven to garner profits. **10**

Nontariff barriers Restrictive standards that detail exactly how a product must be sold in a country. **307**

North American Free Trade Agreement (NAFTA) An agreement that created a free-trade area among the United States, Canada, and Mexico. **311**

O

Objectives Specific statements that detail how to achieve an organization's goals in the short term. **242**

Off-the-job training Internal or external training programs away from the workplace that develop any of a variety of skills or foster personal development. **129**

Oligopoly A form of competition in which just a few businesses dominate a market. **39**

On-the-job training Training at the workplace that lets the employee learn by doing or by watching others for a while and then imitating them. **129**

Online training Training programs in which employees complete classes via the Internet. **129**

Operating expenses The costs involved in operating a business. **226**

Operational planning The process of setting work standards and schedules necessary to implement the company's tactical objectives. **247**

Operations management A specialized area in management that converts or transforms resources (including human resources) into goods and services. **154**

Opportunity cost Refers to what you give up (your next best choice) in order to do or get something else (your chosen decision). **33**

Organization chart A visual device that shows relationships among people and divides the organization's work; it shows who reports to whom. **247**

Organizing A management function that includes designing the structure of the organization and creating conditions and systems in which everyone and everything works together to achieve the organization's goals and objectives. **239**

Outsourcing Assigning various functions, such as accounting, production, security, maintenance, and legal work, to outside organizations. **6**

Owners' equity The amount of the business that belongs to the owners minus any liabilities owed by the business. **223**

P

Par value The dollar amount assigned to each stock certificate on the corporation's charter. **212**

Participative (democratic) leadership A leadership style that consists of managers and employees working together to make decisions. **257**

Partnership A legal form of business with two or more owners. **71**

Penetration strategy Pricing a product low to attract many customers and discourage competition. **103**

Pension A promise made by a company to pay a monthly dollar amount to employees who have worked a minimum number of years. **348**

Perfect competition A market condition in which there are many businesses and no one business is large enough to dictate the price of a product. **38**

Performance appraisal An evaluation that measures employee performance against established standards in order to make decisions about promotions, compensation, training, or termination. **136**

Performance improvement plan (PIP) A detailed document explaining what the employee needs to change and detailed steps on how to accomplish the change. **137**

Personal selling The face-to-face presentation and promotion of goods and services. **111**

PEST analysis An analysis of outside factors that could affect a business: political, economic, social, and technological. **243**

Place In marketing, the process of getting products to the places where they will be sold. **103**

Planning A management function that includes anticipating trends and determining the best strategies and tactics to achieve organizational goals and objectives. **239**

Portal An entry point onto a Web site. **191**

Power of attorney A contract that gives signing power from one person to another to make decisions. **388**

Preferred stock Stocks that offer investors a preference (hence the term "preferred") in the payment of dividends. **213**

Price leadership The procedure by which one or more firms that dominate a market set pricing standards that all the others follow. **103**

Primary research Research collected firsthand by a marketer. **96**

Principle of motion economy A theory developed by Frank and Lillian Gilbreth that every job can be broken down into a series of elementary motions. **285**

Private accountant An accountant who works for a single firm, government agency, or nonprofit organization on the payroll of the company or organization. **216**

Process manufacturing The part of the production process that physically or chemically changes materials. **156**

Producer price index (PPI) A set of monthly statistics that measures prices at the wholesale level. **49**

Product differentiation An attempt to make buyers think similar products are different in some way. **39**, **96**

Product life cycle A theoretical model of what happens to sales and profits for a product class over time. **101**

Product placement Putting products in TV shows and movies, where they will be seen. **110**

Production The creation of finished goods and services using the factors of production: land, labor, capital, entrepreneurship, and knowledge. **154**

Production management The term used to describe all the activities managers do to help their firms create goods. **154**

Productivity The amount of output generated given a particular amount of an input. **14**

Profit The amount of money a business earns above and beyond what it spends for goods, services, salaries, and other expenses. **3**

Program evaluation and review technique (PERT) A method for analyzing the tasks involved in completing a given project, estimating the time needed to complete each task, and identifying the minimum time needed to complete the total project. **167**

Promotion mix The combination of promotional tools an organization uses. **109**

Psychographic segmentation Dividing a market using the group's values, attitudes, and interests. **91**

Psychological pricing (odd pricing) strategy Pricing goods and services at price points that make the product appear less expensive than it is. **103**

Public accountant An accountant who does not work for a specific company. **216**

Public domain software (freeware) Software that is free for the taking. **193**

Public relations (PR) The management function that evaluates public attitudes, changes policies and procedures accordingly, and executes a program of action and information to earn public understanding and acceptance. **111**

Publicity Any information about an individual, product, or organization that's distributed to the public through the media and that's not paid for or controlled by the seller. **112**

Purchasing The function in a firm that searches for high-quality material resources, finds the best suppliers, and negotiates the best price for goods and services. **165**

Q

Quality Consistently producing what the customer wants while reducing errors before and after delivery to the customer. **168**

R

Rack jobbers Wholesalers that furnish racks or shelves full of merchandise to retailers, display products, and sell on consignment. **106**

Ratio analysis The assessment of a firm's financial condition and performance through calculations and interpretation of financial ratios developed from the firm's financial statements. **228**

Reasonable accommodations An adjustment to the work environment that does not have high costs. **139**

Recession A period during which the GDP of a nation declines for two or more quarters. **46**

Recovery A period following a recession during which an economy stabilizes and begins to grow again. **46**

Recruitment The set of activities used to obtain a sufficient number of the right people at the right time; its purpose is to select those who best meet the needs of the organization. **124**

Reinforcement theory The idea that positive and negative reinforcement motivate a person to behave in certain ways. **292**

Relationship marketing A marketing strategy with the goal of keeping individual customers over time by offering them products that exactly meet their requirements. **92**

Resource An input used to produce a good. **14**

Resource development The study of how to increase resources and create the conditions that will make better use of those resources. **34**

Return on investment (ROI) The money gained from taking on a business risk. **2**

Revenue The total amount of money a business takes in during a given period as a result of selling its goods or services. **3, 224**

Reverse discrimination Discrimination against whites or males in hiring or promoting. **139**

Rider Supplemental insurance; also means an amendment to a contract. **381**

Rightsizing Downsizing that takes place with careful matching of resources to needs. **263**

Risk The chance an individual or organization takes of losing time and money on a business or decision that may not prove profitable. **4**

Roth IRA An investment that does not get upfront deductions on taxes, but the earnings grow tax-free and are tax-free when they are withdrawn. **384**

S

S-corporation A legal form of corporation for which the biggest advantage is its tax status, which is the same as a sole proprietorship. **75**

Sales promotion A promotional tool that stimulates consumer purchasing and dealer interest by means of short-term activities. **113**

Sampling Letting consumers have a small sample of a product for no charge. **114**

Sarbanes-Oxley Act Legislation passed in 2002 that set new standards for ethical codes of conduct within organizations. **341**

Scientific management Studying workers to find the most efficient processes and then teaching people those techniques. **284**

Secondary research Research collected by a marketer that has already been compiled by others and published in print or online. **96**

Securities Stocks and bonds that are traded. **208**

Securities and Exchange Commission (SEC) A governmental organization that has responsibility at the federal level for regulating activities in the various exchanges. **209**

Securities market A place where stocks and bonds are traded. **208**

Selection The process of gathering information and deciding who should be hired, under legal guidelines, to serve the best interests of the individual and the organization. **126**

Services Intangible products, such as education, insurance, and travel. **2**

Sexual harassment Unwelcome sexual advances, requests for sexual favors, and other verbal or physical conduct of a sexual nature that creates a hostile work environment. **146**

Shareware Software that is copyrighted but distributed to potential customers free of charge. **193**

Six Sigma quality A quality measure that allows only 3.4 defects per 1 million opportunities. **169**

Skimming price strategy Pricing a new product high to make optimum profit while there's little competition. **103**

Small Business Administration (SBA) A U.S. government agency that advises and assists small businesses by providing management training, financial advice, and loans. 79

Small and medium-sized enterprises Small enterprises employ 50 or fewer people and are managed by their owners on a day-to-day basis, and medium-sized enterprises have 51 to 500 employees. **9**

Social audit A systematic evaluation of a company's progress toward implementing programs that are socially responsible. **353**

Social leader A leader who ensures that everyone in the group is getting along and agrees with the direction the group is going. **281**

Social Security The common name for the Old-Age, Survivors, and Disability Insurance Program, which was established by the Social Security Act of 1935. **382**

Socialism An economic system based on the premise that some, if not most, basic businesses should be owned by the government so profits can be evenly distributed among all people. **41**

Software A set of programs and procedures used to operate a computer and perform specific tasks with the computer. **191**

Sole proprietorship A business operated by a sole proprietor. **59, 69**

Span of control The optimal number of subordinates (employees) a manager supervises. **247**

Staffing A management function that includes hiring, motivating, and retaining the best people available to accomplish a company's objectives. **252**

Stagflation A situation where the economy is slowing but prices are rising. **48**

Stakeholders Any people or organizations who stand to gain or lose from the activities of a business. **10**

Standard of living The amount of goods and services people can buy with the money they have. **4**

Statement of cash flows Reports cash receipts and disbursements related to the three major activities of a firm: operations, investments, and financing. **226**

Statistical process control (SPC) The process of testing statistical samples of product components at each stage of the production process and plotting those results on a graph. Any variances from quality standards are recognized and can be corrected if beyond the set standards. **169**

Statistical quality control (SQC) The process some managers use to continually monitor all phases of the production process to ensure that quality is being built into the product from the beginning. **169**

Stock Shares of ownership in a company. **212**

Stockbroker A registered representative who works as a market intermediary to buy and sell securities for clients. **370**

Strategic alliance A long-term partnership between two or more companies established to help each company build competitive market advantages. **317**

Strategic planning The process of determining the major long-term goals of an organization and the policies and strategies for obtaining and using resources to achieve those goals. **246**

Strike Occurs when workers collectively refuse to go to work. **142**

Strikebreakers Workers hired to do the jobs of striking employees until a labor dispute is resolved. **144**

Supervisory (first-line) management Managers who are directly responsible for supervising workers and evaluating their daily performance. **248**

Supply The quantity of products that manufacturers or owners are willing to sell at different prices at a specific time. **35**

SWOT analysis A planning tool used to analyze an organization's strengths, weaknesses, opportunities, and threats. **242**

T

Tactical planning The process of developing detailed, short-term statements about what is to be done, who is to do it, and how it is to be done. **246**

Target costing Designing a product so it satisfies customers and meets the profit margins desired by the firm. **103**

Target marketing Selecting which market segments an organization can profitably serve. **90**

Tariff A tax on imports. **306**

Task leader A leader who plans activities and helps keep the group on task. **281**

Technical skills Skills that involve the ability to perform tasks in a specific discipline or department. **249**

Telecommuting The practice of working from home. **136**

Term insurance Pure insurance protection with no savings feature for a given number of years that typically costs less the younger you buy it. **378**

Theory X managers Managers who believe the average person dislikes work, has relatively little ambition, and wishes to avoid responsibility, so workers must be forcefully directed or threatened with punishment. Primary motivators are fear and money. **258**

Theory Y managers Managers who believe most people like work and naturally work toward goals to which they are committed. People are capable of using imagination and creativity to solve problems. Each worker is stimulated by rewards unique to that worker. **259**

Theory Z A management theory that focuses on trust and intimacy within the work group. **259**

Time and motion studies Studies of the tasks performed to complete a job and the time needed to do each task. **284**

Title VII A law that prohibits discrimination in hiring, firing, compensation, apprenticeships, training, terms, conditions, or privileges of employment based on race, religion, creed, sex, or national origin. Age was later added to the conditions of the act. **139**

Top management The highest level of management, consisting of the president and other key company executives who develop strategic plans. **248**

Total product offer Everything consumers evaluate when deciding whether to purchase a good or service. **94**

Total quality management (TQM) A management strategy where quality is reviewed at every phase of the production process, even in service organizations. **255**

Tradable currency One country's money that is allowed to be exchanged for another country's money. **13**

Trade deficit An unfavorable balance of trade; occurs when the value of a country's imports exceeds that of its exports. **304**

Trade protectionism The use of government regulations to limit the import of goods and services. **306**

Trade surplus A favorable balance of trade; occurs when the value of a country's exports exceeds that of its imports. **304**

Training and development All attempts to improve productivity by increasing an employee's ability to perform. Training focuses on short-term skills and development of long-term abilities. **128**

Transactional leader A leader who gets people to do things by providing structure and guidelines based on the exchange process. **282**

Transformational leader A leader who can transform the ideas of employees through inspiration, charisma, and a shared vision. **281**

Transparency The presentation of a company's facts and figures in a way that employees could meet the desired standard. **253**

Trial balance A summary of all the financial data in the account ledgers to check whether the figures are correct and balanced. **219**

U

Unemployment rate The number of civilians 16 years of age and older who are unemployed and have tried to find a job within the prior four weeks. **47**

Unencrypted An encryption is a secret code given to information when it is passing through the Internet. An unencrypted piece of data can be seen by anyone; it is not secure. **196**

Union An employee organization that has the main goal of representing members in employee–management bargaining over job-related issues. **140**

Universal life insurance A permanent insurance plan that allows flexibility in one's insurance and savings amounts. **379**

Unlimited liability The responsibility of business owners for all the debts of the business. **70**

V

Value Good quality at a fair price. **16**

Variable life insurance A form of whole life insurance that invests the cash value of the policy in stocks or other high-yielding securities. **379**

Venture capitalists People or companies that invest money in businesses in return for a stake in them. **79**

Vestibule training Training done in schools where employees are taught on equipment similar to that used on the job. **130**

Viral marketing The term used to describe everything from paying people to say positive things on the Internet to setting up multilevel selling schemes whereby consumers get commissions for directing friends to specific Web sites. **114**

Virtual private network (VPN) A private data network that creates secure connections, or "tunnels," over regular Internet lines. **190**

Virtualization A process that allows networked computers to run multiple operating systems and programs through one central computer at the same time. **180**

Virus A harmful piece of programming code inserted into other programming to cause an unexpected and usually undesirable event. **194**

Vision An encompassing explanation of why an organization exists and the direction it's trying to go. **241**

Volume segmentation Dividing a market by usage (volume of use). **91**

W

Web 2.0 The set of tools that allow people to build social and business connections, share information, and collaborate on projects online (including blogs, wikis, social networking sites and other online communities, and virtual worlds). **183**

Whistleblowers Insiders who report illegal or unethical behavior. **341**

Whole life insurance Life insurance where some part of the money paid goes toward pure insurance and another part goes toward savings, so the purchaser is buying both insurance and a savings plan. **378**

Wholesaler A marketing intermediary that sells to other organizations. **105**

Will A document that names a guardian for your children, states how you want your assets distributed, and names the executor for your estate. **388**

Wireless fidelity (Wi-Fi) The technology used to obtain an Internet connection without having to connect to a phone or cable line. **189**

Wireless networking Refers to the ability of a computer or device to transport signals through the air. **189**

Word-of-mouth promotion A promotional tool that involves people telling other people about products that they've purchased. **114**

Work–life balance A person's control over the interactions between his or her work life and family and personal life. **254**

World Trade Organization (WTO) The international organization that replaced the General Agreement on Tariffs and Trade and was assigned the duty of mediating trade disputes among nations. **308**

Chapter 1

1 *Score.* (2009). Retrieved July 27, 2009, from http://www.score.org/explore_score.html

2 Ibid.

3 *History of best Memphis BBQ.* (2007). Retrieved July 27, 2009, from http://www.bestbbqofmemphis.com/history.php

4 The 400 richest Americans. (2008, September 17, 2008). *Forbes.* Retrieved June 6, 2009, from http://www.forbes.com/lists/2008/54/400list08_Michael-Dell_WJOB.html

5 Kroll, L., Miller, M., & Serafin, T. (Eds.). (2009, March 11). *The world's billionaires.* Retrieved June 6, 2009, from http://www.forbes.com/2009/03/11/worlds-richest-people-billionaires-2009-billionaires_land.html

6 Service sector pullback slows, factory orders up. (2009, June 4). *The Los Angeles Times.* Retrieved July 27, 2009, from http://articles.latimes.com/2009/jun/04/business/fi-economy4

7 Lanxon, N. (2007). Top ten terrible tech products. Retrieved July 27, 2009, from http://crave.cnet.co.uk/gadgets/0,39029552,49293700-6,00.htm

8 Brandt, A. (2006, March 31). A brief history of Apple's failed but innovative products. *PC World.* Retrieved June 6, 2009, from http://blogs.pcworld.com/staffblog/archives/001763.html

9 *Top 25 biggest product flops of all times.* (n.d.). Retrieved June 6, 2009, from http://www.walletpop.com/specials/top-25-biggest-product-flops-of-all-time

10 CEO insight: Mixing up the bouquet at 1-800-Flowers.com. (2009, April 7). *BusinessWeek.* Retrieved June 6, 2009, from http://www.businessweek.com/managing/content/apr2009/ca2009047_439174.htm

11 Forbes, S. (2002, December 23). Ignorance is not bliss. *Forbes,* p. 45.

12 Ibid.

13 The quiet Americans. (2009, June 25). *The Economist.* Retrieved July 27, 2009, from http://www.economist.com/world/unitedstates/displaystory.cfm?story_id=13915822

14 Lynn, J. (2007, October 4). *Turn your hobby into a biz.* Retrieved June 6, 2009, from http://smallbusiness.aol.com/start/startup/article?id=20051213184609990012

15 Kelly, M. (n.d.). *Overview of the Industrial Revolution.* Retrieved June 8, 2009, from http://americanhistory.about.com/od/industrialrev/a/indrevoverview.htm

16 U.S. Department of Agriculture. (2009, February) *Farms, land in farms, and livestock operations: 2008 summary.* Retrieved October 1, 2009, from http://latechgovdoc.blogspot.com/2009/03/farms-land-in-farms-and-livestock.html

17 Erickson, K. (2007). Key agricultural industry drivers for the years ahead. *Agri Marketing, 16*(18), 1–5.

18 U.S. Department of Agriculture. (2009, February) *Farms, Land in farms, and livestock operations: 2008 summary.* Retrieved October 1, 2009, from http://latechgovdoc.blogspot.com/2009/03/farms-land-in-farms-and-livestock.html

19 U.S. Department of Agriculture (2008). *2007 census of agriculture: Economics.* Retrieved June 8, 2009, from http://www.agcensus.usda.gov/Publications/2007/Online_Highlights/Fact_Sheets/economics.pdf

20 U.S. Department of Labor. (n.d.). *Databases & tables, Bureau of Labor Statistics.* Retrieved June 8, 2009, from http://data.bls.gov/PDQ/servlet/SurveyOutputServlet?series_id=CES3000000001&data_tool=XGtable

21 Winter, D. (1996, May). The mass-production revolution. *Ward's Auto World, 32,* 101–102.

22 Berr, J. (2009, March 26). Thousands of workers take buyouts at GM – good news, sort of. *DailyFinance.com.* Retrieved June 10, 2009, from http://www.dailyfinance.com/2009/03/26/whats-good-for-gm-is-good-for-america

23 Bureau of Labor Statistics, U.S. Department of Labor. (n.d.). *Employment situation summary.* Retrieved June 10, 2009, from http://www.bls.gov/news.release/empsit.nr0.htm

24 La Monica, P. R. (2009, June 1). Why the market doesn't care about GM. *CNNMoney.com.* Retrieved June 10, 2009, from http://money.cnn.com/2009/06/01/markets/thebuzz/index.htm

25 Toyota beats GM for first time. (2009, January 21). *CBSNews.com.* Retrieved June 10, 2009, from http://www.cbsnews.com/stories/2009/01/21/business/main4742933.shtml

26 Service economy growth below forecast. (2007, October 3). *New York Times.*

27 ISM: U.S. service economy shrinks more slowly in May. *The Associated Press, Oregon Business News.* Retrieved June 10, 2009, from http://www.oregonlive.com/business/index.ssf/2009/06/ism_us_service_economy_shrinks.html.

28 Bureau of Labor Statistics, U.S. Department of Labor. (n.d.). *Tomorrow's jobs. Occupational outlook handbook, 2008–2009.* Retrieved June 10, 2009, from http://www.bls.gov/oco/oco2003.htm

29 Coy, P. (2009, May 11). Help wanted. *BusinessWeek,* 40–46.

30 Clark, M., & Huston, T. (1997). *1992 Directory of microenterprise development programs.* Washington, DC: Nebraska Entrepreneurial Opportunity Network. Retrieved June 7, 2009, from http://neon.neded.org/mbrd/intro.html

31 U.S. Small Business Administration. (n.d.). *Table of small business size standards matched to NAICS codes, effective August 22, 2008.* Retrieved June 6, 2009, from www.sba.gov/size

32 Katz, J.A., & Green, R.P. (2009). *Entrepreneurial small business* (2nd ed.). New York: McGraw-Hill.

33 U.S. Small Business Administration, Office of Advocacy. (n.d.). Retrieved June 7, 2009, from http://www.smallbusinessnotes.com/aboutsb/sbfacts/sbimportance.html

34 Entrepreneur Magazine's 2008 Hot 100: The fastest growing business in America. (2008). *Entrepreneur.* Retrieved June 7, 2009, from http://www.entrepreneur.com/hot100

35 500 Largest U.S. Corporations. (2009, May 4) *Fortune,* p. F-1.

36 Case, S. (2005, May 10). Purpose and profits go together. *The Wall Street Journal,* p. B2.

37 Howard Hughes Medical Institute. (n.d.). Retrieved June 10, 2009, from http://www.hhmi.org/about/

38 Entrepreneur magazine's 2008 hot 100 fastest growing companies in America. (2008). *Entrepreneur.* Retrieved June 7, 2009, from http://www.entrepreneur.com/hot100/details/20084.html

39 Ibid

40 Reingold, J., Caplin, J., & Kowitt, B. (2009, February 16). The new jobless. *Fortune,* 60–69.

41 Chu, K. (2009, April 23). White House and Congress target credit card rates. *USA Today.* Retrieved June 11, 2009, from http://www.usatoday.com/money/perfi/credit/2009-04-22-credit-card-rates-obama_N.htm

42 Green, L. (2009, January 7). More than 1m filed for bankruptcy in 2008. *Credit.com.* Retrieved June 11, 2009, from http://www.credit.com/news/economic-crisis/2009-01-07/more-than-1m-filed-for-bankruptcy-in-2008.html

43 National Conference of State Legislatures. (2009). *2009 proposed state tobacco tax increase legislation.* Retrieved June 11, 2009, from http://www.ncsl.org/IssuesResearch/Health/2009ProposedStateTobaccoTaxIncreaseLegislati/tabid/13862/Default.aspx

44 Tax Foundation (2008, October). 2009 state business tax. *Climate Index,* No. 58.

45 Reza, S. (2007). Privatization and private sector growth in China and Russia: A comparison from the institutional perspective. *China: An International Journal 5*(2)

46 Lemon-Aid. (2007). *State Legislatures, 33*(10), 11–11.

47 *Top most tradable Forex currencies.* (2009). Retrieved June 12, 2009, from http://forexfreedownload.com/top-most-tradeable-

forex-currencies/ and Lee, R. (n.d.). Top 8 most tradable currencies. *Investopedia.com*. Retrieved June 12, 2009, from http://www.investopedia.com/articles/forex/08/top-8-currencies-to-know.asp

48 Plumb, T. (2008, September 17). Corporate fraud on the rise. *Washington Business Journal*. Retrieved June 10, 2009, from http://washington.bizjournals.com/washington/stories/2008/09/15/daily55.html

49 Stone, B. (2005, April 11). High tech's new day. *Newsweek*, 60–64.

50 Barras, C. (2009, May 2). How big is the net? *New Scientist, 202*, 30–31. Retrieved June 8, 2009, from http://web.ebscohost.com/ehost/detail?vid=7&hid=4&sid=2138f2d9-8b5f-41b7-adee-67574870dea9%40sessionmgr8&bdata=JnNpdGU9ZWhvc3QtbGl2ZQ%3d%3d#db=a9h&AN=39344302

51 Bureau of Labor Statistics. United States Department of Labor. (2009). *Occupational outlook handbook, 2008–2009*. Retrieved July 28, 2009, from http://www.bls.gov/oco/ocos111.htm

52 Winsor, S. (2008, February 1). Farming data fields. *Corn and Soybean Digest*. February 1, 2008. Retrieved June 6, 2009, from http://cornandsoybeandigest.com/precision-ag/butler-maps-farm-with-technology-0201/index.html

53 Sloan, P. (2006, March). Retail without the risk. *Business 2.0*, 118.

54 Copeland, M. V. (2006, April). Everyone's investing in B to B. *Business*, p. 30.

55 Netflix.com. (n.d.). Retrieved June 11, 2009, from http://www.netflix.com/HowItWorks

56 Beller, P. C. (2009, June 5). Can Games Save Blockbuster? *Forbes*. Retrieved June 11, 2009, from http://www.forbes.com/2009/06/05/blockbuster-videogames-netflix-cable-markets-media.html?feed=rss_markets

57 Cebrzynski, G. (2008, May 19). Arby's breaks first social-network campaign to generate a brigade of advocates for the brand. *Nation's Restaurant News, 42*(28).

58 Baldwin, C. (2009, June 12). Twitter helps Dell rake in sales. *Reuters News*. Retrieved June 12, 2009, from http://www.reuters.com/article/internetNews/idUSTRE55B0NU20090612?feedType=nl&feedName=usmorningdigest

59 LaGesse, D. (2009, May). Turning social networking into a job offer. *U.S. News and World Report, 146*, 5.

60 Richman, M. (2005, April). The quest for zero defects, *Quality Digest*, 40–43.

61 The Customer Service Champs. (2009, June 12). *BusinessWeek*. Retrieved June 12, 2009, from http://bwnt.businessweek.com/interactivereports/customer_service_2009/index.asp

62 Winstein K. J. (2009, May 14). Massachusetts adopts rules for calorie counts on menus. *Wall Street Journal*. Retrieved June 12, 2009, from http://online.wsj.com/article/SB124225207517116943.html

63 Christie, L (2009, May 14). Census: U.S. becoming more diverse, *CNNMoney.com*. Retrieved June 9, 2009, from http://money.cnn.com/2009/05/14/real_estate/rising_minorities/index.htm

64 *U.S. Census Bureau news*. (n.d.). Retrieved June 12, 2009, from http://www.census.gov/Press-Release/www/releases/archives/population/001720.html

65 Frankel, B. (n.d.).The DiversityInc top ten global diversity companies list. *DiversityInc.com*. Retrieved May 18, 2009, from, http://www.diversityinc.com/public/5862.cfm

66 *History of long term care*. (2008). Retrieved June 30, 2009, from Elderweb.com and *It's 2050…What does your workforce look like?* (2008, February 11).

67 *DiversityInc.com*. Retrieved June 9, 2009, from http://www.diversityinc.com/public/3068.cfm

68 Markson, G. (2006). Dual income: Blessing or curse? *Families.com*. Retrieved June 9, 2009, from http://marriage.families.com/blog/dual-income-blessing-or-curse

69 Herzallah, M. (n.d.).The coming oil crisis, *Newsweek*, Retrieved June 22, 2009, from http://stockinvestguide.com/stock/trading/help/videos/the-coming-oil-crisis-newsweek

70 Gray, S. (n.d.). Chrysler dealer: They're making it impossible. *Fortune*. Retrieved June 12, 2009, from http://money.cnn.com/2009/05/21/magazines/fortune/nola_chrysler_dealer.fortune/index.htm?section=magazines_fortune,

71 Economic Life After College. (2007, June 11) *New York Times*. and Jones, S. D. (2001).*The effect of a college degree on wages: The different experiences of men and women*. The Wyoming Department of Employment. Retrieved June 10, 2009, from http://doe.state.wy.us/LMI/1001/a1.htm9.

72 Williams, K., & Kang, C. (2006, March 22). The Latino small business boom. *Washington Post*, pp.A1 and A10.

73 *HispanicBusiness.com*. (n.d.). Retrieved June 10, 2009, from http://www.hispanicbusiness.com/research/

74 Lowery, Y. (2007). *Minority in business: A demographic review of the minority business ownership*. Washington, DC: U.S. Small Business Administration.

75 Center for Women's Business Research. (n.d.). Retrieved June 10, 2009, from http://www.womensbusinessresearchcenter.org/research/keyfacts

76 National Women's Business Council. (2005, March).*Women business owners and their enterprises*.

77 Davidson, L. (2009, April 29). Women in business are risk takers. *Business Pundit*. Retrieved June 10, 2009, from http://www.businesspundit.com/women-in-business-are-risk-takers

Chapter 2

1 Weinkam, C. (2008, October). Keynote speaker Amilya Antonetti. *Cincy*. Retrieved July 29, 2009, from http://www.cincylifemagazine.com/ME2/dirmod.asp?sid=2CE771F28E0D4281817E2E034A9C57C6&nm=Archive&type=Publishing&mod=Publications::Article&mid=61465020993F438B9FCD60C66CC58CDC&tier=4&id=C85A796AE06649F2ABC19F66EC9652AB

2 Ibid.

3 Isidro, I. (n.d.). Soapworks: How a family need spurred a profitable business. *Powerhomebiz.com*. Retrieved June 9, 2009, from http://www.powerhomebiz.com/vol135/soapworks.htm

4 Gross national income (per capita) by country. (n.d.). *Nationmaster.com*. Retrieved June 16, 2009, from http://www.nationmaster.com/graph/eco_gro_nat_inc_percap-gross-national-income-per-capita

5 Shah, A. (2009). Poverty facts and stats. *GlobalIssues.org*. Retrieved June 15, 2009, from http://www.globalissues.org/article/26/poverty-facts-and-stats#src18

6 The Center for Nursing Advocacy. (n.d.). Retrieved June 17, 2009, from http://www.nursingadvocacy.org/faq/nursing_shortage.html

7 Comrade capitalists. (2006, January 31). *The Wall Street Journal*, p. A14.

8 Too many people: Earth's population problem. (n.d.). *OptimumPopulation.org*. Retrieved June 15, 2009, from http://www.optimumpopulation.org/opt.earth.html

9 Country Profile: Rwanda. (2007, November 2). *WorldVision.org*. Retrieved June 15, 2009, from http://www.worldvision.org.nz/wherewework/profiles/c_rwanda.asp

10 Ohlson, K. (2006, February). Burst of energy, *Entrepreneur*, p. 46–47.

11 King, R. (2008, July 23). Dancing is the new energy generator. *FastCompany.com*. Retrieved June 9, 2009, from http://www.fastcompany.com/blog/rachel-king/geek-style/dancing-new-energy-generator

12 Whitman, D. (2000). *Genetically modified foods: Harmful or helpful*. Retrieved June 17, 2009, from http://www.csa.com/discoveryguides/gmfood/overview.php

13 Slayton, J. T. (2008, November 29). GM Agriculture Pros and Cons. *FastCompany.com*. Retrieved June 15, 2009, from http://www.fastcompany.com/blog/jt-slayton/gm-agriculture-pros-and-cons/gm-agriculture-pros-and-cons

14 *From revolution to reconstruction: Biographies: Adam Smith (1723–1790)*. (n.d.). Retrieved June 15, 2009, from http://www.let.rug.nl/usa/B/asmith/adams1.htm

15 Economics basics: Introduction, (n.d.). *Investopedia.com*. Retrieved June 15, 2009, from http://www.investopedia.com/university/economics/

16 Passmore, N. (2008, February 5). Micro beers brew up big business. *BusinessWeek.com*. Retrieved June 15, 2009, from http://www.businessweek.com/lifestyle/content/feb2008/bw2008025_479685.htm

17 Hottest toys of the 2008 holiday season. (2008, October 7). *NYDailyNews.com*. Retrieved June 15, 2009, from http://www.nydailynews.com/money/galleries/hottest_toys_of_the_200holiday_season/hottest_toys_of_the_2008_holiday_season.html

18 Willis, A. (2009, February 6). Big drop in European steel demand. *BusinessWeek.com*. Retrieved June 15, 2009, from http://www.businessweek.com/globalbiz/content/feb2009/gb2009026_291800.htm

19 McGregor, J. (2009, March 12). Matching prices to demand, in real time. *BusinessWeek.com*. Retrieved June 15, 2009, from http://www.businessweek.com/magazine/content/09_12/b4124064328055.htm

20 Dr Pepper introduces new Dr Pepper Cherry with just a kiss of cherry smoothness. (n.d.). *Entrepreneur.com*. Retrieved June 15, 2009, from http://www.entrepreneur.com/PRNewswire/release/131270.html

21 Moore, J. F. (1999, November 5). MSFT ruled a monopoly. *Money. CNN.com*. Retrieved June 15, 2009, from http://money.cnn.com/1999/11/05/technology/microsoft_finding

22 GlaxoSmithKline agrees to settle Paxil claims for $14 million, (2006, March 29). *Biomedicine.org*. Retrieved June 15, 2009, fromhttp://www.bio-medicine.org/medicine-news/GlaxoSmithKline-Agrees-To-Settle-Paxil-Claims-For--2414-million-8872-1

23 Reardon, M. (2007, October 31). FCC bans exclusive TV deals for cable. *CNET News*. Retrieved June 15, 2009, from http://news.cnet.com/FCC-bans-exclusive-TV-deals-for-cable/2100-1037_3-6216264.html

24 Burrows, P. (2009, January 12).The SEC's Madoff misery. *BusinessWeek*

25 Bernard L. Madoff. (2009, June 29). *The New York Times*. Retrieved August 1, 2009, from http://topics.nytimes.com/top/reference/timestopics/people/m/bernard_l_madoff/index.html?scp=1-spot&sq=madoff&st=cse

26 Ebeling, A. (2009, June 8). States target the rich. *Forbes.com*. Retrieved June 16, 2009, from http://www.forbes.com/forbes/2009/0608/032-taxes-new york states-target-rich.html

27 State sales tax rates. (2008, January 1). Retrieved June 16, 2009, fromhttp://www.taxadmin.org/FTA/rate/sales.html

28 *Key data on world taxes income tax rates tax rates comparison table finance & economy worldwide.* (n.d.). Retrieved June 16, 2009, from http://www.worldwide-tax.com/

29 Ibid.

30 Obama drives U.S. toward socialism, GOP says. (2009, February 28). *Globe Wire Services*. Retrieved June 16, 2009, from http://www.boston.com/news/nation/washington/articles/2009/02/28/obama_drives_us_toward_socialism_gop_says/

31 Forbes, S. (2009, May 18). Real health care. *Forbes.com*. Retrieved June 16, 2009, from http://www.forbes.com/2009/05/15/forbes-healthcare-socialism-intelligent-investing-insurance.html

32 *The world fact book, Cuba.* (n.d.). Retrieved June 16, 2009, from https://www.cia.gov/library/publications/the-world-factbook/geos/CU.html

33 *Key data on world taxes income tax rates tax rates comparison table finance & economy worldwide.* (n.d.). Retrieved June 16, 2009, from http://www.worldwide-tax.com/

34 Lal, D. (2006, March 19). The flat tax for developing countries. *Cato.org*. Retrieved June 16, 2009, from http://www.cato.org/pub_display.php?pub_id=600935

35 Mitchell, D. J. (2007, July/August).The global flat tax revolution. *Cato.org*. Retrieved June 16, 2009, from http://www.cato.org/pubs/policy_report/v29n4/cpr29n4-1.html36

36 Marsden, K. (2008, June 16). New evidence on government and growth. *The Wall Street Journal*.

37 Gage, J. (2009, March 18). The best countries for business, 2009. *Forbes.com*. Retrieved June 16, 2009, from http://www.forbes.com/2009/03/18/best-countries-for-business-bizcountries09-business-washington-best-countries.html

38 The CIA. (n.d.). *The world fact book*. Retrieved June 16, 2009, from https://www.cia.gov/library/publications/the-world-factbook/geos/US.html.

39 List of poorest countries by GDP. (2009, May 5). *EconomicsHelp.org*. Retrieved June 16, 2009, from http://www.economicshelp.org/blog/economics/list-of-poorest-countries-by-gdp/

40 List of richest countries by GDP. (2009, May 4). *EconomicsHelp.org*. Retrieved June 16, 2009, from http://www.economicshelp.org/blog/economics/richest-countries-by-gdp/

41 The CIA. (n.d.). *The world fact book*. Retrieved June 16, 2009, fromhttps://www.cia.gov/library/publications/the-world-factbook/fields/2195.html?countryName=United%20States&countryCode=US&regionCode=na&#US

42 Cooper, J. C., & Madigan, K. (2005, May 16). The GDP report: No reason to sweat. *BusinessWeek*, 21-22.

43 Rooney, B. (2009, February 27). GDP slides 6.2% on slower spending. *CNNMoney.com*. Retrieved June 16, 2009, fromhttp://money.cnn.com/2009/02/27/news/economy/GDP_4Q08_preliminary/index.htm

44 Speilberg, G. T. (2009, January 17). Recession? Not for these businesses. *BusinessWeek*. Retrieved June 17, 2009, from http://www.businessweek.com/bwdaily/dnflash/content/jan2009/db20090116_786365.htm

45 6 Companies born during downturns. (n.d.). *CNNMoney.com*. Retrieved June 17, 2009, from http://money.cnn.com/galleries/2009/smallbusiness/0901/gallery.founded_in_a_recession.smb/index.html

46 Bureau of Labor Statistics, U.S. Department of Labor. (n.d.). Retrieved June 17, 2009, from http://www.bls.gov/news.release/empsit.nr0.htm

47 Your rights when you apply for unemployment benefits. (n.d.). *LARCC.org*. Retrieved June 17, 2009, from http://www.larcc.org/pamphlets/benefits_work/unemployment_rights_to_apply.htm

48 Henderson, N. (2006, January 19). Inflation hit five-year high of 3.4% last year. *Washington Post*, p. D1.

49 Pilling, D. (2005, April 27). Japan still in grip of deflation as prices fall. *Financial Times*, p. 7.

50 U.S. Department of Labor. (n.d.). *Consumer price index*. Retrieved June 18, 2009, from www.bls.gov/cpi/cpifaq.htm

51 Pepitone, J. (2009, June 17). Consumer price index: Largest drop in 59 years. *CNNMoney.com*. Retrieved June 9, 2009, from http://money.cnn.com/2009/06/17/news/economy/cpi_consumer_price_index/index.htm

52 Bureau of Labor Statistics. (n.d.). *Producer price indexes*. Retrieved June 9, 2009, from http://www.bls.gov/ppi/ppifaq.htm

53 Forget rates. Let's print money. (2009, January 5). *BusinessWeek*.

54 *U.S. national debt clock.* (n.d.). Retrieved June 17, 2009, from http://brillig.com/debt_clock

55 Knoller, M. (2009, March 17). National debt hits record $11 trillion. *CBSNews.com*. Retrieved June 17, 2009, from http://www.cbsnews.com/blogs/2009/03/17/politics/politicalhotsheet/entry4872310.shtml

Chapter 3

1 Small Business Administration. (n.d.). *Get ready: Do you have what it takes?* Retrieved July 2, 2009, from http://www.sba.gov/smallbusinessplanner/plan/getready/serv_sbplanner_plan_whatittake.html

2 *JCPenney.net*. (n.d.). Retrieved June 23, 2009, from http://www.jcpenney.net/about/history.aspx

3 EPA names JCPenney 2007 ENERGY STAR(R) retail partner of the year. (2007, March 9). *ir.JCPenney.com*. Retrieved June 23, 2009, from http://ir.jcpenney.com/phoenix.zhtml?c=70528&p=irol-newsCompanyArticle&ID=972300&highlight=

4 Answers.com. (n.d.). Retrieved June 23, 2009, from www.answers.com/topic/jeff-bezos?cat=biz-fin

5 Spaeder, K. E. (2003). Beyond their years. *Entrepreneur.com*. Retrieved June 23, 2009, from http://www.entrepreneur.com/magazine/entrepreneur/2003/november/65006.html

6 Under Armour, Inc. (n.d.). *Hoovers.com*. Retrieved June 23, 2009, from http://www.hoovers.com/under-armour/--ID__106607,ticker__UA--/free-co-fin-factsheet.xhtml

7 About the motley fool. (n.d.). *Fool.com*. Retrieved June 23, 2009, from http://www.fool.com/press/about.htm?source= ifltnvsnv0000001#bod

8 Small business profile, SBA Office of Advocacy. (n.d.). Retrieved June 29, 2009, from http://www.sba.gov/advo/stats/sbfaq.pdf

9 Key facts about women-owned businesses. (n.d.). *Center for Women's Business Research*. Retrieved June 24, 2009, from http://www. womensbusinessresearchcenter.org/research/keyfacts

10 Harris interactive survey. (2009, May). *Entrepreneur*, 67.

11 Ga-ga for Google. (2002, April). *Entrepreneur.com*. Retrieved June 23, 2009, from http://www.entrepreneur.com/magazine/ entrepreneur/2002/april/49804-2.html

12 Kroll, L., Miller, M., & Serafin, T. (2009, March 11). *The world's billionaires*. Retrieved June 23, 2009, from http://www.forbes. com/2009/03/11/worlds-richest-people-billionaires-2009-billionaires_land.html

13 Swak, S (2005, June 3). Students' success as entrepreneurs. *University Wire*; Klein, K. (2005, December 15). Rekindling an entrepreneur's passion. *BusinessWeek*; Gogoi, P. (2006, January 18). Start-up secrets of the successful. *BusinessWeek Online*; and Hatch, J., & Zweig, J. (2000). What is the stuff of an entrepreneur? *Ivey Business Journal, 65*(2), 68–72.

14 Three steps to strategic heaven: Watching the opposition. (2003). *Strategic Direction, 19*(2), 22–24.

15 Challenger, J. (2005). As entrepreneurs, seniors lead U.S. start-ups. *Franchising World*; DeTienne, L. (2005). Prior knowledge, potential financial reward. *Entrepreneurship: Theory and Practice*; List of richest people was topped by Microsoft Corp. founder Bill Gates for 11th year in a row. (2005, March 29). *Capper's*; and Fried, J. (2005, March). How I did it. *Inc.*, 88–90.

16 Petrecca, L. (2009, April 20). Some lose a job and become an entrepreneur. *USAToday.com*. Retrieved June 23, 2009, from http:// www.usatoday.com/money/smallbusiness/2009-04-19-jobless-economy-government-help_N.htm

17 Holden, J. (2008, May 12). Why become an entrepreneur. *America. gov*. Retrieved June 23, 2009, from http://www.america.gov/st/econ-english/2008/May/20080603212324eaifas0.1164362.html

18 Flexman, N., & Scanian, T. (1982). *Running your own business*. New York: Argus.

19 Smith, D. (2003, November). Women of substance. *Entrepreneur. com*. Retrieved June 23, 2009, from http://www.entrepreneur.com/ magazine/entrepreneur/2003/november/65012.html

20 Monosoff, T. (2007, August 22). What inspires people to startup? *Entrepreneur.com*. Retrieved June 23, 2009, from http://www.entrepreneur.com/startingabusiness/inventing/ inventionscolumnisttamaramonosoff/article183286.html

21 Manahan, K. (2009). Baby sitter referral service born of necessity. *Entrepreneur*, 90–91 and Edelhauser, K. (2007, June 20). Starting from scratch. *Entrepreneur.com*. Retrieved August 4, 2009, from http://www.entrepreneur.com/startingabusiness/successstories/ article180652.html

22 Edelhauser, K. (2007, June). Starting from scratch. *Entrepreneur*. Retrieved August 4, 2009, from http://www.entrepreneur.com/ startingabusiness/successstories/article180652.html

23 Ibid.

24 Ibid.

25 Advantages and disadvantages of a start-up business. (n.d.). *BusinessMart.com*. Retrieved June 29, 2009, from http://buying. businessmart.com/advantages-disadvantages-of-a-start-up-business. php

26 Ibid.

27 Wilson, S. (2009, February). Laid off in 2008? Start a business in 2009. *Entrepreneur*, 73–77; and Pollak, P. (2009, March 16). Gen Y entrepreneurs: Here are the first steps to starting your own business. *FastCompany.com*. Retrieved June 29, 2009, from http://www. fastcompany.com/blog/lindsey-pollak/next-generation-career-advice/are-you-gen-y-considering-entrepreneurship-first-s

28 How to buy a business. (n.d.) *Entrepreneur.com*. Retrieved June 29, 2009, from http://www.entrepreneur.com/startingabusiness/ selfassessment/whattypeofbusinessshouldyoustart/article79638.html

29 Franchise 500. (2009, January). *Entrepreneur*, 91–92.

30 The advantages of franchises. (n.d.). *AllBusiness.com*. Retrieved June 29, 2009, from http://www.allbusiness.com/buying-exiting-businesses/franchising-franchises/1434-1.html

31 Starbucks coffee company United Kingdom. (n.d.). *Become a Starbucks partner*. Retrieved June 29, 2009, from http://starbucks. co.uk/enGB/_About+Starbucks/Careers+at+Starbucks.htm

32 Grynbaum, M., & Martin, A. (2008, February 27). Back to basics for Starbucks baristas. *The New York Times*. Retrieved June 29, 2009, from http://www.nytimes.com/2008/02/27/business/ worldbusiness/27iht-27sbux.10458541.html

33 The advantages of franchises. (n.d.). *AllBusiness.com*. Retrieved June 29, 2009, from http://www.allbusiness.com/buying-exiting-businesses/franchising-franchises/1434-1.html

34 Franchise 500. (2009, January). *Entrepreneur*, 147–223.

35 Wu, N. (2006, December 2). Couple takes road to fiscal fitness. *Pacific Business Journal* and Reiser, R. (2006, January 20). Finding a whole new grind. *BusinessWeek Online*.

36 Franchise 500. (2009, January). *Entrepreneur*, 147–223.

37 Chain restaurants charged with promoting x-treme eating. (2007, February 26). *CSPI Newsroom*. Retrieved June 29, 2009, from http:// www.cspinet.org/new/200702262.html

38 Rumor response. (n.d.). *Starbucks.com*. Retrieved June 29, 2009, from http://www.starbucks.com/aboutus/rumor.asp

39 Sterrett, D. (2008, June 18). Giveaways anger McD's franchisees. *Crain's Chicago Business*. Retrieved August 4, 2009, from http://www. chicagobusiness.com/cgi-bin/news.pl?id=29826

40 Del'Re, D. (2005, September 2). Franchisee battles Quiznos over location policy. *Inc.com*. Retrieved June 24, 2009, from http://www. inc.com/news/articles/200509/quiznos.html

41 Del'Re, D. (2005, September 2). Franchisee battles Quiznos over location policy. *Inc.com*. Retrieved June 24, 2009, from http://www. inc.com/news/articles/200509/quiznos.html

42 Galland, Z. (2006, May 2). A stew of small business stats. *BusinessWeek*. Retrieved June 24, 2009, from www.businessweek. com/smallbiz/content/may2006/sb20060502_489185. htm?chan=search.

43 *Sales by business type summary*. (n.d.). Retrieved July 3, 2009, from http://www.bizstats.com/reports/industry-sales-firm-summary.asp

44 Internal Revenue Service, Department of the Treasury. (n.d.). Retrieved June 24, 2009, from www.irs.gov/businesses/small/ article/0id=98202,00.html

45 Fay, J. R. (1998, August). What form of ownership is best? *The CPA Journal, 68*(8), 46–50.

46 *Forbes financial glossary*. (n.d.). Retrieved June 24, 2009, from www. forbes.com/tools/glossary/search.jhtml?term=unlimited_liability

47 Callaway, C. A., Wolf, D., & Kramer, D. (2002). Choosing a business structure. *ASHRAE Journal, 44*(4) 42–46.

48 Elswick, J. (2005, May 1). Loaded statements: Web based total compensation statements keep employees in the know. *Employee Benefit News*.

49 Types of partnerships, (n.d.). *Find Law*. Retrieved June 24, 2009, from http://smallbusiness.findlaw.com/business-structures/ partnership/partnerships-types.html

50 Opdyke, J. (2005, March 17). When business and friendship don't mix. *The Wall Street Journal* and Thomas, P. (2005, March 23). One sweet solution to a sour partnership. *The Wall Street Journal*.

51 Board of Directors. (n.d.). *ir.JCPenney.com*. Retrieved June 24, 2009, from http://ir.jcpenney.com/phoenix.zhtml?c=70528&p=irol-govboard

52 Learn about law. (n.d.). *Types of corporations: S corp versus C corp*. Retrieved June 24, 2009, from www.learnaboutlaw.com/ Corporations/types_of_corps.htm

53 Fay, J. R. (1998). What form of ownership is best? *The CPA Journal, 68*(8), 46–50.

54 Mowrey, M. E. (2005, March 1). Choice of business entity after JGTRRA and AJCA. *Strategic Finance*.

55 Starkman, J. (2007). Advantages of a C corporation. *The Tax Adviser, 38*, 617–618.

56 Ibid.

57 Different types of corporations: Advantages/disadvantages of corporations. (n.d.). *MoreBusiness.com.* March 20, 2009, Retrieved June 30, 2009, from http://www.morebusiness.com/getting_started/incorporating/d934832501.brc

58 Staub, D. K. (n.d.). LLC advantages. *LimitedLiabilityCompany Center.com.* Retrieved June 24, 2009, from http://www.limitedliabilitycompanycenter.com

59 Staub, D. K. (n.d.). LLC advantages. *LimitedLiabilityCompany Center.com.* Retrieved June 24, 2009, from http://www.limitedliabilitycompanycenter.com/llc_advantages.html.

60 Capital, I. (n.d.). *FundIsabella.com.* Retrieved June 30, 2009, from http://www.fundisabella.com/

61 *Angel Capital Association.* (n.d.). Retrieved June 30, 2009, from http://www.angelcapitalassociation.org/

62 Frieswick, K. (2009, August 2). Perfection, Inc. *Boston Globe.* Retrieved August 5, 2009, from http://www.boston.com/bostonglobe/magazine/articles/2009/08/02/perfection_inc/?page=full

63 Senate Report 107-018 – Microloan Program Improvement Act Of 2001. (n.d.). *The Library of Congress: Thomas.* Retrieved June 29, 2009, from http://www.thomas.gov/cgi-bin/cpquery/?&sid=cp107LH9vq&refer=&r_n=sr018.107&db_id=107&item=&sel=TOC_1266&

64 Ibid.

65 CRM: You (should) love your customers, now work to keep them. (n.d.) *StartUpNation.com.* Retrieved June 29, 2009, from http://www.startupnation.com/articles/1533/1/crm-software-strategy.asp

66 Applegate, J. (2001, March 22). Family business challenges need novel solutions. *Entrepreneur.com.*

67 Bluestein, A. (2008, April). The success gene. *Inc.com.* Retrieved June 30, 2009, from http://www.inc.com/magazine/20080401/the-success-gene.html

68 Thurlow, H. (1993, May). A spirit that never gives up-entrepreneur's notebook-column. *Nation's Business.*

69 Sexton, T. (2007, February 9). Why companies should institute policies of promotion from within. *Associated Content.* Retrieved June 30, 2009, from http://www.associatedcontent.com/article/139348/why_companies_should_institute_polices.html?cat=3

70 Canter, J. (2005, February 5). How and why I hired my tax accountant. *The Wall Street Journal.*

71 D'Elia, V. A. (n.d.). *The failure myth revisited.* Retrieved June 30, 2009, from http://www.ihavenet.com/Small-Business-The-Failure-Myth-Revisited.html

72 Schaefer, P. (n.d.). *The seven pitfalls of business failures and how to avoid them,* business know-how. Retrieved June 30, 2009, from www.businessknowhow.com/startup/business-failure.htm; *Why do many small businesses fail?* (n.d.). Retrieved June 30, 2009, from www.allbusiness.com/business-planning-structures/business-plans/1440-1.html; and Sherlock, J. M. (n.d.). How not to fail in business, *Lincoln-Club.org.* Retrieved June 30, 2009, from http://www.lincoln-club.org/business-planning.html

73 Burlingham, B. (1995, July). How to succeed in business in 4 easy steps. *Inc.com.* Retrieved June 30, 2009, from http://www.inc.com/magazine/19950701/2329.html; Schaefer, P. (n.d.). The seven pitfalls of business failures and how to avoid them. *Business know-how.* Retrieved June 30, 2009, from www.businessknowhow.com/startup/business-failure.htm; *Why do many small businesses fail?* (n.d.). Retrieved June 30, 2009, from www.allbusiness.com/business-planning-structures/business-plans/1440-1.html; and Sherlock, J. (n.d.). How not to fail in business. *Lincoln-Club.org.* Retrieved June 30, 2009, from http://www.lincoln-club.org/business-planning.html

74 Manahan, K. (2009). Baby sitter referral service born of necessity. *Entrepreneur,* 90–91 and Edelhauser, K. (2007, June 20). Starting from scratch. *Entrepreneur.com.* Retrieved August 4, 2009, from http://www.entrepreneur.com/startingabusiness/successstories/article180652.html

Chapter 4

1 Williams, G. (2006, July). Top 10 successful marketing stunts. *Entrepreneur.* Retrieved July 6, 2009, from http://www.entrepreneur.com/marketing/marketingideas/article159484.html#ixzz0LEiaxpJa&D

2 Humphreys, J. M. (n.d.). *The multicultural economy 1990–2013, Terry College Selig Center for economic growth, 2008.* Retrieved July 7, 2009, from http://www.terry.uga.edu/selig/docs/buying_power_2008.pdf

3 *Marriott hotels.* (n.d.). Retrieved July 13, 2009, from http://www.marriott.com/corporateinfo/glance.mi

4 Yankelovich, D., & Meer, D. (2006, February). Rediscovering market segmentation. *Harvard Business Review,* 122–131.

5 About Aeropostale. (n.d.). *Aeropostale.com.* Retrieved July 7, 2009, from http://www.aeropostale.com/corp/index.jsp?clickid=bottomnav_about_txt

6 Struck, H. (2009, June 1). Fur flies. *Forbes.com.* Retrieved July 7, 2009, from http://www.forbes.com/2009/06/01/pet-airways-airlines-business-aviation-travel.html

7 M&T Bank. (n.d.). Retrieved July 6, 2009, from https://www.mtb.com/personal/cardproducts/Pages/Visa%C2%AEExtrasRewards.aspx

8 Tierney, J. (2009, May 18). Message in what we buy, but nobody's listening. *The New York Times.* Retrieved July 7, 2009, from http://www.nytimes.com/2009/05/19/science/19tier.html?_r=1

9 Copeland, M. V. (2006, April). Everyone is investing in B-to-C B. *Business 2.0,* 30–31.

10 McCarthy, J. E. (1964, June). The concept of the marketing mix. *Journal of Advertising Research,* 2–7.

11 Lee, L. (2005, August 1). Too many surveys, too little passion. *BusinessWeek,* 38–40.

12 Salter, C. (2008, February 8). Disney–ABC's Anne Sweeney does her own market research. Really. *FastCompany.com.* Retrieved July 2, 2009, from http://www.fastcompany.com/blog/chuck-salter/dash-salt/disney-abcs-anne-sweeney-does-her-own-market-research-really

13 Davenport, T. H. (2008, January). Competing on analytics. *Harvard Business Review,* 99–107.

14 Gallo, C. (2009, May 19). How to sell more than a product. *BusinessWeekOnline.* Retrieved July 6, 2009, from http://www.businessweek.com/smallbiz/content/may2009/sb20090519_058809.htm

15 Mueller industries: Hidden value in industrial goods. (2009, June 16). *SeekingAlpha.com.* Retrieved July 6, 2009, from http://seekingalpha.com/article/143371-mueller-industries-hidden-value-in-industrial-goods

16 Elliott, S. (2009, February 22). Tropicana discovers some buyers are passionate about packaging. *The New York Times.* Retrieved July 3, 2009, from http://www.nytimes.com/2009/02/23/business/media/23adcol.html?_r=1&pagewanted=all

17 Lebor, T. (2001, May 2). FedEx knows brand equity. *The Motley Fool.* Retrieved July 6, 2009, from http://www.fool.com/portfolios/rulemaker/2001/rulemaker010502.htm

18 Gallo, C. (2009, May 19). How to sell more than a product. *BusinessWeekOnline.* Retrieved July 2, 2009, from http://www.businessweek.com/smallbiz/content/may2009/sb20090519_058809.htm

19 Wellner, A. S. (June 2005). Boost your bottom line by taking the guesswork out of pricing. *Inc.,* 72–82.

20 Keizer, G. (2008, December 1). Windows market share dives below 90% for first time. *ComputerWorld.* Retrieved July 2, 2009, from http://www.computerworld.com/action/article.do?command=viewArticleBasic&articleId=9121938

21 Hershey's chocolate bar. (n.d.). *Hersheys.com.*

22 Boom, B. H., & Bitner, M. J. (1981). Marketing strategies for service firms. *Journal of Marketing,* 83–105.

23 RetailPets.com. (n.d.). Retrieved July 6, 2009, from http://www.retailpets.com/

24 Carter, R. (2006, April 3). The FedEx edge. *Fortune*, 77–84.

25 Monthly wholesale trade: Sales and inventories. (2009, April). *U.S. Census Bureau*. Retrieved July 6, 2009, from http://www2.census. gov/wholesale/pdf/mwts/currentwhl.pdf

26 Food Marketing Institute. (n.d.). *Supermarket facts*. Retrieved July 6, 2009, from http://www.fmi.org/facts_figs/?fuseaction=superfact

27 *Internal Revenue Service*. (n.d.). Retrieved July 6, 2009, from http:// www.irs.gov/businesses/small/article/0,id=141426,00.html

28 *Toys R Us*. (n.d.).Retrieved July 6, 2009, from http://www5.toysrus. com/about

29 *Roadside America.com*. (n.d.). Retrieved July 6, 2009, from www. roadsideamerica.com/sights/sightstory.php?tip_AttrId=%3D11761

30 *REI. com*. (n.d.).Retrieved July 6, 2009, from www.rei.com

31 Varner, D. (2009, March 27). Should small companies hire advertising agencies? *AdvertisingAgencies.org*. Retrieved July 6, 2009, from http://www.advertisingagencies.org/article/should_small_ companies_hire_advertising_agencies.html

32 *Ad revenue track*. (n.d.). Retrieved July 6, 2009, from http://www.tvb. org/nav/build_frameset.aspx.

33 Smith, A. (2009, February 3). How $3 million gets you 30 seconds. *CNNMoney.com*. February 3, 2009, Retrieved July 6, 2009, from http://money.cnn.com/2009/01/09/news/companies/superbowl_ ads/index.htm

34 Ibid.

35 Gorman, B. (2009, February 23). Sunday ratings: Academy Awards Up 13% from last year's record low. *TVByTheNumbers. com*. Retrieved July 6, 2009, from http://tvbythenumbers. com/2009/02/23/sunday-ratings-academy-awards-up-from-last-years-record-low/13282

36 Examples of product placement, (2005, August 9). *OCRegister. com*. Retrieved July 6, 2009, from http://www.ocregister.com/ocr/ sections/business/article_627432.php

37 U.S. Department of Labor. (n.d.). *Occupational outlook*. Retrieved July 6, 2009, from http://www.bls.gov/oco/ocos086.htm

38 Kolodny, L. (2005). The art of the press release. *Inc.*, 36–38.

39 American eagle outfitters trades T-shirts for jean try-outs. (2008). *PromoMagazine.com*. Retrieved July 6, 2009, from http:// promomagazine.com/incentives/news/0806-american-eagle-jeans

40 McCarthy, R. (2008). Blessed events. *Inc.com*. Retrieved July 6, 2009, from http://www.inc.com/magazine/20080401/blessed-events.html

41 Creamer, M. (2008, January 23). Word of mouth gaining respect of marketers. *Advertising Age*, 3- 28.

42 J.P. product promotion. (1985, March). *Inc.com*. Retrieved July 6, 2009, from http://www.inc.com/magazine/19850301/8739.html,

43 Rothenburg, R. (2006, March 27). Despite all the talk, ad and media shops aren't truly integrated. *Advertising Age*, 24.

Chapter 5

1 Bureau of Labor Statistics, U.S. Department of Labor. (n.d.). *Occupational outlook handbook, 2008–09 edition*. Retrieved July 8, 2009, from http://www.bls.gov/oco/ocos021.htm

2 Froschheiser, L. (2008, July 1). Business recruitment fundamentals: How to onboard more a players. *Supervision Magazine*.

3 Employers not concerned about loss of baby boomer talent. (2008, September 30). *WorldAtWork.org*. Retrieved July 8, 2009, from http://www.worldatwork.org/waw/adimComment?id=28726

4 John Deere lays the foundation. (2001, April 1). *AllBusiness.com*. Retrieved July 8, 2009, from http://www.allbusiness.com/services/ educational-services/4279727-1.html

5 Wheeler, A. (2005, March). Post-hire human resource practices and person-organization fit: A study of blue collar employees. *Journal of Managerial Issues*.

6 U.S. companies face international hiring dilemma in 2009. (2008, December 17). *VisaNow.com*. Retrieved July 8, 2009, from http:// www.visanow.com/news_events/press-hiring-dilemma.asp

7 Lachnit, C. (2002, April). Going for Generation Y. *Workforce*. Retrieved July 8, 2009, from http://findarticles.com/p/articles/ mi_m0FXS/is_4_81/ai_85698955/ and Welch, D. (2009, August 3). The incredible shrinking boomer economy. *Business Week*, 27–30.

8 Shehan, T. (2005, January 6). How to retain employees: A high turnover rate is costly in both direct and indirect costs and detroiter and hiring is stymied by the search for the perfect candidate. *Business Wire*.

9 Winn-Dixie extends use of kronos solution. (2008, February 12). *Food & Beverage Close-Up*.

10 Kislik, I.. (2005, April 1). A hire authority. *Catalog Age* and HR by numbers: How to hire the right people and then lead them to success. (2006, January 1). *Prosales*.

11 Creps, M. (2005, May 31).What not to ask applicants at a job interview. *Bloomington (Indiana) Herald Times*.

12 McNair, J. (2005, June 5). Ford settles employee suit alleging bias in testing. *The Cincinnati Enquirer*. Retrieved July 14, 2009, from http:// www.whytest.biz/ford.htm

13 Pepper, T. (2005, February 21). Inside the head of an applicant. *Newsweek* and personality assessment tests. *PR Newswire*.

14 Hench, D. (2005, April 18). Maine overwhelmed as background checks balloon. *Portland (Maine) Press Herald*; Hymowitz, C. (2005, March 17). Add candidate's character to boards' lists of concerns. *The Wall Street Journal*; Swann, J. (2005, August 1). Guarding the gates with employee background checks. *Community Banker*; Patton, C. (2006, January 1). To tell the truth: It's an institution's duty to ensure that new hires are who they say they are. *University Business*; and Maytum, M. J.(2006, January 27). Look a little closer: investigators say employers can thwart value of background checks; Some should dig deeper. *Business First*.

15 Myers, D. J. (2005, May 1). You're fired! Letting an employee go isn't easy for any manager. *Alaska Business Monthly*.

16 Overholt, A. (2002, February). True or false: You are hiring the right people. *Fast Company*, p. 110.

17 Stettner, M. (2009, September 15). Select top job candidates while screening out duds. *Investors Business Daily* and Avoid hiring that bad apple. (2009, February 1). *Credit Management*.

18 Tyler, K. (2008, March 1). Treat contingent workers with care: consider both your company's and workers' needs in contingent workforce planning. *HR Magazine*.

19 Horowitz, S. (2009, May 20). The new labor force is out on its own. *Forbes.com*. Retrieved July 14, 2009, from http://www.forbes. com/2009/05/20/freelance-union-benefits-leadership-careers-work. html

20 Raphael, T. (2002, September 22). It's all in the cards. *Workforce*. Retrieved July 9, 2009, from http://findarticles.com/p/articles/ mi_m0FXS/is_9_81/ai_91913073/

21 Bassi, L., & McMurrer, D. (2004, March). How's your return on people? *Harvard Business Review, 82*(3), 18–21.

22 Green, R. (2005, March 1). Effective training programs: How to design in-house training on a limited budget. *CADalyst* and Connelly, L. M. (2005, June 22). Welcoming new employees. *Journal of Nursing Scholarship*.

23 Neag, M. (2008, Setember 16). Great starts: Orientation ovation. *Training Magazine* and Nancherla, A. (2009, February 1). Money matters, but training doesn't? *T + D*.

24 Weiss, T (2009, June 4). Where the jobs are: Physical therapist. *Forbes.com*. Retrieved July 9, 2009, from http://www.forbes. com/2009/06/04/jobs-physical-therapy-leadership-careers-employment.html

25 Bureau of Labor Statistics. (2002). Occupational outlook. *Quarterly Online, 46*(2). Retrieved June 9, 2009, from http://www.bls.gov/ opub/ooq/2002/summer/art01.htm

26 Meyer, H. (2008, August). Apprenticeships enable small firms to grow their own skilled employees. *The Costco Connection*.

27 Troianovski, A. (2008, August 19). Skilled trades seek workers. *The Wall Street Journal*.

28 Weiss, T. (2007, September 19). Lifetime of learning. *Forbes*. Retrieved June 9, 2009, from http://www.forbes.com/2007/09/19/ training-flowers-hamburger-lead-careers-cx_tw_0919universities. html

29 *Cisco Webex*. (n.d.). Retrieved June 9, 2009, from http://www.webex. com

30 Kentucky College training potential army job applicants. (2009, July

4). *Business Week*, July 4, 2009, Retrieved July 9, 2009, from http://www.businessweek.com/ap/financialnews/D997PNA02.htm

31 Goldsmith, M. (2008, September 2). E-tools that help teach leadership. *Business Week*.

32 Walker, S., Davis, J., & Deepesh, D. (2008, February 1). Postural assignments & job rotation: A survey of one company's assembly line supervisors. *Professional Safety*.

33 Weiss, T. (2007, September 19). Lifetime of learning. *Forbes*. Retrieved June 9, 2009, from http://www.forbes.com/2007/09/19/training-flowers-hamburger-lead-careers-cx_tw_0919universities.html

34 *Training and development*. (n.d.). Retrieved July 9, 2009, from http://www.careersatpizzahut.co.uk/html/trainingandDev.htm

35 Employer costs for employee compensation – March 2009. (2009, June 10). *Bureau of Labor Statistics*. Retrieved July 10, 2009, from http://www.bls.gov/news.release/pdf/ecec.pdf

36 Greco, D. (2000, June). Recruiting top talent, one by one. *Inc.com*. Retrieved July 10, 2009, from http://www.inc.com/articles/2000/06/14557.html

37 LaMotta, L. (2007, July). 270. A happy worker won't stray. *Forbes.com*.

38 100 best companies to work for 2009. (n.d.). *CNNMoney.com*. Retrieved July 10, 2009, from http://money.cnn.com/magazines/fortune/bestcompanies/2009/snapshots/1.html

39 Diskin, C. (2008, May 28). Flexible schedules can pay off for employers, too. *The Record (Bergen County, NJ)*.

40 Telework Facts. (n.d.). *The telework coalition*. Retrieved July 10, 2009, from www.telcoa.org/id33.htm

41 Aratani, L. (2008, August 23). Flextime has green appeal and lures younger workers. *The Washington Post*.

42 100 best companies to work for 2009. (n.d.). *CNNMoney.com*. Retrieved July 10, 2009, from http://money.cnn.com/magazines/fortune/bestcompanies/2009/snapshots/1.html

43 Turex, L. (n.d.). Top ten telecommuting questions answered. *Jobsnake*. Retrieved July 11, 2009, from www.jobsnake.com/seek/articles/index.cgi?openarticle&8599&Top_10_Telecommuting_Questions_Answered

44 100 best companies to work for 2009. (n.d.). *CNNMoney.com*. Retrieved July 10, 2009, from http://money.cnn.com/magazines/fortune/bestcompanies/2009/snapshots/1.html

45 Tahmincioglu, E. (2007, October 5). The quiet revolution: Telecommuting. *MSNBC.com*. Retrieved July 11, 2009, from http://www.msnbc.msn.com/id/20281475/

46 IDA.com (n.d.). Retrieved July 13, 2009, from www.incomesdata.co.uk/studies/job-sharing.htm.

47 Kubica, A. J. (2008, March 1). Transitioning middle managers. *Healthcare Executive*.

48 Williams, A. (2008, January 1). Should Black people let affirmative action die? Yes. (Two Sides) *Ebony Magazine* and Cose, E. (2008, January 1). Should black people let affirmative action die? No. (Two Sides) *Ebony Magazine*.

49 Office of Disability Employment Policy, United States Department of Labor (n.d.). *Entrepreneurship: A flexible route to economic independence for people with disabilities*. Retrieved July 13, 2009, from http://www.dol.gov/odep/pubs/misc/entrepre.htm9.

50 CivilRights.org. (n.d.). Retrieved February 17, 2009, from www.civilrights.org and Gillette, B. (2009, January 5). Strong ADA provisions go into effect this year. *The Mississippi Business Journal*.

51 Gregg, B. (2009, January/February). Make sure training isn't ignored. *DiversityInc.com*. Retrieved July 13, 2009, from http://www.diversityinc-digital.com/diversityincmedia/200901/?pg=62&search=disability%20discrimination&per_page=5&results_page=1&doc_id=-1

52 CivilRights.org. (n.d.). Retrieved February 17, 2009, from www.civilrights.org and Riley, A. (2009, January 9). Expansion of ADA law expected to cause windfall of claims. *Arizona Capitol Times*.

53 Robitaille, S. (2008, June 22). Support grows for disabled job seekers. *The Wall Street Journal*.

54 The U.S. Equal Employment Opportunity Commission. (n.d.). *Age discrimination*. Retrieved July 13, 2009, from http://www.eeoc.gov/types/age.html

55 Jackson, M. (2008, June 27). Job market wasted on the young; in an aging society, mature workers still get passed over. *The Boston Globe*.

56 Union history lesson. (2008, June 16). *Bangor Daily News*, June 16, 2008.

57 Kerr, J. C. (2005, June 16). Dissident unions press AFL-CIO. *Capital Times* and John B. Schnapp. (2005, June 16). Auto workers of the world united. *The Wall Street Journal*.

58 *Union members by state*. (n.d.). Retrieved July 14, 2009, from http://www.aflcio.org/joinaunion/why/uniondifference/uniondiff16.cfm

59 Drawbaugh, K. (2008, January 28). Unions gained more members in 2008: Labor department. *Reuters.com*. Retrieved July 14, 2009, from http://www.reuters.com/article/domesticNews/idUSTRE50R6ER20090128

60 Hoerr, J. (2005, June 1). Lucky strike. *Harper's*; and Maher, K. (2006, January 21). Share of the U.S. work force in unions held steady in 2005. *The Wall Street Journal*.

61 Blume, H. (2009, May 13). Judge prohibits L.A. teachers strike. *Los Angeles Times*. Retrieved July 14, 2009, from http://articles.latimes.com/2009/may/13/local/me-lausd-strike13

62 Vives, R. (2009, May 28).Teachers start hunger strike to protest layoffs. *Los Angeles Times*. Retrieved July 14, 2009, from http://articles.latimes.com/2009/may/28/local/me-hunger-strike28

63 L.A. teachers end hunger strike protesting budget cuts. (2009, June 18). *L.A. Now*. Retrieved July 14, 2009, from http://latimesblogs.latimes.com/lanow/2009/06/hunger-strike-1.html

64 Osterman, R. (2005, June 14). UFW ready to boycott Gallo—Again. *Sacramento Bee*.

65 Freeman, S. (2008, January 19). Rail strike averted as Amtrak, unions reach tentative deal. *The Washington Post*.

66 National Mediation Board. (n.d.). Retrieved September 10, 2008, from www.nmb.gov and Fedor, L. (2009, January 8). Mediation board declares Delta, NWA a single system. *Star Tribune* (Minneapolis, MN).

67 Estreicher, S., Heise, M., & Sherwyn, D. (2005, April 1). Assessing the case of employment arbitration: A new path for empirical research. *Stanford Law Review*.

68 Masisak, C. (008, May 21). NHL's cup runneth over: Final matchup is ideal for showcasing league. *The Washington Times* and Jackson, J. (2009, February 1). Another lockout on horizon? *Chicago Sun-Times*

69 DeCarlom S., & Zajac, B. (Eds.). (2009, April 22). CEO compensation. Forbes.com. Retrieved July 14, 2009, from http://www.forbes.com/2009/04/22/executive-pay-ceo-leadership-compensation-best-boss-09-ceo_land.html

70 Lublin, J. S. (2008, April 14). Boards flex their pay muscles. *The Wall Street Journal*.

71 DeCarlo, S. (2008, April 30). Top paid CEOs. *Forbes*.

72 Pfeffer, J. (July, 2005). The pay-for-performance fallacy. *Business, 2*, 64–67.

73 Beck, R. (2008, July 13). Wall Street CEOs should return bloated bonuses. *Telegraph–Herald (Dubuque)*.

74 La Monica, P. (2007, March 5). Google CEO, co-founders stick with $1. *CNN Money*. Retrieved July 14, 2009, from http://money.cnn.com/2007/03/05/news/companies/google_salaries/index.htm.

75 Dvorak, P. (2008, June 23). Firms measure a CEOs (Net) worth. *The Wall Street Journal*, p. B-1 and Welch, J., & Welch, S. (2008, June 14). CEO pay: No easy answer. *Business Week*.

76 Tuna, C. (2009, January 12). Shareholders to focus on executive compensation. *The Wall Street Journal*.

77 Gongloff, M., & Karmin, C. (2009, April 8). Shareholders bring the heat on executive pay. *The Wall Street Journal*.

78 Jayson, S. (2006, December 8). Companies slow to adjust to work-life balance concerns of Generation Y. *USA Today*. Retrieved July 14, 2009, from http://www.usatoday.com/news/nation/2006-12-06-gen-next-life-work-balance_x.htm

79 Rampell, C. (2009, February 9). U.S. women set to surpass men in labor force. *The New York Times*. Retrieved July 14, 2009, from

http://www.nytimes.com/2009/02/06/business/worldbusiness/06iht-06women.19978672.html?pagewanted=1&_r=1

80 U.S. Department of Labor, U.S. Bureau of Labor Statistics. (2008). *Highlight of women's earnings in 2007*. Retrieved July 14, 2009, from http://www.bls.gov/cps/cpswom2007.pdf

81 Williams, E. (2007, September 1). The economic status of women in Michigan: Wide disparities by race and ethnicity. *Briefing Paper Series*.

82 Williams, S., & Luthar, H. K. (2008, November 1). DOTA's software re-engineering group: What's going on in your department, Jimmy? *Journal of the International Academy for Case Studies*.

83 U.S. Equal Opportunity Commission. (n.d.).Retrieved September 10, 2008, from www.eeoc.gov and Liptak, A (2009, January 27) Court expands ability to sue in sexual harassment investigations. *The New York Times*.

84 U.S. Equal Opportunity Commission. (n.d.). *The sexual harassment charges*. Retrieved July 14, 2009, from www.eeoc.gov/stats/harass.html

85 *Sexual harassment in the workplace*. (n.d.). Retrieved July 14, 2009, from http://www.hr-guide.com/data/A07202.htm

86 Holding back women can carry huge cost: Companies end up paying for their bad behavior. (2007, October 4). *Chicago Sun Times*.

Chapter 6

1 Reinartz, W., & Ulaga, W. (2008, May). How to sell services more profitably. *Harvard Business Review*.

2 Frei, F. X. (2008, April). The four things a service business must get right. *Harvard Business Review*.

3 Breyfogle III, F. W. (2008, February). The future of quality management. *Quality Digest*.

4 Cooper, J. C. (2008, May 19). Services: A heavyweight in a hard fight. *BusinessWeek*.

5 Hall, K. (2009, April 8). Sharp adopts global production model. *BusinessWeek*. Retrieved August 3, 2009, from http://www.businessweek.com/globalbiz/content/apr2009/gb2009048_640568.htm

6 Thilmany, J. (2003, October 1). Birth of a new product: Bob Montgomery didn't think he'd need a computer to design his motorized surfboard. Boy, was he wrong. *Mechanical Engineering-CIME*. Retrieved August 3, 2009, from http://www.allbusiness.com/professional-scientific/scientific-research-development/661688-1.html

7 BMW drives Germany. (2007, July 5). *Time*. Retrieved August 3, 2009, from http://www.time.com/time/magazine/article/0,9171,1640398-1,00.html

8 Cooper, R., & Maskell, B. (2008). How to manage through worse-before-better. *Sloan Management Review*.

9 Feingold, J. (2008, May). Lean roots—A quick history lesson. *Quality Digest*.

10 Sowards, D. (2007. November). Lean construction. *Quality Digest*.

11 Cutler, T. R. (2008, May). Bored by lean. *Quality Digest*.

12 Elberse, A. (2008, July/August). Should you invest in the long tail? *Harvard Business Review*.

13 McGregor, J. (2008, May 26). At Best Buy, marketing goes micro. *BusinessWeek*.

14 Rubinkam, M. (2008, May 1). Marketing matriculation. *The Washington Times*.

15 Clemence, S. (2009, March 23). The future of shopping: Custom everything. *Entrepreneur*. Retrieved August 4, 2009, from http://www.entrepreneur.com/growyourbusiness/portfoliocombusinessnewsandopinion/article200894.html

16 Kooser, A. C. (2008, May). Net profits jump in. *Entrepreneur*.

17 Young, L. (2008, October 28). Jackson, Tennessee unemployment will rise with whirlpool plant closing. *Gantdaily.com*. Retrieved August 12, 2009, from http://www.gantdaily.com/news/11/ARTICLE/34956/2008-10-28.html.

18 Tire company buying Whirlpool plant in Tennessee. (2009, July 21). *BusinessWeek*. Retrieved August 3, 2009, from http://www.

businessweek.com/ap/financialnews/D99J2GEO0.htm.

19 Shugart, W. (2009, January 25). Folly of incentives. *The Washington Times*.

20 Lynn, J. (2009, January). Love where you work. *Entrepreneur*.

21 *Facility layout and design*. (n.d.). Retrieved August 4, 2009, from http://www.answers.com/topic/facility-layout-and-design

22 Gomez-Mejia, L. R., Balkin, D. B., & Cardy, R. L. (2008). *Management*. New York: McGraw-Hill.

23 West, J. E. (2008, August). Buyer beware—and in control. *Quality Digest*.

24 Brandt, D. (2007, July 1). Saving lives just in time: DePuy serves health care through orthopedic supply and demand. *Industrial Engineer*. Retrieved August 4, 2009, from http://www.allbusiness.com/services/engineering-accounting-research-management/4499413-1.html

25 Kelly, B. (2009, January 29). ISO 9001 documentation is like a box of chocolates. *Quality Digest*.

26 Bala, S. (2008, July). A practical approach to lean Six Sigma. *Quality Digest*.

27 *Alaska air cargo implements seafood quality control programme*. (2009, March 16). Retrieved August 4, from http://www.allbusiness.com/company-activities-management/operations-quality-control/11815003-1.html

28 National Institute of Standards and Technology. (2008). *Commerce Secretary Gutierrez Joins President Bush in announcing 2008 Baldrige National Quality Awards*. Retrieved May 4, 2009, from http://www.nist.gov/public_affairs/releases/2008baldrigerecipients.htm.

29 West, J. E. (2008, December). Quality improvement is an imperative. *Quality Digest*.

30 West, J. E. (2008, February). Making products better. *Quality Digest*.

31 West, J. E. (2008, March). Beware the mechanical IMS. *Quality Digest*.

32 De Feo, J. A. & Barney, M. (2008, February). The future of manufacturing, *Quality Digest*.

33 Reinartz, W., & Ulaga, W. (2008, May). How to sell services more profitably. *Harvard Business Review*.

Chapter 7

1 Section 508.gov (n.d.) Retrieved August 18, 2009, from http://www.section508.gov/index.cfm?FuseAction=Content&ID=3

2 Hise, P (2008, February 1). Company makes technology accessible for the disabled. *Virginia Business*. Retrieved August 18, 2009, from http://www.virginiabusiness.com/index.php/news/article/tearing-down-barriers/190/

3 TecAccess Pressroom (2008, February 1). Retrieved August 18, 2009, from http://www.tecaccess.net/content/pressroom/awards/vabusinesspr.shtml

4 Zuckerman, L (1995, July 6). Smith Corona, A computer victim, files for bankruptcy. *The New York Times*. Retrieved July 15, 2009, from http://www.nytimes.com/1995/07/06/business/smith-corona-a-computer-victim-files-for-bankruptcy.html

5 Pratt, M.K. (2008, October). IT Careers: 5 tips for charting your 100 day plan. *CIO*. Retrieved July 15, 2009, from http://www.cio.com/article/457517/IT_Careers_5_Tips_for_Charting_Your_100_Day_Plan?page=1

6 Redbox Automated Retail (2009). *How Redbox works*. Retrieved July 15, 2009, from http://www.redbox.com/HowItWorks.aspx

7 Hamm, S (2005, June 20). A virtual revolution. *BusinessWeek*, 98–102; and Mitchell L.R. (2006, March 13). Virtualization's Real Impact. *Computerworld*.

8 Foley, M.O. (2008, December). Hot technologies for 2009. *Inc*.

9 Shambora, J. (2009, January 20). VMware: Good product, uncertain times. *CNNMoney.com*. Retrieved July 15, 2009, from http://money.cnn.com/2009/01/19/technology/shambora_vmware.fortune/index.htm

10 Alexander, P. (2005, November 14). Should your business use instant messaging? *Entrepreneur.com*. Retrieved July 15, 2009, from http://www.entrepreneur.com/technology/

techtrendscolumnistpeteralexander/article81050.html

11 ScienceDaily. (2008, June 4) *Instant messaging proves useful in reducing workplace interruption.* Retrieved July 15, 2009, from http://www.sciencedaily.com/releases/2008/06/080603120251.htm, accessed July 15, 2009

12 www.ecommerceprogram.com. (n.d.). Retrieved July 15, 2009, from http://www.ecommerceprogram.com/ecommerce/Ebusiness-Info.asp

13 U.S. Census Bureau. (2009, May, 28). *EStats.* Retrieved July 15, 2009 from http://www.census.gov/econ/estats/2007/2007reportfinal.pdf

14 Winters, T., King, & C., Davie, W. (2009, May 15). *Quarterly retail E-Commerce Sales.* U.S. Census Bureau. Retrieved July 15, 2009, from http://www.census.gov/retail/mrts/www/data/html/09Q1.html

15 Mehta, S. T. (2009, January 6). Tech memo to team Obama. *Fortune.*

16 Rochester Institute of Technology. (2008, November 12). The next step in health care: Telemedicine researchers broadcast live surgery using Internet2. Retrieved July 15, 2009 from *Ascribe Higher Education News Service.*

17 Juniper Networks (2009, February 11). *Juniper networks powers U.S. Department of Energy's ESnet network supporting global research* [Press release]. Retrieved July 15, 2009 from *Business Wire.*

18 Leary, B. (2009, January). Social media's good, bad, ugly and unexpected. *Inc.*

19 ZDNet (2008, January) *Social Networking: Brave New World or Revolution from Hell?* [White paper]. Retrieved July 15, 2009.

20 Parise, S., Guinan, P. J., & Weinberg, B. D. (2009, January 1). The secrets of marketing in a Web 2.0 world. *The Wall Street Journal.*

21 Hempel, J. (2009, February 8). Web 2.0 is so over. Welcome to Web 3.0. *Fortune.*

22 Sharma, A. & Vascellaro, J. E. (2009, November 28). Companies eye location-services market. *The Wall Street Journal*

23 U.S. Department of Labor (n.d.). *Computer and information systems managers occupational outlook handbook.* Retrieved August 17, 2009, from Bureau of Labor Statistics http://www.bls.gov/oco/ocos258.htm

24 Foley, J. (1995, October 30) *Managing information: Infoglut.* Retrieved July 17, 2009, from http://www.informationweek.com/551/51mtinf.htm,jsessionid=3LC3H52WQCXJ2QSNDLRSKH0CJUNN2JVN

25 MacMillan, R. (2005, April 25). The modern brain, besieged. *The Washington Post.* Retrieved July 20, 2009, from http://www.washingtonpost.com/wp-dyn/content/article/2005/04/25/AR2005042500342.html

26 Gantz, J. F., Chute, C., Manfredtz, A., Minton, S. Reinsel, D., Schlichting, W., et al. (2008, March). The diverse and exploding digital universe. *Emc.com.* Retrieved July 17, 2009, from http://www.emc.com/collateral/analyst-reports/diverse-exploding-digital-universe.pdf

27 Weier, M. H. (2007, April 7). The fight against infoglut. *Information Week.* Retrieved July, 20, 2009, from http://www.informationweek.com/news/software/enterpriseapps/showArticle.jhtml?articleID=198800766&pgno=1&queryText=&isPrev=, accessed July 20, 2009.

28 Ibid.

29 Jana. R. (2007, August 13). Mining virtual worlds for market research. *BusinessWeek,* Retrieved July 20, 2009, from http://www.businessweek.com/innovate/content/aug2007/id20070813_140822.htm

30 Weintraub, A. (2009, June 10). The fight over drug data mining. *BusinessWeek.* Retrieved July 20, 2009, from http://www.businessweek.com/magazine/content/09_25/b4136000501366.htm, accessed July 20, 2009

31 Murray, C. J. (2009, January 4). Faster processors pave way for vision, 3-D TV. *Design News.* Retrieved July 20, 2009, from http://www.designnews.com/article/161452-Faster_Processors_Pave_Way_for_Vision_3_D_TV.php

32 Computer History Museum. (n.d.). *Timeline of computer history. Retrieved July 21, 2009, from http://www.computerhistory.org/timeline/?category=cmptr, accessed July 21, 2009.*

33 Greenberg, A. (2009, February 3). IBM promises world's fastest computer—again. *Forbes.com.* Retrieved July 21, 2009, from http://www.forbes.com/2009/02/02/ibm-supercomputer-sequoia-technology-enterprise-tech_0203_ibm.html

34 DevTopics. (2008, January 11). 101 great computer programming quotes #91. Retrieved July 21, 2009, from http://www.devtopics.com/101-great-computer-programming-quotes/

35 Fishman, C. (2002, July). How to SMASH your strategy. *Fast Company.*

36 Physorg.com (2008, April 21). *Researchers create self-healing computer systems for spacecraft.* Retrieved July 21, 2009, from http://www.physorg.com/news128009580.htm

37 Panera Bread. (n.d.) *Free Wi-Fi hotspots. Retrieved July 21, 2009, from http://www.panerabread.com/cafes/wifi.php*

38 Graham, J. (2004, September 12). Businesses Cast Wi-Fi Lures to Hook Customers. *USAToday.com.* Retrieved July 21, 2009, from http://www.usatoday.com/money/industries/telecom/2004-09-12-wifi-cafes_x.htm

39 USA Today. (2009, January 12). *Popularity of tiny 'Netbooks' set to rise in 2009.* Retrieved August 17, 2009, from http://www.usatoday.com/tech/products/2009-01-12-netbooks_N.htm

40 Pimm, F. (2002, April 8). Plugging into portal returns. *Computerworld.* 38.

41 Cimage. (n.d.). *Intranet users reap rewards* [Press Release]. Retrieved July 21, 2009, from http://www.cimage.com/news/casestudies/inssintranet.htm

42 Correia, A. C., & Menezes De Faria, L. E. (2004, June). An Intranet success story: Auditors at a large financial service organization discover the power of Intra-Enterprise connectivity. *Internal Auditor.* Retrieved July 21, 2009, from http://findarticles.com/p/articles/mi_m4153/is_3_61/ai_n6153201/

43 Standiford, S. S. & Sandvig, J. C. (2002, November 4). Control of B2B commerce and the impact on industry structure. *First Monday, 7.* Retrieved July 21, 2009, from http://firstmonday.org/htbin/cgiwrap/bin/ojs/index.php/fm/article/view/1008/929

44 Kharif, O. (2002, October 1). Brad Boston: No paper. *BusinessWeek Online.*

45 Entrepreneur.com. (2002, January 21). *Arby's connects franchisees via extranet.* Retrieved July 21, 2009, from http://www.entrepreneur.com/franchises/franchisezone/thisjustin/article18406.html.

46 Nolle. T. (2005, June 1). IP VPNs. *Telecommunications Americas;* and Business Wire. (2006, January 4) *Network based IP VPN equipment enabling key services for service providers reports In-Stat.*

47 Mintz Testa, B. (2009, July 17). Small company, big VPN. *Processor.com.* Retrieved July 21, 2009, from http://www.processor.com/editorial/article.asp?article=articles%2Fp3119%2F28p19%2F28p19%2F28p19.asp&guid=, accessed July 21, 2009.

48 Paul, F. (2009, June 23). SMBs do software differently. *Entrepreneur.com.* Retrieved July 21, 2009, from http://www.entrepreneur.com/technology/bmighty/article202390.html, accessed July 21, 2009.

49 Limewire. (n.d.). *About.* Retrieved July 21, 2009, from http://www.limewire.com/about

50 Spendonlife.com. (n.d.). *Official identity theft statistics.* Retrieved July 22, 2009, from http://www.spendonlife.com/guide/identity-theft-statistics

51 Bosworth, M. (2007, January 18). Hackers hit TJ Maxx, Marshalls. *Consumer Affairs.* Retrieved July 22, 2009, from http://www.consumeraffairs.com/news04/2007/01/tj_maxx_data.html

52 Sutter, J.D. (2009, July 16). Twitter hack raises questions about cloud computing. *CNN.com.* Retrieved July 22, 2009, from http://edition.cnn.com/2009/TECH/07/16/twitter.hack/

53 Markoff, J. (2009, January 22).Worm infects millions of computers worldwide. *NYTimes.com.* Retrieved July, 22, 2009, from http://www.nytimes.com/2009/01/23/technology/internet/23worm.html?scp=5&sq=conficker&st=cse, accessed July 22, 2009.

54 Schectman, J. (2009, August 13). Computer hacking made easy. *BusinessWeek.* Retrieved August 21, 2009, from, http://www.businessweek.com/magazine/content/09_34/b4144036807250.htm?link_position=link3

55 Moscaritolo, A. (2008, September 23). U.S. based computers

launch most cyberattacks. *Secure Computing Magazine*. Retrieved July 22, 2009, from http://www.securecomputing.net.au/News/123462,usbased-computers-launch-most-cyberattacks.aspx, accessed July 22, 2009.

56 Schweitzer, D. (2005, March 28). Be prepared for cyberterrorism. *Computerworld*; Mallery, J. (2005, May 1). "Cyberterrorism: Real threat or media hype? *Security Technology and & Design*; Business Wire. (September 20, 2005). *Are we prepared for the latest type of terrorism—cyberterrorism?*; and Bridis, T. (2006, February 10). AP Online. (2006, February 10). *U.S. concludes 'cyber storm' mock attacks.*

57 Malone M. S. (2009, July 10). Cyber-terrorism and how we should respond. *ABCNews.com*. Retrieved July 22, 2009, from http://abcnews.go.com/Business/Technology/Story?id=8045546&page=1

58 American Management Association. (2008, February 28). *2007 Electronic monitoring and surveillance survey*. Retrieved July 22, 2009, from http://press.amanet.org/press-releases/177/2007-electronic-monitoring-surveillance-survey/

59 Black, J. (2002, June 5). Faceless snoopers have upper hand. *BusinessWeek*.

60 Skinner, C. (2008, September 14). Employers admit checking facebook before hiring. *PCWorld*. Retrieved July 22, 2009, from http://www.pcworld.com/businesscenter/article/151044/employers_admit_checking_facebook_before_hiring.html, accessed July 22, 2009.

61 Austin, S. (2008, December 7). Email with a ribbon on it. *The Wall Street Journal*.

62 Songini, M. (2000, November 2). Halloween less haunting for hershey this year. *Computerworld*. Retrieved August 17, 2009, from http://www.computerworld.com/s/article/53214/Halloween_less_haunting_for_Hershey_this_year

63 Freeman, S. (2008, August 27). Flight delays caused by computer failure, FAA says. *The Washington Post*. Retrieved July 22, 2009, from http://www.washingtonpost.com/wp-dyn/content/article/2008/08/26/AR2008082602203.html

64 Zogby, J. (2009, June 18). Why do people trust the Internet more? *Forbes.com*. Retrieved July 23, 2009, from http://www.forbes.com/2009/06/17/media-newspapers-radio-television-opinions-columnists-john-zogby-internet.htm

Chapter 8

1 MBAAssociation.org. (2009, April 13). *The importance of accounting for small business start ups*. Retrieved August 16, 2009, from http://www.mbaassociation.org/Entrepreneurship/The-Importance-of-Accounting-For-Small-Business-Start-Ups.html

2 Costello, M. (n.d.). Why is a good understanding of accounting important for running your business? *Myownbusiness.org*. Retrieved August 16, 2009, from www.myownbusiness.org/videos/html/m_costello_t4.html

3 Visa. (n.d.). *About Visa Inc*. Retrieved August 14, 2009, from http://corporate.visa.com/av/main.jsp

4 Visa. (2009, July 29). *Visa Inc. Posts solid fiscal third quarter 2009 earnings results and updates longer-term guidance* [Press release]. Retrieved August 14, 2009, from http://investor.visa.com/phoenix.zhtml?c=215693&p=irol-newsArticle&ID=1313835&highlight=

5 Gregory, C. (1997). *Savage money*. New York: Routledge Publishing.

6 Flandez, R. (2009, February 17). Barter fits the bill for strapped firms. *The Wall Street Journal*.

7 Detamore-Rodman, C. (2008, December). Care to barter? *Entrepreneur*.

8 Pawlowski, A. (2008, September 2). No cash? No problem, if you barter. *CNN.com*. Retrieved August 14, 2009, from http://www.cnn.com/2008/LIVING/wayoflife/09/02/bartering.rise/index.html

9 Bazar, E. (2009, February 26). Bartering booms during tough economic times. *USAToday.com*. Retrieved August 14, 2009, from http://www.usatoday.com/tech/webguide/internetlife/2009-02-25-barter_N.htm

10 Sennholz, H.F. (2008, April). The origins of money. *The St. Croix Review*.

11 Powers, S. (2005, November 1) Anybody got a ten-spot? *Money*. pp.

166–170; and n.a., (2006, March 3) Government debuts colorful $10 currency. *Washington Times*. p. C11.

12 Johnson, A. (2009, August 7). Funny money no laughing matter in recession. *MSNBC.MSN.com*. Retrieved August 14, 2009, from http://www.msnbc.msn.com/id/32289194/ns/us_news-crime_and_courts/

13 Marks, G. (2008, March 4). The pain of going paperless. *Forbes.com*. Retrieved August 14, 2009, from http://www.forbes.com/2008/03/04/cisco-apple-visa-ent-tech-cx_gm_0305genemarksbillpay.html

14 Savitz, E. (2008, December 11). IPOs in 2008: A year of unenviable statistics. *SeekingAlpha.com*. Retrieved August 14, 2009, from

15 The Motley Fool. (2006, May 26). *Buy or sell MasterCard*. Retrieved August, 14, 2009, from www.fool.com/personalfinance/general/2006/05/26/buy-or-sell-mastercard.aspx

16 http://finance.yahoo.com/q?s=ma, accessed August 14, 2009.

17 http://finance.yahoo.com/q/it?s=MA, accessed August 14, 2009.

18 Ibid.

19 Barr, A. & Andrejczak, M. (2007, November 9). Visa plans $10 bln IPO, following rival MasterCard. *MarketWatch*. Retrieved August 14, 2009, from www.marketwatch.com/news/story/visa-plans-10-bln-ipo/story.aspx?guid=%7B4FB14AF9-B97A-44D6-891A-6D6E0C72E83B%7D

20 Benner, K. (2008, March 19). Visa IPO priced at record $17.9B. *Fortune*. Retrieved August 14, 2009, from http://money.cnn.com/2008/03/18/news/companies/visa_ipo.fortune/

21 Oslund, J.J. (2006, March 24). JARGON; Investment Bankers. *Minneapolis Star Tribune*.

22 Voyles, B. (2008, November 1). Ask not for whom the dow tolls; how will advisors and investors behave after the collapse of 2008. *On Wall Street*.

23 Sasseen, J. (2008, July 21). Why moody's and S&P still matter. *BusinessWeek*.

24 Landis, D. (2006, February 10). Dividends with Room to Grow. *Kiplinger's Personal Finance*.

25 Mueller, J. (2006, March 9). Dividend myths foolishly debunked, part 2. *The Motley Fool*.

26 Yahoo. (n.d.). *Yahoo Finance*. Retrieved August 14, 2009, from http://www.finance.yahoo.com

27 *BusinessWeek*. (2009, July 22). *Amazon Buys Zappos.com for $847M in Stock, Cash*. Retrieved August 14, 2009, from http://www.businessweek.com/bwdaily/dnflash/content/jul2009/db20090722_370605.htm

28 The Motley Fool. (2006, January 26). *Preferred stock, explained*. Retrieved August 16, 2009, from http://www.fool.com/investing/dividendsincome/2006/01/26/preferred-stock-explained.aspx.

29 Fisher, D. (2009, August 4). Accounting tricks catch up with GE. *Forbes.com*. Retrieved August 16, 2009, from http://www.forbes.com/2009/08/04/ge-immelt-sec-earnings-business-beltway-ge.html

30 Heffes, E. (2005, September 1). Accounting trends affecting the next generation of accountants. *Financial Executive*.

31 Douglas, C.B., & Sutthiwan, S. (2008, July 1). The conflicting roles of controllership and compliance. *Strategic Finance*

32 Leibs, S. (2005, May). Who's counting? *CFO*. p. 15; and Duffy, M.N. (2005, October 1). Oh, the places you will go! CPAs today have career options even they never envisioned 100 years ago. *Journal of Accountancy*.

33 Tie, R. (2005, May 1). The case for private company GAAP. *Journal of Accountancy*; and Hauge, I.P.N. (2006, January 1). Convergence: in search for the best: CPAs should understand how U.S. and foreign accounting standards influence each other. *Journal of Accountancy*; and Prince, C.J. (2006, January 1). Closing the GAAP. *Entrepreneur*.

34 Bureau of Labor Statistics. (2008). *Accountants and auditors. Occupational outlook handbook, 2008–09 Edition*. Retrieved August 16, 2009, from http://www.bls.gov/oco/ocos001.htm

35 N.a. (2008, March 10). Qualities to look for in a tax accountant. *Rocky Mountain News*.

36 Katz, H. M. (2008, April 1). Who will pay the cost of government employer retiree health benefits? *Labor Law Journal*; and Lorentz, J.W. (2009, January 1). Report from GASB. *GAAFR Review*.

37 Sostek, A. (2007, March 20). Flexible policies, and a little fun,

put small accounting firm at the top. *Pittsburgh Post-Gazette.* Retrieved August 16, 2009, from http://www.post-gazette.com/pg/07079/770713-334.stm

38 Rahn, R.W. (2005, April 21). Where is the balance sheet? *Washington Times*; and Kianoff, L (2006, January 1). Financial statements: An often unused tool for the masses. *CPA Technology Advisor.*

39 *Entrepreneur.* (2009). *Elements of a business plan.* Retrieved August 17, 2009, from http://www.entrepreneur.com/startingbusiness/businessplans/article38308-7.html, accessed August 17, 2009.

40 Vorster, M. (2005, February 1). Balance sheet basics. *Construction Equipment*; and Eastern, J.S. (2006, January 1). How to read a balance sheet. *Family Practice News.*

41 Whelan, D. (2005, June 20). Beyond the balance sheet: Hot brand values. *Forbes.* pp. 113–115.

42 Clark, S. (2001, January 12). Treat employees like your most valuable asset, because they are. *Houston Business Journal.* Retrieved August, 17, 2009, from http://houston.bizjournals.com/houston/stories/2001/01/15/smallb2.html

43 Logan, J. (2005, July 6). People - the most valuable asset of your business. *BizInformer.com.* Retrieved August 17, 2009, from http://www.bizinformer.com/50226711/people_the_most_valuable_asset_of_your_business.php

44 DW-World.DE. (2009, April 15). *Swiss bank UBS to slash over 8,000 jobs as losses mount.* Retrieved August 17, 2009, from http://www.dwworld.de/dw/article/0,,4178838,00.html

45 Nixon, S. (2009, August 5). For UBS Employee Morale is the Story. *The Wall Street Journal.* Retrieved August, 17 2009, from http://online.wsj.com/article/SB124939108822704607.html

46 Melvin, S.P. (2002, April). It's Payback Time. *Entrepreneur.* Retrieved August 17, 2009, http://www.entrepreneur.com/money/paymentsandcollections/billingandcollections/article49828.html

47 Pleasant, S. (2009, August 17). *The importance of the balance sheet statement.* Retrieved August 17, 2009, from http://www.populararticleo.com/article16388.html

48 Heebner, J. (2005, May 1). Snapshot of an income statement. *Jewelers Circular Keystone*; 2005, April 14). Minority groups of 10 trillion dollar consumer market. *The Bergen County Record*; and (2005, April 14). Here's a sweet lesson on income statements. *The Bergen County Record.*

49 Lacter, J. (2008, August 7). caffeinated, aggressive, and brash Esq. *Fast Company.com.* Retrieved August 17, 2009, from http://www.fastcompany.com/magazine/128/caffeinated-aggressive-amp-brash-esq.html

50 Torres, N. (2005, April). Count me in. *Entrepreneur.* Retrieved August 17, 2009, from http://findarticles.com/p/articles/mi_m0DTI/is_4_33/ai_n13659356

51 Campbell, P. (2005, June 1). How do you define cash flow? *Inc.* Retrieved August 17, 2009, from http://www.inc.com/resources/finance/articles/20050601/cashcrisis.html

52 Lieber, R. (2007, December 19). Numbers Talk! *Fast Company.com.* Retrieved August 17, 2009, from. http://www.fastcompany.com/magazine/28/toolbox.html

53 Eaton, K. (2009, July 7). LG Chocolate's screen secret revealed: Cinema ratio widescreen. *FastCompany.com.* Retrieved August 17, 2009, from http://www.fastcompany.com/blog/kit-eaton/technomix/upcoming-lg-chocolates-screen-secret-revealed-cinema-ratio-widescreen

54 NetMBA. (n.d). *Financial Ratios.* Retrieved August 17, 2009, from http://www.netmba.com/finance/financial/ratios/

55 Judge, T. (2005, March 14). Liquidity ratio can help spot cash gap. *Powersports Business.*

56 Little, K. (n.d.). Understanding earnings per share. *About.com.* Retrieved August, 17, 2009, from http://stocks.about.com/od/evaluatingstocks/a/eps1.htm

57 BusinessWeek.com. (2009, August 12). *SRA forecasts strong 2010 earnings growth.* Retrieved August 17, 2009, from http://www.businessweek.com/ap/tech/D9A1KBGO2.htm, accessed August 17, 2009.

58 Schribefeder, J. (n.d.). Calculating return on sales. *Effective Inventory Management.* Retrieved August 17, 2009, from www.effectiveinventory.com/article2.html

59 Schribefeder, J. (n.d.). The concept of inventory turnover. *Effective Inventory Management.* Retrieved October 15, 2009, from www.effectiveinventory.com/-article2.html

60 Depasquale, E. (2008, January 22). Managing inventory for profitability. *Inc.com.*

Chapter 9

1 Bolsta, P. (2008, December). Consolidated container company: Back in the family. *TwinCities Business.* Retrieved August 5, 2009, from http://www.tcbmag.com/superstars/smallbusinesssuccessstories/106536p1.aspx

2 Ibid.

3 Consolidated Container Company (n.d.). *About us.* Retrieved August 5, 2009, from http://www.containerexperts.com/aboutus.cfm; and Consolidated Container Company (n.d.). *Brothers beat failure by drumming up new business* [Press release]. Retrieved August 5, 2009, from http://www.containerexperts.com/PressDetail.cfm?PressID=5139&REFURL=news.cfm

4 Erickson, T.J. (2008, February). Task, not time: Profile of a Gen Y job. *Harvard Business Review.*

5 Gratton, L., & Erickson, T. J. (2007, November). 8 Ways to build collaborative teams. *Harvard Business Review.*

6 Quittner, J. (2008, March 3). A tech pioneer's newspaper deathwatch. *Fortune.*

7 Sellers, P. (2008, October 13). It's good to be the boss. *Fortune*; and Sellers, P. (2008, October 13). The new valley girls. *Fortune.*

8 Shankar, S., Ormiston, C., Bloch, N., Schaus, R., & Vishwanath, V. (2008). How to win in emerging markets. *MIT Sloan Management Review.*

9 West, J.E. (2006, February). Listening to the customer. *Quality Digest.* p.16.

10 Welch, J. (2005 April, 18). It's all in the sauce. *Fortune.* pp. 78–83.

11 Dogwise.com. (n.d.). *Brief company history.* Retrieved August, 6, 2009, from www.dogwise.com/HelpCont/AboutUs.cfm

12 Sanserino, M.,& Tuna, C. (2009, July 27). Companies strive harder to please customers. *The Wall Street Journal.* Retrieved August 6, 2009, from http://online.wsj.com/article/SB124864862273182247.html

13 Green, B. (2005, March). The clear leader. *Fast Company.* pp. 65–67.

14 Drucker, P. (1974). *Management: Tasks, Responsibilities, and Practices.* New York: Harper & Row.

15 Linberg, B.C. (n.d.). *The growth of E-commerce.* Retrieved August 6, 2009, from http://home.earthlink.net/~lindberg_b/GECGrwth.htm

16 Herbst, M. (2007, August 3). Why oil could be headed even higher. *BusinessWeek*; and Seeking Alpha. (2004, June 24). *Predicting oil and gas prices: 2009-2016.* Retrieved August 6, 2009, from http://seekingalpha.com/article/145069-predicting-oil-and-gas-prices-2009-2016

17 CDC.gov. (n.d.). *Life expectancy.* Retrieved August 6, 2009, from www.cdc.gov/nchs/fastats/lifexpec.htm

18 Census.gov. (n.d.). *Statistical abstract of the United States: 2009.* Retrieved August 6, 2009, from http://www.census.gov/compendia/statab/tables/09s0100.pdf

19 Musil, S. (2007, May 23). Wal-Mart to begin selling Dell PCs. *News.CNET.com* Retrieved August 6, 2009, from http://news.cnet.com/8301-17938_105-9722613-1.htm

20 Olofson, C. (2007, December 19). Rough seas, tough customers. *FastCompany.com.* Retrieved August 6, 2009, from http://www.fastcompany.com/magazine/25/wyp.html, accessed August 6, 2009.

21 Tagliabue, J. (2003, March 15). US brands abroad are feeling global tension. *The New York Times.* Retrieved August, 9 2009, from http://www.nytimes.com/2003/03/15/business/international-business-us-brands-abroad-are-feeling-global-tension.html?pagewanted=1

22 Entrepreneur.com. (2005, November). *Leadership statistics.* Retrieved August 12, 2009, from http://www.entrepreneur.com/encyclopedia/businessstatistics/article81998.html

23 N.a. (June 15, 2009). According to a recent study: small, mid-sized

businesses unprepared for data continuity. *Contingency Planning and Management.com*. Retrieved August 9, 2009, from http://www.contingencyplanning.com/articles/72295/

24 Gumbel, P. (2009, January 9). Gucci group: The ice cream man cometh. *Fortune*. Retrieved August 9, 2009, from http://money.cnn.com/2008/01/08/news/international/Gucci_Polet.fortune/index.htm?postversion=2008010910

25 Armour, S. (2007, August 12). Who wants to be a middle manager? *USAToday.com*. Retrieved August 9, 2009, from http://www.usatoday.com/money/workplace/2007-08-12-no-manage_N.htm

26 3M. (n.d.). *Solutions*. Retrieved August 9, 2009, from http://solutions.3m.com/en_US/

27 Entrepreneur. (n.d.). *Staffing service*. Retrieved August 12, 2009, from http://www.entrepreneur.com/startupguides/staffing/index.html

28 Kellaway, L. (2005, May 23). Beware the senseless dumbing up of management thinking. *Financial Times*. p. 8.

29 Mintzberg, H. (2009, August, 6). The best leadership is good management. *BusinessWeek*. Retrieved August 9, 2009, from http://www.businessweek.com/magazine/content/09_33/b4143068890733.htm

30 Stuart, A. (2006, December 5). Get a life! *Inc.com*. Retrieved August 6, 2009, from http://www.inc.com/articles/2006/12/balance.html

31 Herrick, T. (2005, March 21). Leadership as layup? Lessons from basketball. *The Wall Street Journal Online*.

32 Joyce, A. (2005, May 29). Big bad boss tales. *Washington Post*. pp. F1&F4.

33 Jones, D. (2003, June 5). Autocratic leadership works-until it fails. *USAToday.com*. Retrieved August 9, 2009, from http://www.usatoday.com/news/nation/2003-06-05-raines-usat_x.htm

34 Direct Mag. (1999, February 11). *USPS challenged over autocratic management style*. Retrieved August 9, 2009, from http://directmag.com/news/marketing_usps_challenged_autocratic/

35 King, J. (2001, January 10). *NMSU professors say leaders are known by what they do*. Retrieved August 9, 2009. http://www.nmsu.edu/~ucomm/Releases/2001/Jan2001/leaders.html.

36 Loyalka, M.D. (2007, December 19). Laughing your way to success. *FastCompany.com*. Retrieved August 9, 2009, from http://www.fastcompany.com/articles/2006/01/laugh.html?page=0%2C0&partner=rss

37 McGregor, D. (1960). *The human side of enterprise*. New York: McGraw-Hill.

38 Inc.com (2009, June 1). *Under Armour's Kevin Plank on how to motivate employees*. Retrieved August 9, 2009, from http://www.inc.com/magazine/20090601/under-armours-kevin-plank-on-how-to-motivate-employees.html

39 Kelly, T. (2009, May 28). McShakeup. *Forbes.com*. May 28, 2009. Retrieved August 9, 2009, from http://www.forbes.com/global/2009/0608/japanmcdonalds-den-fujita-mcshakeup.html

40 Steinhauser, P (2009, February 23). Poll: Politicians trusted more than business leaders on economy. *CNN.com*. Retrieved August 12, 2009, from http://www.cnn.com/2009/POLITICS/02/23/poll.economy/index.html

41 *Ethics Resource Center*. (2007). *National business ethics survey*. Retrieved August 12, 2009, from http://www.ethics.org/files/u5/The_2007_National_Business_Ethics_Survey.pdf

42 THQ. (n.d.). *Investor relations*. Retrieved August 12, 2009, from http://investor.thq.com/phoenix.zhtml?c=96376&p=irol-homeProfile&t=&id=&

43 Field, A. (2009, August 7). Is it time for your business to change course? *BusinessWeek.com*. Retrieved August 12, 2009, from http://www.businessweek.com/magazine/content/09_68/s0908046301619.htm

44 Hamm, S. (2007, June 14). Guess who's hiring in America. *BusinessWeek*.

45 Reuters (2009, June 19). *Nissan to make electric cars in U.S.* Retrieved August 12, 2009, from http://www.reuters.com/article/environmentNews/idUSTRE55I5VG20090620

46 Niles, S. (2009, August 12). Layoff tracker. *Forbes.com*. Retrieved

August 12, 1009, from http://www.forbes.com/2008/11/17/layoff-tracker-unemployement-lead-cx_kk_1118tracker.html

47 Irwin, N. (2009, January 10). Jobless rate jumps to 7.2%. *The Washington Post*.

48 Hill, P. (2009, January 27). Top companies slash 70,000 jobs in one day. *The Washington Times*.

49 Ibid.

Chapter 10

1 Donlon, J.P. (2009). Best companies for leaders: 3M shoots to the top of the current ranking. *Entrepreneur*. Retrieved August 6, 2009, from http://www.entrepreneur.com/tradejournals/article/194323583.html.

2 Drucker, P.F. (2004, June). What makes an effective executive. *Harvard Business Review*. pp. 58–63.

3 Rooke, D., & Torbert, W.R. (2005, April). Transformations of leadership. *Harvard Business Review*. pp. 67–76.

4 Stogdill, R.M. (1974). *Handbook of leadership*. New York: Free Press; Cohen, W. (1998). The stuff of heroes: The eight universal laws of leadership Athens GA: Longstreet Press; Dewey, L. (2004). Five Qualities Good Leaders Express, *Girl Scouts*. Retrieved September 17, 2007, from www.girlscouts.org/for_adults/leader_magazine/2004_fall/five_qualities.asp; and Lourie, S. (2004, September 20). Six qualities every great leader needs. *CIO News*.

5 Inc. (2009, January 1). *Ask Yvon Chouinard*. *Inc*. Retrieved August 27, 2009, from http://www.inc.com/magazine/20090101/ask-yvon-chouinard.html

6 Casey, S. (2007, May 29). Patagonia: Blueprint for green business. *Fortune*. Retrieved August 21, 2009, from http://money.cnn.com/magazines/fortune/fortune_archive/2007/04/02/8403423/index.htm

7 Petruccelli, J. (2008, June 9). Optimism knows no slowdown. *Entrepreneur*. Retrieved August 21, 2009 from, http://www.entrepreneur.com/startingabusiness/startupbasics/article194606.html

8 ABC Supply. (n.d.). *About*. Retrieved August 21, 2009, from www.abcsupply.com/About.aspx?id=532&ekmensel=56_submenu_0_link_4

9 Wellner, A. S. (2004, July). Everyone's a critic. *Inc*. Retrieved August 21, 2009, from www.inc.com/magazine/20040701/managing.html

10 Fishman, C. (2007, December 18). Are you listening? *FastCompany.com*. Retrieved August 21, 2009, from http://www.fastcompany.com/magazine/11/helpyou2.html

11 BusinessWeek. (2008). Best places to launch a career 2008. Retrieved August 21, 2009, from http://www.businessweek.com/careers/first_jobs/2008/1.htm

12 NSBA. (n.d.). *National school board association*. *Retrieved August 26, 2009, from www.nsba.org*.

13 The Conference Board. (2008, December 2). Weakening global economy and growing financial pressures are increasing CEO concerns. *CEO challenge 2008: Top 10 challenges-financial crisis edition*. Retrieved August 21, 2009, from http://www.conference-board.org/utilities/pressDetail.cfm?press_id=3529

14 Conley, L. (2005, May). 25 Top business leaders, #11 Julie Rodriguez. *Fast Company*. p. 72; Salter, C. (2005, November). It's never been this hard. *Fast Company*. pp. 72–79; and Berger, J. (2006, April 3). Man on a mission. *Fortune*. pp. 86–92.

15 Goldstein, S. (2007, September). How I did it: Amy Rees Lewis, CEO, MediConnect Global. *Inc*.

16 Swahilya. (2005, July 5). Hard work gets 98 percent but attitude gets 100 percent. *The Hindu*.

17 Petruccelli, J. (2008, June 9). Optimism knows no slowdown. *Entrepreneur*. Retrieved August 21, 2009, from http://www.entrepreneur.com/startingabusiness/startupbasics/article194606.html

18 Fortune. (2009, February 2). *100 Best companies to work for 2009*. Retrieved August 21, 2009, from http://money.cnn.com/magazines/fortune/bestcompanies/2009/snapshots/1.html

19 Pofeldt, E. (2007, July 1). Best bosses. *Fortune Small Business*. Retrieved August 21, 2009, from http://money.cnn.com/2006/09/25/magazines/fsb/betterbosses.fsb/index.htm

20 Seda, C., & Seda, J. (2008, July 2). Go out and play. *Entrepreneur.com*. Retrieved August 21, 2009, from http://www.entrepreneur.com/management/leadership/article195272.html

21 Danelski, D.J. (1967). Conflict and its resolution in the Supreme Court. *Journal of Conflict Resolution*; 11: 71–86, & Ostberg, C.L., Wetstein, M.E., & Ducat, C.R. (2004). Leaders, followers, and outsiders: Task and social leadership on the Canadian Supreme Court in the early nineties. *Polity*. Vol. 36.

22 Picklesimer, P. (2008, October 16). 10 Years on, high school social skills predict better earnings than test scores. Retrieved August 23, 2009, from http://www.innovations-report.com/html/reports/studies/10_years_high_school_social_skills_predict_earnings_120438.html

23 Drummond, D. (2009, January 8). Great social skills give you a 12% raise. Here's proof. Retrieved August 23, 2009 from http://www.leadershipstylesblog.com/2009/01/great-social-skills-give-you-a-12-raise-heres-proof/

24 Morris, B. (2003, June 23). The accidental CEO. *Fortune*. Retrieved August 23, 2009, from http://money.cnn.com/magazines/fortune/fortune_archive/2003/06/23/344603/index.htm

25 Carthen, J.D. (2009). War, warrior heroes and the advent of transactional leadership in sports antiquity. *The Sport Journal*. Retrieved August 23, 2009, from http://www.thesportjournal.org/article/war-warrior-heroes-and-advent-transactional-leadership-sports antiquity

26 Wee, D. (2008). Innovation leadership creates high morale and idea-rich environment: Innovation is the source of competitive advantage and profits because it reduces costs, raises productivity, improves products, and attracts customers. *Today's Manager*. Retrieved August 23, 2009, from http://www.entrepreneur.com/tradejournals/article/183312425.html

27 Wilson, M. (2005). The psychology of motivation and employee retention. *Maintenance Supplies*; Kirby, J. (2005, June 1). Light their fires: Find out how to improve employee motivation and increase overall company productivity. *Security Management*; and Arndt, M. (2006, January 9). Nice work if you can get it. *BusinessWeek*.

28 Chandra, S. (2009). U.S. economy: Worker productivity surges and labor costs drop. *Bloomberg.com*. Retrieved August 24, 2009, from http://www.bloomberg.com/apps/news?pid=20601087&sid aat.iwUe1RmQ; and DiPaolo, R. (2005, June 1). Ergonomically inclined. *Maintenance Supplies*.

29 Velury, J. (2005, May 1). Empowerment to the people. *Industrial Engineer*

30 Priestley, S. (2005, November 7). Scientific management in 21st Century. *Articlecity.com*. Retrieved August 24, 2009, from www.articlecity.com/articles/business_and_finance/article_4161.shtml

31 Frank, R. (1995, May 24). Efficient UPS tries to increase efficiency. *The Wall Street Journal*. p. B1.

32 Fortune. (2009, March 16). *America's most admired companies*. *Fortune*. Retrieved August 24, 2009, from http://money.cnn.com/magazines/fortune/mostadmired/2009/full_list/

33 Accel. (n.d.). *Employee motivation*. Retrieved August 24, 2009, from www.accel-team.com/motivation/hawthorne_03.html

34 Bratman, S. (2005, January 1). The double-blind gaze. *Altadena Skeptic*.

35 Dorsey, D. (2007, December 19). Change factory. *FastCompany.com*. Retrieved August 24, 2009, from http://www.fastcompany.com/magazine/35/benchmark.html?page=0%2C0

36 Maslow, A. (1954). *Motivation and personality*. New York: Harper & Row.

37 Herzberg, F., Mausner, B., & Snyderman, B. (1959). *The motivation to work*. New York: Wiley; and Herzberg, F. (1968, January–February). One more time: How do you motivate employees? *Harvard Business Review*. pp. 54–63.

38 Asia One Business. (2009, August 3). *Is casino job within your reach?* Retrieved August 29, 2009, from http://business.asiaone.com/Business/Office/Hot%2BJobs/Story/A1Story20090802-158552.html

39 Hawaii Business. (n.d.). *Best places to work - Small companies*. Retrieved August 23, 2009, from http://www.hawaiibusiness.com/Hawaii-Business/Hawaii-Data/Best-Places-to-Work/Best-Places-to-Work-Small-Companies/index.php?tableid=5&sort=name&so=asc&view=details&itm=3561

40 Hackman, J.R., & Oldham, G.R. (1976, August). Motivation through the design of work: Test of a theory. *Organizational behavior and human performance*. pp. 250–279.

41 Hymowitz, C. (2009, August 19). More than just a job. *Forbes*. Retrieved August 23, 2009, from http://www.forbes.com/2009/08/18/corporate-executives-careers-forbes-woman-power-women-09-public-sector.html

42 Fortune. (2009, February 2). *100 Best companies to work for 2009*. Retrieved August 21, 2009, from http://money.cnn.com/magazines/fortune/bestcompanies/2009/snapshots/1.html

43 Ibid.

44 Javitch, D. (2009, June 19). 5 Employee motivation myths debunked. *Entrepreneur.com*. Retrieved August 24, 2009, from http://www.entrepreneur.com/humanresources/employeemanagementcolumnistdavidjavitch/article202352.html

45 Watson Wyatt. (2007). *Playing to win in a global economy – 2007/2008 Global strategic rewards report and United States findings*. Retrieved August 25, 2009, from http://www.watsonwyatt.com/research/resrender.asp?id=2007-US-0164&page=1

46 Nestle. (n.d.). *Employee Perspectives*. Retrieved August 25, 2009, from http://www.nestleusa.com/PubCareers/wwuEmployeePerspectives.aspx

47 Drucker, P.F. (1954). *The Practice of Management*. New York: Harper; and Drucker, P.F. (1976, January–February). What results should you expect? A user's guide to MBO. *Public Administration Review*. pp. 12–19.

48 Davis, K, & Newstom, J. (1989). *Human behavior at work*. *Organizational behavior*. New York: McGraw-Hill; and Mendelson, J.L. (1980). Goal setting: An important management tool. *Executive skills: A management by objectives approach*. Dubuque, IA: Brown.

49 Chory-Assad, R.M. (2003, March 1). Motivating factors: Perceptions of justice and their relationship with managerial and organizational trust. *Communication Studies*; and Henle, C.A. (2005, June 22). Predicting workplace deviance from the interaction between organizational justice and personality. *Journal of Managerial Issues*.

50 Lohr, S. (2005, December 5). A new game at the office: Many young workers accept fewer guarantees. *The New York Times*. Retrieved August 25, 2009, from http://www.nytimes.com/2005/12/05/business/businessspecial/05contract.html?pagewanted=1&_r=1

51 Pampered Chef. (n.d.). *About Our Founder*. Retrieved August 25, 2009, from http://www.pamperedchef.com/our_company/doris.html

Chapter 11

1 Murray, L. (2009, May 29). Firm finds growth in overseas arena. *Dayton Business Journal*. Retrieved September 2, 2009, from http://www.bizjournals.com/dayton/stories/2009/06/01/smallb1.html

2 Ibid.

3 Ibid.

4 Bawany, S. (2008, December 1). Transition coaching helps ensure success for global assignments. *Today's Manager*.

5 U.S. Census Bureau. (n.d.). *World population clock*. Retrieved August 25, 2009, from http://www.census.gov/main/www/popclock.html

6 Keating, R.J. (2008, May 23). Global trade benefits small business and economy says leading advocacy group. *Small Business and Entrepreneurship Council*. Retrieved August 25, 2009, from http://www.sbsc.org/content/display.cfm?ID=2703

7 Population Reference Bureau. (2009). *2009 World population data sheet*. Retrieved August 25, 2009, from http://www.prb.org/Publications/Datasheets/2009/2009wpds.aspx

8 Ibid

9 Kelly, E. (2003, January 8). Sanders going to China to battle trade imbalance. *Gannett News Service*.

10 Wal Mart. (n.d.). *About us*. Retrieved August 25, 2009, from http://walmartstores.com/AboutUs/246.aspx

11 N.a. (2008, March 15). A few good machines. *The Economist*.

12 The World Bank. (n.d.). *The World Bank*. Retrieved January 28, 2009, from http://www.worldbank.org

13 Maines, M. (2009, June 22). International trade could boost small business. *Inc.com*. Retrieved August 25, 2009, from http://www.inc.com/news/articles/2009/06/trade.html

14 Coy, P., Carter, A., & Arndt, M. (2005, February 14). The export engine needs a turbocharge. *BusinessWeek*. p. 32; and Ladner, M. (2006, January 13). Trade-offs: Understanding legal basics of importing and exporting. *Houston Business Journal*.

15 Keating, R.J. (2008, May 23). Global trade benefits small business and economy says leading advocacy group. *Small Business and Entrepreneurship Council*. Retrieved August 25, 2009, from http://www.sbsc.org/content/display.cfm?ID=2703

16 Cooper, J.C. (2008, April 22). Strong exports could mean a weak recession. *BusinessWeek*.

17 Rocks, D. (2008, March 8). In praise of not-so-free trade. *BusinessWeek*; and Nyden, P.J. (2008, February 10). Wanna trade? Markets free people more often than armies, WVU professor argues. *Sunday Gazette-Mail*.

18 Smith, C. (2005, April 19). Globalization provides mixed blessings. *University Wire*; and Batterson, R. (2006, February 12). Resolutions for 2006 start with embracing free trade. *St. Louis Post-Dispatch*.

19 Cox, J. (2007, August 7). Sugar cane ethanol's not-so-sweet future. *CNNMoney.com*. Retrieved August 26, 2009, from http://money.cnn.com/2007/08/06/news/economy/sugarcane_ethanol/index.htm

20 Spice Advice. (n.d.). *Encyclopedia*. Retrieved August 26, 2009, from http://www.spiceadvice.com/encyclopedia/index.html

21 FoodReference.com. (n.d.). *Saffron*. Retrieved August 26, 2009, from http://www.foodreference.com/html/artsaffron.html

22 Silk-road. (n.d.). *History of Silk*. Retrieved August 26, 2009, from http://www.silk-road.com/artl/silkhistory.shtml

23 Wild, O. (1992). The silk road. Retrieved August 26, 2009, from http://www.ess.uci.edu/~oliver/silk.html

24 Census.gov. (2009, June 10). *Foreign-trade statistics*. Retrieved August 26, 2009, from http://www.census.gov/foreign-trade/statistics/historical/gands.txt

25 U.S.-China Business Council (n.d.). *U.S.-China trade statistics and china's world trade statistics*. Retrieved August 26, 2009, from http://www.uschina.org/statistics/tradetable.html

26 International Monetary Fund. (n.d.). *The United States model*. Retrieved August 31, 2009, from www.imf.org/external/np/res/mmod/mark3/html/us.htm

27 McGrath, D. (2002, June 24). The high price of setting up or not setting up a global net presence. *International Herald Tribune*.

28 Koppel, N. (2003, February 3). Fifteen countries call for tightening of anti-dumping rules in WTO. *AP World Stream*; Zarocostas, J. (2005, April 1). EU prepared to impose sanctions on the U.S. *WWD*; and (2006, January 10). Mandleson warns China it must crack down on illegal dumping. *AP Worldstream*.

29 Barrett, R. (2005, April 19). Tariffs on foreign steel spark debate. *Milwaukee Journal Sentinel*; and (2005, February 9). Prime minister must take action in the softwood lumber dispute. *PR Newswire*.

30 Murthy, R. (2009, May 15). India, China lead global dumping dance. *Asia Times Online*. Retrieved August 26, 2009, from http://www.atimes.com/atimes/South_Asia/KE15Df01.html

31 Hardy, Q., & Buley, T. (2009, April). Green trade wars. *Forbes*. Retrieved August 26, 2009, from http://www.forbes.com/global/2009/0427/016-opinions-steel-environment-green-trade-wars.html

32 Passel, P. (2003, July 20). Tough U.S. enforcement on trade, is it fair? *New York Times*. Retrieved August 31, 2009, from http:www.query.nytimes.com/gst/fullpage.html?res=9F0CE3DD173BF933A15754C0A965958260&sec=&spon=&pagewanted=print

33 Murthy, R. (2009, May 15). India, China lead global dumping dance. *Asia Times Online*. Retrieved August 26, 2009, from http://www.atimes.com/atimes/South_Asia/KE15Df01.html

34 Burrows, P. (2008, February 12). Inside the iPhone gray market. *BusinessWeek.com*. Retrieved August 26, 2009, from http://www.businessweek.com/technology/content/feb2008/tc20080211_152894.htm

35 Negroni, C. (2009, July 28). Gray market cars—A cash for clunkers stumper. *The New York Times*. Retrieved August 27, 2009, from http://wheels.blogs.nytimes.com/2009/07/28/gray-market-cars-a-cash-for-clunkers-stumper/

36 Bhagwati, J. (2007, October 11). Free trade or protectionism? *Financial Times*. Retrieved August 31, 2009, from www.ft.com/cms/s/2/cb0b204a-7683-11dc-ad83-0000779fd2ac.html

37 Birnbaum, J. (2002, May 27). Business to Bush, let us into Cuba. *Fortune*. Retrieved August 31, 2009, from http://money.cnn.com/magazines/fortune/fortune_archive/2002/05/27/323679/index.htm

38 Reuters. (2009, August 3). *Iran fuel imports possible target in nuclear standoff*. Retrieved August 27, 2009, from http://www.alertnet.org/thenews/newsdesk/N03523563.htm

39 Dawson, C. (2009, August 31). Japan: Mitsubishi moves into high gear. *BusinessWeek International*. p. 16.

40 USTR.gov. (2008). 2008 National trade estimate report on foreign trade barriers. *Office of the United States Trade Representative*. Retrieved August 27, 2009, from http://www.ustr.gov/about-us/press-office/reports-and-publications/archives/2008/2008-national-trade-estimate-report-fo-0

41 Sen, A. (2009, July 22). India to push for nontariff barrier database at WTO's Geneva round. *The Economic Times*. Retrieved August 27, 2009, from http://economictimes.indiatimes.com/News/Economy/Foreign-Trade/India-to-push-for-non-tariff-barrier-database-at-WTOs-Geneva-round/articleshow/4805329.cms

42 Sanders, L.D., Moulton, K.S., Paggi, M, & Goodwin, B. (2009, August 28). *The GATT Uruguay round and the World Trade Organization: Opportunities and impacts for U.S. agriculture*. Retrieved August 28, 2009, from http://www.ces.ncsu.edu/depts/agecon/trade/seven.html

43 World Trade Organization. (n.d.). *Understanding the WTO*. Retrieved August 28, 2009, from www.wto.org/english/thewto_e/whatis_e/tif_e/org6_e.htm

44 Zedillo, E. (2009, August 31). Will the Doha Round implode? *Forbes*. p. 29.

45 Office of the United States Trade Representative. (n.d.). *Free Trade Agreements*. Retrieved August 28, 2009, from http://www.ustr.gov/trade-agreements/free-trade-agreements

46 Europa.eu. (n.d.). *History of the European Union*. Retrieved August 28, 2009, from http://europa.eu/abc/treaties/index_en.htm

47 CIA.gov. (n.d.). *European Union*. Retrieved August, 28, 2009, from https://www.cia.gov/library/publications/the-world-factbook/geos/ee.html

48 Perez, Angel. (2008, May 19). Latin America/EU: Leaders agree to accelerate trade talks. *International Press Service English News Wire*.

49 Arostegui, M. (2008, June 5). Brazil proposes alliance of Latin American nations: Security plan part of larger union without U.S. *The Washington Times*; and (2008, May 31). Speak fraternally but carry a stick; South American defence. *The Economist*.

50 Indonesia's membership in OPEC was suspended in January 2009.

51 OPEC. (n.d.). *Organization of the petroleum exporting countries*. Retrieved August 28, 2009, from www.opec.org/home/

52 Cavanagh, J, & Anderson, A. (2009, August 31). Happily ever NAFTA. *Foreign Policy*. p. 58.

53 Office of the United States Trade Representative. (n.d.). *North American free trade agreement*. Retrieved August 28, 2009, from http://www.ustr.gov/trade-agreements/free-trade-agreements/north-american-free-trade-agreement-nafta

54 Welch, J., & Welch, J. (2008, June 28). A punching bag named NAFTA. *BusinessWeek*.

55 Ibid.

56 Office of the United States Trade Representative. (n.d.). *North American free trade agreement*. Retrieved August 28, 2009, from http://www.ustr.gov/trade-agreements/free-trade-agreements/north-american-free-trade-agreement-nafta

57 Modic, S. (2008, June 1). Export more goods to produce balance:

Do free trade agreements really 'suck' as critic says? *Tooling and Production.*

58 Molaro, R. (2007, April 15). Taste of success. *Global License!* Retrieved August 30, 2009, from http://www.licensemag.com/licensemag/article/articleDetail.jsp?id=416915

59 Lopez, R. (n.d.). Disney in Asia, again [Case study]. *Lubin School of -Business Case Studies.* http://digitalcommons.pace.edu/cgi/viewcontent.cgi?article=1002&context=business_cases

60 N.a. (2008, May 1). Lending a hand: SBA, AICPA partner to help small businesses. *Journal of Accountancy.* N.a. (2008, May 10). Fiscal 2009 appropriations: Commerce, justice, science. *Finance Wire.*

61 Export.gov. (August 30, 2009). *Contact a trade specialist near you.* Retrieved August 30, 2009, from http://www.export.gov/eac/index.asp

62 U.S. Small Business Administration. (2008). *Breaking into the trade game: A small business guide to exporting* (4th ed.). Retrieved September 3, 2009, from http://www.sba.gov/idc/groups/public/documents/sba_program_office/oit_bitg4th_full.pdf

63 Reuters. (2009). *Rocky mountain chocolate factory.* Retrieved August 30, 2009, from http://stocks.us.reuters.com/stocks/fullDescription.asp?rpc=66&symbol=RMCF.O

64 Rocky Mountain Chocolate Factory. (n.d.). *Rocky Mountain chocolate factory.* Retrieved August 30, 2009, from http://www.rmcf.com.

65 The Athletes Foot. (n.d.). *The athletes foot.* Retrieved August 30, 2009, from http://www.theathletesfoot.com/

66 Wharton School of Business. (2006, May 10). *Success and failure in the Chinese fast food industry: It's all about standardization.* Retrieved August 30, 2009, from http://knowledge.wharton.upenn.edu/article.cfm?articleid=1470

67 N.a. (n.d.). *McDonald's Netherlands: Facts and figures.* Retrieved August 31, 2009, from www.alpha-group.biz/content/News/press2000_archiv.asp?Suchen=Nein&Index1=9,

68 Prasso, S. (2007, September 25). India's pizza wars. *Fortune.* Retrieved August 30, 2009, from http://money.cnn.com/magazines/fortune/fortune_archive/2007/10/01/100398841/index.htm

69 Bassak, G. (2005, March 1). Homegrown outsourcing. *Product Design & Development;* and Srinivasan, S. (2006, January 13). U.S. senator supports outsourcing to India. *AP Online.*

70 Reuters. (2002, May 18). *Global markets—U.S. stocks surge on Cisco, bonds drop.*

71 Hull, K. (2009, July 9). TV giants are outsourcing more manufacturing. *BusinessWeek.com.* Retrieved August 30, 2009, from http://www.businessweek.com/globalbiz/content/jul2009/gb2009079_881220.htm

72 Brown, C. (2006, June). Partnering for a profit. *Black Enterprise.*

73 Hawkins Jr., L., & Lublin, J.S. (2005, April 6). Emergency repairman: GM's Wagoner aims to make auto company more global. *The Wall Street Journal.* p. B1; (2005, March 9). N.a. (2005, March 9). Shanghai automotive industry corporation guide to China's auto market. *Automotive News;* and Strathnairn, M. (2006, January 9). SAIC car sales to get boost from GM. *Birmingham Post.*

74 Ho, P.J. (2009, August 30). GM, China FAW form joint venture. *The Wall Street Journal.* Retrieved August 30, 2009, from http://online.wsj.com/article/SB125160989949269941.html

75 Newman's Own. (n.d.). *General Newman's own questions.* Retrieved August 30, 2009, from http://www.newmansown.com/genQA.aspx#q6a

76 Knowledge@Wharton. (2009, July 1). Can we innovate our way out of recession? *Forbes.* Retrieved August 30, 2009, from http://www.forbes.com/2009/07/01/strategic-alliances-innovation-entrepreneurs-technology-wharton.html

77 Simonian, H. (2005, March 4). A case of two heads being better than one. *Financial Times.* p. 9.

78 Small Business Notes. (n.d.). *Strategic alliances.* Retrieved August 30, 2009, from http://www.smallbusinessnotes.com/operating/leadership/strategicalliances.html.

79 Schick, C.L. (2009, February 2). Strategic alliance brings needed financial relief to franchise and small business. *Reuters.* Retrieved August 30, 2009, from http://www.reuters.com/article/pressRelease/idUS170921+02-Feb-2009+PRN20090202

80 Organization for International Investment. (2009, March 18). *Foreign direct investment in the United States.* Retrieved August 30, 2009, from http://www.ofii.org/docs/FDI_2009.pdf

81 Fordahl, M. (2002, June 18). Haagen Dazs scoops up Dreyers in cool deal for shareholders. *Associated Press.*

82 bNet. (2000, May). Unilever Gets Ben & Jerry's for $326 Million. *Dairy Foods.* Retrieved August 30, 2009, from http://findarticles.com/p/articles/mi_m3301/is_5_101/ai_63091154/

83 Srite, M. (2005, April 1). Levels of culture and individual behavior: An integrative perspective. *Journal of Global Information Management.*

84 Bensinger, G. (2009, July 31). GM probably led drop in sales. *Bloomberg.* Retrieved August 31, 2009, from http://www.bloomberg.com/apps/news?pid=20601087&sid=aSdqZKQfQGMo&refer=home

85 Spencer, R. (2006, October 19). University says business students have to take golf lessons. *Telegraph.co.uk.* Retrieved August 31, 2009, from http://www.telegraph.co.uk/news/worldnews/1531853/University-says-business-students-have-to-take-golf-lessons.html

86 Mdchachi. (2006, April 30). Global marketing mistakes [Weblog]. Retrieved August 31, 2009, from www.chachich.com/blog/b.2006-04-30-Global-Marketing-Mistakes.html

87 CETRA. (2008, October 15). CETRA averts potential translation disasters and becomes a member of the Philadelphia 100 [Press release]. *Reuters.* Retrieved August 31, 2009, from http://www.reuters.com/article/pressRelease/idUS142630+15-Oct-2008+BW20081015

88 CNN.com. (1998, November 21). Nike and Islamic group end logo logjam. Retrieved September 3, 2009, from http://www.cnn.com/US/9811/21/nike.islamic/

89 Bellman, E., & Hudson, K. (2006, January 18). The high price of setting up or not setting up a global net presence. Wal-Mart trains sights on India's retail market. *The Wall Street Journal.* p. A9.

90 Kripalani, M., & Clifford, M. (2003, February 10). India: Coke finally gets its right. *BusinessWeek.* p. 18.

91 Trend Watching.com. (2009, September 1). Retrieved September 1, 2009, from *Sachet Marketing.* http://trendwatching.com/trends/SACHET_MARKETING.htm

92 Higgins, M. (2008, February 10). The American greenback is losing universal appeal. *The New York Times.*

93 Aeppel, T., (2005, January 20). Weak dollar, strong sales. *The Wall Street Journal.* pp. B1–B2; and Carew, R. (2006, January 4). China takes further step towards freeing up yuan. *The Wall Street Journal.*

94 Swan, C. (2005, March 22). U.S. exporters fail to reap the full benefits of a weaker greenback. *Financial Times.* p. 3.

95 Nike. (n.d.). *Company Overview.* Retrieved September 1, 2009, from http://www.nikebiz.com/company_overview/

96 Ed Zwirn, "Dollar Doldrums," *CFO,* May 2005, pp. 35–38.

97 HB Fuller. (n.d.). *About us.* Retrieved September 1, 2009, from http://www.hbfuller.com

98 Is4profit. (2009, August 25). *Volatile exchange rates costing small firms.* Retrieved September 1, 2009, from http://www.is4profit.com/small-business-news/20090825-volatile-exchange-rates-costing-small-firms.html

99 Marck, A.C., & Ramachandran, N. (2004, September 6). Wanna swap? *U.S. News & World Report;* Kaiser, R. (2004, October 4). Bartering makes a comeback through evolving business networks. *Chicago Tribune;* and Gutterman, S. (2006, January 4). Russia, Ukraine companies reach deal. *AP Online.*

100 Alex, G.G., & Bowers, B. (2009, September 1). *The American way to countertrade.* Retrieved September 1, 2009, from http://www.barternews.com/american_way.htm

101 Rigby, R. (2005, February 17). The jails where time is money. *Financial Times.* p. 8.

102 Simpson, G.R. (2005, January 27). Multinational companies unite to fight bribery. *The Wall Street Journal.* p. A2.

103 Fritsch, P., & Mapes, T. (2005, April 5). In Indonesia, a tangle of bribes creates trouble for Monsanto. *The Wall Street Journal*. pp. A1–A6.

104 Stone, S., & Helft, M. (2009, April 26). In developing countries, web grows without profit. *The New York Times*. Retrieved September 1, 2009, from http://www.nytimes.com/2009/04/27/technology/start-ups/27global.html

105 CIA.gov. (2009, August 29). *China. CIA World Factbook*. Retrieved August 29, 2009, from https://www.cia.gov/library/publications/the-world-factbook/geos/ch.html

106 Kimes, M. (2009, July 8). China on the march, again. *Fortune*. Retrieved August 29, 2009, from http://money.cnn.com/2009/07/07/news/economy/china_growth_investing.fortune/indcx.htm

107 Poon, T. (2009, August 18). Foreign direct investment in china continues to slide. *The Wall Street Journal*. Retrieved August 29, 2009, from http://online.wsj.com/article/SB125047781996935959.html

108 Russia Today. (2009, August 25). *FDI Into Russia continues slide as talk of economic rebound gathers pace*. Retrieved August 29, 2009, from http://russiatoday.com/Business/2009-08-25/fdi-russia-slide-rebound.html

109 PriceWaterhouseCoopers (2009). *Doing Business in Russia 2009*. Retrieved August 29, 2009, from http://www.pwc.com/ru/en/doing-business-in-russia/index.jhtml

Chapter 12

1 Law.Jrank.org. (n.d.). *Corporate fraud—Enron: An investigation into corporate fraud, further readings*. Retrieved September 1, 2009, from http://law.jrank.org/pages/5759/Corporate-Fraud.html

2 Ethisphere. (2008). *2008 Worlds most ethical companies*. Retrieved September 7, 2009, from http://ethisphere.com/wme2008/

3 Fortune. (2009). *World's Most Admired Companies 2009*. Retrieved September 1, 2009, from http://money.cnn.com/magazines/fortune/mostadmired/2009/snapshots/235.html

4 Trex, E. (2008). Money for (almost) nothing: Fat paychecks for very little work. *CNN.com*. Retrieved September 1, 2009, from http://www.cnn.com/2008/LIVING/wayoflife/10/01/mf.easy.money/index.html

5 Santa Clara University. (n.d.). *A framework for ethical decision making*. Retrieved September 1, 2009, from www.scu.edu/ethics/practicing/decision/framework.html

6 Guttentag, M.D., Porath, C.L., & Fraidin, S.N. (2008, June). Brandeis' policeman: Results from a laboratory experiment on how to prevent corporate fraud. *Journal of Empirical Legal Studies*; and n.a. (2009, January 6). Legal and ethical violations risks seen rising, but not resources to control the risk. *U.S. Newswire*.

7 Pursey P., Heugens, M. A. R., Kaptein, M., & van Oosterhout, J. (2008, January). Contracts to communities: A processual model of organizational virtue. *Journal of Management Studies*; and Martha, P. (2009, January 1). Focus on the fundamentals. *Public Management*.

8 U.S. Census Bureau

9 Turnitin.com. (n.d.). *Welcome to turnitin*. Retrieved September 1, 2009, from http://www.turnitin.com; and Whittle, S.R., & Murdoch-Eaton, D.G. (2008, May). Learning about plagiarism using Turnitin detection software. *Medical Education*.

10 Gurchiek, K. (2008, February 1). Ethics, schmethics, U.S. teens say. *HR News*.

11 Burke, J.A., Polimeni, R.S., & Slavin, N.S. (2007, May). Academic dishonesty: A crisis on campus—Forging ethical professionals gegins in the classroom. *CPA Journal*.

12 Blanchard, K, & Peale, N.V. (1996). *The power of ethical management*. New York: William Morrow.

13 Ethics Resource Center. (2007). *2007 National Business Ethics Survey*. Retrieved September 7, 2009, from http://www.ethics.org/files/u5/The_2007_National_Business_Ethics_Survey.pdf

14 Coughlan, R. (2003, May). Demystifying business ethics. *Successful Meetings*. 5. p33.

15 Stolz, R.F. (2007, May 16). Taking the lead. *Human Resource Executive*; and Floyed, T. (2008, January 25). Executive teams may benefit from coaching on ethics. *Boston Business Journal*.

16 Johnson, A. (2008, February 29). Practicing good ethics gives competitive advantage. *St. Louis Business Journal*.

17 Sullivan, B. (2008, May 13). Can't cancel that service? Blame 'perverse incentives'. *www/redtape/msnbc.com*; and Corkindale, G. (2008, January 30). What the SocGen mess means for your company. *Harvard Business Online*.

18 Bucaro, F.C. (2008, January 4). If good ethics is good business. What's the problem? *Business First*; Blanchard, D. (2008, January 1). How ethical is your supply chain? *Industry Week*; Smigocki, M. (2008, February 8). Complying with new ethics rules. *Set-Aside Alert*; and Powell, K.A. (2008, February 1). More than the math: CFOs should be 'people people' too. *HRMagazine*.

19 United States Department of Labor. (n.d.). *The Whistleblower Protection Program*. Retrieved September 1, 2009, from http://www.osha.gov/dep/oia/whistleblower/index.html

20 Tyler, K. (2005, February 1). Do the right thing: Ethics training programs help employees deal with ethical dilemmas. *HRMagazine*.

21 Sarbanes-Oxley. (2002). *Sarbanes-Oxley 101, Info Guide to the Sarbanes-Oxley Act of 2002*. Retrieved September 1, 2009, from www.sarbanes-oxley-101.com/sarbanes-oxley-compliance.htm

22 American Shredding. (n.d.). *Sarbanes*. Retrieved September 1, 2009, from www.americanshredding.com/index.php?section=sarbanes

23 Olberding, M. (2006, January 8). For some companies, cost outweighs good of corporate fraud law. *Lincoln Journal Star*.

24 Weinberg, N. (2005, March 14). The dark side of whistleblowing. *Forbes*. Retrieved September 1, 2009, from http://www.forbes.com/forbes/2005/0314/090.html

25 National Park Service. (n.d.). *Giving Statistics*. Retrieved September 2, 2009, from http://www.nps.gov/partnerships/fundraising_individuals_statistics.htm

26 Ronald McDonald House. (n.d.). *What we do*. Retrieved September 2, 2009, from http://rmhc.org/what-we-do/ronald-mcdonald-house/

27 Anderson Corporation. (n.d.). Anderson corporation's legacy of giving. Retrieved September 2, 2009, from http://www.andersenwindows.com/servlet/Satellite/AW/Page/awGeneral-3/1104867941491.

28 Business Ethics. (2007). Business ethics 100 best corporate citizens 2007. *Business Ethics*, Retrieved September 2, 2009, from http://www.business-ethics.com/node/75

29 Flandez, R. (2009, September 1). Pro bono work helps firms fight economic slump. *The Wall Street Journal*. Retrieved September 2, 2009, from http://online.wsj.com/article/SB125176720925874609.html

30 Ibid.

31 Murphy, C. (2007, January 22). *Xerox Social Service Leave Press Release*.

32 Hempel, J. (2005, January 31). A corporate peace corps catches on. *BusinessWeek*.

33 Dow Chemical Corporation. (2008). *More than 50 Dow Chemical employees volunteer at New Orleans city park today* [Press release]. Retrieved September 8, 2009, from http://www.news.dow.com/dow_news/manufacturing/2008/20080228a.htm

34 Nobis. (n.d.). *Social responsibility*. Retrieved September 2, 2009, from http://www.nobisengineering.com/social.html

35 Lexmark. (2004, March 24). News releases. Retrieved September 2, 2009, from http://www.lexmark-me.com/lexmark/pressrelease/home/0,6930,204816596_653271419_327265923_en,00.html

36 Allen, S. (2009, July 21). The new ROE: Return on ethics. *Forbes*. Retrieved September 2, 2009, from http://www.forbes.com/2009/07/21/business-culture-corporate-citizenship-leadership-ethics.html

37 Trex. (n.d.) *Policy code of conduct and ethics*. Retrieved September 2, 2009, from http://www.trex.com/governance/Trex_POLICY-CODE_OF_CONDUCT_AND_ETHICS.pdf

38 Barrett, K. (2008, March 3). Airborne to refund consumers. *ABC News*. Retrieved September 2, 2009, from http://abcnews.go.com/

Health/ColdFlu/Story?id=4380374&page=1

39 Suzuki SJ (n.d.). Retrieved September 2, 2009, from Answers.com: http://www.answers.com/topic/suzuki-sj?cat=biz-fin

40 English, A. (1997, June 28). Bouncing baby Benz to get £100M redesign. *Electronic Telegraph*.

41 Gluckert-Menke, W. (1998, February 2). Baby Benz faces the moose. *Europe*. pp. 40–44.

42 Pierson, R., & Pelofsky, J. (2009, September 3). Pfizer to pay $2.3 billion, agrees to criminal plea. *Reuters*. Retrieved September 8, 2009, from http://www.reuters.com/article/businessNews/idUSTRE5813XB20090903?feedType=nl&feedName=usbeforethebell

43 Porretto, J. (2002, July 17). WorldCom files suit against former controller, wants him to repay $800,000. *CRN*.

44 Reh, J. (2009, September 2). What good people really cost. Retrieved September 8, 2009, from http://management.about.com/cs/people/a/WhatPeopleCost.htm

45 Business Ethics. (n.d.). *Business Ethics 100 best corporate citizens*. Retrieved September 8, 2009, from http://www.business-ethics.com/node/75

46 Motorola. (n.d.). *Diversity and inclusion*. Retrieved September 8, 2009, from http://www.motorola.com/staticfiles/Business/Corporate/US-EN/corporate-responsibility/employees/diversity-and-inclusion-performance-and-goals.html.

47 Leung, R. (2003, July 6). The mensch of Malden Mills. *CBS News*. Retrieved September, 2, 2009, from http://www.cbsnews.com/stories/2003/07/03/60minutes/main561656.shtml

48 Tozzi, J. (2009, April 15). The right way to handle layoffs. *Business Week*. Retrieved September 8, 2009, from http://www.businessweek.com/smallbiz/content/apr2009/sb20090415_156982.htm

49 Tozzi, J. (2009, April 15). Playbook: six ways to help your laid-off employees. *Business Week*. Retrieved September 8, 2009, from http://www.businessweek.com/smallbiz/content/apr2009/sb20090415_406885.htm!chan=smallbiz_smallbiz+index+page_small+business+leadership

50 Shore Bank Corp. (n.d.). *Our story*. Retrieved September 3, 2009, from http://www.shorebankcorp.com/bins/site/templates/child.asp?area_4=pages/nav/story/right_side.dat&area_7=pages/titles/shore_story_title.dat&area_2=pages/about/shore_story.dat

51 Shore Bank Corp. (n.d.). *Mission performance*. Retrieved September 3, 2009, from http://www.shorebankcorp.com/bins/site/content/pages/annual_reports/2004AnnualReport/mission.html

52 Green, H., & Capell, K. (2008, March 6). Carbon confusion. *BusinessWeek*.

53 Vonasek, W., & Warnock, M. (2008, February 1). Green building movement continues to grow. *Wood & Wood Products*.

54 Ciba. (n.d.). *Environment health and safety*. Retrieved September 2, 2009, from www.cibasc.com/index/cmp-index/cmp-ehs.htm

55 Seventh Generation. (n.d.). *About Seventh Generation*, Retrieved September 3, 2009, from http://www.seventhgeneration.com/about

56 Coster, H. (2009, June 19). Greener than thou. *Forbes*. Retrieved September 3, 2009, from http://www.forbes.com/2009/06/19/seventh-generation-marketing-cmo-network-seventhgeneration.html

57 Tucker, L. (2008, June 4). Need a job? Look to green economy. *Daily Journal of Commerce*. Portland: OR; and (2009, January 18). UW School of business forums push green economy. *The Capitol Times* (Madison, WI)

58 Rhino. (n.d.). *What is Rhino's mission*. Retrieved September 2, 2009, from www.rhino.com/about/support.html

59 Chandler, M. (2008, April 18). Area cool to social responsibility investing. *Business First of Buffalo*; and Energy Resource. (2009, January 13). *Kellogg company releases first corporate responsibility report*.

60 Gunther, M. (2008, August 21). Eco-police find new target: Oreos. *Fortune*. Retrieved September 3, 2009, from http://money.cnn.com/2008/08/21/news/companies/palm_oil.fortune/index.htm?po

61 N.a. (2007, December 27). Holiday shoppers influenced by 'social conscience'. *Tampa Bay Business Journal*. December 27, 2007; and

62 Crawford, C.F. (2007, December 31). Environment top of mind for holiday shoppers. *Nashville Business Journal*.

62 Kimberley Process. (n.d.). *What is the Kimberley Process*. Retrieved September 3, 2009, from http://kimberleyprocess.com

63 N.a. (2006, June 29). Japan needs to tackle bribery. *BBC News*.

64 Kersnar, J. (2007, June). View from Europe: Global bribery. *CFO*. Retrieved September 4, 2009, from http://www.cfo.com/article.cfm/9211033?f=related

65 Allen, S. (n.d.). *The greening of McDonalds*. Retrieved September 3, 2009, from www.uoregon.edu/~recycle/events_topics_McDonalds_text.htm

66 Fuller, T. (2007, November 14). Boycott clouds gem show in Myanmar. *The New York Times*. Retrieved September 4, 2009, from http://www.nytimes.com/2007/11/14/world/asia/14iht-myanmar.1.8332923.html

67 Barrick. (n.d.). *Supplier code of ethics*. Retrieved September 4, 2009, from http://www.barrick.com/Company/Suppliers/SupplierCodeEthics/default.aspx

68 Lindborg, H. (2008, February 1). Corporations tout social responsibility. *Quality Progress*.

Bonus Chapter

1 Newbart, D. (2008, May 5). College worth cost – To a degree. *Chicago Sun-Times*; and Russell, J. (2008, June 1). *Education remains a sound investment*.

2 Clark, K. (2008, October 30). How much is that college degree really worth? *U.S. News and World Report*.

3 Education-Online-Search. (n.d.). *Education and Income*. Retrieved November 29, 2007, from http://www.education-online-search.com

4 Baum, S., & Ma, J. (2007). Education pays: The benefits of higher education for individuals and society. *The College Board*. Retrieved September 4, 2009, from http://www.collegeboard.com/prod_downloads/about/news_info/cbsenior/yr2007/ed-pays-2007.pdf

5 Cox News Service. (2006, April 5). Americans unprepared for retirement. *Washington Times*. p. C7.

6 Newport, R. (2009, April 20). Americans increasingly concerned about retirement income. *Gallup*. Retrieved September 4, 2009, from http://www.gallup.com/poll/117703/Americans-Increasingly-Concerned-Retirement-Income.aspx

7 Ruffennach, G. (2008, May 3–4). The encore quiz: How much do you know? *The Wall Street Journal*.

8 Nielsen. (n.d.). *Global consumer confidence falls to record low: Nielsen; 56% of global online consumers believe their country is in recession*. Retrieved September 4, 2009, from http://en-us.nielsen.com/main/news/news_releases/2008/may/global_consumer_confidence

9 Goodwin, J. (2009, June 5). How can I create a household budget? Retrieved September 4, 2009, from http://www3.signonsandiego.com/stories/2009/jun/05/1c06questiom145459-smartliving-household-budget/

10 Savage, T. (2009, August 17). Cost of credit card debt soaring. *Chicago Sun-Times*. Retrieved September 4, 2009, from http://www.suntimes.com/business/savage/1719592,terry-savage-credit-debt-081709.savagearticle

11 Trejos, N. (2008, April 13). Majoring in plastic. *The Washington Post*.

12 Kimes, M. (2008, October 13). Credit cards carte blanche. *Fortune*.

13 Bureau of Economic Analysis. (n.d.). *Personal savings rate*. Retrieved September 4, 2009, from http://www.bea.gov/briefrm/saving.htm

14 Spruell, S. (2005, January). Here's to 50 years of DOFT. *Black Enterprise*. pp. 61–64.

15 Greene, K. (2005, April 5). Workers lag on retirement savings. *The Wall Street Journal*. p. D2.

16 Samuelson, R.J. (2005, August 22). Our vanishing savings rate. *Newsweek*. p. 38.

17 Kadlec, D. (1999, June 28). The Prenup Audit. *Time*. Retrieved September 5, 2009, from http://www.time.com/time/magazine/article/0,9171,991358,00.html

18 Realtor.org. (2009, August 21). Strong gain in existing-home sales maintains uptend. *National Association of Realtors.* Retrieved September 5, 2009, from http://www.realtor.org/press_room/news_releases/2009/08/strong_uptrend

19 Christie, L. (2009, July 27). New home sales: 'Really good news.' *CNNMoney.com.* Retrieved September 5, 2009, from http://money.cnn.com/2009/07/27/real_estate/June_new_home_sales/index.htm

20 Epperson, S. (2008, December 31). 10 Ways to save money in 2009. *Msnbc.msn.com.* Retrieved September 6, 2009, from http://www.msnbc.msn.com/id/28436623/

21 Cruz, H. (2008, February 22). Success in investing found in sticking to basic principles. *Triangle Business Journal;* and Alvares, C. (2009, February 8). The emotional investor; investing in the stock market is often influenced by your own personal emotions and short-term market movements. But you can still take control and choose. *Business Today.*

22 Quinn, J.B. (2008, February 18). Your new rebalancing act. *Newsweek;* and Armstrong III, F. (2008, January 1). How much diversification is enough? *CPA Journal.*

23 Bryant Quinn, J. (2008, March 3). Planners wanted ASAP. *Newsweek.*

24 Ody, E. (2008, June 1). The best ways to invest in bonds. *Kiplinger's Personal Finance Magazine.*

25 Browning, E.S. (2008, September 29). Corporate bonds become fund managers' favorite. *The Wall Street Journal.*

26 Marquardt, K. (2008, July 31). Why you should invest in ETFs; They're cheap, transparent, and can easily plug holes in your portfolio. *U.S. News and World Report;* and Mazur, M. (2009, February 1). Mutual funds continue to be popular. *Community Banker.*

27 *M2 Presswire.* (2008, November 3). *Two simple steps to future wealth;* and Marquardt, K. (2009, January 2). 5 smart ways to invest your extra dough; Stash your cash in index funds, ETFS, and Obama stocks. *U.S. News & World Report.*

28 Marquardt, K. (2008, May 15). Ten things you didn't know about ETFs—But should. *U.S. News & World Report;* and Quinn, J.B. (2009, January 18). Exchange-traded funds beat active managers. *The Washington Post.*

29 Dunphy, M. (2005, August). The best credit card for you. *SmartMoney.* pp. 94–99; and Kosofysky Glassberg, B. (2006, April). Go ahead, pick a card, but not just any card. *Budget Travel.* pp. 55–56.

30 Woolsey, B. and Schulz, M. (2009, September 6). Credit card statistics, industry facts, debt statistics. *Credit Cards.com.* Retrieved September 6, 2009, from http://www.creditcards.com/credit-card-news/credit-card-industry-facts-personal-debt-statistics-1276.php#causes

31 Ibid; and U.S. Congress' Joint Economic Committee, (2009, May.). *Vicious Cycle: How unfair credit card company practices are squeezing consumers and undermining the recovery.*

32 Norton, F. (2006, January 31). Buried alive. *Washington Times.* pp. C7 and C8.

33 U.S. Congress' Joint Economic Committee. (2009, May). *Vicious cycle: How unfair credit card company practices are squeezing consumers and undermining the recovery;* Woolsey, B. and Schulz, M. (2009, September 6). Credit card statistics, industry facts, debt statistics. *Credit Cards.com.* Retrieved September 6, 2009, from http://www.creditcards.com/credit-card-news/credit-card-industry-facts-personal-debt-statistics-1276.php#causes

34 Prichard, J. (n.d.). *Government mandates free credit reports to all consumers.* Retrieved September 4, 2009, from http://banking.about.com/od/loans/a/freecreditrpt.htm

35 The Center on Alcohol Marketing and Youth. (n.d.). *Consequences of Underage Drinking.* Retrieved September 6, 2009, from http://camy.org/factsheets/index.php?FactsheetID=29

36 National Association of Insurance Commissioners. (2006, March 28). *NAIC Launches Insure U.* Retrieved September 6, 2009 http://www.naic.org/Releases/2006_docs/insure_u_launch.htm

37 Quinn, J.B. (2006, January 9). Planning for Trouble. *Newsweek.* pp. 57–59.

38 National Coalition on Health Care. (n.b.). *Health insurance coverage.* Retrieved September 6, 2009. http://www.nchc.org/facts/coverage.shtml

39 Institute of Medicine. (2004, January 14). *Insuring America's health: Principles and recommendations. Retrieved September, 6, 2009, from http://www.iom.edu/?id=17848*

40 The American Medical Student Association. (n.d.). *The case for universal healthcare.* Retrieved September 6, 2009, from http://www.amsa.org/uhc/CaseForUHC.pdf

41 Balanced Politics. (n.d.). *Should the government provide free universal health care for all Americans?* Retrieved September 6, 2009, from http://www.balancedpolitics.org/universal_health_care.htm

42 Mitchell, E. (2008, August 29). Renters insurance: Don't live at home without it. *Contra Costa Times.* Retrieved September 6, 2009. http://www.allbusiness.com/insurance/property-casualty-insurance-personal/12122870-1.html

43 Helman, R., Greenwald, M., & Associates, Copeland, C., & and VanDerhei, J. (2009, April). The 2009 Retirement Confidence Survey: Economy Drives Confidence to Record Lows; Many Looking to Work Longer. *Employee Benefit Research Institute.* Retrieved September 7, 2009, from http://www.ebri.org/pdf/briefspdf/EBRI_IB_4-2009_RCS1.pdf

44 Dalrymple, M. (2007, May 1). Want to retire? Start saving now. *The Motley Fool.*

45 Transamerica. (n.d.). *The high cost of procrastination. Retirement planning.* Retrieved September 7, 2009, from http://www.transamerica.com/planning_your_finances/retirement_planning/.

46 Pear, R. (2009, May 12). Recession drains social security and medicare. *The New York Times.* Retrieved September 7, 2009, from http://www.nytimes.com/2009/05/13/us/politics/13health.html

47 Bahnsen, D. (2008.) Accumulation Basics. *World.*

48 Serchuk, D. (2009, August 13). Stocks to rise in five years. *Forbes.* Retrieved September 7, 2009, from http://www.forbes.com/2009/08/12/forecast-stocks-dividends-intelligent-investing-bonds.html

49 Meyers, E.G. (2008). Slow and steady wins the race. *Let's Talk Money.*

50 Morais, R.C. (2008, April 8). The IRA job machine. *Forbes.* Retrieved September 7, 2009. http://www.forbes.com/2009/04/08/ira-robs-startup-personal-finance-retirement-job-machine.html

51 Schurenberg, E. (2008, April). Why we flunked 401(k). *Money.*

52 The Profit Sharing Council of America. (n.d.) *401(k) and profit sharing plan eligibility survey.* Retrieved September 7, 2009, from http://www.psca.org/Portals/0/pdf/research/08%20Eligibility%20All.pdf

53 Bureau of Labor Statistics. (2008). Financial Analysts and Personal Financial Advisors. *Occupational Outlook Handbook, 2008–09 Edition, Bureau of Labor Statistics.* Retrieved September 7, 2009, from http://www.bls.gov/oco/ocos259.htm

54 Lawyers.com (2004, May 24). *Estate planning survey.* Retrieved September 7, 2009, from http://research.lawyers.com/Estate-Planning-Survey.html.

55 Ibid.

56 Ibid.

57 Ibid.

58 Steele, J. (2006, May). How to Make a Million. *Kiplinger's.* pp. 77–85.

59 Data from http://www.icmarc.org/xp/rc/marketview/chart/2008/200 80502SP500HistoricalReturns.html.

Front Matter

Page iii (top to bottom): © Ariel Skelley/Getty Images, © Royalty-Free/Corbis, © Comstock/JupiterImages, © Brad Rickerby/Getty Images; iv: © BananaStock/age fotostock; v top: © Francisco Cruz/SuperStock; v bottom: © Comstock/JupiterImages; vi: © Ariel Skelley/Getty Images; vii top: © BananaStock/JupiterImages; vii bottom: © The McGraw-Hill Companies, Inc./Lars Niki, Photographer; viii: © Photodisc/Getty Images; ix top: © Mikael Karlsson; ix bottom: © Simon Marcus/Corbis; x top: © BananaStock/PunchStock; x bottom: © Royalty-Free/Corbis; xi: © Mike Powell/Getty Images; xii top: Courtesy TOMS Shoe Company; xii bottom: © Stockbyte/PunchStock; xiii top: © Eightfish/Getty Images; xiii bottom: © Photodisc/Getty Images.

Chapter 1

Page 1: © Jack Hollingsworth/Corbis; 2: © Naashon Zalk/Corbis; 4 top: © Burke/Triolo/Brand X Pictures; 4 bottom: © Image Club; 5 left: © Brand X Pictures/PunchStock; 5 right: © Burke/Triolo Productions/Getty Images; 6 top: © The McGraw-Hill Companies, Inc/Ken Karp, Photographer; 6 bottom: © Royalty-Free/Corbis; 7: © BananaStock/PunchStock; 8: Library of Congress; 9: © Dynamic Graphics/Jupiterimages; 10: © Stockbyte/Getty Images; 12: © Burke/Triolo/Brand X Pictures/Jupiterimages; 13: © Lorcan/Getty Images; 15 top: © The McGraw-Hill Companies Inc./John Flournoy, Photographer; 15 bottom: © FoodCollection/Index Stock; 17: © Royalty-Free/Corbis; 18 top: © Burke/Triolo/Brand X Pictures/Jupiterimages; 18 bottom: © Ryan McVay/Getty Images; 19 top: © BananaStock/PunchStock; 19 bottom: © ballyscanlon/Getty Images; 20: © Getty Images; 21: © Stockbyte/Punchstock Images; 22: © Ryan McVay/Getty Images; 23: © BananaStock/age fotostock; 24: © Stockbyte; 25: © Comstock/JupiterImages.

Chapter 2

Page 30: © Royalty-Free/Corbis; 32: Library of Congress Prints and Photographs Division [LC-USZC4-1099]; 33 top: © 1997 IMS Communications Ltd/Capstone Design. All Rights Reserved; 33 bottom: © Digital Vision/PunchStock; 34 top: © Sandra Ivany/Brand X Pictures/Getty Images; 34 bottom: © Harris Barnes/AgStock Images/Corbis; 35: © Royalty-Free/Corbis; 36: © Photodisc/PunchStock; 39: © Royalty-Free/Corbis; 40 top left: © Don Farrall/Getty Images; 40 top right: Dynamic Graphics/JupiterImages; 40 bottom: © Mark Steinmetz/Amanita Pictures; 41 top: © Keith Brofsky/Getty Images; 41 bottom: © Digital Vision/PunchStock; 42: © Francis Dean/The Image Works; 43: © Annie Reynolds/PhotoLink/Getty Images; 44 top: © 1997 IMS Communications Ltd/Capstone Design. All Rights Reserved; 44 bottom: © Royalty-Free/Corbis; 45: © Comstock Images/Alamy; 46: Library of Congress; 47: © Marcio Jose Sanchez/AP Images; 48: © Francisco Cruz/SuperStock.

Chapter 3

Page 56: © Ariel Skelley/Getty Images; 58 left: © Joaquin Palting/Getty Images; 58 right: © RubberBall Productions; 59: © Paul Sakuma/AP Images; 60 top: © Digital Vision/Getty Images; 60 bottom: © Ingram Publishing/SuperStock; 61 left: © Ed Andrieski/AP Images; 61 right: © Ryan McVay/Getty Images; 62: © SW Productions/Photodisc/Getty Images; 63 top: © Tokyo Space Club/Corbis; 63 bottom: © moodboard/Corbis; 64: © Comstock Images/JupiterImages; 66 top: © The McGraw-Hill Companies, Inc./Andrew Resek, Photographer; 66 bottom: © Alexander Nemenov/AFP/Getty Images; 67 top: © The McGraw-Hill Companies, Inc./Jill Braaten, Photographer; 67 bottom: © BananaStock/Alamy; 68: © C Squared Studios/Getty Images; 70: © Stockdisc/Getty Images; 71 top: © Royalty-Free/Corbis; 71 bottom: © Javier Pierini/Getty Images; 72: © BananaStock/JupiterImages; 73 left: © Dynamic Graphics/JupiterImages; 73 right: © Photodisc/Getty Images; 74: © C. Sherburne/PhotoLink/Getty Images; 76: © Creatas/PunchStock; 77: © Ryan McVay/Getty Images; 79: © Royalty-Free/Corbis; 80: Author's Image; 81: © Ingram Publishing/Alamy; 82: © C. Borland/PhotoLink/Getty Images.

Chapter 4

Page 88: © C Squared Studios/Getty Images; 90 left: © The McGraw-Hill Companies, Inc./Jill Braaten, Photographer; 90 right: © Brand X Pictures/PunchStock; 91 top: © Burke/Triolo/Brand X Pictures; 91 bottom: © Jonelle Weaver/Getty Images; 93 left: © Ingram Publishing/Fotosearch; 93 right: © Rob Melnychuk/Getty Images; 94: © Ingram Publishing/Alamy; 95: © Andy Kropa 2006/Redux Pictures; 96 top: © Royalty-Free/Corbis; 96 bottom left: © Paul Burns/Getty Images; 96 bottom right: © The McGraw-Hill Companies, Inc./Jacques Cornell, Photographer; 97: © Janine Wiedel Photolibrary/Alamy; 98 top: © The McGraw-Hill Companies, Inc./Jill Braaten, Photographer; 98 bottom: © Photodisc/Getty; 99: © The McGraw-Hill Companies, Inc./Emily and David Tietz, Photographers; 100: © The McGraw-Hill Companies, Inc./Jill Braaten, Photographer; 101: © James Sparshatt/Corbis; 102: © The McGraw-Hill Companies, Inc./Christopher Kerrigan, Photographer; 103: © Corbis RF/PunchStock; 104: © FoodCollection/PunchStock; 105 left: © Ben Margot/AP Images; 105 right: © Brand X Pictures/PunchStock; 107 top: © Getty Images; 107 bottom: © Royalty-Free/Corbis; 108: © The McGraw-Hill Companies, Inc./John Flournoy, Photographer; 109: © Royalty-Free/Corbis; 111: © M.Becker/American Idol 2009/Getty Images; 113: © Digital Vision/SuperStock; 113 bottom: © pulp/Photodisc/Getty Images; 114: © Jeff Greenberg/PhotoEdit; 115 left: © Comstock/Jupiter Images, 115 right: © USDA.

Chapter 5

Page 120: © BananaStock/JupiterImages; 122: © Photodisc/Getty Images; 123: © Comstock/JupiterImages; 124: © BananaStock/Alamy; 125: © Paula Solloway/Alamy; 126 top: © image100; 126 bottom left: © Brand X/JupiterImages/Getty Images; 126 bottom right: Courtesy of CareerBuilder.com; 128 top: Courtesy of Kronos Incorporated; 128 bottom: © RubberBall Productions; 129 top: U.S. Department of Energy; 129 bottom: © G.K. & Vikki Hart/Getty Images; 130 top: © Burke/Triolo Productions/Getty Images; 130 bottom: © US Air Force photo by Kristina Cilia; 132 left: © Brand X Pictures/Alamy; 132 right: © Royalty-Free/Corbis; 135: © Eric Audras/PhotoAlto/JupiterImages; 136: © The McGraw-Hill Companies, Inc./Lars Niki, Photographer; 138: © Ingram Publishing/Alamy; 139: © Keith Brofsky/Getty Images; 140 top: © Royalty-Free/Corbis; 140 bottom: © The McGraw-Hill Companies, Inc./Andrew Resek, Photographer; 141: © Richard H. Cohen/Corbis; 143 top: © Image Source/PunchStock; 143 bottom: © Ted S. Warren/AP Images; 144-145: © Flying Colours/Digital Vision/Getty Images; 145 top: © BananaStock/JupiterImages; 146 top left: © Stockbyte/PunchStock; 146 top right: © BananaStock/JupiterImages; 146 bottom: © Keith Brofsky/Photodisc/Getty Images.

Chapter 6

Page 152: © Royalty-Free/Corbis; 154: © Digital Vision/PunchStock; 155: © Photodisc/Getty Images; 156 left: © Ingram Publishing/Alamy; 156 right: © Royalty-Free/Corbis; 157: © Aly Song/Reuters/Landov; 158: © Benoit Decout/REA/Redux Pictures; 159 left: © C Squared Studios/Getty Images; 159 right: © Harrison McClary/Bloomberg News/Landov; 162 left: © Siede Preis/Getty Images; 162 right: © Digital Vision/Getty Images; 163: © Siede Preis/Getty Images; 164: © Gary Reyes/San Jose Mercury News; 166 top: © Brand X Pictures/PunchStock; 166 bottom: © Getty Images; 167 left: © Ingram Publishing/Fotosearch; 167 right: © M. Freeman/PhotoLink/Getty Images; 169 left: © Royalty-Free/Corbis; 169 right: © The McGraw-Hill Companies, Inc./Lars Niki, Photographer; 170: © Comstock/Alamy; 171: © Photodisc/Getty Images.

Chapter 7

Page 176: © Simon Marcus/Corbis; 178: © Ingram Publishing/Alamy; 179: © Roz Woodward/Getty Images; 180 left: © The McGraw-Hill Companies Inc./Ken Cavanagh, Photographer; 180 right: © Mikael Karlsson; 181 left: © Photodisc/PunchStock; 181 left: © Tim Pannell/Corbis; 182: © Rune Hellestad/UPI /Landov; 183: © Photodisc/Getty Images; 184: © C Squared Studios/Getty Images; 185 top: © The Mc-

Graw-Hill Companies/Barry Barker, Photographer; 185 bottom left: © Photodisc/Getty Images; 185 bottom right: Eyewire/Getty Images; 186 top: © The McGraw-Hill Companies/Ian Coles, Photographer; 186 middle: © Nova Development; 186 bottom: Digital Vision/Getty Images; 187: © Corbis; 188: © Dinodia Photo Library/Brand X/Corbis; 186 top left: Courtesy of Apple; 189 top right: © Comstock/JupiterImages; 189 bottom: © Arthur S. Aubry/Getty Images; 190: © Stockdisc/Getty Images; 191 top: © Alistair Berg/Getty Images; 191 bottom: © White Packert/Getty Images; 192: © Blend Images/Getty Images; 193: © Pixtal/PunchStock; 194: © Stockbyte; 195 top: © Photodisc/Getty Images; 195 bottom: © Jonathan Kitchen/Getty Images; 196 top: © The McGraw-Hill Companies, Inc./Cadence Gamache, Photographer; 196 bottom: © Photodisc/PunchStock; 198: © RubberBall Productions.

Chapter 8

Page 204: © BananaStock/PunchStock; 206: © Eyewire/Getty Images; 207: © Jim Linna/Photodisc/Getty Images; 208 left: © The McGraw-Hill Companies, Inc.; 208 right: © Newscom Photos; 209: © Ingram Publishing/SuperStock; 210: © JupiterImages; 211: © Stockbyte/Getty Images; 212: © The McGraw-Hill Companies, Inc.; 213: © Stockbyte/Getty Images; 215: © John Lund/Marc Romanelli/Getty Images; 216: © JupiterImages/Getty Images; 217 top: © Image Source/JupiterImages; 217 bottom, 219: © Photodisc/Getty Images; 220: © Royalty-Free/Corbis; 221: © Imagestate Media (John Foxx)/Imagestate; 222: © Steve Allen/Getty Images; 225: © Royalty-Free/Corbis; 226 top: © Chip Litherland/The New York Times/Redux Pictures; 226 bottom: © The McGraw-Hill Companies, Inc., Lars Niki, Photographer; 227 top: © Scott McCloskey/The Wheeling Intelligencer/AP Images; 227 bottom: © Ingram Publishing/Alamy; 229: © Mattew McDermott/Polaris Images; 231: © age fotostock/Superstock.

Chapter 9

Page 236: © Brand X/JupiterImages/Getty Images; 238: © The McGraw-Hill Companies Inc./Ken Karp, Photographer; 240 top: © Comstock Images/Alamy; 240 bottom: © BananaStock/PunchStock; 241: © Comstock Images/Alamy; 242: © Photodisc/Getty Images; 245: Burke/Triolo/Brand X Pictures; 246: © C Squared Studios/Getty Images; 247: © Comstock Images/Alamy; 248: © Hiroko Masuike/The New York Times/Redux Pictures; 249 top: © Erica Simone Leeds; 249 bottom: © Photodisc/PunchStock; 250: © Jules Frazier/Getty Images; 253: © Big Cheese Photo/JupiterImages; 254 top: © BananaStock/PunchStock; 254 bottom: © Photodisc/Getty Images; 255: © Royalty-Free/Corbis; 257: © Eyewire (Photodisc)/PunchStock; 258 left: © Photodisc/Getty Images; 258 right: © blue jean images/Getty Images; 259: © DigitalVision/Punchstock; 260; © Jon Silla; 262: © Janis Christie/Getty Images; 264 top: © PhotoLink/Getty Images; 264 bottom: © Steve Cole/Getty Images.

Chapter 10

Page 270, 272: Digital Vision/Getty Images; 273: © Siede Preis/Getty Images; 274, 275: © Royalty-Free/Corbis; 276: © Ryan McVay/Getty Images; 277, 278: © Royalty-Free/Corbis; 279: © Siede Preis/Getty Images; 280: © Polka Dot Images/Masterfile; 281 top: Comstock Images/Alamy; 280 bottom: Corbis RF/JupiterImages; 282 top: © Mike Powell/Getty Images; 282 bottom: © Radlund & Associates/Getty Images; 284: © Steve Cole/Getty Images; 285 left: © The McGraw-Hill Companies, Inc./John Flournoy, Photographer; 285 right: Property of AT&T Archives. Reprinted with permission of AT&T; 286: © The McGraw-Hill Companies, Inc./Barry Barker, Photographer; 288: © Photodisc/Getty Images; 290: © Royalty-Free/Corbis; 292: © Photodisc/Getty Images; 293: © Stockbyte/PunchStock.

Chapter 11

Page 298: © Royalty-Free/Corbis; 300: © Goodshoot/PunchStock; 301: © Royalty-Free/Corbis; 303 top left & bottom: © C Squared Studios/

Getty Images; 303 top right: © Iconotec/Alamy; 304: © Layne Kennedy/Corbis; 305 left: © Ingram Publishing/Alamy; 305 right: © C Squared Studios/Getty Images; 306: © Comstock/JupiterImages; 307: © Henri Conodul/Iconotec.com; 308 top: © Bullit Marquez/AP Images; 308 bottom: © Prakash Singh/AFP/Getty Images; 309: © Christopher Rolinson/AP Images; 310: © Brand X Pictures/PunchStock; 312: © Paul Sancya/AP Images; 313 top: © Scott Barbour/Getty Images; 313 bottom: © Yoshikazu Tsuno/AFP/Getty Images; 314 top Courtesy of Domino's Pizza; 314 bottom: © Stockbyte/PunchStock; 315: © Thinkstock/Jupiterimages; 316: © Photodisc/Getty Images; 317: © Andy Sacks/Getty Images; 318: © Ingram Publishing/Alamy; 319 top: © The McGraw-Hill Companies, Inc./Christopher Kerrigan, Photographer; 319 bottom: © AP Images; 320 top: © Anderson Ross/Blend Images/Corbis; 320 bottom: © Stockbyte/PunchStock; 321: Author's Image; 323: © European Community 2006; 324: © Charles Gullung/zefa/Corbis; 325: © Antonine Gyori/AGP/Corbis; 326: © Brand X Pictures/PunchStock; 327: © Photomondo/Getty Images.

Chapter 12

Page 332: Courtesy TOMS Shoe Company; 334: © Jack Dempsey/AP Images; 335: © Mike Clarke/AFP/Getty Images; 336 top: © Photodisc/Getty Images; 336 bottom: © John Gress/Getty Images; 337: © Comstock Images/Alamy; 338: © Louis Lanzano/AP Images; 339: Courtesy of turnitin.com; 340 left: © Comstock Images/Alamy; 340 right: © Daniel Hulshizer/AP Images; 341: © Pam Francis/Getty Images; 342: © Stockdisc/PunchStock; 343 top: © Photodisc/Getty Images; 343 bottom: © Laurence Mouton/Photo Alto; 344 top: © Ryan McVay/Getty Images; 344 bottom: © Digital Vision/PunchStock; 345: © Stockbyte/JupiterImages; 346 top: © Dagmar Schwelle/Alamy; 346 bottom: © Reuters/Corbis; 347: © Digital Vision/PunchStock; 348 top: Courtesy of Green Mountain Coffee Roasters; 348 bottom: © Ed Quinn/Corbis; 349 top: © NOAA; 349 bottom: © Brand X Pictures/PunchStock; 350: © Photodisc/Getty Images; 351: © Medioimages/Alamy; 352: © Brand X Pictures/PunchStock; 353: © Ingram Publishing/Alamy; 354: © C Squared Studios/Getty Images; 355: © Royalty-Free/Corbis.

Bonus Chapter

Page 360: © Don Farrall/Getty Images; 362: © Peter Dazeley/Getty Images; 364: © Keith Brofsky/Getty Images; 365 top: © Brand X/JupiterImages/Getty Images; 365 bottom: © Serge Kozak/Corbis; 366 top: © Javier Pierini/Getty Images; 366 bottom: © Dynamic Graphics/JupiterImages; 367: © Brand X Pictures/PunchStock; 368 top: © Stockbyte/Getty Images; 368 bottom left: © AP Images; 368 bottom right: © Ryan McVay/Getty Images; 369: © Comstock/PunchStock; 370 top: © Newscom Photos; 370 bottom: © Thomas Northcut/Getty Images; 371: © Eightfish/Getty Images; 372: © Photodisc/Getty Images; 374 top: © Jack Hollingsworth/Getty Images; 374 middle: © Tony Cordoza/Getty Images; 374 bottom: © Comstock/PunchStock; 377: © Corbis; 378 top: © Stockbyte/JupiterImages; 378 bottom: © Blend Images/Getty Images; 379: © Image Source/JupiterImages; 381: © Lynsey Addario; 382: © BananaStock/Alamy; 384 top: © Brad Rickerby/Getty Images; 384 bottom: Courtesy of Leadfusion; 387 left: © moodboard/Corbis; 387 right: © MedioImages; 388: © BananaStock/Alamy.

Glossary

Page 393: © PhotoAlto/Punchstock; 404: © Andersen Ross/Blend Images/Corbis.

Endnotes

Page 405: © Comstock/PictureQuest.

Credits

Page 423: Photodisc/Getty Images.

connect™ plus+

LESS MANAGING.

MORE TEACHING.

GREATER LEARNING.

What is Connect *Plus+*?

McGraw-Hill Connect *Plus+* is a revolutionary online assignment and assessment solution providing instructors and students with tools and resources to maximize their success.

Through Connect *Plus+*, instructors enjoy simplified course setup and assignment creation. Robust, media-rich tools and activities, **all tied to the textbook's learning outcomes**, ensure you'll create classes geared toward achievement. You'll have more time with your students and less time agonizing over course planning.

Connect *Plus+* Features

McGraw-Hill Connect *Plus+* includes powerful tools and features that allow students to access their coursework anytime and anywhere, while you control the assignments. Connect *Plus+* provides students with their textbook and homework, **all in one accessible place.**

▶ ***Simple Assignment Management***
Creating assignments takes just a few clicks, and with Connect *Plus+*, you can choose not only which chapter to assign but also specific learning outcomes. **Videos, animations, quizzes**, and many other activities bring **active learning** to the forefront.

▶ ***Smart Grading***
Study time is precious and Connect *Plus+* assignments **automatically provide feedback** to you and your students. You'll be able to conveniently review class or individual students knowledge in an online environment.

Connect Plus+ eBooks
▶ McGraw-Hill has seamlessly **integrated eBooks** into their Connect *Plus+* solution with **direct links to the homework, activities, and tools**—students no longer have to search for content, allowing them more time for learning.

McGraw-Hill provides live instructor orientations for Connect *Plus+* to guarantee you will have a worry-free experience.

connect™ plus+

Mc Graw Hill

To learn more about Connect *Plus+*,
go to **www.mcgrawhillconnect.com**
or contact your local representative.